D1320443

Time Out Guides Limited
Universal House
251 Tottenham Court Road
London W1T 7AB
Tel + 44 (0)20 7813 3000
Fax + 44 (0)20 7813 6001
Email guides@timeout.com
www.timeout.com

Editorial

Editor Lesley McCave
Consultant Editor Paul French
Deputy Editor Jan Fuscoe
Listings Checker Annette Bourdeau
Proofreader John Pym
Indexer Jonathan Cox

Editorial/Managing Director Peter Fiennes
Series Editor Ruth Jarvis
Deputy Series Editor Lesley McCave
Business Manager Gareth Garner
Guides Co-ordinator Holly Pick
Accountant Kemi Olufuwa

Design

Art Director Scott Moore
Art Editor Tracey Ridgewell
Senior Designer Oliver Knight
Designer Chrissy Mouncey
Digital Imaging Dan Conway
Ad Make-up Charlotte Blythe

Picture Desk

Picture Editor Jael Marschner
Deputy Picture Editor Tracey Kerrigan
Picture Researcher Helen McFarland

Advertising

Sales Director Mark Phillips
International Sales Manager Ross Canadé
International Sales Executive Simon Davies
Advertising Sales (Toronto) DPS Media
Advertising Assistant Lucy Butler

Marketing

Marketing Director Mandy Martinez
Marketing & Publicity Manager, US Rosella Albanese

Production

Production Director Mark Lamond
Production Controller Samantha Furniss

Time Out Group

Chairman Tony Elliott
Managing Director Mike Hardwick
Group Financial Director Richard Waterlow
Group Commercial Director Lesley Gill
Group Marketing Director Christine Cort
Group General Manager Nichola Coulthard
Group Circulation Director Jim Heinemann
Group Art Director John Oakey
Online Managing Director David Pepper
Group Production Director Steve Proctor
Group IT Director Simon Chappell

Contributors

Introduction Lesley McCave. **History** Hugh Graham (*Messaging the medium, You saw it here first* Paul French; *Crimes and misdemeanours* Kim Gertler). **Toronto Today** Paul French. **Hollywood North** Pamela Cuthbert. **Architecture** Paul French. **Where to Stay** Patchen Barss. **Sightseeing: Introduction** Ruth Jarvis. **Downtown** Kim Gertler; Brent Ledger. **Midtown** Kim Gertler. **West End** Kim Gertler. **North Toronto** Kim Gertler. **East Toronto** Paul French. **Restaurants & Cafés** Pamela Cuthbert. **Bars** Nathalie Atkinson. **Shops & Services** Nathalie Atkinson (*Pick up a picnic* Pamela Cuthbert). **Festivals & Events** Brent Ledger. **Children** Denis Seguin. **Comedy** Andrew Clark. **Film** Pamela Cuthbert. **Galleries** Catherine Osborne. **Gay & Lesbian** Brent Ledger. **Music** Kerry Doole. **Nightlife** Li Robbins. **Sport & Fitness** Perry Stern. **Theatre & Dance** Kamal Al-Solaylee (*Hot peppered soul* Jan Fuscoe). **Trips Out of Town: Getting Started** Steve Veale. **Niagara Falls & Around** Betty Zyvatkauskas (*Falls guys* Jan Fuscoe). **Quick Trips** Betty Zyvatkauskas (*Top five wines* Pamela Cuthbert). **Further Afield** Betty Zyvatkauskas. **Directory** Annette Bourdeau.

Maps JS Graphics (john@jsgraphics.co.uk).

Map on page 288 reprinted by kind permission of TTC.

Photography by Matei Glass except: page 10 Corbis; pages 14, 18 (c) Bettmann/Corbis; page 19 Mike Cassese/Reuters/ Corbis; page 25 Reuters/Andrew Wallace; page 26 The Kobal Collection; page 29 Isaiah Trickey, Toronto International Film Festival; page 44 Tom Sandler; page 45 Alex Legault; page 166 Peter Bregg, PhotoSensitive; page 175 Rex Features; page 185 Kelly Mark; page 218 (c)2004, Joan Marcus; page 220 Guntar Kravis; pages 222, 223 Cylla von Tiedemann; page 226 Hannah Levy; page 228 Lesley McCave; page 231 Hulton Archive/Getty Images. The following images were provided by the featured establishment/artist: pages 32, 123, 170, 200, 206, 215, 240, 243

The Editor would like to thank Dalia Blumenthal, Melanie Coates, Natalie Couto, Mike DeToma, Sylvie Dionne, Peter Fink, Ellen Flowers, Trina Hendry, Ellen Himmelfarb, Melissa Macdonald, Aubrey Marshall, Anne Mortensen, Alka Patel and previous *Time Out Toronto* contributors, on whose work parts of this book are based.

Contents

Introduction

There has never been a better time to visit Toronto. Following the SARS outbreak of 2003, the city took two steps back, did some soul-searching, then rebounded, an improved, more vibrant version of its former self. A new mayor, new boutique hotels, spruced-up neighbourhoods, revamps of major sights... the list goes on. There's even a new museum dedicated to the Olympic Games the city didn't get to host. But the enthusiasm doesn't end there: projects due to come to fruition in the next couple of years include a new opera house, an Aga Khan museum, a huge new sound stage to bolster the local movie industry and a new luxury 70-storey hotel and condo complex, courtesy of Donald Trump. In addition, Norman Foster and local boy Frank Gehry join the growing roster of world-renowned architects who have turned their attention to Toronto; the result is some stunning architecture that you'd be mad to miss.

But don't be fooled into thinking it's a façade, a show for the tourists. Toronto is a living, working city, home to 80 well-established communities and 2.4 million people, and more than that number again in the sprawling suburbs. Indeed, it's one of the world's most desirable places to live,

as the statistics will keep reminding you. But it's also a great place to be a visitor. OK, it's not brimming with traditional tourist attractions – you'll have to make the trip to nearby Niagara Falls for that. Rather, it's a place for exploring on foot (or by streetcar), for wandering around historic neighbourhoods, for delving into markets and local shops, for listening to a local band and for people-watching at the latest hip bar. It's also a great place for tucking in – Toronto has a sizeable clutch of excellent eateries that place it in the gastronomic big league.

Of course, there are downsides too, as with any major city. The suburbs are interminable. The waterfront is a mess. The local film industry is under threat. Clubland is heaving at weekends. But that's not bad going for a city of, yes, we'll say it again, 2.4 million people (which, incidentally, has a relatively low crime rate given its size).

With so little to whinge about, and so much going for it, the city could be forgiven for bragging. But it doesn't. There is no pretension here. What you see is what you get – nothing more, nothing less. Give it time to grow on you and you'll find out for yourself what makes Toronto tick.

ABOUT TIME OUT CITY GUIDES

Time Out Toronto is one of an expanding series of travel guides produced by the people behind London and New York's successful listings magazines. Our guides are all written and updated by resident experts who have striven to provide you with all the most up-to-date information you'll need to explore the city, whether you're a local or first-time visitor.

THE LOWDOWN ON THE LISTINGS

Above all, we've tried to make this book as useful as possible. Websites, telephone numbers, transport information, opening times, admission prices and credit card details are all included in our listings. And, as far as possible, we've given details of facilities, services and events, all checked and correct at the time we went to press. However, owners and managers can change their arrangements at any time. Before you go out of your way, we'd strongly advise you to call and check opening times, dates of exhibitions and other particulars.

While every effort has been made to ensure the accuracy of the information contained in this guide, the publishers cannot accept responsibility for any errors it may contain.

PRICES AND PAYMENT

We have noted whether venues such as shops, hotels and restaurants accept credit cards or not but have only listed the major cards – American Express (**AmEx**), Diners Club (**DC**), MasterCard (**MC**) and Visa (**V**). Lots of businesses will also accept other cards, including Switch/Maestro or Delta, JCB, Discover and Carte Blanche. Many shops, restaurants and attractions will accept travellers' cheques issued by a major financial institution (such as American Express).

The prices we've supplied should be treated as guidelines, not gospel. Fluctuating exchange rates and inflation can cause charges, in shops and restaurants particularly, to change rapidly. If prices vary wildly from those we've quoted, ask whether there's a good reason. If not, go

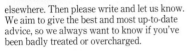

elsewhere. Then please write and let us know. We aim to give the best and most up-to-date advice, so we always want to know if you've been badly treated or overcharged.

THE LIE OF THE LAND
Toronto's geography is easy to grasp. To make it even easier, we have divided the city into areas, which are shown on the Toronto Transport & Areas map on page 287. Our area divisions are based on local usage but as there are no formal boundaries we have occasionally used arbitrary divisions. These areas are defined in our Sightseeing chapters and used throughout the book, both in addresses and chapter subdivisions. We've included cross streets in our addresses, so you can find your way about more easily.

TELEPHONE NUMBERS
Greater Toronto has three area codes: 416, 905 and 647, 416 being the most central. To dial from anywhere within the city to anywhere else, even within the same area code, you need to dial the code followed by the seven-digit number. To dial long-distance numbers, precede the area code with 1 (note that some 905 numbers are long distance). Numbers preceded by 1-800, 1-888, 1-877 and 1-866 can be called free of

charge from Toronto (and usually the rest of Canada and the US) but incur an international charge from abroad.

Canada shares the US's international code of 1 (so calling from the US is the same as making a long-distance national call), followed by 1 and then the area code and number.

For more details of phone codes and charges, *see p264.*

ESSENTIAL INFORMATION
For all the practical information you might need for visiting the city – including visa and customs information, disabled access, emergency telephone numbers, a list of useful websites and the lowdown on the local transport network – turn to the Directory chapter at the back of this guide. It starts on p252.

MAPS
There's a series of fully indexed street maps, along with Southern Ontario and Toronto Overview maps, at the back of the guide, starting on page 274. Venues listed in the book that fall into the area covered have a page and grid reference to take you directly to the right square. There is also a Subway map on page 288.

LET US KNOW WHAT YOU THINK
We hope you enjoy *Time Out Toronto*, and we'd like to know what you think of it. We welcome tips for places that you consider we should include in future editions, and take notice of your criticism of our choices. You can email us on guides@timeout.com.

There is an online version of this book, along with guides to over 45 other international cities, at **www.timeout.com**.

What Londoners take when they go out.

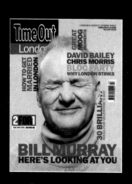

In Context

Yonge Street in the early 20th century.

History

From occupation to invasions, via busts and booms, Toronto still swings.

Toronto means 'meeting place', and the area was so named in the 17th century by the Huron Indians because it it was situated right at the southern end of their forest trails to the Upper Great Lakes. But the region was inhabited long before then. Hunters roamed the icy wilderness where the city now stands at least 13,000 years ago, pursuing caribou and bison with their stone-tipped spears. By 1,000 BC the ice had retreated and the nomadic types had been replaced by Toronto's first settlers: the ancestors of the Iroquois, who built villages along the lake and grew crops. The Huron tribe moved in and brought the first white man to Toronto in 1615…

FRENCH TORONTO

… and that man was a woodsman named Etienne Brûlé, an adventurous young Frenchman sent into the wilds by Samuel Champlain, his fur trader boss in New France (Quebec), to befriend the Indians. Facing frequent attacks from the fierce Iroquois,

the French allied themselves to a rival tribe, the Huron, who showed Toronto to Brûlé on 9 September 1615. During the 17th and 18th centuries French and English fur traders were engaged in a frenetic expansionist rivalry, building trading posts to gain control of the rich hunting grounds around the Great Lakes.

It wasn't until 1720 that the French established a permanent trading post in Toronto, by which time most of the Huron tribe had died from European diseases. Over the next 40 years Toronto's population consisted of a mixture of Mississauga and Iroquois Indians, Jesuit missionaries and French fur traders who exchanged trinkets with the natives in return for pelts. To consolidate their supremacy, the French built Fort Rouillé (also known as Fort Toronto) in 1751, now the site of the Canadian National Exhibition. But in 1756 England and France went to war, and in 1759 the British took Toronto. Rather than surrender their fort, the French burned it to the ground in retreat.

While the 1763 Treaty of Paris brought an end to French rule in Toronto, the British took little interest in their new possession, leaving it undisturbed for 30 years. But when Britain lost the American Revolution in 1783, the city suddenly assumed strategic importance.

BRITISH TORONTO

After the American Revolution, thousands of United Empire Loyalists fled the US to settle in British North America. To handle the massive influx, the British government created a new province in 1791: Upper Canada, to the west of Quebec, which was to have English systems of law, land tenure and politics.

The British appointed John Graves Simcoe, a decorated soldier who had fought in the American Revolution, as the province's lieutenant-governor. His mission was to carve a capital out of the wilderness, and Toronto seemed perfect from a military and naval standpoint. It had a sheltered harbour and a good 20-mile stretch of water separating it from the US. Not only that, but Lord Dorchester, the governor of British North America, had already purchased the site from the Mississauga Indians in 1787 to secure the area for British trappers. For the mighty sum of £1,700, the British gained a portion of land 14 miles across and 28 miles deep.

On 30 July 1793 Simcoe arrived from England – after a brief stint at Niagara – in the forest that was Toronto, with his wife Elizabeth, who fell in love with her new surroundings. One of his first acts was to change Toronto's name to York, in honour of Frederick, Duke of York, a son of King George III. Simcoe, after all, was on a mission to bring English civilisation to the New World. Moreover, he professed an 'abhorrence of Indian names'.

Next Simcoe ordered his regiment, the Queen's Rangers, to build a garrison, Fort York, to protect the settlement from a possible American invasion. He also had his men survey Yonge Street, which replaced the Indian trails to the Upper Great Lakes. Named after the British war secretary, Sir George Yonge, the street would eventually become the world's longest, starting at the lakeshore and running 1,178 miles to the north-west, ending at Rainy River, Minnesota. Yonge Street facilitated fur trade and allowed farmers a route to bring their goods to market. Other roads were also being laid – a very orderly, ten-block grid including King, Front, George, Adelaide and Berkeley Streets – which attracted merchants and craftsmen to the area. But Simcoe's main interest in Yonge Street was strategic: it could prove a useful escape route from marauding Americans.

Simcoe also ordered the construction of the first parliament buildings, which were erected in 1796. To placate grumpy colonial officials, resentful of being transferred to this marshy outpost, he granted them a series of free 100-acre 'park' lots north of Queen Street. The roads that ran between these farms were often given family names, including Finch, Sheppard, Lawrence and Eglinton. This system of land concessions resulted in Toronto's very rectangular, evenly spaced layout. Despite Simcoe's generosity, the new residents were disparaging of the town, referring to it as 'Muddy York' because of its notoriously squishy streets. They were, after all, essentially living in the wilderness: packs of wolves were killing farmers' sheep, bears were attacking horses, and deer were commonly seen on the streets.

> ## 'Within a year of declaring war, York's worst nightmare – an American invasion – became a grim reality.'

THE 1812 OVERTHROW

By 1812 York was positively civilised: it had a tailor, a baker, a brewer, a watchmaker and an apothecary to serve the population of 700. The ruling elite erected dignified mansions along King Street, and a British-style landed gentry was firmly taking shape. York's leaders were all Church of England Tories, and fiercely Loyalist – they were horrified by American notions of democracy. And this anti-American sentiment was about to intensify.

On 18 June 1812 America declared war on Britain. Former president Thomas Jefferson had said that 'the capture of Canada is a mere matter of marching'. President James Madison wanted to establish a trade monopoly on all North America's natural resources. Americans were also furious at the devious British practices of kidnapping their sailors at sea and supplying arms and encouragement to hostile Indian tribes.

Within a year of declaring war, York's worst nightmare – an American invasion – became a grim reality. In April 1813, 14 ships carrying 1,700 American troops invaded the town, and succeeded in blowing up Fort York and burning the parliament buildings to the ground. But although Americans won the Battle of York, the US army suffered devastating losses and failed to take the rest of Canada. By 1814 the British had negotiated an end to the war.

You saw it here first

Inventions, icons and institutions that all call Toronto home.

● Edward Rogers Sr invented the world's first alternating current (AC) radio tube in 1925, which enabled radios to be powered by ordinary household current. The revolutionary 'batteryless' radio became the key factor in popularising radio usage.

● The discovery of the pancreatic hormone insulin by scientists Frederick Banting and Charles Best at the University of Toronto in 1921 is the most famous Canadian medical achievement. Insulin remains the only effective treatment for diabetes.

● Along a similar theme, the pacemaker was invented by Dr John A Hopps at the University of Toronto in 1950. Ironically, Hopps himself later needed the device to regulate his own heart.

● The world's first fully electronic toll highway, Highway 407. A camera records licence plates and a bill is sent in the post.

● MAC Cosmetics, one of the world's most popular brands of make-up, was founded by Torontonians in the 1980s.

● The world's first permanent AIDS memorial was erected in 1993 in Cawthra Park, Church & Wellesley.

● Canada's wealthiest individual – by a long shot – and currently 15th richest in the world, according to *Forbes*, is Torontonian Kenneth Thomson, son of Roy Thomson (*see p18*). He derives his $17.2 billion from a 69 per cent stake in media giant Thomson. As an art lover, he recently pledged $50 million towards the expansion of the Art Gallery of Ontario, and in 2002 famously paid the third highest price ever for a painting (£49.5 million), the *Massacre of the Innocents* by Peter Paul Rubens.

● Though Thomas Edison is widely regarded as the inventor of the electric lightbulb, Henry Woodward of Toronto should really take some credit, as he sold a share in his patent to Edison, who went on to design a more practical version in 1879.

● In nearby Brantford, Ontario, Alexander Graham Bell first outlined the scientific principle that would convey the human voice over wires in 1874, two years before 'inventing' the telephone in Boston. Later that year, Bell made the first long-distance telephone call from his home in Brantford to Paris, Ontario.

THE FAMILY COMPACT

In retaliation for the burning of Fort York, a group of angry local soldiers went down to Washington, DC, in 1814 and set fire to the president's residence. (It was painted white soon after to cover up the charred wood, and subsequently became known as the White House.) American immigrants, who had previously been welcome additions to the town, were now banned by York's staunchly British, aristocratic leaders. Indeed, York's ruling political regime, composed mainly of lawyers, doctors, judges and Church officials, was so tight-knit, and prone to intermarriage, that it became known as the Family Compact. This elite group's stranglehold on politics would come to be resented as the population grew.

And grow the population did. In Britain the demobilisation of 400,000 soldiers following the Napoleonic wars, coupled with a depression and the mass evictions of Scottish crofters, prompted a huge exodus to Canada. In the 20 years following the war, the town's population increased from 700 to 9,250.

The Old Guard suffered a blow in 1834, the year the town became incorporated as a city, when a bill to readopt the name of Toronto. Traditionalists were opposed to the move – York sounded more British.

REBEL YELLS

Around this time, resentment at the Family Compact's political dominance reached fever pitch. Even Charles Dickens, who visited the city in 1842, was moved to comment on the city's Conservative bent. 'The wild and rabid Toryism of Toronto is, I speak seriously, appalling.' Leading the resistance was William Lyon Mackenzie, a Scottish firebrand who had been publishing anti-Tory rants in his own newspaper, the *Colonial Advocate*, since 1825. Mackenzie called the ruling elite 'thieves', arguing that too much money, land and power was held by too few. The main target for his scorn was Bishop John Strachan, whom he dubbed 'the governor's jackal'. Mackenzie's bilious columns became such a worry for the Family Compact that Conservatives broke into his office and tipped his printing presses into the lake. But it was too late: Mackenzie had already amassed a devoted following of farmers, merchants and new immigrants, and in 1834 he was elected Toronto's first mayor.

Mackenzie hoped that a provincial election in 1836 would bring his party, the Reformers, to power in the province of Upper Canada. But the Tories won what was perceived to be a crooked election – one Conservative ploy was to offer free booze to anyone who voted for them – and Mackenzie called for rebellion.

On 5 December 1837 Mackenzie and 700 rebels gathered beyond the city, at what is now Yonge and Eglinton, outside Montgomery's Tavern. The plan was to march on Toronto, seize the 5,000 guns stored in City Hall, and capture the governor. But the sheriff, William B Jarvis, had been tipped off, and his militia crushed the rebellion. Mackenzie fled to America and lived there until 1849, when

he was pardoned. He returned to Upper Canada and was elected to the Legislature, where he served until his death in 1858.

Despite the failure of the rebellion, a new era of more democratic government followed, coinciding with another wave of immigration. In addition to the British influx, scores of freed black slaves arrived from America. Britain officially outlawed slavery in 1834, and by the 1850s blacks made up three per cent of the city's 25,000-strong population.

Another group found refuge in York – the Irish. They arrived in droves, particularly in the 1840s, to escape the potato famine at home, and soon comprised a third of Toronto's population. Many were Catholic, which provoked sectarian tensions with the Irish Protestants. Riots on July 12, the day of the Orangemen parades, became an annual occurrence.

Union Station – still glorious after 80 years. *See p16.*

Crimes and misdemeanours

Go ahead, poke fun at Toronto's squeaky-clean image. But the truth is that the city hasn't always been the civilised, law-abiding, progressive place it is today. It has a dark side, replete with bandits, bootleggers, rebellion, riots, rogues and – if you can bear to imagine it – illegal tobogganing.

Heaven help you if you found yourself on the wrong side of the law in the 18th century. At that time petty crimes were punished with branding on the tongue, and you could be hanged for at least 120 different offences.

In the late 1800s the Toronto police began to enforce an invasive group of strictures to ensure locals conducted themselves with the proper decorum upon the Lord's Day. Known as the 'Sabbath Laws', they banned businesses from serving the public, prohibited streetcars from running and made popular pastimes (including tobogganing) illegal.

Even Toronto's first mayor, William Lyon Mackenzie, was a rebel, leading a mob of hundreds down Yonge Street in an armed revolt to overthrow the government (see p13). Two of his brothers-in-arms were not so lucky. Peter Matthews and Samuel Lount were caught and hanged before a huge crowd at the corner of King and Toronto. (A plaque hangs in the sandwich shop that's now on the site). The rebellion was instrumental in helping to create the reforms that define democratic and legal traditions in Canada to this day.

Not all acts of public rage in Toronto had such noble outcomes. On a hot day in August 1933 a baseball tournament at the Christie Pits in the West End turned into a riot. At the time, Hitler's fascist ideology was gaining currency with the disaffected around the world. The riot broke out when a group of Nazi sympathisers unfurled swastika banners and hurled abuse at a team with a number of Jewish players. Although local papers foreshadowed (and, some say, helped to provoke) the tensions, police were strangely absent as the ensuing fracas swelled into a riot involving 10,000 people, pitting ethnic minorities against each other. Injuries were numerous, but no charges were laid.

A further look into Toronto's crime file will unveil a shadowy cast of infamous evil-doers and troublemakers. Lifelong criminal 'Red' Ryan did such a convincing makeover of himself in prison that the then Prime Minister, RB Bennett, made him a test case for new rehabilitation leniency. Upon his release in 1934 he was given a second chance and landed a job as a journalist for the *Toronto Star*. But early the following year the new poster boy for rehabilitation was shot dead after a robbing a liquor store and murdering a policeman. Apparently, he had been pulling heists – and the wool over everyone's eyes – since the day he got out.

By the late 1940s as many as 50 youth gangs were terrorising the public. Today's newspapers still love to print scary stories about modern gangs, but in reality Toronto is safer than many big cities of a comparable size. Indeed, the closest thing to a brush with the law you're likely to get while in town is a trip to the **Toronto Police Museum** (40 College Street (416 808 7020, www.toronto police.on.ca/museum). Entry is free, and here you'll find, as well as a succinct history of the Toronto force, uniforms, badges and cars, plus interactive displays with radio dispatch calls from notorious local crimes.

If you want to get closer to the underworld, wander past the old **Don Jail** (559 Gerard Street East, at Broadview Avenue, East Toronto). Designed by William Thomas in 1863, and expanded in the 1950s, it is considered by many to be an architectural triumph of its time. Others have called it a dungeon and likened it to the Black Hole of Calcutta. Either way, the prison has a legacy of overcrowding, violence and disease, and there's constant pressure to close or even demolish it. While gazing at the joint, you may get a sense of déjà vu: the Don has featured in dozens of feature films, including several by local shock maestro David Cronenberg.

While immigrants flooded the city, Native Canadians disappeared from the area. Many died of European diseases, while some settled on nearby Indian reserves – such as the Six Nations Reserve near Brantford – that were established in treaties with the British throughout the period.

INDEPENDENCE DAY

As immigrants poured in, Toronto made the transition from rural backwater to bustling industrial city. The construction of a north–south railway line to America in the 1850s, followed by a coast-to-coast national line in the 1880s, further cemented Toronto's prosperity. In addition to the existing industries – sawmills, flour mills, tanneries, furniture, wagons, soap processing, leather goods, brewing, publishing – the city became a centre for ship manufacture and a trading hub for timber imports and exports. Banks appeared everywhere, merchant empires were founded, railroad tycoons emerged and the Toronto Stock Exchange was opened in 1852.

'Leopold Infeld famously said that he hoped he would die on a Saturday "so that I won't have to spend another Sunday in Toronto".'

If it was an age of industry, it was also an age of leisure. In 1858 Toronto's freakish weather for once provided the city with a blessing: the creation of Toronto Island. Formerly a peninsula, the island was created when a storm destroyed the spit of land that joined it to the mainland. Taking a ferry across the harbour soon became a summertime tradition: holiday cottages went up, as did an amusement park, bicycle trails and the Royal Canadian Yacht Club.

In 1867 Canada gained independence from Britain, and Toronto was named the capital of the new province of Ontario. An accolade, sure, but competition was hardly stiff, and locals were (and remain) more than miffed that Queen Victoria, apparently on the basis of a few paintings she'd seen, favoured Ottawa as the national capital. However, as a small compensation, Toronto finally got some decent shopping. In 1869, a young Irishman named Timothy Eaton opened a general store at the corner of Yonge and Queen. His new shop offered a revolutionary and exciting sales technique: satisfaction guaranteed or your money back. The successful shop quickly evolved into a bona fide department store,

spawning a mail-order catalogue that eventually reached all corners of Canada.

During this prosperous Victorian era, Toronto's architecture also became downright glamorous. The opening of the University of Toronto in 1843 was significant for more than just academic reasons: it yielded some of the city's most ornate buildings, most notably the spectacular Romanesque University College (King's College Circle, 1856). Throughout the city, the dignified colonial town of plain Georgian buildings gave way to a new craze for neo-Gothic. Jarvis and St George streets and the neighbourhood of Rosedale became hotbeds of Romanticism in a flurry of gargoyles and turrets. The American author John Updike called these buildings 'lovingly erected brick valentines to a distant dowager queen'. Surviving examples include the Keg Mansion (515 Jarvis Street), the Flatiron building (49 Wellington Street East, 1892), the York Club (135 St George Street, 1892), the Ontario Legislature at Queen's Park (1892) and the Old City Hall (1888-99).

Some of the most striking buildings of the period were Gothic churches, such as St James' Cathedral (65 Church Street, 1850). The city's preponderance of spires, coupled with its puritanical mores, soon earned it the sobriquet 'Toronto the Good'. Anti-vice laws at various times in the city's history would include a ban on alcohol between 1916 and 1927, and Sunday bans on just about everything (*see p14* **Crimes and misdemeanours**). Department stores drew curtains across their windows on Sundays, and public houses were closed on the Sabbath until 1971. Leopold Infeld, Einstein's collaborator, famously said that he hoped he would die on a Saturday 'so that I won't have to spend another Sunday in Toronto'.

The city's rather prissy outlook was coupled with a continued devotion to Queen and country. The Queen's Jubilee was celebrated in spectacular style in 1897, and on 25 October 1899 a massive parade sent off thousands of Toronto troops to fight in the Boer War, in a frenzy of Union Jacks and weeping mothers.

20TH-CENTURY TORONTO

If the 19th century ended in a surge of imperial fervour, then Toronto's 20th century started with a blaze of a different kind. On 19 April 1904, fire broke out at a downtown tie factory on Wellington Street West, and within eight hours, 122 buildings and 20 acres of downtown had been destroyed.

While the Great Fire devastated the city on one level – 6,000 people lost their jobs and the business district was destroyed – Toronto bounced back quickly. How could it not, with the wave of immigrants flooding in? In 1894 the population was 168,000; by 1924 it had risen to 542,000 and by 1934 it was 640,000. And they weren't all British. Jews from Russia and Poland settled in Kensington Market and opened textile businesses around King and Spadina, the garment district; Greeks worked on the railroads and made the Danforth their home. By 1921, more than 8,200 Torontonians were of Italian ancestry, many of whom built roads and bridges. The Chinese settled around Dundas Street West, opening laundries and restaurants.

The New World wasn't all bliss. Many Irish labourers settled in Cabbagetown, an area in the east of the city named for the vegetables they grew to feed themselves. Toronto writer Hugh Garner described Cabbagetown – now a gentrified neighbourhood – as 'North America's only Anglo-Saxon slum'.

WORLD WAR I

As is often perversely the case, war – in this case World War I – brought renewed prosperity to the city, not to mention another bout of imperial zeal. Citizens sang 'Rule Britannia' in the streets, and thousands of volunteers poured into armouries. Seventy thousand men – one seventh of Toronto's population – left Toronto for Europe; 13,000 died.

The city played a major role in Britain's war effort, serving as a training ground for pilots. Toronto companies manufactured aeroplanes, including the famous Flying Jennies, and explosives and munitions. Jewish textile firms made blankets, tents and uniforms. Women went to work in large numbers, in weapons factories and as volunteer Red Cross nurses. In fact, a young Amelia Earhart was a nurse in Toronto during the war, and it was here, while watching pilots at Armour Heights, that she caught the flying bug.

THE ROARING '20S

The end of the war was followed by a mini economic slump, but by 1925 Toronto was roaring, spurred along by the age of the automobile. American firms such as General Motors and Ford set up plants in and around the city to avoid a 35 per cent Canadian tariff on car imports. Not everyone was driving around in Buicks, however: the Toronto Transit Commission was founded in 1921, after the public voted to establish a publicly owned and operated mass transit system. Soon 575 electric streetcars cruised the streets.

The city was also reaping the benefits of a mining boom in Northern Ontario, triggered by the discovery there of gold, copper, nickel and silver. The price of wheat on the international market also rocketed during this period, which meant that the agricultural machinery plants of Massey-Harris flourished.

Such a wealthy city required a spectacular hotel, and in 1929 the Royal York, with its 1,600 rooms, running water and ballroom, opened. The largest hotel in the British Empire, it was built by the Canadian Pacific Railway for easy access to the similarly magnificent Union Station (1927), a Beaux Arts gem that epitomised the grandeur of the railway age.

DEPRESSION, AND WAR AGAIN

Wealth provided riches for culture seekers, who flocked to the Art Gallery of Ontario to see the striking landscape paintings of the Group of Seven, Canada's most famous painters, or view

Flock to the **Eaton Centre**. *See p18.*

Egyptian mummies at the Royal Ontario Museum. Performers such as Al Jolson entertained the masses at the Royal Alexandra Theatre, and hometown girl Mary Pickford, the world's biggest silent movie star, drew the hordes to Shea's Hippodrome.

The good times came to an end with the stockmarket crash of 1929, and by the time the Great Depression hit in 1932, there was 30 per cent unemployment in the city. Queues formed around the block for soup kitchens. Poverty lead to bigotry, with signs that read 'No Jews, Niggers or Dogs' appearing on beaches. The scorching summer of 1936 compounded the misery, with temperatures reaching 41°C (106°F), coinciding with a polio epidemic. World War II brought the city back to life. As in the previous two wars, Toronto rushed to sign up for military duty – 3,300 would ultimately die in combat – but along with the exodus of soldiers, the city experienced its own European invasion: British children and Norwegian men. Eight thousand young Britons were shipped to Toronto to sit out the war safely, while Norway sent its airforce to the city for training. Once again the city functioned as an aviation centre, with local companies manufacturing around 3,000 airplanes, including the Mosquito bombers that some experts believe played a large part in winning the air war. Women once again took up work in the factories, producing 100,000 machine guns. And in the tunnels of Casa Loma – the city's most eccentric architectural folly – anti-submarine weapons were developed.

Behind this industriousness lay a continued fierce loyalty to the Mother Country, which helped Canadian citizens endure rationing on alcohol, sugar, meat and tea, and frequent 'dim-outs'. In 1940, when the Toronto Squadron was shot down in the skies above London, the Toronto Symphony Orchestra played 'There'll Always Be an England' at Massey Hall.

BOOMTOWN STATS

Toronto's white-bread, Little England persona was about to receive a makeover. In 1920, 80 per cent of the city's population was of British origin. By 1960 only 50 per cent of the population could make that claim, and by the 90s, well, the UN had declared Toronto the most multicultural city on earth – Toronto had more Italians than Florence, more blacks than Kingston, Jamaica, and more Chinese than any other city in the world outside China. After the war, Canada had relaxed its immigration laws, and it seemed the world came to Toronto. Russians, Yugoslavs, Poles, Hungarians and other many other Eastern Europeans poured into the city, as did Portuguese, Greeks and West Indians, followed later by further waves of immigration from India, Africa, Central and South America and Asia.

By 1953 the population of the Toronto urban area had mushroomed to 1.2 million. Disputes between the city and the suburbs were growing frequent, and the need for unified social services was so great that an effective administrative solution was required. The result was the establishment of a new, overarching city government: the Municipality of Metropolitan Toronto, which would be comprised of the city of Toronto, plus five suburban boroughs: North York, East York, York, Scarborough and Etobicoke, each with its own mayor. This new government would be responsible for major infrastructure, while the individual municipalities would still retain control over local matters.

> **'It was like finding a Jaguar parked in front of a vicarage and the padre inside with a pitcher of vodka Martinis reading *Lolita*.'**

The mayor of this new super-city, Fred Gardiner, had grand visions of a great North American metropolis with major highways running through it: the first, the monstrous Gardiner Expressway, was laid down during the '50s along the lakeshore, effectively cutting off the city from the lake. The 401, a mega-highway to the north of the city, followed soon after, as did malls, malls, malls and utopian, post-war suburbs, perfect for raising baby-boomers. Don Mills, built in 1952, was a modernist's dream, designed to be a self-contained suburb where the car was king. Scarborough, a pretty farming community, became a nightmare of strip malls, factories and bungalows. This was followed in 1962 by Yorkdale, the first giant mall in North America, adjacent to Highway 401 in the northern suburbs.

In the city centre, developers started ripping down old Victorian and Edwardian buildings – which were seen as fading relics of colonial Toronto and the Depression – and replacing them with high-rise apartment buildings and office blocks. Between 1955 and 1975, 28,000 buildings were torn down in the city.

THE NEW TORONTO

It wasn't a complete travesty. Many pretty, centrally located neighbourhoods – the Annex, Rosedale, Forest Hill and Cabbagetown included – managed to avoid the wrecking ball. And the

Messaging the medium

Canadians, it has been argued, are particularly adept at building media and communications empires. Some say it comes out of necessity, given the country's vast distances. But a company can only grow so big with such a small population, so home-grown titans generally look abroad to build their dynasties. It is then perhaps not a surprise that Canada also produced one of the world's most influential communications gurus of the 20th-century.

Marshall McLuhan (1911–80; *pictured left*), born in Edmonton, looked beyond the confines of his native country to dazzle and confuse the masses, coining some of the most resonant slogans of his era, including 'the medium is the message' and 'the global village'. During his tenure as an English professor at the University of Toronto (1946–79) he expounded on the role of mass media in society during a period when three Canadian newspaper barons were gaining global influence with their expanding empires.

The press magnates in question were William Maxwell Aitken (1879–1964), Roy Thomson (1894–1976) and Conrad Black (born 1944; *pictured right*). Of the three, two were born in Toronto, while the third solidified his base here. During their careers they went on to wield significant influence on Fleet Street, snagging British titles for themselves along the way.

Aitken made a fortune in cement by the time he was 30. He took his riches to London and was elected to the House of Commons as a Conservative. He was granted the title Lord Beaverbrook during World War I while serving in the cabinet of Lloyd George,

and acquired a controlling interest in the *Daily Express*, turning it into the most widely read newspaper in the world. He told his readers his newspaper was 'the prophet of equal opportunity' and railed against a system that bestowed favouritism on an elite class. He founded the *Sunday Express* and in 1929 purchased the *Evening Standard* – securing a significant hold on the English

first subway line, consisting of 12 stations and running for 7.4 miles underneath Yonge Street, opened in 1954. This was to be followed by new lines and extensions throughout the remainder of the century, resulting in today's sprawling underground and suburban rail network.

Moreover, some of the new buildings were stunning. The Toronto-Dominion Centre (1964-9), a cluster of four black steel and glass skyscrapers, was hailed as the crowning glory in the career of Mies van der Rohe, one of the gods of modernist architecture.

The New City Hall, built in 1965, was another modernist classic. Designed by Finnish architect Viljo Revell, this *Star Trek*-style

spectacle – two semi-circular office towers surrounding a UFO-esque council chamber – adjoined by a public square, symbolising the birth of a more civic-spirited city. Other modern gems included the gold-coated Royal Bank Plaza (1976), the atrium-style Eaton Centre shopping mall (1977) and the Toronto Reference Library (1977).

But of all the new buildings, the CN Tower (1976) was the most important symbolically. The world's largest freestanding structure, this majestic television tower became Toronto's Big Ben or Empire State Building, lending the city an instantly recognisable skyline. 'As the tower was being planned, Torontonians were starting

newspaper market – and later served in Winston Churchill's World War II cabinet.

By the time Roy Thomson made it to England's shores in 1952, he too had made a fortune from businesses as diverse as women's hairdressing salons, ice-cream cone manufacturing and 19 Canadian newspapers. He bought *The Scotsman* newspaper, a TV licence and Britain's largest newspaper group, Kemsley, which included the *Sunday Times*. By the time he was made 1st Baron Thomson of Fleet in 1964, he controlled a conglomerate of 200 newspapers and had interests in publishing, TV, travel and oil. When he died his title passed to his son, Kenneth Thomson (*see also p12* **You saw it here first**). Both men shared a disdain for ostentatious displays of wealth: though ranked among the richest men in the world, they took the subway to work.

Such a lack of pretension could scarcely be said of Conrad Black, whose desperate bid to join the House of Lords was finally achieved by relinquishing his Canadian citizenship in 2001 – to become Lord Black of Crossharbour.

Born in Montreal the son of a wealthy brewing executive, he amassed a string of small Canadian newspapers by his mid-20s. By the late 1990s he was the third-largest publisher of newspapers in the world, his portfolio including the *Daily Telegraph*, *Chicago Sun-Times* and *Jerusalem Post*, plus 60 per cent of all Canadian newspaper titles.

Black's empire began to unravel in 2003 when his board levied charges that he had diverted shareholders' funds for personal gain. Accusations piled up, as did the number of alleged missing millions, until in 2004 Black was removed as chairman and Hollinger International filed suit to reclaim $200 million. The US Securities and Exchange Commission has charged him with fraud while class-action suits seek billions of dollars in damages. At the time of writing, Black had retreated to his suburban Toronto mansion to await his fate.

to consider, with shy pleasure, the novel idea that their city might be attractive, even enviable,' wrote journalist Robert Fulford.

THE CITY SWINGS

Along with this great wave of construction and immigration, the once-uptight city was at last outgrowing its starchy, Waspish image. In 1947, the people of Toronto voted to go 'wet', and the city's first cocktail bar, the Silver Rail, opened on Yonge Street, spawning a thriving bar culture. A British writer who returned to this relatively louche city in 1959 said 'it was like finding a Jaguar parked in front of a vicarage and the padre inside with a pitcher of vodka Martinis reading *Lolita*'.

By the 1960s Toronto was becoming positively hedonistic. Spliff-smoking flower children colonised Yorkville, playing acoustic music in coffeehouses and forming Toronto's answer to San Francisco's Haight-Ashbury district. Here, Joni Mitchell, Neil Young and Leonard Cohen all played the circuit. In 1972 Toronto got a hip television station, Citytv, which caused a stir by showing blue movies in the wee hours. Around this time, strip joints and adult movie theatres opened along downtown Yonge Street – even now US tourists flock to the city for its famously permissive nudity and lap-dancing laws – as did bars frequented by Toronto's burgeoning gay community. Jarvis Street, once home to Toronto's wealthiest families, became the city's unofficial red light district. It wasn't all salacious: amid the general buzz, the city became home to an increasing number of renowned writers, including Robertson Davies and Margaret Atwood. The Toronto International Film Festival made its debut in 1975, and the local government poured money into the theatre.

The thriving cultural scene attracted, and was strengthened by, Americans dodging the Vietnam War. Another anti-war protester with vision was Jane Jacobs, the famed urban planning critic who in 1971 led a successful fight against the proposed Spadina Expressway, which would have destroyed several downtown neighbourhoods. This victory spurred a civic reform movement in the '70s that emphasised preservation of historic neighbourhoods, public transport and smart development, including valuable, publicly funded projects designed to lure visitors to the city: Ontario Place (a waterfront park) in 1971, and the Metro Zoo and Ontario Science Centre in 1974.

Tourists certainly discovered Toronto in the '70s, but so also did architects, urban planners and journalists. The US media was impressed that a city of its size had managed to avoid the mistakes of many a crime-ridden, dying American metropolis. *Time* magazine devoted a cover story to 'the world's newest great city', *Harper's* dubbed it 'the city that works' and the actor Peter Ustinov called it 'New York run by the Swiss'. And the *National Geographic* announced that 'the drab stepsister of Montreal has become worldly, wealthy and relatively problem-free'. In fact, Toronto officially took over from Montreal as Canada's most populous city in 1976, when its population hit 2,303,206.

UP, UP... AND DOWN AGAIN

The 'me decade' brought some glamour and decadence to the city. Yorkville, once beatnik central, became the city's most exclusive shopping district, its old Edwardian houses transformed into chi-chi boutiques, while bond traders snorted lines in its embarrassingly flashy bars. Formerly poor immigrant areas like Cabbagetown, Greektown and Little Italy were discovered, and gentrified, by yuppies: great for the restaurant scene, bad for house prices. The gay community colonised the Church & Wellesley district during the 1980s. As the population mushroomed – 65,000 new immigrants arrived in Toronto every year – a development boom saw modest suburban bungalows demolished in favour of gigantic 'monster homes' crammed on to tiny lots.

Architectural showpieces that were erected during the era included Roy Thomson Hall (the new home of the Toronto Symphony, 1982), and SkyDome, an engineering marvel with its retractable roof (1989). Three spectacularly ornate vaudeville theatres from the early 1900s were lovingly restored and reopened as commercial theatres: the Elgin, the Winter Garden and the Pantages (now the Canon), where *Phantom of the Opera* made its debut in 1985, kickstarting a now thriving theatre scene. Toronto's cosmopolitan appeal began to attract US film producers, who discovered Toronto's versatility as a stand-in location for movies set elsewhere.

The conspicuous consumption and glamorous living of the 1980s continued apace in the '90s, but was accompanied by a loss of social conscience; indeed, the 'problem-free 1970s' seemed a distant memory. Toronto elected its very own Margaret Thatcher in the form of the right-wing, neo-conservative Ontario premier Mike Harris, who slashed funding for the city, a move that sent its outward appearance into a downward spiral magnifying myriad problems, from homelessness to potholes. Meanwhile, Harris courted the suburban vote by expanding highways and allowing urban sprawl to fester. The city's five boroughs were amalgamated in 1998 into one massive, 'megacity' government, which effectively removed self-rule from neighbourhoods and resulted in further cuts to public services. As the first mayor of the new Toronto, Mel Lastman proved woefully inept and led a scandal-ridden office while the city suffered.

OUT WITH THE OLD...

Politicians don't solve problems in a vacuum – it takes a city's collective spirit to bring about change. Tossing out the old guard was a good place to start. The deadly outbreak of SARS in 2003 was a rude wake-up call for Toronto, one that continues to impact the economy even now. Many blamed the years of cutbacks in public services for leaving the city vulnerable.

Now midway into the first decade of this century, Toronto has a new mayor, David Miller, a left-leaning dark horse candidate who was swept into office in late 2003 literally clutching a broom as he promised to sweep corruption from City Hall. On a wider scale, Ontario has a Liberal government under Dalton McGuinty that has yet to win over the hearts and minds of 13 million Ontarians.

Meanwhile, Toronto continues to expand, despite of growing pains along the way, the city consistently finishes near the top of the UN world survey of desirable places to live.

Toronto Today

Forget about being world-class: Toronto is starting to shine on its own terms.

You could say Toronto got off to a rough start in the 21st century. The city that had shone for so long as a beacon of tolerance, racial integration, livability and, heck, just a nice place to be, had lost its lustre. The toll from years of raiding the municipal coffers by a rapacious provincial government was evident everywhere, from the growing number of homeless to the mundane nuisances of potholes and mounting garbage – and in Toronto cleanliness is next to godliness. An incompetent mayor let developers run roughshod over the city's attempts at urban planning, and 'growth for growth's sake' was the mantra as the condo towers rose and life down on the street grew a little shabby.

Then came a wake-up call in the nasty form of a killer virus. In spring 2003, citizens were sporting facemasks to protect themselves from SARS (Severe Acute Respiratory Syndrome).

Forty-four people succumbed to the air-borne terror, with paroxysms of fear and loathing gripping the happy city. Ever wanting to be seen as a 'world-class' kind of place, Toronto had finally got the world's attention, though not in the way it intended. And all of a sudden, people stopped coming here. So, what happens then?

THE CITY STRIKES BACK

After quarantines and curfews and a red alert from the WHO, the virus had run its course. In the new, safe dawn that followed, a whole lot of soul-searching began. Among the thorny issues that popped up as a result of SARS was the nagging question: why would anyone come to Toronto anyway? Apart from a new corporate playpen-cum-sports arena, there hadn't been a major new addition to the city's cultural diversions in over a decade. Caught resting

Say cheese! Visitors soaking up the sights (**Nathan Phillips Square**).

on its laurels, Toronto recognised there were a lot of other cities out there vying for the tourist and convention trade.

What was needed was some spit and polish and a new image, a slogan to shout from the rooftops. Something. Anything. The Rolling Stones were wheeled in for some emotional rescue and headlined an all-day concert in Downsview Park dubbed 'SARSstock'. It drew 800,000 people on a warm summer's night, and Mick Jagger proclaimed that Toronto was back in business.

As it happens, a number of developments were already taking shape to put the city back on a solid footing. The cultural sector had been lobbying hard to get the government to pitch in to revamp the tired infrastructure of museums and theatres. And there was a whole lot of money to be coerced from wealthy citizens, for whom the concept of family-crested philanthropy had never quite caught on in the way it has in the US. The taps started to flow, and suddenly Toronto was preparing to blossom with a full-on renaissance that is

unfolding in 2005 and will continue for a number a years, with a programme tentatively titled 'Creative City'.

All the mega-projects under way place an emphasis on architecture. Some of the world's best have been called upon to put a new spin on this modern city. Daniel Libeskind is remaking the Royal Ontario Museum with a dramatic glass pyramid that will loom out over Bloor Street W. Norman Foster is spiffing up a high-profile corner of Queen's Park with an academic building for the University of Toronto. Just down the street, another British architect, Will Alsop, has unleashed the most revolutionary structure since New City Hall opened 40 years ago – at the Ontario College of Art & Design. Around the corner, Toronto-born Frank Gehry is bringing his titanium touch to the Art Gallery of Ontario, while another local, Jack Diamond, has designed the new opera/ballet house at Queen Street and University Avenue. In the suburb of Don Mills, acclaimed Japanese architect Fumihiko Maki will design the Aga Khan Museum and Indian architect Charles

Correa has been commissioned to design for the Ismaili Centre. Add to the list upgrades and new performance and gallery spaces at the Royal Conservatory of Music, the Ontario Science Centre, the Gardiner Museum of Ceramic Art, the National Ballet School, Soulpepper Theatre and the Hummingbird Centre for the Performing Arts (Libeskind, again), and suddenly there's a whole lot of new happening in Toronto.

> **'There is now a desire to commemorate – even flaunt – the accomplishments of the city's staid past.'**

Torontonians were ready for change. To lead the charge they voted in a new mayor, a left-wing, dark-horse candidate with a Harvard degree and experience as a Bay Street lawyer. The English-born David Miller captured the popular imagination with his call to clean up the corruption at City Hall and the filth in the streets. Clichéd as it was, he used a broom as a symbol for his campaign in autumn 2003 and was duly swept into office. The issue that turned the election in his favour was a vow to stop a little bridge from being built at the foot of Bathurst Street to the island airport. That bridge came to symbolise all that had been wrong with the city's priorities: unchecked development over quality of life, and diktat over consultation. The bridge would have brought expansion to the money-losing airport, along with bigger planes and the noise and air pollution that comes with them. For now, the airport remains a privileged playground for recreational pilots and is accessed by what's called the shortest ferry ride in the world.

DON'T LOOK BACK IN INDIFFERENCE

It's fair to say there is a renewed sense of optimism at the mid-point of the decade. The Toronto-based author Margaret Atwood remarked in early 2005: 'Toronto for a while was a city that didn't have any civic pride and destroyed things because nobody seemed to care – that is changing.' Certainly, there is a legacy of demolishing what went before in the name of progress, but several new gestures suggest there is now a desire to commemorate – even flaunt – the accomplishments of the city's staid past to preserve a collective memory. Street signs acknowledging famous Torontonians have sprung up, honouring the likes of media guru Marshall McLuhan, film director Norman Jewison and comedian Mike Myers. Curiously, Oscar Peterson had a square named after him even though the jazz great

hails from Montreal, whereas Toronto-born Gil Evans, who went on to shape the sound of cool jazz as Miles Davis' long-time producer, goes unacknowledged. After losing out to Beijing to host the 2008 Summer Olympics, Toronto was bound by its desperate, 11th-hour promise to erect an everlasting temple to the Olympic spirit. The result is a new museum at Dundas Square. With Vancouver hosting the 2010 Winter Games, it's unlikely Toronto will get another shot for a long time to come.

Civic gestures aside, Toronto has an unstoppable energy that finds new outlets for expression. The music and club scenes thrive as bands come up through the ranks and many take their rightful place on the world stage. The art scene is buzzing with two new destinations, one in the Distillery District and the other across town on the hip West Queen West strip. In the first edition of this guide, they barely rated a mention. Now they are must-see attractions. Visitors also have new options for boutique and unique hotels, including the Drake and Le Germain. And Toronto's restaurants continue to serve up the world on a plate.

GROWTH SPURTS

A magnet for waves of immigrants –
the backbone of the vibrant society that
defines today's metropolis – Toronto remains,
unquestionably, a desirable place to live. To
the city's credit, this assimilation has occurred
hand-in-hand with acceptance, even a sense of
celebration, of diversity. There are around 80
substantial, well-established ethnic groups here.
The challenge now is to manage the continuing
expansion properly. Urban sprawl is a huge
problem as the subtopia grows. Depending
on who you ask, Toronto is home to two or
five million people. The city proper, that is the
part known as Metropolitan Toronto before it
was amalgamated with the suburbs in 1998
into one 'mega-city', has 2.4 million people.
The combined population of the satellite cities
of Mississauga, Brampton, Richmond Hill,
Markham and Pickering is larger, creating two
Torontos that are separated by the symbolically
charged 416 area code of the city and 905
code for beyond. All signs point to another
one million inhabitants in the Greater Toronto
Area (GTA) by 2030.

LET'S TALK IT OVER

A thriving downtown core where people
actually choose to live rather than escape from
at the end of the day has spared Toronto the
post-working hours blight that afflicts many

American cities. This has been reinforced
by a strong sense of neighbourhood and a
collective spirit that seems to keep the place
on the right track. The crime rate remains
well below that of cities of comparable size
in the US, although the number of gun-related
incidents is on the rise. Having attained a
certain level of confidence about what Toronto
is, there is a lot of discussion now about what
the city can be. Such talk would have been
dismissed out of hand a few years ago under
former mayor Mel Lastman (who never
concerned himself with such matters). But
David Miller likes to talk openly about it
and engage citizens in debate on how to make
the city live up to its potential. He loathes
the term 'world class' to describe Toronto:
'It means you're trying to be something else,
like you're trying to be New York. Well,
I don't think that's right. We should just
be us, but just do it brilliantly.'

One way he's getting Toronto to raise the bar
is to address the often-overlooked fact that a lot
of the cityscape looks rather, um, dull. Actually,
plenty of it looks downright ugly, cluttered with
newspaper boxes, transit shelters and garbage
cans that don't exactly blend in well with the
environment. Experiments with new street
furniture will be tried in the next few years
and Miller is determined to let the people have
a say in what's best for the city as part of his

Is it Vegas? No, it's **Dundas Square**.

'clean and beautiful' initiative. In the past, dressing things up often simply meant planting a tree in a sidewalk concrete case. Not surprisingly, of the trees that survived such treatment, few were bigger than bonsais. Toronto loves its trees and the city is looking at ways to give them a fighting chance.

> **'Schemers and dreamers are cooking up plans they hope will be Toronto's waterfront salvation by creating a new urban oasis.'**

FUTURE DREAMS

The city lost its chance to have a waterfront for the people by allowing a concrete curtain of condos to line the shore. Harbourfront, the cultural centre, will try to reclaim some of the space by adding a boardwalk and piers in 2005 that extend out over the lake. But this is minor tinkering compared to the real task ahead of redeveloping the vast and toxic industrial area known as the docklands, which extends east of the downtown core. Schemers and dreamers are cooking up plans they hope will be Toronto's waterfront salvation by creating a new urban oasis, just as many European cities have done with their old port areas.

But don't bet on that happening anytime soon. A short-lived high-speed ferry service between Toronto and Rochester (New York State) in 2004 quickly took on too much debt and sank. The city is now stuck with a new international boat terminal and no customers. There's a slim chance the boat will sail again with a States-side push, but Torontonians could never figure out why anyone would want to go to Rochester in the first place.

With the second-largest public transit system in North America after New York, Toronto knows that coaxing people out of their cars is crucial to the long-term wellbeing of city life. The Toronto Transit Commission remains under-funded and dominated by crisis management. Any long-term plans to further expand the subway system are dreams on a distant horizon. At least there is a plan finally to link Union Station with Pearson International Airport by train. But don't buy a ticket yet: the link won't be in place until 2009.

Home owners have enjoyed the kind of phenomenal upward trend in property prices that makes people feel better off than they may actually be. Property taxes continue to spike as well, which further widens the affordability gap. Locals will say it's expensive to live

Mayor **David Miller**.

in Canada's largest city, but to foreigners Toronto remains an affordable – even a bargain – destination, especially for those coming from European countries.

One new bit of business on the city agenda is a facility that celebrates Toronto's accomplishments and history; somehow no one ever got around to it during the rush to grow up. Just don't call it a museum. 'The word museum tests badly,' according to a consultant to the project, which is still in an embryonic stage. Torontonians have not shown an overly enthusiastic interest in their own past. A mere 180,000 people visited the ten small, city-owned historical museums in 2004. There are vaults crammed full of artefacts and curios that shaped the city and some people want them to have a home. The awkward and unsexy name of Humanitas is being bandied about for this exercise in civic pride, which could cost $200 million. As an alternative, others suggest that an aquarium would revive the dowdy Canadian National Exhibition and Ontario Place grounds. It comes down to this in unruffled Toronto: history or fish. Don't bet on history.

Naked Lunch. *See p27.*

Hollywood North

Toronto's film industry is poised for the biggest comeback of its career.

Like a forgotten movie star, Hollywood North is casting about in search of the cameras, but the crews have all gone away. It's looking more and more as if this saga is turning into a tragedy. But wait, is that a hero riding in through the city gates? (He's wearing a Mountie's uniform, and looks just like Nelson Eddy!) As with many things in Canada's cinema history, Nelson Eddy was American. A singing Yankee of the 1930s ('When I'm calling you-ou-ou-oou ou-ou-ooou'), with a broad smile and even broader shoulders sporting a Mountie hat, with matching scarlet tunic and snappy slacks. A bigger celebrity than any Canadian could hope to be.

These days Toronto's star factor is almost entirely dependent on the Hollywood flicks that come to shoot here. Problem is, the solid decade of booming Tinseltown activity is currently on the wane, losing out to aggressive Canadian competitors, Montreal and Vancouver, which are grabbing more of the location shooting business each year. Toronto, for all its allure

as a chameleon-like locale, needs a mega sound stage to stay in the running for those mega-buck Hollywood productions.

> **'In a good year the city benefits by about $1.5 billion from tarting itself up (or down) as required.'**

Cue those daring investors wanting to thrust the city back on top with grand plans to build one of the world's largest sound stages by 2006. Toronto Film Studios and the Rose Corporation have designs for a complex covering 1.25 million square feet near Cherry Street, in the Port of Toronto, complete with multiple stages, coffee shops and perhaps a hotel. A new treasure box of glam to keep the stars coming. In the meantime, the city is still managing to attract some big deals, such as John 'Boyz N the Hood' Singleton's film *Four Brothers*, starring Mark Wahlberg, and a new *Kojak* TV series.

For now the heyday – still a recent memory – remains the stuff of urban legend. Sidle up to the bartender and hear about Mick Jagger getting down at Revival; Renée Zellweger helping a homeless person; Colin Farrell partying into the night with local folk; Sam Shepard strolling across Bloor Street as if it were his ranch.

ON LOCATION

Perhaps the city's biggest on-screen talent is its ability to disappear. Usually it stands in for New York City (*X-Men*, 2000). Sometimes it's Chicago (as in the film musical of 2002), Boston (*Good Will Hunting*, 1997), or even an exotic destination such as Morocco (*Naked Lunch*, 1991). At the movies, locals can pinpoint familiar restaurants, street corners and parks, but they would mean nothing to outsiders. (Truth be told, even the locals fail to pick out the city in most of its guises.) There is no movie district or landmark as such: Hollywood North is not an area, or a state of mind. It's business.

The crews are polite, talented and numerous and, over the past decade, the city has developed a solid infrastructure for film-makers. The bottom line is money, of course: Toronto offers major tax incentives for foreign productions. In a good year the city benefits by about $1.5 billion from tarting itself up (or down) as required. It's important enough for the prime minister, the mayor and provincial premiers to travel to Los Angeles and New York to promote Hollywood North.

A story – surely apocryphal – from the mid 1980s remains popular folklore, probably because it suggests that Toronto is inherently anonymous. A crew dressed a stretch of pavement to look like a dirty, American street, littering it with rubbish. Then everyone broke for lunch. When they returned, the local sanitation department – no doubt alerted by an outraged citizen – had cleaned up the abomination, and returned the city to its proper state of cleanliness.

Atom antics

Atom Egoyan is a darling of the Toronto arts scene. Mostly known for his artistic, edgy and often disturbing films – *Exotica* (1994), *The Sweet Hereafter* (1997), *Ararat* (2002) – the Egyptian-born, Toronto-raised artist has also proven himself as an opera director both here and in London. His most recent contribution to Toronto is a club on West Queen West – where else but hipster central? – appropriately called Camera Bar (*see p139 and p179*). A combination of art-house cinema, sleek bar and hangout lounge, this is the city's newest and grooviest film destination. The 50-seat theatre, co-owned by local film distributor Hussain Amarshi, screens three truly independent titles daily (admission $10). Be prepared to linger – this is a place where post-screening discussions are de rigueur and gingerbread lattes forbidden.

Working behind a different kind of camera – the kind that rolls when 'Action!' is called – Egoyan has recently been tackling his first near-mainstream film. To date, some of his greatest successes have been adaptations of popular novels (in particular *The Sweet Hereafter* and *Felicia's Journey*, 1999) and perhaps this latest one, *Somebody Loves You*, will follow suit. Adapted for the screen from Rupert Holmes's acclaimed novel *Where the Truth Lies*, the noir-ish murder mystery stars Kevin Bacon, Colin Firth and Alison Lohman. The joint Canada/UK effort was

shot in LA, London and Toronto – good news for the local ailing production biz.

A favourite of French and other European critics' circles, as well as the press at home, Egoyan is Canada's most likely candidate for cinematic ambassador. Although his films don't tend to be hits on local turf, he has emerged as a true and lasting talent.

The Toronto International Film Festival

With the majority of Hollywood production taking place elsewhere, the pile-up of celebs about town has diminished somewhat. But what Hogtown lacks in Tinseltown hysteria most of the year is made up for in ten days each September, when Toronto's film festival rolls out the red carpets.

The festival began life three decades ago, in 1976, as a modest celebration of films culled from other international festivals; since then it has expanded to a bloated movie-thon of more than 300 titles – and about as many parties.

The celluloid extravaganza is now a case study in functional inter-dependence. Buyers and sellers – big and small – come to see titles tested in front of the public, their competitors and members of the press. Studios come for the media coverage. The press and public get up close with celebrities. And they all profit from the line-up of premières, which is important bait to attract both the fish and the sharks. Although primarily a public event, it rates as one of the most important for doing business. (Cannes, with its unbeatably glamorous locale and incomparable French flare, remains both the grande dame and the leading lady.) Often, Oscar contenders, especially foreign-language winners such as No Man's Land (2002) and Antonia's Line (1995), are seen first at the festival. And sometimes major hits are unearthed here, most famously Shine (1996), American Beauty (1999) and Sideways (2004).

If anything, the TIFF has been a victim of its own success. Tickets sell out long before opening night, a situation exacerbated by the loss of cinemas around Bloor and Bay Streets: the former 'Festival Village' in Yorkville is now a handful of multiplexes. Enter the promise of a new home for the fest and its year-round exploits, such as the Cinematheque Ontario's daily screenings of foreign and classic movies. Like any self-respecting cultural institution, the film festival is getting into the condo business, selling little boxes to pay for a new building in the heart of the Entertainment District. You never know, you could end up renting a room next to Annette Bening and hubby (then again, maybe not). The dates keep getting pushed back – the project's ambition heavily outweighs its funding – but Festival Centre might well be open by 2007.

For tickets, contact the box office at 416 968 3456 from mid July, or go to www.bell.ca/filmfest. In 2004 tickets cost $9-$14; a variety of passes are also available, including the all-glitz Gala pass. You can also buy 'Rush Tickets' on the same day, particularly for lesser-known titles.

Canada invited America to dominate its movie scenes and screens from the outset. In the late 1930s the then prime minister Mackenzie King decided not to fund Canadian pictures when Hollywood came knocking with an offer to set American pictures in Canada. This agreement brought about such kitsch-flicks as Rose-Marie (1936), starring Nelson Eddy. Film-making simply wasn't part of the city's cultural identity, unlike literature. Over the decades many of the biggest talents have left for the US: Toronto was too small to hold Jim Carrey, Mike Myers, Lorne Michaels and many others.

Nonetheless, Toronto made a splash in the 1960s when Don Shebib shot Goin' Down the Road (1970), the classic tale of country boys who come to the big city: a kind of Midnight Cowboy (1969), Canadian style (clean). In the greasy '70s Toronto was hit by a wave of so-called 'dentist movies' – low-grade cash-grabs that were financed by teeth-pullers in exchange for whopping tax breaks. The flicks were made to look, sound, feel American. But then the occasional local film talent emerged – and stayed home – against the odds, especially when a government agency (now Telefilm Canada) began handing out money for indigenous production in the 1980s.

'David Cronenberg has been called a pornographer, a sadist – and much, much better.'

BRIGHT LIGHTS, BIG NAMES

As well as actors, the city has also spawned a clutch of world-renowned directors. Arguably the most famous is David Cronenberg, Toronto's king of intellectual creep and subversive sex, who has been called a pornographer, a sadist, a controversial visionary – and much, much better. Whatever the epithets, he accomplishes something unique in the world of Canadian

cinema, over and over again: he makes
mainstream-budget movies, usually at home,
with American and foreign funds, and a mix
of Canadian and foreign talent – and succeeds.

Oscar-winner Norman Jewison – *In the Heat
of the Night* (1967), *Fiddler on the Roof* (1971) –
made a brilliant career in Hollywood, and then
gave his home town of Toronto a unique gift:
the Canadian Film Centre. The film school,
now nearly 20 years old, has a strong list of
graduates, including Clément Virgo (*The Planet
of Junior Brown* won Best Feature Film at the
Urban World Film Festival, 1997). Too bad
more recent efforts have been shaky: Jewison's
The Statement (2003) was a bomb.

Today there is a small local movie industry,
and occasionally it plays up Toronto's cultural
identity. Deepa Mehta celebrated the South
Asian communities here in *Bollywood/
Hollywood* (2002). Don McKellar used local
colour to its fullest in *Last Night* (1998): even
the streetcars played a role. And although the
landscape is often secondary in Atom Egoyan's

films (*see p27* **Atom antics**), the city's
nightclubs did look downright dirty and local
in *Exotica* (1994). Some of *Somebody Loves You*
(2005), his latest movie, was also shot in town.

Sadly, these are rare examples of an industry
that is under-funded and little loved by the
locals. English-language Canadian movies
generally snag less than one per cent of the
national box office. Add to that, the real
Hollywood is frantically trying to discourage
business from working across the border
(New York's film office has claimed that
movie production is down by ten per cent since
Canada introduced its film tax incentives in
1997). Famously, Arnold Schwarzenegger's
Terminator 3 (2003) was headed for production
in Vancouver, but the actor wanted to make a
statement and shot it in California instead.

So it's fair to say that there's a lot riding on
the sound stage – surely it will be the kickstart
the city needs? Until then Toronto will just
have to continue to try to make Hollywood
feel right at home when it comes north.

Toronto-Dominion Centre. *See p31*

Architecture

The CN Tower is everywhere, but you'll have to dig deeper for the smaller gems.

Ask someone why they would visit Toronto and 'for the architecture' is likely to be way down on the list of reasons. That may be about to change. For a place that blithely (and shamefully) bulldozed its past through much of the second half of the 20th century – and put in its place only a handful of buildings of note – there's a new appreciation for the role architecture has in the city's wellbeing. Purse strings have been loosened; visionary thinking has taken flight. Who knows? People may come to Toronto to check out the bricks and mortar and, oh yes, titanium, after all: Frank Gehry, the wizard of shiny surfaces, is finally set to make his mark on his home town.

Let's blame the city's dearth of building design, for argument's sake, on the **CN Tower** (1976, 301 Front Street W; *see also p63*). Once you've built the tallest freestanding structure in the world, where do you go from there? The famous stick is over 30 years old now and the city is searching to make its architectural presence felt anew.

A LITTLE OF EVERYTHING

Without a definitive style to call its own, Toronto's architecture embraces an eclecticism that has referenced other movements and influences as the city has come of age. Humourist Bruce McCall likened Toronto's overriding appearance to 'Early Penitentiary' style. Stone and brick were the city's literal building blocks, quarried from the local hills and kiln-baked in the Don Valley. Stalwart, unadorned homes rose in keeping with the prevailing Presbyterianism of the 19th century. For larger projects, these materials expressed the lofty aspirations of an emerging metropolis. Examples are found in the centre of town: **Old City Hall** (1888-99, 60 Queen Street W; *see also p67*) is a fanciful statement built from Credit Valley red sandstone in the Romanesque Revival style by the legendary EJ Lennox (who also designed **Casa Loma**; *see p88*). Its monumental scope allowed for flourishes such as a 300-foot clock tower, gargoyles and grotesques, one of which is Lennox's own face.

Despite the building's eminent pedigree, it nearly met with the wrecker's ball simply because it fell out of fashion, representing another era from the fast-growing city's past. The original plan for the Eaton Centre was to have included the land where Old City Hall stands today, and the battle to preserve it was a catalyst for the heritage movement. It's now a courthouse, and though security can be tight it's worth getting inside to admire the stained-glass and the grand staircase.

Of the city's remaining original bank towers, **Commerce Court North** (1931, 25 King Street W; *see also p32* **Doors Open Toronto**), a 34-storey limestone-clad skyscraper, has the hauteur that comes from being the tallest building in the British Commonwealth until 1962. Look up to see the giant heads that surround the former viewing platform. Cathedral-like doors lead into the main banking hall modelled after the Baths of Caracalla in Rome, with its vaulted ceiling in blue and gilt mouldings.

Beaux Arts style is interpreted at **Union Station** (1927, 65 Front Street W; *see also p64*) with the façade's imposing Doric colonnade echoed by the main hall's 22 mighty pillars. The pitched, chateau-like roofline is echoed across the street by the **Fairmont Royal York Hotel** (1929, 100 Front Street W; *see also p38 and p64*). Art deco's most expressive example is found at the **Design Exchange** (1937, 234 Bay Street; *see also p65*), the former home of the Toronto Stock Exchange.

The city's push to modernism came in 1957 with a design competition for the **New City Hall**. Finnish architect Viljo Revell won the competition with his two curving towers and central oyster-shaped dome for the city council chambers. The project, completed in 1965, included a much-needed public space (named after the mayor of the day, Nathan Phillips), which symbolically reflected the city's own opening up to new ideas. In 2005, surrounded by concrete buildings in the Brutalist style, City Hall retains a fresh appeal as it turns 40; *see also p71*.

The **Toronto-Dominion Centre** (1964-9, 55 King Street W; *see also p65*) heralded the international style, piercing the skyline with Ludwig Mies van der Rohe's austere twin black towers, the taller at 54 stories. Diverting human traffic from the open plaza at street level to an underground concourse was part of the design, meant to emphasise the inhuman scale of the towers. Fostered by bank rivalries, IM Pei's 57-storey stainless steel box of **Commerce Court West** (1968-72, 199 Bay Street; *see also p64*) quickly rose to prominence across the street.

KEEPING UP APPEARANCES

By the 1980s preservationists were fighting to end the destruction of old buildings, but with unintended consequences. City Hall compromised by allowing developers to incorporate bits of earlier buildings into their designs, creating a strange hybrid known as façadism. This has proved to be a love it or hate it, hit-or-miss proposition. **Queens Quay Terminal** (1983, 207 Queens Quay W; *see also p55*) is a successful early example on the waterfront. **BCE Place** (1992, 181 Bay Street; *see also p64*) displaced an 1840s bank façade that now sits without context amid the wonderful swirling ironwork in the atrium, both by Santiago Calatrava. The **Air Canada Centre** (1990, 200 Bay Street; *see also p63*) retains the charming bas-relief scenes of maple leaves and beavers from a former postal station, proof that the rampant commercialism of professional sport must bow at the altar of such iconic Canadian imagery. With **Maple Leaf Gardens** (1931, 33 Carlton Street; *see also p79*), the revered Art Moderne hockey shrine, set to become a grocery store, one only hopes this incongruous co-mingling of purposes will find a satisfying and ironic expression in its use of façadism.

Successful restorations have brought back to life some stunning architectural gems. For sheer decorative exuberance, the **Elgin & Winter Garden Theatres** (1913, 189 Yonge Street; *see also p68*) are in a gold leaf, cherub-filled,

Summerhill LCBO Store. *See p32.*

faux forest class of their own. The **Carlu** (1930, 444 Yonge Street, once known as the Eaton Auditorium, is back in all its Art Moderne glory, with a distinctly nautical theme. This is the work of the French designer Jacques Carlu, who devised the interiors of ocean liners *Ile de France* and *The Normandie*, favourite ships of his patron, Lady Eaton. The **Summerhill LCBO Store** (1916, 10 Scrivener Square; *see also p90 and p156*) now displays its full marble-laden attributes as a former Midtown train station. Over in the east side, the **Distillery District** (1859-61, 55 Mill Street; *see also p84*) is a work in progress, keeping intact the largest Victorian-era industrial complex in North America as boutiques, galleries and restaurants move in.

Inventive uses of landscape architecture are creeping into public spaces, transforming the notion of city parks, and infusing small parcels of land with imagination. The **Village of Yorkville Park** (1993, Cumberland Street, at Bellair Street; *see also p86*) tantalises with its references to Canada's wilderness – granite boulders, wild grasses and water – contained in an urban setting. **Toronto Music Garden** (2000, 475 Queens Quay, west of Spadina Avenue; *see also p59*) creates a tranquil space for an intimate grass amphitheatre, while **Dundas Square** (2003; *see also p65*) is a stage set without a blade of nature from which to gaze upon the hubbub of city life.

ONWARDS AND UPWARDS

Toronto's skyline continues to bristle with new condominium towers, which, while providing lots of relatively affordable housing, are doing little to build an architectural legacy. The city's lack of vision for the waterfront allowed developers to erect a cement curtain that cuts off the pleasures of the lake to all but those who dwell there. Architecture critics dine out on trashing the inappropriateness to their surroundings of many condo designs, and the fussy trappings used to sell a lifestyle for a 500-square-foot living space. The result: a whole lot

Doors Open Toronto

Seeing Toronto's landmark structures from the outside often tells only half the story. Being able to get inside the buildings, many of which are normally off-limits to the public, is the reason for the popularity of Doors Open, an annual weekend architectural binge held in late May. The concept originated in Europe, and Toronto was the first city in North America to come on board for an event that has now spread around the world.

Every year, over the last weekend in May, Doors Open Toronto focuses on a period or theme, such as modernism. But there are also favourites like the **Gooderham Flatiron Building** (49 Wellington Street E; *see p85*) and the time capsule that is the Crystal Ballroom (which has been closed since the '70s) atop **Le Royal Meridien King Edward Hotel** (37 King Street E; *see p45 and p85*).

You might also get a peek inside landmark buildings like **Scadding Cabin** (now on the grounds of the Canadian National Exhibition), the oldest surviving structure in the city (built in 1794), **Osgoode Hall** (130 Queen Street W; *see p68*), the **Royal Alexandra Theatre** (260 King Street W; *see also p221*), or **Commerce Court North** (25 King Street W; *pictured*; *see p31 and p64*), with its glorious interior. Some private residences also throw their doors open, such as the **Studio Building** (1 Severn Street), once a studio for Canada's famous Group of Seven painters.

Buildings bear silent testament to the eras in which they were born and each has a story that reveals its own chapter in the evolution of the city. When these buildings open once a year, Toronto's architecture comes alive.

In 2005 Doors Open Toronto takes place on 28 and 29 May. For future dates and further information, go to http://www.doorsopen.org.

of condo kitsch. One of the more ambitious undertakings is **City Place**, which, when completed in 2010, will consist of 7,500 condo units in 21 towers, in the space occupied by former railway yards west of **SkyDome** (1989, 1 Blue Jays Way; *see also p63*), that architectural marvel with the world's first retractable roof, whose form has outlived its function (the hulking structure is now a white elephant and was sold in 2004 for a fraction of what it cost to build, before being renamed the Rogers Centre).

The **University of Toronto** enjoys a prized position downtown, with many fine ivy-covered edifices that reflect the halls of learning in neo-Gothic, Romantic and Romanesque expression. A wave of new construction is changing the face of the campus and adding some eye-pleasing architecture. **Graduate House** (2000, 60 Harbord Street; *see also p78*) can be counted a success if inviting polarised opinions is a measure of good design. Some love it; most loathe it and its looming cantilevered 'gateway'. The **Woodsworth College Residence** (2004, Bloor and St George Street) by Toronto architect Peer Clewes works much better as an entrance to the campus, with two-tone glass 'skin' that is both contemporary and mid-century retro at the same time. Britain's Norman Foster is designing the **Leslie Dan Pharmacy Building**, his first commission in Canada, at Queen's Park and College Street. Here, a vertical glass podium supports a low-rise tower, which will make for yet another visually appealing point of entry for the campus when the building opens in 2006. U of T dropped the ball when it decided against building a 25,000-seat stadium to house the new home of the Toronto Argonauts football team. Instead, the team will play at a new stadium to be built on the distant York University campus in the north-west corner of the city.

> **'Daniel Libeskind's prismatic, iceberg-like addition to the Royal Ontario Museum is world-class design writ large.'**

Perhaps the most outstanding and visually arresting addition to the city so far in this century is the vertical expansion to the **Ontario College of Art & Design** (2004, 100 McCaul Street; *see also p69*) – a black and white box that 'floats' 100 feet above street level and appears to be supported by 12 off-kilter stilts in bright crayon colours (the stilts are only decorative; the column housing the lift provides the support). It was British architect Will Alsop who designed this highly appropriate addition for the province's leading school of art.

Of all the projects on the drawing boards or under way, it is in the cultural sector where architecture is taking a star turn. Daniel Libeskind's prismatic, iceberg-like addition to the **Royal Ontario Museum** (Queen's Park; *see also p77*) is startlingly bold. Here is world-class design writ large – just what the city fathers want to fulfil the 'if you build it they will come' approach. Libeskind is also putting his name forward to redevelop the **Hummingbird Centre for the Performing Arts** (1 Front Street E; *see also p85 and p198*), which has plans to become a cultural centre with rotating exhibits. Next door to the ROM, a new 1,000-seat theatre is being added to the **Royal Conservatory of Music** (273 Bloor Street; *see also p77*).

The **National Ballet School** (404 Jarvis Street) is getting a large new venue linked to an existing performance space. Canada's first purpose-built opera house, the **Four Seasons Centre for the Performing Arts** (Queen Street, at University Avenue; *see also p65*) will stage both opera and ballet. All of these projects will open in 2006/07, marking an unprecedented renaissance in the city's cultural life.

Frank Gehry's initial redesign of the **Art Gallery of Ontario** (317 Dundas Street W; *see also p71*) has undergone major revisions after some board members objected to his concept. As this guide goes to print, the master builder who grew up around the corner from the AGO says a billowing glass and titanium façade will stretch 600 feet across the gallery's Dundas Street W side. A titanium-clad tower will house a new contemporary art section facing Grange Park on the south side. But this is not anything like Bilbao: Gehry wants this architecture to fit in with the residential neighbourhood.

Some architecture works best when it's invisible. The new **Terminal 1** (2004; *see also p252*) at Pearson International Airport makes for swift transit for passengers guided through the vast space by giant skylights that flood the halls with natural light.

Understated architecture is not on the horizon for the city's downtown skyline. Not since **First Canadian Place** (1972-5, 100 King Street W; *see also p64*) rose to become the tallest office building in Canada have there been any challengers to the claim. Now two condo developers are poised to rival one another for the title, using designs that cry out for the attention they desperately seek. **Trump International Hotel & Tower** and the **Sapphire Tower** are jockeying with city officials to add those extra inches. It's a fitting fight for a city being transformed by rapid growth in the new century – but to date, one that has often left good architecture behind.

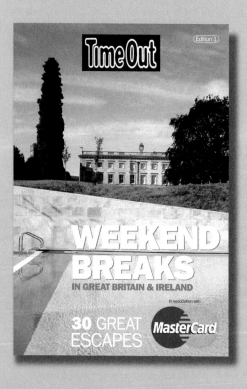

Where to Stay

Where to Stay

Sleeping around – a user's guide.

Toronto's hotel industry took a pounding in 2003, thanks to an outbreak of Severe Acute Respiratory Syndrome, which kept tourists away for an entire season. In truth, SARS was more of a PR problem than an actual health risk for travellers, but the fallout continues to transform the city's accommodation scene.

For many hotels, the SARS crisis was a case of 'that which does not break me makes me stronger'. For others, especially smaller operations, it was more a case of 'that which breaks me leaves me broke and I will now go out of business. Last one out please turn off the lights.' Regrettably, therefore, many long-running hotels and (especially) bed and breakfasts are simply no more.

On the plus side, the past couple of years have seen a mini explosion of small, independent hotels that raise the bar on individualised service and design. Notable properties in this category include the **SoHo Metropolitan** (*see p39*) and the **Hôtel Le Germain Toronto** (*see p41*). This upwards trend looks set to continue: Donald Trump's on-again off-again plans for a new 70-storey five-star hotel and condo complex in the heart of the financial district are back on again. Meanwhile, Yorkville is anticipating the arrival of the **Hazelton**, another entry into the high-end boutique market. Comprising 77 luxury hotel rooms and suites, as well as 18 private residences (starting at $2.7 million), the nine-storey terraced limestone building is designed to set the standard for five-star living when it opens to the public in early 2007.

Many of these boutique hotels – especially those catering to celebrities and executives – will leave your credit card wilting, but there are new interesting options that are within the grasp of the common folk. Indeed, Toronto's 35,000 hotel rooms remain for the most part comparatively good value.

For affordable, alternative places to stay, it's worth investigating old-made-new spots such as the **Drake** (*see p49*), a heavily redesigned former flophouse, or the **Isabella Hotel & Suites** (*see p47*), which has less character but a more central location.

Hôtel Le Germain Toronto, where the chic sleep. *See p41.*

RATES, SEASONS AND GRADINGS

In this chapter we have divided our listings according to the price of the cheapest double room; **Budget** is under $90, **Moderate** $90-$159, **Expensive** $160-$259 and **Luxury** anything from $260 to your life savings; hostels are listed separately. However, hotels tend to quote wide price ranges over the phone because the rate you actually get on the day depends on so many factors, a big one being the season: in slow periods, a 'luxury' hotel might discount itself down into the expensive bracket, and during special events like the film festival or the Molson Indy, everyone's prices shoot through the roof. As a rule of thumb, high season runs from April to October, when deals are hard to come by. However, some places that are heavily oriented towards corporate customers get very quiet in the summer. Hit them while they're down, and ask for a reduced rate. In addition, enquire about deals for students, seniors, CAA, AAA or AA members, teachers, or other groups you belong to. It's always worth finding out if a hotel has any special offers or upgrades. Also, in this post-SARS city, many hotels have partnered with other attractions around town to offer dinner/show or spa/shopping packages that can make your stay cheaper and more enjoyable.

Though we have specified in the listings whether a hotel offers internet access (and if so, whether it's high-speed, wireless or via a dataport), note that some hotels charge for this service. Also be aware that you should specify whether you want a non-smoking room (sometimes staff will place an air purifier in the room after a smoker has checked out; this doesn't always do the job adequately).

Note that rates listed in this chapter do not include federal tax, which is currently seven per cent (though there are ways of claiming this back; *see p262*). Unless otherwise stated, the following rates only include breakfast at B&Bs, not hotels.

BOOKING AGENCIES

Bear in mind that most booking agencies will only hook you up with their own members, so you still need to do a little shopping around. **Tourism Toronto** (416 203 2600, www.torontotourism.com) is the city's official booking service, while the **Greater Toronto Hotel Association** (416 351 1276) maintains comprehensive links on its website, www.gtha.com. **Travellers' Aid Society of Toronto** (416 366 7788, www.travellersaid.ca) can provide shelter and information in emergencies. This society also has booths at many rail and bus stations, as well as the airport. **Bed & Breakfast Homes**

of Toronto (416 363 6362, www.bbht.ca) comprises a handful of independent B&Bs in the Greater Toronto Area. Though basic information and photos are given online, booking should be done direct with the B&B. The **Downtown Toronto Association of Bed & Breakfast Guest Houses** (416 410 3938, www.bnbinfo.com) will be able to match your accommodation preferences – via a detailed online form or by phone – to B&Bs in central Toronto. **Toronto Bed & Breakfast Reservation Service** (1-877 922 6522 or 705 738 9449, www.torontobandb.com) helpfully brings together a handful of B&Bs, mainly in downtown areas.

The best Hotels

For afternoon tea
The **Fairmont Royal York Hotel** (*see p38*) or the **Windsor Arms** (*see p39*), where a nice hot cuppa will bring out the royalist in anyone.

For families
The **Delta Chelsea** (*see p42*): if the waterslide doesn't keep the blighters amused, the real-life rabbits should.

For swinging a cat (theoretically, that is)
The **Comfort Suites City Centre** (*see p47*), whose huge rooms allow visitors to spread out without having to splash out.

For style lovers
The **Hôtel Le Germain Toronto** (*see p41*). All the right design boxes have been ticked at this chic yet unpretentious hotel.

For open affairs
The **Renaissance Toronto Hotel at SkyDome** (*see p41*), which makes guests staying in stadium-facing rooms sign a form promising to be on their best behaviour.

For clandestine affairs
The dingy but funky **Drake Hotel** (*see p49*) – never was a hotel more suited to a secret rendezvous. Appropriately, it opened on Valentine's Day.

For a taste of the country, without leaving town
The historic **Old Mill Inn** (*see p49*) on the edge of town. Forget you're in bustling Toronto as you explore walking trails and meandering paths.

Waterfront & Islands

For a truly unique take on the city, check out the B&B offerings on Toronto's residential island park community. A word of caution, though: in the winter months, ferry services to – and facilities on – the Islands are vastly reduced, and you'd do well to take some supplies with you.

Expensive

Westin Harbour Castle

1 Harbour Square, at Bay Street, Waterfront, ON M5J 1A6 (1-888 625 5144/416 869 1600/ fax 416 869 0573/www.starwood.com/westin/ index.html). Bus 6/streetcar 509, 510. **Rates** $128-$394 single/double. **Credit** AmEx, DC, MC, V. **Map** p279/p280 F9.

Light, spacious rooms and unobstructed harbour views are the big draws here (make sure you request accommodation on the south side of the building). Sunshine glints off the glassed-in pool and bakes the large rooftop terrace. The day spa has a two-storey waterfall and views of Lake Ontario from its treatment rooms. Because of its meeting spaces, the hotel draws a lot of convention business, but it also has better-than-average services for families with children, who appreciate all the leisure facilities. The waterfront area ceases to bustle in the evening, but the Westin operates a shuttle service to downtown, which goes a long way to compensate.

Bar. Business centre. Concierge. Disabled-adapted rooms. Gym. Internet (dataport, high-speed, wireless). No-smoking rooms & floors. Parking ($17; valet $28). Pool (indoor). Restaurants (3). Room service. Spa. TV (DVD/VCR on request, pay movies).

Moderate

Radisson Plaza Hotel Admiral Toronto-Harbourfront

249 Queens Quay W, at Rees Street, Waterfront, ON M5J 2N5 (1-800 333 3333/416 203 3333/fax 416 203 3100/www.radisson.com). Streetcar 509, 510. **Rates** $99-$269 single/double. **Credit** AmEx, DC, MC, V. **Map** p279 E9.

The nautically themed Radisson offers stunning views over Toronto Harbour from the Bosun's Bar, Commodore's restaurant and Promenade deck and outdoor pool area. The lobby is all lacquered wood and brass, with a smattering of interesting marine art and artefacts. Nearby activities – tennis, cycling and sailing – abound during the day, and it's only a short walk to the CN Tower and other sights. At night the surrounding area is a bit of a wasteland, but the hotel runs a complimentary limousine service into downtown.

Bar. Business centre. Concierge. Disabled-adapted rooms. Gym. Internet (wireless). No-smoking rooms & floors. Parking ($18). Pool (outdoor). Restaurant. Room service. Spa. TV (pay movies).

Budget

Studio Apartment

2A Nottawa Avenue, Algonquin Island, ON M5J 2C8 (jeanniep@sympatico.ca). **Rates** per wk $550-$600 single/double. **No credit cards**.

Proud island resident Jeannie Parker rents out this self-contained one-room apartment by the week in the summer and by the month in the winter. With basic kitchen equipment, a private balcony (with a great view of the island) and a new garden, this home is a good base for an extended self-catering stay. *Internet (dataport). No-smoking house. TV (VCR).*

Toronto Island Bed & Breakfast

8 Lakeshore Avenue, Ward's Island, ON M5J 1X4 (416 203 0935/fax 416 203 2646/miriammcfarlane @hotmail.com). **Rates** $58-$75 single/double. **No credit cards**.

Miriam McFarlane rents out her two upper rooms year round (not good for disabled travellers) on the south side of the island. Breakfasts are hot and hearty and there's a large deck where guests are welcome to smoke. Bathrooms are shared, but a private exit in the rear allows you to come and go at any time without disturbing the rest of the household. *No-smoking. TV (in 1 of the 2 rooms).*

Downtown West

Luxury

Fairmont Royal York Hotel

100 Front Street W, at University Avenue, Entertainment District, ON M5J 1E3 (1-800 441 1414/416 368 2511/fax 416 368 9040/ www.royalyorkhotel.com). Subway St Andrew or Union. **Rates** $199-$289 single/double; $379-$469 Fairmont Gold rooms. **Credit** AmEx, DC, MC, V. **Map** p279/280 F8.

When it opened in 1929, this was the largest and tallest building in the British Empire. Although it's now dwarfed by the banking towers of Toronto's Financial District, the hotel's castle-like exterior still merits its royal name (as does the fact that three generations of England's royal family have napped here). Sadly, the once-spectacular lake views from the upper floors of the hotel have been sliced up by a row of condo towers along the shoreline. Chandeliers and a decorated ceiling in the sumptuous lobby set a tone of regal awe (which is impossible to match in the rooms), while, on the other hand, the design of the EPIC restaurant shows grudging acknowledgement that the world has grown hipper (though, thankfully for the traditionalists among us, it still serves tea every day). The gorgeous wood-panelled Library Bar serves a mean Margarita too.

Bars (4). Business centre. Concierge. Disabled-adapted rooms. Gym. Internet (dataport, high-speed). No-smoking rooms & floors. Parking ($24; valet $31). Pool (indoor). Restaurants (5). Room service. Spa. TV (DVD/VCR on request, pay movies).

SoHo Metropolitan

318 Wellington Street, at Blue Jays Way,
Entertainment District, ON M5V 3T4 (416 599
8800/fax 416 599 8801/www.metropolitan.com/
soho). Streetcar 504/subway St Andrew. **Rates**
$350-$650 single/double. **Credit** AmEx, DC, MC, V.
Map p279 E8.

Sister to the original Metropolitan (*see p41*), the
SoHo Met joins a clutch of swanky new(ish) hotels
in the Entertainment District. The ersatz name was
an attempt to brand the neighbourhood; thankfully,
it hasn't caught on. Overall the rooms are generously
size, and feature minimalist yet cosy decor (plenty
of blond wood, and hugely comfy beds), while the
sumptuous marble bathrooms come with Molton
Brown toiletries. Being in party central means it's
not far from bar to bed, but late-night revellers and
traffic can sometimes be heard through the floor to
ceiling windows. As for on-site eating and drinking
options, choose from Senses restaurant (helmed by
superchef Claudio Aprile; *see p108*), the attached bar
(beautifully lit at night) and Senses bakery (frequently half empty, despite the excellent pastries
and cakes). And if you've over-indulged – or vegged
out too much in front of your huge flat-screen TV –
it might be time to burn off some calories in the gym
or pool. Service at the front desk is well-meaning but
occasionally off-key.

Bar. Business centre. Concierge. Disabled-adapted
rooms. Gym. Internet (high-speed). No-smoking
rooms & floors. Parking ($20; valet $25). Pool
(indoor). Restaurants (2). Room service. Spa. TV
(DVD, pay movies, widescreen in some rooms).

Windsor Arms

18 St Thomas Street, at Bloor Street W, University,
ON M5S 3E7 (1-877 999 2767/416 971 9666/fax
416 921 9121/www.windsorarmshotel.com). Bus
4/subway Bay. **Rates** $275-$2,000 single/double/
suites. **Credit** AmEx, DC, MC, V. **Map** p282 F4.

In 1927, this tiny hotel first opened its doors to the
world's celebrities and millionaires. Business
decayed along with the building and in 1991 the
Arms folded. Four years later developer-about-town
George Friedmann bought the property and oversaw a painstaking reconstruction, wrestling the
Arms back to its original neo-Gothic stateliness.
(Only the stained-glass windows and the stone por-
tico of the entrance are original. Everything else
is repro.) Discretion is the better part of service here,
and many rooms have fireplaces and 'private but-
lers' cupboards' through which guests can receive
room service without having to interact with another human being. In the past few years the hotel has
been working hard to shrug off its haughtiness,
repositioning itself to attract a younger, hipper
crowd. The barber shop provides a luxurious shave,
the two-floor spa offers a wide range of treatments,
and entertainment includes live music, dancing and,
possibly, in future, stand-up comedy. For something
more sedate, take tea in the lovely Tea Room just off
the lobby, or enjoy breakfast, lunch or dinner in the
regal Courtyard Café (*see p115*).

Bar. Concierge. Gym. Internet (high-speed).
No-smoking rooms. Parking ($25). Pool (indoor).
Restaurant. Room service. TV (DVD/VCR).

Expensive

Hilton Toronto

145 Richmond Street W, at University Avenue,
Financial District, ON M5H 2L2 (1-800 267 2281/
416 869 3456/fax 416 869 3187/www.hilton.com).
Streetcar 501/subway Osgoode. **Rates** $219-$389
single/double. **Credit** AmEx, DC, MC, V. **Map**
p279/280 F7.

This is a rarity: a modern hotel (built in 1975, with
a major redesign completed in 2000) with character.
The lobby, with its raised wooden floor and hanging curtain, looks as though it was created by stage
designers, which it was. Exit stage left for the
Canadian-themed (both in terms of design and food)
Tundra restaurant, and exit stage right for chunky
glass elevators that carry you to hallways designed
to mimic the flow and activity of a river (note the
abstract fish, stones and ripples in the carpet patterns). The rooms have asymmetrical furniture and
sleek fixtures that are modern, but comfortable and
warm. The Hilton shares its indoor/outdoor pool
with a nearby health club; in return guests get access
to the club's squash courts and aerobics classes.

Bars (2). Business centre. Concierge. Disabled-
adapted rooms. Gym. Internet (high-speed).
No-smoking rooms & floors. Parking ($22;
valet $32). Pools (1 indoor/outdoor). Restaurants
(3). Room service. TV (pay movies).

Fairmont Royal York Hotel.
See p38.

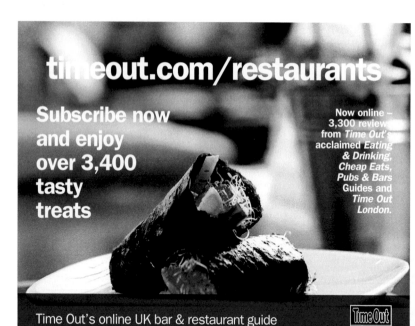

Hôtel Le Germain Toronto

30 Mercer Street, at John Street, Entertainment District, ON M5V 1H3 (1-866 345 9501/416 345 9500/fax 416 345 9501/www.hotelboutique.com). Streetcar 504. **Rates** $220-$295 single/double. **Credit** AmEx, DC, MC, V. **Map** p279 E8.

The Le Germain group already owned award-winning properties in Montreal and Quebec when it opened this Toronto counterpart in early 2003. The designers managed to get every detail right, from the subdued lighting to the luxury showerheads that make you feel like you're soaping up in a tropical rainstorm, to the mixture of natural textures in the furniture and fixtures. The sumptuous rooms are designed to help guests relax, and make them forget about the world outside (though the Hooter's restaurant in the forefront of the view from some north-facing rooms tends to bring reality crashing back in; other rooms overlook faceless office blocks). The lobby boasts a massive glass fireplace, sculptures and paintings, and, on the raised floor above, a 'library', with about 200 art books, plus a self-serve coffee machine. Free net access in the rooms, proper hairdryers and friendly chamber staff are further bonuses. The breakfast buffet isn't to everyone's liking (some feel it's out of place in such a stylish venture), nor is the restaurant, Luce (is it design over substance?; *see p11*), but this is nonetheless one of the city's best hotels by a long shot.

Bar. Concierge. Disabled-adapted rooms. Gym. Internet (high-speed in rooms, wireless in lobby). No-smoking rooms. Parking (valet $25). Restaurant. Room service. TV (DVD/VCR on request, pay movies, widescreen in suites).

InterContinental Toronto Centre

225 Front Street W, at Simcoe Street, Entertainment District, ON M5V 2X3 (1-800 422 7969/416 597 1400/fax 416 597 8128/www.torontocentre. intercontinental.com). Subway St Andrew or Union. **Rates** $200-$250 single/double. **Credit** AmEx, DC, MC, V. **Map** p279/280 F8.

Attached as it is to the Toronto Convention Centre, the 586-room hotel formerly known as the Crowne Plaza attracts a lot of business traffic. Don't let the conference facilities fool you, though: its location in the bustle of the Entertainment District, the deep colours and soft chairs of the Azure bar, as well as the tropical feel of the Victoria Spa (which is operated in the hotel by a separate company) make this hotel well suited for vacationers. Services vary according to the room: touches such as high-speed internet, bathrobes and kitchenettes only come with more expensive ones. Should venturing out seem too much like hard work, there are are several decent restaurants within the hotel.

Bar. Business centre. Concierge. Disabled-adapted rooms. Gym. Internet (high-speed). No-smoking rooms & floors. Parking ($19; valet $30). Pool (indoor). Restaurant. Room service. Spa. TV (DVD/VCR on request, pay movies, widescreen). **Other locations**: 220 Bloor Street W, at Admiral Avenue, The Annex (1-800 327 0200/415 960 5200).

Metropolitan Hotel Toronto

108 Chestnut Street, at Dundas Street W, Chinatown, ON M5G 1R3 (1-800 668 6600/416 977 5000/fax 416 977 9513/www.metropolitan.com/ toronto). Streetcar 505/subway St Patrick. **Rates** $219-$279 single/double; $349-$469 suite. **Credit** AmEx, DC, MC, V. **Map** p279/280 F6.

This Asian-owned Metropolitan is probably a little less stylish than it likes to think itself, but nonetheless it has tasteful and comfortable rooms with nary a floral in sight: think beige and beech, with intelligent touches such as double-decker desks, good lighting and your radio tuned to French *chansons* at turndown time. The rooms aren't huge, but they are lovely. The restaurants are distinctly smart (gourmet Chinese Lai Wah Heen is well regarded, and rightly so; *see p113*) and room service meals of a high standard. The hotel is a little let down by its ordinary public areas, though the nearby city hall dictates that there are a lot of business visitors who probably don't mind it that way. The central location is a bonus too. For the SoHo Met, *see p39*.

Bar. Business centre. Concierge. Disabled-adapted rooms. Gym. Internet (dataport, high-speed). No-smoking rooms & floors. Parking ($19; valet $25). Pool (indoor). Restaurants (2). Room service. TV (pay movies, widescreen in some rooms).

Renaissance Toronto Hotel at SkyDome

1 Blue Jays Way, at Front Street W, Entertainment District, ON M5V 1J4 (1-800 237 1512/416 341 7100/fax 416 341 5091/www.marriott.com). Streetcar 504/subway St Andrew or Union. **Rates** $249-$579 single/double. **Credit** AmEx, DC, MC, V. **Map** p279 E8.

The Renaissance is built into the fabric of SkyDome, the stadium that's home to the Blue Jays baseball team, and the Toronto Argonauts football team (at least until their move to their new home at York University, slated for 2006). But with its combination of business facilities and muted red, gold and green decor, the hotel offers all-round comfort for a wide range of guests. There's no getting away from the fact that 80 of the rooms overlook the stadium (with opening windows), along with the bar and restaurant – it's a great way to see a game, or to stare out at an eerily empty stadium on non-game days. The classy suites are split level, with a comfortable lounge and marbled bathroom.

Bar. Business centre. Concierge. Disabled-adapted rooms. Gym. Internet (high-speed). No-smoking rooms & floors. Parking ($18; valet $25). Pool (indoor). Restaurant. Room service. TV (DVD/ VCR on request, pay movies).

Toronto Marriott Downtown Eaton Centre

525 Bay Street, at Dundas Street W, Dundas Square, ON M5G 2L2 (1-800 905 0667/416 597 9200/fax 416 597 9211/www.marriotteaton centre.com). Bus 6/streetcar 505/subway Dundas. **Rates** $169-$299 single/double. **Credit** AmEx, DC, MC, V. **Map** p279/280 F6.

Love to shop but hate fresh air? If you want never to set foot outside, there is no better place to stay in Toronto than this 435-room Marriott. On the other hand, although the attached shopping mall (not to mention indoor walkways to most of the rest of downtown) is a big selling point, many rooms overlook Trinity Church and the small but peaceful Labyrinth Park, which beckon you to set aside any agoraphobic tendencies. The lobby of the hotel has lots of natural light and plenty of greenery, and skylights illuminate the pool on the 18th floor. Eating and drinking options range from the worryingly entitled Characters Sports Bar to the Parkside Restaurant (international fare) and JW's Steakhouse. *Air-conditioning. Bars (2). Beauty salon. Business services. Concierge. Disabled-adapted rooms. Gym. Internet (dataport, high-speed). No-smoking rooms & floors. Parking ($19; valet $24). Pool (indoor). Restaurants (3). Room service. Spa. TV (DVD/VCR on request, pay movies).*

Moderate

Bond Place Hotel

65 Dundas Street E, at Bond Street, Dundas Square, ON M5B 2G8 (1-800 268 9390/416 362 6061/fax 416 362 6046/www.bondplacehoteltoronto.com). Streetcar 505/subway Dundas. **Rates** $95-$130 single/double. **Credit** AmEx, DC, MC, V. **Map** p278 G6.

The Bond is on a constant self-improvement kick, though it can never fully shrug off the drabness of the neighbourhood in which it towers. Recent renovations, and some expanded services (like hairdryers in every room) give the place a little more style, but still not enough really to be considered classy. In true Toronto fashion, the hotel staff serve travellers in many languages, including Cantonese and Tamil. While prices shoot upwards during special events, this hotel remains good value, especially if your gang can fill a triple or quadruple occupancy, which costs only a bit more than a standard double. *Bar. Business centre. Concierge. Disabled-adapted rooms. No-smoking rooms. Parking ($14). Restaurant. Room service. TV (pay movies).*

Delta Chelsea

33 Gerrard Street W, at Bay Street, Chinatown, ON M5G 1Z4 (1-800 243 5732/416 595 1975/fax 416 585 4375/www.deltachelsea.com). Bus 6/subway College or Dundas. **Rates** $99-$269 single/double. **Credit** AmEx, DC, MC, V. **Map** p279/280 F6.

With 1,590 rooms, the Chelsea is the largest hotel in the British Commonwealth. Indeed, it feels as though an entire village is housed in this one-building complex at the corner of Bay and Gerrard Streets. The restaurants run the gamut from food court to fine dining, and the hotel has an affiliation with a nearby spa, should you be in need of some TLC. The hotel is kid-friendly in the extreme, with a well-equipped childcare centre (with live bunnies), a video arcade, dedicated family suites with bunkbeds and child-compatible fixtures, plus a huge

waterslide dropping into the all-ages pool. But it's also great for parents too, with a second, less frenetic, adults-only pool, which adjoins a fitness centre and a drinks lounge. *Bar. Business centre. Concierge. Disabled-adapted rooms. Gym. Internet (dataport, high-speed). No-smoking rooms & floors. Parking ($25). Pools (2 indoor). Restaurants (4). Room service. TV (pay movies, VCR on request, widescreen in TV lounges).*

Hotel Victoria

56 Yonge Street, at Wellington Street, Financial District, ON M5E 1G5 (1-800 363 8228/416 363 1666/fax 416 363 7327/www.hotelvictoria-toronto.com). Streetcar 504/subway King or Union. **Rates** $110-$170 single/double. **Credit** AmEx, DC, MC, V. **Map** p279/280 F8.

Old and small are good things when it comes to hotels, and this one is both. Built in 1908, the Victoria is one of the oldest continuously operating hotels in the city. The 56 rooms are on the small side and some have vastly better views than others, but this venerable institution has more character than many nearby behemoths. The hotel has a breakfast room, but you'll need to venture outside for sustenance at other times of the day. *Internet (wireless). No-smoking rooms. TV.*

Pantages Hotel

200 Victoria Street, at Shuter Street, Dundas Square, ON M5B 1V8 (1-866 852 1777/416 362 1777/fax 416 368 8217/www.pantageshotel.com). Streetcar 501/subway Queen. **Rates** $149-$309 double/suites. **Credit** AmEx, DC, MC, V. **Map** p280 G7.

The timing was a bit off: to name a boutique hotel after a historic nearby theatre that changed its name before the hotel opened. The theatre schtick lives on in this high-rise condo-like tower. In fact, the top floors are condos, which makes for an odd (but perfectly friendly) mix of people in the lobby. Rooms have a minimalist feel, with fluffy white duvets, and funky leather chairs in the larger rooms, though bathrooms can be a letdown in comparison. Where the Pantages has the edge over others in the price bracket is its mod cons: each room features a generous kitchenette, with hob, full-size refrigerator, dishwasher, microwave, washer and dryer. While the home-from-home comforts might not be everyone's cup of tea (there's nothing particularly romantic about sleeping a few feet away from a fridge), there's no denying that business travellers will find these extras useful. 'Serenity Rooms', come with yoga mats and running water features, and the salon (sorry, 'Anti-Aging & Longevity Spa') provides any necessary beautifying or relaxing treatments. If you're peckish, pop downstairs to Fran's diner, or, a better option, the Senator diner (*see p125* **Grease is the word**) just across the road. *Bar. Business centre. Concierge. Disabled-adapted rooms. Gym. Internet (high-speed, wireless). No-smoking rooms & floors. Parking ($20). Spa. TV (DVD/VCR on request, pay movies).*

SoHo Metropolitan – it's a style thing. *See p39.*

Strathcona Hotel

60 York Street, at Wellington Street, Financial District, ON M5J 1S8 (1-800 268 8304/416 363 3321/fax 416 363 4679). Streetcar 504/subway King or Union. **Rates** from $115. **Credit** AmEx, DC, MC, V. **Map** p279/280 F8.

The Strathcona used to be a bargain spot that took in the overflow of business from the grander (and more famous) Royal York Hotel across the street when it was full. Following recent renovations, it has swum a little further upmarket, though it's still pretty busy when there's a big conference in town. Thanks to a deal with a nearby fitness club, guests get cheap access to hot tubs, squash courts and a fully equipped gym.

Bar. Concierge. Internet (dataport, high-speed). Restaurant. Room service. TV (pay movies).

Sutton Place Hotel

955 Bay Street, at Wellesley Street, University, ON M5S 2A2 (1-800 268 3790/416 924 9221/ fax 416 924 1778/www.suttonplace.com). Bus 6, 94/subway Wellesley. **Rates** $129-$159 single/ double; $299-$329 suite. **Credit** AmEx, DC, MC, V. **Map** p282 F5.

A local newspaper once referred to it as the 'cereal box on Bay', but the blocky, International Style exterior hides some of the most luxurious rooms in the city – and in a central location too. The hotel shoots for a European feel, with a ballroom lit by stunning Venetian-style chandeliers and suites named after great operas. The intersection of Bay and Wellesley is no oil painting, but the hotel is located across the street from Bistro 990, the host restaurant for the Toronto International Film Festival. Sutton Place graciously receives celebrity traffic year-round, especially in its penthouse suites. But even the ordinary rooms are furnished with fine antiques and east-facing rooms have balconies. The hotel opened in 1967, and staff tell us they're still getting return visitors from the first year.

Bar. Business centre. Concierge. Disabled-adapted rooms. Gym. Internet (high-speed). No-smoking rooms & floors. Parking ($24). Pool (indoor). Restaurant. Room service. Spa. TV (DVD/VCR on request, pay movies, widescreen).

Travelodge Motor Hotel

621 King Street W, at Bathurst Street, Entertainment District, ON M5V 1M5 (1-800 578 7878/416 504 7441/fax 416 504 4722/ www.travelodgetorontodowntown.com). Streetcar 504, 511. **Rates** $90-$140 single/double. **Credit** AmEx, MC, V. **Map** p279 D8.

A new name, some radical landscaping and a location in a suddenly trendy area of the city do nothing to quash the retro feel of this classic motor inn. Rates include breakfast and parking, the latter being particularly valuable this close to downtown. With fancy wine bars popping up all over the neighbourhood to serve the new flow of condo-dwelling hipsters, this basic hotel still manages to keep its 1950s cool.

Internet (dataport, wireless). Parking (free). TV (VCR on request).

Pantages Hotel. *See p42.*

Budget

Bay Street Motel

650 Bay Street, at Elm Street, Chinatown, ON M5G 1M8 (1-800 695 8284/416 971 8383/ fax 416 971 8527/www.baystreetmotel.com). Bus 6/streetcar 505/subway College or Dundas. **Rates** $50 single; $65 double. **Credit** AmEx, MC, V. **Map** p279/280 F6.

Recently renovated, this low-end hotel can now officially be upgraded to 'pleasant'. Across the street from the bus station, and close to the Toronto Eaton Centre, it's one of the most affordable ways to sleep in the heart of the action. Staff are friendly, and you can get great bargains on longer stays – commit to a week and cut your room rate by more than a third; staying for a month bring it down by more than two-thirds. Look at your room before you settle in to check the amenities, as they tend to vary. Bathrooms are shared.

Internet (wireless). TV.

Victoria's Mansion Guest House

68 Gloucester Street, at Church Street, Church & Wellesley, ON M4Y 1L5 (416 921 4625/fax 416 944 1092/www.victoriasmansion.com). Subway Wellesley. **Rates** $75-$143 single/double. **Credit** MC, V. **Map** p283 G4.

This sedate Victorian brick mansion, built as a residence in the 1890s, sits on a wide, shady street very close to the Church Street Village. It opened as a tourist hotel in 2000, and makes a nice change from the big international chains. The 23 highly individual rooms all have a fridge and microwave; some are set up with kitchen facilities to suit longer stays.

Internet (dataport, wireless). Parking (free). TV (VCR on request).

as they pass through the soaring marble columns of the four-storey lobby, overseen by a portrait of King Edward VII himself. The King Eddy, as it's known by locals, is a designated historic building and retains all its grandeur, from the original chandeliers in public areas, to the high ceilings in the 292 spacious rooms and suites. The power elite breakfast at the hotel's Café Victoria, where guests are treated like royalty. Although the hotel celebrated its centenary in 2003, it still likes to keep up with the times, offering wireless net access in the lobby and meeting rooms.

Bar. Business centre. Concierge. Disabled-adapted rooms. Gym. Internet (high-speed, web TV). No-smoking rooms. Parking ($30). Restaurant. Room service. Spa. TV (DVD/VCR on request, pay movies, widescreen).

Moderate

B 'R' Guest Bed & Breakfast

367 Ontario Street, between Dundas Street E & Gerrard Street E, Moss Park, ON M5A 2V8 (1-866 928 0187/416 944 8579/fax 416 944 3160/ www.brguesttoronto.com). Streetcar 505. **Rates** $100-$160 single/double; $250-$325 suite. **Credit** MC, V. **Map** p280 H6.

This 19th-century building has recently been renovated, but it still blends in well to the historic Cabbagetown streetscape. Despite the tacky name, this B&B has boutique hotel pretensions. The sitting room is decorated with antiques, and the rooms are designed to maximise seclusion and luxury – many have private balconies, and there's a stand-alone two-bedroom suite that can be used to seal off an entire family from the other guests.

Disabled-adapted rooms. Internet (high-speed, wireless). No-smoking rooms. Parking (free). TV (VCR, widescreen with DVD in lounge).

Clarion Selby Hotel & Suites

592 Sherbourne Street, at Bloor Street E, Church & Wellesley, ON M4X 1L4 (1-800 387 4788/416 921 3142/fax 416 923 3177). Bus 75/subway Sherbourne. **Rates** $119-$199 single/double/suites. **Credit** AmEx, DC, MC, V. **Map** p283 H4.

One of several hotels in town that claims Ernest Hemingway (who used to write for the *Toronto Star* newspaper) as their most distinguished guest, this hotel has changed hands recently, though with very little alteration in service or decor. The red brick hotel was built as a private home in 1880, then served as a girls' school until 1915. Today this historic building comprises 82 basic rooms that provide travellers with a reasonable alternative to the downtown high-rises. It's close to, but not in the exuberant heart of, Toronto's gay village, and also handy for the subway. You'd be wise to steer clear of the home office rooms located in the basement: their windows are so small you might not be able to tell when the sun rises.

Disabled-adapted rooms. No-smoking rooms. Parking ($13). TV (widescreen in suites).

Downtown East

Expensive

Novotel Toronto Centre

45 The Esplanade, at Scott Street, St Lawrence, ON M5E 1W2 (1-800 668 6835/416 367 8900/fax 416 360 8285/www.novotel.com). Subway Union. **Rates** $170-$310 single/double. **Credit** AmEx, DC, MC, V. **Map** p280 G8.

If you can deal with the lack of porters, the unpretentious, solid Novotel offers good facilities and a decent location for the money. A well-kept traditional lobby complete with gift shop, bar and liveried concierge hustling theatre tickets belies rooms that are simple (though well kitted-out) and with maybe one pastel colour too many. The breakfast buffet cuts no corners and the gym, though ill-advisedly muralled with people of a sickly caste, does the job well. Not luxury, then, nor stylish, but reliable, well run and good value (especially as there's room service and a minibar).

Bar. Concierge. Disabled-adapted rooms. Gym. Internet (dataport, high-speed). No-smoking rooms & floors. Parking ($16). Pool (indoor). Restaurant. Room service. TV (pay movies).

Le Royal Meridien King Edward

37 King Street E, at Victoria Street, St Lawrence, ON M5C 1E9 (1-800 543 4300/416 863 0888/ fax 416 863 4102/www.lemeridien-kingedward.com). Streetcar 504/subway King. **Rates** $200-$250 single/double; $350-$450 suites. **Credit** AmEx, DC, MC, V. **Map** p280 G8.

Architect EJ Lennox, who also built Casa Loma and Old City Hall, sure knew how to show off with his work. Even regular guests look up in awe

If these walls could talk

John and Yoko slept here.

Whether they brag about it openly or drop hints surreptitiously, hotels love having celebrities to stay. Not only do they tend to flash their cash but, treated right, they generate excellent publicity.

Often, though, celebrities leave behind more than fond memories. For instance, in one suite at **Le Royal Meridien King Edward** (*see p45*) you'll find the 'Neil Diamond window', whose most exciting feature is that it opens. It seems that Diamond likes to blow off steam by blowing smoke. In Toronto for a gig, he discovered the unpleasant truth about the windows in his digs: they were closed, so no cigars. Hotels don't do renovations for just anyone, but Neil Diamond isn't just anyone. After much huffing about his puffing, the hotel installed an openable window to give the man a place to vent.

Of course, the King Eddy is famous for hosting just about everyone on the planet, but if it's other rock stars you're interested in, you might like to know that John Lennon and Yoko Ono kipped here in May 1969. Only for a night, mind, while they waited for their visas to be processed at the airport. Lennon was apparently so impressed by Canada's willingness to treat him and Yoko as 'human beings' (no doubt a dig at the US, which had refused him entry because of an outstanding marijuana conviction) that he ended up recording his legendary 'Give Peace a Chance' that same week in a Montreal hotel. Maybe they'd been inspired by Peter Fonda, who'd penned the screenplay to *Easy Rider* in Toronto's now-defunct Lakeshore Motel.

Sometimes it's the hotel that leaves the lasting change on the celebrity. The **Isabella Hotel & Suites** (*see p47*), for one, wasn't always the demure place it is today. In the 1980s, it was a centre for Toronto's raucous blues community. One of the bright lights on the scene was the Downchild Blues Band, led by a pair of brothers, Donnie and Hock Walsh. One night when the Walshes were playing the Izzy, a window opened up in the mind of a little-known comedian who was sitting in the audience. A fresh idea blew in: 'Brothers… who play blues! That's brilliant!' thought Dan Aykroyd (or something to that effect). Inspired by the Walshes, Aykroyd teamed up with John Belushi to create the iconic *Saturday Night Live* characters, The Blues Brothers.

Comfort Suites City Centre

200 Dundas Street E, at Jarvis Street, Church &
Wellesley, ON M5A 4R6 (1-877 316 9951/416 362
7700/fax 416 362 7706). Streetcar 506/subway
Dundas. **Rates** *$90-$449 single/double/suites.*
Credit AmEx, DC, MC, V. **Map** p280 G6.
In strict dollar-to-square-foot terms, this is one of the
best values in town. Even the cheapest rooms leave
space to stretch out. Thanks to a pull-out couch, the
standard double can accommodate six people, making them a steal, even with an extra $10-per-person
charge. Aside from cost, it's clean and safe (though
Dundas Street becomes a bit dodgy east of here, so
evening walks are best taken towards Yonge Street).
Bar. Business centre. Concierge. Disabled-adapted
rooms. Gym. Internet (dataport, high-speed). No-
smoking floors. Parking ($18-$20 indoor, $14
outdoor). Pool (indoor). Restaurant. TV (pay movies).

Grand Hotel & Suites Toronto

225 Jarvis Street, at Dundas Street E, Moss Park,
ON M5B 2C1 (1-877 324 7263/416 863 9000/
fax 416 863 1100/www.grandhoteltoronto.com).
Streetcar 505. **Rates** *$159-$269 junior/deluxe suites;*
$399-$599 ambassador suites. **Credit** AmEx, DC,
MC, V. **Map** p280 G6.
Opened in 2000, this boutique hotel caters largely
for the film industry and other business travellers
who require longer stays. Its large, luxurious suites,
complimentary breakfasts, softly lit pool and unpar-
alleled views of the lake and the city from two
rooftop hot tubs – not to mention Citrus, a restaurant that forms a transition between the limestone
lobby and a lush garden – allow such stars as
Gabriel Byrne and Shaquille O'Neal to feel right at
home here. (You'd never know, incidentally, that this
building was formerly the HQ of the Mounties.)
Bar. Business centre. Concierge. Disabled-adapted
rooms. Gym. Internet (high-speed, wireless). No-
smoking rooms & floors. Parking ($16). Pool
(indoor). Restaurant. Room service. Spa. TV
(DVD/VCR).

Ramada Hotel & Suites Downtown

300 Jarvis Street, at Carlton Street, Church &
Wellesley, ON M5B 2C5 (1-800 567 2233/416 977
4823/fax 416 977 4830/www.ramada.ca). Streetcar
506/subway College. **Rates** *$129-$189 single/double;*
$175-$259 1-bed suites; $229-$309 2-bed suites.
Credit AmEx, DC, MC, V. **Map** p280 G5.
Right across the street from Allan Gardens and the
greenhouses of the Toronto Horticultural Society,
this 1929 designated historic building was originally an apartment complex. Some legacies from the
early days remain: the elevator shafts are smaller
than average, while the old (refinished) cast-iron
bathtubs are larger than average, and look even bigger in the small bathrooms. The hotel shares its pool,
fitness room, squash court and billiards table with
an adjacent condo complex.
Bar. Business centre. Concierge. Disabled-adapted
rooms. Gym. Internet (dataport, high-speed). No-
smoking rooms & floors. Parking ($15). Pool
(indoor). Restaurant. Room service. TV (pay movies).

Budget

Isabella Hotel & Suites

556 Sherbourne Street, at Isabella Street, Church
& Wellesley, ON M4X 1L3 (1-888 947 2235/416
922 2203/fax 416 922 2204/www.isabellahotel.com).
Subway Sherbourne. **Rates** *$79-$199 single/double.*
Credit AmEx, DC, MC, V. **Map** p283 H4.
A former flophouse that's riding Toronto's gentrification wave, the Isabella offers a little bit of history
and character for travellers on a budget. The original hotel was built in 1890, with a new tower added
25 years later. Its current incarnation preserves
some of the 19th-century detail, including hand rails
and some of the external ornaments. The hallways
are a bit drab, and the rooms on the small side (especially in the newer section), but still cosy. Some
suites have fireplace and jacuzzi.
Bar. Internet (dataport, high-speed). No-smoking
rooms & floors. Restaurant. Room service. TV.

Neill-Wycik College Hotel

96 Gerrard Street E, at Church Street, Church
& Wellesley, ON M5B 1G7 (1-800 268 4358/416
977 2320/fax 416 977 2809/www.neill-wycik.com/
college_en). Streetcar 506/subway College or Dundas.
Rates *$40-$65 single/double; $80 triple; $95*
quad/suite. **Credit** MC, V. **Map** p280 G6.
During the academic year this is a co-operative students' residence, but from May to the end of August
it becomes a tourist hotel, offering some of Toronto's
best-value rooms for the location. Rooms are
arranged in groups of four or five, with each cluster
sharing two common bathrooms, a kitchen and a
living area. There's no bar on the premises, but the
Love at First Bite restaurant on the ground floor is
licensed and provides a place to drink and socialise
with other travellers. The hotel gives discounts to
students, seniors and hostel members.
Internet (pay terminal). Parking ($10). TV (lounge).

Midtown

Luxury

Four Seasons Hotel

21 Avenue Road, at Cumberland Street, Yorkville,
ON M5R 2G1(1-800 819 5053/416 964 0411/fax
416 964 2301/www.fourseasons.com/toronto).
Subway Museum. **Rates** *$295-$570 single/double.*
Credit AmEx, DC, MC, V. **Map** p282 F4.
Despite having picked up more trophies than
you can shake a stick at (including *Travel & Leisure*
magazine's 'most comfortable bed' award), Toronto's
Four Seasons seems to be missing the X factor. OK,
so the rooms are nice enough, the huge suites are not
bad value, and there's a staff of 600 to serve a max-
imum of 764 guests, but, well, there's just nothing
special about it. That said, it's still the preferred
resting spot for the upmarket Yorkville shopping
crowd, not to mention countless A-list movie and
rock stars, especially during the film festival. The

Ainsley House Bed & Breakfast.

four restaurants include the swanky Truffles, and the light and airy Avenue bar and lounge (*see p137*), which helps the hotel attempt to maintain a youthful image. The mostly outdoor pool is kept at 95°F (35°C) in winter, which means you can swim even when it's snowing.
Bars (3). Business centre. Concierge. Disabled-adapted rooms. Gym. Internet (high-speed, web TV). No-smoking rooms & floors. Parking ($30 valet). Pool (1 indoor/outdoor). Restaurants (4). Room service. TV (DVD/VCR on request, pay movies, video games).

Park Hyatt

4 Avenue Road, at Bloor Street, Yorkville, ON M5R 2E8 (1-800 778 7477/416 925 1234/fax 416 924 4933/http://parktoronto.hyatt.com). Subway Museum. **Rates** *$260-$419 single/double.* **Credit** AmEx, DC, MC, V. **Map** p282 F4.
The Park Hyatt is as classy as you'd expect: marbled halls, capped bellboys, soft carpets and seamless service. It's not a style leader – that would be far too vulgar – but a provider of international top-end comforts, tastefully rendered. Among them are the renowned Roof Lounge (*see p138*), a coffee shop with the standards of an upmarket restaurant, and the very beautiful Stillwater Spa (*see p161*), though guests have to pay to use anything other than the fitness room, including, rather inconveniently, the changing rooms (though it's probably worth the 20 bucks to luxuriate on your own private TV couch while you recover from the exertions of the sauna). Rooms vary in size but all have pleasant, if rather safe decor with good-quality wooden

furniture, marble-topped desks and photos hung under their own lights. Here's a tip: if you can't figure out the tap, pull it towards you.
Bars (2). Business centre. Concierge. Disabled-adapted rooms. Gym. Internet (high-speed). No-smoking floors. Parking ($30 valet). Restaurant. Room service. Spa. TV (DVD/VCR on request, pay movies).

Moderate

Howard Johnson Downtown

89 Avenue Road, at Yorkville Avenue, Yorkville, ON M5R 2G3 (1-800 446 4656/416 964 1220/fax 416 964 8692/www.hojo-canada.com). Subway Museum. **Rates** *$105-$159 single/double.* **Credit** AmEx, DC, MC, V. **Map** p282 F4.
This is the best bet for staying in Yorkville on a budget. Located right next door to Hazelton Lanes, this chain hotel has homely rooms with wooden furniture and exposed brick walls. (The downside is that some rooms have windows that look out on to other brick walls.) It's not cramped exactly, but in the halls, lifts, rooms and bathrooms you'll always wish you had just a little more space. Although there's no restaurant, rates include free breakfast, and coffee and tea (available 24 hours a day in the lobby).
Gym. Internet (dataport, pay terminal). No-smoking rooms. Parking ($10). TV (pay movies).

Budget

Ainsley House Bed & Breakfast

19 Elm Avenue, at Sherbourne Street, Rosedale, ON M4W 1M9 (1-888 423 3337/416 972 0533/fax 416 925 1853/www.interlog.com/~hannigan). Bus 75/subway Sherbourne. **Rates** *$49.50-$109 single/double.* **Credit** MC, V. **Map** p283 H3.
Staying at this century-old European-style guesthouse gives you rare access to a Rosedale mansion, though that access is limited. Guests are steered away from the living room, which is used by the Hannigan family, who run the B&B. Rooms have high ceilings and iron beds, plus en suite bathrooms. Hot breakfast is served every day.
Internet (dataport). No-smoking hotel. Parking (free). TV.

Global Guest House

9 Spadina Road, at Bloor Street W, The Annex, ON M5R 2S9 (416 923 4004/fax 416 923 1208). Streetcar 510/subway Spadina. **Rates** *$56-$66 single; $66-$76 double.* **Credit** MC, V. **Map** p282 D4.
Norman and Rhona Singer run this renovated 1889 house, next door to Spadina subway station. Rhona's paintings decorate each room and Norman has been known to play ragtime on the old piano in the office. With only ten rooms, the hotel is intimate, but it's by no means a hostel, nor is it a B&B. It doesn't serve breakfast, but there are free hot and cold drinks in the common room – that's presumably why the Singers call it a 'Bed and Tea'. Not all rooms have en suite bathrooms. The backyard is available for use.
No-smoking rooms. TV.

Madison Manor Boutique Hotel

20 Madison Avenue, at Bloor Street W, The Annex, ON M5R 2S1 (1-877 561 7048/416 922 5579/ fax 416 963 4325/www.madisonavenuepub.com/ madisonmanor). Subway St George or Spadina. **Rates** $89-$194 single/double/suites. **Credit** AmEx, DC, MC, V. **Map** p282 E4.

This historic Victorian mansion on a quiet road just off Bloor Street W has 23 rooms, each individually decorated by co-owner Isabel Manore. (She and her husband David also own the adjoining Madison Avenue Pub; *see p138*.) Furnished with antiques found in Queen Street boutiques, the rooms vary in size, price and amenities. Four have balconies, and three have fireplaces. (Note that some of the rooms appear disturbingly close to the patios of the bar next door, though staff say they have never had a complaint about it.) The hotel gives discounts to U of T students' parents, but children under 13 are not allowed. Rates include continental breakfast.
Bar. Internet (high-speed). No-smoking hotel. Parking ($10-$15). Restaurant.

West End

Expensive

Old Mill Inn

21 Old Mill Road, at Bloor Street W, ON M8X 1G5 (1-866 653 6455/416 236 2641/fax 416 236 2749/ www.oldmilltoronto.com). Subway Old Mill. **Rates** $195-$375 single/double; $395-$595 suite. **Credit** AmEx, DC, MC, V.

The original mill was built on this site next to the Humber River in 1793, the year that Toronto was founded. Today the wooded valley feels almost as secluded as it would have been then. The Tudor-style hotel, which only opened in 2001, incorporates the stone ruins of a later mill, and exudes history and luxury. The 47 individually designed rooms and 13 large suites encircle a wild, multi-level garden with trickling water. Tennis courts, a spa and easy access to trails and parks make you forget you're even in a city (should you want to). And if you like your fluffy bathrobe, duvet, or even your bed, remember: they're all for sale.
Bar. Concierge. Gym. Internet (high-speed). No-smoking hotel. Parking (free). Restaurant. Room service. Spa. TV (DVD/VCR on request, pay movies).

Moderate

Drake Hotel

1150 Queen Street W, at Beaconsfield Avenue, ON M6J 1J3 (416 531 5042/fax 416 531 9493/ www.thedrakehotel.ca). Streetcar 501. **Rates** $149-$259 single/double. **Credit** AmEx, DC, MC, V. **Map** p278 A7.

If you've spent more than three seconds in Toronto you'll have heard of the Drake. Once a flophouse, the 19-room property was transformed by ex-dot.com-mer Jeff Stober, who devoted $5 million and two years to building something Toronto lacked – a multi-purpose HQ of hipdom. Public rooms nicely blend original trimmings of mahogany, terrazzo

Drake Hotel.

floors and steel railings with rotating art exhibits and the odd performance piece: don't be surprised to catch a striptease on the stairway or a spoken word act over Eggs Benny. Though wired for the 21st century with flat-screen TVs, CD and DVD players and high-speed net access, the rooms are not for the claustrophobe (at least the rates are pretty puny as well). The basement provides a venue for eclectic performances. Queues form to get into the funky street level bar and Sky Yard on the roof (heated in winter, but a great place to relax at any time of year). The Corner Café, a restaurant and raw bar round out the attractions of a destination that anchors the transformation of the West Queen West scene. Naysayers maintain this transformed ugly duckling is trying too hard to be cool, but we say, for once, do believe the hype. *See also p130, p140 and p203.*

Bars (2). Concierge. Internet (high-speed, wireless). No-smoking hotel. Restaurants (4). Room service. TV (DVD/VCR, pay movies, widescreen).

Gladstone Hotel

1214 Queen Street West, at Gladstone Avenue, M6J 1J6 (416 531 4635/fax 416 539 0953/ www.gladstonehotel.com). Streetcar 501. **Rates** from $100. **Credit** MC, V. **Map** p278 A7.

West Queen West's newest – and oldest – landmark hotel came back to life in spring 2005 after a spiffy and expensive restoration that highlights many of the original details (including wooden windows and doors) of this 1889 Victorian railroad hostelry. The alternative crowd have long frequented the ground floor public rooms: the Melody Bar for karaoke, the Ballroom for bands, and the Art Bar for book launches and screenings. Upstairs, 52 rooms now all have their own washrooms. For something different, ask for one of the 15 artist-designed rooms. The large suite has access to the turret and a private rooftop deck. A restaurant and café were due to be opened as this guide went to press. With the Drake Hotel (*see p49*) just up the road, WQW is the hippest place to be seen. *See also p94 and p200.*

Internet (wireless), cable, phone.

East Toronto

Budget

Beaches Bed & Breakfast

174 Waverley Road, at Queen Street E, ON M4L 3T3 (416 699 0818/http://members.tripod.com/ beachesbb). Streetcar 501. **Rates** $85-$120 single/double. **Credit** MC, V.

The character of this longstanding B&B is a direct result of the character who runs the place. Enid Evans, who used to own a lingerie shop called Enid's Underworld, has decked out each of the four guest rooms in this century-old house with eclectic themes, including a jungle room (and jungle bathroom) and a romantic, curtain-shrouded loft bed. The location is great, just a block and a half from the boardwalk. *Internet (shared terminal). No-smoking house. TV.*

Hostels

College Hostel

280 Augusta Avenue, at College Street, Chinatown, ON M5T 2L9 (416 929 4777/fax 416 925 5495/ www.affordacom.com). Streetcar 506, 510. **Rates** $50 single; $65 double; $22 (per person) dormitory. **Credit** AmEx, DC, MC, V. **Map** p279 D5.

Just off College Street on the edge of Kensington Market, this popular hostel is pretty well equipped. The single and double rooms have cable TV and phones, and the games room has a pool table and pinball machine. There's also a decent sushi bar. *Internet (wireless). No-smoking hostel. Parking (free). Restaurant. TV.*

Global Village Backpackers

460 King Street W, at Spadina Avenue, Entertainment District, ON M5V 1L7 (1-888 844 7875/416 703 8540/fax 416 703 3887/ www.globalbackpackers.com/toronto/tor.htm). Streetcar 504, 510. **Rates** $56-$60 private room; $26-$28 (per person) quad; $23-$25 (per person) dormitory. **Credit** MC, V. **Map** p279 D8.

Jack Nicholson slept here. Of course, it was a hotel then, not a hostel. Now it's a bright and friendly option with dorms, quads and a few private rooms. The busy bar is a good place to meet fellow travellers, and the staff organise events such as tours of Niagara Falls in rainbow-painted 'Magic Buses'. *Bar. Internet (pay terminal). No-smoking hostel. TV.*

Hostelling International Toronto

76 Church Street, at Adelaide Street E, St Lawrence, ON M5C 2G1 (1-877 848 8737/416 971 4440/ fax 416 971 4088/www.hostellingint-gl.on.ca/ toronto.htm). Streetcar 504, 501/subway King. **Rates** $70 single/double; $23 (per person) dormitory. **Credit** MC, V. **Map** p280 G7.

This is a basic hostel whose about 188 beds are mostly in dorms, while the few private rooms have en suite bathrooms. It's a social place, with organised walking tours of the city and pub crawls on a Wednesday. Barbecues are held on the roof patio in high season. *Disabled-adapted rooms. Internet (pay terminal). No-smoking hostel. TV (lounge with VCR).*

Planet Traveler's Hostel

175 Augusta Avenue, at Dundas Street W, Chinatown, ON M5T 2L4 (416 599 6789/ www.theplanettraveler.com). Streetcar 505, 510. **Rates** $50-$75 single; $21.50-$25 dormitory. **No credit cards. Map** p279 D6.

There's no sign outside this hostel, so look for the garden planted in a vaguely planetary pattern, and the stained-glass Earth above the door. It's a small place – with a big, friendly attitude. The traditional back-patio drinks parties have been on the wane of late, but they still happen if guests prod a little. The one-hole mini-golf course in the backyard maintains its sad charms. Bathrooms are shared and there's a complimentary breakfast of pastries and fruit. *Internet (shared terminal). No-smoking hostel. TV (lounge with VCR).*

Sightseeing

Features

Introduction

The lie of the land.

Toronto is a walking city where much of the pleasure of visiting it comes from being out on the streets exploring diverse neighbourhoods: riding the streetcars, wandering around markets, stopping for a patio lunch or walking in a historic district or parkland artery.

In terms of sights, however, Toronto has few: the CN Tower, obviously, and depending on your orientation, the Hockey Hall of Fame, Royal Ontario Museum, SkyDome (now the Rogers Centre) and the Art Gallery of Ontario. However, things are changing as heavyweights such as Will Alsop and Daniel Libeskind put their stamp on the city, with bold, must-see designs (for an overview, *see pp30-33*).

Don't miss Toronto

Mainstream sights
CN Tower (*see p63*); **SkyDome** (*see p63*); **Kensington Market** (*see p156*); **Chinatown** (*see p68*); **The Beaches** (*see p102*); **Queen Street West** (*see p63*); **Royal Ontario Museum** (*see p77*); **Distillery District** (*see p84*); **Art Gallery of Toronto** (*see p71*); **Casa Loma** (*see p88*).

Lesser-known sights
Bata Shoe Museum (*see p78*); **RC Harris Filtration Plant** (*see p102*); **Elgin & Winter Garden Theatre Centre** (*see p68*); **Toronto Islands** (*see p56*); **Little India** (*see p103*); **Don Valley Brick Works Park** (*see p90*); **'West Queen West'** (*see p62*).

Quintessential Toronto experiences
A peameal bacon sandwich at St Lawrence Market (*see p82*); watching hockey in a bar; taking a streetcar; a dim sum lunch (*see p69*); strolling a lakeside boardwalk; skating at Nathan Phillips Square (*see p71*).

Viewpoints
CN Tower (*see p63*); **Canoe Restaurant & Bar** (*see p107*); looking back at the waterfront from a Toronto Islands ferry (*see p56*); the **Roof Lounge** (*see p138*); **Panorama Lounge** (*see p136*).

ORIENTATION
It is particularly handy that Toronto is so easy to navigate. First, it borders a lake, so if you sense a slight slope downwards, then that's south. Second, it has the world's tallest freestanding building, acting as a handy marker near the lakefront, just west of centre. Third, it's built largely on a grid system, with just enough variation to keep it interesting, but not so much that getting lost is especially easy.

Point zero for east–west street designation and numbering is Yonge Street (pronounced 'Young'), famously if tenuously the longest street in the world. Yonge starts on the central lakefront and heads north – yes, yes, all the way to the state line. So King Street, for example, which runs east–west, is called King Street West to the west of Yonge, and King Street East to the east, with numbers starting from zero at Yonge and running upwards and outwards along each arm. (North–south numbering starts at zero at the south end of roads and goes up as the road heads north.) On an east–west street, even numbers are on the north side, odd numbers on the south; on a north–south street, even numbers are to the west and odd to the east. Armed with this information, you (or your taxi driver) should seldom get lost. The only mildly confusing factor is that numbers on either side of a street don't necessarily match up, or realign in any predictable way at intersections.

Some major thoroughfares have two names, notably Bloor Street, which turns into Danforth Avenue once you cross the Don River, and College Street, which becomes Carlton Street east of Yonge Street. Spadina ('Spad-*eye*-na') Avenue is arbitrarily downgraded to a mere Road in midtown, despite the presence of the august Spadina ('Spad-*ee*-na') House Museum.

Wandering at will is helped by the fact that you're unlikely to find yourself inadvertently in a dangerous area: there really aren't that many. As usual, keep your wits around you at transport terminals, and don't be tempted to short-cut from Cabbagetown to St Lawrence through the slightly ropey Regent Park/Moss Park area. For more on safety, *see p263*.

OVERVIEW
When Metropolitan Toronto amalgamated its five internal cities into one, it officially dropped the 'Metropolitan' moniker. That was in 1998. Now the whole shebang is simply known as the

CN Tower.

City of Toronto, or the 'mega-city', and stretches some 20 miles (32 kilometres) across and from the lakeshore to Steeles Avenue in the north. The population is 2.4 million and growing by the second, if you believe the statisticians. But there's another world on Toronto's doorstep with a population that threatens to exceed the city's own: the vast expanse of suburbs – Mississauga, Brampton, Richmond Hill, Markham and Pickering, to name a few – strung out on a concrete necklace of freeways and malls. Torontonians dismiss hinterland residents as '905-ers', referring to the telephone area code that surrounds the city proper. Taken together, the city and its 'burbs are now called the GTA, or Greater Toronto Area, which is not a political entity as such and even less of a unified mindset.

This book focuses principally on the area defined by the original city of Toronto, roughly bounded by Eglinton Avenue on the north side, Victoria Park Avenue to the east, the waterfront and Islington Avenue on the west, though we have extended those boundaries where an attraction warrants it.

Toronto has relatively few defined, named areas; often neighbourhoods are marked by a strip of businesses and named after their main artery – Queen West, the Danforth, Yonge & Eglinton, for example – or their character: Entertainment District, Little Italy and so on. Our Sightseeing chapters, and the rest of the book, follow an area schema that sticks closely to local use, but as there are no formal boundaries we have sometimes used arbitrary divisions.

Downtown Toronto, south of Bloor Street and between Bathurst and the Don Valley Parkway, is the business and civic heart of the city. Almost every main sight is here, along with the University of Toronto and the major arts and entertainment venues. People very much still live here, so although Toronto seldom bustles, it is rarely dead, either, day or night (Chinatown and the Entertainment District particularly). Next up is culturally diverse **Midtown**, where the money lives, plays and spends itself in tasteful fashion. Casa Loma and Spadina Historic House are here. The **West End** is the hipper side of town, with independent, individual shops, bars and restaurants and a boho lifestyle mainlining down Queen Street West and, to a lesser degree, College Street (Little Italy). If you go out at night and like to eschew the obvious for the characterful, you'll find yourself here a lot of the time. **East Toronto** (aka the East Side) is a little more unreconstructed, with traditional residential areas, the Greek-influenced Danforth, Little India and the Beaches: exactly what it sounds like, with pleasant eating and drinking and some intriguing residential roads to wander. Finally, **North Toronto** (North Side) has the civic amenities of North York (which, prior to amalgamation, was one of Canada's largest cities) and a lot of suburbia.

KEEP IT CHEAP

Toronto is a relatively cheap city to spend time in. The fact that Americans and Brits usually get a favourable exchange rate helps, of course, but so does the fact that lots of city facilities are free, including swimming pools and ice rinks. If you're planning on doing much sightseeing the **CityPass** ($46 adults, $28.50 children), available from Royal Ontario Museum, CN Tower, Art Gallery of Ontario, Casa Loma, Ontario Science Centre and Toronto Zoo or online at http://citypass.com/city/toronto, allows you in to these six main attractions.

Tours

Toronto is somewhere you can enjoyably explore independently, on foot or by public transport (in particular the reliable, characterful streetcars). **Gray Line** (416 594 3310, www.grayline.ca) and **Toronto Tours** (416 869 1372, www.toronto tours.com) both do guided tours, and the latter also has a hop-on, hop-off bus.

In summer, uniformed touts around the Harbourfront jetties hawk boat tours. **Mariposa Tours** (416 203 0178, www.marip osacruises.com) offers one-hour cruises and dining tours; the **Great Lakes Schooner Company** (416 203 2322, www.greatlakes schooner.com) will take you out on a three-mastered tall ship. **A Taste of the World** (416 923 6813, www.torontowalksbikes.com) runs offbeat, culturally oriented walks, such as foodie tours of Chinatown, and literary walks. For **Toronto Hippo Tours**, see p174.

Sightseeing

Downtown

From island-hopping to market shopping, the city centre is your oyster.

Waterfront

Maps p278, p279, p280 & p281

Streetcar 509, 510/subway Queens Quay, Union.
Despite the fact that Toronto owes its very existence to its natural harbour, in a rush to grow up, the city's downtown core has recently been on a determined course to blot out its most attractive natural asset: Lake Ontario.

Long before the city was founded, the sheltered bay served aboriginal peoples as a base for trade and commerce. In the 18th century the French and English settlers used the inland port as a centre for the fur trade. By the early 1900s the port was chugging with steamboats that used Toronto as a starting point for tours of the Great Lakes. The city was the hub of Ontario's booming economy.

The opening of the St Lawrence Seaway in 1959 brought huge ocean-going freighters into Toronto's harbour. But trade by rail and road soon eclipsed the city's hopes as an inland port, a trend exemplified by the construction of the Gardiner Expressway, an elevated highway that runs beside the waterfront.

Today the Gardiner is considered an eyesore and is the source of much local debate. In fact, many who use the road every day say they'd love to see it torn down. Not because it's ugly, and not because it's crumbling and in a constant state of disrepair (urban legends abound about falling concrete chunks), but because it acts like a giant fence between downtown Toronto and its waterfront dreams (*see p60* **Toronto the Green**).

Meanwhile, visitors to the city tend to wonder what all the fuss is about. While getting to the waterfront (especially on bike or foot) can be an alienating urban experience, once there it's easy to spend time exploring the many treasures along the shoreline. Where once were warehouses, fuel stations and port machinery, now there are shops, cafés, theatres, museums, nature reserves, galleries, gardens and parks.

In addition to the lakefront attractions, one of the best ways to experience (and photograph) the waterfront is by taking the ferry to the Toronto Islands (*see p56* **Walk on**), where a variety of attractions await, including a car-free residential community on Ward's Island.

Though the harbour attractions are spread out across the waterfront, many of the best ones are clustered around a series of quays between Cooper Street and Lower Portland Street. A good central location to begin and to get a close up look at the lake is at the terminus of Yonge Street, the longest street in the world. A small tribute here marks the names of towns along the 1,178-mile (1,896-kilometre) road. The town at the very end of the line is Rainy River, Ontario, on the Minnesota border. The esteemed address 1 Yonge Street belongs to the *Toronto Star*, Canada's largest newspaper.

Looking east, the cityscape quickly devolves into an unattractive industrial stretch, with one sweet exception – the **Redpath Sugar Museum** (*see p61*). The **Waterfront Trail** for joggers, bikers and bladers is here little more than faded paint on patchy asphalt (and therefore a bit hard to follow), but improves further out towards the Beaches (*see p102*). The trail also links up to other substantial recreational paths that meander for kilometres up the Don and Humber river valleys and out into the lake along the **Leslie Street Spit** (*see p60* **Toronto the Green**).

Where Bay Street joins Queens Quay is a path that leads behind the **Westin Harbour Castle** hotel (*see p38*) to the Island ferry docks and to **Harbour Square Park**. If you're looking for quiet green space in which to escape the crowds and the hustle of the city, this is not the place. Towers loom over the busy strip of grass, squeezing it against the water. If you follow the park around Harbour Square back to the main road, you'll find **Pier 6** (145 Queens Quay W, at the foot of York Street), the oldest surviving building on the waterfront. Built in 1907, the former freight shed has had many incarnations, including a stint as the shore station for the Royal Canadian Yacht Club. It now houses a coffee shop and a souvenir store. On warm days the former cargo doors are opened up, allowing visitors to sip their latte while enjoying the sights and sounds of boats going to and fro.

In the 1970s the **Queens Quay Terminal** (207 Queens Quay W, 416 203 0510), just to the west, was a disused food warehouse, a casualty of hard times at the harbour. Today it's an affluent office/shopping mall complex with upscale boutiques and restaurants, some

Walk on Toronto Islands

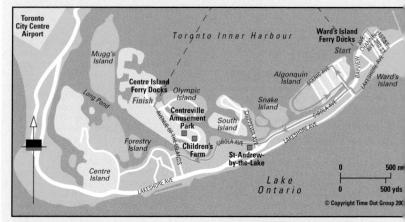

Start: Ward's Island Ferry Terminal
Finish: Centre Island Ferry Terminal
Length: About 4 miles (6km)
Time: 60-90 minutes, not including distractions
General information: 416 397 2628
Ferry timetable: 416 392 8193 ($6; $3.50 concessions; $2.50 under-15s)

The Toronto Islands are like the city's alter ego. Together, they've played a quiet but vital supporting role – protecting the city shores and offering Torontonians (and visitors) an accessible, serene escape with no motorised vehicles. Here wildlife and nature are closer at hand and urban life seems far away – even while savouring some of the best views of the city. These wonderful islands, full of paradox and mystery have always been entwined with the Toronto's history, but they haven't always been islands.

John Graves Simcoe (*see p11*) chose the shores near the sheltered harbour as the perfect location for Upper Canada's new capital. But when John and his wife Elizabeth sailed into the harbour in 1791 they saw a long sandy isthmus adjoined to the harbour's east mainland, dotted with a few tiny islands at the west. As York was being settled, one of Elizabeth's favourite pastimes was to gallop on horseback along the shore of that isthmus. It remained until 1858 when a huge storm flooded and blew out the connection to the mainland.

Part island, part archipelago, part sandbar, ever evolving: these 15 islands, large and small offer predictable amenities like paddleboats, beaches, tennis courts, bicycle rentals and the small amusement park on Centre Island. But in addition there are sprawling breezy parks, a bird sanctuary, a nudist beach and a historic (and heroic) residential community of about 800 people who live on Ward's Island, year round. *Take the Ward's Island Ferry from the terminal behind Westin Harbour Castle Hotel at Bay Street and Queens Quay Boulevard. Walk begins from the ferry dock on Ward's Island.*

Look carefully at the harbour and enjoy the breeze and the seagulls as the city slips away. 'Ah.' That's the first feeling as you disembark into the clean air of the Toronto Islands – instead of cars you're greeted by bicycles, quadricycles, boarders and bladers zipping along the paved pathways that spiral off in different directions.

Bear to the left along the waterside concrete path that turns into Bayview Avenue. Turn right on to Third Street.

These so called 'streets' are just barely wide enough for two people to walk abreast, if you're on a bike walk it or lock it up for this part of the tour. In the 1950s the city tried to chase the locals off the islands to make way for a park. Walking through this quiet paradise, hemmed by flower gardens, picket fences, spreading trees and small

cottages, it's easy to see why these people fought so hard to keep the island community alive. Thanks to them, it's here for all of us to enjoy.

Turn left at Channel Avenue and walk to First Street.

And mind the gap! Behold the infamous 'Eastern Gap', where the islands were truncated by a torrential tempest in 1858. After being dredged and deepened the gap has improved access to the harbour for deeper vessels. It's now an important shipping route, as well as a backdrop for a spectacular garden of lilies, primroses and daisies.

Follow First Street to Lakeshore Avenue, where you turn right.

Lakeshore Avenue, the major east–west thoroughfare, runs like a spine along the south side of the islands. It becomes a boardwalk for a stretch, from which you have a view across the water of a migratory bird sanctuary (on Muggs Island). Several paths to the right tuck neatly through a lush wall of greenery back to the gardens, picnic tables and playgrounds in the interior of the island. A few hundred metres along, take the one that leads to the **Rectory Café** (416 203 2152). This is the best spot to eat on the islands, and offers home-made soups, sandwiches and other tasty treats. The Rectory is also a cultural centre – check the bulletin board near the entrance for details on art exhibitions and musical performances.

Continue along the path to Cibola Avenue. Turn left and then quickly right on to Algonquin Bridge, which turns into Ojibway Avenue after it crosses Omaha Avenue. Keep following it north to the shore.

Swans, ducks, geese and kayakers are all commonly seen paddling through these still waters, while the city rises up in contrast behind them. This is possibly the best view anywhere, of Toronto's skyline.

Turn left on Seneca Avenue. At Wyandot Avenue, a secluded trail leads off the path. This trail loops around and rejoins Omaha Avenue. Recross Algonquin Bridge and continue west on Cibola Avenue. When the path forks, stay to the right.

Just after it crosses Chippewa Avenue, the path runs by **St Andrew-by-the-Lake Church** (416 203 0873). This small Anglican church, built in 1884, still offers regular Sunday services, as well as weddings and baptisms. The humble clapboard exterior forms a contrast with the gothic arches of its stained-glass windows. The shady setting and nearby picnic tables provide an ideal resting spot.

The path continues west to Avenue of the Islands. Turn right.

A small hedge maze just east of the avenue offers a zany diversion.

Follow Avenue of the Islands north over a white and pastel-green bridge, peaking over a quiet canal.

Turn right just after the Iroquois Coffee Shop to enter the **Centreville Amusement Park** (416 203 0405) – a great spot for the kids. Attractions include swan, pedal and bumper boats, plus a miniature train, a petting farm, a video arcade and a bare-bones miniature golf course. Sugary snacks and crispy treats abound. Enjoy the rides, or head off in another direction and find your own little piece of the island. If you stroll down the main path you'll soon reach the Centre Island Ferry dock, where a frequent ferry service awaits. It's nice to wait down the shore for a few minutes to watch the ships go by (and your ferry come in) and meditate on the next adventure that lurks over across the water... back in the smoke and the noise of the urban jungle.

Note that, out of season, this walk is best done with a friend, as some areas are deserted.

Toronto Music Garden.

boasting harbourside terraces for al fresco noshing. The terminal also houses the **Premiere Dance Theatre** (*see p224*).

Next door, the **Power Plant Gallery** (231 Queens Quay W, 416 973 4949) is easy to spot, thanks to its distinctive smokestack, a vestige from its days as a generating plant. Built in 1926, the Power Plant and its conjoined sibling, the Ice House (now the Harbourfront Centre Theatre), provided heating and cooling for the Toronto Terminal Warehouse (which later became Queens Quay Terminal). Its conversion to a gallery began in 1980, but the doors didn't open to the public until seven years later. The Power Plant features contemporary works and installations by Canadian and international artists. A word to the credulous: the **Harbourfront Centre Theatre** (formerly known as the du Maurier Theatre) is said to be haunted by up to three different ghosts.

You won't see any ghosts in the building to the west (yet another converted terminal building), but you will see plenty of live artists, performers and artsy types at the **York Quay Centre** (235 Queens Quay W, 416 973 4000), which is home to a thriving cultural complex run by the Harbourfront Centre.

The York Quay complex also includes indoor and outdoor performance spaces and four art galleries. The Brigantine Room is where the Harbourfront Reading Series takes place (*see p171*). It's also home to a craft studio where you can watch sculptors, glass blowers and artists in other media practising their crafts in an open studio setting. Their works are for sale at the nearby craft shop. On the south side

of the building is an outdoor café with a small pond. Here hobbyists skipper remote-controlled model boats in the summer – in the winter it's a public skating rink. Also facing the lake, the **Harbourfront Centre Concert Stage** (*see p198*) is an outdoor venue that hosts music concerts in summer. While admission to Harbourfront is free, and there are frequent excellent free concerts, many events and venues do require tickets. Check the website and weekly listings.

Heading west will take you to the **Toronto Music Garden** (475 Queens Quay W). Originally planned for Boston, the garden was inspired by Bach's 'Suites for Unaccompanied Cello' as envisioned by cellist Yo-Yo Ma, who collaborated with landscape designer Julie Moir Messervy to interpret the music in a natural garden. The Summer Music in the Garden series presents classical and new music concerts. From June to September visitors can relax and enjoy the garden in bloom with self-guided audio tours.

At the foot of Bathurst Street, behind the last standing grain elevator on the waterfront, is a public boat service that crosses the Western Channel to Toronto City Centre Airport. Dubbed 'the shortest ferry ride in the world', the trip takes less than 60 seconds. In a bold and progressive move, the city recently rejected an airport expansion plan that would have replaced the ferry with a permanent bridge (*see p60* **Toronto the Green**).

A half-hour walk further along the shore takes you to **Ontario Place** and **Exhibition Place** (for both, *see p61*).

Toronto the Green

After several years of booming downtown construction and development there are signs that Toronto is doing some stock-taking, putting into place some sensible measures to conserve its valuable natural resources.

Nowhere is this value shift more evident than along the waterfront. Under mayor Mel Lastman, condo developers had a lakefront feeding frenzy, with high rises forming a concrete curtain across the city's centre core. Lastman's successor, current mayor David Miller, swept to victory based, in good part, on his strong stance on a key waterfront issue: declaring he would not allow the construction of a permanent bridge to the tiny island commuter airport, the candidate swept into office and ceased the bulldozers and cranes, literally on the eve of construction.

In addition to preventing tons of jet fuel from leeching directly into the harbour, Miller has revived the hope of transforming Toronto's waterfront from an industrial heartland into an open, attractive, people-oriented place that is re-integrated with the rest of downtown. In the meantime there are some encouraging signs of intelligent life along Lake Ontario.

The first, heading east along Lake Shore Drive, is a striking new 30-storey-high wind turbine by the Liberty Grand at Exhibition

Place. The Dutch-built windmill has the capacity to power up to 250 households a year, but its presence is more symbolic of future trends in power generation.

One of Toronto's lesser-known environmental triumphs is a crescent-shaped, man-made lake-fill park known as the **Leslie Street Spit**. This three-mile (five-kilometre)-long peninsula is one of North America's most successful urban wilderness reclamation projects. The unique public project began in the 1950s as a harbour upgrade for the expected increase in shipping traffic along the St Lawrence Seaway. As other modes of transport eclipsed the shipping business, the city transformed the spit into an aquatic wilderness preserve. On weekends and holidays walkers, birders, bladers and cyclists enjoy the solitude of this haven, and an incredible variety of flora and fauna – some 400 varieties of plant and about 300 bird species. Beaver, otter, red foxes and coyotes have also been sighted here. In 1974 a lighthouse was established to mark its terminus. Today the 'Spit' is officially known as Tommy Thompson Park, after a former parks commissioner.

Further west is Humber Bay Park, home to the **Humber Bay Butterfly Habitat**, a new ecological restoration project that provides critical habitat for native butterfly species, with native wildflowers, shrubs, trees, grasses, sedges and other physical features known to support butterflies throughout their life cycles.

Humber Bay Butterfly Habitat

Base of Park Lawn Road, south of Lake Shore Boulevard W, Humber Bay Park East, West End (information 416 392 5253). Streetcar 501. **Open** *dawn-dusk daily.*

Leslie Street Spit

South of Lake Shore Boulevard, Harbourfront. Streetcar 501 (get off at Berkshire Street & go south on Leslie Street; it's about 1 mile/ 1.5km to the gate). **Open** *early May-mid Oct 9am-6pm daily. Late Oct-early May 9am-4.30pm daily.*
Cars aren't allowed onto the Spit, but parking is available at the gate. A shuttle van operates from early May to mid October, running to a footbridge about three-fifths of the way out to the lighthouse. Otherwise, the walk from the park entrance to the lighthouse is about two miles (five kilometres). A walking map and brochure are available at the park entrance.

Exhibition Place

Lake Shore Boulevard W, between Strachan Avenue & Dufferin Street (416 263 3600/www.explace.on.ca). Bus 29/streetcar 509, 511. **Open** times vary; phone for details. **Admission** prices vary; phone for details. **Map** p278 B9.

The imposing Princes' Gates (named after Edward, Prince of Wales, and his brother George) rise up to meet you as you approach the grounds from the east and promise the pomp and circumstance befitting the grand old lady, born in 1879, known as the Canadian National Exhibition. The CNE celebrated its 130th anniversary recently and the facilities have been nicely upgraded to host not just the annual late summer festival and amusement park, but over 100 major events, from the Molson Indy car race (*see p169*) to the Canadian National Exhibition (*see p170*). Look out for what is believed to be the oldest building in the city, the Scadding Cabin, which was built in 1794 and moved here from its original location on the east bank of the Don River (*see also p32* **Doors Open Toronto**).

The former Carlsberg building has been buffed up as the Liberty Grand Entertainment Complex (25 British Columbia Road, Exhibition Place, 416 542 3890). The beautiful Beaux Arts building with swooping hallways and 27-foot (10-metre) ceilings is playing a new starring role on the exhibition grounds, as a favoured local venue for huge and glamorous events in the worlds of film, fashion, fundraising, food and wine.

Ontario Place

955 Lake Shore Boulevard W, between Aquatic Drive & Newfoundland Drive (416 314 9900/ www.ontarioplace.com). Bus 29/streetcar 509, 511/subway Union. **Open** Dates & times vary; phone for details. Closed winter. **Admission** $13-$29; $13-$17 concessions; free under-3s. *IMAX* tickets $8-$10, $6 concessions. **Credit** AmEx, MC, V. **Map** p278 B10.

This public amusement park was built in the 1970s, when Canadian nationalism (and, some would say, government spending) was at its zenith. The private sector has since stolen all the thunder at Paramount Canada's Wonderland north of the city (*see p173*), but Ontario Place retains the pleasure of its lakeside location. The walkways, cafés and the world's first IMAX theatre are built out over the water, and many of the rides – from waterslides to a nifty log boat ride – involve getting at least a little wet. The pedal boats, normally the runt of the amusement park litter, are fun, as you can chug in and out of the futuristic structures that criss-cross the water. The park is also home to the Molson Amphitheatre (*see p201*), a 15,000-capacity al fresco venue, where fans spread out on the grass hill or take the reserved seats close to the stage for top summertime touring acts.

Redpath Sugar Museum

95 Queens Quay E, between Yonge Street & Lower Jarvis Street (416 366 3561). Bus 6, 75/streetcar 509. **Open** 10am-noon, 1-3.30pm Mon-Fri. **Admission** free. **Map** p280 G9.

Sightseeing

Ontario Place.

Although its hours don't lend themselves to the weekend tourist trade, free admission makes this unusual attraction a worthwhile stop. The entrance is poorly marked, but when you sign in the gate attendant will point you in the right direction. The museum, housed in a converted sugar bag warehouse, was opened in 1979 and underwent a major revamp in 1996. In addition to generic exhibits on the history of the Redpath dynasty and of the sugar industry in general, there are also special programmes for groups. To the museum's credit, these have often delved in to controversial issues of the sugar trade, including the role of child, immigrant and slave labour and the introduction of women into the workforce. This is a working refinery and sugar boats from the Caribbean are often in port unloading their cargo.

Downtown West

Entertainment District

Maps p279 & p280

Streetcar 501, 504, 510/subway Osgoode, St Andrew, Union.

This area is not misnamed, even if it sounds like something from a Stalinist manifesto on urban planning. This is where Toronto comes to have fun – as do busloads of visitors.

Three major attractions are plonked between the train tracks running into Union Station and the Gardiner Expressway: the **Air Canada Centre** arena, the thrusting needle of the **CN Tower** and the **Rogers Centre** (aka **SkyDome**) stadium (for all three, *see p63*), with its famous retractable roof. All are accessible via indoor walkways from **Union Station** (*see p64*), and if you're on foot they are best approached from there or the walkway's other street junction at Front Street W and the foot of John Street – this is otherwise not a pedestrian-friendly area. Conveniently, the walkway has another exit on to Bremner Boulevard right opposite the **Steam Whistle Brewing** company (*see p63*).

Moving north, many of Toronto's media, music and fashion types work in the cool Queen Street West zone, roughly between Bathurst and University Avenue. It's full of nightclubs, theatres, cafés, designer shops and plenty of beautiful people looking extremely urgent while playing with their cellphones, MP3s and Blackberries. Further west is the new 'West Queen West' area.

At the corner of John Street, the **Canadian Broadcasting Corporation**'s headquarters (250 Front Street W, live tapings 416 205 3700, museum 416 205 5574) is worth a look to get to know Canada's (in)famous public broadcaster (considered either the absolute saviour of Canuck culture, or a complete waste of time and money, depending on which local you ask). A free museum in the lobby depicts the golden age of radio and TV. To get fully with the flow, switch on, tune in or log on to CBC's many media outlets (*see p261*), or catch a free taping of one of programmes done before a live studio audience. The **Glenn Gould Studio** (*see p198*) is also in this building and is an intimate venue for concert recordings.

A few blocks north is the **Paramount Cinema** (259 Richmond Street W; *see also p181*). If you can stand the sensory overload, you'll find an out-of-place and often-overlooked display at the top of the long escalator that leads from the lobby to the cinemas. The Paramount Historic Railing includes sections of the bronze railing from the lobby of the original Paramount Theatre in Times Square, New York. A small collection of old photos and a continuous video presentation help recapture the grandeur of the 1920s movie experience.

Two blocks away is the Toronto home of Canada's well-known **National Film Board** (150 John Street, 416 973 3012), complete with individual screening rooms (*see p180* **Room with a viewing**).

One block north, the **MZTV Museum of Television** (277 Queen Street W, 416 591 7400 ext 2870, www.mztv.com) offers regular guided

View from **CN Tower**. *See p63.*

tours. Founded by the late Moses Znaimer, the museum features what it claims is the world's largest collection of television sets (about 200 in all) and TV memorabilia, including a 1928 General Electric 'Octagon', an experimental model never sold to the public, and the 1939 Phantom Teleceiver, which launched the television age in North America.

Home to the cutting edge arty set in the 1970s and early 1980s, **Queen Street West**, from University Avenue to Bathurst Street, is more about retail than revolution these days. Chain stores have moved in to cash in on the area's vibe, leaving some of the funkier galleries, restaurants and bookshops to emigrate further west in search of cheaper rent. It must be said, however that, though it's glory days are gone, Queen West is still a vibrant spot to walk, to lunch, to people watch and to shop for those offbeat items – including vintage vinyl. Famous clubs like the Beverly have closed, though the **Rivoli** (see p107, p203 and p216), the **Cameron House** (see p203) and the **Horseshoe Tavern** (see p201) keep the Queen West nightlife spirit alive.

The 'new' Queen West ('West Queen West') is further west, west of Bathurst Street.

Air Canada Centre

40 Bay Street, at Front Street W (416 815 5500/ www.theaircanadacentre.com). Subway Union. **Tours** *May-Aug* hourly 10am-4pm daily. *Sept-Apr* hourly 11am-3pm Wed-Sat (dependent on events; phone to check). **Admission** $12; $8-$10 concessions. **Credit** AmEx, MC, V. **Map** p279/p280 F9.

The 21,000-seat arena offers regular behind-the-scenes tours that, schedule permitting, include a glimpse inside the dressing rooms of home teams the Raptors (basketball) and the Leafs (ice hockey), as well as a chance to try on a goalie outfit.

CN Tower

301 Front Street W, at John Street (416 868 6937/ www.cntower.ca). Subway Union. **Open** *Tower* Summer 8am-11pm daily. Winter 9am-10pm Mon-Thur, Sun; 9am-10.30pm Fri, Sat. *Other attractions* phone for details. **Admission** $22-$30; $16-$28 concessions; free under-4s. **Credit** AmEx, MC, V. **Map** p279 E8.

There are those who quip that the best thing about the CN Tower is that it's the only place you can be in Toronto where you don't have to look at the CN Tower. Love it or hate it, there's one thing everybody agrees on: it's very, very tall. Completed in 1976 by the railway giant Canadian National, it's the world's tallest freestanding structure (there's ongoing debate about whether it qualifies as a building, given that most of it is just a pillar of hollow concrete). It stands 1,815 feet (553 metres) high and is basically a big radio antenna – and tourist attraction. Visitors are awed by its height, and locals are pleased to have such clear TV reception. The tower

is about twice as tall as its closest competitor in the city, and it's astounding to watch the surrounding 40- and 50-storey buildings fall away below you from the glass elevator. The basic ticket takes you up to the 346-metre (1,136-foot) Look Out Level, where there are indoor and outdoor observation decks, plus a nerve-jangling section of glass floor. The Horizons Café is cheaper and more casual than the tower's swanky, rotating restaurant, 360 The Restaurant (reservations 416 362 5411).

From here you can pay extra to reach the Sky Pod another 30 storeys up to a height of 1,467 feet (447 metres). The experience is truly breathtaking and, at busy times, can also be mildly claustrophobic. Vertigo sufferers can head to the basement to find a short time-lapse documentary on the construction of the tower, as well as a vast gift store.

SkyDome (Rogers Centre)

1 Blue Jays Way, at Front Street W (416 341 2770/www.rogerscentre.com). Streetcar 504/subway St Andrew or Union. **Tours** *Summer* hourly 10am-3pm daily. *Winter* 11am, 1pm, 3pm daily (dependent on events; phone to check). **Admission** $12.50; $7-$8.50 concessions; free under-5s. **Credit** AmEx, MC, V. **Map** p279 E8/E9.

Looking like a giant white beetle, the SkyDome (which was recently renamed the Rogers Centre after its purchase by Rogers Communications) is a more significant building than the Air Canada Centre, and also has a more arresting tour. The walking tour, which starts with a 15-minute film about the construction, varies according to what's happening in the stadium, but, in addition to the boxes, media centre and memorabilia room, it can include a walk on the field, or even a tour of the amazing roof. When the stadium opened in 1989, the fully retractable roof was the only one of its kind in the world. An efficient, quiet rail system allows it to open or close in only 20 minutes. The stadium holds up to 70,000 people, though few events actually draw that many fans, especially since the fall from success of resident ball team, the Blue Jays. One thing the tour does not cover is Toronto artist Michael Snow's sculpture, *The Audience*, on the outside of the stadium. You can find this frieze of 14 enthused spectators high on the north-east corner of the edifice.

Steam Whistle Brewing

255 Bremner Boulevard, at Spadina Avenue (416 362 2337/www.steamwhistle.ca). Streetcar 509, 510. **Open** noon-6pm daily. **Tours** hourly 1-5pm daily. **Admission** *Tours* $4. **Map** p279 E9.

Of the many microbreweries in Toronto, this one gets top marks for location, sandwiched between the ACC and the CN Tower in a railway roundhouse building. The brewery tour informs about combining hops and malt, as well as providing a glimpse of Toronto's railroading past. Steam Whistle offers tours, pours sizeable samples and hosts various events and exhibits. The products are available here, at most bars and taverns in town, and in the Beer Store (see p156).

Sightseeing

Financial District

Maps p279 & p280

Streetcar 501, 504/subway King, Osgoode, Queen, St Andrew, Union.

Bay Street, the main drag of the Financial District, is synonymous with both Canadian monetary power and the dour Presbyterian work ethic that made Toronto such a dull city for so long. In spite of this, the buildings that are testaments to money new and old make the concrete canyons worth risking neck strain to take it all in.

The **King** and **Bay** area is still money central. Four of the five major Canadian banks scrape the sky here, and the fifth, the Royal Bank, maintains an iconic presence a block south, where its flashy golden towers bring an almost American glitz to the skyline.

Banks have clustered in the neighbourhood at least since the mid 1800s, but the first wave of 'skyscrapers' didn't arrive until the early 20th century, and the first biggies didn't apper until the 1920s and '30s, a period that produced the stunning **Commerce Court North** (the original Canadian Imperial Bank of Commerce building) at 25 King Street W. Built 1929-31 and 34 storeys tall, it has a 65-foot (20-metre) high banking hall modelled on the Baths of Caracalla in Rome, and was once the tallest building in the British Commonwealth. The building dominated the neighbourhood until the mid 1960s, when the three original towers of the **Toronto-Dominion Centre** arose on the south-west corner of King and Bay Streets. Designed by Mies van der Rohe, the giant of modernism, the austere black-steel and bronzed-glass towers quickly became a Toronto landmark.

Other, taller structures soon followed, as rival banks sought to catch the public eye. But none of them equals the T-D Centre's austere pizazz, and today the neighbouring banks are mostly notable for their helpful colour coding: the shiny steel of the 57-storey tower of **Commerce Court West** (the CIBC's current home, designed by IM Pei); the white marble of the Bank of Montreal's **First Canadian Place** tower, with its 72 storeys; and the red granite of the **Bank of Nova Scotia**'s 66-storey tower. A more nondescript tower west of the Bank of Montreal tower, at York and King Streets, houses the **Toronto Stock Exchange**, while the TSE's former home round the corner at 234 Bay Street is now the **Design Exchange** (*see p65*).

Further south on Bay Street, the triangular towers of **Royal Bank Plaza** at 200 Bay Street are shorter (41 and 26 storeys), but more resonant of the Bay Street ethic, their mirrored golden windows an apt metaphor for Bay Street's driving materialism. Built in the mid 1970s, their opulent reflections have enriched the pages of many a corporate calendar.

Across the street, the massive towers of **BCE Place** look like a series of tin cans stacked haphazardly on top of one other. The complex incorporates the façades of several historic buildings on its Yonge Street side, and houses the remains of Toronto's oldest surviving stone structure, the former Commercial Bank of the Midland District (1845), within its bulk. The bank was designed by William Thomas, who is also responsible for two other important structures in old Toronto – **St Lawrence Hall** (built in 1850) and the old **Don Jail** (*see p14* **Crimes and misdemeanours**). The centre's best feature, in fact, is its astonishing galleria. Designed by the Spanish architect Santiago Calatrava, the high white arches of the galleria resembling the ribs of a giant whale or the vaulted roof of an old cathedral.

An underground mall leads to the **Hockey Hall of Fame** (*see p65*), part of which occupies a rococo bank building on the north-west corner of Front and Yonge Streets. Once the main Toronto office for the Bank of Montreal, it dates from 1886 and boasts a 14-metre (45-foot) high banking hall and a stained-glass dome. Too bad that the architecture is now overshadowed by hockey memorabilia.

West on Front Street, the **Fairmont Royal York Hotel** (*see p38*) dominates the area. One of a string of railway hotels that spans the country, it has been one of Toronto's signature hotels since opening in 1929.

Across the street rises the massive colonnade of **Union Station**, a gateway to the city and a landmark in the struggle to preserve its past. Built between 1915 and 1927 in Classical Revival style, the railway hub was slated for redevelopment in the 1970s but was saved by determined preservationists. Today it's both the intersection point of subway, rail and commuter lines and an architectural landmark. It's almost 850 feet (259 metres) long and its celebrated Great Hall is considered one of the finest public rooms in Canada.

At the other, northern end, of the Financial District, the handsome **Hudson's Bay Company**'s department store anchors the south-west corner of Queen and Yonge Streets. Built 1895-6 (with later additions), the former Simpsons store houses both contemporary fashions and part of Ken Thomson's famous collection of Canadian art. West on Queen Street, Toronto's first real opera house opens in 2006 at the corner of Queen Street and University Avenue, just opposite Osgoode Hall. Despite its reputation as an arts centre, Toronto has never had a designated opera house before.

Will Alsop's **Sharp Centre for Design**. See p69.

Designed by Diamond + Schmitt, the **Four Seasons Centre for the Performing Arts** will hold about 2,000 people in a tiered horseshoe-shaped auditorium. *See also p196.*

PATH, a much-ballyhooed system of underground pathways, connects most of the major buildings in the downtown core, providing protection from the winter cold and summer heat. It stretches from the Metro Toronto Convention Centre in the south to the bus terminal at Bay and Dundas Streets in the north. With 16 miles (27 kilometres) of shopping arcades and 1,200 shops and services, the maze-like system can feel disorienting. Despite poor signage, it's a convenient place for shelter.

Design Exchange

234 Bay Street, at King Street W (416 216 2160/ www.dx.org). Streetcar 504/subway King. **Open** 9am-6pm Mon-Fri. **Admission** $8; $5 concessions. **Credit** AmEx, MC, V. **Map** p279/280 F8.
The former home of the Toronto Stock Exchange, this 1937 building is as notable for its deco design as for its collection of post-war Canuck artefacts. Noted Canadian artist Charles Comfort created the eight murals on the former trading floor as well the the exterior stone frieze, which depicts different kinds of workers. Check out the businessman in a top hat (fourth in from the right) apparently picking the pocket of the worker in front of him.

Hockey Hall of Fame

BCE Place, 30 Yonge Street, at Front Street W (416 360 7765/www.hhof.com). Streetcar 504/subway King or Union. **Open** *June-Aug* 9.30am-6pm Mon-Sat; 10am-6pm Sun. *Sept-May* 10am-5pm Mon-Fri; 9.30am-6pm Sat; 10.30am-5pm Sun. **Admission** $12; $8 concessions; free under-4s. **Credit** AmEx, MC, V. **Map** p279/280 F8.

A tribute to Canada's national game, this sports shrine features more than 50,000 sq ft (5,110 sq m) of games, displays and memorabilia, including Olympic artefacts and information on the hall's 300-odd inductees. Most people come to get their photo taken with the Stanley Cup and other hockey trophies, but you can also test your skills against a couple of virtual greats.

Toronto-Dominion Centre

66 Wellington Street W, at Bay Street (416 869 1144/www.tdretail.ca). Streetcar 504/subway King or Union. **Open** 10am-6pm Mon-Fri. **Admission** free. **Credit** varies. **Map** p279/280 F8.
Mies van der Rohe's late modernist masterpiece is a close cousin to his famous Seagram Building in New York, but the black steel and bronze glass towers are now very much a part of Toronto's self-image. Together with new City Hall, the T-D Centre set the pace for the rejuvenation of Toronto in the 1960s. Later additions to the complex, one of them towering over the former Toronto Stock Exchange (now the Design Exchange), have unbalanced the plaza in which the towers are set, but the complex remains one of the few architectural masterpieces in modern Toronto. Most of the centre is off-limits to the public, including the banking boardroom on the 54th floor of the main tower, with its original Mies-designed furniture. But two large outdoor sculptures are noteworthy: Al McWilliams' eerie circle-and-chairs (officially known as *Wall and Chairs*) on the King Street side, and Joe Fafard's exceedingly popular bronze cows in the central plaza. The seven life-size bovines ruminate on a tiny patch of grass indifferent to the urban activity all around them.

Directly to the south of the cows is the celebrated Toronto-Dominion Gallery of Inuit Art (Ground Level, 79 Wellington Street W, 416 982 8473). Housed in the southernmost tower of the T-D complex, this gallery is part of the bank's vast world-wide collection of art.

Dundas Square

Maps p279 & p280

Streetcar 501, 505/subway Dundas, Osgoode, Queen, St Patrick.
Bounded by Gerrard, Jarvis, Queen and Bay streets, the Dundas Square neighbourhood is, in many respects, the true heart of the city. The area, in particular Yonge Street, is filled with a mix of people from all fields of life, plus a wide-ranging combination of retail outlets: porn cinemas, discount electronics shops and music megastores. The latest addition to the area is a granite park that basks in the neon glare of billboards above the intersection of Yonge and Dundas. Many had hoped that grass and trees would replace the tacky low-rise shops that were expropriated in this effort to create a converging point for the city's throngs. So far, though, this square, with its inhospitable hard surface and

Sightseeing (sidebar)

hastily wrought stage, has not in any way supplanted Nathan Phillips Square as a civic showcase of any purport. The new **Olympic Spirit Toronto** (*see p68*) ups the wattage of electronic emission flowing on to the square.

Over on Yonge Street, just outside **Toronto Eaton Centre** shopping mall (*see p68*), the pavement is inscribed with a map of the meandering route traced out by Yonge. In this open area, souvenir shills unload cheap baubles, while Bible-thumpers foretell the Apocalypse. Escape to tranquil **Trinity Square Park** behind the mall, where the groovily progressive Anglican **Church of the Holy Trinity** (10 Trinity Square, 416 598 4521) offers a less intrusive version of Christianity (the activist church makes a point of welcoming marginalised groups). The south entrance of the building opens on to a small grassy copy of the 13th-century stone labyrinth at Chartres Cathedral. Walking the circuitous path is meant to be meditative, not puzzling – the turf grass walls are only a few inches high, so the only place you'll get lost here is in your own thoughts.

North of the Eaton Centre, across Dundas, is the **Atrium on Bay**, a mediocre mini mall that houses the central office of the **Ontario Travel Information Centre** (*see p265*).

South from here, nothing beats Toronto's **Old City Hall** and its wondrous gargoyles (60 Queen Street W, 416 338 0338) for a taste of Toronto's prevalent architectural style of old: Romanesque Revival. Designed by architect Edward James Lennox, who also created Casa Loma and the King Edward Hotel, the castle-like hall opened in 1899 and is now a National Historic Site. The massive stone building features a 341-foot (104-metre) clock tower and highly ornamented Romanesque façades. It costs nothing to visit the grand entrance hall, and it's a worthwhile stop to see its mosaic floor, wrought-iron grotesques, stained-glass windows and scagliola columns. Since 1965, when the new City Hall went up across Bay Street, this building has been used as a courthouse. Across Bay Street to the west is another period piece – the current **City Hall** (*see p71*), whose futuristic spaceship council chambers and arcing office towers made the perfect (1960s) symbol for a burgeoning, confident city on the move.

Back on Yonge Street you'll find two of Toronto's best-known theatres, the **Canon Theatre** (*see p220*) and the **Elgin & Winter Garden Theatre Centre** (*see p68*). Just north-east, at the corner of Shuter and Victoria Streets, is **Massey Hall** (*see p198*), the legendary music venue; heading north along Victoria (passing the lovely **Senator** diner; *see p125* **Grease is the word**) will take you to Ryerson

University, home of **Ryerson Theatre** (44 Gerrard Street E, 416 979 5086). The university's grassy quad, accessible from Gerrard Street, between Yonge and Church, can provide quiet respite from the main thoroughfares.

East of Yonge is worship central. This area puts the 'church' in Church Street (although most of the entrances are in fact on Bond Street). **St George's Greek Orthodox Church** (115 Bond Street, near Gould Street, 416 977 3342) is recognisable by its semi-circular mosaic of George slaying the dragon and by its hemispherical domes capped with distinctive orthodox crosses. Across the road at No.116, the **First Evangelical Lutheran Church** (416 977 4786), erected in 1898 by German immigrants to the Toronto area, still offers services in both English and German.

The Gothic **St Michael's Cathedral** (65 Bond Street, at Shuter Street, 416 364 0234) is the principal church of Canada's largest English-speaking Catholic Archdiocese. Michael Power, Toronto's first Catholic bishop, laid the first cornerstone in 1845, and the building was completed three years later. The design is adapted from 14th-century English Gothic style by English architect William Thomas. Masses are sometimes graced by the boys of the St Michael's Choir School.

Metropolitan United Church (56 Queen Street E, 416 363 0331) places an emphasis on spreading the word through music. The first building on this site was constructed by Methodists and opened its doors in 1872. In 1925 the Methodists merged with the Congregational Union of Canada and most of the Presbyterian Church of Canada to form the United Church. Three years later this church was devastated by fire. Undaunted, the congregation rebuilt on the same foundation, resulting in the cathedral-style church that stands here today. The building was dedicated in 1929, and the following year 'Met United' installed Canada's largest pipe organ, with some 8,000 pipes. In addition to their house (of God) performers, there are regular guest musicians, often with a new-agey, multicultural bent.

Wedged among these sacred institutions, **Mackenzie House** (82 Bond Street, 416 392 6915) is a densely packed museum devoted to the building's former tenant, William Lyon Mackenzie (1795-1861). Mackenzie was the first mayor of Toronto, a radical journalist and political reformer, but he is best known for leading the 1837 Upper Canada Rebellion (*see p13*). The rebellion failed and Mackenzie fled to the United States. Eventually, though, he was pardoned, and in 1850 he returned to Canadian politics and publishing. His humble home was converted into a museum in 1950.

Elgin & Winter Garden Theatre Centre

189 Yonge Street, between Dundas Street E & Queen Street (416 314 2871/www.mirvish.com). Streetcar 501, 505/subway Dundas or Queen. **Tours** 5pm Thur; 11am Sun. **Admission** $7; $6 concessions. **No credit cards. Map** p280 G7.

It's touted as the last operating double-decker theatre in the world, but, whatever the terminology, these theatres are insanely beautiful. They have been painstakingly restored to their original luxury: the Elgin was readorned in ruby fabric and gilt, while the botanical fantasy of the Winter Garden's hand-painted walls was enhanced by thousands of leafy beech branches hung from the ceiling. A tour shows off both of the theatres, the lobbies, as well as an exhibit of vaudeville-era scenery. *See also p221.*

Olympic Spirit Toronto

35 Dundas Street E, at Victoria Street (1-888 466 9991/www.olympicspirit.ca). Subway Dundas. **Open** 10am-6pm daily. *Restaurant* noon-10pm Tue-Thur; noon-11pm Fri, Sat. **Admission** $21; $12.50-$17.50 concessions. **Credit** AmEx, MC, V. **Map** p280 G6.

Olympic Spirit is the first of a proposed worldwide chain of IOC-sanctioned interactive entertainment venues to promote the Olympic Games. The five-floor complex provides a complete history of the Games, with rare film footage, artifacts and user-friendly simulators. Entertaining, informative and centrally located – a solid time-killer if you need one.

Toronto Eaton Centre

1 Dundas Street W, at Yonge Street (416 598 8560/www.torontoeatoncentre.com). Streetcar 501, 505/subway Dundas or Queen. **Open** 10am-9pm Mon-Fri; 9.30am-7pm Sat; noon-6pm Sun. **Admission** free. **Map** p280 F6/G6.

While Dundas Square contains some of Toronto's most important places of worship, the biggest shrine here is devoted to consumerism. The Eaton Centre opened its doors in 1979, transforming Yonge Street from a tavern-lined, seedy street, into a tavern-lined, seedy street with a gigantic shopping mall. Actually, the mall paved the way for many other commercial enterprises in the area and also served as a model for a new breed of upmarket shopping centres across North America. Its offspring have outpaced it: the Eaton is looking a bit dated these days.

The complex stretches a full block from Dundas to Queen Street. At the south end, on upper floors, look up at the sculpture *Flight Stop* by local artist Michael Snow. The flock of life-sized Canada geese (swooping down through the upper five storeys of the atrium) was created by affixing hand-tinted photographs on to fibreglass sculptures.

There are about 300 stores, restaurants and services in the mall. Eaton's, the flagship store, no longer exists. The Eaton Company declared bankruptcy in 1999. Sears Canada Inc bought out the major stores and tried to resurrect the historic Eaton name but that attempt failed and, in 2002, the last Eatons outlets were converted into Sears stores. *See also p144.*

Chinatown

Maps p278 & p279

Streetcar 501, 505, 510/subway Osgoode, Queen's Park, St Patrick.

There are at least three major Chinatowns in the Greater Toronto Area, spawned by the suburban migration of second- and third-generation Asian-Canadians, creating enclaves in Markham's Pacific Mall (*see p143*) and the Chinatown of Broadview and Gerrard. But the original heart and soul of Toronto's dynamic and large Chinese community (*see p70* **Global village**) beats strongest along Dundas Street W and Spadina Avenue. Here you'll find a wonderfully manic, just-off-the-durian-truck intensity. The added bonus is that Chinatown links together some of downtown's major attractions in one neat, dumpling-like package. Nowadays Chinatown spreads up Spadina Avenue from Queen to College and along Dundas Street W from Bay Street almost as far west as Bathurst Street.

There are more than a few other non-Asian attractions in this enclave. **Osgoode Hall** (130 Queen Street W, at University Avenue, 416 947 3300) was built in 1932 and held Canada's first law school (which has since moved to become a part of York University). Named after Ontario's first chief justice, William Osgoode, the building's vintage wrought-iron gates were built in 1868 to prevent grazing cows from entering (and soiling) the hallowed grounds of what was then and remains today the Law Society of Upper Canada. Tours of this classic example of Victorian Classical architecture are free (don't miss the rotunda).

Across University Avenue at 160 Queen Street W, **Campbell House** (416 597 0227, *see p71*) sits in the shadow of the **Canada Life Building** (330 University Avenue, 416 597 1456); known for its famous beacon, the tower lights provide coded weather forecasts, which are updated four times a day. The **Canada Life Beacon** emitted its first signal on 9 August 1951. (Back then the tower was much more visible throughout the city, and by boaters far out on the lake.) A cube-shaped light flashes red for rain, white for snow, shines a steady green for clear conditions and steady red for clouds. If the rows of white lights on the tower flash upwards, it means hotter weather is on the way. Similarly, descending or non-moving patterns indicate dropping or steady temperatures.

The **Textile Museum of Canada** (55 Centre Avenue, at Dundas Street W, 416 599 5321) is another amenity woven into this eclectic neighbourhood, with over 10,000 textile artefacts from all over the world.

Heading west you'll find the **Ontario College of Art & Design** (100 McCaul Street, 416 977 6000), with Will Alsop's must-see, much talked-about, stilt-elevated **Sharp Centre for Design** building. Its neighbour to the north is the **Art Gallery of Ontario** (*see p71*), which is in the midst of receiving a Frank Gehry-designed makeover. Don't miss the Henry Moore sculpture at the corner of McCaul and Dundas Street W. At 2 Grange Avenue is well-known Canadian artist Charles Pachter's **Grange Modern** gallery (open by appointment only; call 416 596 8452).

Behind the gallery is the architectural period museum, the **Grange** and **Grange Park**. At the south end of the park, the ivy-covered **St George the Martyr Anglican Church** (197 John Street, entrance on Stephanie Street, 416 598 4366) is one of Toronto's oldest places of worship, dating from 1844. A fire in 1955 destroyed everything except the tower, which still looms over this urban park today. The congregation meets in the original parish hall, which also holds some objects saved from the fire. This is also the home of the **Music Gallery** (416 204 1080), a publicly assisted centre for the creation and performance of new and unusual music, well known for a vibrant legacy of sonic innovation by the likes of John Oswald, Henry Kaiser and Michael Snow.

A couple of short blocks north of here is the Baldwin Street neighbourhood, between Beverley and McCaul, with its mix of earthy shops, bakeries, upscale bistros and boho cafés. It's a great spot to grab lunch before you head back down to Dundas into the chaotic, exotic flow of Chinatown proper. Year round these busy blocks are crowded with shopkeepers and customers, who haggle and joust among barrels of beansprouts, unending varieties of dried fishes and crate upon crate of wonderful Chinese greens. At Chinese New Year the traditional parade features much noise-making and a giant dragon, which heads down this street and past the **Ten Ren Tea Company** (454 Dundas Street W, at Huron Street, 416 598 7872), one of the world's largest tea producers. It's an excellent place to buy and taste a wide variety of teas, teapots and cute little cups.

For many, the definitive Chinatown experience is the ritual of a leisurely dim sum lunch. While serious aficionados scout for new terrain almost weekly (including in the other Chinatowns), **Yiu Wah** (421 Dundas Street W, 416 979 8833) provides a tempting array of dumplings and other freshly prepared delights. If budget is not an issue, head eastwards to the luxurious **Lai Wah Heen** in the Metropolitan Hotel (108 Chestnut Street; *see also p113*), who many believe serves the finest dim sum in town.

Continuing westbound on Dundas towards Spadina, the stores and trading companies spill out on to the sidewalks, hawking Cantonese CDs with cover versions of Madonna, animé-themed MP3 holders, vials of traditional medicine and Hello Kitty earmuffs.

Sightseeing

Put your skills to the test at **Olympic Spirit Toronto**. *See p68.*

Global village China

Population: 500,000
Home base: Spadina Avenue and Dundas Street W; Gerrard Street E and Broadview Avenue

The Gold Rush brought the first Chinese up from California to Canada (mainly Vancouver), but the construction of the Canadian Pacific Railway transported them to Toronto. After the last track was laid, many decided to stay. Among the challenges of finding work and shelter for those early Chinese Canadians was a degrading and racist 'head tax' of $500 levied solely on Chinese immigrants. When, at the turn of the last century, they began to evolve into restaurant owners and shopkeepers, they found the cheap housing of Spadina Avenue to their liking. After an exclusion act was repealed following World War II, immigration began to surge, and what is now known as Chinatown proper took its shape as a bustling marketplace.

As the city's focus shifted westwards in the 1960s and '70s and Spadina Avenue became a more thriving business centre, cheaper rents lured immigrants to the east side. The intersection of Broadview Avenue and Gerrard Street East is an alternative Chinatown favoured for its superlative restaurants, bakeries and supermarkets. Meanwhile, the second and third generations, and those who came from southern China to invest in Toronto's future, built up suburbs in the north-east of the city like Mississauga, Scarborough and Markham.

Trading places: Markham's Pacific Mall (*see p143*) is the place for bamboo, kitchen supplies, designer knock-offs and dim sum. Experience the wonders of brazen, Asian architecture at its extreme at the Dragon City Mall (280 Spadina Avenue, at Dundas Street W, 416 979 7777).

A taste of: At peak times there are often queues for Lee Garden (331 Spadina Avenue, 416 593 9524), but it's worth the wait. Swatow (309 Spadina Avenue, 416 977 0601) is a less expensive, delicious but alcohol-free alternative down the street, with wonderful soups, greens and dumplings. Serious dim sum-ers will adore Dragon Dynasty (2301 Brimley Road, 416 321 9000). Chinese buns of barbecue pork, shredded beef, chicken curry and more can be found at the Miao Ke Hong Bakery (345 Broadview Avenue, 416 463 6388) –

all reason enough to check out bustling Chinatown east by walking east on Gerrard.
Join in: The city's largest Chinese New Year celebration features the festive and noisy Dragon Dance. A huge dragon winds its way, to the delight of all, slowly down Dundas Street. Held on the last week of January or the first week in February is a related pan-Asian trade fair: Toronto Celebrates Lunar Year (www.torontocelebrates.com) lasts for three full days at Exhibition Place's Automotive Building (105 Prince's Boulevard).
Local luminary: Councillor Olivia Chow – a take-charge politician – immigrated to Canada, from Hong Kong at the age of 13. Since 1985, when she was elected as a school trustee, she has proven herself a force to be reckoned with, speaking out courageously on key issues: the waterfront, health care, law enforcement, youth and child care, and the homeless. Olivia is one half of one of an interesting power couple: she's married to the leader of Canada's (left-wing oriented) NDP party, Jack Layton. She made a bid to join her husband in Ottawa as a federal MP in 2004's election. He won but Olivia lost in a squeaker by less than a thousand votes. Many Torontonians are happy that hard-working Chow is still representing their interests at City Hall.

Spadina

Streetcar 505, 509, 510.
In addition to the diverse regions of China, Toronto's Chinatown is home to a range of Asian cultures, from Thailand to Korea to Malaysia to Vietnam. The latter culture is well represented by the superb restaurants, soup kitchens and sandwich shops on Spadina Avenue. The **Kim Thanh Food Co** (336 Spadina Avenue, 416 979 7928) and the **Pho Hung** (350 Spadina Avenue, 416 593 4274) are two reliable and well-priced options among many.

Once the centre of a booming garment industry Spadina has a funky, industrial feel, with vintage warehouses and retail outlets lining the broad boulevard. At 160 feet (50 metres), it's also one of the widest streets in the city, but on weekends even these super-sized sidewalks are totally jammed. At the intersection of Dundas and Spadina the action really thickens: diminutive women crouch down low selling vegetables and fresh herbs, while seafood is somehow bought and sold from street-side stalls, and young Asian teens gab on cellphones. As you go further up the street, the sidewalks are much less crowded, while the shopping gets even better. In addition to offering the cheapest souvenirs in the city, this section of Spadina is a great source for lots of handy items for the traveller: backpacks, suitcases and camera bags; international phone cards; herbal medicines; hats, inexpensive clothing and footwear. Just up the street at No.448 is another retail institution, **Gwartzman's Art Supplies** (416 922 5429).

Art Gallery of Ontario

317 Dundas Street W, at Beverley Street (416 979 6648/www.ago.net). Streetcar 505/subway St Patrick. **Open** 11am-6pm Tue, Thur, Fri; 11am-8.30pm Wed; 10am-5.30pm Sat, Sun; also 11am-6pm Mon for selected exhibitions. **Admission** $12; $6-$9 concessions; $30 family; free under-6s. **Credit** MC, V. **Map** p279 E6.
The AGO maintains it will be open for the business of enjoying art over the next few years while it undergoes major renovations. But specific galleries and wings will be closed on a rotating basis, so it's best to call ahead if you're keen on the Henry Moore sculpture gallery, the fine European collection, the Group of Seven or other stand-outs from the permanent collection. The Frank Gehry-designed makeover is scheduled to be finished in 2007.

Campbell House

160 Queen Street W, at Simcoe Street (416 597 0227/www.campbellhousemuseum.ca). Streetcar 501/subway Osgoode. **Open** 9.30am-4.30pm Mon-Fri. *May-Oct* noon-4.30pm Sat, Sun. **Admission** $4.50; $2-$3 concessions; $10 family. **No credit cards**. **Map** p279/280 F7.

This is one of the city's older treasures of Georgian architecture, built in 1822 for Sir William Campbell, a judge who later became Chief Justice of Upper Canada. It passed through many hands over the ensuing century, until finally, in 1973, the 300-ton house was moved from its original location on Adelaide Street to its current position. The operation was massive, but it saved the building from demolition. In 1974 it opened as a museum, although parts of the building are used as offices and therefore off-limits to the public. In addition to guided tours, the museum has a herb garden with explanations of how herbs were used for food and medicine.

City Hall & Nathan Phillips Square

100 Queen Street W, at York Street (416 338 0338/ www.city.toronto.on.ca). Bus 6/streetcar 501/subway Osgoode or Queen. **Open** *City Hall* 8.30am-4.30pm Mon-Fri. **Admission** free. **Map** p279/280 F7.
When it was completed in 1965, Toronto's fourth City Hall was one of the city's few modernist buildings. The then-mayor Nathan Phillips held an international competition, won by Finnish architect Viljo Revell. Revell designed the council chamber as a low, round building, embraced by two concave office towers of differing heights. The dramatic design has aged well, remaining bold and futuristic 40 years on. The ground floor is open to the public (check out the scale model of the city) and tours can be arranged by appointment. (Unfortunately, the observation deck at the top is not accessible).

City Hall faces south on to the concrete expanse of Nathan Phillips Square. Phillips' successor as mayor, Phil Givens, fought hard for the Henry Moore bronze on the hall's forecourt, believing high status art conferred a high status world image, but this vision proved his undoing. He won his battle against the philistines but lost the next election due in large part to the outrage of the electorate at what was seen as a waste of public funds. History vindicates him: *The Archer*, as the sculpture is known, is by far the most popular public sculpture in the city.

The square succeeds as a genuine gathering place. It's where Toronto rings in the new year. During the summer it's busy with concerts, dance performances, the annual IRIE Music Festival (*see p100* **Global village**), the Toronto Outdoor Art Exhibition (*see p169*) and a great weekly Wednesday farmers' market (*see p154* **Pick up a picnic**). In winter the reflecting pool becomes a popular ice rink and skaters whisk under the huge concrete arches that span it. Skates are available for hire (*see p214*).

Kensington Market

Streetcar 506, 506, 510.
The landing point for many immigrants beginning their lives in the city, Kensington Market has been the unofficial gateway to Toronto for over 200 years. The district (it's an area rather than a single market) was once

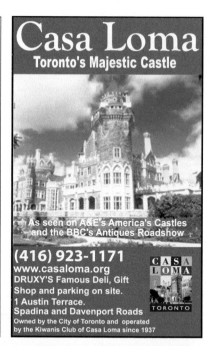

Tall tales

Trawl through the local tourist board's websites and you're unlikely to find any references to **Rochdale**, the notorious tower block at 341 Bloor Street W, at Huron Street (Subway St George or Spadina). Nor will you find any plaques or markers on the building itself.

Now known rather more soberly as the Senator David A Croll Apartments, this innocuous-looking building is a landmark in Toronto's cultural history. Built in 1968 as a bold experiment in alternative education and communal cohabitation, Rochdale quickly became a symbolic beacon of love and general grooviness, attracting like-minded spirits from across the continent: rock stars, draft dodgers, McLuhanites and, especially, dopers. Like nearby Yorkville, it was a thriving stage for the music, art, politics, protest and poetry of the times. Rochdale soon became a hotbed of talent, drawing notable writers, artists, musicians and scholars, hosting poetry slams, nude theatre, underground radio, workshops in civil disobedience and experimental film screenings. Within a few years it had spawned a recording studio, at least one major theatre group, a publisher and a printing press.

Sadly, the good karma didn't last – a combination of drugs, vagrants, vandals and mismanagement ended the trip, and after numerous overdoses and one 'jumper' suicide, the building was closed in 1975 and the remaining tenants forcibly evicted. 'Toronto the Good' was never quite the same again.

After lying dormant for several years, a frenzy of gutting, cleaning, de-stoning and re-zoning began transforming the hippie palace into a seniors' apartment building (as far as we can tell, the new inhabitants are blissfully unaware of their happening habitat's psychedelic past). Other than the outer shell of the building, all that remains of Rochdale now is the sculpture on the south-west corner of Huron and Bloor, a giant slumping bronze called the *Unknown Student* by Dale Heinzerling. (Footnote: following the building's renovation, authorities turned the sculpture around: its back now faces the building and its sordid past.)

For further information on Rochdale, check out Toronto movie-maker Ron Mann's film *Dream Tower* (see www.sphinxproductions.com/pages/film_dreamtower.html).

known as the 'Jewish Market', as it was the centre for the thousands of Eastern Europe Jews. They worked in Spadina's busy garment industry and by the 1920s there were 30 synagogues in the neighbourhood. The market evolved when merchants began selling their wares on their front lawns – and eventually in the converted storefronts that still comprise the actual market today. It continues to have a small Jewish presence, but is an ever-changing cultural mall.

Kensington Market's main thoroughfares are Baldwin Street, Augusta Avenue, Nassau Street and Kensington Avenue. Stores are run by a mixture of Chinese, Italians, Greeks, Portuguese, East and West Indians, Koreans, Vietnamese, Filipinos, Africans from many countries, Mexicans, Spaniards and Latin Americans. The market is ever-changing, but that old market feeling lingers on: you still get the sense that many of the stores and restaurants were set up on a whim, with clothing racks and cardboard signs pitched up in front yards, along sidewalks and even down alleys. There are clubs here too, but Kensington's streets have a music of their own:

dancehall reggae booms out from a Jamaican fruit store, mixing with mandolins emanating from a cheese shop and the discordant twang of Mandarin pop music coming from a greengrocer. Kensington Market's cultural mix means that it has some of the city's best – and cheapest – shopping, including fresh and speciality food stores; an eclectic mix of vintage and discount clothing and snack foods from every continent.

Sanci's Wholesale Produce & Tropical Foods (416 593 9265) has been at its 66 Kensington address since 1914, and is as popular today as it was then. Fans of vintage apparel should check out the crowded stretch of brightly painted brick storefronts along lower Kensington Street, where **Courage My Love** is a virtual museum for obscure vintage clothing and accessories (*see also p152*), while **Exile** (20 Kensington Avenue, 416 596 0827) and **Dancing Days** (17 Kensington Avenue, 416 599 9827) are offbeat, punky and funky alternatives. If you're in that special mood, check out the self-explanatory **Roach-O-Rama** (191A Baldwin Street, 416 203 6990) and its famous **Hot Box Café**.

You're better off visiting the market during the week or on a Saturday, as not all stores are open on Sundays.

For more on the shops at Kensington Market, *see p156*.

Running parallel with Spadina Avenue, **Augusta Avenue**'s formerly dodgy blocks are being spruced up by authors, club promoters and movie types, buying in and setting up shop with upscale new businesses, such as hip bar

Brain gain

Sightseeing

A well-known incubator for eggheads, the University of Toronto has turned out its share of influential characters, in particular a decent clutch of literary giants. Herewith a very list of the biggest names:

Margaret Atwood. Before she won the Booker Prize (once) and the Governor-General's Award (twice), the prolific poet and novelist attended Victoria College at U of T, where she was much influenced by poet Jay Macpherson and critic Northrop Frye. More than 40 years later, she lives on a tree-lined street in the Annex, not far from her alma mater.

Robertson Davies. One of Canada's most popular and esoteric writers, Davies wrote like an impish Oxford don and seemingly found his place when he became first Master of the pseudo-Oxfordian Massey College in 1963. Davies died in 1995, leaving behind 11 novels including *Fifth Business* and *What's Bred in the Bone*, but legends of his high-table hijinks live on.

Morley Callaghan. Though he studied law at the U of T in the 1920s, Callaghan instead went on to become one of the giants of early 20th-century Canadian literature. He was encouraged in his writing by Ernest Hemingway (who worked at the time for the *Toronto Star*), and famously spent time in Paris with Hemingway, James Joyce and F Scott Fitzgerald, among others. American critic Edmund Wilson called him 'perhaps the most unjustly neglected novelist in the English-speaking world', while others find his style earnest, clunky and oddly Sunday school-ish. But there's no denying Callaghan's importance on the Toronto scene. Of the books he wrote during his long life, his most famous include *Such Is My Beloved*, *For They Shall Inherit the Earth* and *More Joy in Heaven*.

Northrop Frye. 'Northrop Frye/Whatta guy/Reads more books than you or I,' wrote a Toronto poet a few years back, and generations of awe-struck students probably felt much the same way. As the author of the fearfully erudite *Anatomy of Criticism* and one of the foremost literary critics of his day, Frye could be an intimidating figure. He taught English at U of T for more than 30 years, later becoming chancellor of Victoria University within U of T. Legend has it that he spoke not just in perfect sentences, but in perfect paragraphs. One of the buildings at Victoria College (73 Queen's Park Crescent E) is named in his honour.

Marshall McLuhan. If McLuhan didn't exactly invent the internet, he certainly prophesised its effects. The first great sage of the media age, the U of T prof coined the phrases 'global village' and 'the medium is the message'. Part of St Joseph Street, which runs through McLuhan's old academic stomping ground of St Michael's College, has recently been renamed Marshall McLuhan Way. It's located between Bay Street and Queen's Park Crescent. *See also p18* **Messaging the medium**.

Embassy (No.223; *see also p135*); upscale bistro **La Palette** (No.256; *see also p114*), vibrant houseware shop **Bungalow** (No.273; *see also p152*) and diner/DJ club **SuperMarket** (No.268, 416 840 0501). If you need refuelling, grab a coffee at a local landmark, **Casa Acoreana & Luis Coffee** (235 Augusta Avenue, 416 593 9717), take a quick look at the wondrous, self explanatory **House of Spice** (190 Augusta Avenue, 416 593 9724), then walk northwards for a taste of the funky new guard. While you're here don't miss the **Pueblan** (Mexican regional) eaterie, or **El Trompo** (277 Augusta Avenue, 416 260 0097) for some tiny, perfect tacos.

The **Kiever Synagogue** (25 Bellevue Avenue, 416 593 9702) is one of Canada's oldest Jewish landmarks. Designed by an architect named Benjamin Swartz, the synagogue served a small congregation of immigrants from Kiev, Ukraine. The formal name of the congregation is the 'First Russian Congregation of Rodfei Sholem Anshei Kiev', but for entirely understandable reasons is generally known simply as 'the Kiever'. The Kiever overlooks **Bellevue Square**, a small but pleasant community park at the corner of Wales and Augusta Avenues. Keep an eye out for a life-sized statue of a smiling Al Waxman. The Canadian actor and humanitarian, who died in 2001, is best remembered for playing Al King, the lead character in *King of Kensington*, a 1970s TV show set here in the market.

University

Map p282
Bus 94/streetcar 506, 510/subway Bay, Bloor-Yonge, Museum, Spadina, Wellesley.

The largest university in Canada comprises some of the choicest real estate downtown and for the tourist in search of either tranquil reflection or architectural interest, the campus is an oasis of old-fashioned beauty in the heart of the city. Thanks to the university's many courtyards, quadrangles and large open spaces, the area feels like a park interrupted by chapels of learning. A stream once ran through the middle of the university, and while the Taddle Creek is long gone, the bucolic atmosphere remains.

The university, founded in 1827 as King's College, is one of the few local institutions that has done a decent job of conserving its heritage – turrets and all. In the past decade it has also been an incubator for new architecture, with talented from Canada and abroad designing dazzling new buildings.

Bordered on the north by Bloor Street and on the east by Bay Street, the St George campus is divided into three almost equal sections by two imposing north–south avenues, Queen's Park and St George Street. Together with two suburban campuses – Erindale and Scarborough – the University of Toronto is the third largest public university in North America.

Bata Shoe Museum – not just for the well-heeled. *See p78.*

Sightseeing

Central

The university's oldest and most iconic buildings lie directly north-west of Queen's Park and the provincial parliament building. **Hart House** was a gift from the wealthy Massey family and named after its chief patriarch, Hart Massey. With its Gothic arches, bay windows and Great Hall, it has a terribly English, terribly Oxbridge feel, yet is comfortably old Toronto. Formerly an undergraduate men's centre, it's now open to women too. A small gallery, the **Justina M Barnicke**, is located in the west wing (*see below*). **University College** is one of the oldest buildings on campus and still very much a landmark. You can see its lone, asymmetrical spire and central tower from as far away as Yonge Street; the interior woodwork is worth a visit in itself. In the Laidlaw Wing is the **University of Toronto Art Centre** (*see below*), housing the eclectic and enjoyable art collection of New York psychoanalyst Dr Lillian Malcove Ormos. Cross the playing field in front of the college and you'll find **Convocation Hall**, a vast domed building from the 1920s that has seen its fair share of graduation exercises. Head further south to College Street and you'll hit the **Faculty of Architecture**, with its sleek modernist gallery, and the very different **Lillian H Smith Public Library** (*see below*), with its distinctly postmodern design.

Two even flashier buildings are close to completion near the corner of College Street and University Avenue: the **Centre for Cellular Biomolecular Research**, and the new **Leslie Dan Pharmacy**, the first Canadian building by British architect Norman Foster.

Justina M Barnicke Art Gallery

Hart House, 7 Hart House Circle (416 978 8398/ www.utoronto.ca/gallery). Subway St George. **Open** *Sept-June* 11am-7pm Mon-Fri; 1-4pm Sat, Sun. *July, Aug* 11am-6pm Mon-Fri; 1-4pm Sat. **Admission** free. **Map** p282 E5.
Great Canadian art hangs in all corners of Hart House – in reading rooms, restaurants, even stairwells – but this is the official gallery, and though it's tiny, it often features interesting art shows.

Lillian H Smith Public Library

239 College Street, at Huron Street (416 393 7746/ www.torontopubliclibrary.ca). Streetcar 506, 510. **Open** *Sept-June* 10am-8.30pm Mon-Thur; 10am-6pm Fri; 9am-5pm Sat; 1.30-5pm Sun. *July, Aug* 10am-8.30pm Mon-Thur; 10am-6pm Fri; 9am-5pm Sat. **Admission** free. **Map** p282 E5.
A postmodern chateau with a dungeon-like basement and giant bronze griffins flanking the central doorway, this public library is a fanciful piece of architecture. It's also a must for fans of science fiction and/or children's literature, as it houses excellent collections of both.

University of Toronto Art Centre

Laidlaw Wing, University College, 15 King's College Circle (416 978 1838/www.utoronto.ca/artcentre). *Bus 94/streetcar 506/subway Queen's Park.* **Open** *Sept-June* 10am-6pm Tue-Thur, Sun; 10am-9pm Fri; noon-4pm Sat. *July, Aug* noon-5pm Tue-Fri. **Admission** free. **Map** p282 E5.
This little-known museum on the north side of the University College quad houses the private collection of New York City psychoanalyst Dr Lillian Malcove Ormos. Medieval ivories and a stunning 1538 panel painting of Adam and Eve by Lucas Cranach are on view, though regular exhibits are occasionally pushed aside by travelling shows, like the recent display of Picasso ceramics.

Queen's Park & east

The provincial parliament building sits in the middle of Queen's Park and the government is often referred to as **Queen's Park**. A fine example of Richardsonian Romanesque, the massive pinky-brown stone edifice was built between 1886 and 1892.

Another fine example of the genre, from 1892, lies north-east of Queen's Park in the middle of the Victoria College quadrangle, and is known as **Old Vic**. On the same quad is the **EJ Pratt Library**, named after the prominent Canadian poet. Check out the polka dot walls of this 1961 building and the famous portrait of literary guru Northrop Frye (*see p74* **Brain gain**). The eminent critic appears to be sitting on air.

To the north lies Charles Street and two of the city's more interesting new buildings – the **McKinsey & Company** building and the **Isabel Bader Theatre**, a gift from Alfred Bader to the college in the name of his theatre-loving wife. The limestone-clad building echoes the scale and colour of Burwash Hall to the east and Emmanuel College to the west. Across Charles Street, on the north side, the rather West Coast-looking **Wymilwood Student Centre** is the creation of Eric Arthur, the influential Toronto architect who helped save such early landmarks as St Lawrence Hall and Old City Hall, and who gave his name to the Faculty of Architecture's gallery at 230 College Street (416 978 5038). Arthur died in 1982 but his posthumously revised *Toronto: No Mean City* remains the bible of the city's historical architecture.

North of Charles Street, two of Toronto's most important museums face each other across the broad lanes of Queen's Park. The **Gardiner Museum of Ceramic Art** (*see below*) was founded by a local philanthropist and his wife in 1984; a big revamp was now nearing completion as this guide went to press. Its older cousin across the street, the **Royal Ontario Museum** (*see below*), explores both natural history and human cultures and is the largest museum in Canada, the fifth largest in North America. While you're in the neighbourhood, take a glance at the **Royal Conservatory of Music** (273 Bloor Street W, 416 408 2825). Originally the Toronto Baptist College, the hulking building does indeed look as if it could rain down hail and brimstone. Walk through the ornate iron gates to the east of the conservatory and down Philosophers Walk and you can usually hear the sound of dozens of piano students practising.

Gardiner Museum of Ceramic Art

111 Queen's Park, at Bloor Street W (416 586 8080/ www.gardinermuseum.on.ca). Subway Museum. **Map** p282 F4.

The first specialist museum of ceramic art in North America, the Gardiner is scheduled to re-open in autumn 2005 with $15 million worth of new space, including three new galleries and a glass-covered atrium. (Phone for admission times and prices nearer the time.) In the meantime, its fantastic collection of Italian maiolica, English delftware and other ceramics from Europe, Asia and the Americas is out of sight. The museum's shop, offices and clay studios, however, are open a few subway stops south, at 60 McCaul Street, at Grange Road, just south of OCAD and the AGO.

Royal Ontario Museum

100 Queen's Park, at Bloor Street W (416 586 5549/www.rom.on.ca). Subway Museum. **Open** 10am-6pm Mon-Thur, Sat, Sun; 10am-9.30pm Fri. **Admission** *Mon-Fri* $15; $12 concessions. *Sat, Sun* $18; $15 concessions; free under-5s. Free to all 1hr before closing daily & 4.30-9.30pm Fri. **Credit** AmEx, MC, V. **Map** p282 F4.

The ROM's new 'crystal' addition doesn't open until some time in 2006 but it's already the most controversial building in Toronto. Designed by Daniel Libeskind, the architect behind Berlin's Jewish Museum and Manchester's Imperial War Museum North, the glass-and-steel structure on the ROM's north side is, depending on your point of view, either a grand gesture or a godawful folly. Fun or fickle, though, it has already kicked some life into the Toronto museum scene and is sure to draw still more visitors to what is already one of Canada's greatest museum collections.

Though it's known for its enormous Chinese collection, the museum surveys everything from natural history to human culture. Kids will love the bat cave, dinosaurs and mummies, not to mention the totem poles beside the main entrance. Adults may prefer the Canadian and indigenous peoples' collections. For a literary view, read Margaret Atwood's *Life Before Man*, which features the ROM as the backdrop.

St George Street & west

A recently relandscaped St George Street is now the principal north–south axis of the university's western campus. Walk north from College Street and you'll pass everything

Allen Gardens. See p80.

from the Beaux Arts splendour of the **Koffler Student Services Centre** (originally a public reference library, now the home of the university's main bookstore) to the brand-new **Bahen Centre for Information Technology**; from the very '60s **Sidney Smith Hall** to the very '70s **Robarts Library**. The latter, sometimes referred to as 'Fort Book', is a bulky concrete structure that looks like a overloaded spacecraft attempting lift-off, but it has a serious purpose and is the largest of the U of T's 30 libraries. The beaked tower at the south end is home to the Thomas Fisher Rare Book Library.

Where St George joins Bloor Street is a collection of somewhat less academic interest, the **Bata Shoe Museum** (*see below*), which makes for a surprisingly fun diversion. Directly opposite lies the new **Wordsworth College Residence**. A yellow-brick podium topped by a checkerboard tower of clear and opaque glass, it's a very sassy addition to a somewhat traditional stretch of Bloor Street. (The 19th century home of the ultra-exclusive York Club is across the street.)

North of Robarts lies **Innis College**, named after the academic who inspired the communications theorist Marshall McLuhan

(*see p18* **Messaging the medium**). East of the library, at the corner of Hoskin and Devonshire Place, lies a celebrated re-imagining of the monastic ideal – **Massey College**. Conceived by former governor-general Vincent Massey, it was designed by Canadian architect Ron Thom.

Spadina Avenue marks the western edge of the university and here, near the junction of Harbord Street, lies the athletics centre and one of the most controversial buildings in the city, **Graduate House**. Built in an almost industrial style by a team of Toronto and Los Angeles architects, the residence offends and attracts people to almost equal degrees. The pivotal point in any discussion is usually the sign-cum-cornice that overhangs Harbord Street and welcomes you to the university.

Bata Shoe Museum

327 Bloor Street W, at St George Street (416 979 7799/www.batashoemuseum.ca). Subway St George. **Open** *Sept-May* 10am-5pm Tue, Wed, Fri, Sat; 10am-8pm Thur; noon-5pm Sun. *June-Aug* 10am-5pm Mon; 10am-5pm Tue, Wed, Fri, Sat; 10am-8pm Thur; noon-5pm Sun. **Admission** $8; $4-$6 concessions; free under-5s & 5-8pm Thur. **Credit** AmEx, MC, V. **Map** p282 E4.
A playful pun on a shoe box, Raymond Moriyama's odd-angled design houses everything from native footwear to celebrity footwear – Marilyn Monroe's red pumps to Elton John's platforms. A permanent exhibition follows the history of western footwear.

Harbord

Map p282
Situated at the western edge of the university, Harbord Street is a bastion of upscale leftish liberalism. The street houses everything from the **Toronto Women's Bookstore** (73 Harbord Street, 416 922 8744) to a women-friendly sex shop **Good For Her** (*see p195*), not to mention some of the city's better restaurants and patios.

Downtown East

Church & Wellesley

Map p283
Bus 75, 94/streetcar 506/subway Bloor-Yonge, College, Wellesley.
Home to the local gay village, or 'the ghetto', as it's most commonly called, Church & Wellesley is also a showcase for some of Toronto's best 19th-century architecture. Church Street was named after **St James's Church** (now a cathedral), one of the loveliest structures in

Historic **Cabbagetown**. *See p80.*

the city, and some of the other buildings in this area (bounded by Yonge, Bloor, Gerrard and Sherbourne Streets) are equally dignified, imposing and graceful.

More obvious, though, at least at first glance, are the massive apartment complexes erected in the 1950s and '60s after the opening of the Yonge Street subway in 1954. Buildings like the **City Park** co-op apartments at 484 Church Street, the city's first high-rise apartment complex, and the conical-shaped **Village Green** building a block north, encouraged the arrival of many a confirmed 'bachelor'. So many, in fact, that Village Green is often known as 'Vaseline Towers'.

But the area only took off in 1984 when the **Second Cup** (*see p193*) opened near the corner of Church and Wellesley. Originally equipped with a broad set of steps suitable for lounging, chatting and cruising, the tiny coffee shop attracted a dedicated gay following and 'the Steps' became a local landmark, mythologised by frequent references on the TV series *Kids in the Hall*. 'The Steps' fell victim to renovation a while back, but their effect lives on. In 1989, five years after Second Cup set up shop, **Woody's** (*see p191*) opened a block further south at Church and Maitland in a Queen Anne rowhouse originally built in 1893, and the gay gold rush was on. Rising rents and a proliferation of upscale condos may yet imperil the village's broad-based demographic, but for the moment it's almost impossible to run a gay business without a Church Street connection.

Tiny **George Hislop Park** acknowledges at least some of this history. Named after the legendary gay businessman and activist, it runs parallel to Yonge Street between Charles and Isabella Streets.

The names of many more gay men are incised on the upright steel markers of the AIDS Memorial, erected in 1993, in **Cawthra Park**, which is located behind the **519 Church Street Community Centre** (*see p258*) at Church and Wellesley Streets. The original home of the ritzy Granite Club, 'the 519' is now home to innumerable support groups, community meetings and legal practices, as well as a popular beer garden during Pride Week (*see p168*) and a phoneline for reporting anti-gay violence.

At its southern end, the ghetto encircles one of Canada's premier jock palaces, **Maple Leaf Gardens**, at Church and Carlton Streets. Built in 1931, the blocky, yellow-brick building, mostly deco with Art Moderne details, was long home to the Toronto Maple Leafs hockey team, not to mention dozens of concerts by everyone from the Beatles and the Rolling Stones to touring circuses and occasional opera. But the Leafs moved to the **Air Canada Centre** (*see p63*) in the late 1990s, and the Gardens awaits redevelopment – most likely as a giant grocery store, which hockey fans decry as sacrilege.

A century ago this area, in particular Jarvis and Sherbourne Streets, was home to some of the city's more eminent movers and shakers. Today it houses an oddball collection of historic homes, high-rise condos and hard-working hookers. The **Massey Mansions** at 515 and 519 Jarvis Street, north of Wellesley Street, are good examples of the old order. Originally designed for a dry goods merchant, the house at No.515, now a **Keg Mansion** restaurant (416 964 6609), was later home to the Masseys, the influential Canadian family who made their money in farm machinery and gave their name to several Toronto landmarks, including **Massey Hall** (*see p198*) and **Massey College** (at U of T; *see p79*). Hart Massey, the 19th-century Methodist patriarch who moved the family firm into the front ranks, lived at No.515. Two of his most famous grandsons resided next door at No.519, a baronial home designed by EJ Lennox, the architect of Old City Hall. Vincent Massey grew up to become Canada's first native-born governor-general, while his younger brother Raymond became an actor famous for his portrayal of Abraham Lincoln.

The **National Ballet School** owns several historic buildings south of the Massey mansions, near the corner of Jarvis and Maitland Streets, including the classically inspired **Quaker Meeting House** at 111 Maitland Street and the Victorian home at 404 Jarvis Street. In a bid to triple its space and add new studios, classrooms and residences, the school is also expanding south on to a heritage site formerly owned by the Canadian Broadcasting Corporation. Look for the twin 30-storey condo towers known as 'Radio City'. Designed by prominent local architect Peter Clewes, they're not part of the ballet school itself, but they do mark the revitalisation of this long-dormant part of the city. To the west of the towers, on Jarvis Street, the ballet school's new facilities wrap themselves around and incorporate two historic buildings.

Northfield House at 372 Jarvis Street was built in 1856 and was an early home of Oliver Mowat, later a Father of Confederation and a long-serving premier of Ontario. The wonderfully Jacobethan pile at **354 Jarvis**, built in 1898, looks like a set for *Jane Eyre* (and a proper perch for a madwoman in an attic), but it was actually once home to the Havergal Ladies College (now located on Avenue Road near St Clair Avenue) and later the Canadian Broadcasting Corporation, from where Canada's first TV broadcast was transmitted in 1952.

Sightseeing

Sherbourne Street houses many excellent 19th-century buildings, but the most interesting is probably the **Clarion Selby Hotel & Suites** (*see p45*) at No.592. At different times it has housed everything and everyone from Ernest Hemingway to a gay backroom bar. The original macho man stayed here in September 1923, when the building was the Selby Hotel and Hemingway was a reporter for the *Toronto Star*. The bar flourished during the building's long stint as a gay bar and hotel complex in the 1980s and '90s. The mansion at the centre of the complex was built in 1883 for a member of the Gooderham liquor dynasty.

At the junction of Sherbourne and Gerrard Streets, **Allen Gardens** contains a complex of conservatories dating back to 1909, beautifully planted with flora from various climatic zones.

Cabbagetown

Map p283

Bus 65, 75/streetcar 506/subway Sherbourne, Castle Frank.

In the 1840s many Irish families flocked to Toronto, fleeing the potato famine that was devastating their homeland. They settled in a working-class district of Toronto, and, mindful of their experience in Ireland, filled their front yards not with potatoes but with cabbages (hence the area's name). New waves of immigrants brought wealthier residents to the area, creating an unusually diverse economic mix that continues into modern times.

During a post-World War II push for urban renewal, Cabbagetown became both a proving ground for low-income public housing projects and a stomping ground for more affluent Torontonians, who were drawn by the beautiful fixer-upper homes at bargain prices. In fact, renovators here set the bar for the tasteful and profitable gentrification of inner-city Toronto. Homes that were purchased for $25,000 in the 1950s are now worth close to half a million. Indeed, the tough, working-class neighbourhood, described by author Hugh Garner as 'North America's largest Anglo Saxon slum', is a thing of the past. The English-born author grew up in the 'hood and his coming of age classic, *Cabbagetown*, sketches a bleak tableau of poverty, unemployment, alcoholism and teen pregnancy.

While there are still a few gritty spots on its periphery, today's Cabbagetown is better characterised by its strong sense of community pride, as vintage hotels, cocktail lounges and industrial spaces are lovingly buffed up with a keen sense of maintaining the area's history

and charm. Today the vast majority of houses have been modernised on the inside, but their historic façades remain.

Toronto's most neighbourly of neighbourhoods is full of hushed, leafy streets lined with red- and yellow-brick houses, thanks to the nearby **Don Valley Brick Works Park** (*see p90*). Parks and cemeteries line much of the northern and eastern borders, creating many cosy cul-de-sacs. As you'll see if you stroll these streets, it's difficult to single out one particular architectural masterpiece, as the entire neighbourhood boasts one of the best collections of 19th-century residences in North America (*see p82* **Walk on**).

The borders of Cabbagetown are somewhat fluid and much disputed, as they have gradually crept north over the decades. Originally extending down to Queen Street East, Cabbagetown is now bounded by Gerrard Street on the south, Bloor/Danforth at its northern extreme, Sherbourne Street on the west, and spills down a wooded slope into the Don Valley on the east.

Although some of the action is on Carlton Street, Cabbagetown's heart and main commercial artery is **Parliament Street**. The street was named after Upper Canada's original parliament buildings, constructed at the base of the street in 1793. Recent efforts to develop the site of those buildings were stymied by archaeological preservationists – not surprising in this part of town, where even new condo developments (such as the one at the corner of Parliament Street and Aberdeen Avenue) are closely regulated to blend in with the local Victorian and Edwardian architectural texture.

Parliament Street retains a lively, urban neighbourhood feel, with many unusual cafés, shops and services. Restaurants are fairly priced for the most part, and boast a smörgåsbord of international cuisine – with Mexican, Sri Lankan, Japanese, Filipino, Indian and French fare available within a few short blocks.

The area is thick with historic buildings, most of them private residences. One exception is the theatre at 509 Parliament Street, home to, among others, the **Canadian Children's Dance Theatre** (416 924 5657).

If you prefer to get your architecture hit during prayer rather than performance, **Saint Luke's United Church** (353 Sherbourne Street, 416 924 9619) makes all the buildings around it seem plain in comparison. Originally known as Sherbourne Street Methodist, the church opened its huge wooden doors to worshippers in 1887. Its castle-like stonework exterior and stained-glass panels are among the nicest in the city. The church stands at the corner of Carlton Street, which boasts many fine examples of Second Empire and Gothic Revival buildings from the 1880s and '90s.

Carlton Street takes a turn north at Parliament and becomes a residential street culminating in **Riverdale Park**. Trails lead from the wooded park down to a footbridge (over the Don Valley Parkway), allowing access to the Don Valley park system and to more parks on the valley's east side.

Just to the north of Riverdale Park is **Riverdale Farm** (*see below*), a friendly farm that's a huge hit with kids of all ages: cows, sheep and pigs rule in the upper part of the farm, while recreated wetlands below are a haven for turtles and ducks. The farm holds all sorts of environmentally conscious community events and family fun, such as pottery lessons, hayrides, cow milking and a weekly farmers' market (*see p154* **Pick up a picnic**).

Within mooing distance of the farm is the **Toronto Necropolis** (200 Winchester Street, 416 923 7911). A cemetery and crematorium opened in 1850, this majestic cemetery replaced Potter's Field, Toronto's first non-sectarian cemetery. Located at Bloor and Yonge, Potter's Field was closed in 1855 as the city expanded. Nearly 1,000 of its esteemed denizens were uprooted and moved to the necropolis, where they now rest in peace once again. Here you'll find some famous Torontonians, including William Lyon Mackenzie (Toronto's first mayor), George Brown (founder of the *Globe*, now the *Globe and Mail*) and world champion sculler Edward Hanlan. Also resting here is celebrated Toronto architect Henry Langley, who designed the chapel at the entrance to the cemetery, as well as the attached lodge and *porte-cochère* – all built in 1872. Langley is noted for his Gothic Revival churches, designing no less than 70 in Toronto alone. (Check out the **Metropolitan Methodist Church** at Queen and Church, or the **Jarvis Street Baptist Church** at 130 Gerrard Street E for nearby examples.) Considered among the best Gothic Revival structures in the country, the necropolis is exemplary of the haunting, ornate style. Note the huge arching stained-glass windows illuminating the nave and sanctuary.

On the north side of the necropolis is **Wellesley Park**, which was once an animal crematorium. A fire destroyed the main building in 1888, and now a row of tidy little homes sits precisely two steps from the park. A paddling pool and small playground make it a popular place for local families.

To its north, **St James' Cemetery** (635 Parliament Street, 416 964 9194) completes Cabbagetown's collection of peaceful green spaces. Impressive crypts with historic Ontario

names such as Brock and Jarvis cast shadows on broken tombstones, whose names have eroded away. Many of Toronto's original Irish immigrants are buried here, along with such luminaries as Sir William Pearce Howland, one of the Fathers of Confederation. At the entrance to the cemetery stands the Gothic yellow-brick Chapel of Saint James-the-Less, built in 1858.

Between Cabbagetown and St Lawrence is **Moss Park**. Apart from a small strip of antique shops along Queen Street East, this neighbourhood, notorious for dopers, and other creatures of the night, is of marginal interest.

Riverdale Farm

201 Winchester Street, east of Parliament Street (416 392 6794/www.friendsofriverdalefarm.com). Bus 65/streetcar 506. **Open** 9am-5pm daily. **Admission** free. **Map** p283 J5.

St Lawrence

Maps p279, p280 & p281

Bus 75/streetcar 501, 504/subway King, Queen.
This historic quarter dates back to the founding in 1793 of what was then called the village of York. Ever since, the area has been entwined with Toronto's history, political life and economic wellbeing. In the early days it

Riverdale Farm.

Walk on Cabbagetown

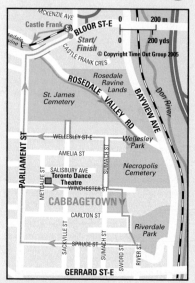

Begin: Castle Frank Station
Finish: Castle Frank Station
Length: 4 miles (6km)
Time: 2 hours, not including distractions

This walk takes in many of the highlights of Cabbagetown's 19th-century construction, and provides ample opportunity for further exploration of side streets and alleys. It also takes you into two of Toronto's most beautiful cemeteries.

Turn left out of Castle Frank Station (away from Bloor Street E). Find the steep unpaved trail leading down and to the west, passing under the subway bridge.
This short trail, leading from one busy street to another, is unexpectedly tranquil, but at the bottom traffic moves quickly. Cross Rosedale Valley Drive and turn left on the paved path. The path takes you deep into a wooded ravine, past St James' Cemetery. Unfortunately, the graveyard's lower gates are locked and there is no way out of the valley until you reach a flight of stairs where Rosedale Valley meets Bayview Avenue. (Note: This is one of the area's where some of Toronto's homeless community reside. They sometimes congregate around the base of the stairs. They're generally friendly, but some can be pretty outgoing. For that reason, many find it's best to do this walk with a friend.) At the top of the staircase is Wellesley Park (*see p81*).
Take Wellesley Street from the north-west corner of the park and turn south on Sumach Street.
Let the architecture fest begin: many fine 19th-century homes can be found on along Sumach. The double house at 420-22 is a well-regarded Second Empire building, recognisable by its mansard roof and dormers whose wooden ornaments are painted a soft, creamy white. Turn left on Winchester Street, to find the entrance to the historic **Necropolis cemetery** (*see p81*). Its name, literally translated means: city of the dead. Public washrooms, for the living, are located across the road from this historic gothic site.
Cross Riverdale Park to Carlton Street.

was designated the market block, and the shoreline of Lake Ontario came right up to the backs of warehouses along Front Street, where ships could dock and unload their merchandise. (The current line of the waterfront crept much further south as debris from building excavations was used as 'lakefill' to accommodate the city's growth.)

The area along Front Street between Church and Sherbourne Streets has been gentrified over the past two decades. Condos, apartments and Crombie Park, a flourishing example of public housing that has been studied by urban planners the world over, have transformed the original market district into one of the liveliest neighbourhoods in the city.

Few experiences in Toronto can match a fossick around **St Lawrence Market** at its heart. Enliven your senses – they will most certainly be stirred – any day of the week except Sunday and Monday (Saturday is probably best) by strolling through this vast two-storey complex. This is where the crowds jostle for supplies and load up for the coming week or a dinner party, continuing a Toronto tradition that began near this location 200 years ago in 1803. You can get a sense of its past at the city-run **Market Gallery** (*see p85*) on the second level. Changing exhibits feature old photos, documents and historical artefacts about the art and cultural history of Toronto.

The park abuts **Riverdale Farm** (*see p81*), which you'll smell on your left, (a worthy distraction, it's not part of this walk).

The easternmost block of Carlton Street, approaching the lip of the lower Don Valley, is paved with red brick that matches the row of townhouses that line its southern side. One of the oldest houses on the street, at No.397, was built for a barrister named James Reeve in 1883, when the area was still essentially rural. White brick highlights and large decks on both storeys make this house as enviable now as it was then. *Follow the path south between the houses and the Don Valley to Spruce Street. Walk west on Spruce.*

The row houses at Nos.74-86 are one of the area's more successful public housing projects, celebrated for their spacious design. Turning north on Parliament Street, you'll emerge in the heart of Cabbagetown. **Jet Fuel** (519 Parliament Street, 416 968 9982 is a local favourite and true to its name, is good spot to get fired up for the rest of the walk. To pick up a terrific lunch (or dinner or snacks), there's the gourmet take-away, **Daniel et Daniel** (248 Carlton Street, 416 968 9275), but Parliament Street offers options galore: from fast food to international fare; juice bars; grocers; butchers; health food shops, as well as a neighbourhood liquor store. *Continue north and turn right on Winchester Street.*

The former Presbyterian Church at 80 Winchester Street now houses the **Toronto Dance Theatre** (416 967 1365; *see p224*) and school. The Romanesque Revival

structure was built in 1891, and its unpretentious red brick motif makes it look like the mother of all the houses around it.

The home at 156 Winchester was originally owned by Daniel Lamb, the founder of the Riverdale Zoo and the son of Peter Lamb, the animal crematorium founder. The wonky porch speaks to the hard times the house has seen, but now the trim is freshly painted blue and the large front garden is well kept and there's not a cabbage in sight. *Turn left back on to Sumach Street and left again on to Wellesley Street.*

Wellesley Street has the quintessential mix of Cabbagetown's Edwardian and Victorian styles. This beautiful section of the street is also where you'll find the classic cottage-styled and bay-and-gable homes, some with perky picket fences. Briefly detour north on Sackville Street to Alpha Avenue. This quaint dead end street is lined with tiny mansard-roofed houses from the 1880s. These dwellings are so small that you half expect a hobbit to emerge from one of them and invite you to tea.

Back on Wellesley Street, No.314 is a number indeed. Completed in 1890, the home's front façade is crammed with carved stone ornaments that must have been great publicity for the original owner, Thomas Harris, who owned a stone cutting company. *Turn right on to Parliament Street.* On this side, you have access to **St James' Cemetery** (*see p81*). *Turning right on Bloor Street E, takes you over the bridge you passed under at the beginning, and back to Castle Frank Station.*

The gallery is also a good place to look down on the bustle of a typical Saturday shopping spree. Permanent vendors including butchers, fishmongers and seafood stands, plus stalls selling fresh breads, spices and cheeses, attract the mall-weary from all over town. Keep your elbows up and your bags at your side as you make your way from stand to stand, sampling as you go.

On the lower level, cooking supplies, pastries and more greengrocers are found, as well as many handmade crafts, often sold by the artist. At **Domino's Foods Ltd** (95 Front Street E, 416 366 2178), the closest thing to a grocery store in the market, stock up on sweets and European foods.

St Lawrence Market is not just about filling the larder. Many people drop in during the week for a breakfast speciality that tastes good any time of day – peameal bacon on a kaiser bun, that famous Canadian delicacy. This is more like a thick slice of ham, salt-and-sugar cured and then rolled in cornmeal and cooked on the grill. Bite into a warm peameal at **Carousel Bakery** (95 Front Street E, 416 363 4247) or **Paddington's Pump** (95 Front Street E, 416 368 6955). Crowds also gather at the little hole-in-the-wall **Churrasco of St Lawrence** (95 Front Street E, 416 862 2867) for slow-roasted, specially seasoned, mouthwatering Portuguese chicken on a bun, usually accompanied by a bag of French fries,

Distillery District

Streetcar 504/ subway King then 15min walk.
Imagine you're living in a city when suddenly a forgotten chapter of history magically emerges before you. In the spring of 2003 Toronto was blessed with just such a gift from the past – the Gooderham & Worts Distillery District, a 20-minute walk east of St Lawrence. Once a booming booze factory, the dilapidated and run-down area is now home to a hive of creative amenities and activities. A time capsule of 19th-century splendour, the immaculately restored project is the largest and best-preserved collection of Victorian industrial architecture in North America.

Dormant (or, at least, unnoticed) for years, this giant block of the city's heritage has been

fully reclaimed as a modern cultural complex. The 44 historic buildings are still configured around the original connected courtyards and alleyways of the former distillery. Dotted around the site are period vehicles, industrial machinery, a vintage weather vane and a set of old grain rollers.

The original state-of-the-art facility was built in 1858 and, after a fire in 1869, rebuilt faithfully. The distillery was operating up until the 1990s and served as a location for several big-budget Hollywood films – and it's easy to see why. Strolling the bricked walkways (it took 340,000 bricks

to pave the district's cobblestone thoroughfares alone), it still has the feel of a Victorian village. This may yet change: a 30-storey condo development has been proposed for the corner of Parliament and Mill Streets.

The pedestrian-only attraction is currently comprised of about 20 art galleries, half a dozen upscale restaurants, plus clubs, cafés, performance venues and some of the city's most rarefied retail. There are lots of places to browse, but our favourite shops and eateries include **Lileo** (*see p151; pictured*); **Balzac's Coffee Roastery** (*see p119*), the **Mill Street Brewery** (*see p139* **Hopping mad**); **Perigee** (*see p119*).

The Gooderham family left other significant landmarks about town: workers' homes still standing at Trinity and Sackville Streets, 'Little' Trinity Church on King Street nearby, a mansion at Bloor and St George Streets, and the classic 1891 Gooderham Building, also known as the Flatiron Building (see *p85*).

In late May the Distillery District Jazz Festival features 150 different performers at various venues around the area. For details, see the website, www.distillery jazz.com. For more information on the district, including tours of the site, visit the **Distillery Visitor Centre** (416 364 1177, www.thedistillerydistrict.com).

a soft drink and a couple of rich custard tarts. For many, this treat is close to an addiction.

On Saturdays the North Market, an annex on the opposite side of Front Street, features a farmers' market selling fresh goods straight from the countryside. It opens at an ungodly hour – many farmers are setting up at 5am. Cured and fresh meats, farm-raised trout, fruit and vegetables, herbs and even Ontario-grown peanuts are sold. But the vendors like to call it a day by 1pm so don't arrive too late. On Sundays the building is transformed into an antiques market. For more shopping tips for both markets, *see p159*.

One of the city's most photographed vantage points lies between the north and south markets. Looking west, the skyscrapers are symmetrically lined up behind the **Gooderham Building** (49 Wellington Street E), or as most people know it, the **Flatiron**. It was constructed in 1891, ten years before its more famous and much larger cousin in New York. On the opposite side of the building is a clever trompe-l'oeil by artist Derek Besant that fills the 'flat' side of the Flatiron. And if you want to get inside, pop into the Flatiron & Firkin pub in the basement (416 362 3444).

Two important theatres are across Berczy Park behind the Flatiron. The 2,000-seat **Hummingbird Centre for the Performing Arts** (*see p198*) hosts both the National Ballet of Canada and Canadian Opera Company until their new home opens in 2006. The **St Lawrence Centre for the Arts** (27 Front Street E, 416 366 7723) presents music and Canadian Stage Theatre Company performances in two smaller, more intimate venues – the **Jane Mallet** and **Bluma Appel** theatres (*see p220*). While on Front Street E, look for the **Dixon Building** (Nos.45-49), with the city's only remaining cast-iron façade. The 1872 structure is a tribute to architectural illusion: what appears to be painted wood and stone is actually cast iron. Also note the 1877 warehouse at 67-69 Front Street E, which underwent a meticulous restoration of its ornate Renaissance Revival style.

To get a real feel for St Lawrence's history head to **Toronto's First Post Office** (*see below*). The last four digits of its phone number – 1833 – correspond with the year it opened. Step across the threshold into this fascinating and perfectly restored working post office. Sit by the fireplace and dip a quill in an ink well to write a letter home on old-fashioned paper. You can learn about the role the first post office played in the Rebellion of 1837 (*see p13*). The postmaster, James Scott Howard, was dismissed for refusing to open the mail to see who was planning the uprising.

Carousel Bakery's peameal sarnie. *See p83*.

Another building not to be missed in this district is the Edwardian classic structure of the King Edward Hotel at 39 King Street E. The 'King Eddie' was the city's most fashionable hotel for some 60 years. The original property was developed in 1901 and received an additional 18 storeys in 1920. Now known as **Le Royal Meridien King Edward** (*see p45*) the grand old hotel suffered decades of skid row neglect before being returned to its former glory. It's a perfect spot for an elegant afternoon tea or tall drink in the stately street-level bar, with its leather chairs and oak panelling.

The **Distillery District** (*see p84*), east of St Lawrence, is well worth a detour.

Market Gallery

95 Front Street E, at Jarvis Street (416 392 7604). Streetcar 504. **Open** 10am-4pm Wed-Fri; 9am-4pm Sat; noon-4pm Sun. **Admission** free. **Map** p2780 G8.

St Lawrence Market

92 Front Street E, at Jarvis Street (416 392 7120/ www.stlawrencemarket.com). Streetcar 504. **Open** *South Market* 8am-6pm Tue-Thur; 8am-7pm Fri; 5am-5pm Sat. *North Market* 5am-2pm Sat (farmers' market); 8am-5pm Sun (antiques market). **Admission** free. **Map** p280 G8.

Toronto's First Post Office

260 Adelaide Street E, at George Street (416 865 1833/www.townofyork.com). Streetcar 504. **Open** 9am-4pm Mon-Fri; 10am-4pm Sat, Sun. **Admission** free. **Map** p280 H8.

Midtown

Where Toronto's Presbyterian past meets its modern-day multiculti self.

The Annex. See p87.

People often remark that Midtown exudes a village-like charm. Indeed it should, as it once comprised several distinct villages and communities, clustered around the fringe of the expanding city. Even today the distinctive personality of each neighbourhood stubbornly persists. Forest Hill still feels like a village, with its centre tidily concentrated around neat florists, prim boutiques, coffee shops and greengrocers along upper Spadina (note that it's Spadina Road up here, not Avenue). Rosedale's deliberate and secretive, spiralling crescents still confound the unsuspecting map-wielding visitor (or shortcut-seeking cab driver) who navigates their way into this ravine lined, tree-heavy pied-à-terre for the privileged. Once rich in hippy heritage, Yorkville is still a happening urban people place on the cusp. Gentle Leaside retains the cottagey, out-of-town charm of a hamlet, where lawn bowling is still a popular pastime.

Note that this guide takes Bloor Street as the dividing line between Downtown Toronto and Midtown: venues on the north of Bloor are covered here but those on its south side (such as the Bata Shoe Museum and Royal Ontario Museum) will be found in the Downtown Toronto section (*see pp55-85*).

Yorkville

Map p282

Bus 6/subway Bay, Bloor-Yonge, Museum.
Incorporated as a village in 1853, Yorkville existed as its own entity for only 30 years before it became part of Toronto. This tiny wedge of an area, bounded by Bloor Street, Yonge Street, Avenue Road and Davenport Road, has played a key role in the development of Toronto's counter-culture personality. In the 1950s planners chose wisely to limit building density and prohibit high-rise development, maintaining the village's original character and encouraging street-level activities. It worked. In the '60s the area mushroomed with artist-run studios, innovative shops and galleries. Buzzing coffee houses showcased the burgeoning talents of folks and folkies such as Gordon Lightfoot, Neil Young, Rick James, Ronnie Hawkins, The Band and a young singer who had just breezed in from the prairies, named Joni Mitchell. These days the tie-dyed Trotskyites and beat poets have moved on, making way for some of the city's most exclusive and expensive boutiques and hotels. The area is giving in to new development pressure with large condos and hotels on the way. But don't let that put you off – Yorkville is still an easy-going place that's great for hanging out.

At Bloor Street and Avenue Road, the **Village of Yorkville Park** (Cumberland) is built on a former parking lot. Designed as a series of themed gardens, it was laid out in 1991 along the original lines of the 12 properties on Cumberland. It's the perfect setting for an impromptu urban picnic, on a 650-ton chunk of pink granite from the Canadian shield. As you reflect on the area's groovy days, you can browse the swingin' souvenirs from the era, like a 'genuine' Beatles lunchbox at the memorabilia candy and curio store, **Retro Fun** (130 Cumberland Street, 416 968 7771).

A series of connecting north–south walkways traverse the area, making the exploring a bit more interesting. Though many galleries have exited recently to trendy West

Queen West (*see p182*), some of the finest and most innovative art in Toronto can be enjoyed (free) in the galleries that cluster along Yorkville's streets, notably on Scollard Street and Hazelton Avenue. Stalwarts including **Mira Godard Gallery** (22 Hazelton Avenue, 416 964 8197) and **Beckett Fine Art** (120 Scollard Street; *see also p184*) consistently present a great variety of top-quality Canadian and international exhibitions.

A small alleyway takes you from 14 Hazelton Avenue to the back entrance of the decadent **Hazelton Lanes** shopping mall (55 Avenue Road; *see also p143*). Inside are upscale temptations in fashion, cars and the first Canadian branch of the trendy, Texas-based supermarket chain **Whole Foods** (*see p158*).

Just up the street from Hazelton Lanes is one of the kookiest buildings in town – the **Toronto Heliconian Club** (35 Hazelton Avenue, 416 922 3618), a rare example of Carpenter's Gothic architecture, where wood rather than masonry reinterprets the grandiose vintage revival style. Originally a church (built in 1876), the building was moved from its first location on the corner just to the south, and was bought by the THC in 1923 to provide a home for women in the arts, which it does to this day. A noticeboard outside announces events and exhibitions.

In Yorkville it's not uncommon to see autograph seekers clustering around the exits of the area's five-star hotels, hoping for a brush with the many celebrities of sport, screen and song who favour Yorkville's upper-crust amenities, particularly during the Toronto International Film Festival, when the neighbourhood serves as a sort of Hollywood North base camp (*see p28*). At the west end of Yorkville, **Alliance Atlantis Cumberland 4 Cinemas** (159 Cumberland Street; *see also p181*) screens quality (non-Hollywood) movies.

At the east end of Cumberland Street is the **Toronto Reference Library** (789 Yonge Street, 416 395 5577), the largest reference library in Canada. **Yorkville Library** (22 Yorkville Avenue, 416 393 7660), around the corner, is a gentler, smaller library, a nice spot to stop to read, and a good place to check out local events. Across the street at No.27, is another landmark, **Lovecraft** (*see also p163*), which opened in 1971 and is the oldest 'adult boutique' in Canada.

The Annex

Map p282
Bus 26/streetcar 510, 511/subway Bathurst, Bay, St George, Dupont, Spadina.
Unlike Yorkville, this area was designed as a suburb of Toronto. In one fell swoop, 259 lots were put up for sale in 1886, which sparked the first of two waves of construction in the area. Many Victorian houses went up before 1910, followed by a second building spurt of Georgian and Tudor residences. But by 1930 the popularisation of the automobile meant that the smart money (well, all the money, really) was moving further out to Rosedale and Forest Hill. Today the Annex is one of Toronto's most diverse communities, mixing up Yorkville's fabulous wealth and the University of Toronto's exuberant student culture.

As well as being the southern boundary of the neighbourhood, Bloor Street is the commercial hub, where most of the Annex's shopping, restaurants and nightlife can be found. The northern boundary, Davenport Road, follows a path that was originally a trail used by Toronto's first inhabitants, the native communities that commuted between the Don and Humber River valleys. Find out more with a visit to the nearby **Native Canadian Centre of Toronto** (16 Spadina Road, 416 964 9087), which organises public gatherings and events to promote First Nations' culture. Indeed, cultural institutions abound in the Annex: there's the **Alliance Française de Toronto** (24 Spadina Road, 416 922 2014), which showcases francophone culture throughout the year, and the **Italian Cultural Institute** (496 Huron Street, 416 921 3802), featuring rotating exhibits and seminars on contemporary Italian culture.

Casa Loma. *See p88.*

On the far side of the railway tracks you'll find the large warehouse and exhibition hall of the **City of Toronto Archives** (255 Spadina Road, 416 397 5000). The downstairs of this clean, modern building has rotating exhibits on Toronto's urban history and geography. To find out more about a particular topic, head upstairs to the research hall; registration is quick and free and the staff are helpful.

Casa Loma

Map p282

Bus 7/streetcar 512/subway Bay, Rosedale, St Clair, St Clair W, Summerhill.
Toronto's grid system suddenly goes all twisty through this hilly neighbourhood, which stretches north from Davenport Road to St Clair Avenue between Yonge and Bathurst Streets. Early on in the city's history, the outstanding view from this hilly summit led many of Toronto's wealthiest citizens to settle here.

Of course at that time this was wooded land, and the city was merely part of a pleasing but distant view. Two remnants from those heady days, **Casa Loma** and **Spadina Historic House** (for both *see below*) are popular public attractions, conveniently located next door to one another. The former is the more famous venue, and it's certainly more spectacular from the outside, but if you only have time to tour one of the two, take a quick photo of Casa Loma from outside, and head into Spadina House: it's actually the more interesting museum. Between the two attractions, a small park leads to **Baldwin Steps**. Named after the family who originally owned the land on which Spadina House now stands, these 110 stairs span a section of hillside that is too steep for a road. Stretch your legs on the way up for a fantastic view of Downtown.

Heading north along Spadina Road takes you to Sir Winston Churchill Park, at the corner of St Clair Avenue W. The park has floodlit tennis courts and a playground, and it's also popular with joggers. You can also gain access to **Nordheimer Ravine** (*see also p91*) from the park, which has many good picnic spots, as well as a long tree-shaded trail.

Casa Loma

1 Austin Terrace, at Spadina Road (416 923 1171/ www.casaloma.org). Bus 7/streetcar 512/subway Dupont. **Open** 9.30am-5pm daily. Last entry 4pm. **Admission** $12; $6.75-$7.50 concessions; free under-4s. **Credit** AmEx, MC, V. **Map** p282 D2.
Some love it, others dismiss it as a kitsch folly. Either way, Casa Loma is a sight to behold, with its corbelled towers and battlements. Late 19th-century magnate Sir Henry Pellatt enlisted architect EJ Lennox to build this medieval-style castle with a stunning view of the city below. It was finished in 1914, but Pellatt hit hard times a decade later and had to move out; the house opened as a tourist attraction in 1937. Inside, the high ceilings and wide-open rooms feel oddly empty, despite the many displays from the heyday of the 'House on the Hill'. Check out the dome in the conservatory, which is made with Italian glass, cut and stained into images of grapes and trellises. Pendulous lights hang down from the dome, resembling bunches of grapes. The house also has a bona fide secret passage to the stables, which were carried out on an equally grand scale and are included in the price of admission. The six acres of gardens at the back of the building are lovely, dark, and steep, with fountains, waterfalls and woodsy pools. Ring the bells on the dragon sculpture in the so-called Secret Garden. If you're pure of heart, legend has it, the dragons will come to life.

Spadina Historic House & Gardens

285 Spadina Road, at Austin Terrace (416 392 6910). Bus 7/streetcar 512/subway Dupont. **Open** *May-Aug* noon-5pm Tue-Sun. *Sept-Dec* noon-4pm Tue-Fri, noon-5pm Sat, Sun. *Jan-Apr* noon-5pm Sat, Sun. **Admission** $6; $4-$5 concessions. Free under-6s. **No credit cards. Map** p282 E2.
This 50-room mansion was built for Toronto financier James Austin in 1866. When they outgrew that in the early 20th century, his son, Albert, created even more space, so it now has elements of both Victorian and Edwardian architecture. The family sold the manse to Ontario Heritage Foundation in 1984, and Austin's descendants donated the contents of the house to the new museum, meaning that each exhibit contains furniture, appliances, crockery, and books that were actually used by the people who lived there.

The museum gives an especially good sense of what high-society life was like a century ago. Enthusiastic staffers provide guided tours, and exhibits are changed frequently to suit a particular theme or season. The extensive historic gardens (free, if you don't enter the museum) are resplendent with the flowers, legumes and herbs of Austin's day. Don't miss the archaeological display on the lower level, which contains items from an even earlier house built on the same foundation by the Baldwin family. On special occasions, appetising period dishes are prepared for visitors in the mansion's working kitchen.

Rosedale

Map p283

Bus 75, 82/subway Rosedale, Summerhill, Davisville, Eglinton, St Clair.
Whether you approach Rosedale from Bloor Street, Mount Pleasant Road or St Clair Avenue, you immediately feel that you've entered a different world, where every citizen is a king or a queen. Rosedale's streets are quiet, shady and lined with stone and brick mansions. In the

Spadina Historic House
& Gardens. *See p88.*

1820s Sheriff William Botsford Jarvis (after whom Jarvis Street is named) settled here with his wife Mary. William is credited with founding Rosedale, but it was Mary who named it, giving a nod to the wild roses that grew on the hills of their large estate. Mary spent many a day wandering these hills on foot and on horseback, and the trails she made are thought to form the template for modern Rosedale's roads. Visitors get lost here more than anywhere else in the city, and most of the locals like it that way.

Many of Toronto's wealthiest and most prominent citizens live in Rosedale. The area's Victorian, Georgian, Tudor and Edwardian mansions were built between 1860 and 1930 and many are listed in the Toronto Historical Board's Inventory of Heritage Properties. Rosedale has a row of gourmet shops and restaurants along Yonge Street north of Church and south of the railway tracks, where you can shop and eat alongside Toronto's rich and famous.

Abutting Rosedale to the west is the pleasant neighbourhood of **Summerhill**, filled with high-end shops and services. Also here is the award-winning **Summerhill LCBO store** (10 Scrivener Square; *see also p156*), the flagship shop for Ontario's publicly owned liquor board, housed in a restored vintage train station.

Back in Rosedale proper, well-manicured **Rosedale Park** has tennis courts, a playing field and a skating rink. This was also the location of Canada's first Grey Cup game in 1909, between the University of Toronto and the Parkdale Canoe Club.

A series of ravines forms a horseshoe shape through Rosedale, cutting it off nicely from the rest of the city. These woody crevasses bear names that further evoke a fairytale atmosphere: the Vale of Avoca, Moore Park and Rosedale Valley. The ravines also lead into the **Don Valley**, which forms the eastern boundary of the neighbourhood. One trail leads you right to the **Don Valley Brick Works Park** (*see below*).

Don Valley Brick Works Park

550 Bayview Avenue, at Pottery Road (416 392 1111/ www.city.toronto.on.ca/parks/parks_gardens/lowerdon 2.htm). Subway Castle Frank then 20min walk.
Don Valley Brick Works Park is one of the most important geological sites in North America. Rich in industrial and ecological history, the area was used centuries ago by indigenous communities as a source of clay, and between 1889 and 1984 the Don Valley Pressed Brick Works Company, one of Canada's biggest brickyards, operated here, pro-ducing bricks that were used for some of the city's best-known buildings (Hart House, Casa Loma, Osgoode Hall and Old City Hall, among others).

It was only in 1995 that the park became a public space, and restoration of the site began. The old quarry has been re-integrated into a nature park with a wildflower meadow and wetlands, paths and boardwalks that are ripe for exploring, and historic buildings with enlightening displays on the making of bricks. There are also plans afoot to develop the site further to include an organic nursey, a rock and rope climbing centre, office space and a restaurant.

Don Valley.

Forest Hill

Bus 32B, 32C/subway Davisville, Eglinton, St Clair, St Clair W.
You won't see a forest, but you will see trees. Forest Hill was incorporated as a village in 1923, succeeding the former community of Spadina Heights. Its snooty status was assured in 1929, when **Upper Canada College** (200 Lonsdale Road, 416 488 1125), one of Canada's most respected private schools, opened its doors to young men. The area developed as a result of the wealthy being able to buy cars and therefore live further from the centre. In 1936, in an effort to keep the place classy, new building practices were introduced, requiring that a tree be planted at the front of each property. From

little bylaws mighty oak trees grow, and Forest Hill, especially the lower part, still feels like an exclusive town in the middle of the country. That said, the area has had many more homes torn down and rebuilt than Rosedale, which gives it a more modern feel. Neo-Georgian, neo-Victorian and other 'neo-traditional' forms are common along Forest Hill Road and Old Forest Hill Road. A cluster of pleasant shops and restaurants just north of St Clair on Spadina Road is a good place to take a break from the flaunting of wealth. Even better, escape to the **Nordheimer Ravine** (*see also p88*), which runs along the south-west section of Forest Hill, with access at **Relmer Gardens**. The Belt Line Trail cuts across the north-east corner. This 2.8-mile (4.5-kilometre) pathway follows the line of a short-lived belt line railroad from the late 19th century and was renamed the **Kay Gardner Belt Line Park** in 2000 in honour of the city councillor who fought for its conversion to a park.

Davisville

Bus 32B, 32C/subway Davisville, Eglinton, St Clair.
This largely residential area takes its name from John Davis, who arrived from England in 1840, and was Davisville's first postmaster.

The neighbourhood, east of Yonge and north of Davisville Avenue to Bayview Avenue, is architecturally less interesting than Forest Hill and Rosedale, and is home to yuppies rather than millionaires. The only real reason for visitors to come to Davisville is to visit **Mount Pleasant Cemetery** (375 Mount Pleasant Road, 416 485 9129). The mile-long graveyard has been an outing destination for everyone from Toronto's unicyclists to its Goth community. (In Toronto, even the Goths have a slogan: 'Making Toronto a darker place.') The cemetery laid its first customer to rest in 1876 and by 1945 more than 117,000 interments had taken place, which is about twice the population of Toronto when the cemetery first opened. Many notable Canadians have found their final resting place here, including William Lyon Mackenzie King, Canada's tenth and longest-serving prime minister. World-renowned pianist Glenn Gould lies here, as do Frederick Banting and Charles Best, whose experiments in the early 20th century led to the discovery of insulin.

The intersection of **Yonge and Eglinton** has become a focus for the bars and restaurants patronised by the new suburbanites who've moved north into Davisville and Forest Hill. Several of these are worth a detour, though there's not a lot else round other than their houses and a neighbourhood feel. Once home to a thriving singles scene, the area is still known as Young & Eligible by some locals.

Leaside

Bus 51, 56, 100/subway Davisville, Eglinton, St Clair.
This neighbourhood is named after a farming family headed by John and Mary Lea, who emigrated here from England in 1819. As often happens, it was the second generation that rose to prominence: their son William Lea opened a tomato cannery, became township counsellor for seven years, and built an octagonal house that he called Leaside. Part residential and part industrial, the streets of Leaside proper don't have much to offer, but this is a gateway into suburbia on the other side of the Don Valley park system. Just north of Eglinton, a bike path leads from Broadway Avenue down into **Serena Gundy Park**. If you cross back south under Eglinton Avenue, you'll end up in **Ernest Thompson Seton Park**. Seton was an eccentric naturalist, and author of *Wild Animals I Have Known*, reputedly one of the inspirations for Rudyard Kipling's *Jungle Book*. When Seton moved to Toronto in 1870, this part of the Don Valley was still wilderness, and it became a natural research laboratory for his zoological studies. Today it's tamer, with picnic tables dotting grassy areas along the West Don River, but scientific endeavour remains integral to the area. Where the park meets Taylor Creek, and where the Don Valley Parkway meets Don Mills Road, sits a series of sculptures that look like giant exposed molars, roots and all, rising from the ground. Filled with soil and plants, they actually make up an experimental water purification system. Further north is the **Ontario Science Centre** (*see below*).

Ontario Science Centre

770 Don Mills Road, at Eglinton Avenue (416 696 1000/www.ontariosciencecentre.ca). Subway Eglinton then bus 34. **Open** *Sept-June* 10am-5pm daily. *July, Aug* 10am-6pm daily. **Admission** $14; $8-$10 concessions; free under-4s. **Credit** AmEx, MC, V.
Sprawling from a suburban boulevard and tumbling down into the lush Don Valley, the multi-level centre houses 800 or so permanent science exhibits, plus Toronto's only planetarium and an Omnimax movie theatre. The centre opened in 1969, and some exhibits now have a distinctly retro feel. But the interactive Science Arcade at the far end of the complex makes the trip worthwhile, and the temporary shows are consistently engaging and topical. The brand new $40-million Weston Family Innovation Centre, described as a 'scientific Times Square', will highlight new developments via multimedia displays, and is a further reason to visit. The excellent gift shop will please any science junkie, but the food services are disappointing. If weather permits, pack a lunchbox and picnic in the park that lies behind the museum.

West End

Welcome to the wild west – Toronto's funky frontier of cutting-edge cool.

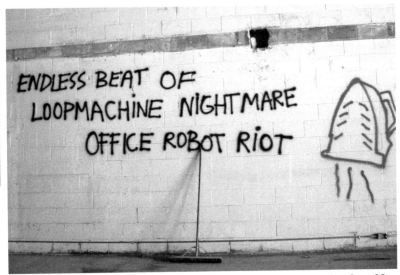

Art speaks for itself (we think) at the **Museum of Contemporary Canadian Art**. See p98.

Map p278

Streetcar 501, 504, 505, 506.

Toronto's West End is one of the city's major crossroads. The expansive and widely varying terrain stretching west from Bathurst Street past the Humber River has plenty of parks, shopping and sights, but best of all its charming neighbourhoods are ideal for charting out the city's kaleidoscopic cultural diversity. Of the 80 or so different communities in the city, a good many started out in the West End.

Artsy types love the West End too: tree-lined blocks, vintage storefronts, industrial warehouse spaces and, most importantly, lower rents, all conspire to allow pockets of bohemiana to arise spontaneously. This phenomenon can happen anywhere out here, at any time: just look at the formerly bleaker-than-bleak strip of **Dundas Street West** (*see p96* **Walk on**). Sandwiched between West Queen West and Little Italy, a small but seminal scene is awakening – offering a fresh alternative to both areas.

The west end of Toronto may be wild but it's also wide. To explore, take it area by area, according to your interests and time frame. For sporty types, the breezy **Waterfront Trail** (*see p55*) allows cyclists and walkers to zip through a corridor of parks, sports facilities, public art and historic sites in one almost seamless, car-free strip. High Park and the Humber River are accessible from the trail.

The West End's four major vectors – Bloor, College, Dundas and Queen Streets – lead to a variety of urban diversions, from vital nightspots to the best pierogi in town.

Bloor Street connects a great diversity of neighbourhoods – with the added bonus of the subway line below. At Bloor and Bathurst Street, both locals and visitors love to shop at the crazy, must-see **Honest Ed's** (*see p144*). Round the corner is Markham Street's **Mirvish Village**, and its funky mix of arty bookstores, restaurants and shops.

Walking west (in the direction of Christie), **Koreatown** – some call it Little Korea – is in your face, with its peppy retail strip (at its most intense at Euclid and Manning Streets). Check out the bakery window at Uni Kim (680 Bloor Street), where tiny walnut cakes pop out of a mechanised mini-assembly line. Koreatown halts abruptly at Christie Street, where **Christie Pits Park** and the Christie subway provide further options: heading westwards on Bloor there are waves of smaller international enclaves to explore – you'll find a mix of Latin, African, Indian and Sri Lankan communities, which are currently adding new life to the strip.

College Street is home to the oldest of several Italian pockets (*see p94* **Global village**). More places to nosh and sip per square foot than probably any other in the city keep this patch of Little Italy buzzing on an espresso-induced high. Some of the quiet, tree-lined residential streets that run off College hide tiny stores, sandwich shops, ice-cream parlours and galleries.

The remarkable transformation of Dundas West near Ossington Avenue is still in its early stages, but it's all upwards. Once the preserve of hardware and plumbing supply stores, sports bars and fish vendors, suddenly the area has sprouted spots like the **Crooked Star** (202 Ossington Avenue, 416 536 7271), the **Communist's Daughter** (1149 Dundas Street W; *see also p140*) and the **Press Club** (850 Dundas Street W; *see also p141*), which bring a street-level rec-room aesthetic all their own.

Today **West Queen West** is the talking point of the town. Oh so chic yet oh so downtrodden, here Toronto's down-and-outers rub shoulders with its up-and-comers and divey hostels have become the city's most desirable hotels. The **Drake Hotel** (1150 Queen W; *see also p140*) offers a myriad of salon-styled diversions and is a starring attraction bringing WQW an influx of business, a touch of glamour and sparkle. But this neighbourhood has been a hotter-than-hot spot before. Back in railroad's glory days, near the turn of the 19th century, there were no less than three different train

Global village Poland

Population: 150,000
Home base: Roncesvalles Avenue, between Lake Shore Boulevard W and Bloor Street W

The first Polish émigrés settled in the city in the 18th century, but it wasn't until 1850 that peasants began to arrive in large numbers, attracted by advertisements for railway and land development (a number headed westwards towards Saskatchewan to take up beet farming). Determined to express themselves religiously and culturally, they established a community of churches, bakeries and butchers, just a few blocks north of the railway yards.

A lull in immigration between the world wars was followed by an influx of political refugees; defecting athletes and performers – along with accredited doctors, engineers and professors – chose this fast-growing Canadian city as their harbour from communist rule. Today Toronto's Polish community supports two daily newspapers and several TV and radio timeslots, and has grown far beyond the confines of Roncesvalles Avenue to the West End (Bloor West Village, Etobicoke) and Mississauga.

Trading places: Though the Roncesvalles neighbourhood, between the churches of St Casimir (156 Roncesvalles Avenue) and St Vincent de Paul (263 Roncesvalles Avenue), continues to trade heavily in Polish delicacies, books and videos, the focus is now shifting to suburban strip malls.

A taste of: Toronto's largest Polish population now resides outside the city proper, in adjacent Mississauga, home to Plaza Wisla (named after the longest river in Poland), at Dundas Street W and Dixie Road, and the cheapest baked goods this side of Warsaw. The downtown pedestrian can find his mecca at Dundas Street W and Roncesvalles Avenue, where 80 per cent of businesses are run by Polish Canadians and residential streets are flooded with the sounds of Polish pop. Threatened by mass gentrification (a trendy antiques strip flourishes at Queen Street West), the strip still remains sausage central. Copernicus Delicatessen (79 Roncesvalles Avenue, 416 536 4054) is the best link to superlative spicy kielbasa, while Czechowski Polish Sausage (935 The Queensway, 416 252 4567) in Etobicoke serves fancy varieties stuffed with foreign cheeses.

Join in: Off-season for the majority of travellers, save for a few hardy northern Europeans, is the Feniks Polish Film Festival. Two theatres – one on Bloor Street W at the Kingsway, the other in Mississauga – promote the films of the two Krzysztofs (Kieslowski and Zanussi).

Local luminary: Late radio and TV broadcaster Peter Gzowski is the great-great-great-grandson of one of Canada's first Polish immigrants, Sir Casimir Gzowski, a military and civil engineer who oversaw the building of bridges, canals and railways across Ontario.

Sightseeing

stations clustered at the bustling junction of Queen and Dufferin. One of the few remaining edifices of the era is the Victorian-styled **Gladstone Hotel** (1214 Queen Street West). The family-run hotel has been (and continues to be) meticulously buffed up to its 1889 splendour. In the glory days of steam and steel, the bustling Gladstone's basement had a sporty transit lounge, where patrons could buy rail tickets and speed through a connecting underground tunnel to Gladstone Station. (You'll find the last remaining pieces of that station just across the street from the hotel at the flower and gardening store.) *See also p96* **Walk on**.

King Street West is a thriving hub for Toronto's graphic arts, design, animation and communication firms. Developers have their sights set firmly on the area too. They're busily converting the area from a trendy studio warehouse district into a trendy studio condominium district.

Further west is **Parkdale**. Once a majestic lakeside village, it spiralled into decline after World War II, as the nearby lake was filled in and developed with tracks and roadways. The current renovation generation is busy rebuilding this classic Toronto neighbourhood, which is still scenic and full of lovely old homes.

Global village Italy

Population: 500,000
Home base: College Street and Bathurst Street, St Clair Avenue W and Dufferin Street

Toronto's Italians originally came from the poverty-stricken Calabria region of southern Italy and settled in the neighbourhood via the Ward – a shanty town of railway workers that grew north from Union station – when, in the early 1900s, accomplishments in railway building were parlayed into constructing the streetcar lines and sewers that branch out from the city centre. In Little Italy, fruit merchants, barbers, tailors and bars served the growing community. After World War II Canada opened up its borders, and Torontonian Italians sponsored the arrival of family members. At the same time, a building boom attracted huge numbers to the construction trade. Another zone consisting of mostly northern Italians formed at St Clair Avenue W and Dufferin Street and is now even bigger and more Italian in flavour than its downtown counterpart. Migration continued northwest into the suburbs of Woodbridge, where many of the city's construction royalty have built their estates. Today the community supports the CHIN television and radio station and a newspaper (*Corriere Canadese*). The Italian Cultural Institute (*see p87*) runs screenings, exhibitions and other events.
Trading places: Motoretta (554 College Street, 416 925 1818) sells enough gelato-coloured Vespas to give you a Federico Fellini flashback. Riviera Bakery (576 College Street, 416 537 9352) has ice-cream, and supplies most of the neighbourhood with baked goods. Grab some Calabrese rolls and head to Centro Formaggio (578 College Street,

416 531 4453), or any of the other great food shops on the street and dine alfresco at the new Piazza Johnny Lombardi (at the intersection of Grace Street south side of College). The new parkette is a loving tribute to the late great CHIN founder – a man who championed both multiculturalism and bikini contests. Venture to Faema (672 Dupont Street, 416 535 7147) for exceptional Italian coffee.

Further west, it's a shopper's haven for all kinds of vintage goods, from serious antiques to much thriftier second-hand stores. At the bottom of the hill Queen Street ends abruptly (the streetcars, however, keep on going) and on your left you'll see Lake Ontario; to the right is Roncesvalles Avenue.

Roncesvalles' strong local community is also bringing new life to the 'hood. It's still lined with plenty of Polish businesses (see p93 **Global village**), but a diversity of shops and services now add a peppy tone.

Further west is **High Park**. At over 200 acres, it's Toronto's biggest city park –

a remarkable gift to the city by John Howard. He purchased it in the 1830s, building his residence, **Colborne Lodge** (see p97), on a fine hilltop overlooking the lake.

The house/museum is one of the many great amenities that complement the unusually diverse park, which is home to an astonishing array of plants, animals and birds. Trails spool through rolling hills, paths are well maintained (but steep and muddy here and there), with informative markers along the way. Nature-loving adults will love Grenadier Pond; the kids may prefer the duck pond over at the park's popular little zoo. See also p173.

Sightseeing

A taste of: Grab a seat on the patio at Café Diplomatico (594 College Street, see also p126) in the heart of Little Italy and savour the streetscape. While you're people watching, check for signs of Old World Italian life. As well as a great espresso, you'll find the soul of Little Italy at places like Sammy Joes, Café Bar Azzurri and local sports bars: as well as Italian people, there's often a good card game or soccer match to watch. For a real veal meal deal head down Clinton Street, taking the alleyway at the bottom for a block, to the original California Sandwich Bar (244 Claremont Street, 416 603 3317). This is one of Toronto's great culinary institutions: these messy buns of meatball, aubergine, steak and veal are revered by all – as testimonials on the walls, from hockey players, police and firemen, celebrities and film crews, gleefully attest.

For serious shopping, strike uptown to the St Clair and Dufferin 'Corso Italia' retail strip. Here you'll find all things Italian – including designer clothing, jewellery and furniture. It's also a sweet haven, with many pasticceria (try Tre Mari Bakery, 1311 St Clair Avenue W, 416 654 8960); or go further west for canoli at Messina Bakery (19 Scarlett Road, 416 762 2496). For a cultural experience and the city's finest gelato, don't miss La Paloma Gelateria & Cafe (1357 St Clair W, 416 656 2340). Try one or more of the 50 varieties of ethereal hand-made gelatos that vary with the seasons, including old world faves like spumoni, fig and glazed chestnut.

Join in: College Street is shut to traffic for two days in June, when the Taste of Little Italy festival (www.tasteoflittleitaly.com) swells with thousands of people enjoying

music and street performances. Special vendors and local businesses offer a feast, from Italian through Brazilian to Thai. Rides for children and beer gardens for adults are further attractions.

Local luminary: Italian-Canadian Nino Ricci, author of Lives of the Saints, has lived in the city for years.

Walk on West Queen West

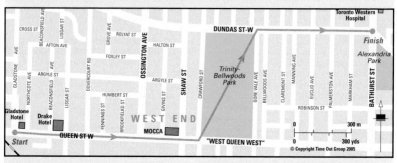

Start: Queen Street West, at Dufferin Street
Finish: Bathurst Street
Length: About 4 miles (6km)
Time: three hours, including gallery time and a meal break

This downtown stroll takes in up-and-coming West Queen West and Dundas Street West, via art, history, street culture and architecture. *Take the subway to Dufferin station, then bus 29 southbound. Get off at Queen Street West. Cross Dufferin to the east at the lights and enter the Gladstone Hotel (see p94).*
Stroll through the lobby to hop aboard the city's oldest and loveliest elevator to the second floor. Gazing to the south from the balcony, railyards and warehouses sprawl down to Lake Ontario. The hotel was founded in 1889 by Susanna Robinson as a family-run hotel; under current owners, the Zeidler family, it is once again a family enterprise. Meticulous heritage restoration, under the eye of proprietor Eberhard Zeidler (the Canadian architect who designed the Eaton Centre), will one day recap the building with its glorious flag-topped cupola. There is also a ballroom and two lounges on the ground floor. *Turn to your left when you exit, heading east.*
As you stroll, be gently forewarned that like the Gladstone, West Queen West is a work in progress. Contrasting forces give the area its gritty energy – appliance stores, flophouses, print shops and greasy spoons of yesteryear underscore the mondo bars and boutiques of the moment. Street life gets a bit spicy around here after dark, so heads up. In this robust culture, dozens of galleries have collectively arisen in a creative cabal. Conveniently, almost all of them are on the north side of the street.

Walking east a block or two, at Beaconsfield Street you'll find the Drake Hotel (see p93). The Drake has been a major contributor to the area's resurgence, and even if you're not staying here, pop in for breakfast or a drink. Alternatively, continue walking east, and try one of the restaurants nearby – Brazilian, Ethiopian, Vietnamese, or even a Canadian classic like **Oyster Boy** (*see p130*).
The migration of **MOCCA** (*see p98*) to its new digs at No.952 is nicely augmented by other art institutions nearby, such as **Edward Day** (No.952; *see also p186*); **DeLeon White** (No.1096; *see also p186*) and **Stephen Bulger** (No.1026, 416 504 0575). Bar-wise, there's **Lot 16** at No.1136 (416 531-6556), plus Atom Egoyan's **Camera Bar & Media Gallery** at No.1028 (*see also p139*). *After Oyster Boy you'll see Trinity-Bellwoods Park stretching to the left (north).*
The park is home to the former Trinity College, as well as another lost treasure: the Garrison Creek, which is now buried deep below. *Head on a loosely defined north-east trajectory through the park until you reach the top at Dundas Street West. Then continue right (heading east).*
Observe how this traditional Portuguese neighbourhood is in upward urban flux. New galleries, cafés and small clubs are staging a mini-revival of their own. Check out the **Chelsea Room** (No.923; *see also p140*), **Cocktail Molotov** (No.28; *see also p140*), the **Press Club** (No.850; *see also p141*) and **Musa** (No.847, 416 368 8484). *For an arty end to your walk, cross over Bathurst Street and continue on to the Grange Modern (see p69), Will Alsop's addition to OCAD (see p69) and the Art Gallery of Ontario (see p71).*

To the west of High Park is **Bloor West Village**. Once a run-down retail strip, it's now a fashionable shopping district. Trendy cafés, upscale markets and classy clothiers join Ukrainian bakeries and Euro-styled delis to make this the perfect place for a post-park wind down. One of the West End's best breakfast spots is the **Bloor-Jane Diner** (2434 Bloor Street W, 416 766 5383).

To the south of Bloor Street, Riverside Drive runs through the neighbourhood of Swansea, and is a trove of Tudor-style houses. Keep an eye out for 210 Riverside, identifiable by the spreading oak tree on the front lawn. The home's first owner was **Lucy Maud Montgomery**, the Canadian author most famous for her *Anne of Green Gables* books. Montgomery nicknamed her house 'Journey's End'. Swansea itself was one of the last independent villages to be assimilated by the city of Toronto, and the hilly, affluent neighbourhood retains its character. Its individuality is aided by its being bounded on three sides by water: Grenadier Pond, Lake Ontario and the Humber River. You can walk – or better still, cycle – along the Humber through an almost unbroken chain of parks all the way to the northern limits of the city.

To explore the western lakefront, walk or bike the **Waterfront Trail** (*see p55*). One option for an excursion is to visit **Historic Fort York** (*see below*) and head down to the lakeside path. You'll see the grand buildings and gates of **Exhibition Place** (*see p61*) as the trail rounds Humber Bay, as well as the vintage arches of the **Sunnyside Pavilion**, with its large public swimming pool (*see p217*) and beachside restaurant. It's a great, surprisingly uncrowded, little-known spot to watch beach volleyball or gaze out on to the lake, where scullers from the nearby Argonaut Rowing Club provide an athletic but leisurely diversion.

The **Palais Royale** (1601 Lake Shore Boulevard W, 416 533 553) is where the giants of swing once swung Toronto crowds. This deco dancehall still hosts regular exhibitions and events; its sprung floor and high-ceilinged wooden structure make it one of the city's most enjoyable live music venues. It was here that the Rolling Stones threw a surprise gig on a hot August night in 2002.

Heading west along the water's edge past picnic tables, green space and ice-cream vendors – at the bay's midpoint, you can cut under the Gardiner Expressway on **Colborne Lodge Drive** for an excursion into High Park (*see p95*).

Look out for two monuments: in **Sir Casimir Gzowski Park** a few miles along from Bathurst you'll find a bust of Sir Casimir himself, along with biographical information (*see p93* **Global village**).

Half a mile further along the trail, the **Queen Elizabeth Monument** commemorates a visit by King George VI and his wife Elizabeth (later the Queen Mother) to Canada in 1939, when they officially opened the stately highway known as the Queen Elizabeth Way.

Way out west – on the outer limits of the city, you'll find the **Montgomery's Inn Museum** (*see p98*). Even further away is the **Black Creek Pioneer Village** (*see below*), a step back in time, and a day trip in itself.

Black Creek Pioneer Village

1000 Murray Ross Parkway, Jane Street at Steeles Avenue (416 736 1733/www.trca.on.ca/ parks_and_attractions/places_to_visit/black_creek). Bus 35, 60. **Open** *May-June* 9.30am-5pm Mon-Fri; 11am-5pm Sat, Sun. *July-Sept* 10am-5pm Mon-Fri; 11am-5pm Sat, Sun. *Oct-Dec* 9.30am-4pm Mon-Fri; 11am-4.30pm Sat, Sun. **Admission** $11; $7-$10 concessions; free under-5s. **Credit** AmEx, MC, V.

This catch-all re-creation of 19th-century village life could easily have become 'Ye Olde Disneyesque Embarrassment', but it's actually an interesting place to spend an afternoon. Indeed, with special events like 'Meet the pigs' and 'Seven uses for a goose', how could you go wrong? The property was a farm that belonged to Daniel Stong and his family in the 1800s (there never was a village of Black Creek). There's a working mill, a blacksmith, a printing house and a weaver's shop. The barns, workshops and other restored buildings are staffed by costumed animators practising traditional trades and crafts.

Colborne Lodge

Colborne Lodge Drive & The Queensway (416 392 6916/www.city.toronto.on.ca/culture/colborne.htm). Streetcar 501/subway High Park. **Open** *Jan-Apr* noon-4pm Sat Sun. *May-Dec* noon-5pm Tue-Sun. **Admission** $4; $2.75 concessions. **Credit** V.

Architect John G Howard knew a thing or two about making a house a home. Shortly after becoming Toronto's first surveyor, he designed a villa for himself and his wife Jemima on the highest point of land overlooking the Humber Bay (prompting Jemima to dub the area 'High Park'). Howard made several additions to the house, including installation of the city's first indoor toilet.

Their home is now a museum, chock full of the Howards' furniture, kitchen gadgets and other possessions, arranged as they would have been in the 1860s. John and Jemima are buried nearby.

Historic Fort York

100 Garrison Road, between Bathurst Street & Strachan Avenue (416 392 6907). Streetcar 511. **Open** *Jan-May, Sept-mid Dec* 10am-4pm Mon-Fri; 10am-5pm Sat, Sun. *May-Sept* 10am-5pm daily. Closed last 2wks Dec. **Admission** $6; $3-$3.25 concessions; free under-6s. **No credit cards**. **Map** p278 C8.

This is where it all began. Lt-Governor John Graves Simcoe founded the fort in 1793 to protect the town of York (which was incorporated the same year). The fort only saw real military action once, at the Battle of York in 1813. It was sacked by the Americans, but rebuilt shortly thereafter. Modern refurbishment began in the 1930s, but by then many of the forts' vintage buildings were destroyed to make way for the Gardiner Expressway. The museum offers guided tours and historical re-enactments, and performances of period music and dance.

Montgomery's Inn Museum

4709 Dundas Street W (416 394 8113). Subway Islington then 10min walk. **Open** 1-4.30pm Tue-Fri; 1-5pm Sat, Sun. **Admission** $4; $1-$2 concessions. **No credit cards.**
It's a shame that this inn, the main part of which dates from 1830, is so far from anywhere else. But if you're in the area, it's well worth a visit. Thomas Montgomery operated the inn and tavern for 25 years. When Thomas's wife Margaret died in 1855,

he took down the sign and closed up shop. The late Georgian stone house fell into disrepair, until it was opened as a museum in 1975.

The old sign emblazoned with a picture of a plough, is one of the few artefacts that have survived from Montgomery's day. It now hangs in the museum.

Museum of Contemporary Canadian Art (MOCCA)

952 Queen Street W, at Shaw Street (416 395 0067/ www.mocca.toronto.on.ca). Streetcar 501. **Open** noon-6pm Tue-Sun. **Admission** phone for details. **Credit** V. **Map** p278 B7.
For years the MOCCA has struggled to find a space that can live up to its ambitious name, but chronic public underfunding has made the battle to find a new home embarrassingly slow. The museum has only recently reopened on Queen West after being sequestered in the northern suburbs for more than two decades. Its new space is relatively modest in size and construction, but the move to a downtown location is without doubt a step in the right direction.

Global village Portugal

Population: 350,000
Home base: College Street and Dundas Street W, between Ossington Avenue and Dufferin Street

Mass Portuguese immigration didn't hit Toronto until the mid 1960s and '70s, yet today the group is the third largest in the city by mother tongue. Originally settling in Kensington Market, where they opened rice, bean and fruit stands, the community soon shifted south to the area around St Mary's Church (589 Adelaide Street W, 416 703 2326), the city's largest Portuguese parish, and westwards to the inexpensive village surrounding Trinity-Bellwoods Park along Dundas Street W. Difficult though it was to find employment in a city teeming with immigrants, the Portuguese eventually rose above their station as construction workers and cleaners, finding jobs in the hospitals, schools and restaurants in their community.

At Dundas Street W and Dovercourt you'll see plenty of mom-and-pop groceries, banks, tiny travel outfits and used-car dealerships.

The local churches reflect the local population. The Santa Cruz Parish Church (142 Argyle Street, 416 533 8425) rivals the Church of St Patrick (at Dundas and Grace Streets) as the neighbourhood's spiritual nucleus; both say Mass in Portuguese.
Trading places: The Mira Mar Fish Store (225 Ossington Avenue, 416 533 5900) also

sells other edibles, plus pottery, tiles and religious artefacts.
A taste of: Start on Dundas, west of Ossington, ordering a beer at one of the local sports bars and it will usually arrive with a plate of marinated beans, shrimp or peanuts. Now that you've had a little taster walk west into carnivore country Little Portugal style: churrasqueiras proffer grilled and roasted chicken with sides, and rows of butcher shops, with bright come-hither signs, boast meat specials. Find snacks aplenty at Caldense Bakery & Pastries (1209 Dundas Street W, 416 534 3847), or back up to Golden Wheat Bakery & Pastry (652 College Street, 416 534 1107), for breads, coffee and ethereal custard tarts. There's plenty to explore along College Street, west of Ossington.
Join in: In the second weekend of June, Trinity-Bellwoods Park and adjoining Dundas Street get jammed with Portuguese Day revellers – expect giant barbecues of chicken and fish, folk-dancing, live music with Brazilian beats, sports and stuff for thekids.

If you fancy watching footie with a cool beer, try College Street. Outlets such as Bairrada Churrasqueira Grill, at No.1000 (416 539 8239), offer spicy grilled meat churrasco-style.
Local luminary: Nelly Furtado moved here from her native Victoria, BC, after launching her pop career.

North Toronto

Get up, get out and get wild on Toronto's northern fringe.

Most visitors to Toronto tend to focus on attractions closer to the city's core, but those who opt to explore the city's northern side will discover that they can get away from it all without leaving town. All that space, though, means distances are spread out and while transit service do exist, you might want to consider renting a bike or a car for places well off the subway lines. The built-up area around Yonge Street and Sheppard Avenue is a busy commuting zone where subway lines meet and Highway 401 cuts across the city.

The North Side grew into a satellite downtown under the stewardship of the mayor of the pre-amalgamation city of North York. 'His Melness', Mel Lastman, deemed his accomplishments of such high regard that he gave the people a central gathering point and named it **Mel Lastman Square** (5100 Yonge Street). A fountain features a bell-ringing, kinetic sculpture nicknamed 'Mel's Bells'. The square is just in front of the over-ballyhooed **North York Civic Centre** (416 338 0338), which, before amalgamation, was North York's City Hall. It's home to a hotel, shopping mall and a popular public library.

Culturally, an infrastructure is in place here so that suburbanites don't have to venture downtown, but there are fewer offerings here than just a few years ago. The **Toronto Centre for the Arts** (5040 Yonge Street, 416 733 9388) houses three theatres, including the acoustically superlative **George Weston Recital Hall** (see p198). The nearby **Museum of Contemporary Canadian Art** moved to West Queen West in 2005 (see p98).

North of the square, **Gibson House** (5172 Yonge Street, 416 395 7432) commemorates David Gibson, one of the major figures from the failed Rebellion of 1837 (see p13). A Scottish immigrant, Gibson built his first family home here in 1826, and following his exile and subsequent pardon, he returned to the site with his wife and children, building the farmhouse that stands here today in 1851, in sharp contrast to the surrounding high-rise landscape. Supplementing the exhibits in the museum, costumed tour guides demonstrate such 19th-century skills as spinning yarn and making ice-cream by hand. Just to the west of all of these sites, **York Cemetery** (101 Senlac Road, 416 221 3404) is a peaceful place to walk.

Grazing cattle was a common sight for the first people who built homes in the **Lawrence Manor** neighbourhood back in the 1950s. Today the section of Bathurst Street north of Briar Hill Avenue up to the 401 expressway is the (very) bustling home to Toronto's Jewish community. David Bezmozgis, a Toronto author, profiles life among Jewish immigrants in this neighbourhood in his award-winning *Natasha: And Other Stories* (2004). Orthodox synagogues and schools abound, and storefronts offer kosher foods (including bagels and deli fare), books, gifts and Judaica. The **Holocaust Centre of Toronto** (4600 Bathurst Street, 416 635 2883) has exhibits, a resource library and an audio-visual presentation. Admission is free, but by appointment only.

Just down the road, at 4588 Bathurst Street, the **Bathurst Jewish Community Centre** (416 636 1880) is a well-equipped complex that houses the respected **Koffler Gallery**, the **Leah Posluns Theatre** and **My Jewish Discovery Place Children's Museum**. South of Sheppard Avenue in **Earl Bales Park** (see p217) stands a **Holocaust Memorial** monument created by Toronto sculptor and Holocaust survivor Ernest Raab. Another monument, also by Raab, commemorates Raoul Wallenberg, the Swedish diplomat who saved the lives of thousands of Jews in Budapest.

Though its name conjures up images of equestrian elegance, the **Bridle Path** is a monument to excess, but worth a good gawk. The homes on this street (near the York Mills neighbourhood) are monsters, costing anything up to $20 million. With that kind of money most people would buy privacy, but on the Bridle Path residents might just as well stand on their massive front lawns and scream out their bank balance to passers-by. Many owners have bought a lot, torn down the existing house and custom-built their new dream home in its place. The resulting pastiche of building styles can only be called Disneyesque. Maybe that's why the Artist Now Known Again As Prince picked up a palatial pad here after marrying Torontonian Manuela Testolini (check out the grey stone mansion at No.61, rumoured to have cost around $7 million). Check out too the colonial brick monster at No.24, which looks like it houses an exiled dictator who can't give up the presidential lifestyle. Discredited newspaper baron Conrad Black has been staying close to his palatial digs on Park Lane Circle. No.18 is a three-storey, neo-Georgian goliath, while No.19 looks rather like a '70s subway station.

The **Toronto Aerospace Museum** (65 Carlhall Road, at Keele Street and Sheppard Avenue W, 416 638 6078) is north-west of here, located in a building that isn't just full of history, but is part of that history – it's the original 1929 home of the de Havilland aircraft company. It's also the oldest aviation heritage building in the Greater Toronto Area, the oldest surviving aircraft factory in Canada and the birthplace of many famous Canadian-designed aircraft. You can see most of them, as well as vintage flight-related paraphernalia and equipment, right here.

Built in 1952, **Don Mills** – named after the Don River – was a modernist's dream. Today, as well as the Don Mills Shopping Centre, the area is home to the striking new **Japanese Canadian Cultural Centre** (6 Garamond Court, at Wynford Drive, 416 441 2345), which houses a performance theatre as well

as a central gallery. In addition to regular exhibitions, the centre hosts a number of events and activities throughout the year.

The **David Dunlap Observatory** (123 Hillsview Drive, at Major Mackenzie Drive, 905 884 9562) is located way up beyond the city proper in **Richmond Hill**. Here students and researchers ponder the astronomical mysteries of the universe – and so can you. Evening tours include a chance to look at the night sky through the largest optical telescope in Canada. The multi-domed observatory is located in a large and airy park, a property the astronomers share with a small population of white-tailed deer. This is a serious research facility, and children under seven are not permitted on the evening tours.

Southbrook Farm (1061 Major Mackenzie Drive, at Bathurst Street, 905 832 2548) provides a chance to visit a country farm, market and winery on the edge of town. In summer and early autumn you can pick your own fresh fruit, and hot baked pies and award-winning fruit wines are sold year-round.

Global village Jamaica

Population: 300,000
Home base: Throughout the Toronto area

As part of a historic peace treaty with the British, the first immigrants from Jamaica came to Canada in 1796 to help build a fort in Halifax. But it wasn't until the 1960s that they started arriving in significant numbers, when new laws were passed, favouring well-educated and highly skilled immigrants.

In the 1970s Toronto became home to an A-list of Jamaican musical talent: Stranger Cole, Jackie Mittoo, Leroy Sibbles, Ernie Smith and Carlene Davis are just a few who left an indelible mark on the local soundscape – you still hear the sound of reggae in the streets.

Today there are many communities living in the far-flung fringes of Toronto: Scarborough, Brampton, Don Mills, Rexdale, Mississauga and Ajax. 'Little Jamaica' proper runs along Eglinton Avenue W (for blocks) past Oakwood.

Trading places: Kensington Market (*see p156*) is an especially vibrant hub, and is home to Patty King Bakery (187 Baldwin Street, 416 977 3191), selling hot patties, pastries and breads, plus stalls offering everything from coconuts to vinyl to hand drums. Another small pocket of Jamaican-run, stores, hairdressers and grocers is found on Bathurst Street, north of Bloor Street...

A taste of: ... which is where you'll also find Wong's Restaurant (930 Bathurst Street, 416 532 8135), which has been dishing up excellent Jamaican cuisine for over three decades.

Join in: Toronto's Jamaicans keep in touch with the island via weekly publications like *Pride*, *The Gleaner*, *Share* and the monthly *Word* magazine (www.wordmag.com), which hosts the annual IRIE Music Festival (www.iriemusicfestival.com); also check out the annual Caribana festival (*see p170*). The Jamaican Canadian Association (995 Arrow Road, 416 746 5772) remains the active hub for the community and hosts frequent events.

Local luminary: Toronto is still home to some high-profile Jamaicans, among them Louise Bennett ('Miss Lou'), who is regarded by many as the first dub poet. Michael Lee-Chin, meanwhile, is undoubtedly the worldwide poster boy for overachieving Jamaicans. One of nine children growing up in Port Antonio, Jamaica, he managed to convince the Jamaican government to sponsor his studies in civil engineering in Hamilton, Ontario. He later switched careers and now runs one of the largest mutual funds companies in Canada, with an estimated personal worth of around $2.5 billion.

East Toronto

For a feast, head east.

The Don Valley cuts through the heart of Toronto, and its wide green gap is more than a geographical division: it separates a mentality. Head east across the graceful five-arch span of the Bloor Viaduct (Prince Edward Viaduct on the map, but nobody calls it that) and you leave downtown behind and enter a world of old-fashioned, small-town neighbourhoods – quiet streets, canopied by lines of trees, sprawling parks, mom-and-pop cornerstores – and some of the best skyline views in the city. East Toronto is also home to a large **Greektown** (*see p104* **Global village**) and **Little India** (*see p103* **Global village**) as well as the most accessible stretch of city shoreline along Lake Ontario in **the Beaches** neighbourhood.

While East Toronto lacks any major attractions, the powers that be hope to draw the crowds by transforming the toxic wastelands of the port district into a model of urban development. Sadly, where other cities have managed to create eye-popping architecture and visionary designs of post-industrial urban renewal, plans for developing this vast site remain mired in a bureaucracy. For now, the **Portlands** offer a strange mix of Great Lakes freighter ships that from a distance appear land-locked, hulking incinerators, scrap heaps and bike trails. It's also home to the city's film district – which sounds like a great tourist attraction – but the stages and back lots remain well-hidden behind high fences.

In 2004 a bizarre and short-lived attempt to make the East Side a new international gateway to Toronto with a high-speed ferry service across Lake Ontario to New York State lasted only a few months before fizzling due to underwhelming public response. The folks in Rochester, New York, who cooked up the plan were banking heavily on the idea while Torontonians couldn't figure out why anyone would want to go there. Still, the backers insist the ferry is not dead in the water and Toronto's Port Authority is seeing through its commitment to build a customs house and terminal for a non-existent ferry near Cherry Beach.

It's a short hop from heavy industry to a scene of bucolic sailboats bobbing on the lake at **Ashbridge's Bay**. This gateway park to the Beaches has acres of sandy expanse that are home to one of the largest sites of beach

Kickin' off at **the Beaches**. *See p102.*

volleyball action in North America (*see p213*). On warm summer nights, buff bodies in skimpy attire take face plants in the sand under a sea of looping volleyballs on 85 courts. A new theatre in the park performs Shakespeare all summer long to compliment the annual summer Bard fest in High Park in the West End.

The Beaches

Bus 64, 92/streetcar 501.
This community was created during the 19th century when the gentry decided they needed homes 'outside' the city and built small mansions by the lake. In summer they would close up their downtown Rosedale homes and relocate here. Since then the city has sprawled out to swallow them, and it's a direct 30-minute trolley ride from Yonge Street straight along Queen Street E. But the Beaches remains a community to itself, with a feeling not unlike a Muskoka resort town up north. In summer, the cottage-less crowds from downtown escape the heat by packing on to the beaches and filling every outdoor patio along Queen Street East.

The area occupies the stretch of Queen Street between Woodbine Avenue and Victoria Park Avenue, after which you will find yourself in Scarborough (a mainly residential district that turns into a land of fast food outlets and strip malls). For years the debate raged over the name. Some called it the Beach, others the Beaches. So confusing. What to do? It's matter of personal choice, really, but as the two miles (four kilometres) of wooden boardwalk pass through stretches of beach with different names (Balmy Beach, Kew Beach, Woodbine Beach), the plural seems more apt.

Whatever its name, it remains the same gentri-fashionable area, filled with chic shops, cafés and bars, casual restaurants serving wings and beer and more well-heeled dining that demands a credit card. Downtowners marvel at the seclusion of cottage homes nestled at water's edge. (Never mind the fact that the boardwalk is a constant parade of strollers, joggers, dog walkers, bikers and zooming bladers.) Perfectly manicured parks with bandstands and gazebos make for idyllic picnics under the shade of weeping willows.

For kicking back, smearing on the suncream and pretending you're on South Beach, Queen Street has several joints with patios, including the **Lion on the Beach** (1958 Queen Street E, 416 690 1984; *see also p141*). The **Sunset Grill** diner (2006 Queen Street E, 416 690 9985; *see also p125*) is unmissable for breakfast. The **Garden Gate** (2379 Queen Street E, 416 694 3605) or 'Goof' as its known from days when its Good Food neon sign was missing some lights,

serves up portions of Chinese-Canadian cuisine. Think chow mein with grilled cheese sandwiches. It's also across the street from a fine rep house, the **Fox Theatre** (2236 Queen Street E, 416 691 7330).

As unlikely as it may seem, fans of art deco will want to pay a visit to the **RC Harris Filtration Plant** (2701 Queen Street E, at the foot of Victoria Park Avenue), the monolithic building prominent at the eastern end of the beaches. Designed by English architect Thomas Pomphrey in the 1930s, this operational water treatment plant, all towers and arched doorways, sits on a grassy knoll in striking contrast to its park setting. Tours are offered haphazardly; call 416 338 0338 for times.

Equally unexpected are the **Scarborough Bluffs**, dramatic cliffs that plunge into the lake a couple of miles east of the water plant and which can be seen from the grounds. Every year a few houses lose their footing to erosion on the Bluffs and have to be rescued. You can scamper about the base of the cliffs at Bluffer's Park (a 10-minute walk down Brimley Road from the Kingston Road 12 bus stop) where there is also a community of houseboat dwellers. The **Guild** (191 Guildwood Parkway, 416 338 8798) is currently closed while the city decides how to revive this unusual assortment of log cabins and artfully placed 'ruins' – pediments and other architectural details of long-gone city buildings – set amid lush gardens on the bluffs.

The Danforth

Streetcar 504/subway Chester or Pape.
Bloor Street changes names to Danforth Avenue (locals call it the Danforth) on the east side of the Don Valley and, typically, the neighbour-hood changes as well. This is where a large Greek immigrant population settled. Peppered with Greek shops, restaurants and cafés, Greektown is not a cutesy, ethnic tourist trap… yet, but as the forces of gentrification have their inevitable effect and the original inhabitants move out it is at risk of becoming a second Little Italy. It already has a similarly fashionable bar and restaurant scene.

The Danforth is a pleasant place to amble at any time, but you do have to be hungry to get the most out of the area. Greeks like to feed you, and the irresistible aroma of souvlaki, feta and moussaka wafts from storefronts all along the street. Most of the restaurants stay open late so you can always get a plate piled high with kebabs, roast potatoes, savoury rice and Village Salad (the 'real' Greek salad of onions, tomatoes, cucumber and feta cheese – no lettuce) after the bars close at 2am. The classic experience, is **Mr Greek** (568

Danforth Avenue, 416 461 5470), serving heaped platters at reasonable prices. For more culinary finesse, *see pp106-141*.

The Danforth is also known throughout the city for a little shopping complex known as **Carrot Common** (348 Danforth Avenue, 416 466 3803), anchored by the **Big Carrot** (*see p158*), which is the original – and still the most extensive – site for health food shopping and natural products in Toronto.

Gerrard Street East

Streetcar 506.

When you start to notice signs with the titles Mo Pa, Hoi Tan and Wing Kee, you know you have wandered into another of the city's authentic ethnic sections. This area east on Gerrard Street was an offshoot of Chinatown but many other cultures including Vietnamese and Cambodian have since joined the neighbourhood. And as it is still not considered as trendy as the central Dundas–Spadina district, the bargains are better in the restaurants, groceries and little speciality shops, especially those dispensing Chinese herbs and medicines, such as **Dai Kuang Wah Herb Market** (595 Gerrard Street E, 416 466 9207). At the **Grand Sea Food House** (615 Gerrard Street E, 416 778 8888) you can order a fresh lobster dinner for a positively meagre $15. You will be at a real advantage if you can decipher the menu, however, as most of these restaurants feature Chinese characters – which at least means the food is authentic.

Global village India

Population: 200,000
Home base: Gerrard Street E, west from Coxwell Avenue

In Toronto, as in cities throughout the world, immigrants tend to flock downtown, settle, prosper, then shift their focus to spacious suburbs while the next displaced culture takes its place. Toronto's Indian community, however, colonised a remote patch of the east end, off the radar of some long-time residents, who managed eventually to detect its presence only once the numbers had exploded and vast tracts of this hitherto ignored slice of suburbia had been developed in the name of Indian progress.

Indian immigration began in earnest in the 1960s and '70s, mostly in the form of young men who drove taxis, took over convenience stores, opened restaurants and laboured in construction while upgrading professional studies that didn't translate from the old country. Families followed – parents, grandparents, cousins, children – and soon the population that still occupies a one-and-a-quarter-mile (two-kilometre) stretch around Gerrard Street E and Coxwell Avenue had fragmented into developments further east in Scarborough, and west by the airport and in the suburb of Bramalea.

Of course, the community itself is fragmented into Sikhs, Tamils and the Hindu majority, the traditional Southern Indians (who adorn their temples with black granite icons) and the more liberal northerners (who prefer lighter marble). In all, there are 45 Hindu temples in the city, the neighbourhood of Richmond Hill claiming the largest – the Hindu Temple Society of Canada (10865 Bayview Avenue, 905 883 9109) – where not a week goes by without some fête.

Trading places: Though more of Toronto's Indians make their home outside the Gerrard/Coxwell community than within it, business there is overwhelmingly Indian, with silks and saris attracting seamstresses and fashion mavens taken with the Bollywood trend. There are dozens of sari shops along Gerrard Street E (most in the 1400s).

A taste of: On Gerrard Street you're best at the simplest end: stalls sell authentic street treats and there are good takeaways and caffs but some of the restaurants proper compare poorly to those in the world's other Indian communities. For pastries and sweets, comb Gerrard Street E or the Albion and Islington area in Etobicoke, the only other predominantly Indian community in Toronto. Madras Palace (1249 Ellesmere Road, 416 759 5400) is a South Indian hotspot in faraway Scarborough, whose thali is worth the dreary drive eastwards.

Join in: Meditate at the Vedanta Society of Toronto (120 Emmett Avenue, 416 240 7262) in Etobicoke, daily from 6pm to 7pm. In mid May, for 15 days, Hindus celebrate Rathotsawam (the Chariot Festival), during which processions of lotus-shaped wood chariots can be seen circling around the neighbourhood.

Local luminary: The novelist Rohinton Mistry emigrated from Bombay to Toronto in 1975.

Little India

Bus 22, 31/streetcar 506.

A few blocks further east along Gerrard Street, between Greenwood and Coxwell Avenues, is Little India. The neighbourhood, with its colourful garish advertising signs, is famous for its **Indian Bazaar**, where you can buy saris, silks and brightly coloured scarves, and spices and foods. Both professional and weekend chefs peruse these markets regularly. Festivals during the year bring a Bollywood excess to the area.

Riverdale/Leslieville

Streetcars 501, 506.

Riverdale faces Cabbagetown across the Don Valley. Favoured by the city's liberal chattering classes, it stretches from Broadview Avenue to

Pape Avenue, and Mortimer Avenue to the lake, although its eastern boundary is constantly expanding. As affordable real estate in Riverdale proper becomes scarce, more families are buying less expensive homes further east in largely immigrant neighbourhoods as far as Coxwell Avenue. If you like to house-browse, take a stroll down any of the streets surrounding the impressive Withrow Park, located between Logan and Carlaw Avenues.

Another nice walk is through **Leslieville** (Queen Street E, between Logan and Connaught Avenues). A range of funky antiques shops strong on 1950s and '60s kitsch, and places to brunch (**Bonjour Brioche**, 812 Queen Street E; *see also p131*; **Edward Levesque's Kitchen** 1290 Queen Street E, 416 465 3600; *see also p132*) are changing the area's long-held reputation as the poor cousin to Queen West.

Global village Greece

Population: 150,000

Home base: Danforth Avenue toward East York; Scarborough, Markham and Mississauga

It would hardly be mistaken for the motherland, but the Danforth, aka Greektown, has that discernible southern Mediterranean feel, especially in the summer, when patios with no concept of last orders spill on to the street and Hellenic music (not just 'Zorba the Greek') can be heard from open kitchens, private homes and passing cars. The neighbourhood of modest homes and shops was settled by Greek immigrants who had escaped Turkish occupation in the early 20th century to toil away – not unlike other ethnic groups – on the Canadian National Railway, and as miners or farmers. Successive waves in the mid-century brought over women sponsored by their husbands and fathers, who worked as domestics for the city's establishment. Whereas in 1907 only two dozen Greek names appeared in the city's phone directories, today the Greek population on the Danforth and beyond is the second largest outside Greece (Queens, New York, is the first). Consequently, the local flavour is unique in its authenticity, with its Greek-language signage, blue-and-white flying flags and Mediterranean banks and manufacturers. Restaurants – the favoured business of first-generation émigrés in the latter half of the century – are considered to be among the best reviewed in the city.

In the 1990s this social scene, along with low house prices, made the area attractive to Toronto's upward mobility, who gutted and reno'ed to yuppie standards. More Greeks have shifted eastwards than remain, with thousands of families shifting to Scarborough, Markham and Mississauga.

Trading places: Those who have forsaken the quarter have nonetheless remained faithful to Mister Greek Meat Market (801 Danforth Avenue, 416 469 0733), purveyor of lamb and pig for backyard spits and wedding feasts.

A taste of: Though Danforth remains the hub (Myth, at 417 Danforth Avenue, is still a hangout; *see p141*), the strip is in danger of becoming a wax museum of Greek life, its souvlaki joints and pastry shops mere kitsch amid new-era coffee dens and health food houses. A few high points remain: Sun Valley Fine Foods (583 Danforth Avenue, 416 469 5227) is a modest fruit shop-cum-produce bazaar in the Danforth's hectic heart.

Join in: Early each August stone ovens and grills are towed on to the pavement for the week-long Taste of the Danforth festival (*see p170*). St George's Greek Orthodox Church (*see p69*) in Downtown West, established in the 1930s, is the pre-eminent venue for experiencing Greek Easter celebrations and St George's Day, both in April.

Local luminary: Greek Prime Minister Andreas Papandreou resided in the Danforth while in exile in the early 1970s, and also taught economics at Toronto's York University.

Eat, Drink, Shop

Restaurants & Cafés

Around the world in 80 dishes.

A quieter moment at Indian favourite **Nataraj**. *See p122.*

See p122.

In Toronto, the world is your oyster. The multicultural fabric brings riches from all parts of the globe to the resto scene. Locals take it in their stride, from the first jolt of authentic espresso in the morning to a late-night nosh-up of Vietnamese barbecue, via crocodile dim sum, tender tandoori, vegan omelettes, oodles of pasta and enough foie gras infusions to keep cardiac wards in business for decades. This banquet of choice is generally a good thing, but be warned: this is sometimes taken a step too far. So watch out that your oyster doesn't come 'painted' in yuzu mignonette and perfumed with offal essence. It could happen, especially in the trendier spots where fashion rules over fare.

Some restaurants are turning this bounty of delights to their advantage, by offering tasting menus. **Susur Lee** has a few; **Perigee** is nothing but, and **Avalon**'s most ambitious showcase is a dazzling performance of succulent surprises with carefully selected wines to match.

Yet, despite its epicurean tendencies, Toronto has no culinary traditions as such. Before World War II, the city's palate was as bland as that of a Midwestern farming community and lived up to its porcine nickname – Hogtown, indeed. Getting oriented to today's foodie scene needs a compass and the easiest way to eat around town is to go by neighbourhoods – the 'hood defines the food. The ethnic patchwork means you can count on finding Chinese in Chinatown, Greek on the Danforth, funky cafés on Queen West and elegant eateries in Midtown – choosing where to go for what is a no-brainer.

True, you can now find a Belgian bistro on the Danforth, French in Little Italy and Mexican on Korean-dominated Bloor Street, though the dominant cultural flavour in each area still remains potent.

Dressing for dinner in Toronto is easy: keep it casual. You'll spot denim and trainers even in the top haunts. You might want to smarten up for places like **Avalon**, **Bymark**, **Scaramouche** or **North 44**, **The Fifth**, **Canoe Restaurant & Bar** and the **Courtyard Café** – though none of these requires men to wear a jacket. Smoking is forbidden in Toronto restaurants. Beware: anyone under 19 is restricted from entering restaurants that declare bar status.

Entertainment District

Cafés & coffeehouses

Rivoli
332 Queen Street W, at Spadina Avenue (416 597 0794/http://rivoli.ca/2003). Streetcar 501, 510. **Open** 11.30am-1am daily. **Main courses** $8-$18. **Credit** AmEx, MC, V. **Map** p279 D7.
The Rivoli was ever-present during the formative years of the now-legendary stretch of Queen West between University and Spadina, and is still a central meeting place for hipsters of all generations. The functions of the space are various: diners gather on the east side of the building, drinkers on the west, and the two mingle on the patio out front. Upstairs is a pool hall, and the back room serves as a venue for up-and-coming bands and DJs. Nourishment is bistro style, with some Asian fusion thrown in the mix. Soups and salads are run of the mill, noodle dishes fare better; burgers and pad Thai are the best bet. This is no gourmet fantasy, but the (fair) price you pay for food includes scenery and music. *See also p134, p203 and p216.*

Continental

Avalon
270 Adelaide Street W, at John Street (416 979 9918). Streetcar 504/subway St Andrew. **Open** 5.30-11pm Tue, Wed, Fri, Sat; noon-2pm, 5.30-11pm Thur. **Main courses** $30-$44. **Credit** AmEx, DC, MC, V. **Map** p279 E7.
Neighbourhood noshing in the Entertainment District is all about pre-show, but at Avalon, dinner *is* the show. Chef/owner Chris McDonald creates new menus daily according to the availability of fresh, top-quality ingredients. The cuisine is inventive and intelligent, a series of happy unions of contrasting textures, flavours and culinary traditions that reflect McDonald's experience in Europe, Mexico and the US. The elegant, unfussy setting and skilled service allow diners to lavish full concentration on the food. Although à la carte is tempting, the

six-course gastronomic menu ($150 per person) is the best choice, especially with accompanying wines. If your wallet doesn't allow for dinner, come for lunch (Thursdays only). This is quite simply one of the city's best restaurants.

Brassaii
461 King Street W, at Spadina Avenue (416 598 4730/www.brassaii.com). Streetcar 504, 510. **Open** 7am-3pm, 5pm-midnight Mon-Fri; 5pm-midnight Sat. **Main courses** $18-$38. **Credit** AmEx, DC, MC, V. **Map** p279 D8.
Finding this sizeable bar/bistro is not exactly a piece of cake, as it's tucked at the back of a courtyard along King Street West. The clubby atmosphere, sofa lounge at the entrance and loft-like layout appeal to young and-comers out to gnaw on steak-frites and swill some New World wine. Named after the master photographer of the 1920s, whose work hangs here, Brassaii is a cut above bland bistro. Nothing too adventurous, but reliable braised meats and roasted birds and consistently tasty veg. The only downside is the kitchen's inability to do justice to fish – a mystery, but there you have it.

The best Eateries

For breakfast or brunch
Aunties & Uncles *(see p115)*; **Edward Levesque's Kitchen** *(see p132)*; **Lai Wah Heen** *(see p113)*; **Pain Perdu** *(see p126)*; **Senator** *(see p125* **Grease is the word***)*; **Verveine** *(see p131)*; **Xacutti** *(see p128)*.

For lunch
Canoe Restaurant & Bar *(see p113)*; **Gallery Grill** *(see p116)*; **Gamelle** *(see p128)*; **Lee** *(see p108)*; **Osgoode Hall** *(see p114)*; **Sidhartha** *(see p132)*.

For afternoon tea
Pangaea *(see p120)*; **Red Tea Box** *(see p126)*; **Senses** *(see p108)*; **Vienna Home Bakery** *(see p127)*; **Courtyard Café** *(see p116)*.

For a patio setting
Allen's *(see p132)*; **Bar One** *(see p128)*; **Boulevard Café** *(see p116)*; **Bymark** *(see p112)*; **By the Way Café** *(see p120)*; **Café Diplomatico** *(see p126)*; **Drake Hotel** *(see p130)*; **Trattoria Giancarlo** *(see p128)*; **The Fifth** *(see p108)*.

For late-night eats
Bar Mercurio *(see p116)*; **Kei** *(see p130)*; **Lee Garden** *(see p113)*; **Mona's Shwarma & Falafel** *(see p126)*; **Ouzeri** *(see p131)*; **7 West** *(see p119)*.

Crush

455 King Street W, at Spadina Avenue (416 977 1234/www.crushwinebar.com). Streetcar 504, 510. **Open** 11.30am-11pm Mon-Fri; 5pm-midnight Sat. **Main courses** $23-$43. **Credit** AmEx, DC, MC, V. **Map** p279 D8.

This industrial-sized bar-restaurant might be a little too cool for some, but time has tested the French fare and the reviews have, on the whole, been favourable . Maybe it's because it's no longer a rarity in this fast-gentrifying neighbourhood of film houses and architecture firms, and these days is surrounded by similarly chic bistros. Chef Masayuki Tamaru's menu features magret of duck, hearty Breton pork and boudin blanc, among other famous French delicacies, and the bar pours more than 30 wines by the glass. Desserts are dazzling. Informal, and very popular.

The Fifth

5th floor, 225 Richmond Street W, at Duncan Street (416 979 3005/www.easyandthefifth.com). Streetcar 501/subway Osgoode. **Open** 6-11pm Thur-Sat. **Set menu** $85; terrace $50. **Credit** AmEx, DC, MC, V. **Map** p279 E6.

It's a warehouse loft, a living room and a dining room, and sits (kind of) quietly above a booming nightclub. The Fifth quickly established a loyal following although the kitchen has suffered through a series of departing chefs. With JP Challet now at the helm you can still expect fine French treats such as filet mignon, foie gras and a wide selection of cheeses. The Fifth is open only Thursday to Saturday, so reservations are highly recommended (especially for the terrace in summer).

Jules

147 Spadina Avenue, at Queen Street W (416 348 8886). Streetcar 501, 510. **Open** noon-9pm Mon-Fri; noon-5pm Sat. **Main courses** $15-$17. **Credit** AmEx, DC, MC, V. **Map** p279 D7.

A simple and simply good French bistro that stands alone in its category on the Queen West strip. Especially popular at lunchtime, the quaint dining room has a distinctively buttery scent (it must be the quiches, crêpes and home-made desserts). Office types take a break from the rat race, dining on flavourful sandwiches and creamy chicken. Most mains are served with crispy fries, and the tarte tatin will leave you humming the *Marseillaise*.

Le Sélect Bistro

328 Queen Street W, at Spadina Avenue (416 596 6406/www.leselect.com). Streetcar 501, 510. **Open** 11.30am-11pm daily. **Main courses** $17-$29. **Set menu** $29. **Credit** AmEx, DC, MC, V. **Map** p279 D7.

This quintessentially Paris-style bistro, long a haunt of the Queen West boulevardier set, packs up in the summer of 2005 and heads to a new locale at 432 Wellington Street W. The French owners insist the ambience won't get left behind (nor the hanging bread baskets or the extensive wine cellar). If the menu stays the same, expect decent French bistro

fare like escargots, pissaladière and smoked whitefish mousse for starters, followed by confit of duck leg, braised oxtail and steak-frites.

Senses

SoHo Metropolitan Hotel, 318 Wellington Street W, at Blue Jays Way (416 935 0400/www.metropolitan. com/soho/restaurants.asp). Streetcar 504/subway St Andrew. **Open** 6-10pm Wed-Sun. **Main courses** $32-$49. **Credit** AmEx, DC, MC, V. **Map** p279 E8.

Chef Claudio Aprile is one of those world travellers who manages to slip styles from sushi to salsa into his cooking without making things seem too nouveau. Now happily ensconced in the SoHo Metropolitan, the restaurant is anything but standard hotel fare. The dining room – all white linen and stiff high-back chairs is a tad formal. A casual, sunny café shows off fresh goods from the in-house bakery.

YYZ Restaurant & Wine Bar

345 Adelaide Street W, at Peter Street (416 599 3399). Streetcar 504, 510. **Open** 4.30-10pm Mon-Wed, Sun; 4.30-11pm Thur-Sat. **Main courses** $25-$29. **Credit** AmEx, DC, MC, V. **Map** p279 E7.

The acronym refers to Pearson International Airport's call letters, but this is more catwalk than runway and the food more jetset than airport lounge. In the epicentre of Downtown, it attracts fabulous people from business and media, darling. It's hard to imagine why, though, when you inspect your bill and wonder how you've spent so much. Best to come in a group and try a bit of everything: you're bound to find something to your liking (food spans western Europe, and is heavy on the seafood).

Fusion

Lee

603 King Street W, at Portland Street (416 504 7867). Streetcar 504, 511. **Open** noon-2.30pm, 6-10.30pm Mon-Fri; 6-10.30pm Sat. **Main courses** $5-$14. **Credit** AmEx, MC, V. **Map** p279 D8.

Susur Lee, the star chef of fusion in Toronto, has made a gift to his fans: an affordable alternative to his next-door restaurant, Susur (*see p109*). But rather than divide his attention between two places, Susur has put well-groomed sous-chef Jason Carter in the driver's seat. Carter deals in the trademark intricate combinations of flavours and textures. Marinated pork loin with celeriac, apples and onions has a depth of sweetness and spice; crab is both spicy with ginger and earthy with pine nuts and toasted orzo. The open, casual room is a bit noisy, but the clatter, combined with lively wait staff and the sensational food, creates an air of excitement. The plates are small, so order many and share.

Rain

19 Mercer Street, at John Street (416 599 7246/www.rainlounge.ca). Streetcar 504/subway St Andrew. **Open** 5.30-10.30pm Mon-Sat. **Main courses** $35. **Credit** AmEx, DC, MC, V. **Map** p279 E8.

Plenty to dance about at **Ultra Supper Club**. *See p111.*

Entrepreneurs Michael and Guy Rubino have created a *Barbarella*-meets-*Tarzan* decor that favours Lucite along with jungle bamboo. Though doormen can be ridiculously brazen, Rain is worth experiencing at least once: nibble for hours on appetisers over expensive drinks, or watch your (Asian fusion) main be brought to your table on a steaming serving stone.

Susur

601 King Street W, at Portland Street (416 603 2205). Streetcar 504, 511. **Open** 6-10pm Mon-Sat. **Dinner** $110. **Credit** AmEx, MC, V. **Map** p279 D8.
Eating at this minimalist haven (behind the stucco façade of the trad Italian eaterie it replaced) is like opening Pandora's box: the overall taste is so much more than the sum of its ingredients. Main courses are standard haute cuisine fare – lamb and pork tenderloin, lobster, roast quail – though chef Susur Lee's use of them is decidedly Asian. His famous dozen-course tasting menu – a $100 affair that can last hours – has its mains at the outset followed by appetisers, soup and dessert. (The less adventurous can dine the traditional way, but pay more for it.) Either way, the foie gras terrine and foie gras mousse with soy aspic and mustard sauce should not be missed.

Indian

Babur

273 Queen Street W, at Duncan Street (416 599 7720). Streetcar 501/subway Osgoode. **Open** 11.45am-2.30pm, 5-10.30pm daily. **Main courses** $8-$11. **Credit** AmEx, DC, MC, V. **Map** p279 E7.
Lunch buffets this good don't come any cheaper: Babur's is just $11 and offers all the standards along with bottomless rice and tender nan. The location is also unparalleled – arty types working along Queen and King enjoy easy access, as do the suits across University Avenue. The butter chicken is a good bet for those who like to go easy on the spice, Goan fish curry is the fish eater's favourite, and shashlik paneer will please the veggie in your party.

Italian

La Fenice

319 King Street W, at John Street (416 585 2377/ www.lafenice.ca). Streetcar 504/subway St Andrew. **Open** 11.30am-2.30pm, 5.30-10.30pm Mon-Fri; 5.30-10.30pm Sat. **Main courses** $18-$21. **Credit** AmEx, DC, MC, V. **Map** p279 E8.

What Londoners take when they go out.

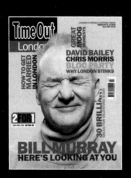

Old-world service in a sleek, modern setting. This is one of Toronto's pioneering northern Italian establishments. Diners slide into comfy leather chairs and tuck into refined pastas and meaty chops and ribs. Antipasti include seafood classics such as calamares and shrimp doused in olive oil from the family grove in Italy. A staggering selection of 350 wines earned La Fenice the nod from *Wine Spectator* in 2003. A pre-theatre fave.

Luce

Hôtel Le Germain Toronto, 30 Mercer Street, at John Street (416 599 5823). Streetcar 504/subway St Andrew. **Open** 5-10pm Mon-Thur, Sun; 5-10.30pm Fri, Sat. **Main courses** $30-$43. **Credit** AmEx, DC, MC, V. **Map** p279 E8.

The Rubino brothers (the partnership behind Rain, *see p108*) have received operatic accolades for their latest venture, a modern ode to Italy. The kitchen's foundation begins in the cantina – just like in the old country; the Rubinos make their own bread, pasta, cured meats, even *gelato* and it all arrives at your table with the contemporary flair of a smart new restaurant in Milan (and all the attitude of that city's tony set). An extremely stylish spot, Luce could do with a less generous approach – something that might fade with time. Officially the restaurant of Hôtel Le Germain Toronto (*see p41*).

Tutti Matti

364 Adelaide Street W, at Spadina Avenue (416 597 8839/www.tuttimatti.com). Streetcar 504, 510. **Open** noon-3pm, 6-10.30pm Mon-Fri; 6-10.30pm Sat. **Main courses** $9-$19. **Credit** AmEx, DC, MC, V. **Map** p279 D7.

Chef Alida Solomon spent years training in Tuscan trattorias, and then returned home to spread the good news: it's not all about tomato sauce and cheese – it's not even all about sun-dried tomatoes and buffalo mozzarella. Solomon's small kitchen excels at rustic soups, fresh pasta (which most of Toronto's chefs cannot master) matched with deep, earthy sauces. Desserts can be a disappointment – it seems that in this case, the chef has taken authenticity a bit too far.

North American

Rodney's Oyster House

469 King Street W, at Spadina Avenue (416 363 8105/www.rodneysoysterhouse.com). Streetcar 504, 510. **Open** 11.30am-1am Mon-Sat. **Main courses** $16-$50. **Credit** AmEx, DC, MC, V. **Map** p279 D8.

A transplant from the east coast, Rodney Clark imported his dad's oysters before a backer helped him open his own joint. Rodney's is one of the city's first, and still most traditional, oyster bars; once you've drizzled a dazzling array of sauces on the molluscs, tuck into Dungeness crab, lobster and other seafood in this cheery maritime ambience. As Rodney is his own middle man, you won't find fish this fresh elsewhere.

Ultra Supper Club

314 Queen Street W, at Peter Street (416 263 0330/ www.ultrasupperclub.com). Streetcar 501, 510. **Open** 6-11pm Mon-Sat. **Main courses** $26-$40. **Credit** AmEx, DC, MC, V. **Map** p279 E7.

As in 'ultra trendy'. If you like your dining room to be a dance-club – and not by simply pushing back some chairs – then this is the spot for you. With a forced sense of poshness, Ultra Supper Club has moved in where the city's old down-and-funky Caribbean nightclub/restaurant, the Bamboo, used to be. The high-ceilinged, open room is fitted with 'privacy curtains' that wrap around tables. It's supposed to make you feel like a classical Roman emperor, but that's not an invitation to wear a toga to dinner. The contemporary menu is suitably rich.

Thai

Queen Mother Café

206 Queen Street W, at Duncan Street (416 598 4719). Streetcar 501. **Open** 11.30am-midnight Mon-Sat; 11.30am-11pm Sun. **Main courses** $10-$15. **Credit** AmEx, MC, V. **Map** p279 E7.

People who have been shopping this strip of Queen West since Elizabeth Bowes-Lyon was a sprightly 85 will tell you that they learned the words 'pad Thai' right here. The Queen Mother is an icon in this community, a symbol of the city's royal past and its

Don't miss Cuisine

Avalon
A destination: here's where you'll find the city's top gastronomic menu. See p107.

Canoe Restaurant & Bar
Proves that form and function can exist together in upscale dining. See p113.

Jamie Kennedy Wine Bar
Exquisite fare in a convivial bistro. See p120.

Lai Wah Heen
Dim sum so fine it has Hong Kong talking. See p113.

Perigee
The Distillery District's outstanding theatre of the gullet. See p119.

Sushi Kaji
Offers the definitive seafood adventure. See p129.

Susur
For complex concoctions that taste simply divine. See p109.

OLD PARIS CAFE : HOME
IVING HAND KLENZE
ALET SERVICE 19601

Queen Mother Café. See p111.

multicultural future. Dishes haven't lost their shape or size over the years: bowls of noodle soup are still deep, skewers fat and filling, and rice dishes heaped high with chunks of chicken, lemongrass and spice. The back patio comes alive over summer lunches.

Financial District

Cafés & coffeehouses

Mövenpick Marché
42 Yonge Street, at King Street (416 366 8986/www.movenpickcanada.com). Streetcar 504/subway King. **Open** 7.30am-2am daily. **Main courses** $9-$15. **Credit** AmEx, DC, MC, V. **Map** p280 G8.
Mövenpick loves Toronto, and in the past few decades several incarnations of this Swiss-owned eaterie have sprung up, from Yorkville and the Eaton Centre to trendified Loblaws grocery outlets. Mövenpick Marché is also the esteemed occupant of BCE Place with seating under the swirling Santiago Calatrava-designed atrium. In the restaurant proper, things are more hectic. The protocol here is to wander with an undersized tray from kiosk to kiosk, and wait for the chef to prepare your meal from scratch – not exactly relaxing. That said, the mostly Swiss delicacies are above par and the desserts are scrummy.
Other locations: throughout the city.

Continental

Bymark
66 Wellington Street W, at Bay Street (416 777 1144/www.bymarkdowntown.com). Subway King. **Open** 11.30am-2.30pm, 5-11pm Mon-Fri; 5-11pm Sat. **Main courses** $35-$45. **Credit** AmEx, DC, MC, V. **Map** p279/p280 F8.
The Toronto Dominion Tower in the heart of the financial district offer some of the best Modernist eye-candy above ground (as well as the room-with-a-view restaurant Canoe on the 54th floor; *see p113*). Now chef Mark McEwen of North 44 has created a split-level dining room at the base of the towers. Sleek and elegant, this is a regular destination for the high rollers of Bay Street who come for contemporary, finely crafted dishes. Even the burger is sumptuous: an eight-ounce beauty topped with melted brie de Meaux and porcini mushrooms. The 5,000-bottle wine cellar guarantees an excellent selection and the menus offer suggested pairings. Foie gras and champagne are daily staples, natch.

North American

beerbistro
18 King Street E, at Yonge Street (416 861 9872/ www.beerbistro.com). Subway King. **Open** 11.30am-1am Mon-Wed; 11.30am-2am Thur, Fri; 4pm-2am Sat. **Main courses** $10-$22. **Credit** AmEx, DC, MC, V. **Map** p279/P280 E8.

For those who don't only like their beer to be poured into a frosty glass, but also braised, basted and barbecued, beerbistro certainly makes a meal out of the stuff. Wonder how? The Belgian Ale burger is caramelised by sugars in the ale; the Coq au Bier substitutes wine with a German-style wheat beer. Perhaps now you get the pitcher. The wait staff suggests pairings from the 20 brews on tap and over 100 kinds by the bottle – just don't ask to smell the cap (though if you fancy extending your knowledge of brilliant brews, beermeister Stephen Beaumont holds a bi-monthly beer school and tasting for between $40 and $50).

Canoe Restaurant & Bar

54th Floor, Toronto Dominion Bank Tower, 66 Wellington Street W, at Bay Street (416 364 0054/ www.canoerestaurant.com). Bus 6/subway King or St Andrew. **Open** 11.30am-2.30pm, 5-10.30pm Mon-Fri. **Main courses** $37-$44. **Credit** AmEx, DC, MC, V. **Map** p279/p280 F8.

Canoe appeals, for the most part, to the CEOs who toil in the walls of the concrete canyons of Bay Street: they habitually hit the bar here between marathon meetings. Even if you're weak of wallet, you too can enjoy the panoramic view and a glass of Niagara chardonnay without committing yourself to a meal (the free nibble selection will fill you up in any case). Should you seek further fulfilment – and you should – we recommend the six-course tasting menu ($85, or $135 with wine pairings). Canoe is Canadian only – that means beef is from Alberta, salmon from Newfoundland, lobster from Nova Scotia, potatoes from Prince Edward Island, cheese from Quebec and greens from local growers. As if to hammer home the point, designers of the bright, wood-panelled space have added a curling stone as a door stopper.

Dundas Square

North American

Torch Bistro

253 Victoria Street, at Dundas Street E (416 364 7517/www.thesenator.com). Streetcar 505/subway Dundas. **Open** 5-10pm Tue-Thur; 5-11pm Fri, Sat. **Main courses** $24-$36.**Credit** AmEx, DC, MC, V. **Map** p280 G7.

In the shadow of the Toronto Eaton Centre, Torch is a good pre-theatre choice: its front windows look out on to the Canon Theatre's stage door and the Elgin and Winter Garden are a short distance further down the street. But the bistro-style food is good at any time of the day. Start with the crab cakes and move on to the steak-frites, served with copious amounts of the latter. Booths along one wall are enclosed by dark wood panelling, with a curtain for seclusion. On the opposite wall are big leather banquettes, and upstairs the Top 'o the Senator jazz club (*see p204*) makes for a good after-dinner – even after-theatre – retreat.

Chinatown

Asian

Matahari Grill

39 Baldwin Street, at Beverley Street (416 596 2832). Streetcar 505, 506. **Open** 11am-3pm, 5-10pm Mon-Fri; 5-10pm Sat, Sun. **Main courses** $15-$20. **Credit** AmEx, DC, MC, V. **Map** p279 E6.

Bordering Kensington Market and Chinatown, this small Malaysian hot-spot offers the best of both worlds: fiery Asian fare in a hip setting. Also, in keeping with the area, it's easy on the pocket. The Matahari Platter – a selection of satays, spring rolls, wontons and pickles – is a good place to start, though curries and seafood are equally tasty. Service is helpful, especially when navigating some of the more exotic menu items. Best to reserve.

Chinese

Lai Wah Heen

Metropolitan Hotel Toronto, 108 Chestnut Street, at Dundas Street W (416 977 9899/www.metropolitan. com/lwh). Streetcar 505/subway St Patrick. **Open** 11.30am-3pm, 5.30-10.30pm Mon-Fri, Sun; 11am-3pm, 5.30-11pm Sat. **Main courses** $20. **Credit** AmEx, DC, MC, V. **Map** p280 G8.

Dim sum trolleys are wheeled out all over Chinatown at the weekend in Toronto, but none is as fine (or as pricey) as the fare at Lai Wah Heen. Although the elegant dining room is somewhat institutional – this is a hotel, after all – the Cantonese cooking is so good that the setting matters little. Sunday brunch's tasting menu comprises six dim sum selections and one noodle dish. Portions and presentation are the epitome of delicate: alligator-loin dumplings, banana-and-shrimp mousse and mini abalones to start. The belle of the dinner menu is crispy Peking Duck.

Lee Garden

331 Spadina Avenue, at Baldwin Street (416 593 9524). Streetcar 505, 510. **Open** 4pm-midnight Mon-Thur, Sun; 4pm-1am Fri, Sat. **Main courses** $12-$16. **Credit** AmEx, DC, MC, V. **Map** p279 D6.

Locals decided long ago that Sunday would be the night for Chinese. And so, while the rest of the city grinds to a halt, Spadina gears up for its biggest evening of the week. Lee Garden is markedly more popular than its competitors, and its dishes are characterised by their freshness rather than by their fiery temperature – this is Cantonese, after all. Prepare to wait, and then to be whisked to a table by staff who deliver your order swiftly and with gusto.

Wah Sing Seafood

47 Baldwin Street, at Henry Street (416 599 8822). Streetcar 505, 506, 510. **Open** 11.30am-10.30pm daily. **Main courses** $8-$15. **Credit** MC, V. **Map** p279 E6.

Seafood junkies with a soft spot for Chinese cuisine are drawn to Wah Sing. Many of the Far East operations in the area claim to serve the best seafood in town (notice the profusion of fish tanks in windows), but none has more of a right to this than Wah Sing, which will draw you in with its two-for-one lobster deal, and keep you there with all manner of low-priced bottom-feeder specialities. You may not want to hang around in this no-nonsense outfit after the last claw or tail, but there's plenty more to enjoy along this endearing local drag.

Continental

Osgoode Hall
2nd Floor, 130 Queen Street W, at University Avenue (416 947 3361). Streetcar 501/subway Osgoode. **Open** noon-2pm Mon-Fri. Closed July, Aug. **Main courses** $13-$17. **Credit** AmEx, DC, MC, V. **Map** p279 F7.
Osgoode Hall is an 1830s building set behind a great lawn and cast-iron fence at the corner of Queen and University. Young, energetic chef Yasser Qahawish has a knack for taking fresh, often organic ingredients and creating delectable dishes. The menu ranges from soups and sandwiches to filling mains such as lamb keftas and cassoulet. This is also your best chance to taste the famous Canadian butter tart.

La Palette
256 Augusta Avenue, at Oxford Street (416 929 4900). Streetcar 506, 510. **Open** 6-10pm Mon-Fri; 11am-4pm, 6-11pm Sat, Sun. **Set menus** $10-$31. **Credit** AmEx, DC, MC, V. **Map** p279 D6.
It was only a matter of time before Kensington Market gave us a reason – other than the purchase of used denim – to hang out. For residents of the market, this classic French boîte for bohemians offers respite from Sichuan beef and the smell of fish (it does creep in now and then, though happily in the form of *moules* soaked in tangy juice). La Palette's set menu has the most agreeable price tag in town, and the quality of the three courses is very high.

Japanese

Sushi Bistro
204 Queen Street W, at St Patrick Street (416 971 5315). Streetcar 501/subway Osgoode. **Open** 11.45am-10.30pm Mon-Sat; 4-10.30pm Sun. **Main courses** $7-$15. **Credit** AmEx, MC, V. **Map** p279 E7.
You may not reckon you're in a local institution, but this is the restaurant that whetted the city's now-insatiable appetite for (cheap) sushi. Justifying its longevity, the Bistro offers the cleanest, most pleasant experience of all bars of its calibre. The sushi slips down a dream and the chicken teriyaki arrives completely skinned – visit the competition and you'll realise just how wonderful that is.

North American

Barberian's Steak House
7 Elm Street, at Yonge Street (416 597 0335/www.barberians.com). Streetcar 505/subway Dundas. **Open** noon-2.30pm, 5pm-midnight Mon-Fri; 5pm-midnight Sat, Sun. **Steaks** $22-$46. **Credit** AmEx, DC, MC, V. **Map** p280 G6.
The golden years are waning for the Barberian family, which has been operating this deep-city cavern for four decades. The celebs, politicians and fat cats have come and gone: steak isn't for everyone these

What's your beef?

Are you feeling lean, mean or like a fighting machine? Any way you cut it, Toronto's burgers are made to suit many moods, from vegan guilt-free impostors to mile-high beauties oozing French cheese. Canada loves its beef, and there are many ways to enjoy it.

In the heart of the financial district, **Bymark** (*see p112*) pays suitable tribute with possibly the most expensive and excessive meat-on-a-bun: eight ounces of ground round topped with melted brie de Meaux and sautéed porcini mushrooms. Very la-di-dah – and it might just call for a glass of the finest red available to mankind. On a more modest scale, **Allen's** pub (*see p132*) has been serving excellent burgers for years; choose from a good selection of toppings, but even the basic version stands up on its own.

Edward Levesque's Kitchen (*see p132*) knows the earthy delights in organics, and his burgers are a nod to diner specials with a contemporary twist. You don't need to read the menu at the unpretentious diner **Lakeview Lunch** (1132 Dundas Street W, West End, 416 530 0871) to guess the speciality; the sweet smell of hamburgers on the grill meets and greets you at the door. And if you want a treat 'but please hold the meat', try the portobello mushroom burgers at **Pulp Kitchen** (*see p131*) or the very chaste miso burger at **Fresh by Juice for Life** (*see p121*). Alternatively, you could go the other way and head for **Langdon Hall** (*see p240* **Spa trek**), where the chef is a dab hand at burgers topped with foie gras. The diet starts next Monday, remember.

Café Nervosa. *See p120.*

days, and only a few old boys hold 'regular' status. That said, this a storied destination for those seeking slabs of red meat with the essential side of starch. Forgo the chain establishments and Bay Street hideaways for this welcome throwback.

Vegetarian

Café 668

668 Dundas Street W, at Bathurst Street (416 703 0668/www.cafe668.com). Streetcar 505, 511. **Open** 12.30-4pm, 6-9pm Tue-Fri; 1.30-9pm Sat, Sun. **Main courses** $10-$13. **No credit cards. Map** p278 C6.
It used to be that eating out for vegetarians meant soggy tofu served in dingy rooms where smelly sandals were barely disguised by burning incense. But we have progressed, thankfully, and herbivores are no longer punished for their food choices. This is strictly veg Chinese fare with a bent for biting spice. There are plenty of mock meats, as well as fine noodles, and the room itself is as clean as can be. Yet another reason to check out Kensington Market.

Vietnamese

Pho Hung Restaurant

350 Spadina Avenue, at St Andrew Street (416 593 4274). Streetcar 505, 510. **Open** 10am-10pm daily. **Main courses** $5-$10. **No credit cards. Map** p279 D6.

There are plenty of Cantonese and Sichuan options in Chinatown, but not much Vietnamese of merit. If you're looking for Asian but want to avoid all those thick, heavy sauces, try a warm tureen of pho washed down with some of the cheapest beer south of College. Noodles are a speciality, but they aren't the only dishes on the menu – other delicacies come wrapped in shrimp rice paper or golden buns, and you can also get a mean curry.
Other locations: 200 Bloor Street W, at Queen's Park, University (416 963 5080).

University/Harbord

Cafés & coffeehouses

Aunties & Uncles

74 Lippincott Street, at College Street (416 324 1375). Streetcar 506, 511. **Open** 9am-4pm Tue-Sun. **Main courses** $7-$8.50. **No credit cards. Map** p279 D5.
Set up to bear an uncanny resemblance to your granny's kitchen, with mismatched Arborite tables and vinyl seats, Aunties is classic 'what you see is what you get' territory. Grilled cheese sandwiches and French toast are made from fresh, chubby chollah bread. Club sarnies are impossible to eat neatly for all their chunky cuts of chicken breast and tomato. Potato salad goes with everything, and the prices are blissfully low.

Courtyard Café

Windsor Arms Hotel, 18 St Thomas Street, at Bloor Street W (416 921 2921/www.windsorarmshotel.com). Bus 6/subway Bay. **Open** 7am-2.30pm Mon; 7am-2.30pm, 6-11pm Tue-Sat; 7am-3pm Sun. **High tea** 1.30-3pm, 3.30-5pm daily. **Main courses** $27-$39. **Credit** AmEx, DC, MC, V. **Map** p282 F4.

The Courtyard Café is the ideal place for a spot of people-spotting: by night it's a fantastical, lofty pillared ballroom with a splendid domed ceiling; by day a milky white garden room full of intimate breakfast nooks. The food is by no means your average hotel fare, either – indeed, the menu is an exciting, ever-changing selection of sophisticated continental classics, while the outstanding dessert list simply cannot be ignored. And in September the Toronto International Film Festival attracts the cream of the Hollywood set to the Café's home, the smart Windsor Arms Hotel.

Continental

Gallery Grill

7 Hart House Circle, at King's College Circle (416 978 2445/www.harthouse.utoronto.ca/English/gallery-grill.html). Bus 94/subway Museum. **Open** *Sept-June* 11.30am-2.30pm Mon-Fri; 11am-2pm Sun. Closed holiday weekends & July, Aug. **Main courses** $15. **Credit** AmEx, DC, MC, V. **Map** p282 E5.

From the vertiginous balcony in this elegant room, you can look down into Hart House's oak-panelled Great Hall and ponder the life of learning while tucking into a menu of earthly delights. U of T faculty and students who can afford it come here to lunch on refined continental fare prepared with a light touch by chef Suzanne Baby. Sunday brunch's smartest pick is the scrambled eggs scented with truffle oil, mixed with brie and served with ham and toast. Other midday options include salmon trout salad and poached chicken. Leave time to tour the grounds.

Italian

Bar Mercurio

270 Bloor Street W, at St George Street (416 960 3877). Subway St George. **Open** 7am-11pm Mon-Sat. **Main courses** $22-$32. **Credit** AmEx, MC, V. **Map** p282 E4.

Along a stretch of Bloor Street West, where there's little other than fast-food chains and pubs spilling over with beer-challenged university students, you'll find this bona fide European bar. You can lean on the marble counter as the day begins, sip a latte and nibble on a brioche. Food is available all day – through lunch and late into the evening for dinner. Best bets are the home-made pastas, especially gnocchi in a gorgonzola sauce and the Pasta Mercurio, broad noodles in a duck ragu scented with black truffle. Wines are plentiful and the place hums with a low-key buzz.

Latin American

Boulevard Café

161 Harbord Street, at Borden Street (416 961 7676). Bus 94/streetcar 510. **Open** 11.30am-4pm, 5.30-11pm Mon-Sat. **Main courses** $18-$27. **Credit** AmEx, MC, V. **Map** p282 D4.

If you're averse to the forceful taste of coriander, stop reading here – it takes over the salsas, sauces and salads that accompany most dishes in this Latin-flavoured resto. But if you're a seafood fan, give it a chance. The culinary atmosphere here is decidedly Mediterranean, and the fish and cornbread good. It also boasts the jolliest patio on the boulevard.

Latitude Wine Bar & Grill

89 Harbord Street, at Spadina Avenue (416 928 0926). Bus 94/streetcar 510. **Open** 11.30am-2.30pm, 5.30-9.30pm daily. **Main courses** $30-$50. **Credit** AmEx, DC, MC, V. **Map** p282 D4.

A bit of Spain, a hint of Mexico, a splash of Asia and a dash of North America. This small, friendly bistro uses these influences to pleasing effect: lamb is rubbed with cinnamon, salmon sweet in a mango sauce. Chipotle pops up here and there, adding a layer of depth to dishes such as braised pork. The patio in the back is charming and quiet. Not enough of a wine list to be called a wine bar, truth be told.

Middle Eastern

Kensington Kitchens

124 Harbord Street, at Robert Street (416 961 3404). Bus 94/streetcar 510. **Open** 11.30am-10pm Mon-Thur, Sun; 11.30am-10.30pm Fri, Sat. **Main courses** $10-$18. **Credit** AmEx, DC, MC, V. **Map** p282 D4.

Popular with nearby university students, this long-standing Lebanese neighbourhood eatery is a notch above most fast-food falafel joints. The pretty dining room, decorated with antique toy planes, used to be family-run, and the falafel platters, fresh fish and desserts were stellar. Now, things here are consistently tasty at best, although staff can be less than helpful. The upstairs patio in the back is set amid the sprawling arms of a lovely old tree.

93 Harbord

93 Harbord Street, at Spadina Avenue (416 922 5914). Bus 94/streetcar 510. **Open** 5.30-10pm Tue, Wed, Sun; 5.30-11pm Thur-Sat. **Main courses** $20-$30. **Credit** AmEx, MC, V. **Map** p282 D4.

The area has known other Middle Eastern restaurants, but none like this. Palestinian chef Isam Kaisi's fusion menu plays front and centre in the demurely stylish room. Start with a plate of wonton wrappers and you'll discover layers of heat (Sometimes it's too much, so ask in advance.) The menu is scattered with liquorice and mint, citrus and chillies, and the juice from pomegranates and red currants. Don't miss the lamb tajine, a piece of slow-cooked meat tossed in an aromatic couscous.

D'ough!

While the Atkins craze is being blamed for
killing business for wheat producers on
the prairies and potato farmers in Prince
Edward Island, Torontonians are obliviously
bucking the trend.

Bakery-restaurants are on the rise here,
so to speak, and the timing couldn't be
better, as these idiosyncratic places are
giving Starbucks a run for its money. These
joints are a microcosm of the city's multiculti
food scene: find Basque specialities at **Pain
Perdu** (*see p126*); fine French pastries at
Patachou (*see p122*); the juiciest berry pies
at **Vienna Home Bakery** (*see p127*); Euro-
Asian creations at **Red Tea Box** (*see p126*);
hearty Ukrainian fare at **Future Bakery**
(*see p121*), Brit basics at the **Brick Bakery**
(*see p119*); and inventive French pastries
at **Bonjour Brioche** (*see p131*).

Toronto's bakery-restaurants were some
of the city's dining-out pioneers. The **United
Bakers Dairy** (Lawrence Plaza, 506 Lawrence
Avenue, North Toronto, 416 789 0519),
which dates from 1912 (in a former location)
has kosher foods and an all-veggie menu.
Slide into a booth and order cheese blintzes
or potato latkes. The atmosphere lacks, but
your stomach won't care.

In terms of liquid refreshment, good coffee
is the norm in these places, though even
home-grown donut chain **Tim Horton's**
(*pictured*) does decent cups of 'steeped tea'.

E CHOCOLATE   CANADIAN MAPLE

VANILLA DIP

Eat, Drink, Shop

HUNGRY FOR NEW PLACES TO EAT?

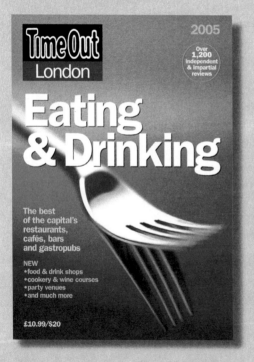

Church & Wellesley

Cafés & coffeehouses

7 West
7 Charles Street W, at Yonge Street (416 928 9041). Subway Bloor-Yonge or Wellesley. **Open** 24hrs daily. **Main courses** $10-$15. **Credit** MC, V. **Map** p283 G4.

Happily for its neighbours in the umpteen condo complexes nearby, 7 West stays open late. It's also open early. In fact, you can count on it being open whenever you pop round. Which is likely to be often, given its location near the crossroads of Bloor and Yonge, and its interesting sarnies, various pastas, the usual salads, Moroccan platters and a meaty selection of mains.

Fusion

Byzantium
499 Church Street, at Wellesley Street E (416 922 3859). Subway Wellesley. **Open** 5.30-11pm Mon-Sat; 11am-3pm, 5.30-11pm Sun. **Main courses** $25. **Credit** AmEx, MC, V. **Map** p283 G5.

Boystown is best known for its rainbow flags, outdoor mingling, late-night parties and traffic, but Byzantium goes to show there are also some keen eaters in the 'hood, as well as a spot of serenity. Also home to a well-regarded Martini bar, Byzantium invites you to sip away before or after your gastronomic adventures. *See also p194.*

St Lawrence/ Distillery District

Cafés & coffeehouses

Balzac's Coffee Roastery
Building 60, 55 Mill Street, at Parliament Street (416 207 1709/www.balzacscoffee.com). Bus 65. **Open** 7am-10pm daily. **Credit** V. **Map** p280 H8.

If entering this post-retro coffee house feels like walking on to a movie set for a Paris café, then Balzac's designers will smile quietly to themselves and perhaps pat themselves on the back. This was ground zero for Hollywood North, before the Distillery District emerged as a tourist destination. The java on offer is made from fresh-roasted beans that are then micro-roasted on the premises. For caffeine addicts with a conscience there are fair-trade and organic blends. A small selection of sweet breads, tarts and cookies is provided by middling pastry shop Dufflet Pastries.

Brick Bakery
Building 45A, 55 Mill Street, at Parliament Street (416 214 4949). Bus 65. **Open** *Summer* 9am-7pm daily. *Winter* 10am-6pm daily. **Main courses** $6-$7. **No credit cards**. **Map** p280 H8.

Another conspicuously conceptualised spot in the smart Distillery District, this British-style pastie-and-pie take-out shop has good grub on offer at fair prices. Especially tasty are the savoury pies – steak and stout, ma'am – and not-too-sweet Eccles cakes. Turkey chilli is an odd, and bad, idea – a low-fat option on an otherwise fine menu that also includes braised lamb sarnies with apricot chutney. The harried but friendly staff will heat your order. Narrow benches favour design over comfort, but outside in fine weather there are two regular picnic tables.

Continental

Perigee
Cannery Building, 55 Mill Street, at Parliament Street (416 364 1397/www.perigee restaurant.com). Bus 65. **Open** from 5.30pm Tue-Sat, closing times vary. **Set menus** $85-$105. **Credit** AmEx, DC, MC, V. **Map** p280 H8.

To date, this is the only fine restaurant in the Distillery District. Although the food-worshipping attitude here could do with a bit of levity, the open-kitchen dining room does offer a memorable, if pricey, experience. Chef Patrick Riley toils away for all to see, and encourages round-table discussions of the finely prepared classical French dishes as they are served. Little more than 30 people can fit, so the concept often works. Tasting menus only.

Italian

Romagna Mia
106 Front Street E, at Jarvis Street (416 363 8370/ www.romagna-mia.com). Subway Union/Streetcar 504. **Open** noon-2.30pm, 5-10.30pm Mon-Fri; 5-10.30pm Sat. **Main courses** $15-$30. **Credit** AmEx, DC, MC, V. **Map** p280 G8.

Named for Emilia Romagna, a region in central Italy that is both the dairy belt and bread basket, this trattoria initially sets off warning bells with its red-checkered tablecloths and bright lighting. But have no fear. The risotto is superior – and in keeping with the region, there are plenty of prosciutto and parmesan dishes. The crisp-skinned roasted chicken attracts cross-towners. Too bad they stopped making those thin-crusted, oven-baked pizzas.

Japanese

Nami
55 Adelaide Street E, at Church Street (416 362 7373). Subway King or Queen. **Open** noon-2.30pm, 5.30-10.30pm Mon-Fri; 5.30-10.30pm Sat. **Main courses** $25-$30. **Credit** AmEx, DC, MC, V. **Map** p280 G7.

A classic Japanese meeting place that tucks diners into sushi bars or discreet alcoves shielded by rice paper or curtains. Long in the running for the freshest sushi in town, at least until sushi became ubiquitous, but it's still up there. A 'sushi pizza' is an

Eat, Drink, Shop

interesting, some might say disturbing, choice. For the purists, there's sashimi, makimono and sushi all present and correct. Tender teriyaki off the menu is perfectly matched by beautifully seasoned, grilled accompaniments from the robata bar.

North American

Jamie Kennedy Wine Bar
9 Church Street, at Front Street E (416 362 5586/ www.jkkitchens.com). Subway Union. **Open** 11.30am-11pm daily. **Main courses** $6-$14. **Credit** AmEx, DC, MC, V. **Map** p280 G8.
Chef Jamie Kennedy is a local legend for his exquisite cooking, but this intimate bistro is remarkably casual and affordable. Pick a seat at one of the two bars – one faces a small, open kitchen where you can watch the maestro at work – and choose from the tapas-style menu. Courses are expertly paired with wines and range from a whimsical, delicious take on Quebec poutine (made with succulent lamb) to a luxurious dish of braised oxtail. A dazzling wall of preserves in mason jars flags the kitchen's commitment to seasonal offerings. Reservations for lunch only; arrive early for dinner.

Yorkville

Cafés & coffeehouses

Café Nervosa
75 Yorkville Avenue, at Bellair Street (416 961 4642). Bus 6/subway Bay or Bloor-Yonge. **Open** 11.30am-11pm Mon-Sat; 11.30am-10pm Sun. **Main courses** $20-$25. **Credit** AmEx, DC, MC, V. **Map** p282 F4.
Celebs in town lounge at the Four Seasons or Windsor Arms hotels. Wannabe celebs loll here, at the gateway to posh Yorkville. If you're coiffed, bleached, manicured and/or animal printed, you'll blend right in – particularly with the leopard-accented upstairs refuge. In good weather, smokers get a prime perch on the terrace. The food takes backstage, although it is fair: pizza is terrifically thin and there are light dishes such as spinach salad and angel hair pasta.

Coffee Mill
99 Yorkville Avenue, at Bellair Street (416 920 2108). Subway Bay or Bloor-Yonge. **Open** 10am-11pm Mon-Thur; 10am-1am Fri, Sat; noon-11pm Sun. **Main courses** $10-$14. **Credit** AmEx, DC, MC, V. **Map** p282 F4.
This Hungarian café is about as old-world as the city gets. It's an institution in a neighbourhood once crowded with the groovy unwashed; now it's the designer divas who squeeze into leatherette banquettes or sip espresso on the pretty outdoor terrace. If you've never had palascinta, an Eastern European sweet crêpe filled with soft cheese, now's your chance. Or leave room for one of the many hot drinks made with chocolate.

Continental

Pangaea
1221 Bay Street, at Bloor Street W (416 920 2323). Bus 6/subway Bay. **Open** 11.30am-11.30pm daily. **Main courses** $24-$39. **Credit** AmEx, DC, MC, V. **Map** p282 F4.
Although this is one of the busiest parts of town, there are precious few places to eat around Bay and Bloor. So Pangaea, upscale as it is, stands out as a rare breed. Join the suits – some of them Chanel – for a taste of the continent on the wild side. Caribou, venison and cattail hearts (the edible parts of bullrushes) are handled with care, and pastry chef Joanne Yolles creates exquisite sweets.

The Annex/Casa Loma

Cafés & coffeehouses

By the Way Café
400 Bloor Street W, at Brunswick Avenue (416 967 4295). Streetcar 510/subway Spadina. **Open** 10am-11pm Mon-Fri; 10am-midnight Sat; 8am-10pm Sun. **Main courses** $10-$17. **Credit** AmEx, DC, MC, V. **Map** p282 D4.

Future Bakery.

The Annex may have been overrun lately by cheap sushi and haughty bistros, but By the Way has managed to stay true to its roots, keeping prices low and servings simple. Dinners are Moroccan in flavour, though the falafel platter can be a bit bland. This is a great place for weekend brunch: their eggs benedict come topped with a supreme hollandaise sauce, and their bagels are always irreproachably fresh. And the patio can't be beat for sun and scene.

Fresh by Juice for Life

521 Bloor Street W, at Bathurst Street (416 537 4573/www.juiceforlife.com). Streetcar 511/subway Bathurst. **Open** 11.30am-10.30pm Mon-Fri; 10.30am-10.30pm Sat, Sun. **Main courses** $10-$15. **Credit** AmEx, DC, MC, V. **Map** p282 D4.

The whir of blenders is an omnipresent background sound in this juice bar-cum-vegan paradise. If you can ignore the noise – and get past the queues by the entrance – you'll find Fresh a welcome departure from the usual bistros and trattorias. The establishment that introduced wheatgrass to Bloor Street (and then to Queen West) has grown into much more than a purveyor of the 50 varieties on its juice menu. Wraps, rice bowls and miso burgers are mainstays; spicy Cajun fries are a calorie-laden relief from the wholesome theme.

Future Bakery

483 Bloor Street W, at Brunswick Avenue (416 922 5875). Streetcar 510, 511/subway Bathurst or Spadina. **Open** 8am-1am daily. **Main courses** $7-$10. **Credit** AmEx, MC, V. **Map** p282 D4.

There's nothing futuristic about it. The food harks back to granny's childhood in Poland, the desserts are enormous, and the beer is basic; wobbly tables are scattered about the vast layout and patio, floors are grungy, walls stained with decades of cigarette smoke (though smoking is no longer allowed). The one thing Future has going for it is its location – on the main strip of the Annex, one of the most eccentric pedestrian corners in the city. And, if you happen to like mashed potatoes and pierogi (dumplings) there's an added bonus in it for you.

Continental

Scaramouche & Scaramouche Pasta Bar

1 Benvenuto Place, off Edmond Avenue, at Avenue Road (416 961 8011). Streetcar 512/subway Summerhill. **Open** *Restaurant* 5.30-10pm Mon-Sat. *Pasta Bar* 5.30-10.30pm Mon-Sat. **Main courses** *Restaurant* $36-$42. *Pasta Bar* $19-$26. **Credit** AmEx, DC, MC, V. **Map** p282 F1.

The old guard of the Toronto restaurant scene stands overlooking the city from a midtown hill. Scaramouche still has the look of a grandiose '80s hotspot: furnishings – and clientele – are brassy. Book ahead for a window seat and all the gloss will be behind you and the view downtown unsurpassed (especially in leafless winter). The food is a stellar accompaniment, as decadent as can be sourced in Toronto in the main dining room, and slightly more modest at the Pasta Bar next door.

Indian

Indian Rice Factory

414 Dupont Street, at Howland Avenue (416 961 3472). Bus 7, 26/subway Bathurst or Dupont. **Open** noon-2.30pm, 5-10.30pm Mon-Fri; 5-10.30pm Sat, Sun. **Main courses** $10-$15. **Credit** DC, MC, V. **Map** p282 D2.

Head north along Howland Avenue through the heart of the Annex and you'll hit on a small island of gastronomy. On an otherwise uneventful residential stretch, the Indian Rice Factory is something of a hub – at least to those who favour clean, classy Indian cuisine over the more rugged, gritty kind you get in Little India. Though some complain that such sophistication comes at too high a price, a bite of the butter chicken usually shuts them up. The lamb is cooked just right, tender and carefully spiced; the light, flaky samosas won't sabotage the main course. Even early in the week this restaurant can be busy, so best call ahead if you don't want to wait.

Nataraj

394 Bloor Street W, at Brunswick Avenue (416 928 2925). Subway Bathurst or Spadina. **Open** noon-2.30pm, 5-10pm Mon-Fri; 5.30-10.30pm Sat. **Main courses** $8-$10. **Credit** AmEx, DC, MC, V. **Map** p282 D4.

As Little India is so far off the subway line, there's much debate over the best Indian cuisine in the city centre. Though fancier spots may get a mention, those in the know vote for Nataraj. Grab a Cobra, then order up the fragrant saffron rice with piquant tandoori and palak paneer, and you'll soon see why it's always busy.

Italian

Mistura

265 Davenport Road, at Avenue Road (416 515 0009/www.mistura.ca). Bus 5/subway Museum. **Open** 5.30-10pm Mon-Wed; 5.30-11pm Thur-Sat. **Main courses** $25-$30. **Credit** AmEx, DC, MC, V. **Map** p282 F3.

Chef Massimo Capra and partner Paolo Paolini have created a restaurant elegant enough for a special occasion but with a warm and friendly atmosphere. The open, airy space is frequented by a neighbourhood crowd – we're in the well-heeled, left-leaning Annex, don't forget. Everyone comes for home-made pastas, traditional fare such as veal scaloppine and

fish soup. Standouts include a red-beet risotto and melt-in-your-mouth gnocchi. There is a fine selection of vino to match your meal.

Korean

Korea House

666 Bloor Street W, at Manning Avenue (416 536 8666). Subway Bathurst. **Open** 11am-midnight daily. **Main courses** $10-$15. **Credit** MC, V.

Restaurants in the Annex tend to be pretty mainstream. But if the occasion calls out for something more exotic than comfort food or continental, stray a few blocks west to Little Korea. Order a soju (Korea's answer to saké) and watch the dishes of kim chee and its cousins appear. Be bim bop gives you all your food groups – and all your calories – in one bowl, while bulgogi beef surpasses your typical Chinese shredded kind. Queues aren't unusual.

Rosedale/Forest Hill

Cafés & coffeehouses

Patachou

1095 Yonge Street, at Price Street (416 927 1105). Subway Rosedale or Summerhill. **Open** 8.30am-7pm Mon-Fri; 8.30am-6pm Sat. **Main courses** $6.50-$7. **Credit** MC, V. **Map** p283 G2.

Few of the New World patrons had ever seen a croissant when Patachou opened its doors a quarter-century ago at the opposite end of Forest Hill. They learned the easy way. Patachou's pastries are fit for aristocracy – indeed, their crumbs can be found on the upholstery of many a well-to-do Range Rover. Bistro tables, outside and in, encourage visitors to enjoy a prepared salad or enchanting slice of gateau on the noisy but charming premises. Or check out the new location on St Clair West for a quieter lunch spot off the beaten path.

Other locations: 835 St Clair Avenue W, at Hendrick Avenue, West End (416 927 1105).

Continental

Fat Cat Bar & Bistro

376 Eglinton Avenue W, at Avenue Road (416 484 4228/www.fatcat.ca). Subway Eglinton West. **Open** 5.30-10pm Mon-Wed; 5.30-10.30pm Thur-Sat. **Main courses** $23-$35. **Credit** AmEx, DC, MC, V.

Fat Cat, as satisfying as the name implies, is not for the faint-hearted: veal tenderloin tends to share the plate with sweetbreads. But the feline feeder in you will almost certainly love the stir-fried calamares, if not all the other substantial meats and treats. This is first and foremost a neighbourhood joint – and a fashionable one at that – so expect your conversation to compete with that of scores of affluent locals discussing their BMWs or forthcoming holidays in Aruba.

Italian

Seven Numbers

343 Eglinton Avenue W, at Avenue Road (416 322 5183/www.sevennumbers.com). Subway Eglinton West. **Open** 5-11pm Tue-Sun. **Main courses** $7-$11. **Credit** AmEx, DC, MC, V.

The atmosphere is at least half of the draw here: staff double blessed with good manners and good looks shoehorn you into a space around a funky cast-off table (a terrace twice the size of the interior successfully accommodates communal seating, a rare thing in this city), in full view of the open kitchen. Rosa Marinuzzi chefs up Old World specialities with a zeal and timing that only an Italian mama can muster. Dishes of grilled veggies, pastas and seafood are filled to overflowing.

Japanese

EDO

484 Eglinton Avenue W, at Avenue Road (416 322 3033). Bus 32/subway Eglinton. **Open** 5-11pm daily. **Main courses** $18-$25. **Credit** AmEx, DC, MC, V.

Hardly the only one of its kind in town that's operated by non-Japanese, this Forest Hill stalwart is helmed by a local restaurateur who nevertheless knows what his peers want: generous portions,

Home cooking

Call them radical. In keeping with one of the smartest food trends around these days, a cabal of Toronto cooks are promoting – even playing with – the pleasures of local foods. Some of these regionalists have been at it long before the notion became stylish. They take the best from here and there and whip them into delicious results.

Jamie Kennedy (**Jamie Kennedy Wine Bar**, *see p120*) proudly displays a dazzling wall of colourful preserves – a cold-climate tradition. But by that we don't mean Depression-era pickled turnips; these savoury and sweet conserves of berries and other fruits, spiced veggies and subtle spreads are tasty accompaniments to the lamb Kennedy gets from a nearby farmer, sheep milk cheeses from local artisans and such novelties as purple carrots, which in fact predate the orange variety.

Kennedy keeps good company. Susur Lee (**Susur**, *see p109*; and **Lee**, *see p108*) brings near and far together in his fusion menus. Chris McDonald (**Avalon**; *see p107*) defers to what's fresh and in season before he writes the carte *du jour*. **Edward Levesque's Kitchen** (*see p132*) fries up local organic eggs, bacon and other treats. Guy and Michael Rubino of **Rain** (*see p108*) and **Luce** (*see p111*) – pioneers that they are – redraw the geography of the area with such specialities as home-cured Italian-style meats. Small French bistro **Gamelle** (*see p128*) pays tribute with succulent roast venison, while **Scaramouche** (*see p121*) features Quebecois foie gras. **Trattoria Giancarlo** (*see p128*) is strong on top-notch produce sourced from nearby organic farms. The all-Canadiana flavours at **Canoe Restaurant & Bar** (*see p113*) come from

Jamie Kennedy

the land: Niagara wines, Alberta beef, Pacific salmon and PEI (Prince Edward Island) potatoes. With **Perigee** (*see p119*) it's tasting menus only, so in a sense you get lots of choice and no choice at the same time.

As diverse as these restos are, the one thing they share is a talent for using ingredients as a launching point for some of the most creative fare in town. *Terroir* at its tastiest.

Eat, Drink, Shop

relaxed, attentive service and none of the harsh lighting and dubious offerings of many fast food sushi joints. On the contrary, you'll want to spend the night picking away at plump sashimi and hand rolls, and tempura that won't wilt in your grasp. And you may learn a thing or two from the staff about saké.

Middle Eastern

Jerusalem

955 Eglinton Avenue W, at Rostrevor Road (416 783 6494). Bus 32/subway Eglinton West. **Open** 11.30am-10.30pm Mon-Fri, Sun; 11am-midnight Sat. **Main courses** $11-$20. **Credit** AmEx, MC, V.

Before falafel became ubiquitous further downtown as a staple pub-crawler's snack, there was Jerusalem, frequented mainly by the hundreds of Jewish families in the neighbourhood. It's not quite as dowdy as its environs would suggest, with a menu that flows from meze to mains to fresh seafood. You won't find dips this tantalising on most of the finer Greek menus. There are more tasting platters than dishes, which appeals to the adventurous diner.

Davisville/Leaside

Continental

Centro Grill & Wine Bar

2472 Yonge Street, at Eglinton Avenue (416 483 2211/www.centrorestaurant.com). Subway Eglinton. **Open** 5-11.30pm Mon-Sat. **Main courses** $28-$42. **Credit** AmEx, DC, MC, V.

Long a destination for uptown A-listers, Centro has the feel of a Hollywood dining room. Enter, past the team of valets, into a multi-tiered playground for the well-coiffed. Linger on the wine list – of which you'll find few rivals north of Eglinton – while the band plays on in the lounge below. If you fancy pasta, it's all home-made and fresh here, accented with smoked chicken and grilled cheese from Treviso, or Taggiasche olives. Purists will opt for the steak, but distinctively flavoured ostrich loin is also on offer.

North 44

2537 Yonge Street, at Eglinton Avenue (416 487 4897/www.north44restaurant.com). Subway Eglinton. **Open** 5-10pm Mon-Sat. **Main courses** $31-$49. **Credit** AmEx, DC, MC, V.

Its name refers to the line of latitude on which Toronto sits, and the mod decor echoes that theme (compass points embedded into flooring, and so on). The menu balances cuisines of several continents (no Canadian focus): pizzas and pastas are Cal-Ital, seafood is Mediterranean-inspired, while Asian and Mexican flavours influence the side dishes. The grand wine list is what lures the locals.

Square

692 Mount Pleasant Road, at Eglinton Avenue (416 486 0090). Subway Eglinton. **Open** 5.30-9.30pm Mon-Wed; 5.30-10pm Thur-Sat. **Main courses** $30-$40. **Credit** AmEx, DC, MC, V.

Red Tea Box. See p126.

Obviously, this place is anything but square. The latest progeny of the Oliver Bonacini union (among others, they also own Canoe Restaurant & Bar, *see p113*) is an overnight sensation. The chic menu is a nod to the British birthplace of chef Neil McCue, but soggy Yorkshire pudding you won't find. Instead, prepare your tastebuds – and your credit card – for an extravagant affair of refined continental with a splash of the fantastical. Monkfish comes with a topping of foie gras, as does an avocado salad. A sign of the chef's playfulness is 'Breakfast for dinner', a silken sausage of crabmeat layered with scrambled eggs and smoked bacon.

Fusion

JOV Bistro

1701 Bayview Avenue, at Eglinton Avenue (416 322 0530). Bus 11/subway Eglinton. **Open** from 5.30pm Wed-Sun; closing times vary. **Main courses** $22-$35. **Credit** DC, MC, V.

Welcome to one of the most talked-about restaurants around, not only for its magical menu but also for its unlikely location in Leaside. The philosophy here is Asian fusion, but ingredients run the gamut from truffles and chestnuts to ostrich and squab. A four-course 'blind' menu ($50) is worth investing in for its entertainment value – don't let the risk factor keep you away, as it's guaranteed to appeal even to the grumpiest of gastronomes. The whimsical and warm decor helps earn JOV a rightful place in Toronto's fine-dining canon.

Italian

Grano

2035 Yonge Street, at Lola Road (416 440 1986/ www.grano.ca). Subway Davisville or Eglinton. **Open** 10am-10pm Mon-Sat. **Main courses** $10-$25. **Credit** AmEx, DC, MC, V.

At once elegant and casual – reference the antique posters, warm-hued walls and a front deli counter – with the service veering between the two, Grano is a something of a tradition in north Toronto, nestled in a decidedly family-oriented neighbourhood by attracting Italophile foodies from across town. You'll find something for everyone here: lively pastas and rich risottos, as well as hearty Mediterranean-style meats. The long display case of antipasti – a cornucopia of Italian salads and starters – is not to be overlooked. Breads are baked on the premises – all the better for soaking up the selection of reasonably priced wines. The festivity continues well past suitable family hours.

West End

Cafés & coffeehouses

Bar Italia

582 College Street, at Manning Avenue, Little Italy (416 535 3621). Streetcar 506, 511. **Open** 10.30am-midnight Mon-Thur, Sun; 10.30am-2am Fri, Sat. **Main courses** $12-$25. **Credit** AmEx, DC, MC, V. **Map** p278 C5.

Grease is the word

Once upon a time Toronto's greatest culinary statement was the diner. Eggs were indulgent, hash browns were hip, bran muffins plump. After the ethnic explosion of the second half of the 20th century, diners lost their allure. Chrome tarnished and Bakelite cracked, and the city's psyche turned to more exotic fare. But urbanites can be a fickle bunch, and once the '40s were distant enough to inspire nostalgia, a lust for kitsch developed, and the most wistful entrepreneurs brought some diners back to life.

The **Senator** (253 Victoria Street, Dundas Square, 416 364 7517) was the first to be rescued, in the '80s – giving the area something to boast about, with its leather booths and New York City fry-ups. Up in the nether regions of Dupont and Shaw, the **Universal Grill** (1071 Shaw Street, West End, 416 588 5928) was recently degreased and revived, kickstarting a widespread

revitalisation of the area. Now it serves huevos rancheros and steak 'n' eggs by day, *moules* and lamb by night. The Queen Street Mental Health Centre across the street did nothing to improve the image of the way **Swan** diner in the '60s (892 Queen Street W, West End, 416 532 0452). Taking pity on the unloved joint was a band of investors who switched on the background jazz and iced the oyster bar. It's great for brunch and coffee, and worth the occasional long queues. Staff are funky, friendly and serve up fine French toast. The crowd is cool, with a few oldsters and tourists thrown in. And it's been a quarter of a century since the **Rosedale Diner** (1164 Yonge Street, 416 923 3122) was transformed into a diner/grill where patrons sip red at the steel bar before delving into their sesame chicken. Also worth a mention are **Sunset Grill** (2006 Queen Street E, The Beaches, 416 690 9985) and **Mars** (432 College Street, Harbord, 416 921 6332).

Before a visit to Little Italy meant dodging pedestrians, prams and poodles – when all that existed here were canoli bakeries, trattorias and old men playing *bocci* – there was Bar Italia. Having changed locations in the past decade, its newest incarnation is as slick as anything on the block. Generous sandwiches include roast pork with garlic mayo. The mushroom and parmesan salad is consistently good. This place is best at Sunday brunch for polenta with poached eggs – arrive early, before crowds of Saturday night revellers start to dribble in.

Café Diplomatico
594 College Street, at Clinton Street, Little Italy (416 534 4637/www.diplomatico.ca). Streetcar 506, 511. **Open** 8am-2am Mon-Fri; 8am-3am Sat, Sun. **Main courses** $5-$15. **Credit** AmEx, DC, MC, V. **Map** p278 C5.

It's a trade-off: the Dip wins hands-down for the best people-watching platform in Little Italy, inside or on the vast patio. But you'll have to contend with poor service and average food. One menu surprise is the French fries, some of the best on the strip. But forget about the eats – the Dip is all about sitting back with a Stella and watching the world strut by.

Mona's Shwarma & Falafel
661 College Street, at Grace Street, Little Italy (416 535 8466). Streetcar 506, 511. **Open** noon-10pm Mon-Thur; noon-3am Fri, Sat; 1-7pm Sun. **Main courses** $4-$10. **No credit cards**. **Map** p278 C5.

Little Italy's best Middle Eastern take-out is one of the friendliest spots along College Street. If the place is hopping, which it often is, you might be offered a hot slice of crispy potato while you wait for that heaped falafel platter. A new addition to the strip just west of the trendiest bars, this small eatery stays open long enough to attract the late-night crowds – and, rumour has it, über-chef Susur Lee.

Pain Perdu
736 St Clair Avenue W, at Christie Street (416 656 7246). Streetcar 512. **Open** 7am-7pm Tue-Fri; 7am-5pm Sat; 8am-4pm Sun. **Main courses** $5-$7. **Credit** DC, MC, V.

Toronto's reputation for offering delights from lesser-known foodie destinations receives another endorsement with this Basque boulangerie. Best to take a healthy appetite to this small and casual neighbourhood café because everything, from buttery croissants to egg-rich quiches and pastries, is tempting. The namesake dish is a type of French toast: yesterday's baguette is soaked in cream, oven baked and served with fruit. Oh, and some of the city's finest gateaux Basque, a custard-filled tart.

Red Tea Box
696 Queen Street W, at Tecumseth Street (416 203 8882). Streetcar 501. **Open** 10am-6pm Mon, Wed, Thur; 10am-7pm Fri, Sat; noon-5pm Sun. **Main courses** $5.50-$17. **Credit** MC, V. **Map** p278 C7.

This once-abandoned coach house tucked in behind Queen West has been transformed into a scented, pretty boîte with exquisite teas that taste of their flowery and leafy origins. Artfully prepared sweets are whimsical and delicious – chocolate cake decorated with lavender, for instance. A limited fusion menu proposes aromatic soups, sandwiches and a good-value bento box. The summertime patio, situated between small front and back dining rooms, is a quiet retreat from the bustling 'hood. Upstairs is a small shop selling fine Asian tableware and linens.

Tavola Calda
671 College Street, at Beattrice Street (416 538 7328). Streetcar 506. **Open** 5-10pm Mon-Thur; 5-11pm Fri; noon-11pm Sat. **Main courses** $10-$12. **Credit** DC, MC, V. **Map** p278 B5.

The name means 'hot table' in Italian, as in cafeteria, but the food is far removed from high school grub. Think generous platters of grilled vegetables and cured meats, steaming bowls of rustic soups, home-made pastas and mile-high eggplant parmigiana. Updated a few years ago from a cosy room to a very big one, Tavola Calda could do with a bit more atmosphere, but as one of College Street's least pretentious spots, the familial greetings and home cooking go a long way to make amends.

Terroni
720 Queen Street W, at Claremont Street (416 504 0320/www.terroni.ca). Streetcar 501. **Open** 9am-10pm Mon-Wed, Sun; 9am-11pm Thur-Sat. **Main courses** $8-$13. **Credit** V. **Map** p278 C7.

Despite its pejorative name, Terroni (Italian for 'bloody southerners') manages to attract countrymen in their droves. Waiting for a table (and wait

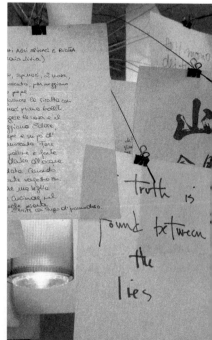

you will at mealtimes) is a lesson in dialect. Perhaps most appreciated here are the pizzas, 23 old-school configurations that average $10 but could feed two and leave scant room left for the famed canoli. Conspicuously absent from Little Italy, Terroni occupies equally trendy ground in all its locations. **Other locations**: 1 Balmoral Avenue (416 925 4020); 106 Victoria Street, Dundas Square (416 955 0258).

Vienna Home Bakery

626 Queen Street W, at Markham Street (416 703 7278). Streetcar 501, 511. **Open** 10am-7pm Wed-Sun. **Main courses** $7-$10. **No credit cards**. **Map** p278 C7.

Everything here is made from scratch, and the menu is short and sweet, offering a few breakfast items such as granola, yoghurt and fruit, plus soups and sandwiches. For pudding there are fab fruit pies, muffins and maple treats. The signature phallic bread loaves add some sauce to the mumsy cooking. The weekend brings regulars who know about the delicious eggs, including Bombay (hollandaise with a whiff of curry). Note that there are just a few tables and the counter, plus a patio that's open in summer.

Fish & chips

Chippy's

893 Queen Street W, at Strachan Avenue (416 866 7474). Streetcar 501. **Open** 11.30am-8pm Mon-Wed, Sun; 11.30am-9pm Thur-Sat. **Main courses** $8-$10. **No credit cards**. **Map** p278 B7.

Most days it's cranked-up Led Zeppelin that keeps the cooks here happy – and happy they must be, because Chippy's take-out fish-and-chips are some of the city's finest. Working with top-grade vegetable oil, halibut, cod and haddock and a stout-spiked batter, Chippy's two-person team fries to order. Potatoes are hand-cut and double-fried, which means crispy and very light on the grease. The garlic mayo is delicious, but tartare is rather dull. Don't stray too far from the mainstream: deep-fried salmon is oily. Opposite scenic Trinity Bellwoods Park, this is a great place for picnic fixings.

Fusion

Mildred Pierce

99 Sudbury Street, at Lisgar Street (416 588 5695/www.mildredpierce.com). Streetcar 501, 504. **Open** noon-2pm, 5.30-10pm Mon-Thur; noon-2pm, 5.30-11pm Fri; 11am-3pm, 5.30-11pm Sat; 10am-3pm, 5.30-10pm Sun. **Main courses** $17-$26. **Credit** AmEx, DC, MC, V. **Map** p278 A7.

This Indian-Mediterranean fusion restaurant has survived countless trends and changed little – and neither should it. It's a stone's throw from the Queen West strip west of Bathurst, but somewhat hidden away, so check your map before setting off. The namesake is the Joan Crawford classic film noir, which should clue you in: drama is embraced here, especially in the rich textiles draping down from high ceilings, rather like a romantic movie set. Favourites include sweet-and-spicy roast chicken

Xacutti. *See p128.*

and roast rack of lamb, as well as some tasty vegetarian dishes. Some items and cocktails are named after movie characters – be prepared to have fun.

Xacutti

503 College Street, at Palmerston Boulevard (416 323 3957/www.xacutti.com). Streetcar 506, 511. **Open** 6.30pm-1am Mon-Thur; 6.30pm-2am Fri, Sat; 10.30am-4pm Sun. **Main courses** $19-$37. **Credit** AmEx, DC, MC, V. **Map** p278 C5.

Pretty Xacutti ('sha-koo-tee') is named after a spicy curry from India's west coast. The dining room downstairs and mood-enhancing bar upstairs, Bird (*see p139*), are bustling with Toronto's young and beautiful crowd, especially weekend nights. It's easy to be distracted by the glamour of it all – orders are taken on Palm Pilots by waiters who are as well turned out as the patrons – but the contemporary Indian-western fusion is surprisingly inventive, even seductive (as in cinnamon-scented pork ribs with guava and lobster in a star-anise champagne butter). Sunday brunch is no more sober: try the macadamia nut pancakes topped with whipped banana butter.

Italian

Bar One

924 Queen Street W, at Shaw Street (416 535 1655). Streetcar 501. **Open** 11.30am-4pm, 5-11pm Tue-Fri; 9am-4pm, 5-11pm Sat; 9am-4pm Sun. **Main courses** $5-$28. **Credit** AmEx, DC, MC, V. **Map** p278 B7.

Now that they've made their mark on Little Italy with Bar Italia (*see p125*), the Barone family are working on still trendier Queen West. This place is more intimate, with communal seating at the marble-topped counter and curved-wood booths. Dinners range from squash-stuffed ravioli to fillet of salmon. The hidden patio out back is a delight; come for brunch, as evenings are more harried.

Gamelle

468 College Street, at Markham Street, Little Italy (416 923 6254/www.gamelle.com). Streetcar 506, 511. **Open** 6pm-2am Mon, Sat; noon-2.30pm, 6pm-2am Tue-Fri. **Main courses** $20-$26. **Credit** AmEx, DC, MC, V. **Map** p278 C5.

Just up the street from Little Italy's collection of middling eateries and fleeting darlings is this charming Mediterranean bistro. Owner Jean-Pierre Centenau has seen the mercurial influences on Toronto's restaurant scene over his long career and he opened Gamelle nearly a decade ago with an eye to keeping it small and constant. So far the plan has worked: the warm room, popular with locals, has a gentle atmosphere that encourages leisurely dining. Soups, local specialities such as roasted venison and finely tuned desserts are prepared in the tiny, open kitchen.

Trattoria Giancarlo

41 Clinton Street, at College Street, Little Italy (416 533 9619). Streetcar 506, 511. **Open** 6-11pm Mon-Sat. **Main courses** $20-$25. **Credit** AmEx, DC, MC, V. **Map** p278 C5.

Under leafy branches, the summertime patio more than doubles the size of this Italian neighbourhood restaurant. The food here is created not for weekend mobs but for regulars who return time after time for lemon-cream pasta, shrimp in delicate broth and a tender veal chop big enough for two. Giancarlo sometimes gets too comfortable with its success, but the kitchen always pulls its socks up and word gets around that all is well again. Local ingredients are sourced from some of the area's finest, small-scale farms. The show-off wine list carries some stand-outs; for smaller budgets, ask about the house wines.

Via Allegro

1750 The Queensway, west of Highway 427, Etobicoke (416 622 6677). Bus 123. **Open** 11.30am-10.30pm Mon-Wed, Sun; 11.30am-11.30pm Thur-Sat. **Main courses** $60. **Credit** AmEx, DC, MC, V.

You have to travel to Etobicoke for this neighbourhood ristorante/pizzeria, but it merits a trip for this bounty of antipasti, pizzas baked in the wood-burning oven, and fine home-made pastas. Chef Lino Collevecchio's creativity soars with mains such as the 'Rabbit Triplets' – an unfortunate name that conjures up families of bunnies, but is in fact a trio of braised rabbit, confit and rilettes. The outstanding cellar has wines to match.

San Korean Restaurant.

Japanese

Sushi Kaji

860 The Queensway, at Plastics Avenue (416 252 2166). Bus 123. **Open** 6-9pm Wed-Sun. **Set menus** $85-$120. **Credit** AmEx, MC, V.

As far as most people are concerned, there wouldn't be much to be gained from schlepping to the Queensway, an extension of King Street that heads westward into the suburbs. But enough locals are raving about Sushi Kaji that it's probably worth alerting intrepid foodies. Still something of a secret, Kaji may yet have space at the intimate eight-seat sushi bar for your party. There you'll watch masters at work slicing seafood in ways you may never see again. There are also plenty of vegetarian options and a couple for meat-and-potato types.

Korean

San Korean Restaurant

676 Queen Street W, at Euclid Avenue (416 214 9429/www.sankoreanrestaurant.com). Streetcar 501, 511. **Open** 11.30am-4pm, 5-10pm Tue, Wed; 11.30am-4pm, 5-10.30pm Thur, Fri; noon-4pm, 5-10.30pm Sat; 5-10pm Sun. **Main courses** $12-$17. **Credit** AmEx, DC, MC, V. **Map** p278 C7.

You don't normally find this kind of thing outside Little Korea: San serves fine Korean fare in a Queen West-style centre that packs customers in nightly, and spits them out satisfied every time. You'll spot the similarities with Japanese food in bento boxes stuffed with dumplings, tempura, tuna rolls and teriyaki. But San also does shredded beef and barbecued ribs with distinctly Korean flavours. And here, you'll linger longer over beer, wine and complimentary goodbye tea.

Latin American

Caju

922 Queen Street W, at Shaw Street (416 532 2550/www.caju.cardinalfactor.net). Streetcar 501, 511. **Open** 11.30am-2.30pm, 5.30-11pm Tue-Fri; 5.30-11pm Sat. **Main courses** $14-$28. **Credit** AmEx, MC, V. **Map** p278 B7.

Every Saturday evening, to the beat of the bossa nova, this Brazilian fusion restaurant goes native and serves feijoada, the nation's signature dish, a stew of pork, black beans and collard greens. To whet your appetite, sip a Caipirinha – mint, lime juice and rum – and sample pao de queijo, puffy popovers made with cassava flour. Other dishes unite Caribbean and Portuguese influences, while desserts draw on exotic fruits.

El Bodegón

537 College Street, at Euclid Avenue, Little Italy (416 944 8297). Streetcar 506, 510. **Open** 11.30am-10pm Wed-Sun. **Main courses** $10-$15. **Credit** AmEx, MC, V. **Map** p278 C5.

We wouldn't blame you for thinking an evening of Peruvian would hold little promise, but think again. Even if you're annoyed after waiting by the entrance for a table (where tables are shoehorned in), you'll have forgotten about it after the first sangria. El Bodegón's extensive menu will be hard to navigate for novices, but staff will talk you through. Seafood eaters have the best of this menu.

Julie's Cuban Restaurant

202 Dovercourt Road, at Foxley Street (416 532 7397). Streetcar 505. **Open** 5.30-11pm Tue-Sun. **Main courses** $11-$17. **Credit** MC, V. **Map** p278 A6.

Word is getting around about this, one of the city's best-kept secrets. But by virtue of its location – on a residential stretch of Dovercourt, north of Queen – Julie's remains untarnished by cruisers of the main drags. If you can't squeeze on to the patio, squeeze into one of the old kitchen tables indoors. Cuba is not lauded for its culinary flair, but Julie's fried green plantains and corn fritters always please. Otherwise, expect the traditional Cuban rice dishes, fried with pork, chicken or beef.

Malaysian

Kei

936 Queen Street W, at Shaw Street (416 534 7449). Streetcar 501. **Open** 6-10pm Mon-Thur; 6-11pm Fri, Sat. **Main courses** $15-$23. **Credit** AmEx, DC, MC, V. **Map** p278 B7.

Subtle Malaysian flavours are key to this restaurant's compact menu of silken miso soups, good gado-gado, light-as-air curry puffs and satisfying main dishes. The singular dessert, in keeping with the minimalist vibe, is a fragrant fried-banana tapioca. An intimate spot, Kei attracts in-the-know locals for a casual supper or an affordable romantic evening. Unselfconsciously cool, it turns into more of a hangout as night melts into morning and the music gets down.

North American

Drake Hotel

1150 Queen Street W, at Beaconsfield Avenue (416 531 5042/www.thedrakehotel.ca). Streetcar 501. **Open** 11am-2.30pm, 6-11pm Mon-Sat; 10.30am-2.30pm, 6-11pm Sun. **Main courses** $16-$36. **Credit** AmEx, DC, MC, V. **Map** p278 A7.

Menu items are as varied as the places to eat at this multi-purpose hot-spot. There's the sidewalk café, lunch and evening lounges, a sushi bar, a dining room, a couple more bars, a terrace and, if all else fails, room service with everything from yummy tuna sandwiches to funky veggie cassoulet to a way-out combo of braised lamb with mint and chocolate.

The Drake is surprisingly low on the attitude barometer and high on value for the globe-trotting menus. Sometimes the relaxed approach can mean impossibly slow or inept service – chalk it up to its boho groove. *See also p49, p140 and p203.*

Lemon Meringue

2390 Bloor Street W, at Jane Street (416 769 5757/www.lemonmeringue.com). Bus 35/subway Jane. **Open** 11am-3.30pm, 5.30-10.30pm Tue-Thur; 11am-3.30pm, 5.30-10.30pm Fri; 9.30am-3.30pm, 5.30-10.30pm Sat. **Main courses** $27-$32. **Credit** AmEx, MC, V.

Popular on the brunch scene in Bloor West village, this pâtisserie also works the night shift with a short list of engaging dinner dishes whose presentation matches the minimalist decor of the small, candle-lit room. Seared calamares with lemon zest and miso-glazed salmon set you up for the eponymous dessert, and very good it is too.

Oyster Boy

872 Queen Street W, at Strachan Avenue (416 534 3432). Streetcar 501. **Open** 5-10pm Mon-Wed; 5-11pm Thur-Sun. **Main courses** $11-$17. **Credit** AmEx, DC, MC, V. **Map** p278 B7.

This narrow hideaway in the heart of West Queen West makes a refreshing change from the raucous male atmosphere of most oyster bars. The menu has few surprises, and not many options for those averse to crustaceans, but Oyster Boy is a great place to slurp your Malpeques, and the convivial atmosphere will tempt you to linger longer.

Phil's Original BBQ

838 College Street, at Ossington Avenue, Little Italy (416 532 8161). Bus 63/streetcar 506. **Open** 5-9pm Mon-Thur; 5-10pm Fri, Sat. **Main courses** $11-$19. **Credit** MC, V. **Map** p278 B5.

The division between Little Italy and Little Portugal is nebulous. But Phil's (formerly Dipamo's Barbeque) clearly occupies the latter. Though the plattered chicken and ribs reference the American South, the experience aligns itself with the churrasquerias of neighbouring Ossington, Dovercourt and Dundas. The dining room is decidedly no-frills but cool jazz on the stereo is a nice touch. Dishes are bursting with flavour, particularly the beef brisket, stewing in its own juices and served with barbecued beans.

Southern Accent

595 Markham Street, at Bloor Street W (416 536 3211/www.southernaccent.com). Streetcar 511/subway Bathurst. **Open** 5.30pm-1am Tue-Sun. **Main courses** $14-$29. **Set menus** $25. **Credit** AmEx, DC, MC, V.

A quick hop across Bathurst from the Annex, tucked in behind Honest Ed's, Southern Accent looks a bit out of place. In fact, it would be out of place anywhere but the Bayou, with its eccentric decoration, quirky staff and resident fortune teller. Offerings are not for the weak of heart: blackened livers and spicy sausage will set your tongue on fire ('heavy' isn't a word that worries the chef). Side orders include fried green tomatoes, crunchy calamares and the bar does a superb bourbon sour.

East Toronto

Cafés & coffeehouses

Bonjour Brioche
812 Queen Street E, at DeGrassi Street (416 406 1250). Streetcar 501, 504. **Open** 8am-5pm Tue-Fri; 8am-4pm Sat; 8am-3pm Sun. **Main courses** $6-$9. **No credit cards. Map** p281 L7.
A beacon in up-and-coming Leslieville, you'll probably spot Bonjour Brioche a mile off from the queues outside the door. Even on slushy winter mornings, supporters of this French-accented bakery-café wait in a huddle on the street outside, dreaming of brioche, buttery croissants and warm baguettes. For brunch, try baked French toast or a croque madame with a bowl of café au lait.

Myth
417 Danforth Avenue, at Arundel Avenue, The Danforth (416 461 8383/www.myth.to). Subway Chester. **Open** 4pm-midnight Mon-Thur; 4pm-2am Fri; noon-2am Sat; noon-midnight Sun. **Main courses** $14-$26. **Credit** AmEx, DC, MC, V.
Brawny Eastsiders with a penchant for the pool cue hangs around for hours with a few beers, while others sip trendy cocktails or dine alfresco. The food is a tasty mix of the Greek Isles (typical of a Danforth joint) and California (read: fish, fish and more fish).

Pulp Kitchen
898 Queen Street E, at Logan Avenue (416 461 4612/www.pulpkitchen.ca). Streetcar 501. **Open** 8am-7pm Mon-Wed; 8am-9pm Thur, Fri; 10am-4pm Sat, Sun. **Main courses** $10-$13. **Credit** MC, V. **Map** p281 L7.
The name is as cheeky as the place. Starting with the disclaimer that 'All references to dairy, egg or meat products are entirely fictional', the vegan menu serves up tofu disguised as an eggless omelette, portobello mushroom burgers, satisfying sandwiches and other superb creations. Although they take their diets seriously here, moralising is left at the door.

Continental

Café Brussel
124 Danforth Avenue, at Broadview Avenue, The Danforth (416 465 7363/www.cafebrussel.com). Streetcar 504, 505/subway Broadview. **Open** 5-11pm Tue-Sat; 5-10pm Sun. **Main courses** $20-$30. **Credit** AmEx, DC, MC, V.
This ambassador of northern Europe specialises in mussels. Just one sniff upon entering will tell you that every table has indulged in satisfyingly rattly mountains of perfectly prepared *moules*. The traditional menu proffers all things Belgian – crisp frites and braised endive, for instance, and chocolate in many forms (but no waffles).

Verveine
1097 Queen Street E, at Winnifred Avenue (416 405 9906). Bus 72/streetcar 501. **Open** 6-10pm Mon-Fri; 10am-3pm, 6-10pm Sat; 10am-3pm Sun. **Main courses** $16-$25. **Credit** AmEx, DC, MC, V.
Verveine is a break in the clouds in an area that offers few high-quality dining possibilities. The decor of calming neutral tones has a few quirks, while the menu is consistently scrumptious, featuring trendy comfort food alongside modern dishes. The pork tenderloin is a highlight.

Fusion

Tomi-Kro
1214 Queen Street E, at Leslie Street (416 463 6677). Streetcar 501. **Open** 6-11pm Tue-Thur; 6pm-midnight Fri, Sat. **Main courses** $18-$26. **Credit** AmEx, DC, MC, V.
The neighbourhood used to be considered dull, but recent arrivals such as this Mediterranean-Asian fusion bistro suggest that things might be looking up. John Coronius, a former partner in Lolita's Lust, named this (in Greek) 'the little place'. A bold sense of fun greets you at the door: lamps covered in hearts, blaring music and nonsense declarations on the menu. The food, thankfully, is usually more serious. Pairings include octopus with saké, duck with kaffir lime leaves; venison with cocoa. Not one for timid palates.

Greek

Ouzeri
500A Danforth Avenue, at Logan Avenue, The Danforth (416 778 500/www.ouzeri.com). Subway Chester. **Open** 11am-midnight daily. **Main courses** $12-$20. **Credit** AmEx, DC, MC, V.
Budget eaters tend to opt for pseudo-Greek platters of souvlaki, fries and salad at generic eateries throughout Greektown. But for just a little more pocket shrapnel you can enjoy the real thing, and all in a clean scheme of white with coloured tiles that makes a welcome change from checked tablecloths. Magnificent dips and oven-warmed pitta are the prelude to a seafood list of Aegean proportions, so pace yourself carefully.

Pan
516 Danforth Avenue, at Ferrier Avenue, The Danforth (416 466 8158/www.panonthedanforth. com). Subway Pape. **Open** 11.30am-11pm Mon-Thur, Sun; 11.30am-midnight Fri, Sat. **Main courses** $13-$23. **Credit** AmEx, MC, V.
At Pan, fine dining of the white tablecloth variety is crossed with southern European attitude. Staff are genuinely glad to see you, and attend to your every whim – even if they're dressed like they're just hanging out. Mains are generally superior to most on this resto-heavy strip; meat and fish platters are generous to overflowing. Appetisers are less ambitious, leaning to the conventional in nature and flavour.

Indian

Madras Durbar

1435 Gerrard Street E, at Ashdale Avenue, Little India (416 465 4116). Bus 22/streetcar 506. **Open** 11am-11pm daily. **Main courses** $3-$7. **Credit** AmEx, DC, MC, V.

Finding Madras Durbar is a treat in itself: the streetcar traverses a lowly stretch of Gerrard Street, approaches the grand-but-grimy Don Jail, then curves into the colourful madness of street markets, bakeries and fabric shops. The restaurant is an even bigger treat, where plates are the size of platters and prices very reasonable. Don't forget to order the excellent samosas.

Sidhartha

1450 Gerrard Street E, at Coxwell Avenue, Little India (416 465 4095). Bus 22/streetcar 506. **Open** 11am-10.30pm daily. **Main courses** $8-$10. **Credit** MC, V.

Little India stretches along Gerrard Street East and like most 'strips' offers more mediocre fare than anyone could hope to eat in a lifetime. Sidhartha, however, with its warm tones and friendly service, presents an appealing and affordable alternative. Skip the buffet, temptingly inexpensive as it is, and go à la carte. An airy pastry filled with sautéed onions (bhaji), the vegetarian biryani and accompanying mint and tamarind sauces are all very fine, as is lamb biryani, or any lamb dish for that matter. Desserts, on the other hand, underwhelm.

Japanese

Akane-ya

2214 Queen Street E, at Fernwood Park Avenue, The Beaches (416 699 0377). Streetcar 501. **Open** 5.30-10.30pm Tue-Sat; 5-10pm Sun. **Main courses** $15-$20. **Credit** AmEx, DC, MC, V.

Fresh-faced and windswept from a day by the boardwalk, you might want decide you want something fresh and fast – and local legend Akane-ya serves both purposes. Sidle up to the sushi bar for the usual fare – so fresh you may forget you're in freshwater territory. A five-course dinner for two can be had for $35.

Lily

786 Broadview Avenue, at Danforth Avenue, The Danforth (416 465 9991). Streetcar 504, 505/subway Broadview. **Open** 5-10pm Mon-Thur; 5-11pm Fri, Sat. **Main courses** $16-$60. **Credit** AmEx, MC, V.

The decor is as close to art deco as Japanese gets – possibly because the venue was formerly a Belgian bistro. Some of the distinctive features have lingered, as has an artistry in the preparation. Every traditional item on the menu has a twist: lime is a favourite, adding a flourish to soups and mains. Ingredients are layered and layered again, and the result is delicious.

North American

Edward Levesque's Kitchen

1290 Queen Street E, at Alton Avenue (416 465 3600/www.edwardlevesque.ca). Streetcar 501. **Open** 6-10pm Tue; 10am-3pm, 6-10pm Wed-Fri; 9am-3pm, 6-10pm Sat; 9am-3pm Sun. **Main courses** $15-$22. **Credit** AmEx, DC, MC, V.

This casual diner/dining room excels at breakfasts (using mostly organic products) and basic fare like burgers. Depending on your perspective, the menu is puzzling or varied: tandoori chicken, grilled sandwiches, fine burgers and hearty salads. Italian dishes are generally the weakest link, especially the heavy-handed pasta sauces. Good homestyle pies.

Tulip Steak House

1606 Queen Street E, at Coxwell Avenue (416 469 5797/www.tulipsteakhouse.com). Bus 22/streetcar 501. **Open** 8am-11pm Mon-Wed; 8am-midnight Thur; 7am-midnight Fri, Sat; 7am-11pm Sun. **Main courses** $15-$18. **Credit** AmEx, DC, MC, V.

This dowdy diner is just off the beaten track, west of the Beaches. Which is probably one reason it hasn't changed in over 50 years. You can dine on scrambled eggs or schnitzel, but the sell-out is the beef: Tulip is actually a steakhouse, without the heavy drapery and white-shirted waiters. Don't leave without sharing one of the giant T-bones, or at least a brisket. And save room for the rich chocolate cake.

Pub food

Allen's

143 Danforth Avenue, at Broadview Avenue, The Danforth (416 463 3086/www.allens.to). Streetcar 504, 505/subway Broadview. **Open** 11.30am-1am Mon-Fri; 11am-1am Sat, Sun. **Main courses** $10-$26. **Credit** AmEx, DC, MC, V.

Toronto has no shortage of Irish pubs; this one, curiously, has a classy, polished-oak Manhattan feel. Regulars crowd the brass rail bar, and tables are tucked into windows, corners and on to platforms; further back is the dining room, where larger parties congregate; the back patio seats dozens more. The menu is sophisticated, including Kerry lamb and bistro specialities such as Atlantic salmon; the burgers are among the best in town.

Vietnamese

Mi Mi Restaurant

688 Gerrard Street E, at Broadview Avenue (416 778 5948). Streetcar 504, 506. **Open** 10am-10pm Mon, Tue, Thur, Fri; noon-10pm Wed; 10am-10.30pm Sat, Sun. **Main courses** $5-$15. **No credit cards.** **Map** p281 K6.

There are only a few good Vietnamese joints in Toronto, and Mi Mi is one of the best. With cheerful atmosphere and pink walls, this family-run place excels in barbecued everything – meats and shrimp – as well as rice and noodle dishes and pho soups.

Bars

For cruising, schmoozing and plain old-fashioned boozing, Toronto is a drinker's playground.

Whether it's sipping a delicately infused, overpriced Martini or crying into a $2 glass of beer, you won't have to go very far to satisfy your thirst in Toronto. When planning a night on the tiles, it's best to choose an area and stick to it – most neighbourhoods have more than enough variety to keep the drinker occupied until the wee small hours. The section of College Street that runs through Little Italy is crammed with more cocktail and wine bars than you can shake a swizzle stick at. The whole area positively glows with the warm light of candles, patios abound and you'd be forgiven for thinking there was a bylaw keeping all the non-attractive people at home after dark. Indeed, many rate Little Italy as Toronto's best drinking region, but other strips, such as the grittier Queen Street West, the student-powered Annex and the Danforth – mixing the area's Greek heritage with a range of newer establishments – compete strongly, as do more recent strips. These new destination zones include low-key drinkeries on the strip of Dundas West north of Trinity-Bellwoods Park, such as the **Chelsea Room** and **Communist's Daughter**, and, further west (and south), anchored by the much-ballyhooed restoration of the **Drake Hotel**, Queen Street West/Parkdale, whose gentrification continues apace, with trendy but cosy hipster bars sprouting every which way. Thankfully, even the city's finest establishments tend to eschew cover charges, obnoxious doormen and fancy dress codes (any exceptions are noted below).

WE'RE ONLY HERE FOR THE BEER

Restrictive provincial laws mean that one area where Toronto comes up short is in the brew-pub department, though recent years have brought developments on the scene (*see p139* **Hopping mad**), and nowadays even run-of-the-mill pubs often have a good selection of imported beers on tap.

Toronto is also near the Niagara wine region (*see p235*), and many bars carry a good selection of Ontario wines. Niagara has an ideal climate for icewine – an extremely sweet dessert wine made from grapes that have been left on the vine to freeze in winter. A glass of icewine from the Strewn or Peller winery is a pricey but delicious local treat, and is highly recommended.

For information on buying alcohol from stores, *see p156*. For bars that also double as music venues, *see p203*.

Black Bull Tavern. See p134.

Entertainment District

For the **Amsterdam Brewing Company**, see *p139* Hopping mad.

Black Bull Tavern

298 Queen Street W, at Soho Street (416 593 2766). Streetcar 501, 510. **Open** noon-2am daily. **Credit** MC, V. **Map** p279 D7.

This British-style pub has one of the largest and best patios in the city: thanks to a parking lot across the street, it gets plenty of afternoon sunshine. The Bull used to be a serious biker bar (in summer you'll still see rows of Hogs parked outside), but these days it's more popular with the regular Queen Street crowd.

Cameron House

408 Queen Street W, at Cameron Street (416 703 0811/www.thecameron.com). Streetcar 501, 510. **Open** 4pm-2.30am daily. **Credit** V. **Map** p279 D7.

Old-cool and new-school Queen Street mix in this dark, friendly bar. Artists and musicians haunt the former flophouse, gaining inspiration from the faded ceiling murals, inexpensive drinks and free conversation. The back room hosts art and music (*see p203*).

Canteena

181 Bathurst Street, at Queen Street W (416 703 9360/www.canteena.ca). Streetcar 501, 511. **Open** 5pm-2am Mon-Sat. **Credit** MC, V. **Map** p278 C7.

Hipsters lounge under gilt mirrors on Moroccan banquettes at this be-seen spot, and nosh on an unusual tapas-style menu that accompanies the heady, trendy cocktails and wines by the glass. DJs change nightly.

Paddock

178 Bathurst Street, at Queen Street W (416 504 9997/www.thepaddock.ca). Streetcar 501, 511. **Open** 5pm-2am Mon-Sat; 5pm-1am Sun. **Credit** AmEx, MC, V. **Map** p279 D7.

The Paddock's has hauled itself up and out of its seedy surroundings, and has all the hallmarks of an upscale pub: a beautiful curved bar, dim lights and cool jazz, plus a clientele of journalists, documentary filmmakers and advertising people, who come to drink posh cocktails and imported and local beer.

Rivoli

332-334 Queen Street W, at Spadina Avenue (416 596 1908/http://rivoli.ca/2003). Streetcar 501, 510. **Open** 11.30am-1am daily. **Credit** AmEx, MC, V. **Map** p279 D7.

A classic Queen Street bar, the Rivoli has one of the best patios in the city, a popular restaurant and a long Martini bar, which is often crowded with fashionable types. The pool hall upstairs has slightly less attitude, and the back room is one of the city's great music venues. *See also p107, p203 and p216.*

Smokeless Joe's

125 John Street, at Richmond Street W (416 591 2221). Streetcar 501, 504/subway St Andrew. **Open** 4pm-2am daily. **Credit** AmEx, MC, V. **Map** p279 E7.

It's easy to miss this lovely little bar, which is overshadowed by the strip of massive meat-market joints that dominates this area. What makes it great is not the abundance of fresh air – even the patio is non-smoking – but the availability of more than 250 types of beer, many of which are not found anywhere else in Ontario.

Squirly's

807 Queen Street W, at Manning Avenue (416 703 0574). Streetcar 501. **Open** 11am-1am Mon, Sun; 11am-2am Tue-Sat. **Credit** MC, V. **Map** p278 C7.

A favourite student and budget watering hole, with time-worn velveteen armchairs and, in summer, a pleasant, spacious back patio stuffed with mid-century furniture that's seen better days.

Wheat Sheaf Tavern

667 King Street W, at Bathurst Street (416 504 9912). Streetcar 504, 511. **Open** 11am-2am daily. **Credit** AmEx, DC, MC, V. **Map** p278 C8/p279 D8.

Situated at the junction of King Street West and Bathurst Street for over 150 years, the Wheat Sheaf (opened in 1849) proudly and loudly trumpets its status as Toronto's oldest bar. A beer-drinking tradition is palpable, especially in the historic neon signs advertising Molson Canadian, not to mention ye olde giant-screen TV.

Rivoli.

The best Bars

The best Bars

For booze with views
Panorama Restaurant & Lounge (see p136).

For people watching from the patio
Black Bull Tavern or the Rivoli (for both, see p134).

To preen and be seen
Bird (see p139).

To go for a song
Melody Bar (see p136 Sing, sing a song).

For dark bar atmosphere
Laurentian Room (see p137) or the Paddock (see p134).

YYZ Restaurant & Wine Bar

345 Adelaide Street W, at Spadina Avenue (416 599 3399/www.yyzrestaurant.com). Streetcar 504, 510. **Open** 4.30pm-2am daily. **Credit** AmEx, DC, MC, V. **Map** p279 D7.
Stepping down from the street into this softly luminescent milky-white and glowing green space it's *Solaris* meets mod 1960s Courrèges. The bar specialises in wines from New World boutique vintners, so expect to find yourself among the financial crowd from nearby Bay Street.

Financial District

For **Canoe Restaurant & Bar**, see *p113*.

Library Bar

Fairmont Royal York Hotel, 100 Front Street W, at University Avenue (416 368 2511/www.royal yorkhotel.com). Subway St Andrew or Union. **Open** noon-1am daily. **Credit** AmEx, DC, MC, V. **Map** p279 F8.
The Library Bar – all wood panelling, leather chairs and literature-laden shelves – is a place for the rich… or at least those who want to feel rich for the length of time it takes to drink a cocktail.

Pravda Vodka Bar

36 Wellington Street E, at Yonge Street (416 306 2433/www.pravdavodkabar.ca). Streetcar 504/ subway King. **Open** 5.30pm-2am Mon-Sat. **Credit** AmEx, MC, V. **Map** p279 F8.
Behind a glacial white façade, Russian dolls nestle under the hammer and sickle flag and portraits of Lenin. There's a sofa lounge at the back, and premium vodkas are served in shot glasses made of ice, with taster trays for the more adventuresome. Caviar and exotic roe feature on the short menu.

Dundas Square

Imperial Pub & Library Tavern

54 Dundas Street E, at Victoria Street (416 977 4667). Streetcar 505/subway Dundas. **Open** 11am-3am daily. **Credit** AmEx, MC, V. **Map** p280 G6.
Few visitors venture the short block east of Yonge Street to visit this slice of faded grandeur. Oh well, their loss. Behind its dull brick exterior, the tavern glows with soft colours, photos of James Dean and paintings of Parisian whores. A well-populated aquarium hangs above the bar – a subtle reminder to drink like a fish.

Chinatown/Kensington Market

Embassy

223 Augusta Avenue, at Baldwin Street (416 591 1132). Streetcar 505, 506, 510. **Open** 4pm-2am Mon-Fri; 1pm-2am Sat, Sun. **No credit cards.** **Map** p279 D6.
A renovated former pet food store, the Embassy features diner booths, pastel walls, blond wood and an unpretentious, unfussy air.

Last Temptation

12 Kensington Avenue, at Dundas Street W (416 599 2551). Streetcar 505, 510. **Open** 11am-2am daily. **Credit** AmEx, MC, V. **Map** p279 D6.
A shady oasis by day, a pool of light on a dark street by night, the Temp is a favourite with Toronto's alternative media people, as well as old-timers who quietly sip their beer and stare into space. The pool table still sees some action from time to time, though the patio is more popular.

Red Room

444 Spadina Avenue, at College Street (416 929 9964). Streetcar 506, 510. **Open** 11am-2am daily. **No credit cards.** **Map** p279 D5.
From the people who brought you the Green Room (*see below*) comes a less overwhelming, but still student-friendly, pub. Old-fashioned street lamps light the patio and inside the casually hip crowd around the booths and tables, or slouch in the couches at the back. If you don't feel like alcohol, try an avocado milkshake instead.

University/Harbord

Green Room

296 Brunswick Avenue, at Bloor Street W (416 929 3253). Subway Bathurst or Spadina. **Open** 11am-2am daily. **No credit cards.** **Map** p282 D4.
The Green Room's back alley entrance leads into a large space cluttered with mismatched chairs and couches, and wobbly tables covered in wax from candles jammed into beer bottles. There's more of the same upstairs, and in the courtyard. It's popular with the alt.student crowd.

Eat, Drink, Shop

Insomnia

563 Bloor Street W, at Bathurst Street (416 588 3907/www.insomniacafe.com). Streetcar 511/subway Bathurst. **Open** 4pm-2am Mon-Fri; 10am-2am Sat, Sun. **Credit** AmEx, DC, MC, V. **Map** p282 D4.
This place started out as an internet café, but the only remaining vestiges are one computer and late hours. The lounge is busiest in the winter, when all the neighbourhood patios are closed. Local DJs play each night between 10pm and 2am. Thursday is cheap Martini night, and beer costs less on Mondays.

Panorama Restaurant & Lounge

51st floor, Manulife Centre, 55 Bloor Street W, at Bay Street (416 967 0000/www.panoramalounge.com). **Open** 5pm-1am Mon-Thur, Sun; 5pm-1am Fri, Sat. **Credit** AmEx, MC, V. **Map** p282 F4.

Panorama lives up to its name, with expansive views over the city. The crowd is conservative: thirtysomething power-suit power-brokers and their arm candy, catching drinks after a movie, thankful for the quiet, civilised Midtown watering hole. The Panorama is best in the summer when the large rooftop patio is open.

Ye Olde Brunswick House

481 Bloor Street W, at Brunswick Avenue (416 531 4635). Subway Bathurst or Spadina. **Open** 4pm-2am Thur-Sat. **Credit** AmEx, MC, V. **Map** p282 D4.
This century-old collegiate drunk tank has cheap pitchers, queues, betting and live music after 10pm on weekends, and recently spiffed up its historic brownstone façade. Inside, the Brunny is still a

Sing, sing a song

Given that Toronto's Asian population numbers half a million, the karaoke had better be good. Traditional bars, public and private, have popped up in most Far Eastern communities – from Little Korea through Kensington Market to the Japanese-style suburban malls. But the current vogue is for karaoke the North American way: country and western, rock 'n' roll and '80s nostalgia. At a host of trendy nightspots-cum-soundstages you'll find barflies and hipsters sharing the stage on virtually any night of the week. Conventional karaoke venues, meanwhile, continue to be popular.

At blind rocker Jeff Healey's eponymous joint **Healey's** (178 Bathurst Street, Entertainment District, 416 703 5882) there's a singalong on Tuesday nights, featuring thirtysomething arty types doing the 'white man's overbite'. It's the best reason most people can give for going out on a Tuesday night, and guests spilling on to the street after their curtain call tend to find themselves in front of the **Paddock** (*see p134*) – a good excuse to have one more for the road.

If all the vocal practice you got as a kid was more Ramones and Sex Pistols than Beach Boys, check out the weekly Kickass Karaoke at the **Bovine Sex Club** (542 Queen Street W, Entertainment District, 416 504 4239), a decade-old hole-in-the-wall that attracts those types you'd expect to eschew such naffness: Goths, ravers and punk rockers. Staff invite the odd celebrity ringer to get the audience going, then open the floor to the public.

Imagine your grandmother's mah-jong buddies next to a bunch of truckstop regulars and you have the eclectic crowd at the

Gladstone Hotel's **Melody Bar** (1214 Queen Street W, West End, 416 531 4635) in Parkdale. Here you'll find a hodge-podge of rhinestone cowboys, welfare mums and young hipsters queuing up from Wednesday to Saturday to belt out mangled versions of hits by the likes of Tammy Wynette, Johnny Cash, Elton and Dr John.

Clinton's Tavern (693 Bloor Street W, West End, 416 535 9541), on the edge of Koreatown, provides a modern Asian take on the hobby (regularly voted one of the top k-joints by the city's alternative weeklies). Karaoke boxes – small rooms with video karaoke machines – are available by the hour. Otherwise, try the private room at **BMB Music Studio** (593 Bloor Street W, West End, 416 533 8786). In these small spaces it's not unusual to find suited business types mixed in with the student patrons, dropping in for a song or two after a lunch meeting. A final authentic karaoke experience comes courtesy of **XO Karaoke Bar** (693 Bloor Street W, West End, 416 535 3734), accessed through an inconspicuous street-level entrance that leads to an upper-floor lair where the poor-quality Asian videos and ridiculous song selection can often be more fun than the singing itself.

Others we love

Peel Pub (276 King Street W, Entertainment District, 416 977 0003, Tuesday); **Spirits Bar & Grill** (642 Church Street, Church & Wellesley, 416 967 0001, Saturday); **Sushi Bistro** (204 Queen Street W, Entertainment District, 416 971 5315, *summer* Monday-Saturday, *winter* Wednesday-Saturday).

Don't look now, but is that Al heading this way? **Laurentian Room**.

binge-drinking favourite, full of rowdy frat boys in baseball caps and soccer jerseys, pool tables, sticky floors and a back-room dancefloor.

Cabbagetown

Laurentian Room
51A Winchester Street, at Parliament Street (416 925 8680). Bus 65/streetcar 506. **Open** 5.30pm-2am Thur-Sun. **Credit** AmEx, MC, V. **Map** p280 H5.
Before it was boarded up, this art deco, prohibition-era saloon was the ladies' and escorts' lounge of the main watering hole downstairs (until 1972, it was illegal for a woman to drink alcohol in Ontario without a male companion). As with the Paddock across town (*see p134*), Al Capone was said to be a regular. Today it's a time capsule of jazz-era nostalgia, with the original mahogany floor and lacquered oak bar, vaulted ceiling and leather banquette. The Mojito is the signature sip here, or the Apple Capone – apple liqueur, bourbon and butterscotch.

St Lawrence

C'est What
67 Front Street E, at Church Street (416 867 9499/www.cestwhat.com). Streetcar 504/subway King or Union. **Open** noon-2am Mon-Fri; 11am-2am Sat; 11am-1am Sun. **Credit** AmEx, MC, V. **Map** p280 G8.
A cosy subterranean bar where *recherché* brew is on tap (over 40 in total), including the house's own hemp ale and coffee porter. It's a place to linger for hours, drinking fancy beers and playing games of backgammon or Scrabble (there are no darts or pool). The bartenders bring in their own CDs, so the music can range from hip hop to Beethoven, and the crowd is just as mixed.

Esplanade Bier Markt
58 The Esplanade, at Church Street (416 862 7575). Streetcar 504/subway King or Union. **Open** 11am-1am daily. **Credit** AmEx, DC, MC, V. **Map** p280 G8.

This faux Belgian brasserie has more than 100 brands of beer and lots of space in which to drink them. On a strip of bars and restaurants that includes Fionn MacCool's (*see below*), it's a popular spot for after-work drinking and flirting.

Fionn MacCool's
70 The Esplanade, at Church Street (416 362 2495/www.fionnmaccoolstoronto.com). Streetcar 504/subway King or Union. **Open** 11am-1am Mon-Thur; 11am-2am Fri, Sat; 11am-midnight Sun. **Credit** AmEx, MC, V. **Map** p280 G8.
It's as if the owners ordered the complete product line from 'The Authentic Irish Pub Catalogue' – Guinness posters, a snug, plenty of dark wood and corned beef and cabbage on the menu. Live Irish music is just as likely to be U2 covers as a traditional reel.

Irish Embassy Pub & Grill
49 Yonge Street, at Wellington Street (416 866 8282/www.irishembassypub.com). Streetcar 504/subway King or Union. **Open** 11.30am-2am Mon-Fri; 11am-2am Sat, Sun. **Credit** AmEx, MC, V. **Map** p279 F8.
This historic British colonial building, dating from 1873, was the first merchant bank in Toronto. Its financial past was not forgotten when it opened as an upscale Irish pub on St Patrick's Day 2000: the vaulted ceiling and marble columns are original. At lunchtime, stockbrokers and corporate lawyers come here to consume Guinness and Irish stew.

Yorkville

Avenue
Four Seasons Hotel, 21 Avenue Road, at Cumberland Street (416 928 7332/www.four seasons.com/toronto). Subway Bay or Museum. **Open** 11.45am-1am Mon-Sat; 10.30am-1am Sun. **Credit** AmEx, DC, MC, V. **Map** p282 F4.
The Four Seasons is, even in the 'off-season' (the other 50 weeks a year it isn't besieged with film festival-goers), a spot for people watching. At ground-level, this wonderful corner space overlooks tony Yorkville. It specialises in Martinis, but also has 25 wines by the glass.

Caren's Wine & Cheese Bar

158 Cumberland Street, at Avenue Road (416 962 5158). Subway Bay or Museum. **Open** noon-1am Mon, Tue, Sun; noon-2am Wed-Sat. **Credit** AmEx, DC, MC, V. **Map** p282 F4.

A new stop for weary Yorkville shoppers and guests from the Four Seasons across the street, the leather wall, glossy interior and tiny, elegant chandeliers make this place posh without being pretentious. Owner Caren Walters is usually on hand to recommend flights of wine, selections by the glass, or a choice of cheese – from platters to fondue.

Hemingway's

142 Cumberland Street, at Bay Street (416 968 2828/ www.hemingways.to). Bus 6/subway Bay. **Open** 11am-2am daily. **Credit** AmEx, MC, V. **Map** p282 F4.

New Zealander Martin McSkimming opened this restaurant and bar in 1980, and you'll still find him hanging around chatting with the regulars. The rooftop patio is open year-round (enclosed in the winter), and there's live music downstairs at weekends.

Lobby

192 Bloor Street W, at Avenue Road (416 929 7169/ www.eatdrinkplay.ca). Subway Bay or Museum. **Open** 4pm-2am Mon-Sat. **Credit** AmEx, DC, MC, V. **Map** p282 F4.

The concept (and name) is stolen from the rash of Hollywood-approved boutique hotels around. The white-on-white palette (marble floor, overstuffed sofas, billowing curtains) is an ode to Philippe Starck's Miami style; bevelled glass mirrors reflect the beachy vibe, which spills on to the boulevard patio. Throughout the year (but particularly during the film festival), this is where the celebrities can be found, with VIPs in the champagne lounge downstairs or behind the gauzy curtain of the semi-private dining room at the back.

Roof Lounge

Park Hyatt Hotel, 4 Avenue Road, at Bloor Street W (416 324 1568/www.parktoronto.hyatt.com). Subway Bay or Museum. **Open** noon-1am daily. **Credit** AmEx, MC, V. **Map** p282 F4.

A mere 18 storeys off the ground, this is by no means the loftiest bar in the city. But it is still one of the nicest of Toronto's high-altitude drinking establishments. The stunning skyline is enhanced by a large fireplace, a leather-lined bar and deep green marble tables. In summer, the terrace is always crowded with patrons enjoying the view of University of Toronto and the skyscrapers beyond.

The Annex

Bedford Academy

36 Prince Arthur Avenue, at Bedford Road (416 921 4600). Subway St George. **Open** 11am-2am daily. **Credit** AmEx, MC, V. **Map** p282 E4.

This old townhouse is one of the more civilised drinking establishments in the Annex. The bar gets plenty of the university trade in the shape of

graduate students sipping local Steam Whistle brew. In addition to a good range of beers on tap and generous Martini portions, the Academy also offers a better-than-average pub menu.

Duke of York

39 Prince Arthur Avenue, at Bedford Road (416 964 2441/www.thedukepubs.ca). Subway St George. **Open** 11am-2am daily. **Credit** AmEx, MC, V. **Map** p282 E4.

Tartan carpet covers one big room after another at this British-style pub. The Duke's quiet vibe attracts teachers and students alike; Thursday's beer-tasting sessions are popular with everyone.

Madison Avenue Pub

14 Madison Avenue, at Bloor Street W (416 927 1722/www.madisonavenuepub.com). Streetcar 510/ subway Spadina. **Open** 11am-2am daily. **Credit** AmEx, MC, V. **Map** p282 F4.

The Frankenstein's monster of the frat scene, the Maddy is made up of three Victorian mansions grafted together into five patios, six rooms (each of which holds about 200 people), 137 beer taps, a kitchen, a scotch bar and, inevitably, a merchandise stand. Like Mary Shelley's creation, this beast isn't quite as scary as it at first seems, and you can enjoy a drink and a meal in relative peace.

Rosedale

Rebel House

1068 Yonge Street, at Roxborough Street (416 927 0704/www.rebelhouse.ca). Subway Rosedale. **Open** 11.30am-2am Mon-Fri; 10.30am-2am Sat, Sun. **Credit** AmEx, MC, V.

This place has a biergarten patio up top, with 17 local brews on tap. Hearty pub grub and easy access from the Rosedale subway station make it a popular destination.

Davisville

Granite Brewery

245 Eglinton Avenue E, at Mount Pleasant Road (416 322 0723/www.granitebrewery.ca). Bus 54/ subway Eglinton. **Open** 11.30am-1am Mon-Sat; 11am-1am Sun. **Credit** AmEx, MC, V.

Dedicated beer aficionados travel great distances for a taste of Peculiar, the strongest of the Granite's many aggressive, own-brewed ales. Unfortunately you can't stock up, as provincial law dictates that all beer must be sold and consumed on the premises. Beer is included in many of the restaurant's dishes.

West End

See also p202 **Lula Lounge** *and p125* **Bar Italia**.

Beaconsfield

1154 Queen Street W, at Beaconsfield Avenue (416 516 2550). Streetcar 501. **Open** 5pm-2am daily. **Credit** MC, V. **Map** p278 A7.

The chandeliers glow and reflect in the stainless steel bar of the Beaconsfield, which is within staggering distance of the Drake (see p140). Housed in the former Molson Bank building, it's a lovely restoration, with a menu of comfort food and a few beers on tap.

Bird
2nd floor, 503 College Street, at Palmerston Blvd, Little Italy (416 323 3957). Streetcar 506. **Open** 8pm-2am Wed-Sat. **Credit** AmEx, MC, V. **Map** p278 C5.
Above trendy Xacutti (see p128), this is where the *très chic, très chic* crowd can be found louching around and sipping pricey cocktails.

Cadillac Lounge
1296 Queen Street W, at Brock Avenue (416 536 7717/www.cadillaclounge.com). Streetcar 501. **Open** 11am-2am daily. **Credit** MC, V.

The Cadillac's interior is beat-up, which makes it perfect for bourbon and denim (often designer), and its patrons' unabashed love of country music. There's a band playing most Saturday nights, and a honkytonk Sunday matinée. *See also p203.*

Camera Bar & Media Gallery
1028 Queen Street W, at Ossington Avenue (416 530 0011). Streetcar 501. **Open** 5pm-2am Tue-Sun. **Credit** AmEx, MC, V. **Map** p278 B7.
Canadian film director Atom Egoyan is co-owner (along with distributor Hussain Amarshi) of this coffee bar and cocktail lounge-cum-cinema, smack in the middle of the newly colonised Queen Street West art gallery strip. The small bar is up front, lying adjacent to the 50-seat independent auditorium, which specialises in suitably Egoyan-like filmic obscurities. *See also p179 and p27 **Atom antics**.*

Hopping mad

Not that we're biased, but Canadian beer is generally far more interesting – not to mention, stronger – than the watery and tasteless stuff found in America. It's a sad fact, then, that the nation's most popular beers are probably also the nation's worst beers.

The good news is that the past decade has seen a jump in the number of microbreweries with their own, superior, varieties that are big on flavour and depth.

Amsterdam Brewing Co (600 King Street W, Entertainment District, 416 504 1040) produces a couple of stalwarts (Natural Blonde and Nut Brown) that are on tap in pubs across the city, as well as at branches of the Beer Store (see p156). On site, try the Framboise (raspberry), the stronger Avalanche, or any of the seasonal specialities. Further east, the cobblestone streets of the Distillery District – former whisky-making centre of James Worts and brother-in-law William Gooderham – now boasts the **Mill Street Brewery** (Building 63, 55 Mill Street, 416 681 0338, www.mill streetbrewery.com). The organic brew (pesticide- and insecticide-free) is crafted in large copper vats, then decanted into delicate little bottles. The Tankhouse Ale

is a fragrant fine ale with zesty malt; Coffee Porter is deep with mocha undertones; and Helles Bock is popular at Christmas.

Housed in the pedigree'd John Street Roundhouse since 2000, microbrewery **Steam Whistle** (255 Bremner Boulevard, Harbourfront, 416 362 2337, www.steam whistle.ca) has just one elixir: a humble and now ubiquitous pilsner. The fleet of delivery folk are dispatched in period trucks decorated with vintage graphics. It offers tours, tastings, private parties and even exhibitions by local artists (see p63).

Drake Hotel.

Chelsea Room

923 Dundas Street W, at Grace Street (416 364 0553/www.canteena.ca). Streetcar 505. **Open** 7pm-2am daily. **Credit** AmEx, MC, V. **Map** p278 C6.
You could easily miss this gently lit space, but it's worth seeking out for its (tiny) patio, brightly tiled Martini bar and comfortable banquette lounge. It's also friendly, and mostly stocked with locals.

Cobalt

426 College Street, at Bathurst Street, Little Italy (416 923 4456). Streetcar 506, 511. **Open** 8pm-2am daily. **Credit** AmEx, MC, V. **Map** p278 C5/p279 D5.
In the borderlands on the eastern end of Little Italy, Cobalt is a romantic option, with soft lighting, deep blue walls and Middle Eastern-inspired cubby-hole booths in the back. The extensive Martini list includes no less than four chocolate varieties.

Cocktail Molotov

928 Dundas Street W, at Grace Street (416 603 6691). Streetcar 505. **Open** 5.30pm-2am daily. **No credit cards. Map** p278 C6.
Blissfully VIP-room free, this simple bar (formerly a design shop) with oak panelling, and repro Eames' stools, is the essence of the city's new laid-back cool, with heavy rock tunes (no bossa nova here), plentiful beer for the thirsty and more elaborate cocktails for the prettier members of the group.

College Street Bar

574 College Street, at Manning Avenue, Little Italy (416 533 2417). Streetcar 506, 511. **Open** 5pm-2am daily. **Credit** AmEx, MC, V. **Map** p278 C6.
Exposed brick and dark wood set the tone for this old favourite. Less formal than some of its swanky neighbours, it's still a place where the young and fashionable come to see and be seen. The seafood-intensive menu has a good reputation.

Communist's Daughter

1149 Dundas Street W, at Ossington Avenue (647 435 0103). Bus 63/streetcar 505. **Open** 5pm-2am daily. **No credit cards. Map** p278 B6.
Tucked away among the area's macho Portuguese soccer bars, lumber centres and Catholic churches is this bustling, tiny bar, with bags of character – right down to the well-curated jukebox.

Drake Hotel

1150 Queen Street W, at Beaconsfield Avenue (416 531 5042/www.thedrakehotel.ca). Streetcar 501. **Open** 8pm-2am daily. **Credit** AmEx, DC, MC, V. **Map** p278 A7.
If you can cut through the nightly line, and the media hype surrounding the restoration of this former railway flophouse, you'll find terrazzo floors, self-conscious art, Rorschach ink-blotted walls. In addition to 19 guest rooms, there's a European-influenced lounge, sushi bar, café, licensed rooftop patio, treatment room, restaurant and a lower-level entertainment space (the Underground), which features an eclectic mix of bands, performance art and retro theme nights. *See also p49, p130 and p203.*

Idoru Wine Bar

331 Roncesvalles Avenue, at Grenadier Road (416 531 2557). Subway Dundas West. **Open** 6pm-midnight Mon; noon-2am Tue-Sat. **Credit** MC, V.
Idoru is named after the William Gibson sci-fi novel, but the decor is thankfully not futuristic; instead, the space is a warmly tealit antidote to the more raucous joints in the 'hood, done in black and white, with tapas-style fare and a lengthy wine list.

Lot 16

1136 Queen Street W, at Lisgar Street (416 531 6556). Streetcar 501. **Open** 5pm-2am daily. **Credit** MC, V.

Low-key in the extreme, this bar is literally and figuratively in the shadow of the Drake (*see p140*). The retro light fixtures, simple cocktails and largely unadorned space make a welcome change from its more polished and contrived neighbour.

Press Club
850 Dundas Street W, at Euclid Avenue (416 364 7183). Streetcar 505. **Open** 6pm-3am daily. **No credit cards**. **Map** p278 C6.
The vintage typewriter in the window may reflect the neighbourhood's gaggle of scribes, but you don't have to be a starving novelist to sidle up to the bar here. Unusual drinks include rare imported liquors from Asia, from snake- through flower- to rice-based, and premium rum and bourbon.

South Side Louie's
583 College Street, at Clinton Street, Little Italy (416 532 1250). Streetcar 506, 511. **Open** 11.30am-2am daily. **Credit** AmEx, MC, V. **Map** p278 C6.
If you've overdosed on Little Italy's fashion-model scene, this casual pub is a good place to recover. A nice cold pint, some solid pub food and a hearty conversation over the pool table will have you feeling like a thousand bucks again in no time.

Souz Dal
636 College Street, at Grace Street, Little Italy (416 537 1883). Streetcar 506. **Open** 8pm-2am daily. **Credit** MC, V. **Map** p278 C5.
This small cocktail bar holds only 50 people (but another 25 can squeeze on to the back patio) and it gets very crowded at weekends. It's dark and seductive, with red plush chairs and candlelight reflecting off the burnished copper wedges that decorate the bar. Down a couple of Martinis from the long list and you can't help but get a romantic glow, even if you're here on your own.

Sutra
612 College Street, at Clinton Street, Little Italy (416 537 8755). Streetcar 506, 511. **Open** 8pm-2am daily. **Credit** AmEx, MC, V. **Map** p278 C5.
This is a date bar *par excellence*, with champagne and oysters, cushion cube seats at the table, and a long, lean sliver of a room. At the back, a heated outdoor patio has a Polynesian theme, with loofah tables, bamboo walls and sand underfoot.

Wild Indigo
607 College Street, at Clinton Street, Little Italy (416 536 8797). Streetcar 506, 511. **Open** 8pm-2am Tue-Sun. **Credit** MC, V. **Map** p278 C5.
In the tranquil backyard patio, a Buddha, lit with blue light, sets the tone for this mellow, convofriendly Martini bar. It also has a reasonable range of wines and imported beers.

East Toronto

Chinchilla Lounge
513 Danforth Avenue, at Logan Avenue, The Danforth (416 465 1751). Bus 72/subway Chester or Pape. **Open** 8pm-2am Fri, Sat. **Credit** AmEx, MC, V.
Upstairs from Lolita's Lust restaurant, the Chinchilla is open only at weekends, when the after-dinner crowd kicks back and relaxes to DJs spin house and funk. The design is evolving, but usually includes geometric paintings by local artist Malcolm Brown.

Dora Keogh Traditional Irish Pub
141 Danforth Avenue, at Broadview Avenue, The Danforth (416 778 1804/www.allens.to/dora). Streetcar 504, 505/subway Broadview. **Open** 4.30pm-2am daily. **Credit** AmEx, MC, V.
The Irish aspect of this pub is kept pleasantly low-key. It's favoured by locals for a pint of Guinness or a glass of Jameson's. The bar has a handsome wood and copper decor, a working fireplace and a snug.

Lion on the Beach
1958 Queen Street E, at Kenilworth Avenue, The Beaches (416 690 1984). Bus 92/streetcar 501. **Open** 11.30am-2am daily. **Credit** AmEx, MC, V.
This informal pub is many people's introduction to the Beaches, and it is a popular gathering spot for larger groups. A bit of a throwback to the area's historic status as a British enclave, it has two quiet patios, and hosts live and lively music at weekends.

Myth
417 Danforth Avenue, at Chester Avenue, The Danforth (416 461 8383/www.myth.to). Subway Chester. **Open** 4pm-midnight Mon-Thur; 4pm-2am Fri; noon-2am Sat; noon-midnight Sun. **Credit** AmEx, DC, MC, V.
The Danforth's nod to the College Street scene, this restaurant and upscale cocktail bar attracts an after-dinner, thirtysomething crowd, as well as some of the Danforth's younger demographic. The dressy bar is a good place to strike up a conversation and the pool tables are a good place to continue it over a rack or two. The bar also occasionally has live jazz.

Eat, Drink, Shop

Shops & Services

Spend, spend, spend.

Even for jaded shoppers, Toronto makes for great retail therapy. There's virtually nothing you can't get hold of here, from cutting-edge electronics to outrageous one-off fashion designs. Sure, there are the department stores, the shopping centres (including the mammoth new Vaughan Mills) and the global chainstores, but there are also some gems that you won't find in every other city around the world: unique boutiques, eminently browsable bookstores, and, thanks to the city's ethnic make-up, a world of gustatory delights.

WHERE TO GO

Fashion shopping areas in Toronto are not particularly well defined, but if you're not in a hurry you can enjoy perusing to your heart's content. The high-end international names – from Gucci to Vuitton – are found along Bloor Street West in Yorkville (*see also p86*), while the streets just north are home to a clutch of lesser-known but equally pricey names. The area around Queen Street West and Spadina Avenue, which earned the moniker SoHo back when safety pins and biker boots were typical attire, has now achieved high-

street status, forcing the lower-rent boutiques that once defined it further west towards Ossington Avenue, and along Queen West of Bathurst Street amid the galleries. A pocket of Canadian fashion has also emerged on the burgeoning Dundas Street West strip (*see p150* **Canuck chic**). The vintage hub remains **Kensington Market** (*see p156*), also a centre for food shopping, along with the indoor **St Lawrence Market** (*see p159*).

PRICES AND SALES

How prices pan out depends on where you come from and how exchange rates are doing. Canadians find Toronto expensive, and now that the Canadian dollar has strengthened somewhat, the American dollar and UK pound allure is less glossy (though Brits, in particular, will still find it cheaper to shop here).

Expect a 15 per cent goods and service tax on most non-essentials (not included in the prices marked) but there is a visitor refund scheme (*see p262*) that is flexible and easy to use.

Sales are generally held in summer (July to August) and winter (from 26 December through January).

Sashaying down the shopping streets of **Yorkville**.

One-stop

Department stores

Holt Renfrew

50 Bloor Street W, at Bay Street, Yorkville (416 922 2333/www.holtrenfrew.com). Subway Bay or Bloor-Yonge. **Open** 10am-6pm Mon-Wed, Sat; 10am-8pm Thur, Fri; noon-6pm Sun. **Credit** AmEx, DC, MC, V. **Map** p282 F4.

New York has Barneys and Toronto has Holt Renfrew, a multi-level temple for high-end attire and pampering products. The Canadian retail dynasty has done some shopping of its own, recently picking up Brown Thomas in Dublin and London's Selfridges. Visiting celebs and local gentry have been known to send their chauffeurs inside to collect goods while they wait in the limo. Titles or not, if you're looking for Armani, Manolo or the latest European jeans, your gold card will lead you here. In 2004 Holt's completed a major redesign, adding more gleaming layers to its designer portfolio. These include USA's Juicy Couture and designer denim, plus Marc Jacobs and his acolytes – such as local wunderkind Mercy. World Design Lab (for emerging and experimental international fashion) and vintage couture are also here, and, on the ground floor, there's a glossy new fragrance and handbags pavilion for Jo Malone, Susanne Lang, Kate Spade, Lulu Guinness and other must-have brands. The food section in the basement stocks scrumptious edibles from Milan's famed Peck emporium.
Other locations: 3401 Dufferin Street, North Toronto (416 789 3261).

Malls

Hazelton Lanes

55 Avenue Road, at Bloor Street, Yorkville (416 968 8680/www.hazeltonlanes.com). Bus 6/subway Bay or Museum. **Open** 10am-6pm Mon-Wed, Fri, Sat; 10am-7pm Thur; noon-5pm Sun. **Credit** varies. **Map** p282 F3/4.

A 1960s monstrosity on the outside, a quaint web of courtyards within, Hazelton Lanes was fashion central for the rich and glamorous until the lean 1990s, when flamboyance went the way of shoulder pads and half the mall lay vacant. Today there's an upscale gym-cum-yoga space, a Rolls Royce dealer and the high-end Whole Foods Market in the basement (celeb spotting in the aisles is now a regular pastime for locals; *see p158*), and construction work continues apace. At Andrew's you'll find well-curated designer sportswear and evening wardrobes for the carriage trade, while Woman apothecary has cult brands like Philosophy and Neal's Yard, and at the expansive über-designed trendy TNT, it's trendy LA-inspired labels and style, plus the tranquil haven of Teatro Verde (*see p162*), an upscale home accessories shop.

Pacific Mall

4300 Steeles Avenue E, at Kennedy Road, Markham (1-905 470 8785/www.pacificmalltoronto.com). Bus 43, 53. By car: Don Valley Parkway northwards to route 404, take Woodbine Avenue/Steeles Avenue exit, turn right on Steeles. **Open** 11am-8pm Mon-Thur, Sun; 11am-9pm Fri, Sat.

 Top ten Shops

The Beguiling
An alternative comics and indie culture emporium that goes way beyond superheroes. *See p147*.

Courage My Love
Vintage treasures and second-hand style in a family-run institution. *See p152*.

Dinah's Cupboard
Delicious seasonal foods. Great for picnic fixings. *See p158*.

Georgie Bolesworth
This fashion-stylist-turned-retailer has her finger on the pulse of emerging Canadian fashion talent. *See p150* **Canuck chic**.

Honest Ed's
What's not to love about a discount store with an eccentric flare for self-promotion. *See p144*.

Lileo
This destination for well-heeled shoppers who are their own lifestyle gurus is a de rigueur stop-off in the emerging Distillery District. *See p151*.

La Paloma Gelateria
A gelato-lover's dream with a constantly evolving roster of new flavours. *See p160*.

San Remo
Out-of-the-way, yes, but this jewel-box of offbeat Canadian-designed, feminine European fashion is well worth a trip. *See p149*.

Shelly Purdy Studio
Whatever your budget when it comes to buying bling, this Canadian diamond specialist will cater to your needs. *See p153*.

Soundscapes
A definitive 411 on the local music scene and neighbourhood hipster nexus. *See p163*.

Eat, Drink, Shop

The name refers to the origin of the stock, though the mall is almost as vast as the ocean itself. Pacific Mall is North America's largest shopping centre selling Asian goods, a sea-blue monstrosity in an industrial area on Toronto's northern fringes. It could take a day to explore this mini-village of toys, togs and treats. On the ground floor, wares are housed in a streetscape of 150 fishbowl-like, glass-enclosed kiosks containing shelf upon shelf of candy-coloured mobile phones, sneakers, T-shirts, school supplies and piles of Hello Kitty products. As payback for the effort you've made to get here, goods are offered at discount prices, and the excitement is almost palpable. A second level is devoted to Far Eastern edibles – pastries, dim sum, noodles – and counters of sticky candy, which ravenous consumers gleefully attack.

Toronto Eaton Centre

220 Yonge Street, at Dundas Street, Dundas Square (416 598 8560/www.torontoeatoncentre.com). Streetcar 501, 505/subway Dundas or Queen. **Open** 10am-9pm Mon-Fri; 9.30am-7pm Sat; noon-6pm Sun. **Credit** varies. **Map** p280 G6.

One of Toronto's top tourist destinations is, ahem, a shopping mall. Long frequented by bargain-hungry Americans spending their super-charged bucks, the mall has retained its sense of retail urgency in the face of a surging canadian dollar. The Eaton name is a vestige of a once powerful family dynasty done in by the dinosaur status of their nationwide department store chain in 1999. Though Sears picked up the pieces of this flagship store, the Eaton name lives on. The south, or Queen Street, end is anchored by the venerable 400-year-old Hudson's Bay Company. Between these retail titans are hundreds of shops, stores, from mid-range international chains (including H&M and Zara) to more pedestrian, home-grown styles like B2 by Browns designer footwear, kitchenware and lifestyle shops such as Williams-Sonoma and Pottery Barn. The basics are covered, including books at Indigo, 100 perfume and cosmetics brands at the new Sephora outlet and Red Earth's north American flagship, a low-key food court, plus a ticket booth and tourist information stand (the latter reflecting the TEC's inexplicable status as a top visitor destination).

Yorkdale Shopping Centre

3401 Dufferin Street, at Highway 401, North Toronto (416 789 3261/www.yorkdale.com). Subway or GO Yorkdale. **Open** 10am-9pm Mon-Fri; 9.30am-9pm Sat; 11am-6pm Sun. **Credit** varies.

Yorkdale, the first mall in North America, can be seen en route into the city. This sprawling neon structure has been expanding since its inception in the mid 1900s, leaving no retailer (local or foreign) uninvited. Once a hangout for teens from local working-class neighbourhoods, Yorkdale has scrubbed up, and now houses a Holt Renfrew, Coach, Harry Rosen, Pottery Barn, Aveda, MAC, Foot Locker, HMV and 200 other shops, plus a multi-screen cinema, restaurants, and professional services, such as car-valeting.

Honest Ed's.

Discount malls

Honest Ed's

581 Bloor Street W, at Bathurst Street, The Annex (416 537 2111). Streetcar 511/subway Bathurst. **Open** 10am-9pm Mon-Fri; 10am-6pm Sat; 11am-6pm Sun. **Credit** AmEx, MC, V. **Map** p282 D4.

For a unique value shopping experience, don't miss Honest Ed's. It's worth a visit even if you don't buy anything. Ed Mirvish, the 90-something proprietor and theatre impresario, and the man who brought London's Old Vic Theatre back to life in the 1980s, decks out his emporium in early Las Vegas vaudeville-meets-old school merchandising style, with oodles of flashing lights and crooked wooden floors. Autographed publicity shots of West End stars from years gone by stare out across the heaps of undergarments and rubber boots. The impresario's artier side can be seen around the corner on Markham Street, where Mirvish Village houses artists' studios, galleries and speciality bookstores.

Vaughan Mills

1 Bass Pro Mills Drive, at Highway 400, North Toronto (1-905 879 1777/www.vaughanmills.com). Subway Yorkdale then Wonderland GO bus (June-Sept only). By car: Highway 400 northwards, exit at Bass Pro Mills. **Open** 9.30am-9.30pm Mon-Sat; 11am-7pm Sun. **Credit** varies.

This $355-million project is the country's first new mall in nearly 15 years, and it's quickly become a bustling tourist attraction since its doors opened in autumn 2004. The 1.2 million sq ft (11,160 sq m) discount mega-mall (that's the same as 70 Olympic-sized hockey rinks), with its gleaming hardwood floors, is home to outlet versions of popular retailers such as American Eagle, Danier Leather, Roots, Mexx, Benetton, Winners, Burlington Coat Factory, BCBG Max Azria and the Bay's Designer Depot. The Bass Pro Shop, a 140,000 sq ft space, complete with three-storey waterfall and huge aquarium, is an outdoorsy outfitter; if it inspires you to indulge in some leisure activities, make a beeline for the Nascar SpeedPark (with five tracks, plus indoor rock climbing) or Lucky Strike Lanes where you can munch on crabcakes and sip Martinis while you mess up the ten pins.

Winners

444 Yonge Street, at College Street, University (416 598 8800/www.winners.ca). Streetcar 506/subway College. **Open** 9am-9pm Mon-Fri; 9.30am-6pm Sat; 11am-6pm Sun. **Credit** AmEx, MC, V. **Map** p282/p283 G5.

After ruling in the suburbs – and drawing downtown denizens out to the sticks for knock-down prices – Winners has arrived in the heart of the city. Designer dresses, casual sportswear and men's and children's clothing can all be found at hefty discounts.

Antiques

Butterfield 8

235 Danforth Avenue, at Playter Boulevard, East Toronto (416 406 5664). Subway Broadview or Chester. **Open** 10am-6pm Mon-Wed, Sat; 10am-7pm Thur, Fri; noon-4pm Sun. **Credit** AmEx, MC, V.

You can comb the Toronto Antiques Centre (*see below*) or stake out the junk shops on Queen, but you're unlikely to come across the high-quality kitsch you get here. True collectibles can be found in cigarette paraphernalia (enamel cases and lighters), and neo-kitsch appears in the form of cute carry-alls and home accessories.

Passion for the Past

1646 Queen Street W, at Wilson Park Road, West End (416 535 3883). Streetcar 501, 504. **Open** noon-6pm Tue-Sun. **Credit** V.

The market atmosphere is pervasive at Passion, where haggling is not the offensive practice it has become elsewhere. The quality Victorian furnishings on which this outlet was founded are becoming scarce – but they do exist, and are fine reminders of Toronto's beginnings.

Sticks & Stones Antiques

1854 Queen Street W, at Roncesvalles Avenue, West End (416 699 9611/www.sticksandstonesantiques. com). Streetcar 501, 504. **Open** 10am-6pm Tue-Fri; 10am-5pm Sat, Sun. **Credit** AmEx, DC, MC, V.

As the name suggests, this family-owned business specialises in gems and furnishings. It's a favourite of the city's fashion stylists: it would take a whole day to peruse the vast rows of vintage jewellery. Thankfully, computerisation means that staff know exactly what they have in stock, even if they can't immediately locate it.

Toronto Antiques Centre

276 King Street W, at Duncan Street, Entertainment District (416 345 9941/www.hfam.com). Streetcar 510. **Open** 10am-6pm Tue-Sat. **Credit** AmEx, MC, V. **Map** p279 E8.

Toronto's most non-European characteristic is its dearth of markets, but this antiques arcade is enough to sate any enthusiast. Two huge floors present the usual china, silver and jewellery – worth sifting through only if you're a collector. Twentieth-century curios include silk-tasselled lamps from vaudeville days, magazines, old tin advertisements, wedding gowns and gloves. There's also a decent selection of antique maps, plus natural-fibre rugs.

Books, newspapers & magazines

Book City

663 Yonge Street, at Charles Street, Church & Wellesley (416 964 1167). Subway St Clair. **Open** 9.30am-10pm Mon-Sat; 11am-10pm Sun. **Credit** MC (over $25), V. **Map** p283 G1.

Even with five locations citywide, Book City is still the ideal small book shop. Sophisticated, hard-to-find literary magazines and low-budget Canadian upstarts all feature, and there are few better places to pick up a Sunday *New York Times* (though copies sell quickly). The rough-around-the-edges decor is charming rather than dusty.

Other locations: 348 Danforth Avenue, East Toronto (416 469 9997); 2350 Bloor Street W, West End (416 766 9412); 501 Bloor Street W, The Annex (416 961 4496); 1950 Queen Street E, The Beaches (416 698 1444).

Chapters

110 Bloor Street W, at Bay Street, Yorkville (416 920 9299/www.chapters.indigo.ca). Bus 6/ subway Bay. **Open** 9am-10pm Mon-Thur; 9am-11pm Fri, Sat; 10am-10pm Sun. **Credit** AmEx, MC, V. **Map** p282 F4.

The first mega-bookstore in Canada, Chapters caused controversy when – nearly a decade ago – it bought Coles and Smith Books and began to multiply, putting the quainter booksellers out of business. It got a taste of its own medicine when rival big-box Indigo set up shop two years later and in 2001 Indigo gobbled up Chapters whole, creating Chapters/ Indigo Inc. The book behemoth has tried to curb the browsing by pumping in the music and removing the more comfortable chairs, but it also offers a healthy discount on popular hardbacks.

Other locations: 2225 Bloor Street W, West End (416 761 9773); 142 John Street, Entertainment District (416 595 7349); 2901 Bayview Avenue, North Toronto (416 222 6323).

Indigo Books & Music

55 Bloor Street W, at Bay Street, University (416 925 3536/www.chapters.indigo.ca). Bus 6/subway Bay. **Open** 9am-10pm Mon-Wed, Sun; 9am-11pm Thur-Sat. **Credit** AmEx, MC, V. **Map** p282 F4.

Kensington Market.
See p156.

It's the better looking of the two huge book outlets, with a clean blue colour scheme and blue accents. Still, rummaging through Indigo is like shopping at IKEA: you're there because you have to be, and lingering is not a great option (even though most locations have a café). Indigo's best asset is its book signing events. Celebrity authors – like Bill Clinton, Michael Douglas and Jamie Oliver – often make pit-stops for crowd-pulling signings or promotions. **Other locations**: 2300 Yonge Street, North Toronto (416 544 0049); Yorkdale Shopping Centre, 3401 Dufferin Street, North Toronto (416 781 6660); Toronto Eaton Centre, 220 Yonge Street, Dundas Square (416 591 3622).

Nicholas Hoare

45 Front Street E, at Church Street, St Lawrence (416 777 2665). Streetcar 504/subway Union. **Open** 10am-6pm Mon-Wed; 10am-8pm Thur, Fri; 9am-6pm Sat; noon-6pm Sun. **Credit** AmEx, MC, V. **Map** p280 G8.

No magazines or newspapers are to be found at Hoare's. A very English-style bookseller, it's all about books, stacked right up to the ceilings and accessed by dark oak ladders on brass rails. Classical music streams out from speakers, while an erudite bunch peruse poetry, coffee table books and the latest in home-grown literature. Skylights illuminate a space that otherwise resembles a well-worn manor study; plush seating is strategically located in front of a stone fireplace that crackles and scents the shop on cold winter days.

Pages

256 Queen Street W, at John Street, Entertainment District (416 598 1447/www.pagesbooks.ca). Streetcar 501/subway Osgoode. **Open** 9.30am-10pm Mon-Fri; 10am-10pm Sat; 11am-8pm Sun. **Credit** AmEx, MC, V. **Map** p279 E7.

It's no surprise that a Queen West bookstore should assume a Queen West sensibility. Pages' forte for a quarter of a century has been heavy art tomes, obscure magazines and quirky postcards. Staff are savvy, just as likely to be poets or novelists in progress as mere supporters of the city's lit scene. The cultural agenda is especially evident with the store's very funky (and very free) This Is Not a Reading Series, held at the nearby Rivoli (*see p134*).

Comics

The Beguiling

601 Markham Street, at Bloor Street, West End (416 533 9168/www.beguiling.com). Streetcar 511/subway Bathurst. **Open** 11am-7pm Mon-Thur, Sat; 11am-9pm Fri; noon-6pm Sun. **Credit** MC, V.

A trip to this two-storey Mirvish Village (*see p92*) boutique, tucked behind elaborate window displays, is true to its name. The feel is avant-garde and underground, the interior dark and clandestine. On the ground floor, expect to find popular graphic novels, mini-comics, children's books, plus European comics like the Tin Tin series, plus alternative gifts such as dolls. More mainstream comics occupy the upstairs, as well as a growing collection of manga and animé. On the walls, a staggering selection of original comic book art is for sale by artists like underground legend Kim Deitch, Paul Pope and internationally renowned locals such as Seth and Chester Brown, who call this shop home. Staff are knowledgeable.

The Silver Snail

367 Queen Street W, at Spadina Avenue, Entertainment District (416 593 0889). Streetcar 501, 510. **Open** 10am-6pm Mon, Tue; 10am-8pm Wed-Fri; 10am-7pm Sat; noon-6pm Sun. **Credit** AmEx, MC, V. **Map** p279 D7.

Amid the cool chaos of Queen West, the Silver Snail is an atypical comic book store, with modern decor and high ceilings on two floors. Staff are suitably opinionated, while stockwise it's small-press reads, mainstream comics and graphic novels, manga and Japanese toys (including figurines and action figures for adults as much as kids), and the requisite back issues for collectors.

Pore over pop culture, politics and poetry at **Pages**.

Used books

The quaint thoroughfare of Harbord Street has developed into something of a used-book haven, owing to its proximity to the University of Toronto. The highest concentration of booksellers runs west from Spadina Avenue. Specialists in texts and academic (**Atticus Books**, 84 Harbord Street, 416 922 6045, www.atticus-books.com; **Caversham Booksellers**, 98 Harbord Street, 416 944 0962, www.cavershambooksellers.com) and women's studies (**Toronto Women's Bookstore**, 73 Harbord Street, 416 922 8744, www.womensbookstore.com) can be found among the stores selling new books. Walk north on Spadina for a browse among the speciality indies; a little further west on Markham Street in Mirvish Village, you'll find tiny **Ballenford Books on Architecture** (600 Markham Street, 416 588 0800, www.ballenford.com) and its airy, skylit neighbour **David Mirvish Books on Art** (596 Markham Street, 416 531 9975, www.davidmirvishbooks.com), selling signficant new releases and out-of-print art books under a giant pop art mural by Frank Stella. East along Bloor to Yorkville, there's **TheatreBooks** (11 St Thomas Street, 416 922 7175, www.theatrebooks.com), housed in an elegant Victorian brownstone, and, a few blocks along, the self-explanatory **Cookbook Store** (850 Yonge Street, 416 920 2665, www.cook-book.com), with friendly, food-loving and knowledgeable staff who regularly host signings with visiting authors and chefs.

Electronics

Bay Bloor Radio

55 Bloor Street W, at Bay Street, University (416 967 1122/www.baybloorradio.com). Bus 6/ subway Bay. **Open** 10am-7pm Mon-Wed; 10am-9pm Thur, Fri; 10am-6pm Sat. **Credit** AmEx, MC, V. **Map** p282 F4.

One of those shops that puts out ads on rock radio that are so annoying you can't help but remember them, Bay Bloor is probably the best-known purveyor of audio and visual equipment in the city. You'll rarely hit a weekend without a sale.

Brack Electronics

44 Wellington Street E, at Church Street, St Lawrence (416 366 3636). Streetcar 504/subway King. **Open** 10am-6pm Tue-Wed, Fri, Sat; 10am-9pm Thur. **Credit** AmEx, MC, V. **Map** p280 G8.

Housed in a heritage building in St Lawrence, Brack is no budget shop, but it draws in customers with excellent sales throughout the year. Those for whom sound quality is sacred will appreciate the store's attention to the latest models and elite foreign brands.

Future Shop

355 Yonge Street, at Elm Street, Dundas Square (416 971 5377/www.futureshop.ca). Streetcar 505, 506/subway College or Dundas. **Open** 10am-9pm Mon-Fri; 10am-6pm Sat, Sun. **Credit** AmEx, MC, V. **Map** p280 G6.

First-time renters are Future's desired customer base, and B-rated models its stock in trade. If you just need a functional VCR or a boom box for the beach, Future is the place. But, as with any budget shop, ask about any extra costs before laying down plastic.

Other locations: 2400 Yonge Street, North Toronto (416 489 4726); 10 Old Stock Yards Road, West End (416 766 1577).

PCUsed & CPUsed

488 Dupont Street, at Bathurst Street, The Annex (416 537 2001/533 2001/www.pcused.com or www.cpused.com). Subway Bathurst or Dupont. **Open** 9am-6pm Mon-Wed; 9am-8pm Thur, Fri; 10am-6pm Sat; noon-5pm Sun. **Credit** AmEx, MC, V. **Map** p282 D2.

This store carries a good selection of PCs and Macs, but often the best deals are on second-hand goods: notebooks go for a song. Technicians speak in layman's terms (thankfully), and can also do repairs.

Fashion

See also p156 **Kensington Market**.

Boutiques

Anne Hung Boutique

829 Queen Street W, at Claremont Street, West End (416 364 7251/www.annehung.com). Streetcar 501, 511. **Open** 12.30-7pm Tue-Fri; 12.30-6.30pm Sat; noon-5pm Sun. **Credit** MC, V. **Map** p278 C7.

Behind the wooden façade, designer Anne Hung's boutique is a tall, narrow space decorated only with racks of slinky, sexy jersey pieces and more. A few years back, she was singled out by Paris *Vogue* as the most promising Canadian designer, with a colour palette that takes no prisoners. On the way out you'll want to pick up Anne's signature men's boxer-brief, with her last name emblazoned on the seam.

Clandestino

249 Crawford Street, at Dundas Street W, West End (647 436 4761). Streetcar 505. **Open** noon-6pm Tue-Sun. **Credit** MC, V. **Map** p278 B6.

In season, a cherry-red Mayan hammock beckons from under a multi-coloured garland flapping gently in the breeze. Inside, it's a riot of colour and cheap 'n' cheerful kitsch worthy of a Mexican fiesta, from the terracotta tile floors to painted tin decorations. Figurines of *luchadores* (Mexican wrestlers) and human-sized wrestling masks share space with handmade wooden toys and *lotería* (lottery) boards; a display case houses handmade silver and turquoise jewellery. In addition to clothing from Nepal and beyond, the shop also carries a selection of silk-screened Ts and separates by local micro-designers.

Clandestino. *See p148.*

Kitsch Boutique

325 Lonsdale Road, at Spadina Road, Forest Hill (416 481 6712). Subway St Clair West. **Open** 10am-8pm Mon-Fri; 10am-6pm Sat; noon-5pm Sun. **Credit** AmEx, MC, V.

It's worth a jog to this neighbourhood shop for 11th-hour cocktail attire by mostly US labels. A few minutes here will net everything you require for an impromptu soirée, including wrap, shoes and faux jewels. A 'bargain' basement has designer duds at a significant discount.

Lilith

541 Queen Street W, at Augusta Avenue, Entertainment District (416 504 5353). Streetcar 501, 511. **Open** 11am-7pm Mon-Wed; 11am-8pm Thur-Sat; noon-6pm Sun. **Credit** AmEx, MC, V. **Map** p279 D7.

Few local designs make it out of the country, but the funkiest find their way to Lilith, the authority on urban frocks and accessories to set them off. If basic black is your thing, you might want to miss out this lively den of mauve, turquoise, orange and all tones except black. The Yummy Mummy line of maternity wear defies the norm.

Peach Berserk

507 Queen Street W, at Spadina Avenue, Entertainment District (416 504 1711/ www.peachberserk.com). Streetcar 501, 510. **Open** 10am-7pm Mon-Sat; noon-5pm Sun. **Credit** AmEx, MC, V. **Map** p279 D7.

Boutique owner and designer Kingi Carpenter is the undisputed monarch of Queen Street, working the mosaic floors and full-on fabulousness of her shop for the past 15 years. The fare is girly, kitschy and catchy, with house-created theme silkscreen prints such as I Love A Man in Uniform, punk rock ephemera and excerpts from Helen Gurley Brown's best-selling 1962 novel *Sex and the Single Girl*, found on everything from oven mitts to velvet coats and kicky bias-cut skirts.

Propaganda

686 Yonge Street, at Isabella Street, Church & Wellesley (416 961 0555/www.propaganda.bz). Subway Wellesley. **Open** 11am-7pm Mon-Sat; 1-5pm Sun. **Credit** AmEx, MC, V. **Map** p283 G4.

Regulars know to grace the orange door on a regular basis to see what hip designer or niche brand buyer/owner Regina Sheung has uncovered next. It might be kitschy, sparkly, pop culture icon belts, buckles and brooches by locals Barbie's Basement Jewellery or perhaps an appliqué leather bag emblazoned with 'I Heart Bacon' or a unique silk-screened T. Unusual accessories rule here, and Sheung's canny eye means the selection is always ahead of the curve.

Risqué

404 Bloor Street W, at Brunswick Avenue, The Annex (416 960 3325). Subway Bathurst or Spadina. **Open** 11am-7pm Mon-Fri; 11am-6pm Sat; noon-6pm Sun. **Credit** AmEx, MC, V. **Map** p282 D4.

The Annex is better known for patchouli and batik than the cleavage-enhancing blouses and hip-hugging trousers that are Risqué's stock in trade, so the boutique has become a welcome addition to the area. Here, the designer denim is by Dish, a Vancouver label with a loyal following. Prices are a bit higher than one would expect for the quality, but the clothes are so pretty, you're unlikely to resist.

San Remo

23 St Thomas Street, at Sultan Street, University (416 920 3195). Bus 6/subway Bay or Museum. **Open** 10am-6pm Mon-Wed, Sat; 10am-8pm Thur, Fri; 1-5pm Sun. **Credit** AmEx, MC, V. **Map** p282 F4.

A ready-to-wear antidote to mass-produced designer collections, San Remo's house label is created by the boutique's down-to-earth owner, with input from Italian artisans. With the return to ladylike glam, it's currently silk velvet blazers and bouclé tweed, rhinestone-studded denim and animal prints, supplemented only by the best cashmere cable pieces from Twin Set by Simona Barbieri. Killer metallic *Barbarella* boots or 100mm stilettos covered in chantilly lace, sparkles and velvet bows complete the look, and friendly staff help take the sting out of the prices.

Scarlet

363 Eglinton Avenue W, at Avenue Road, Forest Hill (416 480 0330). Bus 32/subway Eglinton. **Open** 10am-4pm Tue-Fri; 10am-6pm Sat. **Credit** AmEx, MC, V.

This upscale but funky wardrobe is for modern career women, with a comfy sofa and kid-friendly area near the changing rooms. The selection is witty, with Peter Som mixed in with Canadian Lida Baday, and Brit designers Alice Temperley and Ann-Louise Roswald's unique textiles.

Children

Chocky's

352 Queen Street W, at Spadina Avenue, Entertainment District (416 977 1831). Streetcar 501, 510. **Open** 10am-7pm Mon-Sat; noon-6pm Sun. **Credit** AmEx, MC, V. **Map** p279 D7.

Canuck chic

With home-grown designers like Dean & Dan Caten of DSquared, Arthur Mendonça, Paul Hardy and Lida Baday cutting a swathe internationally, it's safe to say that Canadian fashion isn't all mukluks and parkas. A new wave of boutiques has sprouted up around the city (especially in the newly trendy West Queen West area of the West End) showing, and often dedicated exclusively to, local style.

The renaissance in Canadian-only chic boutiques began with **Georgie Bolesworth** (891 Dundas Street W, 416 703 7625) on an up-and-coming downtown strip surrounded by Portuguese soccer bars and karaoke rooms. Designers are sourced – and often discovered – by bohemian fashion stylist Georgia Groome (the shop is named after her grandfather), way before they make it on to the radar of the mainstream fashion press. From Cincyn's sexy jersey to Lydia K's folk costume-inspired salvaged skirts and boleros and Mercy's vintage-look creations, there's plenty to please, plus exotic jewellery mixed in, and Véronique Miljkovitch's wearable textile art.

A few doors down at the darling boutique **Skirt** (903 Dundas Street W, 647 436 3357, www.skirtclothing.ca; *pictured*), owner Jamie Dowdles will regale you with the cottage-industry story behind each and every label. The stock is more afford-able and everyday than Georgie, with gauchos by Quip, Dagg & Stacey's cute culottes, Tryna's exotic jewellery – all displayed in a whitewashed space capped with a pink chandelier.

Further south-west in the West Queen West art and design district, **Willow Grant** (960 Queen Street W, 416 533 7553, www.willowgrant.com) is a Canadian fashion gallery named after the shop's two iguanas, which roam the front window when there's sunshine. The focus is on Toronto, Montreal and Vancouver designers, with Domistyle aprons, one-of-a-kind handbags from My Old Pants, and SDG 033. The core labels remains the same, with refreshing additions changing monthly, as fashion designers rent individual racks devoted to their works of style.

See also p148 **Boutiques**.

Eat, Drink, Shop

Chocky's former location in Chinatown was a local institution for parents of kids stocking up on mini versions of underwear, T-shirts, pyjamas and rain gear. At this smaller downtown space, the cut-rate pricing system remains, along with trendier clothing at great prices.
Other locations: 2584 Yonge Street, North Toronto (416 483 8227).

Misdemeanours
322½ Queen Street W, at Spadina Avenue, Entertainment District (416 351 8758). Streetcar 501, 510. **Open** 10am-7pm Mon-Wed; 10am-8pm Thur; 10am-9pm Fri; 10am-8pm Sat; noon-6pm Sun. **Credit** AmEx, MC, V. **Map** p279 D7.
Like their mums, who wear the theatrical Fashion Crimes label from mother label across the street, little girls just wanna have fun. Expect to see a feather boa paired with these outfits, trimmed with marabou, faux fur or other amusing synthetics. Proper colours make a change from run-of-the-mill pastels, and tutus and crinolines are everyday wear.

Designer

The strip of Bloor Street West from Yonge Street to Avenue Road, once known to locals as the 'mink mile', is heaven for lovers of luxury labels, with branches of everything from Chanel to Tiffany, via Gucci, Prada, Hermès, and more.

General

Club Monaco
157 Bloor Street W, at Avenue Road, Yorkville (416 591 8837/www.clubmonaco.com). Subway Bay or Museum. **Open** 10am-8pm Mon-Wed; 10am-9pm Thur, Fri; 10am-7pm Sat; 11am-7pm Sun. **Credit** AmEx, MC, V. **Map** p282 F4.
CM was one of the first fashion chains to recognise the elegance of Japanese lines and simple, patternless colour. What then made it an international star was its outstanding pricing. Designs are wearable and affordable: buy a pair of jeans and a ribbed turtleneck and you'll have them for life – and neither will you suffer embarrassing out-of-fashion stigma. Sale items are ubiquitous, as are locations – in every mall and shopping district in the city, but this Bloor Street flagship, in a Greek Revival heritage building, has the best pedigree and selection.
Other locations: throughout the city.

Lileo
Building 35, 55 Mill Street, at Parliament Street, Distillery District (416 413 1410/www.lileo.ca). Bus 65. **Open** 11am-7pm Mon-Wed; 11am-8pm Thur-Sat; 11am-6pm Sun. **Credit** AmEx, DC, MC, V. **Map** p280 H8.
A sprawling space in the historic Distillery District, this lifestyle and fitness emporium is named after Galileo (with a juice bar christened for his daughter Livia). From glitter-encrusted cashmere hoodies to faux-retro Ts, to the trendy revival of classic

brands like Lacoste, Original Penguin and Frye Boots, to recherché garments hand-dyed and woven in Africa, handmade soaps and skincare, to designer Birkenstocks – it's all here. The yoga wear is worn by urbanites as much for work as for workouts, while some of the price tags prove that chic healthy living comes at a premium.

Over the Rainbow
101 Yorkville Avenue, at Hazelton Avenue, Yorkville (416 967 7448). Subway Bay or Museum. **Open** 10am-6pm Mon-Wed, Sat; 10am-8pm Thur, Fri; noon-5pm Sun. **Credit** AmEx, MC, V. **Map** p282 F4.
Push past bratty teens with mums in tow to discover the latest in denim (the fact that the kids actually want to shop here proves that the jeans are up-to-date at least). Styles are stacked with precision from floor to ceiling. Also available are fun and sporty T-shirts, sweats and accessories from Juicy, Paul Frank, Triple Five Soul, Chip & Pepper, Miss Sixty and Diesel.

Roots
Toronto Eaton Centre, 220 Yonge Street, at Dundas Street, Dundas Square (416 593 9640/ www.roots.ca). Streetcar 505/subway Dundas. **Open** 10am-9pm Mon-Fri; 10am-7pm Sat; 11am-6pm Sun. **Credit** AmEx, DC, MC, V. **Map** p280 G6.
You won't meet anyone in the city who doesn't remember a favourite Roots possession, whether it's a sweatshirt, a fleece or a pair of clunky boots. The Canadian icon started cobbling reverse-heel shoes in the '70s, then branched out into leisurewear – to the joy of outdoor folk everywhere. Today styles are spicier, but you can still find the basics.
Other locations: throughout the city.

Menswear

Boomer
309 Queen Street W, at John Street, Entertainment District (416 598 0013). Streetcar 501/subway Osgoode. **Open** 10.30am-7pm Mon-Wed, Fri; 10.30am-8pm Thur; 10.30am-6pm Sat; 1-5pm Sun. **Credit** AmEx, DC, MC, V. **Map** p279 E7.
Boomer offers the best (Boss, Ted Baker et al) of what you'd find at the finer department stores, and stock is chosen with the Queen Street crowd in mind. Their own-brand output is restricted to French-cut dress shirts.

Grreat Stuff
870 Queen Street W, at Massey Street, West End (416 533 7680). Streetcar 501. **Open** 11am-7pm Tue, Wed, Fri; 11am-8pm Thur; 10am-6pm Sat; noon-5pm Sun. **Credit** DC, MC, V. **Map** p278 B7.
The offerings at Grreat Stuff look like a vintage clothes store but the retro feel comes from the choice of designer samples and line ends from Kenneth Cole, Mexx, Tony Bahama and others. Fitted shirts, silk sweaters and Swedish suits are part of a constantly changing inventory, with prices well below the norm.

Eat, Drink, Shop

Harry Rosen

82 Bloor Street W, at Bellair Street, Yorkville (416 972 0556/www.harryrosen.com). Subway Bloor-Yonge. **Open** 10am-7pm Mon-Wed; 10am-9pm Thur, Fri; 10am-6pm Sat; noon-6pm Sun. **Credit** AmEx, DC, MC, V. **Map** p282 F4.

Some might snub Harry Rosen for being on the conservative side of the spectrum (let's face it, he's been around for 50 years), yet there was a time when he was the only game in town for respectable styling – one brogue-shod step from Savile Row. Service is also top-notch.

Other locations: throughout the city.

Street/clubwear

Châteauworks

340 Queen Street W, at Spadina Avenue, Entertainment District (416 971 9314/www.le-chateau.com). Streetcar 501, 510. **Open** 10am-9pm Mon-Fri; 9.30am-7pm Sat; noon-6pm Sun. **Credit** AmEx, MC, V. **Map** p279 D7.

The Montreal-based trend machine Le Château claimed this as its Toronto flagship years ago. Anything the clothier offers can be had here: men's polyester club shirts with collars that could cut bread, floor-length faux-suede coats with faux-fur trim, kids' hipsters… If you don't mind the patchy quality, you can get away with buying a season's wardrobe for under $300.

Vintage/second-hand

Bungalow

273 Augusta Avenue, at Nassau Street, Kensington Market (416 598 0204). Streetcar 506, 510. **Open** 11am-6.30pm Mon, Tue; 11am-7pm Wed-Sat; 11am-6pm Sun. **Credit** MC, V. **Map** p279 D6.

This Kensington Market shop is an ode to mid-century modern, with outrageously affordable teak furnishings, shag rugs, sofas and barware scattered among its racks of second-hand clothing. Regular browsing pays off: in among the rockabilly cowboy shirts, Levi's cords and leather jackets you might unearth a Lilly Pulitzer shirtwaist or a Halston jersey dress, at well below market prices. The airy open-concept space means there's no telltale musty smell, just a clean, well-edited selection.

Courage My Love

14 Kensington Avenue, at Dundas Street W, Chinatown (416 979 1992). Streetcar 505, 510. **Open** 11.30am-6pm Mon-Fri; 11am-6pm Sat; 2-5pm Sun. **Credit** AmEx, MC, V. **Map** p279 D6.

Courage came along (decades ago) and made Kensington Market a centre for vintage chic. It's a family affair, and still the cheapest ticket in town for frumpy but fabulous eveningwear, tuxedoes, cufflinks, leather, crafts, exotic costume jewellery and whimsical buttons. The store also creates very on-trend, limited runs of re-tailored threads, made from charity shop odds and ends.

Paper Bag Princess

287 Davenport Road, at Bedford Road, The Annex (416 925 2603/www.thepaperbagprincess.com). Bus 26/subway Dupont. **Open** 11am-7pm Mon-Fri; 11am-6pm Sat. **Credit** AmEx, MC, V. **Map** p282 E3.

Collector and owner Elizabeth Mason was dealing in vintage couture long before it became a red-carpet staple (Julia Roberts, Madonna, Jennifer Aniston and SJP are just a few of her famous fans). Happily, Mason keeps her Toronto outpost as well stocked as her LA shop. Alaia, Pucci and Missoni are recent favourites.

Preloved

613 Queen Street W, at Bathurst Street, Entertainment District (416 504 8704/www.preloved.ca). Streetcar 501, 511. **Open** 10am-7pm Mon, Tue, Sat; 10am-8pm Wed-Fri; noon-6pm Sun. **Credit** AmEx, MC, V. **Map** p279 D7.

Though Preloved's prices have shot up in recent years, they're still reasonable considering their cachet. The signature collection is creatively cut and pasted from clothing discards. The T-shirts are the most fun, bearing logos and embellishments from defunct bands and summer camps.

Fashion accessories

Handbags

Jeanne Lottie Fashion

106 Yorkville Avenue, at Bay Street, Yorkville (416 975 5115/www.jeannelottie.com). Bus 6/subway Bay. **Open** 10.30am-6pm Mon-Sat; noon-5pm Sun. **Credit** AmEx, MC, V. **Map** p282 F4.

Designer Jane Ip is Canada's answer to Kate Spade – and her perky must-have bags are sold at her Yorkville store, and shops around the country. Thankfully (because it's difficult to leave with less than two), Ip's on-trend accessories – tweed, fun fur or faux shearling – cost less than $100.

Hats

Lilliput Hats

462 College Street, at Bathurst Street, Harbord (416 536 5933). Streetcar 506, 511. **Open** 10am-6pm Mon-Fri; 11am-6pm Sat; by appointment Sun. **Credit** MC, V. **Map** p279 D5.

Milliners are an endangered breed in Toronto, but the lust for vintage has brought hats back. Lilliput makes the classic cloche and the mohair fedora redux, along with other hip headwear.

Jewellery

Birks

55 Bloor Street W, at Bay Street, Yorkville (416 922 2266/www.birks.com). Bus 6/subway Bay. **Open** 10am-6pm Mon-Thur, Sat; 10am-7pm Fri; noon-5pm Sun. **Credit** AmEx, DC, MC, V. **Map** p282 F4.

Celebrating over 125 years in the business, this venerable Canadian jewellery house occupies a stately corner of the otherwise modern ManuLife Centre. In an attempt to shed its mumsy reputation, the company recently hired noted fashion journalist Holly Brubach (former style editor of the *New York Times Magazine*). The 'new Birks' now offers more showy bling, from over-the-top glam charm bracelets studded with jewels to sleek everyday silver. An ever-changing selection of fine vintage jewellery and homeware is also a draw.

Other locations: Toronto Eaton Centre, 220 Yonge Street, Dundas Square (416 979 9311); First Canadian Place, 100 King Street W, Financial District, 416 363 5663.

Experimetal Jewellery

588 Markham Street, at Bloor Street, West End (416 538 3313/www.experimetal.com). Streetcar 511/subway Bathurst. **Open** 11am-6pm Tue, Wed; 11am-7pm Thur, Fri; 10am-6pm Sat; noon-5pm Sun. **Credit** AmEx, MC, V.

Even if organic shapes and unusual settings aren't your thing, this petite boutique is still worth a peek for undulating metal studded with stones. Designer Anne Sportun's hands and rings have even been featured on a Canadian postage stamp.

Other locations: 742 Queen Street W, West End (416 363 4114).

Made You Look
Jewellery Studio & Gallery

1338 Queen Street W, at Dufferin Street, West End (416 463 2136/www.madeyoulook.ca). Streetcar 501, 504. **Open** 10am-6pm daily. **Credit** MC, V. **Map** p278 A7.

Just a block from the new hipster central of Parkdale lies Sarah Dougall's treasure trove of over 40 homegrown jewellery designers. Prices cover the range, and each artist is a find, working in such materials as resin, copper, glass, pearls and crystal. Look out for local darlings Cinelli & Maillet.

Mink

550A College Street, at Euclid Avenue, Little Italy (416 929 9214). Streetcar 506, 511. **Open** 11am-7pm Tue-Fri; 11am-6pm Sat. **Credit** AmEx, DC, MC, V. **Map** p278 C5.

A pink sliver of a shop, replete with fabulous faux baubles, for diamond lovers who can't afford the real thing. Fake flash comes in the form of rhinestone rings and monogram necklaces, but daintier pieces are sold too. Call to check opening times before setting off.

Shelly Purdy Studio

Suite 501, 296 Richmond Street W, at John Street, Entertainment District (416 340 7581/www.shellypurdy.com). Streetcar 501/subway Osgoode. **Open** 10am-6pm Tue-Fri; 11am-5pm Sat. **Credit** MC, V. **Map** p279 E7.

Since 1987 Shelly Purdy has been specialising in beautiful diamonds, particularly AURIAS diamonds (from the Ekati mine in the chilly Canadian tundra),

Pick up a picnic

Torontonians are masters at making the most of the good weather. From the first day of spring right through to crisp autumn days, you'll spot picnickers of all varieties. Families spread across the lawns on Centre Island, four generations in tow, with brimming baskets, portable grills and tape players for cranking out tinny sounds. Couples share gourmet sandwiches and fruit smoothies on a bench; schoolkids snack in the sun; and lone sightseers tuck into ripe juicy peaches while mooching around downtown.

If you want to join the crowds and shop for your own fixings, any of the farmers' markets will do. There's one on a Saturday at **St Lawrence Market** (*see p159*), with vendors selling fresh fruit and veg. Alternatively, grab a back bacon sarnie at the Carousel Bakery, while perusing the goodies at the more than 50 food stands, including cheese shops and deli counters. Try the flavoured mustards at Anton Kozlik's Mustard Emporium, the smoked fish at Domino's or the soft breads at Future Bakery (*see also p117* **D'ough!** for this and more of our favourite bakeries).

Across town, **Kensington**'s outdoor bazaar (*see p156*) stretches for blocks. Perfect for organic coffees, samosas, cheeses,

falafels and wholesome breads – and with a little reggae thrown in for atmosphere, you might decide to have your picnic right here, concrete be damned. Fresh produce ranges from the local to the exotic and prices are generally reasonable.

Throughout the week, afternoon farmers' markets pop up in parks around town. Tuesdays is **Riverdale Park** (Winchester and Sumach Streets, 416 961 8787, 3-7pm, early May to late October); Wednesdays is **Nathan Phillips Square** (Bay and Queen Streets, 416 338 0338, 10am-2.30pm, June-Oct) and Thursdays is **Dufferin Grove Park** (875 Dufferin Street, 416 392 0913, 3-7pm, year-round).

For a picnic that will have people hovering over you in awe, try something more adventurous. How about samplings of maple vinegar, spicy cedar or chokecherry jelly and wild rose petal syrup, for instance? These are some of the discovered delights in Jonathan Forbes' wild and wonderful cupboard. Stop in at **Magnolia Fine Foods** (548 College Street, 416 920 9927) in Little Italy for the best selection of Forbes Wild Foods (www.wildfoods.ca). Toronto indeed has a *sauvage* side. Dig in!

---

which are coveted by her luxe international clientele. Thankfully, however, she can cater to most price brackets: the Achievement (stackable nesting diamond) rings created to celebrate each of life's milestones, start at a reasonable $350. Collections include Celtic Rune (inspired by symbols of fertility and love) and Canadian Jungle (ornate foliage surrounding cultured pearls and coloured stones).

Leather

Augustina
5 Old York Lane, 138 Cumberland Street, at Avenue Road, Yorkville (416 922 4248). Bus 6/subway Bay. **Open** 10am-6pm Mon-Wed, Sat; 10am-7pm Thur, Fri; noon-5pm Sun. **Credit** AmEx, MC, V. **Map** p282 F4.
Most designer handbags have a knock-off twin somewhere in the world. But few pirates could mimic Augustina's imports – gasp-worthy bags that are rarely spotted elsewhere, from some of the world's most underrated designers. Lauren Merkin is a perennial favourite, along with perfumes from Miller Harris and whisper-soft cashmere separates. A good selection of top-end accessories also includes costume jewellery, belts and underwear.

Lingerie

Nearly Naked
749 Queen Street W, just west of Palmerston Avenue, West End (416 703 7561). Streetcar 501, 511. **Open** 11am-6pm Mon-Wed, Sat; 11am-7pm Thur, Fri; noon-5pm Sun. **Credit** AmEx, DC, MC, V. **Map** p278 C7.
Nearly Naked is a hip but no-fuss neighbourhood lingerie haunt. Everything is here, from boy-cut briefs to the boulder holders of the reputable (but not always cheap) speciality brands, plus hosiery, comfy sleep and loungewear, a dash of ruffled satin and racy black lace, and jersey camis of local label Sister Underwear.

Secrets From Your Sister...
476 Bloor Street W, at Bathurst Street, The Annex (416 538 1234). Streetcar 511/subway Bathurst. **Open** 11am-7pm Mon-Wed, Fri; 9.30am-8pm Thur; 10am-6pm Sat; noon-6pm Sun. **Credit** AmEx, MC, V. **Map** p282 D4.
Another neighbourhood favourite, especially with busty gals and those with a thirst for the exotic who prefer pretty and funky to department store fare. The styles, fabrics and outlandish colours are unlike anything your mother ever recommended, though sensible nursing bras and cosy flannel Nick & Nora pyjamas ensure things don't get out of hand.

Shoes

B2

*399 Queen Street W, at Spadina Avenue,
Entertainment District (416 595 9281). Streetcar
501, 510.* **Open** 10am-7pm Mon-Wed, Sat, Sun;
10am-9pm Thur, Fri. **Credit** AmEx, MC, V.
Map p279 D7.
This boutique's parent company, Browns, can be
found in swish department stores and upscale malls.
But B2 is more fun – if only for gawking at eccen-
tric four-inchers you know you can't afford. It car-
ries the international – Costume National, Miu Miu,
Hush Puppy, Camper and Frye – along with its own
Euro-looking brands at more reasonable prices.

Bootmaster

*609 Yonge Street, at Gloucester Street, Church
& Wellesley (416 927 1054/www.bootmaster.com).
Subway Wellesley.* **Open** 10am-7pm Mon-Sat; noon-
5pm Sun. **Credit** AmEx, MC, V. **Map** p283 G5.
The giant red cowboy boot has been parked on the
sidewalk here since 1986; staff often ship to loyal
customers worldwide, and the walls are lined with
photos autographed by celeb clients. They're
known for fair prices and a comprehensive selection of cowboy leather gear, from jackets and accessories, such as hand-tooled silver belt buckles
inlaid with lapis and turquoise, to the main event:
boots from Tony Lama, Justin and Boulet, all types
of Frye (plus Small Frye for the kids), Chippewa for
the motorcycle set, and the colourful, elaborate
handmade boots from the Old Gringo.

Davids

*66 Bloor Street W, at Yonge Street, Yorkville (416
920 1000). Subway Bloor-Yonge.* **Open** 9am-6pm
Mon-Wed, Sat; 9am-8pm Thur, Fri; noon-5pm Sun.
Credit AmEx, MC, V. **Map** p283 G4.
If the currency exchange is working in your favour,
you'll find Davids more rewarding than the average foot fetishist shoe shops. The spotlight is on
high Italian designs – including impressively high
stilettos – in buttery leathers.

John Fluevog Shoes

*242 Queen Street W, at John Street, Entertainment
District (416 581 1420/www.fluevog.com). Streetcar
501/subway Osgoode.* **Open** 11am-7pm Mon-Wed,
Sat; 11am-8pm Thur, Fri; noon-6pm Sun. **Credit**
AmEx, MC, V. **Map** p279 E7.
The Vancouver-based cobbler with goth beginnings is now something of a legend, as much for
his inventive, colourful curlicues and oddball
shapes as his irreverent marketing and kitschy
style names. The fact that the shoes (men's,
women's and unisex) are also surprisingly comfortable enhances their cult fashion status.

Zola Shoes

*1726 Avenue Road, at St Germain Avenue, North
Toronto (416 783 8688). Bus 61/subway Lawrence.*
Open 10am-6pm Mon-Wed, Fri, Sat; 10am-8pm
Thur; noon-5pm Sun. **Credit** AmEx, MC, V.

This uptown boutique is for the well-heeled, in both
senses, with offerings from Alexandra Neel,
Franklin Elman, Hollywould, Edmundo Castillo,
Emma Hope and Rodolphe Menudier – in short,
everything to make an unrepentant designer shoe
fetishist quake in her Sigersons, with bags (and
price tags) to match.

Fashion services

Dry-cleaners

Dove Cleaners

*1560 Yonge Street, at Heath Street, Forest Hill (416
413 7900/www.dovecleaners.com). Subway St Clair.*
Open 7.30am-8pm Mon-Fri; 9am-6pm Sat. **Credit**
AmEx, MC, V.
With home and office pick-up and delivery (an easy
net-based system is in place), Dove's high-end
service is ideal for the moneyed customer.
Other locations: 40 King Street W, Financial
District (416 869 3000).

Splish Splash

*590 College Street, at Clinton Street, Little Italy
(416 532 6499). Streetcar 506.* **Open** 8am-10pm
Mon-Fri; 9am-8pm Sat, Sun. **No credit cards**.
Map p278 C5.
This launderette/convenience store is a friendly
meeting place for young urban types.

Shoe repair

Nick's Shoes & Custom Footwear

*169 Dupont Street, at St George Street, The Annex
(416 924 5930/www.nickscustomboots.com). Subway
Dupont.* **Open** 8am-6.30pm Mon-Fri; 9am-5pm Sat.
No credit cards. **Map** p282 E2.
Nick is known for his reliability and skill: you're
unlikely to lose a heel twice if he's in your little black
book. His auxiliary talent is for imitation – he can
craft fancy footwear for a snip of the usual price.

Novelty Shoe Rebuilders

*119 Yonge Street, at Adelaide Street, St Lawrence
(416 364 8878). Streetcar 501, 504/subway King or
Queen.* **Open** 8.30am-5.30pm Mon-Fri; 8.30am-5pm
Sat. **Credit** MC, V. **Map** p280 G7.
Shoe styles come and go but this institution has been
taking care of wayward soles for 70 years at the
same location in the Financial District. Repairs are
done while you wait or slip into one of the funky
wooden booths for a quick polish.

Flowers

The strip of sidewalk along Avenue Road just
south of Davenport Road is known for its
buckets of fresh and flamboyant cut flowers.
Also doubling as mini grocers, the Chinese
shops that line the west side of the street teem
with inexpensive stems and bunches.

Eat, Drink, Shop

Kensington Market

Kensington Market isn't everyone's cup of tea. If your budget is suited more to a Chanel store than a charity shop, head instead for the designer shops of Yorkville. If, on the other hand, you like to browse among bargains, you'll be in your element. A cluster of narrow, shop-lined streets, the market is home to a mixed bag, from the dowdy (bike mechanics, racks of rags and kiosks of cheap luggage) to the delightful.

Begin with brunch at the **Bellevue Diner** (61 Bellevue Avenue, 416 597 6912) or at the lovely **La Palette** (*see p114*), then find your way to the top of Augusta Avenue for a logical entry point. Knitwear specialist **Fresh Baked Goods** (274 Augusta Avenue, 416 966 0123) is a punchy start, with its shocking-hued angora. Styles are funky by nature, sleeves fashionably long and hems flared. Next door is **Bungalow** (*see p152*), a must for fossickers of mid-century modern. The oddest corner shop in town is **Casa Acoreana** (235 Augusta Avenue, 416 593 9717), a general store stocked with numerous glass jars of candy, nuts, grains and baking goods on one side, the other side, called **Louie's Coffee Stop**, is an open coffee hut, inviting shoppers to pull up a stool for a quick cup of joe. A holdover from the market's days as a Jewish textile centre, **Tom's Place** (190 Baldwin Street, 416 596 0297) is a famed no-frills discount fashion outlet. Women's clothing (German sportswear classics Kasper and Gina B) and Italian designer samples from brands like Versace hold court on the ground floor, but the upstairs men's department is the real draw, offering suits by Zegna, Boss and Armani at prices lower than a department store's summer sale.

If you haven't already enjoyed the market's pungent odour, you'll find an interesting mix of aromas at neighbouring **My Market Bakery** (172 Baldwin Street, 416 593 6772), **European Quality Meats & Sausages** (174 Baldwin Street, 416 596 8691) and **Cheese Magic** (182 Baldwin Street, 416 593 9531). Kensington 'proper' is where the sartorial grit begins, with a string of vintage boutiques virtually indistinguishable from each other, with racks of denim and leather displayed on the sidewalk (**Asylum**, 62 Kensington Avenue, 416 595 7199, is the prime offender). One of the best, and under the same ownership as Asylum, is **Exile** (20 Kensington Avenue, 416 596 0827), a forum for outlandish retro and new fetish wear, with its own press for iron-on T-shirts. The legendary **Courage My Love** (*see p152*) is at the end of the row.

Note that Monday to Saturday is generally the best time to visit the market, as not every outlet is open on a Sunday.

Food & drink

Alcohol

Every now and then the provincial government considers the possibility that Ontarians are responsible enough to buy their booze from the private sector. But then that $1-billion-a-year dividend generated by the Liquor Control Board of Ontario (**LCBO**) brings them back to their senses. Efforts to spruce up the stores are impressive, but there never seems to be one open when you need one. The newly refurbished LCBO store in a landmark train station (10 Scrivener Square, Rosedale, 416 922 0403) boasts vintage rooms and cooking classes. LCBOs stock a full range of wines and spirits, plus some domestic and imported beers, and can be found at 87 Front Street E, St Lawrence (416 368 0521), 337 Spadina Avenue, Chinatown (416 597 0145), in the Atrium on Bay (595 Bay Street, Dundas Square, 416 979 9978), 545 Yonge Street, Church & Wellesley (416 923 8498) and in the Manulife Centre, Yorkville (416 925 5266). For general information, call 1-800 668 5226. Most shops open at 10am weekdays and noon on weekends.

The only competition comes from **Wine Rack** (560 Queen Street W, Entertainment District, 416 504 3647), a small chain licensed to sell Ontario wines.

Beer Stores are a separate monopoly, owned and operated by the big breweries. Downtown branches include 572 Church Street (Church & Wellesley 416 921 6036); 452 Bathurst Street (Little Italy, 416 923 4535); 614 Queen Street West at Bathurst (416 504 4665) and 534 Parliament Street (Cabbagetown, 416 925 1915).

Bakeries

Clafouti

915 Queen Street W, at Gore Vale Avenue, West End (416 603 1935). Streetcar 501. **Open** 8am-6pm Tue-Sat; 9am-5pm Sun. **No credit cards. Map** p278 C7.

Tarts come in individual or family size, glazed and quivering with freshness. There's a selection of imported French jams, jellies and candies, and the fabled buttery croissants (plain, or with rose or cinnamon flavourings) are gone by 11am on weekends.

Harbord Bakery

115 Harbord Street, at Major Street, Harbord (416 922 5767). Bus 94/streetcar 510. **Open** 8am-7pm Mon-Thur; 8am-6pm Fri, Sat; 8am-4pm Sun. **Credit** MC, V. **Map** p282 D4.

This Jewish bakery has been here since the mid 1900s, when Eastern Europeans began arriving in the neighbourhood. You can still find some of the city's freshest chollah, rye bread and bagels (with huge, twisted variations), and a selection of pastries, strudels and tarts.

Confectioners

Nostalgia is a sweet thing, and various sugary testaments to childhood times past have cropped up around town over the past ten years. The first **Sugar Mountain** opened in clubland (320 Richmond Street W, Entertainment District, 416 204 9544, www.sugarmountain.net), but soon expanded into the Yonge Street, St Clair and Queen West areas. The copycat **Suckers** (450 Danforth Avenue, East Toronto, 416 405 8946) tends to be patronised by Greektown yuppies. Chocolate and fudge nuts in the Beaches head for the **Nutty Chocolatier** (2179 Queen Street E, 416 698 5548, www.nuttychocolatier.com), while in the Distillery District, **Soma** (Building 47, 416 815 7662, www.somachocolate.com) serves up the brown nectar in the form of Mayan hot chocolate, spiced with chilli and cinnamon, as well as more mainstream (but equally glorious) flavours. **Laura Secord** (Yorkdale Shopping Centre, 3401 Dufferin Street, North Toronto, 416 789 5697, as well as other mall locations) is a local institution as a purveyor of bite-size candy bars. **JS Bonbons** (811 Queen Street W, West End, 416 703 7731, www.jsbonbons.com) is a local favourite for hand-sculpted works of chocolate art with a contemporary twist on flavourings; it also has a branch in Midtown.

Gourmet grocers

Dinah's Cupboard
50 Cumberland Street, at Bay Street, Yorkville (416 921 8112). Subway Bay, Bloor or Yonge. **Open** 9am-7pm Mon-Fri; 9am-6pm Sat. **Credit** AmEx, MC, V. **Map** 282 F4.
This deceptively small boite is stocked with treasures for the discerning palate. In addition to the delicious prepared foods – from cheesy lasagne to fragrant Asian salads – the deli counter packs foie gras, fine terrines and artisan cheeses. There's also a good selection of spices, teas and coffees and select oils.

Pusateri's
57 Yorkville Avenue, at Bay Street, Yorkville (416 785 9100/www.pusateris.com). Bus 6/subway Bay. **Open** 10am-8pm Mon-Wed; 10am-9pm Thur, Fri; 8am-8pm Sat; 10am-7pm Sun. **Credit** AmEx, MC, V. **Map** p282 F4.
Uptown society matrons send their nannies here for groceries, or pop by themselves for gourmet take-away. It's a pricey one-stop for folk who value time over money, but the downtown location's sleek new design and outstanding imported foods, plus ready-made food service, make it a favourite for everyone, even those who can't regularly afford to shop here. **Other locations:** 1539 Avenue Road, North Toronto (416 785 9100).

Grocers

Dominion
89 Gould Street, at Church Street, Dundas Square (416 862 7171/www.freshobsessed.com). Streetcar 505/subway Dundas. **Open** 24hrs daily. **Credit** AmEx, MC, V. **Map** p280 G6.
Dominion's motto proclaims they're fresh obsessed, but it's not as pretty nor expansive in layout as its yuppie competitor, Loblaws. At some locations you'll queue for a cashier or get lost in the labyrinth and odd organisation, but the flexible hours (some outlets are open 24 hours) make it a favourite among students, shift workers and all-night revellers. **Other locations:** throughout the city.

Loblaws
650 Dupont Street, at Christie Street, West End (416 588 4881/www.loblaws.ca). Bus 26/subway Christie or Dupont. **Open** 8am-10pm Mon-Sat; 9am-8pm Sun. **Credit** MC, V.
It's been around since 1919, but until recently Loblaws was just your average grocer. Then the stores began a clean-up process and expanded into veritable mini-malls: well lit, with in-house cafés, culinary classes, kids' cookery programmes, wine depots, exotic fresh fish, sushi chefs and dry-cleaners. Service is swift and, despite its gilded appearance, Loblaws keeps prices competitive.

Other locations: 10 Lower Jarvis Street, at Queen's Key, St Lawrence (416 304 0611); 396 St Clair W, at Bathurst Street, Casa Loma (416 651 5166).

Health food

The Big Carrot
348 Danforth Avenue, at Hampton Avenue, East Toronto (416 466 2129/www.thebigcarrot.ca). Subway Chester. **Open** Shop 9.30am-8pm Mon-Wed; 9.30am-9pm Thur, Fri; 9am-7pm Sat; 11am-6pm Sun. Juice Bar 9am-8pm Mon-Wed; 9am-9pm Thur, Fri; 9am-7pm Sat; 10.30am-6pm Sun. **Credit** MC, V.
Social consciousness and groceries didn't mix back when this worker-owned cooperative opened 20 years ago. Today, even though prices are what you'd expect in a niche market, it's near impossible to squeeze in here – especially at weekends – even though it's the biggest natural food store in the city. Expect to find free-range chicken and eggs, sustainably harvested fish, supplements, organic meat, and just about anything else you can imagine.

Noah's Natural Foods
322 Bloor Street W, at Spadina Avenue, The Annex (416 968 7930). Streetcar 510/subway Spadina. **Open** 10am-8pm Mon-Wed; 10am-9pm Thur, Fri; 10am-7pm Sat; 11am-6pm Sun. **Credit** AmEx, MC, V. **Map** p282 D4.
A favourite pitstop for Annex dwellers on their way home from yoga, Noah's has been around these parts for decades. The growing obsession with organic and all-natural foods has no doubt brought about its recent growth, and now you can find your alfalfa sprouts, carob chips and oatmeal cleansers at several handy points in the city. There's also a vegan café for those of you who simply can't wait to tuck in. **Other locations:** 667 Yonge Street, Church & Wellesley (416 969 0220); 2395 Yonge Street, North Toronto (416 488 0904).

Whole Foods Market
Hazelton Lanes, 55 Avenue Road, at Bloor Street, Yorkville (416 944 0500/www.wholefoods.com). Bus 6/subway Bay. **Open** 9am-10pm Mon-Fri; 9am-9pm Sat, Sun. **Credit** AmEx, MC, V. **Map** p282 F3/4.
This Texas-based healthy foods conglomerate has more than 130 stores in North America. To date this is the only Canadian outpost, offering a rainbow of fresh produce, striking seafood displays, a sushi bar, preservative-free baked goods, natural meats, international cheeses and a gourmet deli. Some gripe that the prices are as high as the level of health consciousness, but you get what you pay for.

Speciality

Greg's Ice Cream
750 Bloor Street W, at Spadina Avenue, The Annex (416 962 4734). Subway Spadina. **Open** 11.30am-10pm Mon-Thur, Sun; 11.30am-11pm Fri, Sat. **No credit cards. Map** p282 D4/E4.

After 22 years in a basement location, Toronto's favourite ice-cream parlour has moved to a new location – behind a plate-glass storefront at the Jewish Community Centre in the Annex near U of T – and it's line-up central come summertime, as they dish out pints of the most evocative and unusual handmade flavours. The palate-pleasing roasted marshmallow is famous far and wide, and the coffee toffee is made with real cream, real coffee and chunks of bittersweet brittle. Divine.

Kristapsons

1095 Queen Street E, at Winnifred Avenue, East End (416 466 5152). Bus 72/streetcar 501. **Open** by appointment only Mon; 9am-4pm Tue-Thur; 9am-noon Sat. **Credit** V.

In this age of diversification, you'll be hard-pressed to find another Kristapsons. Andris Grinbergs continues Adolph Kristapson's Latvian tradition selling cold-smoked BC salmon. Order ahead and your catch will be smoked on the premises.

St Lawrence Market

fresh maritime LOBSTER 11 99 lb

Named one of the world's 25 best food markets by *Food & Wine* magazine, St Lawrence doesn't disappoint. The market has come along way since it opened two centuries ago; 'market' used to mean cheap eats, but today's vendors have cottoned on to the going rates and now prices match the mainstream. But that doesn't seem to put anyone off: the market is as popular now as ever, with a huge range of fresh local produce, plus international and deli items.

It can be hard for an outsider to evaluate the mass of similar stalls, so it's best to tour the premises before making your choices. On the ground floor, sample from the wheels and wedges of international cheeses from **Alex Farms** or **Chris Cheesemonger**, a specialist in Quebecois provisions who also dishes out fantastic Middle Eastern dips. The **Mustard Emporium** is, not surprisingly, the place to pick up the hot stuff – more than 80 gourmet varieties, in fact (our tip: Rib-B-Que). Seafood is everywhere; if you're here for a quick bite, buy slice or two of freshly smoked salmon or Arctic char at **Seafront**, then queue up for a bagel at **St Urbain**, one of the few bakers in the city offering the Montreal style: dense, chewy and salty. **Churrasco of St Clair**, a satellite of the famed uptown take-out churrasqueira, makes a killer chicken sandwich on a kaiser roll.

The traditional fast food offering here is a peameal sandwich – thick slices of cornmeal-crusted bacon on a doughy kaiser, best smothered in mustard. You can't miss the queues at **Carousel** bakery along the west wall, though they are served at other stands too. Fruit and veg are downstairs, and some stalls present exotic picks. But the top-notch nosh is found in the furthest reaches of the basement, where barrels of bulk food – nuts, chocolate, confectionery – beg to be bagged at **Domino's**. Across the street, in a building characterised by the cheerful mural painted along its side, a farmer's market takes place on Saturdays (5am-5pm), hosted by a motley crew of overalled and aproned visitors from small towns in the area. On Sundays the space is taken over by an antiques fair.

Special events and exhibitions are held frequently on site, and two-hour guided tours of the market and surrounding area set off daily, Wednesday to Saturday at 10am (tickets $20; call 416 392 0028 for reservations).

St Lawrence Market

92 Front Street E, at Jarvis Street, St Lawrence (416 392 7219/www.stlawrence market.com). Streetcar 504. **Open** 8am-6pm Tue-Thur; 8am-7pm Fri; 5am-5pm Sat. *Antiques market* 8am-5pm Sun. **Map** p280 G8.

Eat, Drink, Shop

Sanko Trading Co

*730 Queen Street W, at Niagara Street, West End
(416 703 4550). Streetcar 501, 511.* **Open** 10am-
7pm Mon, Wed-Sun. **Credit** V. **Map** p278 C7.
It keeps a veritable library of Japanese mags and
weird-looking videos, but you're more likely to leave
Sanko with a jar of miso soup or a wad of seaweed.
Kids are kept enthralled by confectionery, cookies
and drinks imported from the Far East, while health-
conscious shoppers head for the macha powder.

La Paloma Gelateria

*1357 St Clair Avenue W, at Lonsdale Avenue, Forest
Hill (416 656 2340). Subway St Clair West.* **Open**
7am-11.30pm daily. **No credit cards**.
With 200 flavours of authentic Italian ice-cream in
its repertoire, and about 50 on hand at any given
time, this classic gelateria is the choice of local
Italians. Though the prices are higher than competitors, so is the quality. Chestnut or fig, Ferrero
Rocher or traditional zabaglione… the list is deli-
ciously and deliriously overwhelming. For savoury
treats, there's a traditional panino counter out back.

Gay & lesbian

See p195.

Gifts & specialist

Art Interiors

*Unit 205, 446 Spadina Road, at Lonsdale Avenue,
Forest Hill (416 488 3157). Subway St Clair West.*
Open 10am-5pm Mon-Sat. **Credit** MC, V.
It takes an experienced eye to spot quality artwork,
but the owners of Art Interiors make it their business to scout around. They celebrate the finest new
and unknown artists in town, then push their pieces
at this loft boutique in Forest Hill Village. Prices are
remarkably low for originals this appealing.

Frank Correnti Cigars Ltd

*606 King Street W, at Portland Street,
Entertainment District (416 504 4108).
Streetcar 510.* **Open** 8am-8pm Mon-Sat.
Credit AmEx, MC, V. **Map** p279 D8.
Walking inside this place is like to stepping on to the
set of *Carmen*. Hand-rolled cigars are fashioned from
Cuban raw leaf, so as well as more casual puffers
clientele includes movie stars and politicians, some of
whom request their own custom-made sticks.

Japanese Paper Place

*887 Queen Street W, at Walnut Avenue, West
End (416 703 0089/www.japanesepaperplace.com).
Streetcar 501.* **Open** 10am-6pm Mon-Wed, Sat;
10am-8pm Thur, Fri. **Credit** AmEx, MC, V.
Map p278 C7.
For those who take paper seriously, there are origami classes, invitation workshops and lectures at
weekends. But this is really just a pretty place to
wander, feeling paper samples, filling Christmas
stockings and getting whiffs of inspiration.

Whole Foods Market. *See p158.*

Health & beauty

Beauty shops

Iodine + Arsenic

*867 Queen Street W, at Niagara Street, West
End (416 681 0577/www.iodineandarsenic.com).
Streetcar 501.* **Open** 11am-7pm Mon-Fri; 11am-6pm
Sat; noon-5pm Sun. **Credit** MC, V. **Map** 278 C7.
The vibe here is playfully medicinal, from the hair
studio (called the OR), the Arsenic 'Anti-Spa' at the
back, and clinical white walls and prescription-
inspired fare, to the IV bag-packaging of the products (handcrafted bath salts, massage products and
atomisers). Choose from inexpensive novelty items
like red devil rubber duckies, or lotions and potions
with attitude (the Bitch line is especially popular).

PIR Cosmetics

*25 Bellair Street, at Cumberland Avenue, Yorkville
(416 513 1603/www.pircosmetics.com). Bus 6/
subway Bay.* **Open** 11am-6pm Mon, Tue, Sat;
11am-6.30pm Wed-Fri; 1-5pm Sun. **Credit** AmEx,
MC, V. **Map** p282 F4.
This boutique is a hub for talked-about and hard-to-
find Japanese, Italian and French brands. Also on
offer are make-up application lessons, eyebrow
shaping, nail treatments and the requisite coif stuff.
Other locations: 77 Front Street E, St Lawrence
Market (416 703 2480).

Complementary medicine

Toronto is a established haven of alternative
medicine. The **Toronto Healing Arts
Centre** (717 Bloor Street W, West End,

416 535 8777) enlists licensed homeopaths, hypnotists and other holistic professionals for a range of therapies. Or you can regroup, rebalance and rejuvenate at the **Centre for Life Essentials** in Forest Hill (416 238 7213, 705 742 7475, www.life-essentials.com; phone for an appointment), specialising in stress-, pain- and fatigue-management through a variety of therapies, including reflexology, aromatherapy and meditation. Find you way to the **Yellow Brick Road** on Dupont Street (*see p162*) to cleanse your system, and for aromatherapy, reflexology, ear candling and other therapies.

Hairdressers

First Choice Haircutters
1730 Bloor Street W, at Indian Grove, West End (416 766 7222/www.firstchoice.com). Subway Keele. **Open** 9am-9pm Mon-Fri; 8am-6pm Sat; 11am-5pm Sun. **Credit** MC, V.
The $11 snip may not be ideal for some of the girls who brush through town, but to others it means a competent cut that leaves you enough cash for a night out afterwards. And the first-come, first-served policy will suit those on the fly.
Other locations: throughout the city.

John Steinberg & Associates Salon
585 King Street W, at Portland Street, Entertainment District (416 506 0268/ www.johnsteinberghair.com). Streetcar 501, 504, 510. **Open** 11am-4pm Mon; 10am-6pm Tue; 10am-4pm Wed; 10am-6pm Thur, Fri; 10am-3pm Sat. **Credit** MC, V. **Map** p279 D8.
This salon was a fixture on King Street W before the area became trendy, so the snippers have a loyal following among actors and media types. While you're getting a new, stylish look, check out the art exhibits, which change every six weeks.

Nail bars

Lux Spa
25 Bellair Street, at Cumberland Street, Yorkville (416 921 1680/www.lux-spa.com). Subway Bay. **Open** 10am-6pm Tue, Wed; 10am-8pm Thur, Fri; 9am-5pm Sat. **Credit** MC, V. **Map** p282 F4.
This posh Manhattan-style nail bar is no-nonsense – both speed and hygiene being paramount. The decor is crisp, cool white, with a single treatment room for reflexology and massage and elegant potted orchids along the lean, gleaming manicure table. A white banquette along one wall for pedicures can accommodate several customers at once. Brands used include (from Monaco) Ecrinal, Akileine, OPI and the house label. Prices start at $28 for a mani-LUX and $48 for a pedi-LUX. The spa also does a full range of waxing (for him and her), as well as brow-shaping and lash-tinting.

Opticians

Josephson Opticians
60 Bloor Street W, at Bay Street, Yorkville (416 964 7070/www.josephsonopt.com). Bus 6/ subway Bay. **Open** 9.30am-6pm Mon-Wed, Fri, Sat; 9.30am-8pm Thur. **Credit** AmEx, MC, V. **Map** p282 F4.
This family operation has been around since the '30s. Never a stodgy mom-and-pop outfit, it stocks the cream of Lacroix, Chanel, Mikli and Prada, along with funkier styles from LA Eyeworks. Turnaround on glasses is between two and four days, but emergency lenses are available in less than a day.
Other locations: throughout the city.

Pharmacies

Shoppers Drug Mart (360 Bloor Street W, The Annex, 416 961 2121) is the most prevalent of Toronto's pharmacies, with many locations open until midnight. **Pharma Plus** (concourse level, 55 Bloor Street W, University, 416 923 0570), formerly known as Boots, is slightly less ubiquitous, and hours are less flexible. The same is true for another chain, **IDA** (66 Avenue Road, The Annex, 416 922 5555). For more information, *see p259*.

Spas

See also p160 **Iodine + Arsenic**.

Estée Lauder Spa
Holt Renfrew, 50 Bloor Street W, at Bay Street, Yorkville (416 960 2909/www.esteelauder.com). Bus 6/subway Bay or Bloor-Yonge. **Open** 10am-6pm Mon-Wed, Sat; 10am-8pm Thur, Fri; noon-6pm Sun. **Credit** AmEx, MC, V. **Map** p282 F4.
This is comfort incarnate, right down to the high-quality robe you'll be idling in. Estée Lauder staff run a tight ship, getting their hands to the problem area in record time, though they can be strict about your usual 'routine'. Treatments run from single manicures via facials and make-up to elaborate whole-body day packages.

The Stillwater Spa at the Park Hyatt
4 Avenue Road, at Bloor Street W, Yorkville (416 926 2389/www.stillwaterspa.com). Subway Bay or Museum. **Open** 9am-10pm Mon-Fri; 8am-10pm Sat; 10am-5.30pm Sun. **Credit** AmEx, MC, V. **Map** p282 F4.
Both locals and visitors flock to this subterranean oasis of pampering and white noise (an underfoot stream beneath glass). After a hot stone massage or a wrap (choose from detoxifying seaweed or mud), you'll want to linger in the steam room and sauna, or relax in front of the fire in the Asian-inspired tea lounge. The boutique upstairs carries cult cosmetics and new discoveries.

Yellow Brick Road

258 Dupont Street, at Spadina Avenue, The Annex (416 926 1101). Subway Dupont. **Open** 10am-7pm Mon-Sat. **Credit** MC, V. **Map** p282 E2.

A modest juice bar occupies the storefront; upstairs, earthy Annex folk flush your system – be it your ears or your colon – to a calming soundtrack of Enya. There's a neurotherapist in residence.

Home

L'Atelier

1224 Yonge Street, at Alcorn Avenue, Rosedale (416 966 0200). Subway St Clair or Summerhill. **Open** 10.30am-6pm Mon-Sat. **Credit** AmEx, MC, V. **Map** p283 G2.

Part bachelor pad, part French chateau, part garden of delights, L'Atelier has plenty of gems in store, whether gilded Italian birdcages, Lucite loungers or thick marble mantels. Dramatic dressers and lighting set the scene, and lesser knick-knacks are on hand for the weak of budget. Explore this stretch, between Rosedale and Summerhill stations, for a slew of French antiques and modern look-alikes.

Caban

262-264 Queen Street W, at Beverley Street, Entertainment District (416 596 0386/www.caban.ca). Streetcar 501/subway Osgoode. **Open** 10am-7pm Mon-Wed, Sat; 10am-8pm Thur, Fri; 11am-6pm Sun. **Credit** AmEx, DC, MC, V. **Map** p278 E7.

Looking for bath salts and a computer desk? How about that sexy top to go with some porcelain bowls. Caban's approach to retail tries to be all things to all people, provided you want a trendy minimalist touch to adorn your lifestyle.

Du Verre

188 Strachan Avenue, at Queen Street W, West End (416 593 4784/www.duverre.com). Streetcar 501. **Open** 11am-6pm Tue-Sat; 1-5pm Sun. **Credit** AmEx, MC, V. **Map** p278 B7.

In an old coach house off Queen West, Du Verre sells tribal imports characterised by clean, contemporary lines. Japanese screens shield tables from Tibet and accessories from India. Brand-new metal hardware from home-grown artists offers a mod sheen.

LA Design

788 King Street W, at Tecumseth Street, West End (416 363 4470). Streetcar 504. **Open** 10.30am-6pm Mon-Fri; 10.30am-5pm Sat; noon-5pm Sun. **Credit** AmEx, MC, V. **Map** p278 C8.

The initials stand for Living Arts, but the feel is Californian home-on-the-ocean aesthetic. Colour reigns supreme, with materials such as Mongolian lambswool (throws) and hammered silk (upholstery).

Teatro Verde

Hazelton Lanes, 55 Avenue Road, at Bloor Street, Yorkville (416 966 2227/www.teatroverde.com). Bus 6/subway Bay. **Open** 10am-6pm Mon-Wed, Fri, Sat; 10am-7pm Thur; noon-5pm Sun. **Credit** AmEx, MC, V. **Map** p282 F3.

Once a fashionable florist, this dealer now represents everything 'home', from sari-covered cushions and throws to kitchen gear and cookbooks to boudoir accessories. And, naturally, you'll still find the odd vase, planter and recliner for the garden. Fresh, the New York home and fragrance line, is also here.

UpCountry

310 King Street E, at Parliament Street, St Lawrence (416 777 1700/www.upcountry.ca). Streetcar 504. **Open** 10am-6pm Mon-Wed, Sat; 10am-7pm Thur, Fri; noon-5pm Sun. **Credit** AmEx, MC, V. **Map** p280 H8.

The anchor of the King Street East design corridor, UpCountry was here before the avant-garde Italian set moved in. But it's still a big draw with sleek Canadian designs in sumptuous fabrics and rich woods. Many of the collections are entirely custom-made. Find sofas, chairs, beds, lighting as well as garden furniture. There is also a smattering of classic and vintage furniture downstairs.

Other locations: 214 King Street E, St Lawrence (416 777 1700).

William Ashley

55 Bloor Street W, at Bay Street, Yorkville (416 964 2900/www.williamashley.com). Bus 6/subway Bay. **Open** 10am-6pm Mon-Wed, Sat; 10am-7.30pm Thur, Fri. **Credit** AmEx, MC, V. **Map** p282 F4.

Sooner or later, everyone comes through the door of Ashley's, whether buying gifts, contemplating the purchase of gourmet necessities, or creating wedding lists (stressed-out couples by the dozen wander the maze of china). Staff are notably well informed, and seem to enjoy discussing the finer points of white bone china and crystal goblets, and helping select from the daunting array of patterns.

Music

HMV

333 Yonge Street, at Gould Street, Dundas Square (416 586 9668/www.hmv.ca). Streetcar 505/subway Dundas. **Open** 9am-10pm Mon-Thur; 9am-midnight Fri, Sat; 11am-7pm Sun. **Credit** AmEx, MC, V. **Map** p280 G6.

HMV can afford to offer some enticing deals, and this flagship carries everything you could possibly want in the way of audio entertainment. Staff are helpful. **Other locations:** throughout the city.

Play de Record

357A Yonge Street, at Dundas Street, Dundas Square (416 586 0380/www.playderecord.com). Streetcar 505/subway Dundas. **Open** noon-8pm Mon-Wed; noon-10pm Thur, Fri; noon-9pm Sat; 1-6pm Sun. **Credit** AmEx, MC, V. **Map** p280 G6.

Squeeze past shelves of video tack to the vinyl haven at the back, where local DJs and hooded club kids come to spin rare editions and the latest releases from the worlds of hip hop, rap, Latin, electronica and jazz. Prices aren't cheap, but you're paying for records unavailable elsewhere in town. Tickets to small-venue shows can be bought at the counter.

Check out local talent at **Soundscapes**.

Soundscapes

572 College Street, at Manning Avenue, Little Italy (416 537 1620). Streetcar 506, 511. **Open** 10.30am-11pm Mon-Thur; 10.30am-midnight Fri, Sat; 10am-11pm Sun. **Credit** AmEx, MC, V. **Map** p278 C5.

The speciality here is not a particular genre, but rather 'good' music. A former accountant and passionate listener, Greg Davis started this venture to promote new local talent (which is hand-sold without being pushy), classic rock, electronica and international beats that aren't getting satisfactory recognition elsewhere. Find the latest concert tickets (and heartfelt recommendations), plus there's enough space at the entrance to display lists of employee favourites. You'll also find a selection of local indie labels at the back, like Paper Bag Records, and might even discover the next Broken Social Scene or Metric.

Rotate This

620 Queen Street W, at Markham Street, Entertainment District (416 504 8447/ www.rotate.com). Streetcar 501. **Open** 11am-7pm Mon-Thur, Sat; 11am-8pm Fri; noon-6pm Sun. **Credit** MC, V. **Map** p278 C7.

Aesthetics are of little interest, the staff have attitude and vinyl is in abundance. Obscure comic books at the front offer reading to those awaiting the headphones at the counter for a record preview. The CD selection is good, though prices tend to be higher than average, even for used stuff. The recently and regularly updated website will show you what you can expect to find here.

Sam the Record Man

347 Yonge Street, at Gould Street, Dundas Square (416 646 2775/www.samtherecordman.com). **Open** 9am-10pm Mon-Thur; 9am-midnight Fri, Sat; 11am-7pm Sun. **Credit** AmEx, MC, V. **Map** p280 G6.

The giant spinning neon platters above this legendary record (and video) store reflect the glow of better days – Sam went bust in 2002 and the national chain shut up shop. But the flagship store survived on a bail-out from Sam's sons, who now run the place. Known for the encyclopaedic staff, its high-quality classical and jazz sections and for promoting Canadian artists, Sam's keeps the competitors on their toes in this music-heavy block of Yonge Street, where prices are the lowest in the city.

Second-hand

Second Spin

386 Bloor Street W, at Spadina Avenue, The Annex (416 961 7746). Streetcar 510/subway Spadina. **Open** 11am-11pm Mon-Fri; 10am-11pm Sat; 11am-9pm Sun. **Credit** MC, V. **Map** p282 D4.

If you're selling, you stand to make a decent sum at Second Spin: staff offer as much as $7 for a well-kept CD. Then again, you're sure to spend your winnings on something from the remarkably extensive dance collection, or a rock classic.

Photography

For developing holiday snaps on the quick and cheap, the best deals are at the supermarkets. But if you're fussy about the finer points, it's probably best to stick with the specialists, the most prominent of which are **Black's** (20 Dundas Street W, Dundas Square, 416 595 0326; and other locations), **Henry's** (119 Church Street, St Lawrence, 416 868 0872) and **Japan Camera** (48 Front Street W, St Lawrence, 416 363 7476; and other locations). They can be pricey, but offer alternatives to the basic matt and gloss with border options and custom alterations (along with the machines that print zoom images of your pics). Professionals or aspiring photographers tend toward **West Camera** (514 Queen Street W, Entertainment District, 416 504 9432) and **Vistek** (496 Queen Street E, Moss Park, 416 365 1777), where you can also buy new or used equipment.

Sex shops

In the '60s, when Toronto was young, inexperienced and bursting with potential, there was only one sex shop to satisfy its impulses. **Lovecraft** (27 Yorkville Avenue, Yorkville, 416 923 7331) was disconcertingly open-concept, with romantic rose-coloured walls and brazen dildo displays. Now the city has grown up, and it's easy to find… well, almost anything you require. **Condom Shack** (729 Yonge Street, Yorkville, 416 966 4226; 231 Queen Street W, Entertainment District, 416 596 7515) is the McDonald's of pleasure and protection, with a bright, scrubbed feel; **Come As You Are** (701 Queen Street W, Entertainment District, 416 504 7934) is more modern in its sensibility, with 'get-to-know-yourself' manuals, oils and toys geared toward same-sex partners. Across the street, get your bondage gear and trampy undergarments at **Miss Behav'n** (650 Queen Street W, Entertainment District, 416 866 7979), featuring live window models at weekends.

Sport & outdoor

Mountain Equipment Co-op (MEC)
400 King Street W, at Peter Street, Entertainment District (416 340 2667/www.mec.ca). Streetcar 504, 510/subway St Andrew. **Open** 10am-7pm Mon-Wed; 10am-9pm Thur, Fri; 9am-6pm Sat; 11am-5pm Sun. **Credit** MC, V. **Map** p278 C8.
This Canadian company is renowned for the quality and scope of its outdoor gear. A co-op (so you have to pay a nominal joining fee), it has motivated staff and a family feel (there's even a rock-climbing wall for kids). Prices on outdoor equipment (tents, sleeping bags, even canoes) and hiking wear (fleeces galore) go down to bargain levels off-season.

Sporting Life
2665 Yonge Street, at Lytton Boulevard, North Toronto (416 485 1611). Subway Eglinton or Lawrence. **Open** 9am-9pm Mon-Fri; 9am-6pm Sat; 10am-6pm Sun. **Credit** AmEx, MC, V.
Top-of-the-range kit for a broad selection of sports, and also a necessary destination for trendy sportswear. Range Rovers line up for the small parking lot at weekends ; inside it's madness – shoes, jackets and bathing suits piled everywhere. Great sales.

Tobacconists

Thomas Hinds Tobacconist
8 Cumberland Street, at Yonge Street, Yorkville (416 927 0797/www.thomashinds.ca). Subway Yonge or Bloor. **Open** 9am-7pm Mon-Wed; 9am-9pm Thur, Fri; 9am-6pm Sat; noon-5pm Sun. **Credit** AmEx, MC, V. **Map** p283 G4.
The maligned breed of humanity known as smokers can find refuge at this 19th-century yellow-brick shop in Yorkville, where sweet trails of wafting pipe and cigar smoke are part of the allure. Another attraction is the frequent presence of Hollywood types – Dennis Hopper, Matt Dillon, Mark Wahlberg – in the upstairs smoking lounge and walk-in humidor. Hinds stocks 150 brands of cigars, most of them Cuban and thus out of reach to Americans at home.

Toys & gadgets

See also p143 **Pacific Mall**, *p147* **The Silver Snail** *and p148* **Clandestino**.

Kidding Awound
91 Cumberland Street, at Bay Street, Yorkville (416 926 8996). Subway Bay. **Open** *Summer* 10.30am-6pm Mon-Wed; 10.30am-7pm Thur-Sat; noon-5pm Sun. *Winter* 10.30am-6pm Mon-Sat; noon-5pm Sun. **Credit** AmEx, MC, V. **Map** p282 F4.
Not exactly cheap, but worth a look for one-of-a-kind trinket shopping. You'll find things to be wound, spun, coloured and laughed at, and a selection of antique toys for big kids.

Science City
Holt Renfrew, 50 Bloor Street W, at Bay Street, Yorkville (416 968 2627/www.sciencecity.ca). Subway Bloor-Yonge. **Open** 10am-6pm Mon-Wed, Sat; 10am-8pm Thur, Fri; 1-5pm Sun. **Credit** AmEx, MC, V. **Map** p282 F4.
From telescopes to gyroscopes, brain-teasers to insect tweezers, this is paradise for junior geeks.

Travellers' needs

Photocopying
With all the expat neighbourhoods in the city, it's likely you'll come across the odd corner store with a mini office out back for phoning, faxing and copying. Or you could opt for **Kinko's**, which has branches in the Annex (459 Bloor Street W, 416 928 0110, www.kinkos.com), the Financial District and Yonge Street (at several junctions), or **Alicos Digital Copy Centre** (66 Gerrard Street E, at Church Street, 416 977 6868, www.alicos.com), which also has outlets around town in addition to this Dundas Square location.

Shipping
Shippers will collect your purchases, pack, crate and haul them overseas – to your door – quicker (and more cheaply) than you'd think. **Alliance Services International** (416 469 5252) and **Worldwide Shipping & Forwarding** (1-905 673 9244) are both tried and tested.

Travel agents

Flight Centre
55 Yonge Street, at King Street, St Lawrence (416 304 6170/www.flightcentre.ca). Streetcar 504/subway King. **Open** 9am-6pm Mon-Fri; 10am-4pm Sat. **Credit** AmEx, MC, V. **Map** p280 G8.
As close to a bucket shop as you'll get in Canada, Flight Centre tries to undercut any price on any flight you've been quoted. Both international and internal flights are available.
Other locations: throughout the city.

Arts & Entertainment

Festivals & Events

A packed calendar of knees-ups, from the hokey to the heart-warming.

All the fun of the fair at **Caribana**. *See p170.*

At certain times of the year it seems you can't move for festivals in Toronto. At other times you wonder where everyone is, it's so quiet (tip: they've all gone off to their holiday cottages). But whatever month it is, there will always be something going on, and taking part in one or more of the festivities is a good way to get a feel for the city. It's certainly true that because the summer is short, locals make the most of it, filling the calendar with large- and small-scale events from Victoria Day (May) through Labour Day (September). But the rest of the year isn't neglected: autumn and winter play host to many indoor pursuits.

Below we review our perennial favourites, but it pays to keep an eye out in the local press too, or go online (for a range of useful websites, *see p266*). It's also wise to book hotels well in advance of any major events, such as the renowned **Toronto International Film Festival** (*see p171*).

Spring

Canada Blooms
South Building, Metro Toronto Convention Centre, 222 Bremner Boulevard, at Simcoe Street, Entertainment District (416 447 8655/ www.canadablooms.com). Subway St Andrew or Union. **Map** p279 E8. **Date** Mar.
A massive flower and garden show running from Wednesday to Sunday, this floral wonderland attracts hordes of local green-fingered fans desperate for a first glimpse of spring. The main attractions are the display gardens and the prize-winning flower arrangements.

Good Friday Parade
College Street/Little Italy. Streetcar 506, 511. **Map** p278 C5. **Date** Good Fri.
Flagellating Roman centurions, candle-bearing worshippers, even the odd donkey, take to the streets of Little Italy for this sombre re-enactment of Christ on his way to the Crucifiction.

Images Festival of Independent Film & Video

Various venues (416 971 8405/www.images festival.com). **Date** Apr.

The most adventurous of the mini film fests, the week-long Images offers lots of dazzling innovations, sometimes at the price of narrative coherence.

National Hockey League Play-offs

Date mid Apr-mid June.

For 2005 it's game over due to a player lock-out (for future information visit www.nhl.com), but this rite of spring usually whips the city into a frenzy. Bars and cafés do brisk business as long as the Maple Leafs are still in the running. They haven't won the Stanley Cup since 1967, a drought that's sated each year by plenty of beer and consternation. Tickets are near impossible to get, except through scalpers.

Hot Docs Canadian International Documentary Festival

Various venues (416 203 2155/www.hotdocs.ca). **Date** late Apr-early May.

North America's biggest documentary festival lasts ten days and features more than 100 films from around the world, from classics to the best of the current scene. Workshops and masterclasses are available, though not all are open to the public.

Contact Photography Festival

Various venues (416 539 9595/www.contact photo.com). **Date** May.

A month-long festival of Canadian and international photography exhibited in galleries, bars and restaurants across the city. Photographers discuss their craft in workshops and seminars.

Inside Out Toronto Lesbian & Gay Film & Video Festival

Various venues (416 977 6847/www.insideout.on.ca). **Date** May.

A social occasion as much as a cinematic experience, this popular ten-day event brings out the lesbian and gay community's arty elite. The second-largest film festival in the city, Inside Out plays everything from commercial stuff to obscure documentaries.

Toronto Jewish Film Festival

Various venues (416 324 9121/www.tjff.com). **Date** May.

The largest event of its kind in North America outside San Francisco, this ten-day fest features films, shorts and documentaries from around the world.

Victoria Day Long Weekend

Date Mon closest to 24 May.

Victoria Day weekend is a national holiday and the unofficial launch of summer. Gardeners get busy, people head off to their cottages, and crowds gather for firework displays... all in honour of a queen who might very well have disapproved. The date recognises the royal birthday, but also (coincidentally) the traditional mode of celebration, the 'two-four' or case of 24 beers, the largest you can buy.

Fashion Cares

South Building, Metro Toronto Convention Centre, 222 Bremner Boulevard, Entertainment District (416 340 2437/www.fashioncares.com). Subway St Andrew or Union. **Map** p279 E8. **Date** late May.

Toronto fashionistas turn out in droves for this enormous AIDS fundraiser, an outrageous fashion show that doubles as an alternative society ball. The after-party goes on until the wee hours. Good-hearted B-list entertainers usually headline.

Doors Open Toronto

Various venues (416 338 3888/www.doorsopen.org). **Date** last weekend in May.

Many of the 100-plus sites on this two-day tour are normally off-limits to the public, so this a good chance for both locals and tourists to discover Toronto's history and architecture. There is no formal tour: participating buildings simply hang out a welcoming blue banner (check local papers for a map). Best of all, it's free. *See also p32.*

Summer

Rhythms of the World

Harbourfront Centre, 235 Queens Quay W, Waterfront (416 973 4000/www.harbourfront centre.com). Streetcar 509, 510. **Map** p279/p280 F9. **Date** June-Sept.

This summer-long series of weekend festivals spotlights different cultures through food, dance, art, film and, most importantly, music. The (mainly free) concerts are surprising, intriguing, offbeat and of an amazingly high quality, and often feature inter-

Top five Festivals

Doors Open Toronto

Your chance to get a proper look at places that are normally off-limits to the public. *See above.*

Pride Week

Don't miss this week-long extravaganza, celebrating gay and lesbian life. *See p168.*

Beaches International Jazz Festival

Kick back and enjoy those lazy, hazy days of summer. *See p169.*

International Festival of Authors

Your chance to eavesdrop as the big names gather for a natter. *See 171.*

Santa Claus Parade

Guaranteed to bring out the child in anyone. *See p171.*

Arts & Entertainment

nationally known stars such as Youssou N'Dour and the Neville Brothers, while the open-air lakeside venue makes this one of the best places in town to hear music on a hot summer's evening. Kick off with the JVC Jazz Festival in June and dance your way through to autumn.

North by Northeast Music & Film Festival

Various venues (416 863 6963/www.nxne.com). **Date** early June.

The sounds of independent music, the kind unfettered by those big record label contract obligations, tear up the city centre during this popular three-day event. Tens of thousands of music fans prowl dozens of clubs, catching the hot talent from Canada, the US and around the world. You can bet the musicians treat the whole thing as an audition for the ears of all those record company execs who trawl the festival in search of the next big sound.

Pride Week

Various venues (416 927 7433/www.pride toronto.com). **Date** late June.

What started out as a small political picnic in 1970 has turned into a brash commercial success that lasts a week and is more celebration than march. There are beer gardens and entertainment on several stages in Church & Wellesley throughout the weekend – everything from disco to alterna-queer to lesbian folk. Off-site, local promoters usually offer a series of massive circuit parties and the local queer theatre company, Buddies in Bad Times (*see p220 and p192* **Good times at Bad Times**), holds a week of plays, staged readings, dances and drag shows. For something really different try Cheap Queers, several nights of cabaret featuring local theatre and comedy stars. Late-night events are adult-oriented, but the big parade itself (always on the last Sunday in June) is increasingly family-friendly, with up to a million people ogling the equally outrageous antics of drag queens, muscle boys, activists and politicians. The parade is long, the weather hot and the crowds enormous – so bring lots of water. The smaller Dyke March takes place the day before. For more information, check out *Xtra!*'s stand-alone guide, usually published in early June.

Queen's Plate

Woodbine Race Track, 555 Rexdale Boulevard, at Highway 427 (416 675 7223/www.woodbine entertainment.com). Bus 37A, 191. **Date** late June.

Three-year-old Canadian-bred thoroughbreds compete in the country's oldest and most famous horse races at Woodbine Race Track. Royalty – or at least their stand-ins– usually put in an appearance.

Toronto Downtown Jazz Festival

Various venues (416 928 2033/www.tojazz.com). **Date** late June-early July.

During this fest, hundreds of artists perform all styles of jazz at dozens of clubs, theatres and outdoor stages throughout the downtown area.

Toronto International Dragon Boat Race Festival

Centre Island (416 595 1739/www.dragonboats.com). **Date** late June.

The colourful dragon boats are the centrepiece of this Chinese festival, which takes place over a weekend. With food, games, music and dance, it attracts more than 100,000 people to the sylvan shores of the Toronto Islands, just across the water from the city.

Canada Day

Nathan Phillips Square
100 Queen Street W, at Bay Street, Chinatown (416 338 0338/www.city.toronto.on.ca/special_events). Streetcar 501/subway Queen. **Map** p279/280 F7.
Mel Lastman Square
5100 Yonge Street, at Sheppard Avenue, North Toronto (416 338 0338/www.city.toronto.on.ca/ special_events). Subway North York Centre.
York Quay Centre
235 Queens Quay W, Waterfront (416 973 4000/ www.harbourfrontcentre.com). Streetcar 509, 510. **Map** p279/280 F9.
Downsview Park
John Drury Drive, at Sheppard Avenue, North Toronto (416 952 2222/www.pdp.ca). Subway Downsview.
All Date 1 July.

Torontonians celebrate Canada's birthday (1 July 1867) with a very Canadian mixture of deference and pride, usually by leaving town for the long weekend. Best bets for fun-filled activity are Nathan Phillips Square, Mel Lastman Square, Harbourfront Centre and Downsview Park; most feature Canuck entertainers and night-time fireworks displays.

Canadian National Exhibition.
See p170.

Toronto Fringe Theatre Festival

Various venues (416 966 1062/www.fringe
toronto.com). **Date** early July.

Here the trick is seeing the hit shows before they're
over. Venues are tiny and the grapevine quick, so
getting in can be tricky, but with more than 100
troupes from both Canada and abroad on hand over
the 12 days, there's plenty of choice, and a very good
chance of high quality. The Annex home base for
the festival has a beer tent, where you can pick up
the buzz on the hits and misses.

Beaches International Jazz Festival

Queen Street E, east of Woodbine Avenue, East
Toronto (416 698 2152/www.beachesjazz.com).
Streetcar 501. **Date** 3rd wk in July.

More than 50 bands perform from street corners,
rooftops and parks in one of Toronto's most bucolic
neighbourhoods. The main stage is located in Kew
Gardens, and with its beach and boardwalk, it's
worth it for the ambience alone.

Celebrate Toronto Street Festival

Various venues (416 338 0338/www.city.toronto.on.
ca/special_events). **Date** July.

Locals hate the traffic jams, but visitors love the free
entertainment at this weekend-long event – everything from world to classical to hip hop, on a series
of stages situated at key intersections on Toronto's
main drag (Dundas Street, Bloor Street, St Clair
Avenue, Eglinton Avenue and Lawrence Avenue).
It's good, cheap fun, with carnival rides for the kids
and beer gardens for the adults.

Molson Indy

Exhibition Place, Lake Shore Boulevard W, between
Strachan Avenue & Dufferin Street, Waterfront
(416 872 4639/www.molsonindy.com). Bus
29/streetcar 509, 511. **Map** p278 B9. **Date** July.

Over a weekend in July, drivers burn rubber on the
streets through Exhibition Place. Expect lots of
testosterone-driven music and street parties.

Toronto Outdoor Art Exhibition

Nathan Phillips Square, 100 Queen Street W,
at Bay Street, Chinatown (416 408 2754/
www.torontooutdoorart.org). Streetcar 501/
subway Queen. **Map** p279/280 F7. **Date** July.

If beauty is in the eye of the beholder, there's plenty
to gaze upon at this large, weekend-long outdoor
expo. Artists range from established to students.

Fringe Festival of Independent Dance Artists

Distillery District (416 410 4291/www.ffida.org).
Bus 65. **Map** p281 J8. **Date** Aug.

This ten-day festival features short works by experienced and emerging choreographers, with some
site-specific works. It's a gamble, but worth it for the
variety alone. Styles run the gamut from modern
dance through ballet to belly dancing.

Tennis Masters Canada & the Rogers Cup

Rexall Centre, York University, 1 Shoreham Drive
(416 665 9777, ext 4333/www.tenniscanada.com).
Subway Downsview then bus 106/subway Keele
then bus 41. **Date** late July-early Aug.

Christmas lists at the ready – it's the **Santa Claus Parade**. *See p171.*

The name changes to suit the event: one year it's the Canadian men's tennis championships, the next it's the women's. Either way, lots of top-seeded players take part. And the new Rexall Centre (11,500 seats), in the city's northern suburbs, is a pleasant place to catch all the action.

Caribana

Various venues (905 799 1630/www.caribana.com). **Date** Simcoe Day long weekend, late July-early Aug. North America's largest Caribbean festival attracts a million-plus tourists and sends what little remains of Toronto's stodgy Anglo past into a happy tailspin. Thousands of colourfully costumed revellers participate in events like the King and Queen of the Bands competition, usually held at Lamport Stadium (1155 King Street W, West End) and the climactic parade that sees dozens of 'mas' (masquerade) bands floating west on Lake Shore Boulevard. For the next two days a cool down-cum-arts festival takes place on Olympic Island, just a short ferry ride across the harbour. You can't miss the parade (or the thumping car stereos on Yonge Street at night), but the many spin-off events are sometimes hard to find. Your best bet is to check the local weeklies for last-minute details.

Taste of the Danforth

Various locations along Danforth Avenue, East Toronto (416 469 5634/www.tasteofthedanforth. com). Subway Broadview, Chester or Pape. **Date** early Aug.

During this weekend event up to a million people sample all kinds of food provided by the restaurants in this nominally Greek neighbourhood. Top entertainers perform on three stages. All in all, a big, bustling people-friendly event.

SummerWorks Theatre Festival

Various venues (416 410 1048/www.summer works.ca). **Date** Aug.
A ten-day event featuring a mix of established and emerging theatre companies presenting 40-odd plays. New work is encouraged.

Canadian National Exhibition

Exhibition Place, Lake Shore Boulevard W, between Strachan Avenue & Dufferin Street, Waterfront (416 263 3800/www.theex.com). **Map** p278 B9. **Date** mid Aug-early Sept.
A cross between an old-fashioned agricultural fair and a modern-day expo, the CNE (or the Ex, as it's known locally) mixes sheep shearing and milking demonstrations with pop entertainment and theme days devoted to Toronto's various ethnic communities. Some folks come just for the sideshows, but the real thrill is the nostalgia – they just don't make 'em like this anymore. Stick around for the last three days of the two-week fair, when high-flying acrobats take to the skies on Labour Day Weekend for the the Canadian International Air Show. It's a blue-sky wonder, with Canada's own performing poodles of the sky, the Snowbirds aeronautic squad, always drawing plenty of cheers.

Autumn

Cabbagetown Festival

Various locations around Carlton & Parliament Streets, Cabbagetown (416 921 0857/ www.oldcabbagetown.com). Streetcar 506. **Map** p280/281 H/J 5/6. **Date** early Sept.

A tribute to a working-class neighbourhood turned affluent enclave, this weekend-long fest offers corn roasts, street dances, pancake breakfasts, an arts and crafts fair, a parade and tours of some of the neighbourhood's unique bay and gable houses.

Toronto International Film Festival

Various venues (416 967 7371/www.bell.ca/filmfest). **Date** early Sept.

After 30 years in business, the ten-day TIFF now rivals Cannes and Sundance for PR power, and that means loads of celebrities and miles of celluloid – everything from Hollywood blockbusters to obscure Eastern European angst-fests. Even work-obsessed Torontonians take time off for this one. The giddiness is pervasive. Public screenings run through the day, starting at 9am, and go well past midnight at some venues. With 300-plus features on display, there's always something to see, but popular items sell out quickly. The complete schedule doesn't usually appear until late August, but avid fans start buying passes and tickets in mid July. *See also p28.*

Word on the Street

Queen's Park, north of Ontario Parliament Buildings, University (416 504 7241/ www.thewordonthestreet.ca). Subway Museum or Queen's Park. **Map** p282 F5. **Date** late Sept.

More than 100,000 people stroll 'neath the oaks and elms of Queen's Park during a street-savvy Sunday celebration of literacy that sees publishers and writers promoting their wares with readings and signings. Kids get their own special tent.

International Festival of Authors

Harbourfront Centre, 235 Queens Quay W, Waterfront (416 973 4000/www.readings.org). Streetcar 509, 510. **Map** p279/280 F9. **Date** 10 days in late Oct.

From the four corners of the world they come, trailing their Bookers, Pulitzers and Nobels – novelists, poets and biographers from the top tiers of the literary firmament. The ten-day event was founded in 1980 by Greg Gatenby, who was determined to promote a cosmopolitan literary culture. A poet and former book editor, he went on to write a literary guide to Toronto and edit two books collecting foreign literary views of Canada. It's a prestigious affair, but the readings, talks and on-stage interviews are surprisingly intimate. The venues are usually the Harbourfront Centre's Premiere Dance Theatre and York Quay Centre, but check nearer the time. If you can't make it to the big event, there other readings at Harbourfront, generally on Wednesday nights, from September to December, and February to June.

Toronto International Art Fair

South Building, Metro Toronto Convention Centre, 222 Bremner Boulevard, at Simcoe Street, Entertainment District (information 1 800 663 4173/604 925 0330/booking 416 872 1212/1 800 461 3333/www.tiafair.com). Subway St Andrew or Union. **Map** p279 E8. **Date** 5 days in early Nov.

It's not Basel or Venice but this four-day art binge gets stronger with each outing and is proving to be a must-see event for the contemporary art scene.

Santa Claus Parade

Bloor Street & University Avenue, Entertainment & Financial Districts (416 249 7833/www.thesanta clausparade.com). Streetcar 501, 504, 505/subway King, Museum, Osgoode, Queen's Park, St Andrew, St Patrick or Union. **Date** late Nov.

Started more than a century ago as a publicity stunt for a local department store, the Santa Claus Parade is now a Toronto institution. More than 500,000 people – mostly parents with kids on their shoulders – watch dozens of floats, storybook characters, marching bands and, of course, Santa and his sleigh, as they parade through the city centre.

Canadian Aboriginal Festival

Rogers Centre (SkyDome), 1 Blue Jays Way, at Front Street, Entertainment District (519 751 0040/ www.canab.com). Streetcar 504/subway Union. **Map** p279 E8. **Date** late Nov-early Dec.

North America's largest multi-disciplinary aboriginal arts event is a three-day affair featuring fashion, films, lacrosse, music awards and a giant powwow.

Cavalcade of Lights

Nathan Phillips Square, 100 Queen Street W, at Bay Street, Chinatown (416 338 0338/www.city. toronto.on.ca/special_events). Streetcar 501/subway Queen. **Map** p279/280 F7. **Date** late Nov-late Dec.

A hundred thousand lights illuminate the city's central square, kicking off a month of skating parties and other events, which culminate in a televised New Year's Eve party with top Canadian acts.

Winter

WinterCity

Mel Lastman Square
5100 Yonge Street, at Sheppard Avenue, North Toronto. Subway North York Centre.
Nathan Phillips Square
100 Queen Street W, at Bay Street, Chinatown. Streetcar 501/subway Queen. **Map** p279/280 F7. **Both** *416 338 0338/www.toronto.ca/special_events.* **Date** late Jan-early Feb.

Toronto in the depths of winter can be harsh. Hence this city-sponsored attempt to make a cold month cool – two weeks of flashy outdoor entertainment (mostly at Nathan Phillips Square), discounted admission to dozens of local landmarks (with a WinterCity passport; check the website for details) and discounted prices at local restaurants via the popular Winterlicious promotion. Fun stuff, but be sure to pack your mittens.

Arts & Entertainment

Children

Big fun for little people.

Toronto is kid-friendly all year-round, from the water park of Ontario Place to the free ice rinks at Harbourfront and Nathan Phillips Square. While hipsters may decry the city's lack of urban edginess, parents can relax in an environment of cleanliness and safety within a big-city setting. An easy-to-navigate streetscape and transit system make most outings a breeze, and those behind a pram will be relieved to see that most major subway stops have lifts, and that all significant destinations have ramp access.

An obvious first stop is an orienting visit to the **CN Tower** (*see p63*), followed by souvenir hunting at the consumer's paradise that is the **Toronto Eaton Centre** (*see p68*) or, for a shift in gears, a ferry ride to the bucolic **Toronto Islands** (*see p56*).

Babysitting & daycare

Any number of websites (www.helpwevegot kids.com is a good one) will provide a list of daycare centres in the Toronto area – many, such as **It's Playtime** (416 465 6688), provide drop-in babysitting services, some up to eight hours. Visit the above website for more information about supervised playgrounds, community centres that cater for single parents and emergency services. For a directory of downtown drop-ins and times, call **Community Information Toronto** (416 397 4636). Otherwise, the **YMCA** (Family Development Centre, 416 928 9622) runs groups throughout the city, is open from dawn till dusk and will take kids from 18 months to 12 years. Major hotels will be able to arrange babysitting (services are listed under individual hotels; see *pp36-50*); alternatively, call a reputable agency such as **Christopher Robin** (416 483 4744, $65 for first three hours, then $15 per hour thereafter).

Indoor attractions

Art Gallery of Ontario

For full listings, see *p71*.
It ain't the Louvre, but then again the AGO works on a scale that is well-suited to families – not too big to exhaust you, but enough quirky material to satisfy neophyte art critics (handy tip: head for the giant hamburger). The AGO is due to begin its extensive renovation from March 2005, so call ahead for schedules and closures.

CBC Broadcasting Centre

250 Front Street W, at John Street, Entertainment District (museum 416 205 5574/www.cbc.ca/ museum). Streetcar 504/subway Union or St Andrew. **Open** 9am-5pm Mon-Fri; noon-4pm Sat. **Admission** free. **Map** p279 E8.
Admittedly Canadian TV history isn't going to mean much to visitors from abroad, but CBC Centre's big-box architecture, giant atrium and main-floor museum are well worth a look. Interactive stations feature newsreels, children's shows and sports trivia. Sadly guided tours were discontinued in 2004.

Hockey Hall of Fame

For full listings, see *p65*.
How many museums have their own ice rink where you can test your slap shot skills? This impressive building houses the world's greatest hockey memories and lets you record your own broadcast.

Lorraine Kimsa Theatre for Young People

165 Front Street E, at Sherbourne Street, St Lawrence (416 862 2222/www.lktyp.ca). Streetcar 504. **Open** *Box office* 9am-5pm Mon-Fri. **Shows** *Matinées* Sat, Sun. **Tickets** $19-$29. **Credit** AmEx, MC, V. **Map** p280 H8.
Toronto's premier venue for children's theatre offers productions that are aimed at kids but will also appeal to their adult escorts. Shows are aimed at specific age groups, so call ahead or check the website.

Ontario Science Centre

For full listings, see *p91*.
This 1970s-era shrine to science and technology is undergoing a much-needed overhaul. Its distance from the city centre, and the admission price, makes this more of a day trip than an afternoon, but once inside kids like the hands-on approach to making science and engineering fun. It also features an Omnimax Cinema for those really big close-ups in science and nature films. Best of all, you can touch practically everything – except the liquid nitrogen.

Paramount Toronto

For full listings, see *p181*.
If cinema is on your offspring's agenda, this movie madhouse is the place to go. Small children may feel overwhelmed, but with more than 12 screens, including an IMAX, there's bound to be something suitable. Be warned: the 'waiting lounge' is a noisy video arcade surrounded by junk food kiosks, with prices far outstripping quality. If your film buffs are old enough to be left alone, take 90 minutes' refuge in the giant Chapters bookstore below (for details, see *p145*).

Royal Ontario Museum

For full listings, *see p77*.

All of Toronto's biggest and most important cultural institutions have recently undergone – or are still undergoing – renovations, but the ROM's is the most transformative and will continue through to 2007. The good news is that the bat cave, every child's favourite, will be open throughout. The permanent collection offers 'Hands-on Biodiversity' rooms with interactive displays.

Outdoor fun

Toronto has several large parks where restless young legs can run wild. The Toronto Islands provide the largest getaway (with a fun ferry ride to boot) and, from May to September, the **Centreville Amusement Park** (*see p57*) offers tyke-friendly pony and train rides. **High Park** (*see p95*) over in the West End features bicycle and inline skating paths, forest walks, a large pond, a small zoo, a tractor-train and a huge children's play castle that's a must for the 4-12 set. **Riverdale Park** is smaller, but has a petting zoo and various barnyard demonstrations. **Harbourfront Centre** (*p59*) on the city's lakeshore always has something going on, from tall ships to craft fairs. Catch a blown-glass demonstration in the craft studio.

For something simple and handy, check out the Yorkville rock (Cumberland Avenue between Avenue Road and Bay Street), a giant chunk of Canadian shield granite plonked down in the centre of the city. Kids love climbing it and parents love the nearby shopping.

And if your kids are sporty, the city has many public swimming pools and beaches, as well as tennis courts and golf courses. In winter public ice-skating rinks, indoor and outdoor, abound. There are also two ski runs in Earl Bales and Centennial Parks (*see p217*).

Ice-skating in Nathan Phillips Square

For full listings, *see p71*.

If you want to do something very Toronto, grab some skates and take a twirl before the landmark City Hall towers. Weekdays, when the coast is clear, are best for beginners. Rentals and sharpening services are positioned by the snack bar. Open from late November to late March, weather permitting.

Ontario Place

For full listings, *see p61*.

This is the mega playground kids dream about. Water activities include slides and bumper boats, and a huge concrete field where massive features spray water and serve as jungle gyms. Dry delight can be had with the indoor maze funhouse, fast food and various amphitheatres (including an IMAX which is built out over the water).

Paramount Canada's Wonderland

9580 Jane Street, at MacKenzie Drive, Vaughan (905 832 7000/www.canadas-wonderland.com). Yorkdale or York Mills subway then GO bus/Highway 400, exit Rutherford Road (just north of Highway 401). **Open** *Late May-mid June 10am-6pm daily. Mid June-Aug 10am-10pm daily. Sept-mid Oct 10am-8pm Sat, Sun. Closed mid Oct-late May.* **Admission** $50; $25 3-6s, concessions. **Credit** AmEx, MC, V.

Ontario Place

Situated out of town but well worth a family visit, this does all the things giant amusement parks do, from stomach-churning roller-coasters to inhabited cartoon characters. For a more authentic midway experience, the Canadian National Exhibition (*see p170*) operates for two weeks up to Labour Day (first Monday in September) at Exhibition Place.

Speaker's Corner

ChumCity Building, 299 Queen Street W, at John Street, Entertainment District (416 591 5757/ www.citytv.com). Streetcar 501/subway Osgoode. **Open** 24hrs daily. **Admission** $1. **No credit cards. Map** p279 E7.

A good first stop before heading to the Paramount (*see p173*), especially for older kids who need to vent some attitude. Named after its London counterpart in Hyde Park, though it's a bit more high tech. A video soapbox ensconced in the Citytv building encourages passers-by of all ages to speak their minds. Depositing a dollar triggers the video camera; pull back the curtain and you're a pundit. Citytv (Channel 7) airs the best comments on a show called *Speaker's Corner*; the money goes to local charities.

Toronto Hippo Tours

416 703 4476/www.torontohippotours.com. Tours leave from 151 Front Street W, at Simcoe Street, Entertainment District. Subway St Andrew or Union. **Tours** May-Oct hourly 11am-6pm daily. Closed Nov-Apr. **Admission** $35; $30 students 13-17; $23 3-12s; free under-3s; $100 family. **Credit** AmEx, MC, V. **Map** p280 F8.

Even residents are tempted to ride this amphibious tour bus, which morphs into a raft at the Toronto harbour. Meet the crew at the south-east corner of Front and Simcoe Streets for a street tour followed by a fishing boat's-eye view from the harbour.

Toronto Zoo

361A Old Finch Avenue, Meadowvale Road, north of Highway 401, North Toronto (416 392 5900/ www.torontozoo.com). Bus 85/GO Rouge Hill Station (weekends only). **Open** Jan-early Mar, early Oct-Dec 9.30am-4.30pm daily. *Early Mar-late May, early Sept-early Oct* 9am-6pm daily. *Late May-early Sept* 9am-7.30pm daily. **Admission** $18; $12 concessions; $10 4-12s; free under-4s. **Credit** AmEx, MC, V.

The zoo is terrific for animals, who have plenty of room to roam, and for their human interlopers, who can make a day of it with outdoor fun and adventure. Call ahead for feeding times, particularly for the polar bears, whose giant enclosure features an underwater observatory. All the big beasts are here, as well as their littl'uns – this zoo's inhabitants are remarkably fecund. Hop on to the Zoomobile when energy begins to wane. A safari simulator ride makes a nice treat as you leave. Last admission one hour before closure.

Eating out

When it comes to refuelling your youngsters in Toronto, there's a wide range of options. You can spend loads on crappy fried stuff available in emporium-style restaurants or go cheap if not cheerful at one of the zillion fast-food outlets. But you'll be missing out on the city's smörgåsbord of ready-to-eat ethnic flavours, from Lebanese shwarmas to Chilean empanadas. For a sit-down meal, Chinatown offers a large and inexpensive selection. Toronto is famous for the quality of its dim sum, and the finger-friendly delicacies need not break the bank. Over in the University District, and convenient after a visit to the Royal Ontario Museum, is the airy and spacious **Dynasty** (131 Bloor Street W, 416 923 3323).

If the tykes insist on the tired but true, **Planet Hollywood** (277 Front Street W, 416 596 7827) is located between the two major tourist spots, the CN Tower and SkyDome. The Entertainment District is lined with bustling eateries catering to large groups. **Wayne Gretzky's** (99 Blue Jays Way, 416 979 7825), named for and owned in part by Canada's greatest hockey player, makes a kid-friendly detour after a visit to the Hockey Hall of Fame. **Alice Fazooli's** (294 Adelaide Street W, 416 979 1910) serves the requisite wings, burgers and bottomless Cokes.

Keg Steakhouse & Bar

12 Church Street, at Front Street, St Lawrence (416 367 0685/www.kegsteakhouse.com). Streetcar 504/ subway Union. **Open** 4pm-1am Mon-Sat; 4-11pm Sun. **Main courses** $14-$32. **Credit** AmEx, DC, MC, V. **Map** p280 G8.

Steak and chicken, steak and ribs, steak and lobster – you get the picture. All the combinations for the little carnivore are at your saucy fingertips, with burgers for the pickiest. Quality is high, and service smiley, American-style.

Old Spaghetti Factory

54 The Esplanade, at Yonge Street, St Lawrence (416 864 9761/www.oldspaghettifactory.ca). Streetcar 504/subway Union. **Open** 11.30am-11pm Mon-Thur, Sun; 11.30am-midnight Fri, Sat. **Main courses** $9-$18. **Credit** AmEx, DC, MC, V. **Map** p280 G8.

Toronto's answer to Chuck-E-Cheez has been filling kids with 'pasghetti and meat bulbs' for more than three decades. Good for filling up en route to the nearby St Lawrence Centre for the Arts (*see p85*).

Shopping

The 'Kids' suffix is catching on everywhere, from Gap to Pottery Barn, but if you don't want your littl'uns looking like walking billboards, there are some decent alternatives, such as **Misdemeanours** (*see p151*), where Pam Chorley fits out little girls in styles that mothers will love. For brand names at a discount, check out **Chocky's** (*see p150*). For outdoor gear for the entire family, try **Mountain Equipment Co-op** (*see p164*). For shops selling toys and gadgets, *see p164*.

Arts & Entertainment

Comedy

Plenty to smile about.

Next to ice hockey, comedy is Canada's number one cultural export. Beginning in the silent movie era, when actress Mary Pickford and Keystone Cops' creator Mack Sennett blew down to Hollywood, northern yuksters have made an enormous impact on the worldwide comedy industry. In fact, so many Canadians have found success over the years that the average Torontonian can reel off a list of the all-time home-grown greats: Jim Carrey, Mike Myers, Rich Little, Michael J Fox, Tom Green (that one's debatable), Martin Short, John Candy and *Saturday Night Live* producer Lorne Michael.

Toronto is the launching pad for their exodus, and ranks as one of the three most important comedy centres in North America (New York and San Francisco being the other two). On any given night you can see seasoned stand-ups practising their craft at **Yuk Yuk's**, the legendary sketch comedy of **Second City**, or, if you're feeling more adventurous, seek out some experimental laughs. It was Toronto comedians, after all, who in the mid 1990s produced the world's only 'Jekyll and Hyde' show: the comics performed a feature show, took a two-hour intermission in which they drank and ingested drugs, and then performed the very same material in an altered state.

Such antics prove that while on the surface Toronto may appear to be a grey city where ambitious residents of the Great White North go to 'make money', beneath the Calvinist veneer beats a bawdy, mischievous heart, one that finds expression in the dozens of comedy venues around town.

Those wanting to venture into this world are best armed by picking up a copy of the local free listings rags: *eye* or *NOW*, which provide a guide to who's appearing at which venue on any given week. Of course, comedy is subjective, so you can never guarantee laughs, but if you frequent these establishments you're sure to at the very least have a few chuckles and at the very most, wet your pants. It may not even be your own liquid: in 1999 shock comic and MTV star Tom Green sprinkled a Toronto comedy crowd with a mixture of his own vomit and barbershop clippings. Nice.

Venues

ALTdotCOMedy Lounge

The Rivoli, 332-334 Queen Street W, at Spadina Avenue, Entertainment District (416 596 1908/ www.altcomedylounge.com). Streetcar 501, 510. **Show** 8.30pm Mon, 1st & 3rd Tue of mth. **Admission** pay what you can. **Credit** AmEx, MC, V. **Map** p279 E7.

Every Monday night the versatile back room at the Rivoli (*see also p107, p203 and p216*) is transformed into a cabaret, where Toronto's self-declared alternative comedians come out to play. On some nights it seems 'alternative' is a metaphor for 'poorly rehearsed', but admission is on a 'pay what you can' basis, which means it's normally good value for money, at least. If you're lucky you'll catch a visiting celebrity dropping in to blow off some mainstream steam. Scott Thompson, Janeane Garofalo, Will Ferrell and Tom Green have all made appearances here. The first and third Tuesday of each month are now devoted to sketch comedy.

Bad Dog Theatre Company

138 Danforth Avenue, at Broadview Avenue, East Toronto (416 491 3115/www.baddogtheatre.com). Subway Broadview. **Shows** 8pm Wed-Fri; 8pm, 10pm Sat. **Tickets** prices vary. **Credit** MC, V.

Toronto is known for its comedic improvisers, the most famous of whom are Mike Myers, the Kids in the Hall, Colin Mochrie and improv guru Bruce Hunter. The font of this talent was Theatresports, which, after a turbulent run at Toronto's Poor Alex

Home-grown chuckle-meister **Mike Myers**.

Theatre, went under and has been replaced by Bad Dog Theatre. This full-time improvisational venue presents an eclectic range of shows – everything from Harry Potter parodies ('Hairy Patter & the Improvisers Stone') to an open comedy jam such as Midweek Mayhem. They offer a weekly free 'drop-in' one-hour improv class, so adventurous types can try their hand. The atmosphere is warm and friendly, tinged with a bit of inventive agitation.

Laugh Resort

Holiday Inn Hotel, 370 King Street W, at Peter Street, Entertainment District (416 364 5233/ www.laughresort.com). Streetcar 504/subway St Andrew. **Shows** 8.30pm Wed, Thur; 8.30pm, 10.45pm Fri, Sat. **Tickets** $7-$15. **Credit** MC, V. **Map** p279 E8.

This cosy 100-seat theatre is in the basement of a Holiday Inn, but it feels like the basement of someone's house. The club moved to this smaller theatre a few years ago, and now it's a great place to get within spitting distance of some of comedy's finest. The intimate setting means the heckling can be fast and furious, and there's no place to hide if a performer sets their satirical sights on you. In addition to hosting local stars, the venue has traditionally

been a good spot to see international acts just before they hit the big time. Adam Sandler, David Spade and Ellen DeGeneres all performed here shortly before they became household names.

Second City

56 Blue Jays Way, at King Street W, Entertainment District (416 343 0011/www.secondcity.com). Streetcar 504/subway St Andrew. **Shows** times vary. **Tickets** $20-$34; $12-$27 concessions. **Credit** AmEx, DC, MC, V. **Map** p279 E8.

Founded in 1973, this is actually the second Second City, an offshoot of the original club in Chicago. Toronto's oldest and most famous comedy venue is still the best place in town to take in an evening of sketch comedy. The main productions at the theatre are loosely interlocked sketches with at least some attempt made at narrative continuity. After the show, members of the audience can stick around to watch the same performers hone their improvisation skills. The resident comedians use these improv nights to develop material for the next big show. Lists of alumni are etched on the theatre's main doors, and include Dan Aykroyd, Eugene Levy, Dave Thomas, Martin Short, Gilda Radner and John Candy. The building also houses the Tim Sims Playhouse (*see p177*).

Paying for laughs

Spurred on by Canada's comedy legacy, in 1999 Toronto's **Humber College** founded the world's first degree-granting comedy school. Aspiring cut-ups with university diplomas can take a one-year post-graduate programme; those fresh out of high school can join the two-year undergraduate stream. Each spring thousands of hopefuls audition for the school, and from this pool of prospective talent 140 students are chosen. But they have to be serious about being funny: courses cost upwards of $3,900 a year.

The school is located at Humber's Lake Shore campus, which is (ironically) housed in a renovated 120-year-old insane asylum. The curriculum is a class clown's dream. A typical schedule might include a morning class in sketch comedy followed by a few hours of stand-up, improv and bit of shtick. It boasts a faculty that has plenty of industry experience. Instructors include television producer Lorne Frohman, who in the 1970s won eight Emmy awards for his work with the likes of Richard Pryor and Lily Tomlin; SCTV alumnus Joe Flaherty; Yuk Yuk's (*see p177*) owner Mark Breslin and veteran Canadian stand-up Larry Horowitz. Humber also brings in guest speakers. In past semesters luminaries such as Seinfeld

producer George Shapiro, Chevy Chase, Steve Allen, Joan Rivers and the Smothers Brothers have all spoken to Humber students.

When it opened, the school of comedy was greeted with open disdain by the comedy community in general. The typical line being that 'you can't teach funny'. The idea of getting a degree in comedy seemed to contradict everything that being a comedian entailed – the rebellious, anti-authoritarian edge. The school's dean, author Joe Kertes, argued that Humber's goal was to help 'funny people get funnier'.

Today Kertes' assertion is being borne out. Humber graduates such as stand-up Levi McDougall and sketch comedian Ryan Belleville are making waves both north and south of the border and each night Toronto's comedy clubs are full of Humber grads plying their trade. Comedy fans wishing to see what Humber has to offer can check out Yuk Yuk's Tuesday night shows, which feature sets from current comedy programme students.

Humber School of Comedy

Humber Lakeshore Campus, 3199 Lake Shore Blvd W, at 23rd Street, West End (416 675 6622/www.humber.ca). Subway Kipling then bus 44.

Second City. *See p176.*

Spirits Bar & Grill

*642 Church Street, at Hayden Street, Church
& Wellesley (416 967 0001/www.spiritsbarand
grill.com). Subway Bloor-Yonge.* **Shows** 9pm
Wed. **Admission** free. **Credit** AmEx, DC, MC, V.
Map p283 G4.
Hosted by the irrepressible stand-up comedian Jo-
Anna Downey, Spirits is the city's longest-running
independent new material night. Located just up the
street from Boystown, it's homo-friendly and every
Wednesday offers a mix of beginners trying to gain
their feet and seasoned comics testing out new bits.
The atmosphere is warm and wacky and the emphasis is on experimentation. Admission is free, so don't
even think about asking for your money back.

Tim Sims Playhouse

*56 Blue Jays Way, at King Street W, Entertainment
District (416 343 0011/www.secondcity.com).
Streetcar 504/subway St Andrew.* **Shows** times
vary. **Tickets** average $10. **Credit** AmEx, MC, V.
Map p279 E8.
Named after the talented Toronto comedian who died
in 1995, the Tim Sims Playhouse is dedicated to providing a venue for one-person shows, avant-garde
sketch comedy and aspiring comic playwrights. It
is located inside the Second City complex (and is
funded by the comedy Goliath) but operates independently. Every month a new bill of comedians is
presented and the mix is as eclectic as it gets. It is a
favourite spot for the city's more talented comedians
to workshop television ideas and to break a few rules.

Yuk Yuk's

*224 Richmond Street W, at Simcoe Street,
Entertainment District (416 967 6425/www.yuk
yuks.com). Streetcar 501/subway Osgoode.* **Shows**
8.30pm Wed, Thur, Sun; 8pm, 10pm Fri, Sat; phone
for details Tue. **Tickets** $2-$17. **Credit** AmEx, MC,
V **Map** p279/280 F7.
'Back in 1976,' stand-up Mike Bullard used to say,
'there was a young man with $200 and the dream of
starting Canada's first chain of comedy clubs. Well,

Mark Breslin knocked that man out, took the $200
and Yuk Yuk's was born.' It's a telling dig, because
Yuk Yuk's – the world's largest chain of comedy
clubs – is a direct reflection of its founder Mark
Breslin's manic artistic vision. Yuk Yuk's is where
such big names as Jim Carrey, Howie Mandel and
Norm Macdonald learned their craft and it is where
(thanks to Breslin) alternative American comedians
like Bill Hicks and Sam Kinison found refuge when
club owners in the United States wouldn't book them.
Tuesday nights feature a mix of amateurs, including
students from the Humber School of Comedy (*see
p176* **Paying for laughs**). The rest of the week presents the best stand-up Canada has to offer.

Film

Toronto's love affair with cinema is on permanent rerun.

Sceptics claim Toronto moviegoers are undiscerning – that they'll see anything, anywhere. Others take a different approach, holding up local audiences as passionate, educated cineastes. Either way, it's true that this city is movie mad; full of fans who haul themselves off to cinemas weekly – come rain, sleet or snow.

Torontonians get to see the latest Hollywood hits before most Americans do. The big studios launch most of their offerings in New York, Los Angeles and Toronto. The city is also home to a few significant firsts in film-going, including the world's first multiplex shoebox built in the 1970s, an 18-screen warren now thankfully relegated to the dustbin of cinema lore. But like some mutating alien in its death throes, it spawned the movie monsterplex that is the industry standard today.

Another innovation that predates the glut of giant home entertainment centres is the **Varsity Cinema**'s VIP screening rooms. With just 30 or so comfy seats and concession stand wait staff, it's popular with moviegoers, who pour in and pay a premium for the pleasure of seeing current movies in an exclusive setting. And then there is the eye-popping phenomenon of IMAX, the giant-screen format that was invented and launched in Toronto in the 1970s and has since circumnavigated the globe with its spectacular nature docs.

To keep appetites satiated, there are a hundred or so film festivals of every rank (*see pp166-171*), including the highly hyped and hugely attended **Toronto International Film Festival** (*see p28*) in September. There's an excellent cinematheque, a healthy chain of rep houses (with screenings from midday to midnight), a drive-in on the waterfront, outdoor screenings and a guy with two rooms and a projector who has become a local legend.

Any week of the year, the lights dim for Shanghai samurai, retro romances, art cinema, dirty cartoons, documentaries, and kids' classics – on top of the newest releases. One thing you probably won't see is a Canadian movie: each year home-grown fare racks up as little as 0.02 per cent of screen time. But the city usually finds a way of satisfying most movie urges, so if you're determined to see something local, check out Cinematheque Ontario, the rep houses or the chic **Camera**

Royal Cinema. *See p181.*

Bar & Media Gallery, co-owned by local film director Atom Egoyan.

Although film content is abundant and varied in Toronto, the cinemas themselves often leave something to be desired. The great old houses are gone. Even in the heart of the city, it's usually a choice between going to a small or large box cinema – places where people with limited attention spans and unlimited cellphone time struggle with pizza and other viscous foods not meant to be eaten in the dark. They may have gathered for the latest Hollywood franchise flick but, together with the legions of dedicated cinephiles and the crowds of Bollywood fans in the suburbs, they're keeping the city's reputation as a buzzing movie hive alive and well.

TICKETS AND INFORMATION

The cost of going to the pictures keeps climbing (though foreigners, especially Brits, will still find it cheap). Tickets at a first-run cinema cost up to $13.95; the best deals are to be had on Tuesdays (when discounts are offered) and on weekday matinées. The rep circuit and the Cinematheque Ontario tickets are slightly cheaper than the norm, ranging from $7.25 to $10.50. There are also free screenings during the summer in Nathan Phillips Square, at the CHUM/Citytv parking lot on Queen Street West and in other neighbourhood venues (mainly parks).

For details of these, as well as weekly film listings, check the local press. The daily papers publish movie sections on Fridays, while the two free weeklies – *eye* and *NOW* – both have reviews as well as listings in their Thursday editions.

Art-house & rep

Bloor Cinema

506 Bloor Street W, at Bathurst Street, The Annex (416 516 2330/www.bloorcinema.com). Streetcar 511/subway Bathurst. **Admission** $7.25; $3.50-$4 concessions; $5.50 Mon-Fri before 4pm. **No credit cards. Map** p282 D4.

After an accident (when chunks of ceiling fell on the audience) steps were taken by the owners to pay attention to this old cinema's flaws. Even now, after repairs, it's a little ragged round the edges, but has a lot of character as the last standing commercial single-screen venue downtown. Expect to find a mix of first-run releases on their last stop before video/DVD, classics and foreign titles. The cinema is also home to many a mini fest, the One-Minute Film Festival and the Jewish Festival among them.

Camera Bar & Media Gallery

1028 Queen Street W, at Ossington Avenue (416 530 0011). Streetcar 501. **Open** 5pm-2am Tue-Sun. **Credit** AmEx, MC, V. **Map** p278 B7.

Director Atom Egoyan and distributor Hussain Amarshi are behind this new lounge with a 50-seat video theatre. Expect programming of avant-garde shorts and nascent festivals such as Monitor, a showcase of new South Asian short film and video. *See also p139 and p27* **Atom antics**.

Carlton

20 Carlton Street, at Yonge Street, Church & Wellesley (416 598 2309/www.cineplex.com). Streetcar 506/subway College. **Admission** $10; $6 concessions; $6 before 4pm Mon-Fri, all day Tue. **Credit** AmEx, MC, V. **Map** p283 G5.

This civilised little art-house multiplex, owned by the Cineplex Galaxy chain, shows the latest foreign films, commercial-free. The nine theatres are small and the walls are thin, but if you want to see the latest Godard, this might be your only choice in the city.

CineForum

463 Bathurst Street, at College Street, Kensington Market (416 603 6643). Streetcar 506, 511. **Admission** $20; $10 concessions. **No credit cards. Map** p279 D6.

Owner Reg Hartt claims he was the first to screen the porn classic, *Deep Throat* (admission was free if you showed up naked). His 'theatre' is in his modest home near modish College Street, where he revels in the weird. Hartt was once called 'a perv with a projector', but others hail him as local hero. Cartoons are his speciality: his Animation series highlighting obscure gems from the likes of Tex Avery, Bob Clampett and Friz Freleng comes around frequently.

Cinematheque Ontario

Advance ticket box office: *Manulife Centre, 55 Bloor Street W, at Bay Street, Yorkville (416 968 3456/www.e.bell.ca/filmfest/cinematheque). Bus 6/subway Bay.* **Open** noon-6pm Mon-Sat. **Map** p282 F4.

Screenings: *Jackman Hall, Art Gallery of Ontario, 317 Dundas Street W, at McCaul Street, Chinatown. Streetcar 505/subway St Patrick.* **Admission** $10.50; $5.50-$6 concessions. **Credit** AmEx, MC, V. **Map** p279 E6.

For now still housed in the Art Gallery of Ontario, which is undergoing long-term renovation, this year-round cinematheque is one of the best anywhere. Programmers offer movie masterpieces, children's classics, foreign rarities and new discoveries from some of the world's finest film-makers.

Fox Theatre

2236 Queen Street E, at Beech Avenue, East Toronto (416 691 7330/www.festivalcinemas.com). Streetcar 501. **Admission** $8; $3.50-$4 concessions. **No credit cards.**

The Fox is an old single-screen cinema that's seen better days, but for the Beaches crowd it's a reliable place to catch recent releases and foreign films.

Ontario Place Cinesphere

955 Lake Shore Boulevard W, Harbourfront (416 314 9900/www.ontarioplace.com/en/Cinesphere). Bus 29/streetcar 509, 511/subway Union. **Admission** $8-$10; $6 concessions. **Credit** AmEx, MC, V. **Map** p278 B10.

The world's first permanent IMAX theatre is inside a geodesic dome perched over Lake Ontario at this government-run amusement park (*see also p61 and p173*). A year-round schedule mixes purpose-made IMAX thrillers with Hollywood blockbusters.

Paradise Cinema

1006 Bloor Street W, at Ossington Avenue, West End (416 537 7040/www.festivalcinemas.com). Bus 63/subway Ossington. **Admission** $8; $4 concessions. **No credit cards.**

Situated in a nondescript part of town – between the Annex and Bloor West Village – this single-screen movie house has little character, but is comfortable and benefits from the shared programming of the rep house circuit.

Regent Theatre

551 Mount Pleasant Road, at Davisville Avenue, Davisville (416 480 9884). Subway Davisville then bus 28. **Admission** $10; $5 concessions. **No credit cards.**

One of the city's few independent theatres, the Regent has had a long and distinguished career. Today it's a modest cinema with a warm atmosphere, and is much loved by its neighbourhood supporters. It screens beyond-first-run releases.

Room with a viewing

Toronto's own media guru, Marshall McLuhan, coined the phrase 'The medium is the message.' Is it purely by accident, then, that his adopted city now has a video arcade of pure Canadiana packaged in McLuhanesque proportions?

NFB Mediatheque (*pictured*) is a screening room run by the National Film Board of Canada, a 65-year-old public film-making institution. Anyone can pop in, slip into an 'interactive personal viewing station' – aka a comfy chair facing a monitor – and choose from more than 1,000 movies. Mostly it's the NFB's own-produced films on offer: beautiful and often bizarre animation, plus a wealth of classic documentaries. But no matter what you end up watching, it will amount to an anthropological dig into Canada's cinematic psyche – executed with digital tools. And like some of this country's better ideas, it's free.

Over the years the NFB has produced over 10,000 titles, a number of which are decidedly educational. So the Mediatheque visitor could just as easily tune into a dead-straight account of developments in 1940s prairie farming as an Oscar-winning cartoon about a pernickety cat. There's plenty of appeal in both, so be prepared to sample and explore – you're in charge, after all. Look out for some of the most brilliant animation anywhere – from the creations of experimental mastermind Norman McLaren to recent cutting-edge hits such as Chris Landreth's *Ryan*, a film that overlays live action with animation. Documentaries cover just about everything imaginable. If you like what you see, NFB videos and DVDs are for sale on site.

The Mediatheque has six individual and eight double personal viewing stations. A conventional cinema upstairs also shows films. If you're heading to Montreal, be sure to pay a visit to the Mediatheque's older brother, CineRobotheque.

NFB Mediatheque

150 John Street, at Richmond Street W, Entertainment District (416 973 3012/ www.nfb.ca). Streetcar 501, 504. **Open** 1-7pm Mon, Tue; 10am-7pm Wed; 10am-10pm Thur-Sat; noon-5pm Sun. **Map** p279 E7.

Arts & Entertainment

Revue Cinema

*400 Roncesvalles Avenue, at Dundas Street W,
West End (416 531 9959/www.festivalcinemas.com).
Subway Dundas West.* **Admission** $8; $4
concessions. **No credit cards.**
The Revue is a long-standing favourite among art-
house fans and neighbourhood moviegoers. Tucked
in the heart of Roncesvalles Village, this classic cinema retains some characteristics of its 1920s origins.

Royal Cinema

*606 College Street W, at Clinton Street, Little Italy
(416 516 4845/www.festivalcinemas.com). Streetcar
506, 511.* **Admission** $8; concessions $4. **No credit
cards. Map** p278 C5.
Another neighbourhood spot, this single-screen
cinema has a great location slap bang in the heart of
trendy College Street. Pity the programming doesn't
reflect the identity of the Italian neighbourhood,
but at least there are plenty of places to sip a decent
espresso while discussing the film afterwards.

Mainstream & first-run

Alliance Atlantis Cumberland 4 Cinemas

*159 Cumberland Street, at Avenue Road, Yorkville
(416 646 0444/www.allianceatlantiscinemas.com).
Subway Bay.* **Admission** $12.75; $7.75 concessions;
free under-3s; $8 all day Tue; $9.50 before 6pm Mon-
Fri; $10 before 6pm Sat, Sun. **Credit** MC, V. **Map**
p282 F4.
Once this was the only theatre in Canada with
reserved seating, but that gimmick has long died
out. Today the comfortable multiplex shows a mix
of foreign and independent movies, with the occasional mainstream hit.
Other locations: Alliance Atlantis Beach
Cinemas 1651 Queen Street E, East Toronto (416
646 0444); **Alliance Atlantis Bayview Village
Cinemas** 2901 Bayview Avenue, North Toronto
(416 646 0444).

Canada Square

*2190 Yonge Street, at Eglinton Avenue, Davisville
(416 646 0444/www.famousplayers.ca). Subway
Eglinton.* **Admission** $11.75; $7.50 concessions;
$7.75 before 6pm Mon-Fri, all day Tue; $8.75
before 6pm Sat, Sun. **Credit** AmEx, MC, V.
This 13-screen theatre offers a sensible mix of foreign
films and first-run mainstream pictures. It's a classic
example of the 1980s cookie-cutter multiplex, but
somehow everything fits, and no one feels cramped.

Colossus

*3555 Highway 7 W, at Westin Road, North Toronto
(905 851 1001/www.famousplayers.ca). Subway
Wilson then bus 165.* **Admission** $13.95; $8.50
concessions; free under-3s; $9.25 before 6pm Mon-
Fri; $9.25 all day Tue; $11.50 before 6pm Sat, Sun.
Credit AmEx, MC, V.
During the 1990s movie exhibitors kept on building
them larger and larger, until they finally hit their
max. For the Famous Players group, this 18-screen

stadium-seating emporium is it. How many screens
of entertainment, rows of concession stands, games
and other distractions can you handle? The answer
lies across the street, where rival exhibitor AMC
went one bigger with something called Interchange
30 (at Highways 400 and 7). The name refers to the
number of booming screens it delivers.

The Docks Drive-In

*11 Polson Street, at Cherry Street, East Toronto
(416 461 3625/www.thedocks.com). Bus 72.* **Open**
Tue, Fri, Sat; phone for details. Closed Oct-late Apr.
Admission $13; $4 concessions; $6.50 all day Tue.
Credit AmEx, MC, V.
Golf driving range by day, drive-in by night. This
nightclub/theme park on the waterfront shows double bills of mainstream movies to 500 cars three times
a week in summer, on what's billed as the largest
drive-in screen in North America. Pull in, spin the
FM dial to the show and kick back. Even if you don't
like the features, the Docks' bars and other attractions will keep you happy. *See also p214* **Tee time.**

Paramount

*259 Richmond Street W, at John Street, Entertainment
District (416 368 5600/www.famousplayers.ca).
Streetcar 501, 504.* **Admission** $13.50; $7.50
concessions; free under-3s; $8.50 before 6pm
Mon-Fri, all day Tue; $11.50 before 6pm Sat, Sun.
Credit MC, V. **Map** p279 E7.
This theatre complex delivers a bruising assault on
the senses. Among the midway atmosphere of video
games and concessions stands, there are 13 screens,
plus an IMAX 3D theatre that shows pop-up versions of mainstream Hollywood fare.

SilverCity Yonge-Eglinton Centre

*2300 Yonge Street, at Eglinton Avenue, Davisville
(416 544 236/www.famousplayers.ca). Subway
Eglinton.* **Admission** $13.95; $8.50 concessions;
free under-3s; $9.25 before 6pm Mon-Fri, all day
Tue; $11.50 before 6pm Sat, Sun. **Credit** MC, V.
There is a collection of SilverCity cinemas around
town: multiplexes with all the noise, bright lights,
games and junk food you'll (n)ever want.
Other locations: SilverCity Yorkdale 3401
Dufferin Street, at Highway 401, North Toronto
(416 787 2052); **SilverCity North York at
Empress Walk** 5095 Yonge Street, north of
Sheppard Avenue, North Toronto (416 223 9550).

Varsity Cinemas

*Manulife Centre, 55 Bloor Street W, at Bay Street,
Yorkville (416 961 6303/www.cineplex.com). Subway
Bay.* **Admission** *Main theatre* $13.95; $8.50
concessions; $9.25 before 6pm Mon-Fri, all day
Tue; $11.50 before 6pm Sat, Sun. *VIP theatres*
$16.95; $12.25 before 6pm Mon-Fri; $14.50 before
6pm Sat, Sun. **Credit** AmEx, MC, V. **Map** p282 F4.
This eight-screen mutiplex on the 'mink mile' boasts
top facilities and a good mix of mainstream, independent and foreign fare. In addition, two VIP
screening rooms offer some of the most intimate
viewing experiences outside a home theatre system.
The VIP theatres range from 28 to 36 seats.

Galleries

A flourishing scene that shows no sign of slowing down.

401 Richmond Street West. *See p183*.

Since the late 1990s the Toronto art scene has been experiencing a remarkable resurgence and enthusiasm not seen since the boom years of the 1980s. Over the past five years or so, dozens of new galleries have opened and an ever-increasing number of artists are jumping into the fray. A high proportion of the art seen around town is by young emerging artists, which isn't exceptional in itself – this is a global phenomenon for artists working in new digital- and time-based media – but in Toronto's case a couple of other factors are also at play. The city's art market was one of the casualties of the recession of the early 1990s, so for a good ten years it wasn't much fun being an artist or running a gallery, to say the least. And anyone who's already an established Canadian art star is likely to be based in either New York or Los Angeles. But the emergence of two major new gallery areas may indeed signal a positive trend for the local art scene.

NEW KIDS ON THE BLOCK

Artists and galleries often lead the way in revitalising neighbourhoods – and in the case of Toronto most of the new spaces that have sprung up are in the hyper-trendy stretch of Queen Street west of Bathurst Street (known simply as West Queen West or Queen Street West) where it seems like someone is blowing the paint dry on a new space every week. The **Clint Roenisch Gallery** has recently opened here, and the fledgling **MOCCA** (Museum of Contemporary Canadian Art; *see p98*) has finally landed in a spacious though structurally modest building in the heart of the action. MOCCA's move to the neighbourhood is the strongest sign that Queen West's art district is not likely to disappear with the next economic downturn.

Most of the galleries in this area are small converted storefronts, and on Friday evenings, when many exhibition openings are in full gear, you will see crowds of trendies spilling on to the streets and whole posses of artists hopping from one gallery to the next. In addition, in the past couple of years, two renovated hotels have opened, both catering to the art crowd: the ultra-hip **Drake Hotel** (*see p93*) and the more earthy **Gladstone Hotel** (*see p94*). Both have rooms for artists-in-residence, and their event spaces are constantly occupied with arty gatherings of every kind. It's best to check their websites for calendar listings, but even if you just turn up you're likely to find yourself in the midst of something worthwhile, such as an indie film festival screening or the popular Trampoline Hall night (www.trampolinehall.net), where guest speakers are invited to talk about something they know nothing about.

While the West Queen West scene is taking hold in a neighbourhood dotted with used appliance stores, across town an arts scene is springing up alongside some interesting commercial outlets. Developers of the east end's Distillery District (*see p184*) have enticed several high-end galleries to fill the vast warehouse spaces left from a Victorian-era booze factory. The area has quickly become touristy, with bars, coffee shops and designer furniture stores bringing a crowd slightly more well-heeled than the hipsters along Queen West. Likewise, the galleries are upscale and housed in some of the most beautiful industrial spaces in the city. **Robert Birch**, **Monte Clark** and **Sandra Ainsley** galleries were among the first to arrive; more recently they have been joined by **Artcore** and the stunningly renovated **Corkin Shopland Gallery**, a labyrinth of big and small viewing areas housed under one very high ceiling with skylights that cast richly atmospheric shafts of light.

So what about the traditional arty areas? Before the emergence of Queen Street West and the Distillery District the gallery scene was focused in and around the Yorkville area at Bloor Street and Avenue Road. Once upon a time this neighbourhood was a hippie hangout, before gradually moving upscale. Yorkville's art market heyday was in the 1980s, but there are still a number of galleries on and around Hazelton Avenue. Many of them, however, are beginning to show the conservatism and inertia that comes with age.

If you're a fan of photography, meanwhile, the city is also home to several galleries for whom it is a speciality. These include the **Stephen Bulger Gallery** (1026 Queen Street W, 416 504 0575), **Tatar Alexander Gallery** (183 Bathurst Street, Suite 200, 416 360 3822) and **LEE fotogallery** (Unit 116, 993 Queen Street W, 416 504 9387).

FURTHER INFORMATION

The listings in this chapter are a broad sample of the fare to be found around the city. In addition to those reviewed here, there are several warehouses around town: **401 Richmond Street West** (its best individual galleries are listed below), and still more across the road at 80 Spadina Avenue, which includes the excellent artist-run photography space, **Gallery TPW**. For comprehensive listings of current exhibitions, read *NOW* (www.nowtoronto.com; out on Thursdays) and the monthly *Slate Art Guide*, free in most galleries or online at www.slateartguide.com. For reviews, check out the 'Gallery Going' section of the *Globe and Mail* or the Saturday edition of the *National Post*.

For the **Toronto International Art Fair**, *see p171*, and the **Toronto Outdoor Art Exhibition**, *see p169*.

Apart from Ydessa Hendeles Art Foundation, all the following galleries have free entry.

Entertainment District

Archive Gallery

110 Spadina Avenue, at Adelaide Street (416 703 6564/www.archivegallery.com). Streetcar 504, 510. **Open** noon-5pm Tue-Fri; by appointment Sat. **No credit cards**. **Map** p279 D7.
This one-room space was designed by architect Johnson Chou and, as its name might suggest, it has a sizeable computer database of artists, mostly from Toronto and Montreal. It also holds exhibitions compiled from the works of artists in the archive by guest curators. Oddly enough, its website does not link to the artist database, but it does show pictures of its current exhibition.

Prefix Institute of Contemporary Art

Suite 124, 401 Richmond Street W, at Spadina Avenue (416 591 0357). Streetcar 501, 510. **Open** noon-5pm Wed-Sat. **Credit** MC, V. **Map** p279 D7.
Prefix Photo started out in 2000 as a high-quality contemporary art-photography magazine. The twice-yearly magazine is still being published, but the Prefix name has morphed into an institution for photo-based art by such artists as Stan Douglas and China's Wang Qingsong. Like the magazine, the gallery is sleek and up-to-the-minute on all things new media. They've even built a sound-proof room for audio works.

Wynick/Tuck Gallery

Suite 128, 401 Richmond Street W, at Spadina Avenue (416 504 8716/www.wynicktuckgallery.ca). Streetcar 501, 510. **Open** 11am-5pm Tue-Sat. **Credit** AmEx, MC, V. **Map** p279 D7.
The prevailing style at this long-reigning gallery is contemporary with a pop-culture streak. You'll find conceptual painter Gerald Ferguson's canvases that

Arts & Entertainment

are painted with a rope dipped in black paint, and Angela Leach's paintings of bright wavy stripes that can do strangely optical things to your eyes. *See also p185* **Space oddities**.

YYZ Artists' Outlet

Suite 140, 401 Richmond Street W, at Spadina Avenue (416 598 4546/www.yyzartistsoutlet.org). Streetcar 504, 510/subway Osgoode. **Open** 11am-5pm Tue-Sat. **Credit** MC, V. **Map** p279 D7.
An artist-run centre that aims to show work not being displayed by commercial galleries and institutions. Like Mercer Union (*see p186*), it's a forum for smart artists like Tim Lee to exhibit works that you can't hang above your couch.

Distillery District

Artcore Gallery

Building 62, 55 Mill Street, at Parliament Street (416 920 3820/www.artcoregallery.com). Bus 65. **Open** 10am-6pm Tue-Sat; noon-5pm Sun. **Credit** V. **Map** p280 H8.
Artcore is one of a handful of galleries in the city with international pretensions, showing both Canadian artists such as figurative sculptor Evan Penny, and international talents like Joseph Beuys and Enzo Cucchi.

Corkin Shopland Gallery

Building 61, 55 Mill Street, at Parliament Street (416 304 1050/www.corkinshopland.com). Bus 65. **Open** 10am-6pm Tue-Sat. **Credit** V. **Map** p280 H8.
Jane Corkin is known internationally as a leader in historic and contemporary photography, but since pairing up with Martin Shopland and moving into this massive gallery in the Distillery District her eye has turned to painting, sculpture, video-based works, and, oddly, Victorian-era antiques.

Gibsone Jessop Gallery

Building 4, 55 Mill Street, at Parliament Street (416 360 6800/www.gibsonejessop.com). Bus 65. **Open** 10am-6pm daily. **Credit** V. **Map** p280 H8.
Devoted solely to international artists who have not shown before in Canada, Gibsone Jessop displays a keen eye for trend-spotting in painting, mixed media and digital art.

Monte Clark Gallery

Building 2, 55 Mill Street, at Parliament Street (416 703 1700/www.monteclarkgallery.com). Bus 65. **Open** 10am-6pm Tue-Sat; noon-5.30pm Sun. **Credit** V. **Map** p280 H8.
The style of this gallery is cool, wry and luscious to the eye. The artists it represents are mainly drawn from the original Monte Clark Gallery in Vancouver, and the prevailing school of concept photography including Roy Arden, Scott McFarland, and author-artist Douglas Coupland.

Robert Birch Gallery

Building 3, 55 Mill Street, at Parliament Street (416 365 3003/www.robertbirchgallery.com). Bus 65. **Open** 11am-6pm Tue-Sat; noon-5pm Sun. **Credit** MC, V. **Map** p280 H8.
Robert Birch has an excellent band of mostly local artists who share a healthy sense of post-modern smarts, including Lee Goreas, Eric Glavin and Euan Macdonald. Like the gallery itself, works here are often deceptively simple.

Yorkville

Beckett Fine Art

120 Scollard Street, at Hazelton Avenue (416 922 5582/www.beckettfineart.com). Subway Bay. **Open** 10.30am-5pm Wed-Sat. **Credit** V. **Map** p282 F3.

Monte Clark Gallery.

Space oddities

Kelly Mark (at Wynick/Tuck; *see p183*) has a gift for making art out of almost nothing. Take her video performance series of her cat Roonie, who is far too sedate and overweight to actually perform. Roonie videos are the antithesis of the cute family pet home movie where Fido bounces happily around for the camcorder. In one series Roonie sleeps soundly on a couch while two stereo speakers beside him blare out pop tunes by Tom Jones and AC/DC. Mark's various forms of work – which also include photography, performance, drawing, sculpture and installation – are studies in spare and wasted time. She has made origami out of subway tickets, videos where she stares blankly into a camera for 33 minutes, and she has photographed, with obsessive keenness, irregularities in road markings. Each work is a pondering on the virtues of slowness, boredom, inane observation and *dolce far niente*.

A **Kelly Mark** demonstration.

Yet Mark can hardly be accused of being idle. Lately she has been busy building a website (www.samplesize.ca) of works by other artists, including critical writings, QuickTime videos, and a collection of photographs that are distinct for having 'absolutely no content' (according to Mark herself). The site has become one of the best resources for tapping into the country's indie art scene.

Other notable mentions on the art scene include **David Acheson** (at Christopher Cutts; *see p186*), who is one of the best sculptors around, depicting superheroes in states of anxiety. Photographer **Ed Burtynsky** (at Nicholas Metivier, 451 King Street W, Entertainment District, 416 205 9000) is known for stunning and disturbing images of man's intrusions into nature through deforestation, mining and quarrying. **Arnaud Maggs** (at Susan Hobbs; *see p187*) is another photographer of international calibre, revered for his serial portraits in black and white. **Jay Isaac** (at Greener Pastures; *see p186*) is a master of turning bad taste into good, and mining the hideous to extract the sublime. If you can picture it, he's made a Cubist-type sculpture of a speed-boat and painted it in powder pinks and blues. The latest to wrestle with the Canadian tradition of attempting to interpret the beauty of the Great White North is **Brad Phillips**, who paints leaves and skies, then switches to portraits of famous faces such as Winona Ryder. One local who finds a happy medium between high-brow art and low-end craft is **Allyson Mitchell**, who has exhibited at Paul Petro (*see p186*), among others. Her fun-fur wall works are hilarious and socially attuned. Last year, one of her female fun-fur nudes showed up on the cover of the national magazine *Canadian Art*.

Established in 1966, this gallery keeps a fresh perspective on contemporary art showing works by local painter and sculptor John Coburn, First Nations' artists David General and Arthur and Travis Shilling, and it exhibits emerging and established artists from Japan, the UK and the US.

West End

Angell Gallery
890 Queen Street W, at Crawford Street (416 530 0444/www.angellgallery.com). Streetcar 501. **Open** noon-5pm Wed-Sat & by appointment. **Credit** V. **Map** p278 B7.

Angell was among the first galleries to anticipate the boom of West Queen West, which makes the flamboyant proprietor, Jamie Angell, something of an elder statesman on the scene. Angell is not afraid to give his walls over to those fresh out of art school; including Kim Dorland, who paints wild, goofy clichés of cattlemen and pin-up girls, and Kristine Moran, whose enamel paintings of cars flying though buildings sell out faster than she can paint them.

Art Metropole
2nd floor, 788 King Street W, at Bathurst Street (416 703 4400/www.artmetropole.com). Streetcar 504, 511. **Open** 11am-6pm Tue-Fri; noon-5pm Sat. **Credit** V. **Map** p278 B7.

This gallery and art bookstore was created in 1974 by the celebrated General Idea collective. There is usually an installation with a conceptual bent here and always a lot of clever little multiples and publications on display. Exhibitions also delve into video, audio and electronic media not found anywhere else in the city. Watch for works by Martin Creed, David Shrigley, Yoko Ono and Lawrence Weiner.

Christopher Cutts Gallery

21 Morrow Avenue, at Dundas Street W (416 532 5566/www.cuttsgallery.com). Streetcar 505/subway Dundas West or Lansdowne. **Open** 11am-6pm Tue-Sat. **No credit cards**.

This immaculate establishment is well worth the time it will take you to find it. It's off the beaten track in a small complex of galleries, which also includes the Olga Korper Gallery (*see below*). It exhibits work by pioneers of modern Canadian painting like Kazuo Nakamura and Ray Mead, founding members of Painters Eleven from the 1950s, as well as an excellent bunch of younger artists such as Janieta Eyre, Richard Stipl and David Acheson.

Clint Roenisch Gallery

944 Queen Street W, at Shaw Street (416 516 8593/www.clintroenisch.com). Streetcar 501. **Open** noon-6pm Thur-Sat; 1-5pm Sun. **Credit** AmEx, MC, V. **Map** p278 B7.

One of the newest galleries on the strip, Roenisch was a curator before becoming a dealer, so his exhibitions lean towards interesting groupings with works like delicate, Renaissance-inspired landscape paintings by Douglas Walk, photography by Nan Goldin and weird little drawings and dolls made from wool socks by local artist Seth Scriver.

DeLeon White Gallery

1096 Queen Street W, at Dovercourt Road (416 597 9466/www.eco-art.com). Bus 29, 63/streetcar 501. **Open** *Summer* noon-6pm Wed-Sun. *Winter* 11am-5pm Wed-Sat; 1-4pm Sun. **Credit** MC, V. **Map** p278 A7.

DeLeon White Gallery's digs are the most elegant and spacious in a neighbourhood that's best known for far more modest storefront renovations. Its mandate is to show artists who work with environmental or ecological paradigms and explore issues revolving around nature, culture and society. It's about eco-art, not landscape art. Check out the roof deck in good weather.

Edward Day Gallery

952 Queen Street W, at Shaw Street (416 921 6540/www.edwarddaygallery.com). Streetcar 501. **Open** By appointment Mon; 10am-6pm Tue-Thur, Sat; 10am-7pm Fri; noon-5pm Sun. **Credit** AmEx, MC, V. **Map** p278 B7.

Edward Day used to be ensconced in the blue-chip Yorkville district. When the gallery moved to Queen West it doubled its floor space to make room for large-scale sculptures and installations. This is a buffet-style gallery – a whole lot of different tastes in close proximity. The styles and artistic tempera-ments range from the high to the low, with every-thing in between. And, just like a buffet, it usually leaves you feeling full – and sometimes satisfied.

Greener Pastures Contemporary Art

1188 Queen Street W, at Dovercourt Road (416 535 7100/www.greenerpasturesgallery.com). Bus 29, 63/streetcar 501. **Open** noon-6pm Thur-Sat & by appointment. **No credit cards**. **Map** p278 A7.

Dealer Kineko Ivic has taken everything he learned working at Stux gallery in New York and applied it to his own gallery, optimistically named Greener Pastures. Some of the best young painters in the city show here: Elizabeth McIntosh's mod abstracts, Jay Isaac's bizarre landscapes in candy-floss colours and Jennifer Murphy's collages of insects, flowers and patterns made from bits of fabric and sequins. If the door's locked, knock: Ivic might be downstairs working on some of his own glitter and splash paintings.

Mercer Union

37 Lisgar Street, at Queen Street W (416 536 1519/www.mercerunion.org). Streetcar 501. **Open** 11am-6pm Tue-Sat. **Credit** V. **Map** p278 A7.

A long-standing ideologically and theoretically driven artist-run space, Mercer Union is actually more fun than it sounds, having seen many of Canada's best artists pass through. The exhibition space is divided into three distinct areas, allowing for concurrent exhibitions, lectures, video screenings and performances.

Olga Korper Gallery

17 Morrow Avenue, at Dundas Street W (416 538 8220/www.olgakorpergallery.com). Streetcar 505/subway Dundas West or Lansdowne. **Open** 10am-6pm Tue-Sat. **Credit** AmEx, V.

Established in 1973, this is one of most beautiful galleries in the city – a cavernous and nicely lit space that was once a foundry, then a garbage repository for a mattress factory. Olga Korper has become some-thing of an institution on the art scene in Toronto and has a strong group of artists, including Lynn Cohen, Marcel Dzama, Paterson Ewen and Tim Whiten.

1080BUS & Katharine Mulherin Gallery

1080 & 1086 Queen Street W, at Brookfield Street (416 537 8827/www.kmartprojects.com). Bus 63/streetcar 501. **Open** noon-5pm Thur-Sun & by appointment. **Credit** V. **Map** p278 B7.

Katharine Mulherin works with a large number of young artists, and though she owns three galleries (the third being an exhibit site for the Ontario College of Art & Design sculpture/installation students) and is therefore a large figure on the scene, the pieces she shows tend to have a humble and personal feel.

Paul Petro Contemporary Art

980 Queen Street W, at Ossington Avenue (416 979 7874/www.paulpetro.com). Bus 63/streetcar 501. **Open** 11am-5pm Wed-Sat. **No credit cards**. **Map** p278 B7.

Ydessa Hendeles Art Foundation.

There is a tiny, easy-to-miss sign outside the gallery; there may be art in the window to clue you in, but if there isn't you could easily walk straight past it. Inside, artwork centres on personal identity and identity politics by the likes of Paul P, Julie Voyce and Stephen Andrews.

SPIN Gallery

2nd floor, 1100 Queen Street W, at Dovercourt Road (416 530 7656/www.spingallery.ca). Bus 29, 63/streetcar 501. **Open** noon-6pm Wed-Sat; 1-4pm Sun. **No credit cards. Map** p278 A7.
Voted best gallery by both *eye* and *NOW* magazines in 2004, SPIN is located on the second floor of a building that once housed a wholesaler of industrial kitchen appliances. From the outside it's nothing special. But inside the upstairs gallery has been sandblasted to a charming ruggedness, with creaky wooden floorboards, exposed brick and arching windows looking out to the lake. The speciality here is local artists but national and the occasional international artist also gets a look-in. Well-known names who have had exhibitions include Michael Stipe (REM), photographer, music video director and filmmaker Floria Sigismondi, and fashion photographer George Whiteside.

Susan Hobbs Gallery

137 Tecumseth Street, at Richmond Street W (416 504 3699/www.susanhobbs.com). Streetcar 501, 504, 511. **Open** 1-5pm Thur-Sat & by appointment. **No credit cards. Map** p278 C7.
On a side street off the main Queen Street strip, Susan Hobbs hosts mainly sculpture and installation by some of the more established Canadian artists such as Ian Carr-Harris, Robin Collyer, Max Dean and Shirley Wiitasalo, many of whom are very well known in Canada but not necessarily elsewhere.

Ydessa Hendeles Art Foundation

778 King Street W, between Niagara & Tecumseth Streets (416 413 9400). Streetcar 504, 511. **Open** noon-5pm Sat or by appointment. **Admission** $4. **No credit cards. Map** p278 C8.
When Ydessa was a dealer, representing artists like Jeff Wall and Jana Sterbak, she began collecting art herself. And when the line between curating and collecting blurred, she opened up her remarkable and ever-developing collection to the public. An installation in its own right, exhibits include Maurizio Cattelan's sculpture of a praying Hitler, and a room covered in thousands of black and white photographs of teddy bears with their owners.

Gay & Lesbian

If you like cruising, your ship's come in.

Despite its varied ethnic make-up, the Toronto gay scene is a very Waspish mixture of raunch and respectability. Unlike most American cities, Toronto never closed its bathhouses – even at the height of the AIDS epidemic – and, somewhat to the surprise of locals, the city has gradually developed a vaguely sexy reputation. There are now at least eight bathhouses, not to mention a strip joint where the boys bare all. At the same time, the city's gay scene can sometimes feel like a sleeper cell for domesticated gay couples. A 2003 judicial decision legalised gay marriage in the province of Ontario, and in many quarters gays are no longer regarded as sexual outlaws or rabid activists, but simply folk with the same concerns as everybody else – a big-screen TV and a mortgage-free home in which to put it.

The community came of age during the legendary bath raids of the early 1980s and still cherishes its activist past, but in-your-face antics have largely been exchanged for establishment clout. Prosperous queer couples have colonised the left-liberal neighbourhood of Riverdale (east of downtown on the far side of the Don River), the formerly raunchy Queen West area of Parkdale, and the up-and-coming artsy enclave of Leslieville (near Queen Street East and Pape). While there's still some friction with the police, the local community has political push and a very visible presence. An openly gay councillor represents the local ghetto at City Hall, the mayor sometimes joins the **Pride Week** parade, and the public library keeps a collection of gay and lesbian books at its Yorkville branch (22 Yorkville Avenue, 416 393 7660).

As for 'flaunting' your gayness, most Torontonians are pretty blasé about homos, but attitudes vary within the city. Gay couples hold hands quite openly downtown, particularly in the gay 'hood around Church & Wellesley, but are more circumspect in the 'old suburbs' of Etobicoke or Scarborough, or even in the straight part of the Entertainment District–Richmond–Adelaide, where testosterone can sometimes get in the way of tolerance.

The bar action is concentrated on Church Street, one block east of Yonge Street, and on the side streets in between. It's a small, compact scene that's close to the subway (both College and Wellesley stations on the Yonge Street line) and easily toured on foot. So if you don't like one bar you can easily walk to another.

Crews, Tango & The Zone. See p189.

Not everyone enjoys the bar and bath scene, of course, and many local gays organise their social lives around volunteer organisations or the city's many active sports leagues, a couple of which are among the largest gay organisations in the city.

Women especially often prefer to socialise outside the bars, either through sports leagues or in some of the city's trendier, gay-friendly neighbourhoods. Both the studenty Annex and Queen Street West west of Bathurst Street, including Parkdale, are popular. Lesbians have been more visible on Church Street in recent years, but the action is still hard to find. There are only a couple of dedicated lesbian bars in the city, and while many mainstream and gay male bars host women's nights, the events come and go with the speed of a press release. Try Wednesdays at **Lüb Lounge**, some Fridays at **5ive** and the second-last Saturday of the month at **Andy Poolhall** (489 College Street; *see also p208*). Called Savour, the latter event is under the tutelage of popular local DJ Denise Benson (*see p206* **Beats babe**). For further details, check out the **Lesbian Social and Business Network** (www.lsbntoronto.com) or the bulletin board at the Good For Her sex shop (*see p195*).

Note: unless otherwise stated, venues in this chapter are in Church & Wellesley.

MEDIA

The key local paper is *Xtra!*, 'Toronto's Lesbian & Gay Biweekly' (www.xtra.ca). A direct descendant of an influential activist paper called *The Body Politic* that flourished in the 1970s, *Xtra!* has a political pedigree that makes it the local paper of record. It focuses on art, entertainment and politics and runs listings of local events, both clubby and cultural. For a lighter, more hedonistic guide to the local scene, try *fab* (www.fab magazine.com). It's the one with cute boys on the cover and loads of party dish inside. Both papers are distributed free in bars, shops and restaurants within the ghetto, as well as further afield. *Xtra!* has its own pink newspaper boxes on street corners throughout the city. Online, Gay Guide Toronto (www.gay guidetoronto.com) offers comprehensive listings, plus tips on upcoming events. Features are updated monthly.

Bars & clubs

In the past decade the bar scene has grown both more specialised (leather, bears, twinks) and more diffuse. Young dance queens in particular tend to head out to one-night-only events at otherwise straight clubs like the **Guvernment** (132 Queens Quay E, Harbourfront; *see also p206*), **Boa Redux** (270 Spadina Avenue; *see also p208*) and various clubs on Queen Street West. The best example of this trend is Will Munro's Vazaleen, the insanely popular alt/rock/glam night held the last Friday of the month at **Lee's Palace** (529 Bloor Street W; *see also p202*). Queues can be long but the crowd is hip, mixed and very funky.

That said, don't believe all the guff about life outside the ghetto. There are all kinds of gay events at West End hotspots such as the **Drake** (*see p49, p130, p140 and p203*), but finding them can be tricky, even for insiders. Plus, many of them are gay-cruisey without necessarily being gay-cruisey; in other words, there may not be enough of your kind to approach lift-off. Check the local gay media for further information, or stand around Church Street and wait for a young 'un to give you a promo flyer.

Licensing laws dictate that bars officially close at 2am and all alcohol must be 'off the tables' within half an hour. Therefore after-hours partying tends to be limited, except at weekends, when places like **5ive**, **Fly** and the **Barn** stay open late.

As well as the following, *see also p194* **Byzantium** *and p209* **El Convento Rico**.

Bar 501

501 Church Street, at Wellesley Street E (416 944 3272). Bus 94/subway Wellesley. **Open** 11am-2am daily. **Credit** AmEx, V. **Map** p283 G5.
Friendly, down-home bar known for its drag shows.

The Barn & The Stables

418 Church Street, at Granby Street (416 977 4702/ www.thebarntoronto.com). Streetcar 506/subway College. **Open** 9pm-4am Mon-Sat; 4pm-3am Sun. **Credit** AmEx, MC, V. **Map** p280 H6.
The Barn is old, dark, grungy and very, very cruisey, especially late on Friday and Saturday nights. Once a backroom bar, the down and dirty atmosphere lingers, particularly on the crowded dance floor. It's open late and is even popular among people who claim to hate it. Sunday evening's underwear party is a big draw.

The Black Eagle

457 Church Street, at Alexander Street (416 413 1219/www.blackeagletoronto.com). Bus 94/subway Wellesley. **Open** 2pm-2am daily. **No credit cards.** **Map** p283 G5.
A leather and denim cruise bar with dress codes (and more) to match, this two-storey bar varies from casual to intense depending on the day of the week. Watch the signs at the door: it can be disconcerting to walk in on a watersports night when you just wanted some boot lickin'. The second-floor deck is a pleasant oasis of quiet during the summer.

Ciao Edie

489 College Street, at Bathurst Street, Little Italy (416 927 7774). Streetcar 506, 511. **Open** 8pm-2am Mon-Sat; 9pm-2am Sun. **Credit** AmEx, MC, V. **Map** p279 D6.
This funky bar hosts a long-running women's night on a Sunday, attracting a fashionable young crowd.

Crews, Tango & The Zone

508-510 Church Street, at Alexander Street (416 972 1662/www.crews-tango.com). Streetcar 506/subway Wellesley. **Open** noon-2am daily. **Credit** AmEx, MC, V. **Map** p283 G5.
A motley crowd of twinks, dykes, queens and sight-seers mingles in a shared space of two Victorian homes. Entertainment ranges from drag through dancing to karaoke, and the vibe is down to earth.

Cube

529 Yonge Street, at Maitland Street (416 963 5196/http://cubenightclub.com). Bus 94/subway Wellesley. **Open** 11am-2am daily. **Credit** AmEx, MC, V. **Map** p283 G5.
The former Trax has a new name, new management and a cleaner feel. Find steady drinkers at the front, dancing queens at the rear and drag aficionados upstairs. Plus bingo players every afternoon, 2-6pm.

5ive LifeLounge & DanceClub

5 St Joseph Street, at Yonge Street, University (416 964 8685/www.5ivenightclub.com). Bus 94/subway Wellesley. **Open** 10.30pm-3.30am Wed, Fri-Sun. **Credit** MC, V. **Map** p283 G5.

This slick, design-conscious dance club attracts just about everyone, from twinks to leathermen.

Fly

8 Gloucester Street, at Yonge Street (416 925 6222/ www.flynightclub.com). Bus 94/subway Wellesley. **Open** 10pm-7am Sat. **Credit** AmEx, MC, V. **Map** p283 G5.

Once a week the boys turn up in droves, eager to shed their shirts in honour of top DJs. Cover charges can be high, but the party goes on till morning.

George's Play

504 Church Street, at Alexander Street (416 963 8251). Streetcar 506/subway Wellesley. **Open** 11am-2am daily. **Credit** AmEx, MC, V. **Map** p283 G5.

A lively Latin bar with lots of drag, dancing and hip-swivelling enthusiasm.

Hair of the Dog

425 Church Street, at Wood Street (416 964 2708). Streetcar 506/subway Wellesley. **Open** 11.30am-2am daily. **Credit** MC, V. **Map** p283 G5.

Cosy pub with a quiet patio (in summer) and a good selection of beer. Men and women, gay and straight.

Lüb Lounge

487 Church Street, at Wellesley Street E (416 323 1489/www.lub.ca). Bus 94/subway Wellesley. **Open** 4pm-midnight Mon-Wed; 4pm-2am Thur, Fri; noon-2am Sat; noon-1am Sun. **Credit** AmEx, MC, V. **Map** p283 G5.

Tiny but terribly chic, this two-storey lounge-cum-dance bar attracts a hip crowd eager to show off their designer sneakers. Line-ups on weekends.

Pegasus Bar

489B Church Street, at Wellesley Street E (416 927 8832/www.pegasusonchurch.com). Bus 94/subway Wellesley. **Open** noon-2am daily. **Credit** AmEx, MC, V. **Map** p283 G5.

Comfortable, well-lit, second-floor pool hall attracting both men and women.

Red Planet

7 Maitland Street, at Yonge Street (416 920 0946). Bus 94/subway Wellesley. **Open** 6pm-2am Wed-Fri; 7pm-2am Sat; 5pm-midnight Sun. **Credit** MC, V. **Map** p283 G5.

A tiny new lounge that, not surprisingly, is all red.

Remington's

379 Yonge Street, at Gerrard Street, Dundas Square (416 977 2160/www.remingtons.com). Streetcar 505/subway Dundas. **Open** 5pm-2am daily. **Credit** AmEx, MC, V. **Map** p280 G6.

The infamous Sperm Attack on Mondays is no more, but numerous hunky strippers continue to bare all on two stages and in private sessions. Get your fun in early; the cover starts at 7pm.

Slack Alice

562 Church Street, at Wellesley Street E (416 969 8742/www.slackalice.ca). Bus 94/subway Wellesley. **Open** 4pm-2am Mon-Fri; 11am-2am Sat, Sun. **Credit** AmEx, MC, V. **Map** p283 G5.

Post-twink lesbians dominate this bar-restaurant on weekends, but the rest of the time it's a real mix, not to mention a hoot.

Woody's/Sailor. See p191.

Sneakers

*502A Yonge Street, at Grosvenor Street, University
(416 961 5808). Subway Wellesley.* **Open** 11am-2am
daily. **Credit** AmEx, MC, V. **Map** p283 G5.
Skinny young guys, hefty older men.

Statlers

*471 Church Street, at Alexander Street (416 925
0341). Streetcar 506/subway College.* **Open** 4pm-
2am daily. **Credit** AmEx, MC, V. **Map** p283 G5.
A tiny piano bar with older but still lively clientele.

Tallulah's Cabaret

*Buddies in Bad Times Theatre, 12 Alexander Street,
at Yonge Street (416 975 9130/www.buddiesin
badtimestheatre.com/tallulahs/index.cfm). Streetcar
506/subway Wellesley.* **Open** 10.30pm-2am Fri, Sat.
Credit MC, V. **Map** p283 G5.
Hip young tikes in graphic Ts dance to chart hits
every Friday and Saturday night at Tallulah's. They
look like they learned their moves from a Britney
video, but that's half the appeal. It's both men and
women, in a 70/30 split.

Woody's/Sailor

*465-467 Church Street, at Maitland Street (416
972 0887/www.woodytoronto.com). Bus 94/
subway Wellesley.* **Open** 2pm-2am daily.
Credit AmEx, MC, V. **Map** p283 G5.
One of the most popular bars in the city. Don't let
the name fool you. Everyone calls it Woody's and
everyone goes there sooner or later. The bar was
famous long before it became a recurring character
on the American *Queer as Folk* and, in a market
known for fickleness, has demonstrated an astonishing longevity. Patrons tend to cower in cliques,
making it difficult for newcomers to make their
entrance, but guys turn out in droves, especially on
weekends and Thursday nights, when the famous
Best Chest Contest draws some of the cutest speci-
mens in town. Be warned, though: it's usually the
out-of-towners who take off their shirts.

Zipperz

*72 Carlton Street, at Church Street (416 921 0066/
www.zipperz-cellblock.ca). Streetcar 506/subway
College.* **Open** noon-2am daily. **Credit** AmEx,
MC, V. **Map** p283 G5.
Sedate types settle at the piano bar in the front, while
beat-mongers bop to often retro tunes in the dance
club in the back. No attitude, all ages, lots of fun.

Bathhouses

Barracks

*56 Widmer Street, at Richmond Street W,
Entertainment District (416 593 0499/www.
barracks.com). Streetcar 504/subway St Andrew.*
Open 24hrs daily. **Credit** AmEx, MC, V. **Map**
p277 D7.
Edgier sex with leather accessories in a small town-
house not far from the establishment arts palace,
Roy Thomson Hall.

Bijou

*370 Church Street, at Gerrard Street E (416 971
9985). Bus 94/subway Wellesley.* **Open** 9pm-4am
Wed, Thur, Sun; 9pm-5am Fri, Sat. **No credit
cards.** **Map** p280 G6.
Home of the infamous 'slurp ramp' (don't ask), this
former backroom bar is now a cross between a porno
palace and a stand-up bathhouse. Most of the 'rooms'
are a bit too narrow for true horizontal action.

Good times at Bad Times

Theatre is too stuffy a word for an institution as salacious as Buddies in Bad Times. A theatre-cum-social centre, Buddies offers everything from a serious subscription series to dances, queer comedy and lesbian cabaret. But whatever form it takes, it's always tinged with a colourful queer vibe.

Co-founded by controversial local playwright Sky Gilbert, it still bears the stamp of his outrageous personality. A prolific playwright, Gilbert has written a string of plays with titles like *Suzie Goo: Private Secretary* and *Drag Queens in Outer Space*, and he has maintained a very high profile in the local media as an outspoken proponent of a certain kind of sex-positive gay chauvinism. Woe betide anyone who suggests gays are just like anyone else – Sky just won't have it. A scourge of the gay middle class, he inveighs against sexual hypocrisy and often appears as his drag alter-ego, a big-busted, big-haired blonde named Jane.

So that's Sky, and that for most of his 18-year tenure as artistic director of the theatre, was Buddies. In the years since his resignation in 1997, Buddies has moved a little closer to the mainstream, emphasising the provocative as much as the sexual, but most productions still feature some kind of queer angle.

A women's festival called Hysteria appeared for the first time in 2003, and Rhubarb! (February), the theatre's long-running festival of shorter works, continues to be one of Toronto's most avid promoters of young, dramatic talent. It's also just giddy, good fun. Most of the plays are so short and produced so fast – licketysplit, one after another – that you can get high just from the sense of creative free-fall. Quality varies, but the best of these dramatic short stories give you the sense of being there at the moment of creation.

Buddies moved to its present location in 1994, and instantly became a centre of local society. The theatre attracts a young, hip crowd late on Friday and Saturday nights, when the smaller of its two spaces, Tallulah's Cabaret, turns into an intimate dance club (*see p191*). In addition, Buddies hosts even larger dance events on most of the major gay holidays – Pride, Halloween and New Year's Eve. For Pride, Buddies usually programmes a week to ten days of queer comedy, staged readings and other performances, with an extra heavy dash of parties. On the Pride weekend (*see p168*), the small park beside the theatre often turns into a mini festival for queer youth.

Buddies in Bad Times Theatre

12 Alexander Street, at Yonge Street, Church & Wellesley (box office 416 975 8555/www.buddiesinbadtimestheatre. com). Streetcar 506/subway Wellesley. **Open** *Box office* noon-5pm Tue-Sat. **Credit** MC, V. **Map** p283 G5.

Cellar

78 Wellesley Street E, at Church Street (416 975 1799). Bus 94/subway Wellesley. **Open** 24hrs daily. **No credit cards. Map** p283 G5.
Widely regarded as the darkest bathhouse in town, this is where you go when you don't want to meet anyone you know. It doesn't even have a sign, just a black door.

Club Toronto

231 Mutual Street, at Carlton Street (416 977 4629/ www.clubtoronto.com). Subway Wellesley. **Open** 24hrs daily. **Credit** V. **Map** p280 G6.
Old and rambling, this attractive Victorian mansion has a whirlpool and a tiny outdoor swimming pool. In addition, it occasionally hosts a women's night known as the Pussy Palace.

St Marc Spa

4th floor, 543 Yonge Street, at Wellesley Street E (416 927 0210). Subway Wellesley. **Open** 24hrs daily. **Credit** AmEx, MC. **Map** p283 G5.

Not as popular as it once was, this huge spa still has a near-perfect location, close to the Yonge Street subway and late-night bus. Hop on, hop off.

Spa Excess

105 Carlton Street, at Jarvis Street (416 260 2363/ www.spaexcess.com). Streetcar 506. **Open** 24hrs daily. **Credit** AmEx, DC, MC, V. **Map** p280 G6.
A maze of dark corners and cubicles provides much room for groping on part of the top floor. Elsewhere there are private rooms, a licensed lounge and a deck.

Steamworks

2nd floor, 540 Church Street, at Wellesley Street E (416 925 1571/www.steamworks.ca). Bus 94/subway Wellesley. **Open** 24hrs daily. **Credit** AmEx, MC, V. **Map** p283 G5.
With high ceilings, glass-walled showers and industrial chic decor, Toronto's newest bathhouse feels more boutique hotel than erotic emporium. The entrance is so discreet you may have to ask for directions (hint: it's directly across from Zelda's patio).

Cafés

The local **Second Cup** started the Church Street revolution back in 1984, and coffeeshops have played a crucial role ever since. Each has its distinct clientele, but all are popular with folk looking for an alternative to the bars.

Bull Dog Coffee

89 Granby Street, at Church Street (416 606 2275/ www.bulldogtoronto.com). Subway College. **Open** 7am-7pm daily. **No credit cards. Map** p280 G6.
A coffee shop with a subtle leather vibe, Bull Dog sports a side-street location (at the southern end of the ghetto near the Barn; *see p189*), a pleasant tree-shaded patio and decent signature drinks.

Lettieri Espresso Bar & Café

77 Wellesley Street E, at Church Street (416 944 3944/www.lettiericafe.com). Bus 94/subway Wellesley. **Open** 7am-11pm Mon-Thur, Sun; 7am-2am Fri, Sat. **Credit** MC, V. **Map** p283 G5.
The prettiest coffee chain on the block, and the least busy (so far). Nice chrome tables on the patio.

Second Cup

546 Church Street, at Wellesley Street E (416 964 2457/www.secondcup.com). Bus 94/subway Wellesley. **Open** 6.30am-11pm Mon-Thur; 6.30am-3am Fri; 7am-3am Sat; 7am-11pm Sun. **Credit** MC, V. **Map** p283 G5.
A ghost of its former all-night self, this Church Street institution still attracts a diverse clientele.

7 West Café

7 Charles Street W, at Yonge Street, University (416 928 9041). Subway Bloor-Yonge. **Open** 24hrs daily. **Credit** MC, V. **Map** p283 G4.
A rambling three-storey hot-spot where students, film-lovers and bohemian types nurse coffees into the wee hours. Known for its desserts and salads.

Timothy's World Coffee

500 Church Street, at Alexander Street (416 925 8550/www.timothys.ca). Streetcar 506. **Open** 7pm-12.30am daily. **No credit cards. Map** p283 G5.
Bears, deaf gays and older guys in search of a quiet place to talk make this one of the busiest rendezvous on Church Street. In summer, hordes of polite cruisers line the front of the store (where there's a small patio) and along public benches around the corner.

Cruising

Gays are visible everywhere in the downtown core and cruising can happen anywhere from the main **Canadian Tire** store (839 Yonge Street, 416 925 9592) – especially popular with home-making couples – to **H&M**'s flagship store in the Eaton Centre, where the twinks turn out to pick up their club gear. But a few spots retain a special hold on the popular imagination, notably **Hanlan's Point** on the Toronto Islands, where there's a 'clothing optional' beach with a great view of the outer harbour; the wooded ravines of **David Balfour Park**, in posh Rosedale, where legends of late-night orgies linger on; **Riverdale Park** on the eastern edge of the Don Valley, where there's a spectacular view of the city, not to mention a dazzling outdoor pool favoured by homos in the summer; the bike trails around **Cherry Beach** on the Toronto waterfront, where the action starts as early as eight in the morning; and **High Park** in the west end of the city. All at your own risk, of course: visits from the police are always a possibility.

Culture

Queer culture is found in many mainstream venues, from established alternative theatres like the **Factory** (*see p221*) and the **Tarragon** (*see p222*) to the local art house **Carlton** multiplex (20 Carlton Street, at Yonge Street, Church & Wellesley, 416 598 2309; *see p179*).

But it's the queer-run venues that set the pace for cutting-edge culture. In addition to the following, the **Metropolitan Community Church of Toronto** (*see p263*) is very vocal on the gay scene, organising events and supporting the local fight for gay marriage.

See also p192 **Good times at Bad Times**, *and p167* **Inside Out Toronto Lesbian & Gay Film & Video Festival**.

Canadian Lesbian & Gay Archives

Suite 201, 56 Temperance Street, at Bay Street, Financial District (416 777 2755/www.clga.ca). Streetcar 501. **Open** by appointment. **Admission** free. **Map** p279/280 F7.
The second-largest lesbian and gay archive in the world, the CLGA has a new home in an historic house in the heart of the gay village (34 Isabella Street) but it won't be moving in for a couple of years yet. In the meantime, its enormous collection of books, T-shirts and queer periodicals resides in an out-of-the-way space on the edge of the Financial District. Call before you turn up as hours are limited.

We're Funny That Way

Buddies in Bad Times Theatre, 12 Alexander Street, at Yonge Street, Church & Wellesley (416 975 8555). **Date** May. **Map** p283 G5.
Queer comedy so good it's been filmed for TV, producing at least two specials. Everyone from Maggie Cassella to Lea DeLaria performs here.

Gyms

Bally Total Fitness

80 Bloor Street W, at Bay Street, Yorkville (416 960 2434/www.ballyfitness.com). Subway Bay. **Open** 6am-11pm Mon-Fri; 8am-7pm Sat, Sun. **Credit** AmEx, MC, V. **Map** p282 F4.

Arts & Entertainment

Brutal lighting doesn't dissuade a very gay clientele at Bally. Maybe it's because the entrance is next to Banana Republic.
Other locations: throughout the city.

Epic Fitness
9 St Joseph Street, at Yonge Street, University (416 960 1705). Subway Wellesley. **Open** 6am-midnight Mon-Thur; 6am-11pm Fri; 7.30am-8pm Sat; 7.30am-7pm Sun. **Credit** AmEx, V. **Map** p283 G5.
The closest thing in the city to an all-gay gym, this minimalist wonder caters to the circuit boy crowd.

Metro-Central YMCA
20 Grosvenor Street, at Yonge Street, University (416 975 9622/www.ymcatoronto.org). Streetcar 506/subway Wellesley. **Open** 6am-11pm Mon-Fri; 7am-8pm Sat, Sun. **Credit** AmEx, MC, V. **Map** p283 G5.
A very gay place, even though most of its 11,000-plus members are straight. A two-year, $4 million renovation has enlarged the main floor conditioning room. It's friendly and relaxed, with one of the city's most beautiful indoor pools and a lovely rooftop running track.

Restaurants

With few exceptions, it's safe to say that nobody goes to Church Street for the food. So if you're looking for something beyond burgers, pasta and other culinary mainstays, you might look elsewhere. That said, recent arrivals are trying to buck the trend and raise standards.

Byzantium
499 Church Street, at Wellesley Street E (416 922 3859). Bus 94/subway Wellesley. **Open** 5.30-11pm Mon-Sat; 11am-3pm, 5.30-11pm Sun. **Main courses** $25. **Credit** AmEx, MC, V. **Map** p283 G5.
The swankiest spot on the strip, the pale green room serves upscale bistro-style fare early on, then morphs into a very loud bar, complete with mirror ball and Martinis, later on. The floor-to-ceiling windows offer a great view of the strip. *See also p189.*

Churchmouse & Firkin
475 Church Street, at Maitland Street (416 927 1735/www.firkinpubs.com). Bus 94/subway Wellesley. **Main courses** $6-$18. **Open** 11am-1am daily. **Credit** AmEx, DC, MC, V. **Map** p283 G5.
Standard pub grub – pasta, curry and so forth – plus lots of draught beer and a great patio facing north (so you get a view of who's coming into the ghetto – as opposed to who's leaving in despair).

5 Alarm! Diner
555 Church Street, at Gloucester Street (416 972 1708/www.5alarmdiner.ca). Bus 94/subway Wellesley. **Open** 8am-11pm Mon-Thur; 8am-4am Fri, Sat; 8am-midnight Sun. **Main courses** $4-$13. **Credit** AmEx, DC, MC, V.
So-so burgers and the like, but very gay – and open late for emergency hangover-aversion therapy.

Garage Sandwich Co
509 Church Street, at Alexander Street (416 929 7575). Bus 94/subway Wellesley. **Open** 11am-8pm Mon-Fri; 11am-7pm Sat; noon-7pm Sun. **Main courses** $5-$10. **No credit cards**. **Map** p283 G5.
A tiny, funky sandwich place that's best known for its vegetarian and meat-based chilli con carne.

Il Fornello
491 Church Street, at Wellesley Street E (416 944 9052/www.ilfornello.com). Bus 94/subway Wellesley. **Open** 5-11pm Mon-Fri; 10.30am-3pm, 5-11pm Sat, Sun. **Main courses** $7-$25. **Credit** AmEx, DC, MC, V.
A member of a successful local chain, this mid-price Italian eaterie offers a fail-safe combo of comforting food (pizza, pasta, etc) at affordable prices.
Other locations: throughout the city.

Mitzi's Café
100 Sorauren Avenue, at Pearson Avenue, West End (416 588 1234). Streetcar 501. **Open** 7.30am-5pm Tue-Fri; 9am-4pm Sat, Sun. **Main courses** $7-$11. **No credit cards**.
Big on brunch and popular with women, this retro '50s diner is situated in newly trendy Parkdale over on the west side, near High Park.

Mitzi's Sister
1554 Queen Street W, at Dowling Avenue, West End (416 532 2570). Streetcar 501. **Open** 3pm-midnight Mon; 3pm-2am Tue-Fri; 10am-2am Sat; 10am-midnight Sun. **Main courses** $7-$12. **Credit** V.
A bigger version of Mitzi's Café, with a licence, lots of local artwork and a big female following.

O'Grady's Tap & Grill
518 Church Street, at Maitland Street (416 323 2822). Bus 94/subway Wellesley. **Open** 11am-2am daily. **Main courses** $10-$16. **Credit** AmEx, MC, V. **Map** p283 G5.
Skip the food, go for the street scene. The gigantic patio is the best people-watching place on the strip.

Trattoria Al Forno
459 Church Street, at Alexander Street (416 944 8852). Bus 94/subway Wellesley. **Open** 5-10pm Mon-Thur; 5-11pm Fri-Sun. **Main courses** $9-$18. **Credit** AmEx, DC, MC, V. **Map** p283 G5.
Pizza and pasta place with a family atmosphere and a gay clientele.

Zelda's Restaurant Bar Patio
542 Church Street, at Maitland Street (416 922 2526/www.zeldas.ca). Bus 94/subway Wellesley. **Open** 11am-2am Mon-Sat; 10am-2am Sun. **Main courses** $7-$14. **Credit** AmEx, MC, V. **Map** p283 G5.
A must-see, if only for the zany gay atmosphere, cute servers and kitsch decor. A tongue-in-cheek tribute to trailer park trash (check out the pink flamingos), Zelda's is lively even when it's half full, which isn't often. There are often massive queues for the summer patio, and half the time they're worth it.

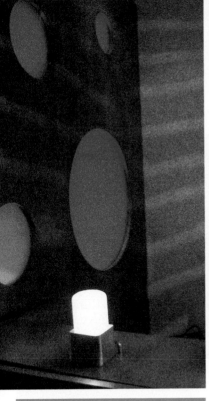

Byzantium. *See p189 and p194.*

Shops

Glad Day Bookshop

598A Yonge Street, at Dundonald Street (416 961 4161/www.gladday.com). Bus 94/subway Wellesley. **Open** 10am-6.30pm Mon-Wed; 10am-9pm Thur, Fri; 10am-7pm Sat; noon-6pm Sun. **Credit** AmEx, MC, V. **Map** p283 G5.

The second-oldest gay and lesbian bookstore in the world (established 1970), Glad Day is a pain to find and no fun to browse (the second-floor space is quite cramped), but it does have an astonishing range of queer titles – everything from fiction to parenting and transgender issues, plus a good selection of queer videos and DVDs, both arty and mainstream.

Good For Her

175 Harbord Street, at Bathurst Street, Harbord (416 588 0900/www.goodforher.com). Bus 94/ streetcar 511. **Open** 11am-7pm Mon-Thur; 11am-8pm Fri; 11am-6pm Sat; noon-5pm Sun. *Women & trans only* 11am-2pm Thur; noon-5pm Sun. **Credit** MC, V. **Map** p282 D4.

Known for educational workshops on everything from G-spots to female ejaculation, this women-centred sex shop is also a good source of information on local lesbian events. It's open to everyone, but some periods of the week are set aside for women and transsexuals only.

Out on the Street

551 Church Street, at Gloucester Street (416 967 2759). Bus 94/subway Wellesley. **Open** 10am-8pm Mon-Wed, Sun; 10am-9pm Thur-Sat. **Credit** AmEx, MC, V. **Map** p283 G5.

Aimed squarely at gay men, this three-level shop carries casual clothing, plus a broad selection (over 100) of T-shirts with catchy queer slogans.

Priape

2nd floor, 465 Church Street, at Maitland Street (416 586 9914/www.priape.com). Bus 94/subway Wellesley. **Open** 10am-9pm Mon-Sat; noon-6pm Sun. **Credit** AmEx, DC, MC, V. **Map** p283 G5.

A squeaky clean sex store, Priape stocks everything from huge dildos to leather harnesses, but some people come just for the sexy streetwear or the latest porn release. Tickets for local events are also sold.

Where to stay

There's no need to worry about a frosty reception at local hotels: the major ones are fully aware of the value of the pink dollar. But for a specifically queer ambience, try one of the gay-friendly B&Bs found within striking distance of the Church & Wellesley ghetto. One pick of the bunch is Dundonald House, 35 Dundonald Street (416 961 9888, www.dundonaldhouse.com).

Arts & Entertainment

Music

Rock, roots, reggae and... *The Ring*.

Classical

Being the biggest fish in the small pond of Canada has helped Toronto's classical ensembles gain international stature. In fact, the city boasts a higher number of top-quality performing groups than most American cities of equivalent size. These groups, such as the **Toronto Mendelssohn Choir** and the **Toronto Symphony Orchestra**, may have had financial and creative ups and downs, but have managed to overcome the challenges coming their way, and continue to present prime quality music.

In 2002 the Ontario and federal governments finalised one of the largest-ever investments in Canadian arts: more than $200 million to fund a decade-long project of building and rebuilding many structures housing Torontonian cultural institutions. Dramatic improvements to **Roy Thomson Hall**, home of the TSO and a key venue for a wide range of performing groups, have resulted in a long-overdue acoustic upgrade. Even more significant is the green light given to the construction of a much-needed opera house (to be called **Four Seasons Centre for the Performing Arts**). The 2,000-seat venue will be the first purpose-built opera house in Canada, and will serve as the new home of both the Canadian Opera Company and the National Ballet of Canada when it opens in 2006. The $20 million donation from Four Seasons Hotels & Resorts to the opera house is the largest single gift ever made to a Canadian arts organisation.

Also in 2006, the **Royal Conservatory of Music** will move into a brand-new facility, the **TELUS Centre for Performance & Learning**. This arts and education venue – all 215,000 square feet (20,000 square metres) of it – will feature an acoustically perfect 1,000-seat concert hall.

A new spirit of optimism exists within the city's cultural community. The election in 2003 of a more progressive and arts-friendly mayor (David Miller) and provincial regime (the Liberal party replacing the neo-conservative Tories) has also boosted that spirit. An excellent time, then, to check out Toronto's classical offerings.

Performing groups

Canadian Opera Company

416 363 8231/www.coc.ca.

The largest producer of opera in Canada, the COC has clearly been invigorated by the impressive plans for a new opera house in the heart of Toronto's theatre district. Response to its capital campaign to build the Four Seasons Centre has been strong, and the company believes the new home will attract larger audiences and high-calibre international stars. With greater backstage space, it will also be able to mount more simultaneous repertory productions.

Building on this momentum, director Richard Bradshaw has announced some adventurous new programming. The inaugural production, set for September 2006, will be the first complete Canadian production of Richard Wagner's Ring Cycle. Local film-maker Atom Egoyan will direct *Die Walküre*.

While awaiting the unveiling of its new home, the COC remains at its Hummingbird Centre base, presenting a wide-ranging repertoire, including crowd-pleasing staples like *Oedipus Rex*, as well as daring work such as an operatic treatment of Margaret Atwood's *The Handmaid's Tale*.

The COC also takes a populist approach by staging charity concerts and shows on the waterfront.

Tafelmusik Baroque Orchestra & Chamber Choir

416 964 6337/www.tafelmusik.org.

This choir and ensemble manages to make baroque chamber music sexy with their witty, entertaining and technically superb shows. Since forming in 1970, they have rightfully earned major popular and critical acclaim at home and abroad. When not touring internationally, Tafelmusik presents more than 40 concerts a year at Trinity-St Paul's Centre, as well as performing at such venues as the George Weston Recital Hall and Royal Ontario Museum. The leadership of musical director and award-winning violinist Jeanne Lamon has been crucial to their success.

Toronto Mendelssohn Choir

416 598 0422/www.tmchoir.org.

This mostly volunteer ensemble, with a core of about 20 professional singers, has been a Toronto mainstay since 1894. Under artistic director Noel Edison, it continues to seek out innovative ways to present choral music. The ensemble is a regular companion of the TSO, Les Grands Ballets Canadiens and the National Arts Centre Orchestra, and its performances have taken in such adventurous works as David Fanshawe's *African Sanctus*. TMC concerts are frequently heard on CBC Radio, and and they have recorded on EMI and Naxos.

Toronto Symphony Orchestra

416 598 3375/www.tso.on.ca.

Founded in 1992 as the New Symphony Orchestra, Canada's most prominent philharmonic ensemble almost sank under the weight of heavy debt a decade later. Increased private and federal government support sees the TSO in much happier shape these days, with increased ticket sales (over 400,000 annually) and a significant improvement in the acoustics of its home base, Roy Thomson Hall. Artistic director Jukka-Pekka Saraste provided a creative boost during her tenure (1994-2001), while current music director and conductor Peter Oundjian is keeping things ticking over nicely. The orchestra has a reputation for diversity and accessibility, having in the past brought in as guests such musical and vocal greats as Yehudi Menuhin, Yo-Yo Ma, Kathleen Battle and Jessye Norman. Renowned composers Henri Dutilleux, R Murray Schafer and the late Sir Michael Tippett have all attended the orchestra's presentations of their music, and Igor Stravinsky once guest-conducted his own work.

The best Venues

To scratch an itch for Canadiana

Every Wednesday night upstairs at the **Rivoli** (*see p203*), the Maple Lounge series plays only Canadian songs, and features a live set by a top local songsmith.

To see a local guitar god

A tie – the **Orbit Room** (*see p203*) and **Healey's** (*see p203*). The former is co-owned by Rush axeman Alex Lifeson, the latter by blues-rocker Jeff Healey.

To buy a beer from a rockabilly star

The **Horseshoe Tavern** (*see p201*), where Teddy Fury is regularly voted the best bartender in Toronto. He often graces the stage as leader of the city's best 'billy band, the Royal Crowns.

To sip a Mojito while listening to a musical cult hero

Lula Lounge (*see p202*) at a 'Gary Topp' presents concert. On other nights, tango-dancing Latin lovelies are a key attraction.

To park your scooter before listening to Britpop

Head along to College Street and the **Mod Club Theatre** (*see p202*) to celebrate all things Anglo.

To drown your sorrows on a Sunday afternoon

Cry in your beer to the sounds of honkytonk country at **Cadillac Lounge** (*see p203*) or the **Cameron House** matinées (*see p203*).

Smaller performing groups

The **Royal Conservatory of Music** (416 408 2824, www.rcmusic.ca) organises symphonic and small ensemble recitals (as well as world music events) at various venues around town. Its 2006 move into the **TELUS Centre for Performance & Learning** will boost its profile significantly. Founded in 1974, the **Toronto Symphony Youth Orchestra** (416 593 7769 ext 372, www.tso.on.ca/season/youth/youth02.cfm) has alumni performing all over the world. The large **Orpheus Choir of Toronto** (416 530 4428, www.orpheus.on.ca) was founded in 1964 and has a reputation for accomplished and adventurous performances of choral work. Its themed concerts are always popular. The **Nathaniel Dett Chorale** (416 340 7000, www.nathanieldettchorale.org) was founded in 1998 by artistic director and conductor Brainerd Blyden-Taylor. Inspired by early 20th-century African-Canadian composer Dett, the Chorale explores Afrocentric styles, including classical, spiritual, gospel, jazz and blues. Its infrequent performances are well worth investigating. The **Amici Chamber Ensemble** (416 368 8743, www.amiciensemble.com) has become one of the city's most popular small classical ensembles. Together since 1985, it has an annual series at the Glenn Gould Studio (*see below*), with the four core members bringing in distinguished guests. Founded in 1968, the **Toronto Chamber Choir** (416 699 8121, www.geocities.com/torontochamberchoir) is a 40-voice ensemble with a repertoire that originally just covered Renaissance music, but now ranges from medieval to modern.

Venues

George Weston Recital Hall

5040 Yonge Street, at Hillcrest Avenue, North Toronto (416 733 9388/www.tocentre.com). Subway North York Centre or Sheppard. **Open** *Box office* 11am-6pm Mon-Sat; noon-4pm Sun. **Tickets** prices vary. **Credit** AmEx, MC, V.

Loved by performers and concert-goers alike, this hall is one of Canada's (and the world's) finest. Located far from the city centre in the Toronto Centre for the Arts in North York, the elegant 1,032-seat theatre is modelled on European concert halls like Amsterdam's Concertgebouw, and has outstanding acoustics and sightlines. In addition to many outstanding international performers, the Canadian Opera Company and Tafelmusik perform concert series here.

Glenn Gould Studio

Canadian Broadcasting Centre, 250 Front Street W, at John Street, Entertainment District (ticketline 416 205 5555/www.glenngouldstudio.cbc.ca).

Streetcar 504/subway St Andrew. **Open** *Box office* 11am-6pm Mon-Fri. **Tickets** prices vary. **Credit** AmEx, MC, V. **Map** p279 E8.

Named after the Canadian piano virtuoso, this theatre continues to be one of Toronto's favourite concert venues. It is home to CBC Radio's flagship live series OnStage, which covers classical, jazz and world music. The 340-seat auditorium has a pleasingly intimate atmosphere and pristine sound.

Harbourfront Centre Concert Stage

235 Queens Quay W, at Lower Simcoe Street, Waterfront (416 973 4000/www.harbourfrontcentre.com). Streetcar 509, 510. **Open** *Box office* 1-8pm Tue-Sat. **Tickets** $20-$60. **Credit** AmEx, Disc, MC, V. **Map** p279/p280 F9.

The fan-shaped outdoor summer stage looks out on to Lake Ontario and the Toronto Islands. It usually hosts folk or pop music, but you can sometimes catch the Canadian Opera Company or other classical ensembles here. The view makes this a memorable place to catch a show, although noise laws mean that the fun has to end by 11pm so the condo-dwellers can get some shut-eye. The seats are notoriously uncomfortable, so bring a cushion.

Hummingbird Centre for the Performing Arts

1 Front Street E, at Yonge Street, St Lawrence (416 393 7469/www.hummingbirdcentre.com). Streetcar 504/subway King or Union. **Open** *Box office* 10am-6pm Mon-Fri; 10am-5pm Sat. **Tickets** $20-$150. **Credit** AmEx, MC, V. **Map** p280 G8.

This is where the Canadian Opera Company has hung its helmet since 1961 (back then it was known as the O'Keefe Centre). The 3,000-seat theatre lacks the intimacy needed for operatic performance, and the COC will fly the coop to the new opera house in 2006. Expect the Hummingbird to continue to host a wide range of pop and classical performers. The stage in this multi-purpose theatre has been trodden by such diverse stars as the Clash and Björk.

Massey Hall

178 Victoria Street, at Shuter Street, Dundas Square (416 872 4255/www.masseyhall.com). Streetcar 501/subway Queen. **Open** *Ticketline* 9am-8pm Mon-Fri; noon-5pm Sat. **Tickets** $20-$100. **Credit** AmEx, MC, V. **Map** p280 G7.

The first concert at this historic auditorium took place in 1894 and featured Handel's *Messiah*, performed by a 500-member choir and 70-piece orchestra. Today the 2,765-seat hall is still one of the most rewarding places in the city to hear classical music. Sightlines vary, and the upper seats are hard and cramped, but the acoustics and intimacy more than compensate. Before Roy Thomson Hall opened, this was home to the Toronto Symphony Orchestra. Classical concerts are not as common now at Massey Hall, but you can still see the best of folk, blues, country and jazz. There is simply no better place to catch such acts as Wynton Marsalis, Alison Krauss and BB King.

Give a big hand to **Roy Thomson Hall**.

Roy Thomson Hall

60 Simcoe Street, at King Street W, Entertainment District (416 872 4255/www.roythomson.com). Streetcar 504/subway St Andrew. **Open** *Ticketline* 9am-8pm Mon-Fri; noon-5pm Sat. *Box office (in person)* 10am-6pm Mon-Fri; noon-5pm Sat. **Tickets** $29-$135. **Credit** AmEx, MC, V. **Map** p279 E8.

This big snare drum-shaped building is best known as the place to catch the Toronto Symphony Orchestra, but the 2,812-seat theatre also hosts many other classical ensembles, along with occasional visits from the likes of Bonnie Raitt and Tony Bennett, to name but two. Opened in 1982, the hall was supposed to be acoustically perfect, but it didn't live up to expectations. Major renovations completed in 2002 replaced the austere concrete interior with warm wood tones that have given it the acoustics it was always intended to have.

Trinity-St Paul's Centre

427 Bloor Street W, at Robert Street, Harbord (416 964 6337/www.tspucc.org). Streetcar 510/subway Spadina. **Open** *Box office* 10am-1pm, 2-6pm Mon-Fri. **Tickets** $18-$69. **Credit** MC, V. **Map** p282 D4.

Intimate, sacred and mellow. With those qualities, it's no surprise that this has been Tafelmusik's main stage for almost 25 years. It is also the favourite venue of local roots heroes Cowboy Junkies. Musicians say the acoustics are good, but audiences say they're great, and the deep horseshoe layout means that everyone gets close to the stage. The church is also used by many other chamber music ensembles, as well as by such contemporary artists as Rufus Wainwright.

Rock, Roots & Jazz

Toronto is unlikely to become the new Seattle or Athens, Georgia, or Manchester, and that can only be a good thing. The music scenes of those cities became synonymous with one sound, which eventually – inevitably – crashed and burned. The Toronto music community is simply too large, diverse and vibrant to be easily commodified, labelled and sold.

At times guilty of ignoring the talent within, while fawning over imported flavours of the month, Toronto's media and audiences alike are now rightfully brimming with pride that the rest of the world has been catching on to the city's near-embarrassment of musical riches (*see p200* **Talent spotting**). The thriving live scene gives emerging talents the opportunity to showcase their wares in public, and though the Toronto-based branches of the multinational record labels exert a dwindling influence on the scene, far more adventurous and creative independent labels (Maple, Arts & Crafts, Paper Bag, True North) have stepped into the void.

On any given night in Toronto, there is live music to be found in at least 30 different clubs, many being on the lively Queen West and College Street strips. Very few cities anywhere can boast that level of activity. New additions to the scene are frequent, with existing venues often taking on a new life. A striking example

Arts & Entertainment

of this is the **Gladstone** on West Queen West. One of the city's most historic hotels (claiming to be the oldest continuously operating hotel in Toronto), it has recently been renovated, and now hosts a wide range of music, theatre, visual arts and literary events. Along with its neighbour the **Drake**, the Gladstone has rejuvenated the Parkdale area.

Things get especially hectic twice a year via 'club crawl' components of Canada's two largest music conference/festivals. Every March Toronto hosts **Canadian Music Week** (CMW), while **North by Northeast** (NXNE; *see also p168*) takes place every June. CMW is more industry-oriented, while NXNE is a little more populist in approach. Each event brings in

Talent spotting

The large and vibrant live music scene in Toronto has served as a fertile incubator of talent since the early '60s, but it is right now that the city is surfing a wave of artistic self-confidence and creativity, gaining it the international recognition that has previously been elusive.

New stars in a wide variety of genres are making an impact, not just locally and domestically, but internationally. They may not be platinum-selling acts (though **Barenaked Ladies** and **Sum 41** have scaled those heights), but their musical originality is giving Toronto real respect.

On the rock side, look out for the aggressive yet soul-fuelled **Constantines**, the Joy Division-influenced **Uncut** and **Controller Controller**, the fiery **Tangiers**, and femme trio **Magneta Lane**.

The sprawling **Broken Social Scene** collective has helped galvanise the local sound, and its fluid membership has included members of other ensembles on the move such as **Metric**, **Apostle of Hustle**, **Stars**, and Montreal's **The Dears**. Keep an eye on Metric, fronted by the charismatic Emily Haines, a Patti Smith for the new era. Soft

pop revolutionaries Stars and their offshoot **Memphis** also merit close scrutiny, as does gay chamber-pop troupe **Hidden Cameras**.

Since the '60s heyday of the Yorkville scene (Joni Mitchell, Neil Young and Gordon Lightfoot), Toronto has been known for producing talented singer/songwriters. Over the past 15 years, **Jane Siberry** and **Ron Sexsmith** are just two of the acts who have earned worldwide followings, and a younger crop is poised to follow suit.

The flamboyant **Hawksley Workman** is well known in Britain and France, and the latter territory has also embraced the sultry stylings of **Feist**. *Time* magazine declared **Sarah Slean** 'Canada's brightest talent', melancholy minstrel **Howie Beck** has charmed the English music press, **Hayden**'s quirky stylings are also getting recognised abroad, while **Royal Wood** and **Reid Jamieson** are showing real promise.

On the roots side, the success of veterans **Cowboy Junkies** and **Blue Rodeo** has helped inspire the likes of the **Sadies**, **Luke Doucet** and **Oh Susanna**.

Toronto hip hop artists have historically found it difficult to break into the US market, but the eclectic **k-os** is now a proud ambassador for the genre.

Jazz-pop songstresses **Molly Johnson** (pictured) and **Holly Cole** were peers on Queen Street, during the late '80s and have gone on to significant success in France and Japan, respectively. The city's active electronica action is spawning such credible artists as **Junior Boys**, **Polmo Polpo**, and **Solvent**, and its multicultural make-up influences the work of world music artists, including **Jane Bunnett**, the **Flying Bulgar Klezmer Band** and **Kiran Ahluwalia**.

Perhaps none of the above will ever become 'the next big thing' – though you never know – but they have at least all helped instil a genuine and justifiable pride in Toronto's musical community.

Open your air... **Molson Amphitheatre**.

hundreds of bands from across the country and beyond, as well as music industry execs scouting the next big (or at least interesting) thing.

TICKETS AND INFORMATION

The city's two major free entertainment weeklies, *eye* and *NOW*, feature extensive listings sections. The information is generally the same, although *NOW*'s listings are marginally easier to use for those unfamiliar with particular venues or acts. The monthly *Toronto Life* magazine has very good listings for classical and jazz concerts.

Expect most club shows to get under way at 10pm or later, even on a school night. Most are pay-at-the-door, but expect club shows with currently hot acts to sell out well in advance. It is prudent to book ahead, or at least show up early. Most stadium and arena shows, as well as some events at smaller venues, are handled through **Ticketmaster** (416 870 8000, www.ticketmaster.ca), which has outlets at most **Sunrise** record stores (336 Yonge Street, Dundas Square; call 416 498 6601 for branches) and at the **Rogers Centre/SkyDome** box office (*see below*), among other locations. Tickets for many of the club shows can be found at two of the city's best record shops, **Soundscapes** (572 College Street; *see also p163*) and **Rotate This** (620 Queen Street W; *see also p163*).

Venues

Stadiums/arenas

Phone or check the local press for ticket prices and opening times for the following.

Air Canada Centre

40 Bay Street, at Front Street W, Entertainment District (416 815 5500/ticketline 416 870 8000/ www.theaircanadacentre.com). Subway Union. **Credit** AmEx, DC, MC, V. **Map** p279 E8. This modern 21,000-seat arena alternates between major name concerts, hockey and basketball games. This is where you're likely to find Madonna, Elton John or Eminem when they're playing in town. The centre can be reconfigured (by pulling a giant curtain across the auditorium) into a comparatively intimate 5,200-seat venue.

Molson Amphitheatre

909 Lake Shore Boulevard W, at Dufferin Street, West End (416 260 5600/www.hob.com/venues/ concerts/molsonamp). Bus 29/streetcar 509, 511. **Credit** AmEx, MC, V. **Map** p278 B10. Many locals still sing the blues over the demolition of their beloved revolving stage at Ontario Place, but its larger replacement remains the city's best outdoor venue for the big names in rock and pop. The amphitheatre has 9,000 seats, while another 7,000 can sprawl on the hillside grass. Even though it's only open in summer (May to September), the lakeside setting occasionally brings a chill, but on a warm evening this is a great place to be.

Rogers Centre (formerly SkyDome)

1 Blue Jays Way, at Front Street W, Entertainment District (416 341 3663/ticketline 416 870 8000/ www.rogerscentre.com). Streetcar 504/subway St Andrew or Union. **Credit** AmEx, DC, MC, V. **Map** p279 E8. With the arrival of the Air Canada Centre, the oft-maligned and cavernous SkyDome (recently renamed Rogers Centre) now hosts fewer concerts, but it's the one place in town for stadium shows, and remains an occasional stomping ground for such dinosaurs as Rod Stewart and the Rolling Stones. Baseball, football, monster truck rallies and wrestling events are its chief clients now.

Mid-sized venues & clubs

Horseshoe Tavern

370 Queen Street W, at Spadina Avenue, Entertainment District (416 598 4226/ www.horseshoetavern.com). Streetcar 501, 510. **Open** 9pm-1am Mon-Thur; 9pm-2.30am Fri-Sun. **Admission** free-$25. **Credit** MC, V. **Map** p279 E7. The rough-and-ready yet legendary Horseshoe has been serving up pints and kick-ass tunes since 1947. It has had colourful incarnations as a country and punk bar, and now books rock and roots acts. Smack in the middle of Queen Street's trendy strip, the

Hitting the **Top o' the Senator**. See p204.

climbing the rock 'n' roll ladder. On the second floor, the 250-capacity Dance Cave hosts DJs spinning alternative rock, retro new wave, and dance hits.

Lula Lounge

1585 Dundas Street W, at Dufferin Street, West End (416 538 7405/www.lula.ca). Bus 29/streetcar 505. **Open** 7pm-2am Fri, Sat; phone for details Mon-Thur, Sun. **Admission** free-$25. **Credit** AmEx, MC, V. **Map** p278 A6.

A refreshing addition to the club scene, Lula's is on the edge of Little Brazil, and has a Latin vibe to its drinks (fine Mojitos), food (tasty tapas) and decor. It looks like an old-style banquet hall, but has a top-notch sound system and great sightlines. Regular bookings stress the Latin and world music side, but veteran local promoter Gary Topp has also brought in cult heroes like Jonathan Richman and Sarah Jane Morris; Norah Jones and Jason Mraz have also performed in the 250-capacity room. Well worth the trip.

Mod Club Theatre

722 College Street, at Shaw Street, Little Italy (416 588 4663). Streetcar 506. **Open** phone for details. **Admission** free-$25. **Credit** AmEx, MC, V. **Map** p278 B5.

Further confirmation of Toronto's long-standing Anglophilia is provided by this new club, which was named after and founded on the success of the long-running Mod Club series previously held at other local clubs. Boasting good sightlines, excellent sound and a locale on the edge of the busy College strip, it has rapidly become one of the city's leading mid-sized club venues. Such big-name English acts as Jamie Cullum, the Stranglers and Dizzee Rascal have packed the joint, while American acts (Blues Explosion, Matthew Sweet) have also been hosted.

Opera House

735 Queen Street E, at Broadview Avenue, East Toronto (416 466 0313/www.theoperahouse toronto.com). Streetcar 501, 504, 505. **Open** phone for details. **Admission** $8-$40. **Credit** AmEx, MC, V. **Map** p281 K7.

This former vaudeville theatre, built in the early 1900s, was converted into a multi-level, multi-purpose venue in 1990. On a run-down section of Queen Street East, it has had to work hard to compete with more central venues. That it has, hosting sell-out gigs from the likes of Björk, Blur and Radiohead.

Phoenix Concert Theatre

410 Sherbourne Street, at Carlton Street, Church & Wellesley (416 323 1251). Streetcar 506/subway Wellesley. **Open** 8pm-2.30am Fri-Sun; phone for details Mon-Thur. **Admission** $5-$50. **Credit** MC, V. **Map** p283 H5.

Part nightclub, part concert venue, the Phoenix boasts impressive sightlines and sound, and has a more opulent feel than many of its peers. It rose from the ashes of the Diamond in 1991, and regularly hosts top Canadian and international pop and rock acts, plus occasional 'all ages' shows.

unpretentious 'Shoe keeps its feet on the ground. It can hold 520 people, and has regularly featured such major acts as Wilco, Los Lobos and Ryan Adams; it even hosted a secret Stones gig in 1997. The no-cover Tuesday New Music nights shows up-and-coming bands from across Canada and abroad.

Hugh's Room

2261 Dundas Street W, at Bloor Street W, West End (416 531 6604/www.hughsroom.com). Streetcar 504, 505/subway Dundas West. **Open** 6pm-2am Tue-Sun. **Admission** $10-$25. **Credit** AmEx, MC, V.

This classy folk club was a dream of Richard and Hugh Carson. Hugh died before the dream was realised, but his name and spirit lives on in this West End venue. Hugh's Room attracts attentive, if sometimes slightly uptight, audiences, many of whom come for dinner plus the show. The booking policy includes world beat, blues and singer-songwriters alongside traditional artists in its broad definition of folk. Such big draws as the McGarrigle Sisters and the Strawbs have played here.

Lee's Palace & the Dance Cave

529 Bloor Street W, at Bathurst Street, Harbord (416 532 1598/www.leespalace.com). Streetcar 511/subway Bathurst. **Open** 9pm-2am Thur-Sat; phone for details Mon-Wed, Sun. **Admission** $2-$20. **No credit cards. Map** p282 D4.

Helped by its proximity to the University of Toronto, this has long been one of the city's premier rock clubs. The high, wide stage, rockin' bartenders and very good sightlines are other assets of the 600-capacity venue. Nirvana played their first Toronto gig here, and it remains a great place to see those

Bars

Cadillac Lounge

*1296 Queen Street W, at Brock Street, West End
(416 536 7717). Streetcar 501.* **Open** 11am-2am
daily. **Admission** free-$10. **Credit** MC, V.

Yes, that really is a Cadillac embedded in the wall
above this bar's front entrance. Inside you'll find
Elvis memorabilia, old country music posters,
and better-than-average bar food and brews. The
popular 4,000 sq ft (372 sq m), 200-capacity heated
patio out the back occasionally hosts bands, but it
is the intimate indoor lounge (holds 120) that regularly features rock, blues and country acts from right
across Canada. The occasional big name like
American rockabilly legend Robert Gordon will
pack the joint. A long-running Sunday matinée features honkytonk troubadour Scotty Campbell. Best
to think of this as a cosy neighbourhood bar with a
diverse clientele that just happens to have reliably
high-quality music.

Cameron House

*408 Queen Street W, at Cameron Street, Chinatown
(416 703 0811/www.thecameron.com). Streetcar
501, 510/subway Osgoode.* **Open** 4pm-2am daily,
plus performances 6-8pm Sat, Sun. **Admission**
Front room pay what you can. *Back room* $5-$10.
Credit V. **Map** p279 D7.

After more than two decades, the Cameron remains
the favourite haunt of Queen West bohemian
hipsters. The eclectic booking policy meanders
through cabaret, country, jazz, swing, folk and rock
territory, but experimental theatre troupes, poets
and spoken word artists are also hosted. You can
catch music in both the front bar (Kevin Quain's
Mad Bastards Sunday night residency is highly recommended) and the separate back room. There's no
cover charge in the front room, but be ready when
they pass the hat round.

Drake Underground

*1150 Queen Street W, at Beaconsfield Avenue,
West End (416 531 5042/www.thedrakehotel.ca).
Streetcar 501.* **Open** 8pm/9pm-2am daily.
Admission free-$15. **Credit** AmEx, DC, MC,
V. **Map** p278 A7.

Part of the Drake Hotel complex, this is one of the
most exciting recent innovations on the city's noc-
turnal scene. The basement club is also the segment
closest to the underground artistic sensibility of the
rejuvenated Parkdale neighbourhood. Local artists
and musicians have taken to this cosy, well-designed
space, which features superior sound and such top-
line technology as a video jukebox. The vibe is especially suited to cabaret-styled or maverick acts,
and the room has hosted memorable performances
from the likes of Broken Social Scene and Juana
Molina. It is also used regularly for performance art,
comedy, film, spoken word, and even board game
nights (a faddish new pursuit for the bohemian scen-
esters). If it all gets too much, retire to the swanky
bar. *See also p49, p130 and p140.*

El Mocambo

*464 Spadina Avenue, at College Street, Harbord (416
777 1777/www.elmocambo.ca). Streetcar 506, 510.*
Open phone for details. **Admission** free-$15. **No
credit cards. Map** p282 D5.

The Elmo has been the city's most internationally
known live music club for over three decades. The
Rolling Stones played an infamous gig (Margaret
Trudeau in tow) here in the '70s, and the likes of
Elvis Costello and U2 have also graced the stage.
It fell on hard times and briefly closed, but a major
renovation has placed it back on the map. Most of
the action takes place on the more spacious ground
level, which sports a Moroccan vibe, expanded
stage, improved sound, and room for 250 clubgo-
ers. An eclectic booking policy ranges from rock to
hip hop to roots (Billy Bragg, Alejandro Escovedo
and Jet have all appeared here). It's good to have
music back at the Elmo.

Healey's

*178 Bathurst Street, at Queen Street W,
Entertainment District (416 703 5882/www.jeff
healeys.com). Streetcar 501, 511.* **Open** 8pm-
2am Mon-Fri; 3pm-2am Sat. **Admission** $5-$20.
Credit AmEx, MC, V. **Map** p279 D9.

Situated next to trendy watering hole the Paddock
(*see p134*), this club takes its name from co-owner
Jeff Healey. The blues-rock guitar ace has a hands-
on approach here, frequently headlining or guesting
with many acts. The booking is heavy on the classic rock and blues side. The basement room can get
a little uncomfortable when packed, but respite is on
hand in the lounge area at the entrance. For the
Tuesday singalongs, *see p136* **Sing, sing a song**.

Orbit Room

*580 College Street, at Manning Avenue, Little Italy
(416 535 0613). Streetcar 506, 511.* **Open** 10.30pm-
1.30am daily. **Admission** free-$35. **Credit** AmEx,
MC, V. **Map** p278 C5.

This small, second-floor bar is a happy place to hear
upbeat Hammond organ funk and jazz. It occasionally brings in stars like Brian Auger and Joey
DeFrancesco, but relies on shining local talents (guitar wizard Kevin Breit's Sisters Euclid and Doug
Riley, for instance). It can get crowded even on
Sunday nights, so be prepared to wriggle into place.
You want intimate? The Orbit Room is so cosy you
have to walk through the band to get to the washrooms and small terrace out back. Retro decor and
friendly staff keep it pleasingly unpretentious.

Rivoli

*332-334 Queen Street W, at Spadina Avenue,
Entertainment District (416 596 1908/http://
rivoli.ca/2003). Streetcar 501, 510.* **Open**
Bar/restaurant 11.30am-1am daily. *Back room*
phone for details. **Admission** $5-$10. **Credit**
AmEx, MC, V. **Map** p279 E7.

The back room at the Rivoli has been a key component of the Queen Street scene since the late '70s,
and is a favoured venue for all things alternative,
whether it's rock, comedy, jazz, funk or punk. The

Arts & Entertainment

club is often used by record labels for industry parties, which adds to the hip factor. The cosy pool hall upstairs also hosts the Maple Lounge series every Wednesday, featuring top Canadian singer/songwriters. *See also p107, p134 and p216.*

Jazz & blues

Toronto has one of the continent's best live jazz scenes, thanks both to clubs featuring it year-round and to some well-attended summer festivals. The **Toronto Downtown Jazz Festival** (*see p168*) brings in top names to perform in the big tent erected in Nathan Phillips Square, as well as in the clubs. The **Beaches International Jazz Festival** (*see p169*) literally stops traffic in the east end, as hundreds of thousands of fans check out the free and eclectic musical fare on the street and in Kew Gardens.

Toronto is blessed with many fine female jazz vocalists (**Laura Hubert**, **Alex Pangman**, **Sophie Milman**, **Heather Bambrick**, to name just a few) and talented instrumental ensembles that traverse classic be-bop, contemporary and avant-garde territory. The blues is a style better heard live than on disc, and it has long been a key component of the city's music scene. Local heroes like **Downchild**, **Jack DeKeyzer** and **Paul Reddick** are always worth catching. The following are among the noteworthy venues.

Grossman's Tavern

379 Spadina Avenue, at Cecil Street, Chinatown (416 977 7000/www.grossmanstavern.com). Streetcar 506, 510. **Open** 11am-2am Mon-Fri; noon-2am Sun. **Admission** free. **Credit** V. **Map** p279 D6.
On the edge of Chinatown, this tavern was opened in 1949 and some of the seasoned regulars look as though they came with the original furniture. Beery and a little grimy, the bar specialises in loud blues played by locals and visiting dignitaries. The likes of Jeff Healey and Downchild (the inspiration for the Blues Brothers) paid their proverbial dues here. It can also be a good place for Dixieland.

Montreal Bistro

65 Sherbourne Street, at Adelaide Street, St Lawrence (416 363 0179/www.montrealbistro.com). Streetcar 504. **Open** 11.30am-midnight Mon-Fri; 5.30pm-1am Sat. **Admission** $10-$15. **Credit** AmEx MC V. **Map** p280 H8.
A jazz club and restaurant long-favoured by the serious jazz fan. The owners have a rigidly enforced 'no whispering' policy during sets by top international and local artists. The club features artists ranging from solo pianists to big bands, covering the spectrum of jazz styles; Diana Krall (her first local club gig), Oscar Peterson, Marian McPartland and The Rob McConnell Tentet have all played here. Make a beeline for the bar area to get the best sightlines.

Reservoir Lounge

52 Wellington Street E, at Church Street, St Lawrence (416 955 0887/www.reservoirlounge.com). Streetcar 504/subway King. **Open** 9pm-2am Mon; 8pm-2am Tue, Wed; 5pm-2am Thur, Fri; 7.30pm-2am Sat. **Admission** free-$10. **Credit** AmEx, DC, MC, V. **Map** p280 G8.
The swing revival may be doornail-dead in most places, but it lives on in this basement lounge. Close to St Lawrence Centre for the Performing Arts and the Hummingbird Centre, it is an ideal place to kick back with a post-theatre Martini and listen to Toronto's best swing bands and such fine singers as Tory Cassis and Alex Pangman. Low ceilings and brick pillars, high tables and long, velvet couches set the scene. The food's a tad pricey, but worth it. The place gets packed at weekends, but there's always a couple or two who find space to dance.

Rex Hotel Jazz & Blues Bar

194 Queen Street W, at University Avenue, Entertainment District (416 598 2475). Streetcar 501/subway Osgoode. **Open** 6.30pm-1.30am Mon-Fri; noon-1.30am Sat, Sun. **Admission** free-$12. **No credit cards**. **Map** p279 E7.
If you're tired of the elitist and snobbish atmosphere of some jazz clubs, then the Rex is for you. The casual atmosphere, friendly regulars and a wide range of beers on tap make this a social place to hear the best local jazz artists. Two, sometimes three, acts play daily, and stars such as Harry Connick Jr have also been known to jam here. A great budget venue.

Silver Dollar Room

486 Spadina Avenue, at College Street, Chinatown (416 763 9139/www.silverdollarroom.com). Streetcar 506, 510. **Open** 10pm-1.30am daily. **Admission** free-$15. **No credit cards**. **Map** p282 D5.
It doesn't look like much from the outside… or much more on the inside. That's part of its grungy charm. Top-notch blues acts from Chicago, and the best local practitioners of the 12-bar form, are showcased here. Another plus is that if it's not full, there's room to dance. The High Lonesome Wednesdays series helped spark a bluegrass revival in Toronto, while garage rock bands from Canada and the US occasionally hit the stage too.

Top o' the Senator

253 Victoria Street, at Dundas Street E, Dundas Square (416 364 7517/www.thesenator.com). Streetcar 505/subway Dundas. **Open** 8.30pm-1am Tue-Sat; 8pm-midnight Sun. **Admission** $8-$25. **Credit** AmEx, MC, V. **Map** p280 G6.
Deco lights and long, leather seats give this much-loved club a touch of 1920s elegance that enhances the emphasis on contemporary jazz. The bar is heavy on bebop, booking well-known names Branford Marsalis and Marcus Roberts. Such A-list vocalists as Diana Krall and Holly Cole have also graced the room. Covers are often high, but students get in for half price on Wednesdays. Top o' the Senator also does dinner-and-show deals in conjunction with Torch Bistro downstairs (*see p113*).

Nightlife

Toronto beats the drum into the wee small hours.

A few short decades ago, you had to order food if you a wanted a drink in a bar on a Sunday in Toronto. 'Toronto the Good' kept its citizens in check with antiquated laws that didn't blend well with an emerging generation that was born to have fun. The party people won the day and now keep the city rocking, if not entirely around the clock, at least with a nightclub scene that thumps to the beat of many different drummers. Clubland in the Entertainment District is one of the most concentrated party scenes on the planet. Warehouses converted into cavernous clubs attract the after-five set looking to unwind, then rev up when the suburban kids descend on weekends.

The area roughly bordered by Queen Street, Spadina Avenue, King Street and University Avenue is ground zero for a scene that draws upwards of 30,000 clubbers on any given Saturday night. This means heavy traffic, outlandish parking fees, promotional litter, public drunkenness, and a relentless thumping from clubs that stay open long past the 2am last call. Queues are a given at most spots after 11pm on Thursdays to Saturdays, regardless of the actual size of crowd within: the velvet rope is all about illusion, and behind it may lie a club

Perfectly **Lucid**. See p207.

packed with revellers, or one that is still struggling to find its groove. Advance planning (surfing the club's website) may get you on the VIP list, allowing you to swagger past the herd. Alternatively, just show up looking glam; the days when jeans were acceptable are largely gone (except at clubs catering to the frat crowd).

In terms of tunes, anything goes – the city's numerous DJs vie for residencies, constantly inventing new speciality nights. On most days of the week you can groove to old school, classic, progressive and deep house, or hip hop, R&B, techno and drum 'n' bass. Stray from deepest downtown and you'll also find clubs and lounges playing the sounds of the world, from Latin through African to Caribbean beats.

LOCATION, LOCATION, LOCATION

Thankfully, club owners concentrate their holdings in a few key neighbourhoods, which means you don't have to totter too far in your sexy shoes, or spend the equivalent of a mortgage down-payment in taxi fares.

Next after Clubland is College Street, the main artery of the city's oldest Italian and Portuguese neighbourhoods. For several giddy blocks you can effortlessly slide from drink to food and back again, as lounges and restaurants and more than a few hybrids (some including dancefloors) vie for attention. Dining morphs effortlessly into full-on nightlife, as the College strip becomes a carnival of bright lipstick on young (as well as aging) lovelies. On that point, note that the distinction between bar and club is often blurred in Toronto, with some venues straddling both categories. **Panorama Restaurant & Lounge** and **Lobby** are two examples (for these and others, *see pp133-141*).

Third in line is King Street West, which is becoming quite a contender in the nightclub stakes – though you may have to search a little harder for the entrances (concealed down alleyways, round the back of buildings, or simply too tiny to be highly visible).

Another attraction of Toronto's clubland is the fact that the city lies on the flight path between Chicago, home of house, and music-loving New York, with techno-centre Detroit a mere four-hour drive away. With a friendly drinking age and a still friendlier exchange rate, the city has become both a favoured destination for south-of-the-border partiers, as well a magnet for high-profile DJs.

To find out what's on in any given week, grab a copy of freebie weeklies, *NOW* or *eye*, from one of the ubiquitous sidewalk boxes. They're both published on a Thursday.

Waterfront

The Guvernment

132 Queens Quay E, at Lower Jarvis Street (416 869 0045/www.theguvernment.com). Streetcar 509. **Open** 10pm-3am Thur, Fri; 10pm-6am Sat. **Admission** $10-$15. **Credit** AmEx, MC, V. **Map** p280 G9.

While its current clientele were still crawling, this venue – as the celebrated RPM – held marathon parties for mods, Goths, punks, the lot. It eventually morphed into this equally enduring clubbing complex that attracts Toronto's top house DJs (Mark Oliver's been spinning here for eight years), along with international turntablist royalty. Bouncers won't turn away the shabbily dressed, but they will make you wait: it's a rare night that doesn't see a queue wrapped around the block. The hangar-like space is also home to concert venue Kool Haus, which attracts international DJs and eclectic acts (Kruder and Dorfmeister, Tenacious D) as well as bands that can play good old-fashioned instruments. Lounge spaces galore, plus two rooftop patios.

Entertainment District

C Lounge

456 Wellington Street, at Spadina Avenue (416 260 9393). Streetcar 510. **Open** 10pm-2am Mon-Wed, Fri; 5pm-2am Thur; 9pm-2am Sat. **Admission** $5-$10. **Credit** AmEx, MC, V. **Map** p279 D8.

Liberty Group, which owns a clutch of other spots around town, specialises in clubs that mix decadence with elegance. The 'C' is a nod to Miami: multiple water features (including waterfalls and a wading pool), plus 'bottle service' (the price of two bottles for a group of your best friends gets you a private

Beats babe

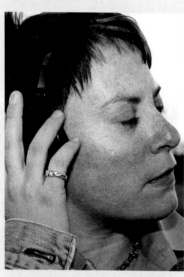

'Music + words + passion' is the phrase that Denise Benson (*pictured*) uses to describe what she's all about. One of the first women to spin in Toronto (and gain huge credibility in the boys' club that pre-dated her), the diminutive Benson is one of the city's top eclectic DJs. The music and passion began early: at age four, to be precise, when a well-intentioned parental bribe – 'you stop sucking the thumb, kid, and we'll give you a turntable' – sent her down a path she would never stray from. As a teen she fell in love with punk, followed by dub, then hip hop, acid-house, techno, acid jazz, acoustic jazz and on and on. Benson takes a stance not so different from one espoused long ago by Duke Ellington: 'There's only two kinds of music: good and bad'. This means she's open to all kinds of music, and she has had to find several ways of expressing the passion – radio, the clubs and the written word. In the late '80s she started the much-loved radio show Mental Chatter, on hip community station CKLN (11am Mondays, 88.1 FM). A source for underground dance information and a place for Benson-ites to hear her play during the day, it's one of the station's top-rated programmes. But for visitors to Toronto wanting a live taste of her club mix of nu-jazz, down tempo, deep house, dub and more, check *eye* for details of her whereabouts. (Benson pens two club culture columns for the weekly entertainment mag.) Over the years Benson has played countless clubs in the city (as well as in Ottawa, Montreal, New York and elsewhere). Most recently, she has been spinning at the popular Synchro Fridays at Andy Poolhall, a pop art, retro hotspot in Little Italy (*see p208*). She is also resident at Andy's for Savour the Flavour, a monthly Saturday gig.

enclave to lounge in). These attractions seem to attract both Beamer types and young wannabes. The unisex loo isn't such a great idea, however: boys have been known to hog the mirrors.

Fluid Lounge
217 Richmond Street W, at Duncan Street (416 593 6116). Streetcar 501. **Open** 10pm-3am Wed-Sun. **Admission** $10-$15. **Credit** AmEx, V. **Map** p279 E7.
Body-glittered bare shoulders mark Fluid out as sexy and not so subtle – but then you don't drop by the joint to discuss Foucault. Fluid is about sliding off the shoulders of your neighbours on the crowded dancefloor, or merely lounging and watching… followed by some lounging and watching.

Hotel Boutique Lounge
77 Peter Street, at King Street (416 345 8585/ http://hotelboutiquelounge.com). Streetcar 504. **Open** 10pm-3am Thur-Sun. **Admission** prices vary. **Credit** AmEx, MC, V. **Map** p279 E7.
Acting like the lounge of an upscale boutique hotel where people just happen to end up dancing after midnight, Hotel knows how to throw a party, despite its compact size. The clientele – monied urbanites with a taste for champers – are out to be seen.

Joker
318 Richmond Street W, at Widmer Street (416 598 1313/www.libertygroup.com). Streetcar 501. **Open** 10pm-3am Thur-Sat. **Admission** $10. **No credit cards. Map** p279 E7.
One of the pioneers of the mega-club continues to attract crowds of debauched clubkids. It's well past its peak of credible popularity, but still knows how to put on a show when it wants to: there are four floors with music ranging from chart hits to classic house; the lights are entrancing; and a rooftop patio is a sweat reducer. Queues can get very long.

Lucid
126 John Street, between Adelaide & Richmond (416 345 843). Streetcar 504, 501. **Open** 10pm-4am Thur-Sat. **Admission** $10-$20. **Credit** AmEx, MC, V. **Map** p279 E7.
Try this one for size: 70 plasma and LCD displays, DL1 Catalyst projectors (as seen on the Grammy Awards) and a capacity of 3,000. Punters explore the four floors via escalator, squeezing into the multiple rooms dedicated to sundry dance music styles – house, hip hop and reggae, to name but three. Oh, and did we mention Lucid has nine – count 'em – nine bars? No wonder the queues are so long. Visitors from Manchester might recognise the original Lucid in this successful spin-off.

Mad Bar
230 Richmond Street W, at Duncan Street (416 340 0089). Streetcar 501. **Open** 10pm-3am Fri, Sat. **Admission** $10. **Credit** MC, V. **Map** p279 E7.
It's actually quite sane, inasmuch as a nightclub can be. Faintly futuristic decor makes an easy backdrop for stylin' hip hoppers and snowboarders with cash to burn, flaunting their Prada shoes.

Money Nightclub/Wallpaper Room
199 Richmond Street W, at Duncan Street (416 591 9000/www.moneynightclub.ca). Streetcar 501. **Open** 10pm-3am Fri-Sun. **Admission** $10. **Credit** AmEx, MC, V. **Map** p279 E7.
Some navel-baring babes think that the first step to marrying a millionaire (or a man who wants you to think he is) is lining up for Money, where looking rich, drinking rich and acting rich is practically a religion. You can ask him to show you the money on any its four floors, or even strike it rich yourself by taking part in Money's own reality TV show, *The Party Maker.*

NASA Dance Pub
609 Queen Street W, at Bathurst Street (416 504 8356/www.nasadancepub.ca). Streetcar 501. **Open** noon-3am daily. **Admission** free. **No credit cards. Map** p279 D7.
This club stays true to its Queen Street school and appeals to a mixed young crowd intent on their tunes and down on the clubland attitude a few blocks south. Inexpensive drinks, and progressive DJs keep the system cranked up.

RoxyBlu
12 Brant Street, at King Street (416 504 3222/ www.roxyblu.com). Streetcar 504, 510. **Open** 10pm-3am Fri, Sat. **Admission** $10-$15. **Credit** AmEx, MC, V. **Map** p279 D8.
Roxy remains a bona fide member of the underground music culture – you might hear groovalicious jazzy Brazilian sounds in one room, the best house music in Toronto in the next. Watch for the monthly Movement events, where the city's celebrated DJ collective play all manner of music – even (gasp) something approaching actual jazz.

Schmooze
15 Mercer Street, just south of King Street W (416 341 8777/www.schmooze.ca). Streetcar 504. **Open** *Restaurant* 4-9pm Fri; 7-9pm Sat. *Club* 9pm-2am Fri; 10pm-2am Sat. **Admission** $7-$20. **Credit** AmEx, MC, V. **Map** p279 E8.
Early evenings see a crowd of lawyers and bankers, (the club's 'over-25' policy makes this inevitable), which means little dancing and a lot of schmoozing. If you stay late enough the romance of the place (1930s cathedral ceilings, chandeliers) may encourage you to take to the floor, or perhaps it will be the draw of a crowd which has clearly followed the club's suggestion: 'Dress as if you're expecting to meet someone, because chances are you will.'

Sound Emporium
360 Adelaide Street W, at Peter Street (416 408 2646). Streetcar 504. **Open** 10pm-3am Thur-Sat. **Admission** prices vary. **Credit** AmEx, MC, V. **Map** p279 E7.
Formerly Turbo, Sound Emporium features a rather limited selection of house, R&B and Top 40 tunes, but it's renowned for being 'anti-dress code', which means you can turn up in your basketball jersey and trainers. Hurrah!

System Soundbar

117 Peter Street, at Richmond Street (416 408 3996/www.systemsoundbar.com). Streetcar 501, 504. **Open** 10pm-3am Wed, Thur; 10pm-7am Fri, Sat. **Admission** $5-$15. **Credit** AmEx, MC, V. **Map** p279 E7.

Enduring in the land of quick turnover, the industrial-looking System Soundbar boasts, appropriately enough, a superb sound system. It's put to good use – international and local DJs have 'em lining up for jungle, hip hop, drum 'n' bass, house and more. As underground as it gets on Richmond Street.

This is London

364 Richmond Street W, at Peter Street (416 351 1100/www.thisislondonclub.com). Streetcar 501. **Open** 10pm-3am Sat. **Admission** $20. **No credit cards**. **Map** p279 E7.

You get a more refined kind of hedonism at This Is London, which is styled after a velvet-roped Soho palace. Sophisticates sip Veuve or premium vodka in the upstairs lounge, while bouncers oversee the lower-level party with military tenacity. The women's loo is possibly the swankiest in town, with beauticians waiting to trim or style, and racks of magazines. Free bottled water compensates for the hefty cover – another London byproduct.

Una Mas

422 Adelaide Street W, at Spadina Avenue (416 703 4862/www.unamas.net). Streetcar 504, 510. **Open** 10pm-3am Fri, Sat. **Admission** free-$10. **Credit** AmEx, MC, V. **Map** p279 D7.

Located on the fringes of clubland, seemingly turning its back on the vulgar hordes, Una Mas has innate cool. Booths along one wall are big enough to seat eight, while low lounges at the back are more intimate. A long, lean bar is the perfect propping post while you nod along to rare groove, funk and hip hop. The basement serves as a sweaty dance pit.

Up & Down Lounge

270 Adelaide Street W, at John Street (416 977 4038). Streetcar 501, 504. **Open** 9pm-3am Wed-Sat. **Admission** free. **Credit** AmEx, MC, V. **Map** p279 E7.

This perennially cool, intimate bi-level club continues to be a favourite with both the beautiful people and regular folk (with a certain *je ne sais quoi*, that is). More of a cocktail lounge than a dance club, it nonetheless has a club vibe. Go fashionably late.

Chinatown

Boa Redux

270 Spadina Avenue, at Dundas Avenue (416 977 1111/www.boa-redux.com). Streetcar 510. **Open** midnight Sat-noon Sun; phone for details Mon-Fri. **Admission** prices vary. **Credit** AmEx, MC, V. **Map** p279 D6.

This is the deal: it Boa 'Let there be sound' Redux opens at midnight on Saturdays and closes at noon on Sundays. It's in an old Chinatown porn theatre, now a two-level dance club. It has a great big honk-

ing sound system. The catch? They can't serve booze until Sunday brunch – this is a non-licensed venue (although you can get expensive juice and water at any old time).

University/Harbord

Comfort Zone

486 Spadina Avenue, at College Street (416 763 9139/www.comfortzone.to.com). Streetcar 501, 510. **Open** 11pm-6am Thur; midnight Fri-1pm Sat; 6am Sun-6am Mon. **Admission** prices vary. **Credit** MC, V. **Map** p279 D5.

The party after the after-party. The Comfort Zone won't score points for form over function – it's basically a dingy basement – but that doesn't stop it being a favourite of DJs, local and imported, who save their best sets for the Zone. Rave on.

Yorkville

Babalúu

136 Yorkville Avenue, at Avenue Road (416 515 0587/www.babaluu.com). Bus 6/subway Bay. **Open** 6pm-3am Tue-Sun. **Admission** $5-$12. **Credit** AmEx, DC, MC, V. **Map** p282 F4.

Babalúu is Toronto's upscale gem of a Latin club, ensconced down a small flight of stairs in the heart of monied pretty people land, aka Yorkville. Simply being able to dance isn't quite enough – here you want to be able to spring for the Moët at the same time. Still, expect to see some seriously sexy dancing to salsa, merengue and cumbia, as well as less dexterous moves from well-heeled amateurs.

West End

Alto Basso

718 College Street at Crawford Street, Little Italy (416 534 9522/www.altobasso.com). Streetcar 506, 511. **Open** 5pm-2am Fri-Sun. **Admission** free. **Credit** AmEx, DC, V. **Map** p278 B5.

Alto Basso was one of the first to make its name on the hybrid scene, as a lounge/restaurant/bar/dance club. Early evening it's mostly a laid-back resto and lounge, but by evening's end the joint is jumping (or at least pulsing to house). Everyone goes, from fashionistas to locals just wanting to join the party.

Andy Poolhall

489 College Street, at Markham Street (416 923 5000). Streetcar 506, 511. **Open** 2pm-2am daily. **Admission** prices vary. **Credit** AmEx, MC, V. **Map** p278 C5.

As in Andy (Warhol) and Edie (Sedgwick). At Andy's, kitsch white plastic bubble chairs and red pool tables help to create an irrepressible groovy groove, drawing an eclectic funky clientele. Watch out for special events (such as the 'sex and perv positive' cabaret). Music covers everything and anything, with soul, house, hip hop, electro and new wave. *See also p188 and p206* **Beats babe.**

BeBa Lounge

614 College Street, at Bathurst Street, Little Italy (416 533 2322/www.bebalounge.com). Streetcar 506, 511. **Open** 8pm-3am Thur-Sat. **Admission** free. **Credit** AmEx, MC, V. **Map** p278 C5/D5.

One of the newest of the many Little Italy newcomers, BeBa is partly late-night lounge (featuring several shadowy curtained-off dens), and partly dance club, albeit with a small floor. Still, it's big enough to witness one of the city's entertaining oddities – DJs accompanied by live electronic percussion courtesy of 'THC, the drumming DJ'. Cheap Martinis early evenings add to the equation.

Cervejaria Downtown Bar & Grill

842 College Street, at Ossington Avenue, Little Italy (416 588 0162). Streetcar 506. **Open** *Restaurant* 11am-2am daily. *Club/music* 10pm-2am Fri, Sat. **Admission** $5. **Credit** MC, V. **Map** p278 B5.

Timing is key at this hybrid beer hall/haven. Saturdays typically bring live local salsa bands, or sometimes Brazilian beats. Either way the crowd will be on its feet spinning and swaying two by two. Otherwise, it's Euro disco mixed with overplayed Latin pop. Still, there's always cheap Portuguese eats, football highlights and pitchers o' beer in the front bar to compensate.

El Convento Rico

750 College Street, at Crawford Street, Little Italy (416 588 7800/www.elconventorico.com). Streetcar 506, 511. **Open** 10pm-3am Thur; 8pm-4am Fri, Sat. **Admission** $7. **No credit cards**. **Map** p278 B5.

On weekends you'll find a mixed bunch here: singles making their moves, marrieds remembering how the other half lives, couples of various sexual predilections on the dancefloor. They've all come for one thing: the heady mayhem leading up to the midnight drag show. Before and after, Latin music and Euro dance tunes are the order of the day. It's all very kitsch, of course, but that's why the crowd has a ball.

Matador Club Country Music

466 Dovercourt Road, at College Street (416 533 9311). Streetcar 506, 511. **Open** 2am-5am Fri, Sat. **Admission** prices vary. **No credit cards**. **Map** p278 A5.

While the rest of the city is running out of gas, this barn-like arena on an obscure residential block, is revving up for a marathon of reckless dancing. Music is country of some description, sometimes proffered by amateur musicians quick with a Stones cover, occasionally by some of North America's finest. The hints of lawlessness and the late hours have made it a cult institution for all-night types of various stripe.

Revival

783 College Street, at Shaw Street (416 535 7888/ www.revivalbar.com). Streetcar 506. **Open** phone for details Mon-Fri, Sun; 9.30pm-2am Sat. **Admission** $5-$10. **Credit** AmEx, MC, V. **Map** p278 B5.

The building is both a former Polish Legion Hall and Baptist church, rescued from uncertain fate by entrepreneurs betting on its value as a club. DJs tend towards soul, funk and newly mixed Brazilian beats. Live acts, jams and special events (fashion shows, CD release parties) plus the old faithful, Saturday Mod Night, keep the place constantly reviving.

East Toronto

The Docks

11 Polson Street, at Cherry Street (416 469 5655/ www.thedocks.com). Bus 72. **Open** 9pm-3am Fri, Sat. **Admission** $10-$15. **Credit** AmEx, MC, V. **Map** p281 J10.

This 'Waterfront Entertainment Complex' also includes a drive-in and driving range: its contribution to Toronto's nightlife is as a theme park – waterslides, Jell-O wrestling rings and bungee towers. But it's the only place in town where you can dance under the stars. Call ahead to ensure the venue is open to the public (they sometimes host private events).

Matador Club Country Music.

Sport & Fitness

Toronto is kickin'... and hittin', throwin' and skatin'.

Take me out to the ball game...

Despite weather that is, at its extremes, unbearable (bitter, bone-shatteringly cold in the winter, swelteringly hot and humid in the summer), the extent of outdoor sports enthusiasm in Toronto is astounding. Day and night, year-round, streets and sidewalks are cluttered (sometimes dangerously so) with cyclists, joggers and in-line skaters. The city's well-run and well-maintained recreation system boasts dozens of free tennis courts, pools, tracks, skating rinks, playing fields and basketball hoops for the citizenry (and visitors) to enjoy, and the proliferation of gyms and exercise studios is a testament to a populace enamoured with fitness and wellbeing.

Hockey is the city's predominant sport obsession, but just about every activity from badminton and horse racing to cricket and windsurfing can be enjoyed and/or observed at a highly competitive level. And if you're willing to spend up to 90 minutes on the road, world-class skiing and golfing facilities are yours.

When they're not on strike, professional sports are played throughout the year, with Toronto being the only city in Canada with teams in three

out of the four major US-dominated sports leagues (baseball, basketball and hockey, the lone exception being NFL football – a slightly different Canadian version is played here). The protracted National Hockey League stoppage of 2004/5 had legions of fans wondering what to do with themselves on Saturday nights across Canada. But Toronto's investment in pro sports remains big business. Recent years have seen major venue upgrades including the Air Canada Centre for hockey, basketball and lacrosse, and the Rexall Centre for tennis. And football's Toronto Argonauts are foresaking SkyDome (which was renamed Rogers Centre as this guide went to press) and moving to a new 25,000-seat stadium on the grounds of York University in time for the 2007 season.

The city's enthusiasm for sports has even led it to create a new museum, **Olympic Spirit Toronto** (*see p68*), which opened on Dundas Square in autumn 2004. Billed as the 'first permanent Olympic Spirit Center in the world', the 52,000-square foot building features interactive and multimedia displays, a restaurant and rooftop patio.

Spectator sports

American football

To understand where the **Argonauts** stand in the pantheon of sports in Canada, you only need to know this: during the 2004 season the owner of a rival team felt compelled to offer a reward to the hometown devotee who could come up with a cheer that would prove more ubiquitous than the longtime fan favourite: 'Argos Suck!'.

Football, as it is played in Canada, is nowhere near the high-priced glamour sport seen south of the border. With three downs (instead of four as in the US game), and fields that are both wider and longer, the Canadian game is arguably faster and more dramatic than its American cousin. Salaries are closer to that of a supply teacher than a CEO, and player ranks are studded with has- and never-beens from the NFL. The missing glamour of the American game can account for the locals' general indifference to the Argos through most of the '90s, but the perseverance of former player, one-time president and current coach of the team, Mike 'Pinball' Clemons, has turned things around. Based on the boosted popularity of other Canadian Football League franchises that have moved to smaller venues, the Argos look forward to leaving the draughty, half-empty Rogers Centre come the 2007 season.

Toronto Argonauts

Rogers Centre (formerly SkyDome), 1 Blue Jays Way, at Front Street W, Entertainment District (information 416 341 2700/tickets 416 341 2746/ www.argonauts.on.ca). Streetcar 504/subway St Andrew or Union. **Season** June-Nov. **Tickets** $18-$65; $15-$60 concessions. **Credit** AmEx, MC, V. **Map** p279 E8/E9.

Baseball

Toronto has joyously embraced America's pastime since the first snow-blanketed game, played at (the now-demolished) Exhibition Stadium back in 1977. Fan fervour grew through the late 1980s and exploded during the World Series-winning seasons of '92 and '93, but since the strike-shortened season of 1994 attendance has steadily declined. Even so, there's no more relaxing way to spend a sunny afternoon or a steamy summer night than at an open-roof game at the Rogers Centre.

Toronto Blue Jays

Rogers Centre (formerly SkyDome), 1 Blue Jays Way, at Front Street W, Entertainment District (information 416 341 1000/tickets 416 341 3000/ www.bluejays.com). Streetcar 504/subway St Andrew or Union. **Season** May-Sept. **Tickets** $26-$37. **Credit** AmEx, MC, V. **Map** p279 E8/E9.

Basketball

While generous observers will call the current state of affairs for the **Raptors** a 'rebuilding period', others will question the use of 're-' as part of the phrase. Launched in 1995, the team has suffered the indignity of losing just about every widely acclaimed player who ever wore the uniform. The revolving door for superstars (and superstars to be) have included Damon Stoudamire, Tracy McGrady and Vince Carter, as well as coaches Isiah Thomas and Lenny Wilkens. The team has actually made it to the playoffs several times, but never to the later rounds. A note of optimism marked the beginning of the 2004 season – the departure of pouty player Vince Carter freed up his huge salary and got the team two future first-round draft picks, along with three players from the New Jersey Nets, a move that could lead to a more team-oriented, well-rounded lineup.

Toronto Raptors

Air Canada Centre, 40 Bay Street, at Front Street W, Entertainment District (info 416 815 5600/ tickets 416 872 5000/www.nba.com/raptors). Subway Union. **Season** Oct-June. **Tickets** $36-$665. **Credit** AmEx, DC, MC, V. **Map** p279/p280 F8/F9.

Cricket

Cricket is certainly the oldest organised sport played in Toronto, although it's fair to say many of the game's participants and observers are among the city's newest arrivals. Beloved by Commonwealth expats, the game in many ways exemplifies Toronto's multiculturalism, with over 100 clubs bringing together members of the Asian, West Indian, British and Australian communities in particular. The **Toronto & District Cricket Association** (www.cricketstar.net) is the largest league in North America, and regularly supplies upwards of 80 per cent of the players on the Canadian national team. The city is also a regular host to international tests, providing neutral ground (and sell-out crowds) for matches.

There are several dozen cricket pitches throughout the Toronto parks system, with at least 20 devoted exclusively to the game. One of the most idyllic locations to enjoy a match is at **Sunnybrook Park** (Eglinton Avenue E, at Leslie Street) in North Toronto, which is home pitch for the West Indian Cricket Club of Toronto. The **Canada Cricket Online** website (www.canada cricket.com) also has information on current tours and tournaments, as well as details of Canada's cricketing history.

Horse racing

Located out by the airport in the north-west corner of the city, **Woodbine Racetrack** is the only game in Toronto. But it's the only racetrack in North America that can offer both thoroughbred and standard-bred horse racing on the same day, as well as providing video links to several other major racetracks, including Churchill Downs and Aqueduct. The track is also home to a number of $1 million-plus races, including North America's oldest stakes race, the **Queen's Plate** (which has been run without interruption since 1860; see also p168), the **ATTO Mile** and harness racing's **North America Cup**. More recently slot machines have been added to the mix so you can really work on your gambling. There are a couple of out-of-town alternatives at **Mohawk** (a 45-minute drive away in Campbellville, near Guelph, for harness racing) and **Fort Erie** (just over an hour's drive from the city).

Fort Erie Race Track

230 Catherine Street, Fort Erie (1-800 295 3770/ 905 871 3200/www.forterieracetrack.ca). **Open** *Racetrack* May-Oct; phone for details. *Slots* 9am-3am Mon-Thur; 24hrs Fri-Sun. **Admission** free. **Credit** AmEx, MC, V.

Mohawk Racetrack

9430 Guelph Line, Campbellville (416 675 7223/ www.woodbineentertainment.com). **Open** *Racetrack* June-Oct; phone for details. *Slots* 9am-3am Mon-Thur; 24hrs Fri-Sun. **Admission** free. **Credit** AmEx, MC, V.

Woodbine Racetrack

555 Rexdale Boulevard, at Highway 427, Rexdale (416 675 7223/www.woodbineentertainment.com). Subway Islington. **Open** *Racetrack* Jan-Dec; phone for details. *Slots* 24hrs daily. **Admission** free. **Credit** MC, V.

Ice hockey

Win or lose, Toronto loves its **Leafs** – almost as much as everyone else in the country hates them. They are the most watched, most analysed, most adored and most reviled team in NHL history. They have won more league championships than any team aside from their long-standing rivals the Montreal Canadiens, but sadly all the wins were prior to 1967, the last time Lord Stanley's Cup was hoisted in victory by a Leaf (just to rub it in, the Cup lives at the Hockey Hall of Fame; see p65) just up the road from the ACC). Oddly enough, the decades-long absence of a championship team is about equal to the length of time you'd have to wait to get a decent season ticket – the Leaf's legendary waiting list is more accurately measured in

generations than in years. Virtually every game is sold out. Attendance remains constant even after the team moved from the venerable nostalgia of grotty, old Maple Leaf Gardens to the sanitised confines of the high-tech, antiseptic Air Canada Centre in 1999. The best tickets for games are generally only attainable through ticket agencies and scalpers at inflated prices.

Toronto Maple Leafs

Air Canada Centre, 40 Bay Street, at Front Street W, Entertainment District (information 416 815 5700/tickets 416 872 5000/www.torontomaple leafs.com). Subway Union. **Season** Oct-Apr. **Tickets** $24-$390. **Credit** AmEx, DC, MC, V. **Map** p279/p280 F8.

Lacrosse

Lacrosse is the official national sport of Canada, protestations from hockey enthusiasts aside. But for a city that adores champions, Toronto has inexplicably ignored its winning pro Lacrosse team, the **Toronto Rock**. Since its inception in 1998, the team has won three league titles, yet its triumphs have gone largely unnoticed by the masses. Perhaps it's the difficulty of the game. It's an extremely rough-and-tumble sport with little glamour, but also one of the most exciting and physically challenging contests a human can endure.

Toronto Rock

Air Canada Centre, 40 Bay Street, at Front Street W, Entertainment District (information 416 596 3075/tickets 416 872 5000/www.torontorock.com). Subway Union. **Season** Jan-Apr. **Tickets** $10-$53. **Credit** AmEx, DC, MC, V. **Map** p279/280 F8.

Soccer

In terms of individual participation, soccer is the fastest-growing team sport in Canada. Nonetheless, observing the game locally seems to be confined to those who play it (and their relatives). Over the years, leagues have swiftly blown in and out of town. Street celebrations ensue during every World Cup, but the TV-viewing fans have yet to materialise into support for Toronto's pro team, the **Toronto Lynx**. The Lynx has fielded a competitive team since its inception in 1997, but the demolition of central Varsity Stadium in 2002, relegating them to Centennial Park Stadium in the West End, hasn't helped their profile.

Toronto Lynx

Centennial Park Stadium, 256 Centennial Park Road, at Renforth Drive, West End (416 251 4625/www.lynxsoccer.com). Subway Royal York then bus 48. **Season** May-Sept. **Tickets** $15; $7.50 concessions. **Credit** V.

Celebrating Canada's victory in the 2004 World Ice Hockey Championships.

Active sports & fitness

Beach volleyball

A decade ago it was illegal to play beach volleyball at Toronto's **Ashbridge's Bay Park** on the shore of Lake Ontario (*see p102*). Today the flat sandy expanse is home to one of the largest collections of beach volleyball courts in North America, a place where thousands of recreational players and those with Olympic dreams pursue their passion. As a spectator sport, what's not to like about watching buff bods in skimpy clothing take face plants in the sand? It's as much fun to play as it is to watch. The **Toronto East Sport & Social Club** runs the programme at Ashbridge's Bay, where 85 permanent courts are marked in the sand for 690 teams and close to 6,000 players. To catch some tournament action or get in on a game of pick-up – dating is a big draw for participants – see www.tessc.com.

Cycling

Toronto is a fantastic city for cycling. Most major thoroughfares have bike lanes and, on the whole, drivers respect them. Of course there are exceptions, but generally speaking you can cross the entire city by bike without a scratch. Travel east–west (most spectacularly along the often scenic lakeshore) and the ride is mostly flat. Head north and things start

getting hilly, but at least that means the ride back is downhill. For route maps check out www.city.toronto.on.ca/parks/maps.htm or visit a bike shop.

Try the **Martin Goodman Trail** along the lakeshore, or head over to the **Toronto Islands** for fresh air and spectacular views of the city; rental is available on Centre Island (call 416 203 0009 for details) . If you think you'll want a bike for more than a day, you might want to investigate **Bikeshare** at 761 Queen Street W in the West End (416 504 2918, www.bikeshare.org), the yellow bike-lending programme, which has hubs around the city. **Wheel Excitement** (249 Queens Quay W, 416 260 9000, www.wheelexcitement.ca) is another reputable bike rental outfit.

Golf

See p214 **Tee time**.

Gyms

From Pilates to spinning, yoga to stretching, you can choose pretty much any form of sweat extraction in Toronto. Good-value daily rates are available at several excellent gyms in the heart of downtown. The **YMCA** (*see p194*) and **Bally Total Fitness** (*see p193*) both have locations within easy walking distance of many centrally located hotels. The University of Toronto's massive

Athletic & Physical Education Centre (55 Harbord Street, at Spadina Avenue, 416 978 3437, www.utoronto.ca/physical) also has a day rate. Known as the AC, it has several gyms, pools, a strength and conditioning centre and an indoor running track. Bally also has personal trainers available.

Ice-skating/'shinny'

The city has many indoor rinks with designated skating hours at affordable prices, but also more than two dozen well-maintained free outdoor rinks, including two that are especially popular. You can fall around to your heart's content in the dramatic shadow of City Hall at **Nathan Phillips Square**, or down by the lake at the **Harbourfront Centre**. Skate rental is available at both. The outdoor skating season runs from roughly December through to the beginning of March.

Hockey enthusiasts don't have to look far to find a great game of 'shinny' (the informal, non-contact, 'be nice' version of the game) at any public rink, particularly at weekends. All you need is your stick and skates.

Tee time

By winning the 2003 Masters Tournament in Augusta, Georgia, Ontario-born Mike Weir catapulted golf on to the front pages of the city's papers. The sport is long regarded as prohibitively expensive, and only afforded by the rich, but Weir's victory democratised the game and pushed its popularity over the top. That year also saw the re-opening of the Muskoka Sands Resort as **Taboo**, a lavish resort that Weir now calls his home course. Although it's a bit of a trek north of the city, the grounds and accommodation are world-class and you can make a memorable trip out of it by accessing the club's helicopter services. For listings, *see p246*.

The most famous local course is **Glen Abbey**, which was designed by Jack Nicklaus and was the home of the Canadian Open when Tiger Woods made his dramatic winning shot to take the title in 2000. It's a short drive west of town (in Oakville) and open to all. *ScoreGolf* magazine, Canada's golf bible, rates the much more affordable **St George's Golf & Country Club** in the West End as the country's No.1 (Glen Abbey came in at No.13). You'll need a letter of reference from your home club, but non-members are welcome by advance arrangement.

For those with less time (or shallower pockets) there are all manner of courses and driving ranges both inside the city limits and within easy driving distance, though, of course, they vary widely in quality. A popular destination is the **Uplands Golf Club & Ski Centre** (don't let the '& Ski Centre' part scare you) in the city's north end. Consisting of nine holes set in a gorgeous forested valley, it includes some enjoyable surprises and challenges. Otherwise, many affordable public courses are found throughout the city, as listed below.

If checking out the occasional celebrity duffer is to your liking, the coolest course in the neighbourhood is **Wooden Sticks**, just outside of town in Uxbridge. Said to be owned by several hockey players, this is where sport freaks go to see and be seen. Wooden Sticks has been hailed because it has several holes inspired by classic courses like Augusta National and the Old Course at St Andrews.

Closer to downtown, the big entertainment complex at **The Docks** includes several golf activities, such as sand traps, a chipping green and an 18-hole Pro Putt course as well as 75 hitting stations at the driving range (which doubles as a drive-in cinema at night).

For more information on local courses call Toronto Parks & Recreation on 416 392 8186 or visit www.city.toronto.on.ca/parks/golf. Note that the golf season runs from mid April to mid November, and that fees tend to be higher at weekends.

Dentonia Park Golf Course

781 Victoria Park Avenue, at Danforth Avenue, East Toronto (416 392 2558/ www.city.toronto.on.ca/parks/golf/dentonia. htm). Subway Victoria Park. **Fees** *$9-$25.* **Credit** *AmEx, MC, V.*

The Docks

11 Polson Street, at Cherry Street, East Toronto (416 469 5655/www.thedocks.com). Bus 72. **Open** *Sept-May 9am-9pm daily. May-Aug 8am-dusk daily.* **Fees** *$6-$10.* **Credit** *AmEx, MC, V.*

Don Valley Gold Course

4200 Yonge Street, just south of Highway 401, North Toronto (416 392 2465/ www.city.toronto.on.ca/parks/golf/donvalley. htm). Subway York Mills. **Fees** *$16-$55.* **Credit** *AmEx, MC, V.*

Harbourfront Centre
235 Queens Quay W, at York Street, Harbourfront (416 973 4866/www.harbourfrontcentre.com). Streetcar 509, 510. **Open** 10am-10pm daily. **Rentals** $5-$7. **No credit cards.** **Map** p279/p280 F9.

Nathan Phillips Square
100 Queen Street W, at York Street, Chinatown (416 338 7465/www.city.toronto.on.ca/parks/ recreation_facilities/skating/skating.htm). Bus 6/ streetcar 501/subway Osgoode or Queen. **Open** 9am-10pm daily. **Rental** $9; $7 concessions/ 2hrs (deposit ID or $40). **No credit cards.** **Map** p279/280 F7.

In-line skating

Not surprisingly for a hockey-mad town like Toronto, in-line skating is hugely popular. During rush hour cyclists have to share their bike lanes with all manner of skaters gliding to and from work. The city's hiking and bike trails are perfect for the sport, and rental skates are available at many bike hire outfits, including **Wheel Excitement** (*see p213*), which also offers training. Rates for skates start at $12 for the first hour; $3 for each additional hour.

Glen Abbey Golf Club
1333 Dorval Drive, Oakville (1-800 288 0388/905 844 1811/www.glenabbey.com). **Fees** $130-$235. **Credit** AmEx, MC, V.

Humber Valley Golf Course
40 Beattie Avenue at Albion Road, West End (416 392 2488). Subway Royal York then bus 73. **Fees** $15-$46. **Credit** AmEx, MC, V.

Scarlett Woods Golf Course
Eglinton Avenue W, at Jane Street, West End (416 392 2484). Bus 32, 35, 79. **Fees** $11-$35. **Credit** AmEx, MC, V.

St George's Golf & Country Club
1668 Islington Avenue, at Eglinton Avenue W, Etobicoke (416 231 9350/www.stgeorges. org). Streetcar 505/subway Islington. **Fees** $100-$240. **Credit** AmEx, MC, V.

Tam O'Shanter Golf Course
2481 Birchmount Road at Sheppard Avenue E, North Toronto (416 392 2547/ www.city.toronto.on.ca/parks/golf/ tamoshanter.htm). Bus 17, 85. **Fees** $15-$46. **Credit** AmEx, MC, V.

Uplands Golf Club & Ski Centre
446 Uplands Avenue, Thornhill (905 889 3291). **Fees** $24-$26. **Credit** MC, V.

Wooden Sticks
Elgin Park Drive, between Main & Toronto Streets, Uxbridge (905 853 4379/ www.woodensticks.com). **Fees** $160-$220. **Credit** AmEx, MC, V.

Taboo.

Ashbridge's Bay Park. *See p213.*

Pool/billiards

Pool playing is well-loved and readily available throughout Toronto. An array of specialised pool halls have sprouted up for the more practised player; the most exotic establishment being the luxurious **Academy of Spherical Arts**, located in the former Brunswick Billiards factory. The Academy boasts 15 sumptuous antique billiard tables, some valued at over $100,000. Fast-forward a century or so and you'll find a modern counterpart at the pool hall at the **Rivoli**, upstairs from one of Queen Street's trendiest night spots. It's stocked with 13 vintage pool tables (smaller for faster games). There's also a bar/restaurant (*see p107*) and DJ lounge, plus live jazz on Sundays (*see p203*).

Academy of Spherical Arts

38 Hanna Avenue, at King Street W, West End (416 532 2782/www.sphericalarts.com). Streetcar 504. **Open** noon-2am Mon-Fri; 5pm-2am Sat. **Credit** AmEx, DC, MC, V. **Map** p278 A8.

Rivoli

332-334 Queen Street W, at Spadina Avenue, Entertainment District (416 596 1501/http:// rivoli.ca/2003). Streetcar 501, 510. **Open** 4pm-1am Thur-Sun. **Credit** AmEx, MC, V. **Map** p279 D7.

Rock climbing

Joe Rockhead's, Canada's largest indoor climbing facility, with over 50 ropes and 3,000 square feet (278 square metres) of bouldering, is deep in the heart of Toronto. **Toronto Climbing Academy** in the east of the city has ten different climbing areas, which include caves and overhangs; instruction is available. For the real thing, travel west of town to the Niagara Escarpment. **Mountain Equipment Co-op** is the city's best resource for both climbing equipment and information (*see p164*).

Joe Rockhead's Indoor Rock Climbing

29 Fraser Avenue, at Liberty Street, West End (416 538 7670/www.joerockheads.com). Streetcar 504. **Open** 10am-9pm Sat; 10am-7pm Sun. **Admission** $9-$15. **Credit** MC, V.

Toronto Climbing Academy

100A Broadview Avenue, at Queen Street, East Toronto (416 406 5900/www.climbingacademy.com). Streetcar 501, 504. **Open** noon-11pm Mon-Fri; 10am-10pm Sat, Sun. **Admission** $14; $12 concessions. **Credit** V.

Skiing

You'd almost think Southern Ontario was nestled at the foot of the Rockies for all the downhill and cross-country skiing enthusiasts in the region. Although there are no nose-bleed-inducing heights to slide (fall) down, there are still many entertaining, and even challenging, slopes surrounding the GTA to provide a season's worth of enjoyable skiing (snow permitting; many runs rely on snow-making equipment). Snow-boarding has also become readily available at most ski resorts and many public parks, while cross-country skiers can choose from a wealth of trails across the city.

Skiing inside Toronto's borders is pretty much confined to the cross-country variety on bike trails and in city parks, although families and learners can pick up the basics (downhill, cross-country and snowboarding) at two parks, **Earl Bales** (4169 Bathurst Street, 416 395 7934) and **Centennial** (256 Centennial Park Road, 416 394 8750), in Toronto's northern reaches. Call 416 338 6754 for information on public skiing or visit www.city.toronto.on.ca/parks/recreation_facilities/skiing/skiing.htm.

For longer runs, there are many downhill resorts to choose from once you leave town and head north. Less than an hour's drive from the city centre, near Barrie, is **Horseshoe Resort** (1-800 461 5627, www.horseshoeresort.com), a well-maintained facility with seven lifts and 22 runs. It also has 35 kilometres (22 miles) of cross-country trails, as well as snowboarding areas and lessons. It would be worth it, though, to drive an hour further, to Collingwood, to hit Ontario's largest resort, **Blue Mountain** (705 445 0231, www.bluemountain.ca). Here you'll find 34 trails and 12 lifts that accommodate all manner of skiing for beginners, as well as challenging double black diamond runs for experts, three half-pipes for snowboarding and a snowtubing park.

Swimming

The City of Toronto operates more than 30 public pools in just the central core alone, and more than half of those are indoors and open all year round. Of the many outdoor pools, the most significant one is the **Gus Ryder Sunnyside Pool** next to Budapest Park on the lakeshore. Originally built as part of a vast amusement complex in the 1920s, Sunnyside was the city's most popular destination for outdoor summer fun for decades. If you'd rather not deal with the general public, both the **YMCA** (*see p194*) and U of T **Athletic & Physical Education Centre** have pools (*see p214*). For more information on public pools call 416 392 8189 or visit www.city.toronto.on.ca/parks/recreation_facilities/swimming/index.htm.

Gus Ryder Sunnyside Pool
1 Faustina Drive, West End (416 394 8726). Streetcar 501. **Open** phone for details. **Admission** $1. **No credit cards.**

Tennis

In 2004 Toronto's huge (and growing) tennis-playing populace celebrated the opening of the world class **Rexall Centre** at York University as the new home for **Tennis Masters**

Canada, the country's premier event in the sport (*see p169*). With its 3,000-seat grandstand court, the venue heralds the acceptance of tennis as a major spectator sport, as well as one actively enjoyed by many people.

While there are many private tennis clubs in Toronto (you'll need a member to get you in), there are also over 30 courts in public parks, some of them covered in the winter (for example, **Eglinton Flats Park** in the West End), which have slots available to one and all. Generally from 9am to 5pm on weekdays you can use these courts at will, while at weekends and in the evenings they become semi-private – which means if a club member shows up, you have to relinquish your court. As for the free courts, the best maintained ones are in the more upmarket neighbourhoods such as Rosedale and Forest Hill. Moore Park, at Bayview and St Clair avenues, also has particularly nice courts.

If the club life is what you desire, then among the best are the **Toronto Lawn Tennis Club** and the **Boulevard Club**.

For a list of public courts, call 416 392 1111 or visit www.city.toronto.on.ca/parks/recreation_facilities/tennis.

Boulevard Club
1491 Lake Shore Boulevard W, at Dowling Avenue, West End (416 532 3341/www.boulevardclub.com). Streetcar 501. **Open** 7am-11pm Mon-Fri; 7am-10pm Sat, Sun. **Membership** phone for details. **Credit** MC, V.

Toronto Lawn Tennis Club
44 Price Street, east of Yonge Street, Rosedale (416 922 1105/www.torontolawn.com). Subway Summerhill or Rosedale. **Open** 8am-10pm Mon-Fri; 8am-8pm Sat, Sun. **Membership** phone for details. **Credit** MC, V.

Watersports

Although there are times when the pollution dissipates to a non-toxic level, you don't ever really want to swim in Lake Ontario. But that doesn't mean you can't enjoy some fun on the water – in season, of course. Marinas dot the entire lakeshore, and there are several places where visitors can enjoy all kinds of wet recreation, from canoes, kayaks and sailboards to round-the-lake tours. For family fun head over to Centreville on the Toronto Islands for rowing and pedal boats (*see p56* **Walk on**). For a good list of local windsurfing sites consult the website www.torontowindsurfingclub.com.
Harbourfront Canoe & Kayak Centre (283A Queens Quay W, 1 800 960 8886, 416 203 2277, www.paddletoronto.com) provides rentals and lessons.

Theatre & Dance

The independent scene is thriving, while bigger productions fall by the wayside.

Mamma Mia! at the **Royal Alexandra Theatre**. *See p221.*

Theatre

For the past 20 years Toronto has been passing itself off as the third-largest theatre centre in the English-speaking world, after London and New York. This holds true in terms of the number of venues and independent theatre companies in the city, but is debatable in terms of quality or government support – compared to, say, the standard of work and public funding that Chicago theatres receive. Indeed, Toronto residents themselves are not known for their love of the stage in the way Londoners and New Yorkers are. In fact, the third-place status often comes as a surprise to average Torontonians, who couldn't name a single Canadian playwright or stage actor (unless they made a transition to US film or TV; Eric McCormack of *Will & Grace* fame, for instance).

According to some onlookers, nobody has contributed more to this state of affairs than Mirvish Productions, Canada's largest commercial theatre producer, which is responsible for bringing such shows as *Les Misérables* and *The Lion King* to Toronto. Such musical theatre may employ many hundreds of actors and stagehands, but that's little consolation to Canadian playwrights or composers whose work rarely makes it to the Mirvish subscription seasons.

Moreover, in the wake of 9/11, SARS, the rise of the Canadian dollar against the American greenback and the attendant drop in US visitors, the 'third-largest' claim is now more wishful thinking than reality. In 2004 alone, two major American musicals closed prematurely (*The Producers*, *Hairspray*) once tourists from Toronto's neighbours to the south stopped coming by the busload. Broadway-style commercial theatre, with Canadian-cast versions of long-running shows, is either dead or being given the last rites as you read this. In fact, the only long-running musical left standing in Toronto (and likely to survive for a few more seasons thanks to its inherent appeal to baby boomers, the main demographic of Canadian theatre) is *Mamma Mia!* The decline of commercial theatre is such that Toronto has gone from being regarded as the 'Broadway of the North' to just another pit-stop for national tours originating from the US, alongside the likes of Dayton, Ohio, or Memphis, Tennessee.

It's not all doom and gloom, however. The slump in mainstream productions is coinciding with an increase in business in the independent and not-for-profit mid-size theatres. Others still, like **CanStage**, probably the largest of all regional theatres in Canada, are competing for a slice of that elusive commercial-theatre dollar with programming that mixes edgy works with nods to popular, but not overtly populist, fare.

So why is there such a sizeable independent theatre scene in Toronto? One reason is the concentration of Canadian cultural production here. Like New York and London, the city is a magnet for artists. There are five theatre schools in the Greater Toronto Area alone, churning out hundreds of aspiring actors, playwrights, directors and designers. Many new theatre companies have been started over the past two decades by these graduates.

Indigenous theatre as an identifiable movement is a relatively new phenomenon that can be traced back to the late 1960s. Until then, Toronto played host to touring companies from the UK and the US where a repertoire of musicals, variety shows and mid-brow fair was the norm. The establishment of **Theatre Passe Muraille** in 1967, the oldest alternative theatre in Toronto, marked a turning point in what can be safely termed Canadian-themed theatre. The 1970s saw an explosion of other local companies (**Tarragon Theatre, Factory Theatre, Buddies in Bad Times Theatre**); the busy scene today is a direct result of those formative years. For these theatres, commercialism is a dirty word.

All this translates to very lively, sometimes groundbreaking, sometimes insufferably sophomoric efforts. When theatre in Toronto is good, it's thrillingly so. But quality varies wildly, so check local newspapers for reviews and feature articles (see the list below). Bigger theatres do not mean better plays and the best of Toronto theatre is found in smaller venues dotted around town, where creativity abounds, even if money is in short supply.

TICKETS AND INFORMATION

Most performances are at 8pm Tuesday to Saturday, with Sunday matinées at 2.30pm, for which many small and mid-size theatres run a ' pay what you can' (PWYC) policy. Larger theatres also have shows on Monday and Saturday and Wednesday matinées. Prices range from $9.99 in the independent sector to up to $100 for such crowd-pleasers as *Mamma Mia!* (tickets for most mid-size theatres average $30). For all theatre bookings, call the box office directly to reserve seats and, for mid-size theatres, arrive early (most don't have numbered seating). You can also buy tickets to big shows from **TicketKing** (416 872 1212, www.ticketking.com) and **Ticketmaster** (416 870 8000, www.ticketmaster.ca).

TO TIX, located in Yonge-Dundas Square, across from the Toronto Eaton Centre (416 536 6468 ext 40, www.totix.ca), sells day-of-performance tickets (usually discounted by 50 per cent), Tuesdays through Saturdays, noon-6.30pm (and also online, noon-5pm).

As well as the free listings magazines *eye* and *NOW*, an excellent website for information is www.scenechanges.com, which has both reviews and previews on current plays, updated weekly.

FESTIVALS

Toronto's theatre scene is supplemented by serious contributions from the classical repertoires of two popular out-of-town festivals: the **Shaw Festival** in Niagara-on-the-Lake (*see p237*) and the **Stratford Festival** (*see p242*), both of which have a wide appeal.

If you're in Toronto in July, check out the ever-expanding **Toronto Fringe Theatre Festival** (*see p169*). Breakaway shows that started here and went on to greater things include *Top Gun! – The Musical, The Drowsy Chaperone* and *Pond Life*. The smaller but more consistently rewarding and now completely juried festival, **SummerWorks** (*see p170*), is held in the first week of August.

Venues

With the exception of **Soulpepper** (*see p220* **Hot peppered soul**), whose new purpose-built theatre is slated to open in 2005, none of Toronto's theatres has a resident company as such. Every season (September to May), each venue offers a selection of plays, some of which are co-productions with local or regional theatre companies, some produced individually in-house, and some touring. As a result, quality varies.

Artword Theatre

75 Portland Street, at King Street W, Entertainment District (416 408 2783/artword.net). Streetcar 504, 511. **Open** *Box office varies.* **Tickets** $15-$30. **Credit** *varies.* **Map** p279 D8.
Independently run, with a hit-or-miss programme of plays and dance performances. In the last couple of years it has acquired an unfortunate 'home of the lost causes' reputation among the theatre community because of its admirably multicultural but often hokey productions. The main theatre seats 150. A smaller space, Artword Alternative, seats about 60 and is a favourite for upcoming theatre companies.

Berkeley Street Theatre

26 Berkeley Street, at Front Street E, St Lawrence (416 368 3110/www.canstage.com). Streetcar 504. **Open** *Box office 10am-6pm Mon-Sat.* **Tickets** $25-$80. **Credit** AmEx, MC, V. **Map** p280 H8.

CanStage (*see p222*) sends its edgier work to this 240-seater. Patrick Marber's *Closer* (2002) and Joe Penhall's *Blue/Orange* (2003) played here as well as American 9/11 polemic *Omnium Gatherum* in 2004.

Bluma Appel Theatre

St Lawrence Centre, 27 Front Street E, St Lawrence (416 368 3110/www.canstage.com). Streetcar 504/ subway King or Union. **Open** *Box office* 10am-6pm Mon-Sat. **Tickets** $40-$75. **Credit** AmEx, MC, V. **Map** p280 G8.

This 875-seater is where CanStage's flashier productions are mounted (*Proof, Take Me Out, Sweeney Todd*). It's a relatively large space, but excellent sightlines make it feel quite intimate.

Buddies in Bad Times Theatre

12 Alexander Street, at Yonge Street, Church & Wellesley (416 975 8555/www.buddiesinbadtimes theatre.com). Streetcar 506/subway Wellesley. **Open** *Box office* noon-5pm Tue-Sat. **Tickets** $18-$25. **Credit** MC, V. **Map** p283 G5.

North America's largest queer theatre (call it gay and lesbian at your peril) dates back to 1979 and is a focal point for the gay community, at whose heart it resides. Its heyday was the 1980s, when its then artistic director Sky Gilbert made it home to grungy, postmodern gay-themed plays that had edge but insufficient audience appeal. After a few years in the artistic wilderness of gay low-brow fare, the company has changed mandate, starting with its 2004-5 season, to focus on risk-taking theatre, straight, gay and in-between. There's a small cabaret theatre too. *See also p192* **Good times at Bad Times**.

Canon Theatre

244 Victoria Street, at Dundas Street, Dundas Square (416 872 1212/www.mirvish.com). Streetcar 505/ subway Dundas. **Open** *Box office* 10.30am-6pm Mon, Tue; 10.30am-8.30pm Wed-Sat; 11am-3pm Sun. **Tickets** $44-$94. **Credit** AmEx, DC, MC, V. **Map** p280 G7.

Hot peppered soul

Before Soulpepper set up in 1998, local fans of classical theatre had to travel further afield, to the Stratford or Shaw festivals, for performances with such attention to emotional and physical detail. Of course, the Stratford and Shaw festivals are still major crowd-pullers, but with Soulpepper's new 44,000-square-foot venue, due to open in the Distillery District in late 2005, the company is going from strength to strength.

Artistic director Albert Schultz is a prime example of a go-go theatre person who also happens to be a top-notch arts administrator. Savvy marketing has a lot to do with Soulpepper's success: a typical season runs from June to October, in direct competition with Shaw and Stratford, but also when most other Toronto theatres are on their summer hiatus.

Although the company has staged a wide range of well-received and award-winning productions, its raison d'être is 20th-century, particularly Absurdist, theatre (Samuel Beckett and Harold Pinter, to name but two). In contrast, its forays into Shakespeare, Goldoni and Sheridan have been criticised by some for being embarrassingly ham-fisted. But there's certainly no doubting Soulpepper's longevity: its youth training and mentoring programmes, to be staged in nine teaching studios in the new facility, show its commitment to home-grown treatments of classical theatre.

Soulpepper Theatre Company

416 203 6264/www.soulpepper.ca.

The Zoo Story.

This exquisitely restored theatre (which was previously known as the Pantages) is now owned by Mirvish Productions. When the venue is not used as part of the Mirvish subscription season it becomes the location of choice for box-and-truck touring musicals. Productions slated for 2005 included the Broadway smash *Wicked*, based on the *Wizard of Oz*.

Elgin & Winter Garden Theatre

189 Yonge Street, at Shuter Street, Dundas Square (416 314 2884/www.ticketmaster.ca). Streetcar 505/ subway Dundas or Queen. **Open** Box office 11am-5pm Mon-Sat. **Tickets** from $25. **Credit** AmEx, DC, MC, V. **Map** p280 G7.

North America's only remaining double-decker theatre complex (a popular design in the early 1900s), the Elgin and the Winter Garden were restored in the 1980s after decades of neglect. The larger Elgin is richly appointed, with ornate fabrics and gilt cherubs. The Winter Garden sits above, festooned in Arcadian watercolour scenes. The theatres are now home to productions that vary from Baroque opera in the grand Elgin, to one-woman shows in the Winter Garden. It draws international touring productions, such as *Umoja*, and well-to-do north Toronto crowds for whom theatre is a diversion after dinner and before nightcaps. The Elgin also doubles as a cinema during the Toronto film festival.

Factory Theatre

125 Bathurst Street, at King Street W, Entertainment District (416 504 9971/www. factorytheatre.ca). Streetcar 501, 511. **Open** Box office noon-4pm Mon; 1-8pm Tue-Sat. **Tickets** $20-$34. **Credit** AmEx, MC, V. **Map** p279 D8.

The quintessential Canadian theatre. Established in 1970 by Ken Gass, who returned in 1997 as artistic director, it was the first in Canada to focus exclusively on works by indigenous playwrights, who have a soft spot for the venue since many got their first break here. A Victorian building on the edge of the Garment District, it defines shabby genteel. Historical significance aside, approach with care: each season the Factory plays host to a clunker or two in the name of national pride and its 2003-4 season was diabolical.

Harbourfront Centre

235 Queen's Quay W, Waterfront (416 973 4000/ www.harbourfrontcentre.com). Streetcar 509, 510/ subway Union. **Open** Box office 1-8pm Tue-Sat. **Tickets** $20-$60. **Credit** AmEx, MC, V. **Map** p279/280 F9.

The Harbourfront Centre is known as a producer of major festivals (jazz, authors', children's). Its bi-annual World Stage Festival in the spring is to local theatre aficionados what the Toronto International Film Festival is to film buffs: a chance to experience a rush of theatre from around the world. (That said, its future is currently in doubt due to financial instability, but a smaller version of the festival is likely to take off in 2005.) The Centre also rents out its

three performing-art venues when they're not in use for its own programming: Harbourfront Theatre Centre, Premiere Dance Theatre and Studio Theatre.

Hummingbird Centre for the Performing Arts

1 Front Street E, at Yonge Street, St Lawrence (416 393 7469/www.hummingbirdcentre.com). Streetcar 504/subway King or Union. **Open** Box office 10am-6pm Mon-Fri; 10am-5pm Sat. **Tickets** $20-$150. **Credit** AmEx, MC, V. **Map** p280 G8.

Named after a sponsoring Toronto software firm, this barn-like (3,000-seater) home of the Canadian Opera Company and the National Ballet of Canada has an uncertain future, as its prestigious tenants are planning a move to the new Four Seasons Centre for the Performing Arts by the end of 2006. Until then, the theatre will no doubt continue to mount a mishmash of shows: everything from *Tap Dogs Rebooted* and performances by the likes of Dionne Warwick and Morrissey, to the umpteenth tour of *Grease*, earning it the unfortunate reputation as the venue that 'time and taste forgot'.

Panasonic Theatre

651 Yonge Street, at Isabella Street, Church & Wellesley (Ticketmaster 416 872 1111). Subway Bloor-Yonge. **Open** Box office phone for details. **Tickets** average $60. **Credit** AmEx, DC, MC, V. **Map** p283 G4.

The New Yorker Theatre was once the home of such popular franchises as *Puppetry of the Penis* and other mid-brow commercial shows but, at the time of writing, this 425-seat downtown theatre was undergoing extensive renovation (and a name-change, to Panasonic), which is tailor-made for the Toronto première of the performance art ensemble, Blue Man Group. The theatre's new owners, Clear Channel Entertainment, hopes BMG and their gallons of body paint will stay there for an indefinite run beginning, tentatively, May 2005. Phone for details of tickets nearer the time.

Princess of Wales Theatre

300 King Street W, at John Street, Entertainment District (416 872 1212/www.mirvish.com). Streetcar 504/subway St Andrew. **Open** Box office 10.30am-6pm Mon, Tue; 10.30am-8.30pm Wed-Sat; 11am-3pm Sun. **Tickets** $26-$94. **Credit** AmEx, DC, MC, V. **Map** p279 E8.

This venue in the heart of the Entertainment District is the first privately owned theatre built in Canada since 1907. With Peter Smith as its architect, Yabu-Pushelberg as its interior design firm and Frank Stella responsible for its murals, this place is noted as much for its design as its productions. It opened in 1993 with *Miss Saigon*. Its future, however, is dependent on what happens to commercial theatre in general.

Royal Alexandra Theatre

260 King Street W, at University Avenue, Entertainment District (416 872 1212/www. mirvish.com). Streetcar 504/subway St Andrew.

Open *Box office* 10.30am-6.30pm Mon, Tue; 10.30am-8.30pm Tue-Sat; noon-7pm Sun. **Tickets** $44-$86. **Credit** AmEx, DC, MC, V. **Map** p279 E8.

Once described as an 'Edwardian jewel box', this 1907 theatre encapsulates grand chapters of Toronto theatre history. In its environs John Gielgud and Ralph Richardson played; Piaf belted, and Fred Astaire put on the Ritz. In 1962 it was bought by Ed Mirvish and served as the premier venue of his subscription season until *Mamma Mia!* came along.

Tarragon Theatre

30 Bridgman Avenue, at Howland Avenue, Casa Loma (416 531 1827/www.tarragontheatre.com). Bus 7/subway Dupont. **Open** *Box office* 10am-5pm Mon; 10am-7pm Tue-Sat. **Tickets** $15-$33. **Credit** MC, V. **Map** p282 D2.

By far the most reliable – artistically and financially – theatre in Toronto and, probably, Canada. Here you're likely to see Canadian theatre at its best as well as some fine productions of, say, David Hare, David Mamet or Tony Kushner. English translations of major works from Quebec are a house speciality. The programming emphasis remains on well-established Canadian playwrights. Tarragon has two auditoriums: the main theatre, a 205-seater for works of wider appeal, and the Extra Space, one of the best small venues in town, where experimental or small-scale plays are staged.

Theatre Passe Muraille

16 Ryerson Avenue, at Wolseley Street, Entertainment District (416 504 7529/www. passemuraille.on.ca). Streetcar 501, 511. **Open** *Box office* noon-5pm Mon-Fri; later hours & also weekends during performances. **Tickets** $16-$38. **Credit** AmEx, MC, V. **Map** p279 D7.

The who's who of Canadian theatre started here. Some of them, like Ann-Marie MacDonald and Michael Ondaatje, have since become internationally renowned novelists. Of late, however, hits have been the exception rather than the rule, though *The Drawer Boy* by Michael Healey in 1999 made up for a dearth of popular or critical successes. Productions in 2003 included Sean Reycraft's O*ne Good Marriage* and Trey Anthony's *Da Kink in My Hair*. The main stage has a jazz bar feel with an open balcony and well-stocked bar; the small Backspace is notoriously uncomfortable (patrons are provided with cushions) but has seen some important independent productions.

Companies

On current estimates, Toronto has 250 theatre companies of all stripes and sizes. Below is a select list of those tested by time and critics.

Bluemouth Inc

www.bluemouthinc.com.

A visionary theatre company, quietly but spectacularly producing environmentally staged plays that mix history and psychoanalysis, dance and text, theatre and anti-theatre in a powerful package. Outdoor theatre in a chilly Toronto November? Only Bluemouth can do it and win a Dora Award (Toronto's equivalent of the Oliviers or the Tonys) for Outstanding Independent Production in 2004.

Canadian Stage Company

416 368 3110/www.canstage.com.

With an annual operating budget of $8 million, CanStage (as it likes to be known) is the envy of every theatre company in town. Recent seasons have included an overwhelming number of US, British and Irish plays that make light of the fact that this is the nearest Canada has to a national theatre. Still, productions are always polished, and cast and directors are the city's crème de la crème. CanStage operates two auditoriums, with its main roster in the Bluma Appel (*see p220*) and edgier stuff in the Berkeley Street (*see p219*).

Da Da Kamera

416 586 1503/www.dadakamera.com.

One of Canada's best and most original theatre companies is a showcase for its artistic director's writing and acting talent. Daniel MacIvor (also a film director and actor) creates plays with a heightened sense of theatricality and deceptive simplicity. The work ranges from multi-character dramas to McIvor's own one-man brand of performance-art-meets-theatre.

(sidebar) Arts & Entertainment

macIDeas

416 294 9239/www.macideas.com.

This once-small company leaped into the big time when it hired Woody Harrelson to direct Kenneth Lonergan's *This Is Our Youth* in 2003. It's now made up of a consortium of producers and financial advisers with an eye to bridge gaps: between the independent $10 fringe show and the more commercial $100 Broadway musical, and between stage and screen work. Its shows, which included the American comic satire *Matt & Ben*, have youth and hip appeal written all over them. Quality, however, is more elusive.

Modern Times Stage Company

416 790 1016/www.moderntimesstage.com.

Artistic director Soheil Parsa's company fuses Middle Eastern theatrical traditions with Western ones to create a uniquely bi-cultural experience. Emphasis on movement and imagistic theatre results in an evocative experience – even if the work suffers from over-stylisation. Still, expect to be dazzled.

Native Earth Performing Arts

416 531 1402/www.nativeearth.ca.

The first theatre company dedicated to developing and creating works that express the aboriginal experience in Canada. Its most famous alumnus is Tomson Highway, whose *The Rez Sisters* and *Dry Lips Oughta Move to Kapuskasing* are Canadian (not just Native) classics. The company continues to hand-hold a number of playwrights and performers with various degrees of success.

Necessary Angel Theatre Company

416 703 0406/www.necessaryangel.com.

A company whose name is associated with serious and intellectually stimulating theatre – a reputation it has lived up to. Founding artistic director Richard Rose has moved to Tarragon Theatre (*see p222*), leaving the company in the hands of director and writer Daniel Brooks. Playwrights whose works it has presented include Jason Sherman, Colleen Murphy and David Young, all Toronto theatre A-listers.

Nightwood Theatre

416 944 1740/www.nightwoodtheatre.net.

Nightwood focuses on work by women writers and has a strong feminist bent but has emerged over the last 20 years as a home of good theatre, period. Examples include Sonja Mills' *The Danish Play* (2002) and, to a lesser extent, Marjorie Chan's *China Doll* (2004).

Theatre Smith-Gilmour

416 504 1277/www.theatresmithgilmour.com.

Since 1980, artistic directors Dean Gilmour and Michele Smith have been creating original, improvisational theatre inspired by sources as various as clown theatre and Dante. But it was only once they

National Ballet of Canada.

let their imagination loose on the work of Anton Chekhov that they became local heroes, collecting eight Dora Awards for productions in 2000 and 2002 based on the Russian master's fiction. Another piece, *Dr Chekhov: Ward 6*, followed in 2004 and a fourth, *Chekhov's Children*, in April 2005. A European influence pervades but the talent is wholly Canadian.

Dance

In terms of size and cultural significance, Toronto's contemporary dance scene is small fry compared to Montreal's, the dance capital of Canada. The biggest event to hit the dance scene was Mikhail Baryshnikov's defection from the USSR while performing in Toronto in 1974. The National Ballet of Canada may have their headquarters in Toronto, but dance in general (and contemporary dance in particular) is an elite art form here. Those who remain active work on the edge of creative and financial anxieties which lend a compelling roughness to the scene. This, combined with visits from touring groups, means there is enough here for the dance-loving traveller. See p219 for ticket information.

Venues

Buddies in Bad Times Theatre (*see p220*) is another major dance-friendly venue. Every August it hosts fFida, fringe Festival of Independent Dance Artists (www.ffida.org).

Betty Oliphant Theatre
404 Jarvis Street, at Wellesley Street, Church & Wellesley (416 964 5140/enquiries 416 964 5148/ www.nbs-enb.on.ca). Subway Wellesley. **Open** phone for details. **Map** p283 G5.
Part of National Ballet School of Canada, this 300-seat space was designed with dance performance (in particular, ballet) in mind – which explains why local and touring dance companies return to it year after year. On the downside, its massive stage can overwhelm more minimalist choreography.

Premiere Dance Theatre
Harbourfront Centre, 235 Queens Quay W, Waterfront (416 973 4000/www.harbourfront centre.com). Streetcar 509, 510. **Open** *Box office* 1-8pm Tue-Sat. **Tickets** $21-$38. **Credit** AmEx, MC, V. **Map** p279/280 F9.
Home to World Moves Dance series, which features the best in contemporary dance from around the world. The curated series runs from October to May and always has spots showcasing Canadian companies as well as international troupes.

Theatre Centre
1087 Queen Street W, at Dovercourt Road, West Toronto (416 538 0988/www.theatrecentre.org). Streetcar 501. **Open** *Box office* noon-5pm Mon-Fri. **Tickets** $10-$20. **Credit** MC, V. **Map** p278 A7.

After six months of renovations, the Theatre Centre unveiled its new look and attitude in December 2004 with a double bill of works by and about Beckett and Brecht. Under new artistic director, Franco Boni, the space will continue to support multidisciplinary creations (many relying on movement and choreography), but will slowly reduce the commitment to modern dance shown by previous directors.

Winchester Street Theatre
80 Winchester Street, at Parliament Street, Cabbagetown (416 967 1365/www.tdt.org). Bus 65/streetcar 506. **Open** *Box office* 10am-5pm Mon-Fri. **Tickets** $15-$35. **Credit** MC, V. **Map** p283 J5.
This Cabbagetown theatre is operated jointly by Toronto Dance Theatre (TDT; *see below*) and the School of Toronto Dance Theatre. With 115 seats, it may be a small venue, but its medium-sized stage is ideal for a mixture of choreographic styles.

Companies

Dancemakers
416 367 1800/www.dancemakers.org.
Toronto's most challenging dance company, physically and intellectually, has had French émigré poet Serge Bennathan as artistic director since 1990. The company's work reflects his poetic vision.

Danny Grossman Dance Company
416 408 4543/www.dgdance.org.
A living legend, Grossman choreographs and presents at least two shows a year. Physical storytelling is the best description of his politicised-in-theme work. In November 2004 he presented the world premiere of *Two for the Road*.

National Ballet of Canada
416 345 9595/www.national.ballet.ca.
The standards may be international but artistic director James Kudelka has been infusing his programming with works by local choreographers. Yes, expect to see the standard (but lavish) interpretations of *Swan Lake* or *Giselle* but keep an eye open for the groundbreaking choreography he sneaks up on his blue-rinse audiences.

Peggy Baker Dance Projects
416 462 4164.
The grande dame of contemporary dance has previously worked with the Lar Lubovitch Dance Company and Mikhail Baryshnikov's White Oak Dance Project. Recent productions include *The Disappearance of Right and Left*, based on landmark moments in Baker's life.

Toronto Dance Theatre
416 967 1365/www.tdt.org.
Formed in 1968, TDT has been part of the evolution of dance culture in Toronto. Current artistic director Christopher House adds wit as well as visual and dramatic appeal to a controversial company that has as many hardcore fans as it has detractors.

Trips Out of Town

Getting Started

A great outdoors.

Map pp274-275

With close to 13 million people, Ontario may be the most populous province in Canada, but, like the rest of the country, around 85 per cent of its inhabitants live within 100 miles (161 kilometres) of the US border, which leaves a lot of space for uninhabited wilderness. Attractions include rugged campgrounds, provincial parks, luxury tennis retreats, family resorts, fly-in fishing camps, winter ski hills, miles of quiet cross-country trails and 20 per cent of the world's fresh water supply dispersed among half a million lakes and rivers (give or take a couple of thousand).

The province is also both the geographical and the political centre of the nation (separating the constant and often fractious 'east–west' national positions), the country's main base for industry and trade and home of two capital cities: Toronto is the capital of Ontario, while Ottawa is the capital of the Canada (though the 'Capital City Region' does extend into Quebec to appease the never-ending Anglo-French rivalry).

It seems that the province's name, given by the native tribes, was a reference to water. The word either comes from the Huron ('beautiful or sparkling water') or from an Iroquois term meaning 'rocks standing near the water', which referred to the now-famous Falls of the Niagara Escarpment. Either way, the word describes Ontario's original transport system.

The province is a little too big to experience in one weekend, with an area of approximately 400,000 square miles (a million square kilometres). To put that in perspective, you could fit France, Germany and Italy within its borders. If you decided to spend the weekend driving north from Toronto to Thunder Bay, on the north shore of Lake Superior, it would take you, well, all weekend, just to get there. And then if you really wanted to drive north to the province's furthest border – forget it, there are no roads. Destinations in the following chapters, then, are a manageable distance away from town, covering the nearby Niagara area, the choicest day trips and samplings of the most easily accessed country and wilderness areas.

McMichael Canadian Art Collection. *See p239.*

Visitors should keep in mind that half the urban population seems to have a summer cottage, while the other half cultivates friends who do, so there's a mass exodus from the city on summer Fridays and major roads can get clogged, especially out towards the Muskokas and Haliburton Cottage Country. Niagara Falls is heaving from Friday to Sunday. So if you can, plan your getaways during the week.

GETTING AROUND

Public transport is patchy, and a car is the only option for many trips out of town. For rental offices, *see p256*. However, **VIA Rail** (65 Front Street W, 1-888 842 7245, www.viarail.ca) provides an excellent service along the well-travelled 'corridor' route from Windsor through Toronto, Kingston, Ottawa, Montreal and Quebec City (it also covers the Toronto–Niagara Falls route, though both the train and bus station at the latter aren't especially convenient for the Falls themselves).

Greyhound buses (1-800 661 8747/416 594 1010, www.greyhound.ca) are more likely to serve the smaller places on the map, and will be cheaper as well. They are the cheapest public transport to Niagara Falls. Greyhound's main Toronto terminal is centrally located at 610 Bay Street, at Edward Street (*see p252*).

Camper vans are a good way of exploring the Ontarian vastness. **CanaDream Campers** hire out all kinds of moving accommodation. The office is near Pearson International Airport at 5315 General Road, Mississauga (1-800 461 7368/416 243 3232, www.canadream.com).

TOURIST INFORMATION

Information on the province is available from **Ontario Travel Information Centre** (*see p265*). Particularly useful are its tours and accommodation brochures. **Ontario Tourism Marketing Partnership** (1-800 668 2746, www.ontariotravel.net) and **Resorts Ontario** (1-800 363 7227/705 325 9115, www.resorts-ontario.com) also offer information on travel and destinations in the province.

For information on parks and camping, contact the **Ministry of Natural Resources** (1-800 667 1940) or **Ontario Parks** (1-888 668 7275, www.ontarioparks.com); for information on Ontario's many heritage sites, contact the **Ontario Heritage Foundation** (416 325 5000, www.heritagefdn.on.ca).

TELEPHONE CODES

When calling lost-distance from Toronto, you will need to dial 1 before the area code. This goes for the Niagara region's 905 code, although some 905 numbers in the Greater Toronto area have the same prefix and are local calls.

Inniskillin winery. *See p236.*

Niagara-on-the-Lake. *See p237.*

Niagara Falls & Around

Somewhere over the rainbow… there are wineries and pretty villages.

The view from the **Maid of the Mist** is pure gold. *See p232.*

Niagara Falls

Surprisingly, many Torontonians aren't much interested in Niagara Falls, seeing them as nothing more than a convenient way of getting rid of houseguests for the day. But watching half a billion gallons of water a second slide off a cliff right in front of you is pretty impressive by any standards, and if you're in Toronto, you should make the trip. Cynical though the surrounding town's exploitation might be, hell, some people *like* viewing towers, sightseeing 'experiences' and tourist attractions of an entirely unashamed nature. Millions certainly come; over 12 million a year, in fact, to the Canadian side alone (and 35,000 people a day to the town's two casinos). If you're not expecting to commune with nature, it can be, well, fun.

The first European to witness the spectacle in 1678 was Jesuit Louis Hennepin, who was introduced to the then-sacred site by local native tribes. The missionary was awestruck by what he saw and immediately sent word of this wonder back to Europe, effectively launching a form of eco-tourism. But it wasn't long before the tacky trappings that have long been associated with the Falls kicked in. The first record of a couple spending their honey-moon at this site was in 1801; in 1803 Jérôme Bonaparte, Napoleon's little brother, brought his bride here, sparking off a fad: the city of Niagara Falls now issues 13,000 honeymoon certificates a year. Oscar Wilde famously summarised the visit to Niagara by newlyweds as 'a bride's second great disappointment'. Border skirmishes in the early 19th century deterred visitors, but by 1827, when the three hotels of the time combined to float a boatful of animals over the Horseshoe Falls, 10,000 people turned up to watch. When the railway arrived in 1840, tourists swarmed in and the sideshow culture started properly to evolve. In 1859 Blondin made the first of his nine tightrope crossings; ever since then a rash of the rash have jumped, plunged and barrelled over, across or into the Falls and rapids (*see p231* **Falls guys**).

With 'experiences' rather than stunts taking over in the later 20th century (the *Maid of the Mist*, Journey Behind the Falls, IMAX, cable cars) and death-defying plunges firmly outlawed (though not altogether knocked on the head), Niagara has became increasingly sanitised. Recently the region has undergone a transformation, expanding from purely Falls-oriented attractions into more general tourist activity – shopping, golf, gambling, miscellaneous mainstream attractions – in an attempt to keep visitors overnight and fill those thousands of hotel rooms. Niagara Falls is Canada's number one tourist attraction. You can take that to the bank.

THE FALLS

The Niagara river is the border between Canada and the US. It is effectively a drainage channel between Lake Erie and Lake Ontario, transporting 200,000 cubic feet of water per second for 34 miles (55 kilometres), with a total drop of 350 feet (108 metres). It runs over the Niagara Escarpment, in which sedimentary layers of hard and soft rock from the ancient Michigan Sea are tilted at an angle. The Falls occur at a bend in the river about halfway along its length, where its total width is about a mile. Goat Island sits on the US side, dividing the two main attractions: the American Falls (184 feet/56 metres) and the smaller Bridal Veil Falls on one one side; the more impressive Canadian (Horseshoe) Falls (177 feet/54 metres) link the island to the Canadian bank in a 2,125-foot (675-metre) arc. The geology here is in a continual state of flux: turbulence at the foot of the Falls erodes the soft rock layer, digging out a deeper drop; periodically, the increasingly unsupported upper, heavier layer breaks off, with the result that the Falls retreat very gradually upstream, at a rate of about a foot every ten years. At the end of the last ice age, 10,000 years ago, the Niagara Falls were seven miles (11 kilometres) closer to Lake Ontario, as high cliffs testify.

A couple of miles downstream (and visible as you look at the Falls) is the Niagara Power Project. This joint Canadian/US enterprise generates 2.4 million kilowatts by diverting part of the flow through its turbines. A hard-argued 1950 pact requires it to leave at least 100,000 cubic feet per second in the original river during daylight hours in the visitor season, half the average total flow (thus helping to limit erosion). Take time to imagine how the Falls would be naturally without any intervention: twice as much crashing water in a world with 24 million fewer lightbulbs.

ORIENTATION

Falls activity centres on two spots on the river, the Falls area itself and the Whirlpool Basin area three miles (five kilometres) north. A road and a strip of parkland with a railed walkway and viewing platforms built along the cliffs link the two. The town of Niagara Falls and its tourist attractions are set on a rise above the river with a hotel hinterland stretching west; you could walk between the two, but people seldom do. There's a funicular (the Falls Incline Railway) near the Horseshoe Falls; hotels run shuttle buses and most tours take you straight to the Falls. In summer the city wheels out its 'people movers', frequent shuttle buses run between the Falls and various points in town; out of season you'll have to manage on normal city buses. The train and Greyhound stations are at the far end of town and a five-minute walk from the nearest bus stop, which is at the corner of Bridge and Erie Streets.

The Niagara Parkway runs the whole length of the river on the Canadian side. North and south of the Falls are, yes, more attractions, plus parks, picnic areas and viewpoints. It's pretty, in a regulated sort of a way.

You can cross over to the US side of the river on foot or by car on either the Rainbow Bridge (near the Falls) or the Whirlpool Rapids Bridge. Take your passport and any visa documents (*see p253* **US passport regulations**) and be prepared for security checks and body searches. Queues are longer since 9/11. Given that the views are less impressive from the American side, it's not really worth it.

WHAT TO SEE

First – and quite possibly only – the Falls themselves. There are always crowds, often dozens deep, at the main Table Rock site, where you can stand (behind a strong stone and metal railing) a mere metre away from the edge of the Horseshoe Falls. There is a spot where you are literally at the peak of the cascade as it rushes by your toes, plummeting 177 feet (54 metres) down into the foaming, misty gorge. In high season you may have to jostle a while to get into position by the railing, but it's worth the wait.

The Table Rock Complex has a restaurant, snack bar and souvenir shops filled with tacky trinkets, and is also the entry point for the Journey Behind the Falls. Visitors take a lift down 125 feet (38 metres) through solid rock, don yellow rain macs and then walk through a tunnel directly behind the curtain of water plunging over the Horseshoe Falls. There is also an outdoor observation deck at the side, where you can watch the thundering waters hit the gorge and turn into white mist. Pretty dramatic stuff, it has to be said.

Trips Out of Town

Half a mile north is the departure point for the **Maid of the Mist**, at the bottom of Clifton Hill, opposite the American Falls. There's a direct road from town, or you can take the crowded, scenic and invariably damp riverside walk through **Queen Victoria Park**. There's no advance booking, so prepare for a lengthy queue in busy times, or get there early – the first cruise leaves at 9.45am – but this is one water ride that is well worth the wait. At the bottom of the cliffs you get suited up in blue slickers. The little ship chugs past the American Falls and Cave of the Winds before it charges straight for the horseshoe of water. Passengers aboard the bucking boat will find the world turns totally white as they disappear into the mists of Niagara. Make no mistake, you will get wet. But it's worth it for the thrill.

Three more river-centric attractions are based in the Whirlpool Basin area, a couple of miles downstream. The **Great Gorge Adventure** (905 371 0254, closed Nov-late April) takes you down in a lift to a boardwalk beside the seething rapids; the **Niagara Whirlpool Aero Car**, built in 1913, spans the dramatic whirlpool (subject to weather conditions) – the ride is lovely, but pretty tame. For a real thrill, book a flight over the Falls with Niagara Helicopters (905 357 5672).

Many people prefer to visit Niagara during the frigid, white winters. For one thing, there are no crowds. But the main reason is that the entire area around the Horseshoe Falls turns into a stunning winter tableau of ice and snow. The mist covers buildings, trees, railings and coats everything with layers of ice. It is a beautiful spectacle, especially at night, when the Niagara Light Show (year round after dusk) bathes the water, mist and ice in startling white, red and blue. Note that many attractions (and restaurants) will be closed, though, or operating on reduced opening hours.

In the town itself you can pretty much take your pick of international tourist franchises, viewing towers and assorted attractions. The **Skylon Tower** is not hard to find. Take one of the little 'yellow bug' exterior lifts for a ride to the indoor or outdoor Observation Deck. This will give you another view of the Falls – and it is breathtaking – from some 775 feet (236 metres) above ground level. You can see the perfect horseshoe shape of the Canadian Falls and the plume of mist spilling up hundreds of metres from the rolling waters of the Niagara river. It's also fun to watch the toytown-tiny *Maid of the Mist* fight its way towards the Horseshoe Falls and then disappear into the white swirls.

Clifton Hill, the steep street that runs up into town from the *Maid of the Mist* departure point, is a glorious concentration of tacky attractions.

Here you will find Dracula's Haunted Castle, the Mystery Maze, the Movieland Wax Museum of Stars, Ripley's Believe It or Not, the Great Canadian Midway, the House of Frankenstein and the Dinosaur Park putting course.

The **IMAX Theatre Niagara Falls & Daredevil Gallery** showcases the largest collection of barrels and home-made contraptions used to challenge the Falls, successfully and otherwise. To save you making the leap yourself, there is some incredible video footage filmed by a daredevil through the reinforced window of his barrel. Don't miss the photos of Blondin as he crossed the gorge on the highwire. The stunning IMAX film, *Niagara: Miracles, Myths and Magic*, plays regularly.

MarineLand is one of the town's most popular attractions. The show features killer whales, sea lions and leaping dolphins; there's also a zoo with elk, bear and buffalo.

When Niagara's city fathers looked for ways to boost tourism in the area, gambling was the obvious way to go. The town has always had the ersatz ambience of an Atlantic City or Las Vegas and slot machines certainly put those places on the map. Gambling is now as much a part of the Niagara culture as fudge factories and snow domes.

Casino Niagara has a massive 96,000 square feet (9,000 square metres) of gaming space. It was eclipsed, however, in spring 2004 by the opening of the **Niagara Fallsview Casino Resort** (*see p234*), a huge hotel/casino with more than double its rival's gambling space. Both establishments are open daily, round the clock.

At the opposite end of the tourist spectrum is **Niagara Parks Butterfly Conservatory**, about five miles (eight kilometres) north along the Niagara Parkway and just south of the Floral Clock (a free attraction that is exactly what it sounds like). This living museum features more than 2,000 butterflies from around the globe. It's an explosion of hues in a lush, climate-controlled rainforest setting. Wear colourful clothing and the butterflies will land on you for the perfect photo op. The Butterfly Conservatory is part of the **Niagara Parks Botanical Gardens** (905 371 0254). Nature lovers also flock to the **Niagara Falls Aviary**, where free-flying toucans, hornbills and some 350 other species of birds reside in a faux jungle temple ruin.

Niagara has some gorgeous green spaces. One is the **Niagara Glen Nature Reserve**, a tranquil antidote to some of the more raucous Niagara attractions. Located on the Niagara Parkway, the Glen is a haven mostly missed by tourists who are put off by the steep, rugged

Falls guys

The fact that it's illegal hasn't stopped numerous 'daredevils' over the years from attempting to cross Niagara Falls. There have been 16 known attempts at it (only ten people have survived) and, whichever method they choose – in a barrel, on a tightrope, or simply in the clothes they stand up in – they have all in their different ways been memorable.

The first person known to have survived a plunge was Sam Patch (aka the Yankee Leaper), who in October 1829 jumped over Horseshoe Falls and lived.

But perhaps the most famous crosser was the Great Blondin (*pictured*), a French tightrope walker, who in 1859 crossed the gorge on a specially made rope. Such was his confidence that he made the crossing several times more – once with his manager on his back, and once with a small stove which, halfway across, he used to cook an omelette.

The first successful 'barrel-crossing' was Annie Taylor, back in 1901, who climbed into an air-tight wooden barrel. She survived (albeit a little bruised and battered), hoping to make some hard cash from her fame. She died in poverty. Then there was Bobby Leach who, in 1911, plunged over the falls in a steel

barrel. He broke both kneecaps but survived – only to die 15 years later from gangrene after slipping on an orange peel. In 1920 Charles G Stephens thought that the way to go was to tie himself to an anvil (which he was using as ballast) within his barrel. Unfortunately, when the barrel 'hit the deck' the anvil (with Stephens attached) kept going. No trace of him was ever found... unless you count his right arm, which was still in the barrel. In 1930 poor George L Stathakis, a Greek waiter, suffocated after his barrel was trapped in the current behind the falls for 14 hours. The story has a happy ending of sorts: George's pet turtle, Sonny Boy, who'd come along for the ride, survived.

The most recent attempt was in October 2003, when Kirk Jones from Michigan made the jump – and survived – wearing only the clothes on his back. He and a friend bought a video camera to record the event. He was fined $2,300 dollars for the offence and banned from entering Canada ever again. Unfortunately, the pair were so inebriated at the time of this historic event that Kirk's friend couldn't work out how to operate the camera; the entire stunt went unrecorded.

paths. Those willing to make the effort are rewarded with rare wildflowers, ferns and mosses that grow on boulders tumbled from the eroding Falls, a centuries-old stand of rare tulip trees and close-up views of the surging Niagara river. Maps are available from the Niagara Glen gift shop (905 371 0254).

Casino Niagara
5705 Falls Avenue (1-888 946 3255/905 374 3598/ www.casinoniagara.com). **Open** 24hrs daily. **Admission** free. **Credit** AmEx, MC, V.

IMAX Theatre Niagara Falls & Daredevil Gallery
6170 Fallsview Boulevard (905 374 4629/ www.imaxniagara.com). **Open** 11am-8pm daily. **Admission** $12; $8.50-$9.50 concessions. **Credit** MC, V.

Journey Behind the Falls
6650 Niagara River Parkway (1-877 642 7275/ 905 371 0254/www.niagaraparks.com). **Open** *Summer* 9am-5.30pm Mon-Fri, Sun; 9am-6.30pm Sat. *Winter* phone for details. **Admission** $10; $6 concessions; free under-6s. **Credit** AmEx, MC, V.

Maid of the Mist
5920 River Road (905 358 5781www.maidof themist.com). **Departures** vary. Closed Nov-Mar. **Admission** $13; $8 concessions; free under-6s. **Credit** AmEx, MC, V.

MarineLand
7657 Portage Road, Niagara Falls (905 356 9565/ www.marinelandcanada.com). **Open** *Late May-late June* 10am-5pm Mon-Fri; 10am-6pm Sat, Sun. *Late June-early Sept* 9am-6pm daily. *Early Sept-early Oct* 10am-5pm daily. Closed mid Oct-early May. **Admission** $16.95-$24.95; $12.95-$21.95 concessions; free under-4s. **Credit** AmEx, MC, V.

Niagara Falls Aviary
5561 River Road (866 994 0090/905 356 8888/ www.niagarafallsaviary.com). **Open** *Early Sept-mid June* 9am-6pm daily. *Mid June-early Sept* 9am-9pm daily. **Admission** $14.95; $9.95-$13.95 concessions. **Credit** MC, V.

Niagara Glen Nature Reserve
Niagara River Parkway (905 371 0254/ www.niagaraparks.com). **Open** phone for details. **Admission** free.

Take a hike

Niagara Falls marks the southern end of one Ontario's most-loved ecologically protected areas, the Niagara Escarpment. Niagara Falls may be the largest but it's only one of dozens of waterfalls that tumble over these limestone cliffs that stretch north some 1,430 miles (2,300 kilometres) towards Georgian Bay and beyond. In 1990 it was designated a UNESCO World Biosphere Reserve. Although urban sprawl has encroached somewhat in recent years, the Niagara Escarpment is still home to ancient cedars and rare ferns.

The best way to explore the escarpment's scenic vistas is to hike a section of the Bruce Trail, which traces the escarpment from Queenston (just north of Niagara Falls) to Tobermory and Bruce Peninsula National Park. Local clubs each maintain a section of the 497-mile (800-kilometre) long trail, marking the route with white blazes. Along the route are assorted conservation areas and parks.

Highlights include **Balls Falls Conservation Area**, where Twenty Mile Creek tumbles over the escarpment into the verdant Jordan Valley. The creek takes its name from the distance Loyalists travelled from the border when fleeing the United States, during the

revolutionary war. They looked for waterfalls like these to establish mills and settlements, the remains of which have been preserved in this historic park.

Dundas Valley, on the outskirts of Hamilton, is situated in a corner of the escarpment where it bends around the western end of Lake Ontario. A network of over 25 miles (40 kilometres) of inter-connecting trails wind through the valley, past moss-covered rocks that have tumbled from the cliffs.

At **Crawford Lake Conservation Area**, near Milton, the trail skirts a reconstructed Iroquoian longhouse and winds down a canyon where turkey vultures nest.

For dramatic scenery, the northernmost section of the trail near Tobermory can't be beat. It undulates along white limestone cliffs overlooking the sky blue waters of Georgian Bay, past gravel beaches, caves and towering flowerpot islands that have broken away from the cliffs. Some of Ontario's best hiking is found in Bruce Peninsula National Park (www.pc.gc.ca/pn-np/on/bruce/index_e.asp).

Copies of the official Bruce Trail guide are available through the **Bruce Trail Association**, PO Box 857, Hamilton L8N 3N9 (905 529 6821, www.brucetrail.org).

Niagara Parks Butterfly Conservatory

2405 Niagara River Parkway (905 358 0025/ www.niagaraparks.com). **Open** phone for details. **Admission** $10; $6 concessions; free under-6s. **Credit** AmEx, MC, V.

Niagara Whirlpool Aero Car

3850 Niagara River Parkway (905 262 4274/ www.niagaraparks.com). **Open** 10am-5pm Mon-Fri; 9am-5pm Sat, Sun. Closed late Nov-early Mar. **Admission** $10; $6 concessions; free under-6s. **No credit cards**.

Skylon Tower

5200 Robinson Street (1-877 475 9566/905 356 2651/www.skylon.com). **Open** *Observation deck* May-Sept 8am-midnight daily. Sept-Apr 10am-10pm daily. **Admission** $10.50; $6-$9.50 concessions. **Credit** AmEx, MC, V.

Where to eat

Niagara Falls isn't known for its fine dining. This is not the place to visit for a deluxe five-star meal. Fast and theme food is the order for the day (here you will find Denny's and the Hard Rock Café, plus all the other usual suspects). However there are two places that are always busy, if not for the food then for the views. The **Table Rock Restaurant** serves decent casual meals and snacks at fair prices, but it has a constant queue because it is only 100 metres from the Horseshoe Falls (hence you are not encouraged to linger over coffee). You can reserve a table, but not a window seat.

The **Skylon Tower** (*see above*) has two eateries, the best of which is the revolving **Skylon Tower Restaurant**. The food is of the rich, international type that aims to impress, and fairly pricey; the views are the attraction.

Skylon Tower Restaurant

Skylon Tower, 5200 Robinson Street (1-877 475 9566/905 356 2651/www.skylon.com). **Open** *May-Sept* 11.30am-2pm, 4.30-9pm daily. *Oct-Apr* 11.30am-2pm, 4.30-10pm Mon-Sat; 11.30am-3pm, 4.30-10pm Sun. **Main courses** $36-$64. **Credit** AmEx, MC, V.

Table Rock Restaurant

6650 Niagara Parkway (905 354 3631/www.niagara parks.com). **Open** phone for details. **Main courses** $25-$40. **Credit** AmEx, MC, V.

Where to stay

If you're here to see the Falls themselves, you will not need or be likely to want to stay in Niagara. Either you'll be carless and on a day trip or driving, with the option, therefore, of staying downriver in the far more pleasant **Niagara-on-the-Lake** (*see p237*). However, if you're going along with the whole pleasure-

Niagara Fallsview Casino Resort. *See p230.*

cruise ethos and here for a few days, you have a choice between one of the the many uniform chain hotels, the down and dirty 'no tell motel' strip above Clifton Hill or the opulence of a palatial suite overlooking the Falls (with, perhaps, a fireplace and heart-shaped jacuzzi. Such things are almost de rigueur in the honeymoon suites). Downtown, try one of the period B&Bs lining the road towards the Falls, such as the **Lion's Head B&B**, a lovely Arts and Crafts house with stylish rooms. Contact **Niagara Falls Tourism** (*see p234*) for comprehensive suggestions. Always ask about deals and packages, particularly off-season.

Two of the most prominent hotels in the city are the **Brock Plaza Hotel** and the adjacent **Sheraton on the Falls**. They stand side by side a block from the Niagara Parkway in the giant Falls Avenue complex (along with the casino and various theme restaurants), and both have views of the American Falls. For a room in the shadow of the Skylon Tower, check out the **Holiday Inn by the Falls**, or if you want a less anonymous location, try the **Travelodge Clifton Hill** in the colourful carnival atmosphere of Clifton Hill.

Sweet as a... grape that's been frozen on the vine. Icewine at **Inniskillin**. *See p235.*

If gambling's your thing and you like to be close to the slots, you might want to consider staying at the new **Niagara Fallsview Casino Resort** (*see also p230*), which contains various restaurants (smart and casual), as well as shopping and gambling. Many of its 368 guest rooms command stunning views of the Falls.

Brock Plaza Hotel
5685 Falls Avenue, ON L2E 6W7 (1-800 263 7135/905 374 4444/www.niagarafallshotels.com). **Rates** *Oct-Mar $50-$259. Apr-Sept $179-$360.* **Credit** AmEx, DC, MC, V.

Holiday Inn by the Falls
5339 Murray Street, ON L2G 2J3 (1-800 263 9393/905 356 1333/www.holidayinn.com). **Rates** *$69-$265.* **Credit** AmEx, DC, MC, V.

Lion's Head B&B
5239 River Road, ON L2E 3G9 (905 374 1681/www.lionsheadbb.com). **Rates** *$95-$165.* **Credit** MC, V.

Niagara Fallsview Casino Resort
6380 Fallsview Blvd, ON L2G 7X5 (1-888 325 5788/www.fallsviewcasinoresort.com). **Rates** *$109-$500.* **Credit** AmEx, MC, V.

Sheraton on the Falls
5875 Falls Avenue, ON L2G 3K7 (1-888 229 9961/905 374 4444/www.niagarafallshotels.com). **Rates** *$99-$529.* **Credit** AmEx, DC, MC, V.

Travelodge Clifton Hill
4943 Clifton Hill, ON L2G 3N5 (1-800 668 8840/905 357 4330/www.falls.com). **Rates** *Sept-June $99-$299. July, Aug $99-$329.* **Credit** AmEx, DC, MC, V.

Tourist information

Hotel concierges tend on the whole to be better sources of information than the following. To save money when visiting attractions, it's worth investing in an all-in-one pass.

Niagara Falls Tourism
5705 Falls Avenue, PO Box 300, Niagara Falls, ON L2E 6T3 (1-800 563 2557/905 356 6061/905 356 5567/www.discoverniagara.com). **Open** *mid May-Aug 8am-8pm daily. Sept-mid May 8am-6pm Mon-Fri; 10am-6pm Sat; 10am-4pm Sun.*

Niagara Parks Commission
Table Rock Complex, 6650 Niagara Parkway, Niagara Falls (1-877 642 7275/905 371 0254/www.niagaraparks.com). **Open** *phone for details.*

Getting there

By car
When traffic co-operates (avoid setting out during the afternoon rush hour), Niagara is a 90-minute drive on one highway, the Queen Elizabeth Way from the city, rounding Lake Ontario. Take the well-signed Highway 420 to drive the last few miles into town.

By public bus

Greyhound buses (1-800 661 8747/416 594 1010, www.greyhound.ca) run throughout the day from Toronto. But at $55 return, they're not much cheaper than a tour bus, and less convenient at both ends.

Bus tours/day trips

Several companies run scheduled tours from Toronto to Niagara. Their literature is ubiquitous, their attraction packages manifold (from transport only to the full excursion/attraction monty) and their differences negligible. Your best bet is to ask at your hotel; staff should know which are the most convenient and may have deals going. Standard operators include Gray Line (416 594 0343, www.grayline.ca) and Niagara & Toronto Tours (416 868 0400, www.torontotours.com).

The Magic Bus Company (416 516 7433, www.magicbuscompany.com) sends a funky, brightly coloured school bus round the hostels before trundling down to Niagara, where it stops at a winery for a free tasting, gives the trippers three to five hours at the Falls and stops at the whirlpool and other attractions before heading back for a bottom-dollar $38.

Casino Niagara (see p232) and Niagara Fallsview Casino Resort (see p234) both have contracts with several companies.

By train

There are two VIA Rail (1-888 842 7245, www.viarail.ca) trains a day in either direction, taking just under two hours to make the journey. One-way fares are $30 for adults, $27 concessions. You can book a cheaper fare with five days' advance reservation for as little at $19 each way.

Getting around

By bus

The green-and-white people movers (available to those buying all-in-one visitors' passes; see p234), are sometimes hard to spot among the numerous tour buses. They're convenient, however, dropping off visitors at the different sights around town.

Wine Country

The fertile southern part of the Golden Horseshoe that wraps around Lake Ontario from Toronto to Niagara is home to one of the largest wine industries in Canada (the other being the interior of British Columbia).

Until 20 years ago the reputation of Canadian wine would have been reason enough to keep on driving through to Niagara Falls. Thankfully, though, all that has changed. Niagara is well on its way to thinking of itself as the 'Napa of the North'. The climate, moderated by the lake and protected by the Niagara Escarpment, is comparable to Burgundy or the Loire Valley. Wine making has been practised here for 200 years, but was hampered by government regulations forcing the wine makers to use the very harsh and acidic local Lambrusca grape. In the late 1970s wine growers were finally allowed to blend classic varietal grapes from Europe and around the world. The vines found a happy home in the Niagara soil. Perhaps the most successful transplant to date is the Riesling, which does well in northern climes. Wines made from pinot noir and chardonnay are also worth seeking out.

The Vintners Quality Alliance (VQA), was established in 1989 to control standards of wine production in the province, and has since done a great deal, through its public recognition of quality, to consolidate Ontario's current reputation for viticulture.

The first to experiment and first to achieve global recognition for its blends was **Inniskillin** wines. **Château des Charmes** was also very important in the development of Niagara wine making. It is a great place to visit, in the nearby village of St David's. Inniskillin is also one of many wineries to produce icewine, which is made from grapes that are pressed

Top five Wineries

Cave Spring Cellars

Like many of Niagara's best wineries, this is a family affair. The finest wines are the Estate Bottled and outstanding are the Cave Spring Vineyard chardonnays and rieslings. See p236.

Château des Charmes

One of Canada's oldest winemakers is winning praise for its chardonnay. Look for the Paul Bosc Estate Viognier. See p236.

Inniskillin

Set Canada's icewine industry in motion when it won top honours at the 1991 VinExpo Bordeaux – and never looked back. See p236.

Jackson-Triggs

Even if it started as a wine spin-off of beer giant Labatt, Jackson-Triggs has proven itself a producer of good vino, especially big and meaty New World wines. See p236.

Vineland Estates Winery

One of the province's most elegant wineries. Beyond the glam are some excellent wines, including Vidal icewines, semi-dry rieslings and cabernet merlots. See p237.

Trips Out of Town

while still frozen, producing a very sweet – and pretty expensive – wine. You can sample it at the historic Brae Burn Barn on the Inniskillin estate, as well as at local restaurants. The **Henry of Pelham Family Estate Winery** also features some excellent VQA products in its cellars. The highlight of its winery and vineyard tours is wine tasting on its patio, next to Short Hills Provincial Park.

There are many other fine wineries and winery restaurants in the region known as 'the Bench', the pick of them is **Vineland Estates**.

The main wineries to visit in Niagara-on-the-Lake are **Peller Estates**, for its elegant old-world-style chateau with vaulted cellars, and **Jackson-Triggs**, a sleek modern winery. Huge industrial doors roll up in fine weather to reveal an expansive view – right through the winery – of vineyards. A classical-style amphitheatre seats up to 500 people for summer concerts.

Away from Niagara-on-the-Lake, it's worth making the 25-mile (40-kilometre) trip to the **Cave Spring Cellars** in the village of Jordan, in the Bench. The winery has its own sumptuous 26-room hotel, **Inn on the Twenty**, with jacuzzis and fireplaces in each suite, as well as one of the Niagara area's best dining spots, **On the Twenty**.

The recommended time to go wine touring is from May to October, though if you visit in January you can catch the annual **Icewine Festival**, where the liquid gold is served outdoors at a bar made of – you guessed it – carved ice. For more information, www.niagara winefestival.com. The major event of the year is the annual late September celebration of the harvest, the **Niagara Grape & Wine Festival** (905 688 0212, www.grapeandwine. com). Over 100 events include tours, tastings, concerts and seminars and food samplings, set off by the autumn foliage. Also look out for the **Niagara New Vintage Festival** in June.

Wineries are now the top places to eat in Niagara. **Jackson-Triggs** is great for light, bistro-style cheese and fruit plates served alongside a flight of wines in a tasting room overlooking the vineyard. **Peller Estates** offers a lavishly praised formal dining room (with prices to match). It, too, has a great patio overlooking the vineyard. **Hillebrand Estates** winery was one of the first to develop a first-rate restaurant, with the **Vineyard Café**. It is famous for its summer jazz and blues concerts held in the vineyard. Also very pleasant is **Strewn Winery**, with its restaurant, **Terroir La Cachette**. All serve great wine-country food. In Vineland, **Vineland Estates Winery** (*see p237*) boasts an award-winning restaurant and top-notch accommodation.

Cave Spring Cellars

3836 Main Street, Jordan (905 562 3581/www.cave springcellars.com). **Open** *Tours* July-Oct 3pm daily. Nov-June 3pm Sat, Sun. *Shop* May-Oct 10am-6pm Mon-Sat; 11am-6pm Sun. Nov-Apr 10am-5pm Mon-Thur; 10am-6pm Fri, Sat; 11am-5pm Sun. *Restaurant* 11.30am-3pm, 5pm-late daily. **Admission** *Tours* $5. **Main courses** $10-$16. **Hotel rates** $149-$355. **Credit** AmEx, MC, V.

Château des Charmes

1025 York Road, Niagara-on-the-Lake (905 262 4219/www.chateaudescharmes.com). **Open** 10am-6pm daily. *Tours* 11am, 3pm daily. **Admission** *Tours* $2. **Credit** AmEx, MC, V.

Henry of Pelham Family Estate Winery

1469 Pelham Road, St Catharines (905 684 8423/ www.henryofpelham.com). **Open** *Tours* May-Oct 1.30pm daily. Nov-Apr phone for details. *Shop* May-Oct 10am-6pm daily. Nov-Apr 10am-5pm Mon-Sat; 11am-5pm Sun. **Admission** *May-Oct* free. *Nov-Apr* phone for details. **Credit** AmEx, MC, V.

Hillebrand Estates

Niagara Stone Road, off York Road, Niagara-on-the-Lake (1-800 582 8412/905 468 7123/ www.hillebrand.com). **Open** *Tours* 10am-6pm daily. *Tasting tours* phone for details. *Restaurant* phone for details. **Admission** *Tours* free. *Tasting tours* $8-$10. **Main courses** $13-$24. **Credit** MC, V.

Inniskillin

RR 1, Niagara Parkway, south of Niagara-on-the-Lake (1-888 466 4754/905 468 3554/www.innis killin.com). **Open** *Tours* Nov-Apr 10.30am, 2.30pm Sat, Sun. May-Oct 10.30am, 2.30pm daily. *Shop* May-Oct 10am-6pm daily. Nov-Apr 10am-5pm daily. *Tasting bar* Nov-Apr 11am-4.30pm daily. May-Oct 11am-5.30pm daily. **Admission** *Tours* free. **Credit** AmEx, MC, V.

Jackson-Triggs

2145 Regional Road 55, Niagara-on-the-Lake (1-866 589 4637/905 468 4637/www.jacksontriggs winery.com). **Open** *May-Oct* 10.30am-6.30pm daily. *Nov-Apr* 10.30am-5.30pm Mon-Fri, Sun; 10.30am-6.30pm Sat. *Tours* May-Oct 10.30am-5.30pm daily. Nov-Apr 10.30am-4.30pm Mon-Fri; 10.30am-5.30pm Sat, Sun. **Admission** $5-$75. **Credit** MC, V.

Peller Estates

290 John Street E, Niagara-on-the-Lake (1-888 673 5537/905 468 4678/www.peller.com). **Open** 11.30am-5.30pm daily. *Tours* 11.30am-5.30pm daily. *Restaurant* noon-3pm, 5.30-8.30pm Mon-Thur, Sun; noon-3pm, 5-9pm Fri, Sat. **Admission** *Tours* free. **Main courses** $25-$38. **Credit** MC, V.

Strewn Winery

1339 Lakeshore Road, Niagara-on-the-Lake (905 468 1229/www.strewnwinery.com). **Open** 10am-6pm daily. *Tours* 1pm daily. *Private tours* phone for details. *Restaurant* phone for details. **Admission** free. *Private tours* $4-$25. **Main courses** $21-$35. **Credit** MC, V.

Vineland Estates Winery

3620 Moyer Road, Vineland (1-888 846 3526/905 562 7088/www.vineland.com). **Open** phone for details. *Tours* late May-Oct 11am, 3pm daily. Nov-late May 3pm Sat, Sun. *Restaurant* phone for details. **Main courses** $15-$36. **Hotel rates** $135. **Credit** AmEx, MC, V.

Wine tours

Wine tourism has come of age, with many wineries now proud to show off their liquid assets and many punters happy to leave their cars behind and indulge in a spot of risk-free tasting. Both scheduled and custom tours are available; they usually include a meal as well as several winery visits and a knowledgeable guide. You will usually need to arrange a pick-up in the Wine Country or Niagara-on-the-Lake area, though sometimes transport from Toronto or elsewhere can be provided. Tour companies include **Crush on Niagara Wine Tours** (1-866 408 9463, www.crushtours.com); **Wine Country Tours** (905 892 9770, www.wine countrytours.ca) and **Niagara Nature Tours** (1-888 889 8296, www.niagaranaturetours.ca), which has an eco slant and can also cover regional cooking, history, agriculture and gardens. For something a little more challenging, sign up for the bike tours of Niagara wineries with **Steve Bauer** (905 563 8687, www.stevebauer.com).

Tourist information

The tourist offices in Niagara Falls and particularly Niagara-on-the-Lake also have information on Wine Country.

Wine Council of Ontario

110 Hannover Drive, St Catharines (1-888 594 6379/905 684 8070/www.winesofontario.org).

Getting there

You can't properly experience Wine Country without your own transport, though several Niagara tours (*see p235*) include a winery stop as part of their itinerary.

Niagara-on-the-Lake

If you've made it all the way to Niagara Falls, it's well worth considering spending a day or two in the pretty village of Niagara-on-the-Lake – if for no other reason than to make the journey from Niagara Falls along the precipice of the Niagara Gorge, which is one of the most scenic routes in the country. The towering cliff faces reveal the extent of the erosion that has seen the Falls steadily carve their way backwards through this dramatic setting.

The Niagara Parks Commission has controlled development and growth along the Canadian side of the river since 1885. The result is the Niagara Parkway, a verdant green belt through which a leisurely winding drive brings you to the perfectly preserved 19th-century village of Niagara-on-the-Lake.

In 1792 Niagara-on-the-Lake became the first capital of Upper Canada, later the Province of Ontario, and was a major site in the occasional conflicts with the American forces just across the river. Just south of the town, **Historic Fort George** national park is a restored version of the original fort (1797), where costumed staff provide the history lessons.

Upon leaving the fort, you will find yourself in the village. The first major building you pass, set back on the left, is the Shaw Festival Theatre, one of the province's most important professional theatres (the season runs from April to November).

The company's mandate is to present plays written by George Bernard Shaw 'and his contemporaries' – although that has been stretched somewhat to include plays set in the Shaw era. The company has performed such varied fare as Shaw's *Caesar and Cleopatra*, Noël Coward's *Hay Fever* and a revival of Stephen Sondheim's musical *Merrily We Roll Along*. The **Shaw Festival** has turned this sleepy hamlet, formerly a retirement community, into one of the province's most popular tourist and theatre communities.

After you have picked up your tickets (best to order some months in advance; *see p238*) park your car anywhere you can find a space and then stroll around town. It isn't very big and you can't really get lost. The Clock Tower, in the middle of the main road, Queen Street, marks the centre.

On the corner opposite the clock is the **Niagara Apothecary Museum** (5 Queen Street, 905 468 3845), a perfectly preserved 'drug store' from 1866, operated and maintained by the Ontario College of Pharmacists. Note the original walnut and butternut fixtures and rare collection of apothecary glass.

Shopping and browsing is not a problem here: you can indulge yourself with fudge, chocolate, wine, candles, deli goods, antiques and paintings. Or, at **Greaves Jams & Marmalades** (55 Queen Street, 905 468 3608, www.greavesjams.com) flavoured spreads made with local fruit.

The area's lengthy history is explained in detail at the **Niagara Historical Society Museum** (43 Castlereagh Street, 905 468 3912, www.niagara.com/~nhs/), one of Ontario's oldest local history museums. Founded in 1907, it contains over 20,000 artefacts from the periods of the Loyalists, the War of 1812 and the Victorian age, including some gripping first-hand accounts of the American occupation of 1812, and virtual Canadian icons such as Laura Secord's beaded Iroquoian purse.

Historic Fort George
905 468 4257/www.niagara.com/~parkscan. **Open** *Apr-Oct* 10am-5pm daily. *Nov-Mar* by appointment only. *Tours* by appointment. **Admission** $8; $5-$7 concessions; free under-6s. *Tours* $5. **No credit cards**.

Where to eat

This little town is a diner's delight – the culinary antithesis to Niagara Falls. Forget the conventional wisdom that the restaurant in your hotel is just there as a promotional exercise; the inns of this community are known nationally for their cuisine and service. Some of the best places to eat are also the best places to stay. Prime examples include the Prince of Wales Hotel, where you can have dinner in the gorgeous **Escabèche** restaurant or lunch in its Churchill Bar. Pub fare is served all day in the bar of the **Olde Angel Inn** (*see below*), which features plenty of draught beer and local wines. If there's no time for a leisurely lunch before the theatre, you can grab a sandwich or salad in the **Shaw Café & Wine Bar**, directly across from the Royal George Theatre.

Other than the winery restaurants (*see p236*), one of the best choices is the dining room at the **Charles Inn** (*see below*), an elegant 1832 former residence with tables on the verandah during summer.

Escabèche
6 Picton Street (1-888 669 5566/905 468 3246/ www.vintageinns.com). **Open** noon-2pm, 5-9pm Mon-Fri; noon-2pm, 5-10pm Sat, Sun. **Main courses** $16-$36. **Credit** AmEx, DC, MC, V.

Shaw Café & Wine Bar
92 Queen Street (905 468 4772). **Open** phone for details. **Main courses** phone for details. **Credit** AmEx, MC, V.

Where to stay

The quaintness of this little 18th-century community has earmarked it as a favourite weekend getaway. Billed as one of the world's finest heritage hotels, the **Prince of Wales Hotel** with new spectacular spa facilities is everyone's first choice for deluxe accommodation right in the middle of town. The **Olde Angel Inn** is the town's oldest inn, with cosy but sometimes colonial-style guest rooms above the bar and two rental cottages. The cottages are lovely, but if you wish to

catch a glimpse of the Olde Angel's famous wandering ghost, you should stay in the main inn. The **Moffat Inn** is an affordable 22-room, two-storey historic inn just off the main street with an elegant penthouse suite. The **Charles Inn** has 12 guest rooms furnished with antiques. The **Harbour House** is a lovely new 31-room boutique hotel with feather beds, Frette bathrobes and oversized whirlpool tubs.

Niagara-on-the-Lake has perhaps more B&Bs and private lodgings than any other village its size in Ontario. Check with the local tourism office and the Shaw Festival office (for both, *see below*) for more information.

Charles Inn
209 Queen Street, ON L0S 1J0 (905 468 4588/ www.charlesinn.ca). **Rates** *Winter* $99-$165. *Summer* $170-$200. **Credit** AmEx, MC, V.

Harbour House
85 Melville Street, ON L0S 1J0 (1-866 277 6677/ www.harbourhousehotel.ca). **Rates** *Winter* $195-$400. *Summer* $275-$500. **Credit** AmEx, MC, V.

Moffat Inn
60 Picton Street, ON L0S 1J0 (905 468 4116/www.moffatinn.com). **Rates** *Nov-May* $69-$149. *Apr-Oct* $89-$169. **Credit** AmEx, DC, MC, V.

Olde Angel Inn
224 Regent Street, ON L0S 1J0 (905 468 3411/www.angel-inn.com). **Rates** *Nov-Apr* $79-$169. *May-Oct* $119-$229. **Credit** AmEx, DC, MC, V.

Prince of Wales Hotel
6 Picton Street, ON L0S 1J0 (1-888 669 5566/ 905 468 3246/www.vintageinns.com). **Rates** *Nov-Mar* $195-$295 single/double; $495 suites. *Apr-Oct* $295-$360 single/double; $495 suites. **Credit** AmEx, DC, MC, V.

Tourist information

Niagara-on-the-Lake Chamber of Commerce and Visitor & Convention Bureau
26 Queen Street, PO Box 1043, ON L0S 1J0 (905 468 1950/www.niagaraonthelake.com). **Open** *Nov-Mar* 10am-5pm daily. *Apr-Oct* 10am-7.30pm daily.

Shaw Festival
10 Queen's Parade (1-800 511 7429/905 468 2172/ www.shawfest.com). **Open** *Box office* 9am-5pm Mon-Sat. *Season* Apr-Nov 9am-8pm daily. **Tickets** $42-$82; $20-$30 concessions. **Credit** AmEx, MC, V.

Getting there

By car
This drive is 80 miles (129 kilometres) from Toronto. Follow the same directions as for Niagara Falls, but turn off the QEW on to Highway 55 just past the St Catharines turn-off.

Quick Trips

History, art and a dollop of fresh air.

Destinations in this chapter are recommended as the best local day trips, but if you want to spend the night the tourist offices listed will be able to recommend a variety of places to stay.

For theme park fun at **Paramount Canada's Wonderland**, *see p173*; for skiing and snowboarding at **Barrie** and **Collingwood**, *see p217*; for **Black Creek Pioneer Village**, *see p97*.

Woodbridge & Kleinburg

Although the former farming village is now more of a suburban bedroom community, the town of Kleinburg is still a favourite day trip for Torontonians, who come for the cafés and boutiques. The annual **Binder Twine Festival** (www.mcmichael.com/klein burg.shtml), held in September, dates back to the days when farmers would come to town to pick up twine for their wheat sheaves.

But Kleinburg is better known for its rich artistic patrimony. It's home to the **McMichael Canadian Art Collection**, an impressive gallery situated in a forest on the edge of a valley, a setting that blends perfectly with the principal theme of its permanent collection: the Canadian landscape. Philanthropists Robert and Signe McMichael constructed an immense building of rough stone and raw timber to showcase their collection of paintings by Tom Thomson and the Group of Seven. These early 20th-century artists spent years in the wilderness capturing the majestic scenery and brilliant colours of a country few of their contemporaries had ever experienced. More recently, landscapes by Doris McCarthy, a pre-eminent Toronto-based painter who studied with Group of Seven member Arthur Lismer, have been added to the gallery's collections. There are also Inuit and Native Canadian artworks, including paintings and soapstone sculptures; most notable are the bold designs of Morriseau, who captured the ancient legends of warriors and gods on canvas.

Join in a guided tour, then take a hike down into the woods to refresh the senses for a slice of real Canadiana. And before you leave, pay homage to six members of this famed group of painters at their burial sites, which are marked by jagged, pink and grey boulders.

As you head out of town, the first destination of major interest – especially if you're a nature lover – is the **Kortright Centre** in Woodbridge, which features ten miles (16 kilometres) of hiking trails, plus all manner of outdoor attractions and seasonal programmes from dog-sledding to autumn colour walks. There's an information centre where you can get trail maps and a gift shop selling nature books and products. Films are screened in a 130-seat theatre and a café offers lunches, snacks and drinks.

Kortright Centre
9550 Pine Valley Drive, Woodbridge (416 661 6600/ www.trca.on.ca/parks_and_attractions/places_to_visit/ kortright_centre). **Open** 9am-4pm Mon-Fri; 10am-4pm Sat, Sun. **Admission** $5-$7; $3-$5 concessions; free under-5s. **Credit** MC, V.

McMichael Canadian Art Collection
10365 Islington Avenue, Kleinburg (905 893 1121/ www.mcmichael.com). **Open** 10am-4pm daily. *May-Oct* 10am-5pm daily. **Admission** $15; $12 concessions; free under-5s. **Credit** AmEx, MC, V.

Where to eat & drink

The Doctor's House is Kleinburg's most historic building, dating from 1867. It's now a classy venue for banquets and weddings, with a restaurant that's open to the public (Sunday brunch is a speciality). If tea time with country cuisine and fresh desserts is in order, drop into **Mr McGregor's House**.

The Doctor's House
21 Nashville Road, (905 893 1615/416 234 8080/ www.thedoctorshouse.ca). **Meals served** noon-3pm, 5.30-11pm Mon-Sat; 10:30am-3.30pm, 5.30-11pm Sun. **Main courses** $18-$36. **Credit** AmEx, MC, V.

Mr McGregor's House
10503 Islington Avenue, Kleinburg (905 893 2508). **Meals served** 10am-5pm Mon-Fri; 10am-6pm Sat, Sun. **Main courses** $5-$10. **Credit** MC, V.

Getting there

By car
For Kortright, drive north from the city on Highway 400, exit west at Major MacKenzie Drive and south on Pine Valley. For Kleinburg, continue on Major MacKenzie Drive to Islington Avenue. For more information, see www.kleinburgvillage.com.

Trips Out of Town

Spa trek

The soothing delights of massage and hydrotherapy meet the comforts of fine food and gracious grounds at many of Ontario's top destination spas. For the energetic there are walking trails through woods and clean country air. For those who simply wish to be indulged there are relaxing mud wraps, soothing massage and skin-softening facials.

A one-hour drive north-west will take you to the rolling Caledon Hills, and the **Millcroft Inn & Spa**, where the stone and timber architecture of the historic mill is echoed in the new spa facility. Guests enjoy a full range of services including *ofuro*, a Japanese bath ritual that begins with an exfoliating body polish and is followed by a relaxing herb-scented session in a Japanese soaking tub or an al fresco massage on the private patio.

Just outside Cambridge, an hour west of Toronto is the august **Langdon Hall Country House Hotel & Spa** (*pictured*), a Federalist Revival mansion that was once home to a scion of New York's Astor family. Meticulously groomed grounds, excellent dining and elegant rooms are topped off with all the spa comforts. Try the hot stone therapy for the ultimate in stress relief. Do plan on staying for lunch or dinner: the dining room is one of the province's best and has a superb wine list.

Cottage Country's newest spa is **Avalon**, in the Inn at Christie's Mill in Port Severn. Guests float in the indoor mineral salts pool with picture windows overlooking the Trent Severn waterway just outside.

Ontario's largest destination spa **Ste Anne's Country Inn & Spa** seems to undergo constant redevelopment to bring in the latest luxuries to its expansive guest rooms and 30 treatment rooms, offering everything from full immersion mud baths to Thai massage, all on a sprawling 570-acre property.

An hour and a half east of Toronto, **Elemental Embrace Wellness Spa Retreat** incorporates traditional practices from East India under the supervision of two Ayurvedic doctors. Start the day with meditation and yoga, followed by a woodland walk or *shirodhara* (oil drip massage).

Our suggestions are simply a tasting: for a complete guide to spa facilities throughout the province, contact **Premier Spas of Ontario** (176 Napier Street, Barrie, ON L4M 1W8, 705 721 9969, 1-800 990 7702, www.premierspasofontario.ca).

Avalon, the Spa at Christie's Mill
263 Port Severn Road North, Port Severn (1-800 465 9966/705 538 2354/ www.christiesmill.com). **Rates** $330-$390. **Credit** AmEx, MC, V.

Elemental Embrace Wellness Spa Retreat
255 Georgina Street, Brighton (613 475 9941/1-800 212 9355/www.elemental embrace.com). **Rates** $765-$3,070. **Credit** AmEx, MC, V.

Langdon Hall Country House Hotel & Spa
1 Langdon Drive, Cambridge (519 740 2100/ 1-800 268 1898/www.langdonhall.ca). **Rates** $259-$609. **Credit** AmEx, DC, MC, V.

Millcroft Inn & Spa
55 John Street, Alton (519 941 8111/1-800 383 3976/www.millcroft.com). **Rates** $240-$355. **Credit** AmEx, DC, MC, V.

Ste Anne's Country Inn & Spa
1009 Massey Road, north of Grafton (905 349 3704/1-888 346 6772/www.spa village.ca). **Rates** $375-$680. **Credit** AmEx, DC, MC, V.

Elora & St Jacobs

With its scenic gorge and historic stone buildings, the 19th-century town of **Elora**, situated on the Grand River 90 minutes west of Toronto, is a favourite destination for a Sunday drive. A century and a half ago mills sprang up alongside the waterfalls and limestone cliffs in the area that is now the **Elora Gorge Conservation Area** (www.grandriver.ca). Today the fast-flowing waters attract tourist and fishermen. In summer months inflatable tubes can be rented for a bouncy ride down the river rapids. Every spring the river is stocked with brown trout; **Grand River Troutfitters Ltd** (519 787 4359) offers guiding services.

The busiest time of year is during the second and third weeks of July, when the **Elora Festival** (519 846 0331, 1-800 265 8977, www.elorafestival.com) of choral, classical and contemporary music is staged in some striking venues, including St John's Anglican Church – which is locally famous for its connection to Florence Nightingale, who was reputedly romantically attached to the man who became a pastor here. Sadly, he was her first cousin, so marriage was impossible, and she headed off to the Crimea.

A free walking tour map is available from the information centre in the nearby town of Fergus. It directs visitors to many of the historic buildings, including an 1856 former school, now the **Elora Centre for the Arts** (519 846 9698, www.eloracentreforthearts.ca). One of the best ways to enjoy the scenery is from the seat of a horse-drawn carriage, similar to those used by local Mennonite farmers. From March to October schoolteacher Jacque Dion (519 638 5079) offers 30-minute jaunts around town

The area to the west is dotted with Mennonite farms. Many of the regional roads have extra-wide shoulders to accommodate their black, horse-drawn buggies. **St Jacobs**, with its shops selling quilting supplies, scented candles and crafts, has become a popular bus tour destination, but anyone interested in authentic Mennonite culture can learn about it on one of the horse-drawn trolley rides offered by **Country Livery Services & Heritage Harvest Farm** (519 888 0302, www.country livery.com), which takes passengers to a Mennonite farm to see a maple syrup bush, while describing how the Mennonites came to settle here after purchasing land from the Six Nations Iroquois in the early 1800s. Alternatively, visit **Telling the Mennonite Story**, a multimedia museum in **St Jacobs Visitor Centre** (*see below*).

Where to eat & drink

Elora has various high-quality restaurants. The **Desert Rose Café** is known for its vegetarian menu. **Summerhayes Bistro** boasts a popular riverfront patio. The Penstock Lounge in the **Elora Mill Country Inn** serves up a sense of history with its ploughman's lunches, while the white linen tablecloths in the main dining room contribute to an elegant atmosphere.

Desert Rose Café
130 Metcalfe Street, Elora (519 846 0433). **Open** hours vary. **Main courses** $5-$15. **Credit** MC, V.

Elora Mill Country Inn
77 Mill Street W, Elora (519 846 9118/1-866 713 5672/www.eloramill.com). **Open** 8-10am, 11am-4pm, 5-9.30pm daily. **Main courses** $25-$40. **Credit** AmEx, MC, V.

Summerhayes Bistro
13 Mill Street E (519 846 8738). **Open** 11am-9pm Mon-Wed, Sun; 11am-2am Thur-Sat. **Main courses** $13-$23. **Credit** AmEx, DC, MC, V.

Tourist information

Centre Wellington Chamber of Commerce
400 Tower Street S, Fergus (519 846 9841/1-877 242 6353/www.ferguselora.com). **Open** 10am-5pm Mon-Fri; noon-4pm Sat, Sun.

St Jacobs Tourism Office
1-800 265 3353/519 664 1133/www.stjacobs.com. **Answerphone** 24hrs daily.

St Jacobs Visitor Centre
1408 King Street N, St Jacobs (519 664 3518/www.st jacobs.com). **Open** 11am-4.30pm Sat; 2-4.30pm Sun.

Getting there

By car
Elora and St Jacobs are about 90 minutes west of Toronto by car (the only option). Take Highway 401 for about 60 miles (96km), turn north on to Highway 6, then take Wellington County Road 7 right to Elora. St Jacobs is a lovely meandering 15-mile (24km) country drive away, south on County Road 18, which turns into CR 22, then west on CR 17. Just follow the signs.

Stratford & St Marys

One of Toronto's main attractions is its diverse and flourishing theatre scene. Rural Ontario also has its own network of more than 30 summer-stock theatres, **ASTRO** (the Association of Summer Theatre's 'Round Ontario, www.summertheatre.org), but it is the town of **Stratford** that put the province on the map for theatre-goers. Since the first season in

1953 with Alec Guinness starring in *Richard III* in a sweltering tent, the **Stratford Festival** has grown into a celebrated cultural event set on four stages, including the Festival (modelled on the original Globe's apron stage), the Avon, the Tom Patterson (named after the local journalist who founded the festival) and the Studio (the most intimate theatre, with only 260 seats). Each season, from April through November, a stellar cast (which in past years has included the likes of Peter Ustinov, Christopher Plummer and Maggie Smith) performs a roster of more than a dozen plays, ranging from Shakespeare to high-kicking Broadway musicals with mass appeal. In addition to its plays, the festival hosts Monday evening concerts.

With its 19th-century main drag (Ontario Street), its distinctive yellow brick churches and numerous parks, Stratford is one of the most picturesque small towns in Ontario. Then there's the added bonus of five-star restaurants, excellent accommodation and more than 1,000 acres of parkland lining the swan-dotted Avon River.

While wandering east through the park, stop at the little **Gallery Stratford**. Located in a former 1833 pump house, it offers changing displays of contemporary and traditional Canadian art (hours vary according to the season, so phone ahead). Free 90-minute heritage walks and garden tours depart from the riverside branch of the tourist office most summer mornings. The double-decker bus trip by Festival Tours (519 273 1652) is also a hoot. Enthusiastic young guides point out the homes of famous actors, the best places for coffee and tell amusing anecdotes about Stratford's history.

Just 15 minutes' drive west of Stratford is the sleepy town of **St Marys**, often dubbed 'Stonetown' for its many 19th-century limestone buildings, including a spectacular town hall, a faux medieval opera house-turned-condo and several residences, one of which is now the Westover Inn, set in 19 acres of grounds, convenient to riverside trails. The quarry that provided the stone is now Canada's largest outdoor swimming pool.

Gallery Stratford

54 Romeo Street S, Stratford (519 271 5271/ www.gallerystratford.on.ca). **Open** Tue-Sun; hours vary. Closed 2wks Dec/Jan. **Admission** *May-Sept* $8; $6 concessions; free under-12s. *Oct-Apr* $5; $4 concessions; free under-12s. **Credit** MC, V.

Where to eat & drink

With half a million hungry theatre-goers to feed each year, Stratford has an embarrassment of culinary riches and now boasts some of the country's finest restaurants; its gastronomic reputation received a further boost with the advent of the Stratford Chefs School (68 Nile Street, 519 271 1414), which has produced some of the country's acclaimed culinary wizards.

Rundles restaurant always makes top ten lists of the best restaurants in Canada. It overlooks the park and river, though you may not notice the scenery when the food reaches the table. The **Church** serves up divine dishes in a deconsecrated building with seating under the vaulted ceiling, and upstairs in the more casual Belfry. The cosy **Old Prune** is a favourite with theatre fans (note that it serves dinner at various 'sittings'); those in the know ask for a table in the sun room. **Balzac's Coffee** has the best latte in Stratford, while stylishly sleek **Pazzo Ristorante** serves high-end Italian food upstairs and great pizza downstairs. Festival actors favour **Down the Street**, a friendly bar with good food. The budget-conscious opt for **York Street Kitchen** (take-out fare for riverside picnics), the **Principal's Pantry** (a deluxe café) and **Boomers Gourmet Fries** (superior fish and chips). Note that many restaurants and cafés in Stratford operate limited hours out of season (or even close altogether), so it's always best to phone ahead to check.

In St Marys, the **Westover Inn** (*see above*) serves specialities using such local ingredients as cheese and pork in its attractive dining room.

Balzac's Coffee

149 Ontario Street, Stratford (519 273 7909/ www.balzacscoffee.com). **Open** *Summer* 7am-8pm daily. *Winter* 7am-9pm daily. **Credit** V.

Boomers Gourmet Fries

26 Erie Street, Stratford (519 275 3147). **Open** hours vary. **Main courses** $5-$10. **No credit cards**.

Church

70 Brunswick Street, Stratford (519 273 3424/ www.churchrestaurant.com). **Open** 11.30am-1am Tue-Sat; 11am-1.30pm, 5-8.30pm Sun. Closed Jan-mid Mar. **Main courses** $29-$44. **Credit** AmEx, DC, MC, V.

Down the Street

30 Ontario Street, Stratford (519 273 5886). **Open** *Summer* 5pm-1am Mon; 11.30am-1am Tue-Sun. *Winter* 11.30am-1am Thur-Sat. **Main courses** $18-$25. **Credit** AmEx, MC, V.

Old Prune

151 Albert Street, Stratford (519 271 5052/ www.oldprune.on.ca). **Open** phone for details. **Closed** late Oct-late May. **Main courses** *Lunch* $9.50-$30. **Set dinner** $65.50. **Credit** AmEx, MC, V.

Pazzo Ristorante

70 Ontario Street, Stratford (519 273 6666/www. pazzo.ca). **Open** *Summer* 11.30am-12.30pm daily. *Winter* 11.30am-10pm Tue-Thur; 11.30am-11pm Fri, Sat. **Main courses** $10-$27. **Credit** AmEx, MC, V.

Principal's Pantry
*270 Water Street, Stratford (519 272 9914/
www.principalspantry.com).* **Open** hours vary.
Closed Nov-mid May. **Main courses** $10-$14.
Credit MC, V.

Rundles
9 Cobourg Street, Stratford (519 271 6442).
Open 5-7pm Tue; 5-8.30pm Wed-Fri; 11.30am-
1.15pm, 5-8.30pm Sat; 11.30am-1.15pm, 5-7pm
Sun. Closed Nov-Apr. **Set dinner** $67.50-$79.50.
Credit AmEx, DC, MC, V.

Westover Inn
*300 Thomas Street, St Marys (519 284 2977/
www.westoverinn.com).* **Open** 7.30-10.30am, 11.30-
2pm, 5-8pm Mon-Thur; 7.30-10.30am, 11.30-2pm,
5-8.30pm Fri, Sat; 7.30-10.30am, 5-8pm Sun.
Main courses $8.95-$29. **Credit** AmEx, MC, V.

York Street Kitchen
41 York Street, Stratford (519 273 7041). **Open**
Summer 8am-8pm daily. *Winter* 8am-3pm daily.
Main courses $7-$14. **Credit** AmEx, MC, V.

Tourist information

St Marys Tourist Information
*5 St James Street N, St Marys (1-800 769 7668/
www.townofstmarys.com).* **Open** 8.30am-4.30pm
Mon-Fri.

Stratford Festival
*55 Queen Street, Stratford (1-800 567 1600/
519 271 4040/www.stratfordfestival.ca).* **Season**
late Apr-early Nov. **Tours** year-round; phone for
details. **Tickets** $45-$100; $24-$50 concessions.
Credit AmEx, MC, V.

Tourism Stratford
*47 Downie Street, Stratford (1-800 561 7926/
519 271 5140/www.city.stratford.on.ca).* **Open**
8.30am-4.30pm Mon-Fri.

Getting there

By bus
Greyhound bus service runs throughout the
day from the main bus terminal in Toronto
(610 Bay Street, 1-800 661 8747, 416 594 1010,
www.greyhound.ca).

By car
From Toronto, drive west along Highway 401,
turn north on Highway 8 to Kitchener-Waterloo,
then follow signs west to Stratford along
Highway 7/8.

By rail
VIA Rail trains to both Stratford and St Marys
(1-888 842 7245, www.viarail.ca) operate from
Toronto's Union Station.

Cor blimey! It's 'My Fair Lady' at the **Stratford Festival**.

Further Afield

Take a walk (camp, canoe, cruise, drive or swim) on the wild side.

Cottage Country

The beautiful wilderness region north of Toronto – actually, north of Barrie – is known as Cottage Country. However, the term is most often applied to the combined holiday areas of **Muskoka**, **Parry Sound** and **Haliburton** that stretch to **Algonquin Provincial Park**, across the rugged terrain of the Canadian Shield – a landscape known for its granite outcrops, myriad lakes, pine and maple forests. City dwellers craving a weekend wilderness escape have turned many of the once-rustic lakefront cottages into palatial playgrounds. Purists grumble about the roar of jet skis and the overwhelming summer traffic (for this reason, visit during the week if you can), but there are still many quiet corners where the calls of the wild can be heard at sunset. Cottages both palatial and plain are traditionally opened up on the long weekend in May and keep lucky Torontonians in the swim through to Labour Day at the start of September.

Bethune Memorial. See p245.

MIDLAND

The mission fort of **Sainte-Marie Among the Hurons** in Midland was built by Jesuits in the 17th century. It was their most westerly outpost and the largest inland European settlement north of New Orleans. It became home to the indigenous Hurons, who converted to Christianity and was the site of Ontario's first church, hospital, blacksmith shop and farm. Guides clad in 17th-century costume will be able to answer your questions about the pioneer era.

GRAVENHURST

This pretty Muskoka town is best known as the birthplace of Dr Norman Bethune, whose 1890s home, the **Bethune Memorial House National Historic Site**, charts his career as a pioneer of innovative surgical techniques: he developed a mobile blood transfusion procedure during the Spanish Civil War. Bethune also became a hero to the Chinese people when he laboured on their battlefields; indeed, he is buried in China and is commemorated as a hero of the Communist Revolution. A must for anyone visiting the area is a cruise through the Muskoka lakes on the spectacular 1887 **RMS Segwun**. This 99-passenger vessel is the oldest operating coal-fired steamship in North America. Cruises range in length from one to seven hours. Back on shore, the **Gravenhurst Opera House** is a landmark heritage building from 1901, restored to its original splendour and with perfect acoustics. It hosts musical productions, touring shows and local theatre groups.

ALGONQUIN PROVINCIAL PARK

There are many provincial campgrounds throughout Cottage Country where you can pitch a tent and commune with nature or the people in the campsite next to you. But to escape from it all, nothing comes close to the wilderness of **Algonquin Provincial Park**: its 3,000 square miles (7,725 square kilometres) of forests, lakes and rivers make it the biggest in southern Ontario.

Algonquin provides visitors with two very different experiences. For car campers the 35-mile (56-kilometre) Highway 60 corridor that runs through the park from the West Gate at Oxtongue Lake to the town of Whitney in the east offers easy access to drive-up camp grounds, numerous hiking trails and the **Algonquin Visitor Centre**, **Logging Museum** and **Algonquin Museum**.

Wilderness seekers who want to immerse themselves in Algonquin's rugged landscape of maple and pine forests, bogs, granite ridges and lonely lakes can spend weeks or weekends exploring the waterways by canoe. Explore the wilderness on guided canoe trips. **Canadian Wilderness Trips** (416 960 2298) organises all-inclusive canoe and camping weekends with transportation from Toronto. **Algonquin Outfitters** (1-800 469 4948) organises day-long excursions to Hailstorm Creek, where moose are often sighted. The reward for a day of paddling and portaging is the haunting sound of a loon call across a still lake.

The park is located about 175 miles (275 kilometres) north of Toronto. There are roughly 1,300 campsites in 11 different campgrounds, accessible by car, and another 2,100 wilderness sites for those paddling through the canoe routes. The prettiest time of year here is late September, when the maples turn brilliant shades of red, gold and yellow and the black flies and mosquitoes have died off.

In recent years the Muskoka region has become famous for its scenic golf courses designed by some of the sport's biggest names. Granite ridges lend an extra challenge to the forest-lined fairways and it's not unusual to spot a white-tailed deer on many of the area courses. Favourites include Deerhurst Highlands Golf Club which is part of the **Deerhurst Resort** (*see p246*) and **Taboo**. Many of the top courses can only be accessed through the **Muskoka Golf Trail**, which pairs championship courses with resorts (1-800 465 3034).

Algonquin Provincial Park

Box 219, Whitney, ON K0J 2M0 (entrances off Highway 11, 17 & 60), (reservations 1-888 668 7275/information 705 633 5572/www.algonquin park.on.ca). **Open** *Reservations* 7am-11pm daily. *Information* Summer 8am-4.30pm daily. Winter 9am-4pm daily. **Admission** $12 per vehicle per day.

Bethune Memorial House National Historic Site

235 John Street N, Gravenhurst (705 687 4261/ www.friendsofbethune.on.ca). **Open** *June-Oct* 10am-4pm daily. *Nov-May* by appointment only Mon-Fri. **Admission** $3.50; $2-$3.25 concessions. **Credit** V.

Gravenhurst Opera House & Arts Centre

295 Muskoka Road S, Gravenhurst (1-888 495 8888/705 687 5550/www.gravenhurst.ca/ townoffice/operahouse). **Box office** 10am-4pm Mon-Fri; hours extended on show days. **Admission** phone for details. **Credit** MC, V.

RMS Segwun

Muskoka Fleet, 820 Bay Street, Gravenhurst (705 687 6667/www.segwun.com). **Cruises** June-mid Oct. **Rates** $14-$77. **Credit** AmEx, MC, V.

Sainte-Marie Among the Hurons

Highway 12, at County Road, Midland (705 526 7838/www.saintemarieamongthehurons.on.ca). **Open** 10am-5pm daily. Closed mid Oct-mid May. **Admission** $10; $7-$8 concessions; free under-5s. **Credit** AmEx, MC, V.

Where to eat & drink

Gourmet offerings in Cottage Country are largely found at the resorts such as **Taboo** (*see p246*). Its legendary Wildfire restaurant recently closed but a replacement was due to open as this guide went to press. En route to and from Cottage Country via Highway 11, **Weber's** is a legendary if overrated burger joint where cottagers brave long line-ups for burgers hot off the grill.

Weber's Original Hamburgers

Highway 11 N, near Orillia (705 325 3696/ www.webersrestaurants.com). **Open** phone for details. Closed Dec-Apr. **Main courses** $2.39-$4.59. **Credit** MC, V.

Where to stay

One of the pleasures of Cottage Country is the variety of resorts, lodges, country inns, hotels, motels and family lakeside cabins for rent. The choice ranges from five-star accommodation

Trips Out of Town

Gravenhurst. *See p244.*

with culinary aspirations, to a basic getaway bunkhouse, with beer and burgers at the local pub. For a full list, check with **Resorts Ontario** (*see p227*).

On the shore of Lake Muskoka near Gravenhurst, **Taboo** (*see below*) offers a wide range of condo-style town homes and hotel rooms in a huge resort property that includes 1,200 acres of parks and woodland. Guided nature hikes, a bird-watching cruise to an island sanctuary and a spectacular golf course (*see p214* **Tee time**) add to the mix. For something more rustic, **Pow-Wow Point Lodge** has five lakefront cottages on Pen Lake.

The acclaimed **Arowhon Pines** resort, in Algonquin Provincial Park, has huge log cabins with cathedral ceilings and a gorgeous wilderness setting on Little Joe Lake. Also in Algonquin, **Killarney Lodge** has vintage Canadiana cabins, each with a waterfront view and a canoe for exploring Lake of Two Rivers. Campers will need to contact Algonquin Provincial Park for reservations on eight public campgrounds, or to obtain maps on wilderness canoe routes.

The **Boat House B&B** in Gravenhurst has lakefront rooms (including some with private balconies) in a renovated boathouse across the water from the *Segwun* dock. Hosts Ron and Bette White run sunset cruises.

Arowhon Pines Summer Resort & Restaurant
Summer address: Box 10001, Algonquin Provincial Park, Huntsville, ON P1H 2G5 (705 633 5661/ www.arowhonpines.ca). Winter address: 297 Balliol Street, Toronto, ON M4S 1C7 (416 483 4393/ www.arowhonpines.ca). **Closed** mid Oct-late May. **Rates** $200-$330 per person incl 3 meals daily & recreational facilities. **Credit** MC, V.

Boat House B&B on Lake Muskoka
130 One Road, Gravenhurst, ON P1P 1V5 (705 687 0103/www.boathousebb.ca). **Rates** phone for details. **No credit cards**.

Deerhurst Resort
1235 Deerhurst Drive, Huntsville, ON P1H 2E8 (1-800 461 4393/705 789 6411/www.deerhurst resort.on.ca). **Rates** $99-$239 single/double; $169-$899 suite. **Credit** AmEx, DC, MC, V.

Killarney Lodge
Box 10005, Algonquin Provincial Park, Huntsville, ON P1H 2G9 (705 633 5551/www.killarney lodge.com). **Open** May-Oct. **Rates** $149-$279 cabins. **Credit** MC, V.

Pow-Wow Point Lodge
207 Grassmere Resort Road, Huntsville, ON P1H 2J6 (1-800 461 4263/705 789 4951/www.powwow pointlodge.com). **Rates** $199-$375 for 2-night packages. **Credit** MC, V.

Taboo
1209 Muskoka Beach, Gravenhurst (1-705 687 2233/1-800 461 0236/www.tabooresort.com). **Rates** vary. **Golf fees** (plus taxes) $110-$195; $110 concessions. **Credit** AmEx, DC, MC, V.

Tourist information

Gravenhurst Chamber of Commerce
685-2 Muskoka Road N, Gravenhurst, ON P1P 1N5 (705 687 4432/www.gravenhurst chamber.com). **Open** 9am-5pm Mon-Fri.

Huntsville–Lake of Bays Chamber of Commerce
Unit 1, 8 West Street N, Huntsville, ON P1H 2B6 (705 789 4771/www.huntsvillelakeofbays.on.ca). **Open** 9am-5pm Mon-Fri; 10am-3pm Sat.

Southern Georgian Bay Chamber of Commerce

208 King Street, Midland, ON L4R 3L9 (705 526 7884/www.southerngeorgianbay.on.ca). **Open** 9am-5pm Mon-Fri.

Getting there

By car

For Midland, drive north from Toronto on Highway 400, then take the 93 north-west. For Gravenhurst and Huntsville, drive north on Highway 400 past Barrie, then Highway 11 north. Continue past Huntsville for Algonquin Provincial Park, then take Highway 60 W straight through the park.

By bus

For Gravenhurst and Huntsville, there is an Ontario Northland bus daily from Toronto (416 393 7911, www.ontc.on.ca).

By rail

For Gravenhurst and Huntsville, take the Ontario Northland (Northlander) from Toronto (1-800 461 8558, www.ontc.on.ca).

Prince Edward County

Unlike the granite landscapes and rugged pines of the north, Prince Edward County (or The County, as locals call it) is a place of pastoral beauty: farms of asparagus, strawberries, peas and apples abound, as do century-old farmhouses, many of which are being snapped up by Toronto media types who have turned their attentions to the County when word got out that it might be suited to viticulture. It's quite a turnaround for a part of the province once dubbed the 'Ozarks of Ontario' for its echoes of hillbilly lifestyle. Although it's not quite the south of France, the County is becoming known as a place to enjoy locally

produced foods and vineyards. To celebrate the bounty, local tourism officials organised a **Taste Trail** – a driving tour route that steers visitors to more than two dozen points of culinary interest, and past some of the area's best scenery, particularly the eastern shoreline, where County Road 8 offers vistas of orchards overlooking Lake Ontario. **Lake on the Mountain Park** provides a marvellous panorama. **Taste the County** (613 393 2796), a day-long festival in October, is exactly what you would expect it to be – a celebration of the County's riches.

Separated from the rest of Ontario by the Bay of Quinte and a canal that follows an ancient portage route, the County seems a world apart. Its quiet roads beg for leisurely exploration. The Taste Trail includes such favourite stops as the **Black River Cheese Company** (913 County Road 13, 1-888 252 5787), which has been producing award-winning cheddar for more than a century; **County Premium Cider** (657 Bongards Crossroad, at County Road 8, 613 476 1022), where visitors sip a range of fine ciders in a historic stone building overlooking Lake Ontario; and **Slickers Homemade Ice Cream** (189 Main Street, Wellington or 254 Main Street, Bloomfield, 613 393 5433), where fresh local strawberries and cream are frozen into delicious treats.

One of the first local wineries to produce its own grapes **Waupoos Estates Winery** (3016 County Road 8, 613 476 8338) welcomes visitors to the quintessential County experience: fresh lamb sausages served with a glass of crisp Pinot Gris in an al fresco restaurant with views of lush vineyards sloping down to Lake Ontario. Not surprisingly, many folk are inclined to take one of the evening wine-tasting sessions or three-hour cooking courses at the **Waring House Cookery School** in Picton (1-800 621 4956).

Long before the gourmet gang arrived, the County was a popular summer destination for its spectacular beaches, the most notable of which are found at **Sandbanks Provincial Park** (County Road 12, south-west of Bloomfield, 613 393 3319), where prevailing westerly winds have deposited towering dunes of white sand at the mouths of several bays. Nature lovers explore trails winding through the sensitive habitats, or climb five-storey-high sand dunes, where marram grass, cottonwood poplars and wild roses grow. Sun worshippers, on the other hand, head straight for any of the park's three excellent beaches. Campgrounds here are notoriously busy so reservations are a must. Less busy is **North Beach Provincial Park** (Consecon, 613 399 2030), whose pristine beach is for day use only.

Where to eat & drink

Many of the area's small hotels also feature excellent dining rooms. **Angeline's** remains a long-standing favourite for chef William Fida's French cuisine served in a lovingly restored historic home. Work by local artists adorns the walls, produce from local farmers fills the plate. Fresh produce presented with flair is the order of the day at **Merrill Inn Restaurant**, under the auspices of former Toronto chef Michael Sullivan. The **Devonshire**'s dining room features simple, quality food served with a spectacular view of Lake Ontario sunsets. Also known for its scenic vistas and excellent food, the new **Claramount Inn** on the outskirts of Picton houses an elegant dining room with wrap-around summer patio.

Angeline's
433 Main Street, Bloomfield (613 393 3301/1-877 391 3301). **Open** *Summer* 11.30am-2pm, 5.30-9pm daily. *Winter* 5.30-9pm daily. **Main courses** $18-$25. **Credit** AmEx, MC, V.

Claramount Inn
97 Bridge Street, Picton (613 476 2709/1-800 679 7756/www.claramountinn.com). **Open** 11am-2pm, 5-8pm Wed-Sat; 11am-2pm Sun. **Main courses** $20-$30. **Credit** AmEx, MC, V.

Devonshire on the Lake Restaurant
24 Wharf Street, Wellington (613 399 1851/ 1-800 544 9937/www.devonshire-inn.com). **Open** phone for details. **Main courses** $17-$28. **Credit** AmEx, MC, V.

Merrill Inn Restaurant
343 Main Street, Picton (613 476 7451/1-866 567 5969/www.merrillinn.com). **Open** 5-9pm Tue-Sat. **Main courses** $19-$30. **Credit** AmEx, DC, MC, V.

Where to stay

Although **Angeline's** accommodation (*see above*) looks like a motel on the outside, the rooms are individually decorated, there's a spa and prices are some of the best in the County. The **Devonshire** (*see above*) also has six rooms.

Several of the grand historic homes in Picton are now small hotels, including the luxurious **Claramount Inn** (complete with spa and restaurant; *see above*), and the **Merrill Inn** (*see above*). Prince Edward County also boasts some of the province's finest B&Bs, including **Suites-on-the-Lake Bed & Breakfast**, a fully renovated 1880 house on Lake Ontario, and, a few miles north of Picton, **Timm's Grandview Manor**, a spacious and elegant home with sweeping gardens overlooking the Bay of Quinte to the north.

Suites-on-the-Lake Bed & Breakfast
229 Main Street, Wellington, ON K0K 3L0 (613 399 1717/www.suites-on-the-lake.com). **Rates** phone for details. **Credit** V.

Timm's Grandview Manor
RR 2, Picton, ON K0K 2T0 (off Highway 49) (613 476 8875/1-800 538 9659/www.pec.on.ca/timms). **Rates** $85-$160. **Credit** V.

Trips Out of Town

Taboo. *See p246.*

Head for heights

Walking through the tree-tops is Ontario's latest adventure craze, with thrill-seekers treading narrow plank paths suspended in the forest canopy, swaying 60 feet (18 metres) above the ground. Although they sound dangerous, the canopy walks can be easily managed by almost anyone old enough to manoeuvre the mountaineering-style safety harness clips. At **Haliburton Forest & Wildlife Reserve**, south of Algonquin Park, the 'walk in the clouds' canopy tour begins with a short drive to a riverside trail, a half-kilometre walk to Marsh Lake, then a 15-minute paddle in a canoe to a stand of old growth pines. After a practice session, participants climb a ladder up to the walkway. It doesn't take long to get used to the slow, steady gait necessary to prevent excessive swaying and become familiar with the system of clips and safety lines. Walking slowly, it takes close to two hours to complete the walkway. The tour includes a visit to the local wolf centre.

More vertigo-inducing thrills can be had at **Scenic Caves Nature Adventures**, perched on the cliffs of the Niagara Escarpment overlooking Georgian Bay and Collingwood (*see also p217*), two hours north of Toronto. Here the adventure begins with a walk over the suspension bridge then a wagon ride through the woods to reach the start of the walkway. A system of safety lines secures walkers on the 1,969-foot (600-metre) plank path suspended as much as 46 to 66 feet (14 to 20 metres) above the ground in a leafy canopy of 200-year-old oaks and maples. A thrilling descent along zip lines follows, then it's time to visit the caves and limestone rock formations.

For both tours, reserve in advance.

Haliburton Forest & Wildlife Reserve

RR 1, Haliburton, ON K0M 1S0, off Highway 118 (705 754 2198/www.haliburton forest.com). **Open** 8am-5pm daily. **Admission** $15. *Canopy tour* $95. **Credit** MC, V.

Scenic Caves Nature Adventures

Blue Mountain, Collingwood, ON L9Y 3Z5 (705 446 3515/www.sceniccaves.com). **Open** 9.30am-4.30pm daily. **Admission** $12-$15; $10-$12 concessions; free under-8s. *Treetop walk* $95; $85 concessions. **Credit** MC, V.

Getting there

By car

From Toronto Prince Edward County it is a 2½hr drive east via Highway 401. At Trenton, exit Highway 33 south towards Wellington, Bloomfield and Picton.

South-western Ontario & Lake Erie

Roughly two hours west from Toronto, the beaches of Lake Erie's north shore have long attracted tourists. Some come for the carnival atmosphere of towns like Port Dover, where the smell of hot dogs and French fries hangs in the summer heat. Others come to experience the joys of nature, particularly in spring and autumn when migrating birds and swarms of Monarch butterflies follow the peninsulas jutting south into Lake Erie to shorten their dangerous journey over the open waters of the Great Lakes. This is a region of small towns, flat farmlands, summer resort villages and miles of white sand beaches.

Long Point is a 19-mile (30-kilometre) finger of sand that juts into Lake Erie, and is filled with row upon row of cottages and trailer parks along its white sands. A number of people live here year round, but it's chiefly a summer vacation spot with few full-time amenities bar one or two restaurants and a couple of general stores. That said, it is a popular beach resort for families, and **Long Point Provincial Park** (519 586 2133) is always full of campers.

You can't drive to the end of Long Point – the road ends at the provincial park – or even hike there. In fact, only park rangers and the lighthouse keeper can walk to the tip of the peninsula, as the park is a protected World Biosphere Preserve. For ordinary mortals, the best way to see the stunning tip is to rent a boat or become friends with someone who has one.

If Long Point is more suitable for family holidays, then **Turkey Point** (take Highway 24, then head south on 10) is a swinging beach town for the younger set. Campers can book one of the 235 sites at **Turkey Point Provincial Park** (519 426 3239).

The central community for the area is **Port Dover**. Unlike the two resorts mentioned above, this is an actual town – with grocery and video stores, bars and restaurants, hotels and inns, a credible summer theatre (the **Lighthouse Festival Theatre**) and tourist attractions including the **Port Dover Harbour Museum**, whose nautical treasures include artefacts from Lake Erie's numerous shipwrecks. You won't find accommodation on any Friday 13, when some 100,000 bikers descend on the little town (a tradition which started back in 1981). If you want to see 'the hidden Dover', take the **RiverRider**, a 40-passenger pontoon boat that sails past fishing tugs, yacht clubs, million-dollar homes and nature reserves. Tickets can be purchased at the pier.

Port Dover Harbour Museum

44 Harbor Street, Port Dover (519 583 2660). **Open** 10am-4.30pm Mon-Fri; noon-4pm Sat, Sun. **Admission** by donation.

Where to eat & drink

Belworth House in Waterford is a rare gem of a restaurant in a converted house, where the proprietor-chef prepares every meal herself. Not only is the house beautifully decorated, so is the food.

Fried Lake Erie Perch fillets are not as common as they once were, but can still be found in heaping platters at the **Erie Beach Hotel**, where the menu hasn't changed in 50 years. Half a century ago big name musicians like Louis Armstrong played at **Callahan's Beach Restaurant**. Today its beachfront patio and year-round restaurant serve reliable pub food.

Belworth House

90 St James Street Street, Waterford (519 443 4711). **Open** 5-10pm Tue, Wed, Sat; 11.30am-2.30pm, 5-10pm Thur, Fri. **Main courses** $18-$32. **Credit** MC, V.

Callahan's Beach House Restaurant

2 Walker Street, Port Dover (519 583 0880). **Open** *Summer* 11am-11pm daily. *Winter* 11am-9pm Mon-Thur, Sun; 11am-10pm Fri, Sat. **Main courses** $6-$15. **Credit** MC, V.

Erie Beach Hotel

Walker Street, Port Dover (519 583 1391/www.erie beachhotel.com). **Open** noon-1.30pm, 5-8pm Mon-Sat; 4-7pm Sun. **Main courses** $16-$24. **Credit** AmEx, MC, V.

Where to stay

Every little beach community has rental cottages for longer stays, but many of the nicer rooms are found in B&Bs. Port Dover's **Erie Beach Hotel** rooms emphasise utility over decor. **Bucks Cottages** have been a favourite of beachgoers since 1887. The rows of identical, tidy blue clapboard cottages arranged around the swimming pool look like they're right out of a 1950s tourism brochure.

For a more elegant ambience, **Clonmel Estate B&B** is a stately 1929 home. Of the six guest rooms – all non-smoking – several have private baths. Guests may also play the massive pipe organ in the living room or lounge in the library with its walnut panelling and leather sofa in front of the fireplace. It is handy to the **Lynn Valley Trail**, a scenic spur of the Trans-Canada walking trail.

Note that rooms are at a premium in the area: people often book a year in advance. Contact the local tourist office for a complete list of B&Bs. You'll also need to reserve early for one of the 235 campsites in **Turkey Point Provincial Park** (*see p249*).

All information and bookings at provincial park campgrounds throughout the province are handled through one website, www.ontario parks.com, and one central telephone number, 1-888 668 7275.

Bucks Cottages

519 583 2263/www.portdovercottages.com. **Rates** $350-$850 per wk. **Credit** MC, V.

Clonmel Estate B&B

11 Mill Road, Port Dover, ON N0A 1N1 (519 583 0519/www.kwic.com/~clonmel). **Rates** $99-$125. **Credit** AmEx, MC, V.

Whispering Pines Cottages

230 Cedar Drive, Turkey Point, ON N0E 1T0 (519 426 0959/www.turkeypointbeach.com/wispine/ wispine.html). **Rates** $375-$850 per wk. **Credit** MC, V.

Tourist information

South Coast Tourism

395 Queensway W, Suite 31, Simcoe, ON N3Y 2M9 (1-800 699 9038/519 426 1693/www.ontarios southcoast.com). **Open** 9am-5pm Mon-Fri.

Getting there

By car

The North Shore of Lake Erie is approximately 90 miles (140km) from Toronto. Take the Queen Elizabeth Way (QEW) west for about 40 miles (64km). The highway forks: take the right turn, which becomes Highway 403. Keep driving for 25 miles (40 km) to Brantford; turn south on to Highway 24; and then drive about 25 miles (40km) through Simcoe and follow the signs to the beach community of your choice.

Directory

Directory

Getting Around

By air

Lester B Pearson International Airport

Terminals 1 & 2 416 247 7678;
Terminal 3 416 776 5100;
www.torontoairport.ca.
Pearson, around 16 miles (25km)
north-west of downtown, is in
the middle of a massive $4.4 billion
reconstruction project designed
to improve the airport's ability
to cope with the rising number
of passengers (projected to increase
from 29 million in 2000 to 50 million
by 2020). The new Terminal 1
opened in July 2004 for Air Canada's
domestic and international flights
and a number of foreign airlines.
Terminal 2, which is used for Air
Canada flights to the US, and West
Jet will eventually be torn down
to make way for more Terminal 1
gates. Terminal 3 is home to charters
and some American airlines. All
passengers are currently charged
an airport improvement fee (the fee –
$15 for passengers departing from
the airport, $8 for passengers
making connecting flights – is
included in your ticket price).

The best way to get to
Pearson by bus is Pacific Western
Airport Express (1-800 387 6787,
www.torontoairportexpress.com).
Buses and vans pick up/drop off
passengers at many downtown
hotels and the Greyhound bus
terminal every 30 minutes from 4am
to 2pm and 10pm to 1am, and every
20 minutes from 2pm to 10pm. The
trip takes 20-40 minutes, depending
on where you get on and the time
of day, and costs $15.50 one-way
or $26.75 return. Seniors and
students with valid ID get a ten
per cent discount on one-way trips.
Two children, aged 11 and under,
per adult ride for free.

City buses also serve the
airport, but the routes are long and
circuitous and there's nowhere to
put your luggage. If that excites the
masochist or the penny-pincher in
you, yes, it is possible to get to the
airport for the baseline TTC fare
of $2.25. The designated 192 airport
shuttle runs from Kipling subway
station between 5.20am and 2am;
alternatively, take the 58 from
Lawrence subway station (departing
every 15 minutes). The 307 Eglinton
night bus will also get you to the
airport and back, it runs between
1.30am and 5am.

If you want a quicker way to
connect with the subway, the GO
bus service runs between Terminals
1 and 2 and the Yorkdale and
York Mills subway stations ($3.65
one way).

Most taxi companies offer a flat
rate to the airport of around $40.
Confirm the price before you set off.

Toronto City Centre Airport

416 203 6942/www.torontoport.com.
Map p278 C10/p279 D10.
The only commercial service from
this downtown airport is Air Canada
Jazz flights to Ottawa. Shuttle buses
from Union Station are available
for Jazz passengers, and there's
a ferry service to and from the foot
of Bathurst Street.

Major airlines

Air Canada *1-888 247 2262/*
www.aircanada.ca.
Air Canada Jazz *1-888 247*
2262/www.flyjazz.com.
Air Canada Tango *1-888 247*
2262/www.flytango.com.
Air France *416 922 5024/*
www.airfrance.com.
American Airlines *1-800 433*
7300/www.aa.com.
America West Airlines *1-800*
235 9292/www.americawest.com.
British Airways *416 250*
0880/www.britishairways.com.
CanJet Airlines *1-800 809 7777/*
www.canjet.com.
Continental Airlines *1-800 784*
4444/www.continental.com.
Delta Air Lines *1-800 221 1212/*
www.delta.com.
Northwest Airlines *1-800 441*
1818/www.nwa.com.
United Airlines *1-800 241*
6522/www.united.com.
US Airways *1-800 943 5436/*
www.usairways.com.

By bus

Greyhound Canada (416
594 1010/1-800 661 8747,
www.greyhound.ca) runs
many routes to Toronto from
other parts of Canada and
the US. The main terminal
is located very centrally
at 610 Bay Street, at Dundas
Street, Downtown, and is open
from 5am to 1am daily. Note
that arrivals come in to the
smaller terminal directly
across Elizabeth Street from
the main terminal.

By rail

VIA Rail trains (general
number 1-888 842 7245,
www.viarail.ca) operate from
Union Station (65 Front Street
W, at University Avenue,
which is on the Yonge-
University-Spadina subway
line. The phone number for
enquiries about VIA Rail
trains from the station is
416 366 8411. In addition
to setting off on the three-
day journey westward to
Vancouver, you can board via
trains for Ottawa, Montreal
and the Maritimes. You can
also climb aboard for New
York City and Chicago. Tickets
are available at most travel
agents in Canada or the US.
In the UK, contact Thomas
Cook Signature (0870 443
4442, www.tcsignature.com).

By sea

A new terminal is due to
open in spring 2005 at Cherry
Beach in anticipation of the
high-speed ferry to Rochester,
New York, which was
launched amid much fanfare
in 2004 but quickly declared
bankruptcy. For information,
call the Toronto Port
Authority (416 863 2000).
It is hoped that cruise

ships will come to Toronto once the terminal is in place.

For the latest information on passport regulations when entering the US, *see below* **US passport regulations**.

Public transport

Toronto has an efficient and easy-to-use public transport service run by the Toronto Transit Commission (TTC). In the central city frequent subway services, buses and streetcars ply the major arteries.

Subway services generally start around 6am Mon-Sat, and the last train runs at around 1.30am. On Sundays, service starts at about 9am and ends near 1am. Buses and streetcars generally run from 6am to midnight or 1am daily. The Blue Night Network of buses, identified by a blue stripe on the kerbside sign, takes over at night.

If you need to transfer from one mode of transport to another, be sure to obtain a transfer/proof of purchase when you start your trip. They're available from the red machines in subway stations or from the streetcar or bus driver. If you leave it too long before starting

the second stage of your journey, TTC staff may not accept the transfer ticket, though it's a rather ad hoc system. (You're supposed to take the next connecting vehicle but locals often dash into a shop between legs of a commute.)

The TTC takes safety seriously. Subway trains have alarms in every car, and there is a Designated Waiting Area on each platform that is brightly lit and has a 'push for help' button. It's also the spot where the conductor's car always stops. Women using buses between 9pm and 5am can ask to get off between stops to minimise the walk to their final destination.

TTC INFORMATION
Call 416 393 4636 or log on to www.city.toronto.on.ca/ttc. Network maps are free from all subway station offices.

FARES AND TICKETS
Cash fare for adults is $2.25. Travellers aged 65 and older, or students under 19 pay $1.50 (with photo ID); children 12 and under pay 50¢ for a one-way trip. (Kids aged two and under are free.) Subway fare collectors can give change,

but it's exact fare only on streetcars and buses (pay on board for both).

Fares are nominally cheaper if you buy tickets or tokens in bulk. Adults can buy five for $9.50 or ten for $19. Five senior or student tickets are $6.25 and ten $12.50 (again, take photo ID), and ten children's tickets are $4.25. Tokens are available only at subway stations, while tickets are sold at convenience and other stores.

If you're going to be covering a lot of ground, your best bet is a day pass for $7.75, allowing unlimited travel from 9.30am Mon-Fri and all day on Sat and Sun. The same pass, for the same price, can be used for groups of six, with no more than two adults, for unlimited travel on Sundays and public holidays.

A monthly pass gives you unlimited travel at any time of day. It's $98.75 for adults or $83.25 for seniors and students, but can only be purchased between the 24th of the month and the fourth business day of the following month.

Subway

There are four main subway lines. The Bloor–Danforth line runs from Kipling Station

US passport regulations

As part of the programme to tighten border security, the United States now requires visitors travelling under the Visa Waiver Program (VWP) to present a machine-readable passport in order to be admitted to the country. VWP countries include the UK, Australia and New Zealand. Machine-readable passports contain either a magnetic strip or barcode. The standard-issue EC/EU maroon passport is machine readable. Each traveller, including all children, need their own passport, which must be valid for at least a further six months.

Passports issued to VWP travellers on or after 26 October 2005 must contain

biometric data; for the US's purposes, index finger prints and a digital photo. Prior to that date, officials will be 'enrolling' VWP travellers at borders, by taking fingerprint scans and a photo. Whether the countries concerned can sort out the administration and technology required to issue biometric passports, and the US to read them, by this date is still subject to question: one deadline extension has already been necessary.

If you intend on making a trip across the US border once in Canada, check the situation before you travel, at www.travel.state.gov/visa (click on 'temporary visas').

We've made Canada as easy as falling off a log

Take it easy. Let Air Canada fly you to Toronto, Montreal, Vancouver, St John's, Halifax, Calgary, or Ottawa. That's seven major cities, every day of the week, thanks to the best flight schedule by far. But then we're Air Canada – and making Canada easy is what we do best. To book your flights, call us on 0871 220 1111 or see your IATA travel agent.

aircanada.com

AIR CANADA

A STAR ALLIANCE MEMBER

in the west to Kennedy Station in the east. The north–south line is divided into two parallel arms – the Yonge line, which runs from Union Station to Finch Station, and the University–Spadina line, which runs from Union Station to Downsview Station. The new fourth line runs east–west along Sheppard Avenue, from Yonge-Sheppard Station to Don Mills Station on the north side. (Don't be fooled into thinking there is something to see up there just because there's a subway – aside from a nearby IKEA and a hospital, it's mostly suburban housing.)

The major transfer points between these east–west and north–south lines are Bloor-Yonge, St George and Yonge-Sheppard stations, where the lines run over each other, with platforms linked by stairs. You don't need a transfer to change subway trains.

Bus

Bus stops are marked by red and white poles or bus shelters and are often just before an intersection. Many – but not all – shelters have posted route timetables. Generally, buses arrive every 10-30 minutes. Currently around ten per cent of Toronto's current fleet are so-called 'kneeling' buses, which allow for easier access for the elderly and disabled; all new buses introduced are of this type.

Streetcars

Toronto's streetcars are the best way to get around the city. Because many run on rail tracks in dedicated central lanes, they usually run to schedule. And they retain a feeling of nostalgia, romance, even. Conveniently

for visitors, many of the main central arteries – Queen, College, Dundas, King and Spadina – are served by streetcars (whose numbers start with a 5) and lumber well into the suburbs.

To take the streetcar, wait at the stop (they look the same as bus stops) and cross in front of stopped cars to board by the front door. Sometimes you'll need to look for a shelter in the middle of the road, especially along the 510 Spadina route. (Passengers who have a transfer or pass may board by the back door along the busy 501 Queen line only – you must use the front door on all other lines.) To disembark, step down into the stairwell and push open the doors using the bars. Cars are supposed to stop well behind streetcar doors but it's always a good idea to look right before getting out. Streetcars are not wheelchair accessible.

Rail

The Scarborough Rapid Transit line is a suburban above-ground extension of the Bloor–Danforth subway line that most visitors only see en route to the Toronto Zoo. GO Transit, the province-run company, runs a commuter rail network, but it's of little use to visitors.

Water transport

The city operates ferries from Harbourfront to Centre Island (summer only), Hanlan's Point and Wards Island. Call 416 392 8193 for schedule information or log on to www.city.toronto.on.ca/parks/to_islands/ferry.htm. Return fares are $6 for adults; $3.50 for seniors 65 and older and students 19 and younger; $2.50 for children 15 and younger; kids aged two

and younger go free. The ferry terminal is at the foot of Bay Street, at Queens Quay W, by the Westin Harbour Castle. Ferries generally run from 6.30am to midnight daily at 30-minute to 2.5-hour intervals but services change depending on the season and the weather: always call ahead, and be careful not to miss the last boat back.

Taxis

Toronto taxis operate under a standard system of fees and rights as set out by the city. The meter starts at $2.75 and increases by 25¢ for every 0.190km driven or 31 seconds of waiting. As usual, check it's been reset when you get into the cab.

Drivers are not allowed to recommend restaurants or hotels to you unless you make a request, and they must follow any route you suggest or otherwise take the most direct route.

If you think you have left an item of property in a taxi, call the company directly.
Beck Taxi *416 751 5555.*
CO-OP Cabs *416 504 2667.*
Crown Taxi *416 750 7878.*
Diamond Taxicab *416 366 6868.*
Royal Taxi *416 777 9222.*
Yellow Cab *416 504 4141.*

The taxi complaints line is 1-877 868 2947, and operates 24 hours daily.

Driving

As with most big North American cities, you should avoid having to drive in Toronto if you can help it. During morning and afternoon rush hours especially, jams are long and tedious, and public transport or your own two feet will always get you where you're going quicker.

You need to be at least 16 years old and have a valid licence from your

Directory

home country to drive in Toronto. The city speed limit is generally 50kmph (about 31mph) while the major highways are 80kmph (50mph) to 100kmph (62mph). While you can drive close to 120kmph (75mph) on the major 400-series highways to keep up with the pace of traffic without getting a ticket, don't try that on city streets. Police enforce speed limits strictly, especially in marked school zones where the limit is reduced to 40kmph. In Toronto, it's legal to make a right turn on a red light (unless signs say otherwise) if you first come to a full stop.

As in most cities, drivers are required to stop for school buses picking up and dropping off passengers. You must stop for a school bus on either side of the road unless you're on a divided highway, and you should also stop for streetcars picking up passengers. It's illegal to drive around one, and you'll not only get a ticket but also run the risk of getting an earful from disgruntled commuters.

Pedestrians always have the right of way at crosswalks, which have painted markings and a string of lights, but they can be tricky to spot in congested areas.

Breakdown services

Canadian Automobile Association

461 Yonge Street, at Carlton Street, Church & Wellesley (416 221 4300/emergencies 416 222 5222/www.caa.ca). **Open** 8.30am-6pm Mon-Fri; 9.30am-4pm Sat. *Emergency line* 24hrs daily. **Map** p283 G5.
Breakdown services for members and members of reciprocal organisations, depending on their level of cover.
Other locations: throughout the city.

Fuel stations

Esso

241 Church Street, at Dundas Street, Dundas Square (416 703 4556/ 1-800 567 3776/www.imperialoil.ca). **Open** 6am-midnight daily. **Credit** AmEx, MC, V.
Other locations: throughout the city.

Petro-Canada

55 Spadina Avenue, at King Street W, Entertainment District (416 977 3653/1-800 668 0220/www.petro-canada.ca). **Open** 24hrs daily. **Credit** AmEx, MC, V. **Map** p279 D7.
Other locations: throughout the city.

Parking

Steep: you'll pay as much as $4 for half an hour or $20 for a day of parking in a privately run downtown lot. City-operated lots are a little less expensive at $3 an hour (look for the green 'P' emblem).

Parking on most major city streets is illegal without feeding a nearby meter (costing between $1 and $2 an hour), and parking enforcement officers are ever vigilant. Street parking privileges are withdrawn during rush hour on busy roads, usually 7-9am and 3.30-6.30pm.

Vehicle hire

You must be 21 to rent a car in Ontario. Rental companies will offer you accident and collision insurance and although it may seem expensive, you'd be wise to take it if not covered by your own policy.

Alamo

920 Yonge Street, at Davenport Road, Yorkville (416 935 1533/ 1-800 462 5266/www.alamo.com). Subway Bloor-Yonge. **Open** 7am-9pm Mon-Fri; 7am-6pm Sat; 9am-5pm Sun. **Credit** AmEx, MC, V. **Map** p283 G3.

Budget

556 St Clair Avenue W, at Bathurst Street, Forest Hill (416 651 0020/ 1-800 561 5212/www.budget toronto.com). Subway St Clair.

Open 8am-6pm Mon-Fri; 8am-4pm Sat. **Credit** AmEx, MC, V.
Other locations: throughout the city.

Discount Car & Truck Rentals

243 Danforth Avenue, at Broadview Avenue, East Side (416 465 8776/ 1-866 310 2277/www.discountcar. com). Streetcar 504, 505/subway Broadview. **Open** 8am-6pm Mon-Fri; 8am-4pm Sat. **Credit** AmEx, MC, V.
Other locations: throughout the city.

Enterprise Rent-a-Car

700 Bay Street, at Gerrard Street, Chinatown (416 599 1375/1-800 736 8222/www.enterprise.com). Bus 6/streetcar 506/subway College. **Open** 7.30am-6pm Mon-Fri; 9am-noon Sat. **Credit** AmEx, MC, V. **Map** p279/p280 F6.
Other locations: throughout the city.

Cycling

Experienced city cyclists will find Toronto a doddle, with easy navigation and about 37 miles (59 kilometres) of bike lanes. But don't start your career here – you need street smarts, and accidents are a regular occurrence. For details of city bike programmes, call 416 392 9253 or go to www.city.toronto. on.ca/cycling. *See also p213.*

Walking

Toronto is a city made for walking, with lots of wide sidewalks. For off-street strolls, take one of the city's self-guided Discovery Walks through parks and points of interest – contact the Parks and Recreation department (www.city.toronto.on.ca/parks).

A useful map is 'The *OTHER* Map of Toronto' to guide you to green options throughout the city – available free at Tourism Toronto (*see p265*) and the TO TIX booth in Yonge-Dundas Square. Most bookstores carry commercial maps to the city. We've also included street maps of central Toronto at the back of this book (*pp278-283*).

Resources A-Z

Addresses

Addresses in Toronto are pretty straightforward as most of the central city is arranged on a grid. Generally, street numbers start at 0 at Lake Ontario and increase as you head north. Even numbered addresses are on the west side and odd numbers on the east side of all north–south streets. Similarly, even numbered addresses are on the north side and odd numbers on the south side of east–west streets. The east and west designation of streets running east–west change at Yonge Street.

Throughout this guide, we give the nearest cross street within each listing, as per local usage, though note that the venue in question is not always right on the corner itself.

Age restrictions

To drink and purchase alcohol in Ontario, and to buy tobacco products, you must be 19. Note that fines for buying tobacco for minors are steep. To drive a car or truck, you must be 16 or over (21 to hire one).

The age of consent for heterosexual sex, according to Canada's Criminal Code, is 14, or 18 if one party is in a position of legal authority over the other. The age of consent for gay sex in Ontario is also 14 (18 in most other parts of the country).

See also p259 **ID**.

Attitude & etiquette

Toronto is a casual, relaxed city, and while Torontonians more than other Canadians may bristle at the idea that Canadians are polite to a fault, it's mostly true. Unless you're meeting with the CEO of a major corporation, casual dress is de rigueur for most business situations, especially on Fridays. While wearing jeans to a business function may be pushing your luck, men are rarely required to wear suits (khakis or dress pants are fine) and women wear pretty much what they please.

Greeting friends, women kiss once on the cheek. Guys tend to go for as little contact as possible – a stiff handshake is usual.

Business

For copy shops, *see p164*.

Conventions & conferences
International Centre
6900 Airport Road, at Derry Road, North End (905 677 6131/www.internationalcentre.com). Subway Lawrence West then bus 58B.
Metro Toronto Convention Centre (North Building)
255 Front Street W, at John Street, Entertainment District (416 585 8000/www.mtccc.com). Streetcar 504/subway Union or St Andrew. Map p279 E8.

Couriers & shippers
FedEx
215 Lake Shore Boulevard E, at Sherbourne Street, Waterfront (1-800 463 3339/www.fedex.ca). Bus 75. **Open** 9am-10pm Mon-Fri; noon-5pm Sat. **Credit** AmEx, MC, V. Map p280 H9.
Purolator Courier
335 Bay Street, at Adelaide Street, Financial District (1-888 744 7123/www.purolator.com). Subway King/streetcar 504. **Open** 8am-9pm Mon-Fri. **Credit** AmEx, MC, V. Map p279/p280 F7.
Quick Messenger Service
296 Richmond Street W, at John Street, Entertainment District (416 368 1623/www.qms-tor.com). Streetcar 501, 504. **Open** 7.30am-6.30pm Mon-Fri. **No credit cards.** Map 277 D7.

Secretarial services
BBW International
2336 Bloor Street W, at Windermere Avenue, West End (416 767 3036/www.bbwinternational.com). **Enquiries** 9am-5pm Mon-Fri. **No credit cards.** This is the mailing address only; call to make an appointment.

Translators & interpreters
ABCO International Translators & Interpreters
330 Bay Street, at Adelaide Street W, Entertainment District (416 359 0873). Streetcar 504. **Open** 9am-5pm Mon-Fri. **No credit cards.** Map p279/p280 F7.

Consumer

Ontario has strong consumer protection laws. To lodge a complaint against a business

---

Travel advice

For up-to-date information for travelling to a specific country – including the latest news on safety and security, health issues, local laws and customs – contact your home government's department of foreign affairs. Most have websites packed with useful advice.

Australia
www.dfat.gov.au/travel

Republic of Ireland
www.irlgov.ie/iveagh

USA
http://travel.state.gov/travel

New Zealand
www.mft.govt.nz/travel

UK
www.fco.gov.uk/travel

South Africa
www.dfa.gov.za/

or obtain further information, contact the Ontario Ministry of Consumer & Business Services, General Inquiry Unit (416 326 8800, www.cbs.gov.on.ca).

Customs

Canadian customs regulations allow you to bring the following into the country without paying tax: 200 cigarettes or 50 cigars, plus 1.5 litres of wine, 1.14 litres of liquor or 24 cans of beer.

You are prohibited from carrying firearms, weapons (including knives of any sort), drugs, endangered species (plant or animal) and cultural property (as in antiquities).

Canada Customs & Immigration can provide more information (1-204 983 3500 outside Canada; 1-800 461 9999 in Canada, www. ccra-adrc.gc.ca).

UK Customs & Excise (www.hmce.gov.uk) allows returning travellers to bring home £145 worth of gifts and goods and any sum of money they can prove is theirs. US Customs (www.customs. ustreas.gov) allows Americans to return home from Canada with US$800 worth of gifts and goods duty-free.

Disabled

Toronto is fairly well set up for people with disabilities in terms of having accessible buses and public buildings. Many restaurants and shops are also accessible, but it's always best to call ahead. On the street, the vast majority of kerbs are dropped at an intersection, enabling easy wheelchair access.

Note that not all subway stations and city buses are wheelchair-equipped, and that streetcars are not wheelchair-accessible. **Wheel-Trans** (416 393 4111, www.city.toronto. on.ca/ttc/special.htm) provides door-to-door services at normal

TTC rates. VIA Rail (*see p252*) and most long-distance bus companies can accommodate wheelchair users with enough notice. Many car rental agencies (*see p256*) have disabled-adapted cars, though you'll need to book well in advance. **Kino Mobility** (416 635 5873, 1-888 495 4455, www.kinomobility.com) has various specially-adapted vehicles. Vans are available for able-bodied drivers at $125 a day. Discounts apply for longer than five-day rentals.

The website www.enable link.org is an online guide to accessible locations in Ontario, with useful info and links.

Drugs

Drug offences are taken very seriously in Canada, so it's best to avoid the use of narcotics while in the country.

Electricity

Just like the US, Canada uses 110-volt electric power with two- or three-pin plugs. Visitors from the UK and Europe will need adaptors, available at most hotels and department stores, to use their appliances from home.

Embassies & consulates

American Consulate General
360 University Avenue, University (416 595 1700). Subway Osgoode or St Patrick. Open 8.30am-1pm Mon-Fri.
Australian Consulate General
Suite 1100, 175 Bloor Street E, south tower, at Jarvis Street, Church & Wellesley (416 323 1155). Subway Sherbourne. Open 9am-1pm, 2-4.30pm Mon-Fri. Map p283 G4.
British Consulate-General
777 Bay Street, at College Street, University (416 593 1290). Subway College/streetcar 506. Open 9am-4pm Mon-Fri. Map p279/p280 F5.
Consulate General of Ireland
20 Toronto Street, St Lawrence (416 366 9300). Streetcar 501. Open 10am-4pm Mon-Fri. Map p280 G7/G8.

New Zealand Consulate
Suite 2A, 225 MacPherson Avenue, at Avenue Road, Midtown (416 947 9696). Bus 5/subway St George. Open 8am-4.30pm Mon-Fri. Map p282 F2.
South African Consulate
2 Bloor Street W, at Yonge Street, Yorkville (416 944 8825). Subway Bloor-Yonge. Open 8am-4.30pm Mon-Fri. Map p283 G4.

Emergencies

If you require emergency assistance from police, firefighters or medical services, call 911. It's free from all phones.

For hospitals, *see p259* **Health**. For other emergency numbers, *see p259* **Helplines** and *p262* **Police stations**.
Poison Information Centre
416 813 5900.

Gay & lesbian

Toronto is a very gay-friendly city. You can freely hold hands with your partner in the Church & Wellesley neighbourhood and make out to your heart's content. You may even get away with it along some parts of Queen Street W, but otherwise, it's best to play it cool. Toronto is, by and large, an accepting city, but gay bashing is not unheard of.

For details of gay-and lesbian-friendly accommodation, *see p195*.

Help & information

For HIV/AIDS information, *see p259* **Health**.
519 Church Street Community Centre
519 Church Street, at Dundonald Street, Church & Wellesley (416 392 6874/www.the519.org). Subway Wellesley. Open 9am-10pm Mon-Fri; 9am-5.30pm Sat; 10am-5pm Sun. Map p283 G5.
Gay Bashing Reporting Line
416 392 6878 ext 337.
Lesbian Gay Bi Youth Line
416 962 9688. Open 4-9.30pm Mon-Fri, Sun.
Trained youth volunteers provide support for callers under the age of 27 with problems associated

with sexual orientation, and are a wealth of information on related social services and social groups.

Health

Accident & emergency

If you need immediate medical attention, dial 911 (free) from any phone.

If you need medical information but it's not a life-threatening situation, call **Telehealth Ontario** on 1-866 797 0000. Registered nurses take calls 24 hours a day, seven days a week, and can help diagnose your problem over the phone. They can't send out prescriptions but can refer you to a pharmacy and help decide if you need hospital attention. The service is free to everyone, including visitors, and provides help in English and French, with translation support for 110 other languages.

To contact the police in a non-emergency situation, call 416 808 2222.

See also p260 **Insurance**.

Contraception & abortion

Hassle Free Clinic
66 Gerrard Street E, at Church Street, Church & Wellesley (416 922 0566 women; 416 922 0603/www.hasslefreeclinic.org). Streetcar 505/subway Dundas. **Open** call for hours. **Map** p280 G6.
Planned Parenthood of Toronto
36B Prince Arthur Avenue, Yorkville (416 961 0113/www.ppt.on.ca). Subway Bay or Museum. **Open** 9am-4.30pm Mon, Tue, Thur, Fri; 9am-noon Wed. **Map** p280 D4.

Dentists

For emergency dental service, contact **Dental Emergency Clinic** (1650 Yonge Street, 416 485 7121, 8am-noon daily).
Ontario Dental Association
416 922 3900/www.dental.oda.on.ca.
This organisation can supply information about local dentists.

Doctors

College of Physicians & Surgeons of Ontario
416 967 2603/www.cpso.on.ca.
For references to local doctors.

Hospitals

The hospitals listed below all have emergency wards open 24 hours daily.
Hospital for Sick Children
555 University Avenue, at Gerrard Street E, Chinatown (416 813 1500). Streetcar 506/subway St Patrick. **Map** p279/p280 F6.
Mount Sinai Hospital
600 University Avenue, at College Street, University (416 586 4800). Streetcar 506/subway Queen's Park. **Map** p279/p280 F5.
North York General Hospital
4001 Leslie Street, at Sheppard Avenue E, North Toronto (416 756 6000). Subway Leslie.
St Joseph's Health Centre
30 The Queensway, at Roncesvalles Avenue, West End (416 530 6000). Streetcar 504.
St Michael's Hospital
30 Bond Street, at Queen Street E, Dundas Square (416 360 4000). Streetcar 501/subway Dundas or Queen. **Map** p280 G7.
Sunnybrook & Women's College Health Science Centre
2075 Bayview Avenue, at Lawrence Avenue E, Don Mills (416 480 4207/www.sunnybrookandwomens.on.ca). Bus 11, 124.
Toronto East General Hospital
825 Coxwell Avenue, at Mortimer Avenue, East Side (416 461 8272). Subway Coxwell.
Toronto General Hospital
200 Elizabeth Street, at University Avenue, Chinatown (416 340 3111). Subway Queen's Park. **Map** p279/p280 F6.
Toronto Western Hospital
399 Bathurst Street, at Dundas Street W, Chinatown (416 603 2581). Streetcar 505, 511. **Map** p278 C6/p279 D6.

Opticians

See p161.

Pharmacies & prescriptions

Pharmacies are allowed to set their own dispensing fee, which can range from $6 to $14 on top of your drugs cost. The cheapest drugs are available from department stores such as Zellers (www.hbc.com/zellers) or Wal-Mart (1-800 328 0402).

Pharmacies are ubiquitous in Toronto. Most open between 9am and 10am and close between 10pm and midnight, though some open 24 hours a day. For locations and hours, contact Shoppers Drug Mart (1-800 746 7737, www.shoppersdrugmart.ca); see p161 for some of our recommendations.

STDs, HIV & AIDS

AIDS Committee of Toronto
4th floor, 399 Church Street, at Carlton Street, Church & Wellesley (416 340 2437/www.actoronto.org). Streetcar 506/subway College. **Open** 10am-9pm Mon-Thur; 10am-5pm Fri. **Map** p280 G6.

Helplines

Alcoholics Anonymous
416 487 5591/www.aatoronto.org.
Assaulted Women's Helpline
416 863 0511/www.awhl.org.
Crisis counselling, shelter referrals, legal advice.
Distress Centres of Toronto
416 408 4357.
Trained volunteers are available 24 hours daily for people who need to talk to someone or are feeling suicidal.
Kids Help Phone
1-800 668 6868/http://kidshelp.sympatico.ca.
Narcotics Anonymous
416 236 8956/www.torontona.org.
Toronto Rape Crisis Centre
416 597 8808.
Victim Support Line
416 325 3265.
Advice from the provincial attorney general's office on what to do if you are the victim of a crime.

ID

You must be 19 or older to buy tobacco products, and most corner stores will ask for photo ID if you look 25 or younger.

Carding is rare in gay bars but more common in straight bars and (especially) clubs, so it's a good idea to carry some photo ID with you.

Directory

Insurance

Canada does not provide health or medical services to visitors for free, so travel and health insurance is a must. Hospitals and walk-in clinics will want the name of your insurer and policy number, so be sure to keep them handy.

Internet

Toronto hotels are very switched on to internet access, and usually provide sockets in rooms for laptop users (though speed and reliability vary, and at some a charge is levied); some rooms have ethernet access. In cheaper hotels access may only be via consoles in the lobby. Public access is available at most public libraries and many cafés. For library locations, contact the Toronto Reference Library (416 393 7131; *see also below*).

For useful Toronto websites, *see p266* **Further Reference.**

Bell Sympatico
416 310 7873/www.sympatico.ca.
A reliable, reasonably priced internet service provider that offers dial-up or DSL connections.

Insomnia Internet Bar/Café
563 Bloor Street W, at Bathurst Street, The Annex (416 588 3907/ www.insomniacafe.com). Streetcar 511/subway Bathurst. **Open** 4pm-2am Mon-Fri; 10am-2am Sat, Sun. **Credit** AmEx, DC, MC, V. **Map** p280 C3.

Language

English is the main language used in Toronto, although with such a vast multicultural population, you're likely to hear everything from Mandarin to Punjabi on the streets. Business is conducted largely in Canadian English, which is only subtly different from US and British English.

That said, some common expressions vary from US and UK English, or use one over the other. You'd get in the line-up to order food to go (put the wrapper in the garbage), or eat in and ask for the bill (though 'check' is creeping in). You may need to visit the washroom. If you bump into someone on the sidewalk, say 'sorry'. You fill your car with gas at a gas station, put your luggage in the trunk and may need to look under the hood. Although Canada is officially bilingual, French-speaking travellers will have trouble getting good service.

Left luggage

There are lockers at Terminals 1, 2 and 3 at Lester B Pearson International Airport (*see p252*), and at the downtown Greyhound terminal (*see p252*), but none at City Centre Airport or Union Station (though if you're travelling with VIA Rail you can check bags in for same-day pick up).

Legal help

If you run into legal trouble, contact your insurers or your national consulate (*see p258*).

Libraries

Toronto Reference Library
789 Yonge Street, at Cumberland Street, Yorkville (416 393 7131/ www.tpl.toronto.on.ca). Subway Bloor-Yonge. **Open** *July, Aug* 10am-8pm Mon-Thur; 10am-5pm Fri, Sat. *Sept-June* 10am-8pm Mon-Thur; 10am-5pm Fri, Sat; 1.30-5pm Sun. **Map** p283 G4.
Unlike all the other branches in the city, you can't sign books out from the Reference Library.
Other locations: throughout the city.

Lost property

Airports

Report lost luggage claims to your airline immediately. If you've lost property in the airport itself, call 416 776 7750 (Terminal 1 and 2) or 416 776 4816 (Terminal 3). For City Centre Airport, call 416 203 6942.

Public transport

All lost property found on subways, buses and streetcars ends up at Bay Station, at Bloor Street W and Bay Street. You may visit the Lost & Found office in person from 8am-5pm Mon-Fri or call 416 393 4100 (noon-5pm Mon-Fri).

Taxis

Call the company itself (for a list, *see p255*).

Media

Torontonians love their media. They're permanently plugged in, switched on or buried in newsprint. The largest media market in the country is thriving. Where many big cities in North America are now one-newspaper towns, Toronto boasts four big dailies: the *Toronto Star*, the *Globe and Mail*, the *Toronto Sun* and the *National Post*. Old-fashioned newspaper wars rage on, with free copies handed out liberally.

Newspapers & magazines

Dailies and monthlies

Globe and Mail
The *Globe and Mail* is considered the paper of record for the country. Smart columnists and strong international coverage make it *The New York Times*-lite. Business is its strength. The 'Seven' section on Fridays has selective listings for the week ahead.

Metro/Toronto 24 Hours
Strap-hangers have an even cheaper way to absorb the day's headlines. Toronto has two freebie tabloids that offer news in pre-digested, bite-sized bits. Find them in the subway or in garbage bins.

National Post
It's still in business and there's talk of a new HQ by the lake. Who knew this money-losing upstart launched by Conrad Black would still be around. It's now owned by Winnipeg-based Canwest Media.

Toronto Life
A monthly glossy with upscale attitude reflecting Toronto's expanding bourgeoisie. Its listings are useful for planning ahead.

Toronto Star
The *Star* is Canada's biggest daily paper, yet unlike two of its cross-town rivals (the *Globe* and the *Post*) it doesn't have national distribution. It's small 'l' liberal in outlook, claims to defend the working stiff and covers city news like no one else. The 'What's On' section on Thursdays is a good heads-up for weekend attractions.

Toronto Sun
'The little paper that could' is a feisty tabloid rag with knee-jerk conservatism as its guiding light. Cheesecake and beefcake photos are part of the daily diet.

Alternative papers
They're called alternatives but *NOW* and *eye* have established themselves squarely in the mainstream. Both are free weeklies that come out on Thursday. *NOW* is more granola and *eye* hipper to the downtown music scene. Both have extensive entertainment listings. You'll find them in street boxes and pubs, cafés and stores.

Xtra! and *Fab* compete on the gay scene. At least they've co-ordinated their publication dates, coming out every two weeks on alternating Thursdays. Other freebies include *Exclaim!* (www.exclaim.ca) which covers the indie music scene every month and can be found in bars and clubs downtown. *Slate* (www.slateart guide.com) is a free monthly listings guide to art shows, available in most galleries. *WholeNote* (www.thewhole note.com) is a free bi-monthly about the classical scene, new music and jazz. *Word* (www.wordmag.com) covers the urban music scene and is available ten times a year at music and Caribbean shops.

Foreign-language press
Pick a country and there's probably a Toronto-based publication that caters to its expat community. Weekly papers can be had in French, German, Greek, Spanish, Ukrainian, Hindi and Malaysian, to name a few. The Portuguese community is served by a bi-weekly and papers appear daily in Italian and Korean; there are three daily newspapers in Chinese.

Newsstands carry lots of UK and US press, or try **Book City** (*see p145*).

Radio & television

Radio
The competitive radio field means that formats change as often as station managers' underwear on ratings day. The battle to win the ear of Toronto listeners keeps things interesting, if rarely innovative. There are 33 stations (AM frequencies are difficult to tune to downtown because of interference from office towers – the CN Tower notwithstanding). Talk rules – in many tongues – on AM with all sports (**The Fan 590**), all news (**CFTR 680**), more talk (**CFRB 1010**) and oldies (**AM 0, 1050 CHUM** and **CKOC 1150**). **Mojo Radio 640** pioneered a new format for guys only. You've been warned.

Flick over to FM where you'll find adult contemporary dominates on barely distinguishable stations: **Jack Radio 92.5, Easy Rock 97.3, CHFI 98.1, CKFM 99.9** and **CHUM FM 104.5**. Hip hop can be found on **Flow 93.5**. Classic rock blares on **Q107**, while **The Edge 102.1** tries to be just that amid the morass of contemporary pop and rock music. One of the more interesting newcomers to the dial is **Aboriginal Voices Radio**, 106.5. There's nothing like listening to a frantic pow wow chant in your car to release traffic tension.

The CBC, the taxpayer-funded national service, doesn't draw the numbers in Toronto that it commands elsewhere. **Stereo One** (99.1) is predominantly talk, with national shows that go in search of the Canadian identity blended with local and regional programmes. It's about the only place you'll hear new radio drama. The flagship current affairs programme, *As It Happens*, is a much-loved national institution. **Stereo 2** (94.1) plays light classics mixed with Cape Breton fiddlers and weekend jazz and opera. **CJBC** (90.3) is CBC's French service with superb classical, jazz and contemporary music content. More classics are on the commercial **CFMX** (96.3), which has a penchant for waltzes. **Jazz FM** (91.1) is finding its way now that it runs commercials (it was previously funded by donations).

As is often the case, it is left to campus radio to push the frontiers of programming. Their wildly eclectic tastes make them unlistenable over long stretches, but dropping in on **CKLN** (88.1), **CIUT** (89.5) and **CHRY** (105.5) is certain to refresh.

Television
Torontonians like to watch, and they've developed their thumbs into lean, mean channel-flipping machines. There has always been an embarrassment of channels, even in pre-cable days when US signals beamed across the lake. Now things may have gone too far. The 500-channel universe was a nice metaphor for the wired future, but when you're faced with such a staggering selection, video paralysis sets in.

Speciality channels cater to niche tastes and generalised topics – history, speed, golf, hockey, news, more news, just local news, food, the home and the great outdoors, which most viewers aren't seeing much of. A rash of digital channels launched in 2001 break down the market even further and in some cases spawned entire channels from an existing TV show (Fashion Television – the Channel). Whether anyone is watching is rather beside the point as broadcasters grasp to control their corner of the TV band.

So, when you flick on the set and want a dose of Canadian TV, here are some of the better options: **CBC** (Channel 5) keeps Canadian content up front along with strong news and sports coverage. **CTV** (Channel 9) is the largest private broadcaster and relies heavily on US programming, as does **Global TV** (Channel 6,41). **Citytv** (Channel 57) has shaped cultural coverage with intelligent shows on film, media, fashion and music. The latest entry into the crowded field is **Toronto 1**, an eminently forgettable service that, despite its name, fills the time with American trash.

Money
Each dollar is made up of 100 cents. Coin denominations include the one-cent penny (copper in colour), the five-cent nickel (silver, featuring a beaver) the ten-cent dime (silver, with the Bluenose schooner depicted), the 25-cent quarter (which usually features a caribou), the one-dollar loonie (gold-bronze in colour) and the two-dollar twoonie (two-tone nickel and aluminium with a polar bear). Notes, or bills, come in denominations of $5 (blue), $10 (purple), $20 (green), $50 (pink) and $100 (brown). Shops have recently begun refusing $50 and $100 bills because of counterfeit worries. In the last few years the Bank of Canada has changed the design of its $5, $10 and (most recently) $20 bills, and it's still common to use both designs.

ATMs/ABMs
Known in Canada as ABMs (automatic bank machines), bank machines are ubiquitous.

Directory

Your best bet is to use one operated by a major bank. Privately owned and operated machines are popping up in bars and shops and while they may be handy, most charge an additional user fee of $1-$2.

Most ABMs are part of either the Interac, Plus or Cirrus network, so non-Canadians shouldn't have any trouble accessing their home account. But it's best to check in advance with your bank to find out what the charge bands are.

Banks

CIBC
2 Bloor Street W, at Yonge Street, Yorkville (416 980 4430/www.cibc. com). Subway Bloor-Yonge. **Open** 8am-4pm Mon-Wed; 8am-5pm Thur, Fri; 10am-3pm Sat. **Map** p283 G4.
Other locations: throughout the city.

Metro Credit Union
800 Bay Street, at College Street, University (416 252 5621/www. metrocu.com). Streetcar 506/subway College. **Open** 9.30am-4pm Mon-Wed; 9.30am-6pm Thur, Fri. **Map** p279/p280 F5.
Other locations: throughout the city.

Royal Bank
200 Bay Street, at King Street, Financial District (416 974 3940/ www.royalbank.ca). Streetcar 504/ subway King. **Open** 9am-5pm Mon-Fri. **Map** p279/p280 F8.
Other locations: throughout the city.

Scotiabank
222 Queen Street W, at McCaul Street, Entertainment District (416 866 6591/www.scotiabank.ca). Streetcar 501/subway Osgoode. **Open** 10am-4pm Mon-Thur; 10am-5pm Fri. **Map** p279 E7.
Other locations: throughout the city.

TD Canada Trust
65 Wellesley Street E, at Church Street, Church & Wellesley (416 944 4135/www.tdcanadatrust.com). Bus 94/subway Wellesley. **Open** 9.30am-4pm Mon-Thur; 9.30am-5pm Fri. **Map** p283 G5.
Other locations: throughout the city.

Bureaux de change

American Express
Fairmont Royal York Hotel, 100 Front Street W, at University Avenue, Financial District (416

363 3883/www.americanexpress.ca). Subway Union.* **Open** 8.30am-5.30pm Mon-Fri. **Map** p279/p280 F8.
Other locations: throughout the city.

Thomas Cook
2300 Yonge Street, at Eglinton Avenue, Davisville (416 486 7055/ www.thomascook.ca). Subway Eglinton. **Open** 9.30am-7pm Mon-Thur; 9.30am-5.30pm Fri; 9.30am-5pm Sat.
Other locations: throughout the city.

Credit cards

Most businesses in Toronto take Visa, MasterCard and American Express. High-end shops and restaurants also accept Diners Club. You can make toll-free calls to report lost or stolen cards at the numbers below 24 hours a day, seven days a week:

American Express
1-800 668 2639.
Diners Club
1-800 663 0284 Standard card; 1-800 563 4653 Gold card; 1-800 363 3333 Silver card.
Discover
1-801 902 3100 (long-distance call).
MasterCard
1-800 307 7309.
Visa
1-800 847 2911.

Tax

Most goods and services bought in Ontario are subject to two taxes – the seven per cent federal Goods and Services Tax and the eight per cent Provincial Sales Tax. Both taxes are levied on just about everything you can imagine, other than books and most groceries, and even those are PST exempt only.

The good news is visitors are eligible for a GST refund on goods and short-term accommodation. You must have spent at least $200 to qualify. For more information, contact the Visitor Rebate Program at 1-800 668 4748 (within Canada) or 1-902 432 5608 (outside Canada), or visit the Canada Customs and Revenue Agency website at www.ccra-adrc.gc.ca/visitors.

Major shops will have information and claim forms on hand. Present these at the tax refund booth at the airport for an immediate refund.

Opening hours vary depending on the business and time of year. Shops tend to open at around 10am and close around 6pm. Many stay open till 9pm from June to August. Banks generally open 9am to 5pm during the week, while a few offer evening and weekend hours. Post offices generally open between 10am and 5pm Mon-Sat.

Police stations

To report an emergency, dial 911. If it's not an emergency, call the police at 416 808 222. Toronto Police Service headquarters is at 40 College Street, at Bay. See also www.torontopolice.on.ca.

Postal services

Mailing a standard-sized letter within Canada costs 49 cents for anything up to 30 grammes. Standard letters and postcards to the US cost 80¢ up to 30 grammes and standard letters anywhere outside Canada and the US $1.40 up to 30 grammes and $1.96 for between 30 and 50 grammes. For couriers, *see p257*.

Post offices

Canada Post
260 Adelaide Street E, at George Street, St Lawrence, M5A 1N1 (416 865 1833/www.canadapost.ca). Streetcar 504. **Open** 9am-4pm Mon-Fri; 10am-4pm Sat, Sun. **No credit cards. Map** p280 G7.
Toronto's first post office – and one of its last. The days of the stand-alone post office are numbered here, so check pharmacies and corner stores for post office counters (use the website to find addresses). Stamps, however, are available in most corner stores and pharmacies.
Other locations: throughout the city.

Poste restante/
general delivery

If you want to receive mail
while in Toronto, but don't
have a permanent address,
you can have it sent to you
'care of General Delivery' to
any post office with a postal
code. You must retrieve it
within 15 days of it being
received and show at least
one piece of photo ID.

Religion

Anglican
Church of the Holy Trinity
*10 Trinity Square, next to Toronto
Eaton Centre, Dundas Square
(416 598 4521/www.holytrinity
toronto.org). Streetcar 505/subway
Dundas.* **Services** 9am, 10.30am
Sun; 12.15pm Wed. **Map** p279/
p280 F7.

Baptist
Walmer Road Baptist Church
*188 Lowther Avenue, at Spadina
Avenue, The Annex (416 924 1121/
www.walmer.ca). Streetcar 510/
subway Spadina.* **Service** 11am Sun.
Map p280 C3.

Catholic
St Michael's Cathedral
*65 Bond Street, at Shuter Street,
Dundas Square (416 364 0234).
Streetcar 505/subway Dundas.*
Services 7am, 8.30am, 12.10pm,
5.30pm Mon-Fri; 7am, 8.30am,
12.10pm, 5pm Sat; 8am, 9am,
10.30am, noon, 5pm, 9pm Sun.
Map p280 G7.

Jewish
Adath Israel Congregation
*37 Southbourne Avenue, at Bathurst
Street, North Toronto (416 635
5340/www.adathisrael.com). Bus
7/subway Wilson.* **Services** usually
7am, 8pm daily; call for details.

Lutheran
Redeemer Lutheran Church
*1691 Bloor Street W, at Keele
Street, West End (416 766 1424).
Subway Keele.* **Service** 11.15am
Sun.

Metropolitan
**Metropolitan Community
Church of Toronto**
*115 Simpson Avenue, at Broadview
Avenue, East Side (416 406 6228/
www.mcctoronto.com). Streetcar 504,
505.* **Services** 9am, 11am Sun.
Map p281 K6.

A key player in the fight for gay
marriage, MCC goes downtown for
Pride Day services and a big Xmas
Eve service at Roy Thomson Hall.

Muslim
Madina Masjid
*1015 Danforth Avenue, at Donlands
Avenue, East Side (416 465 7833).
Subway Donlands.* **Services** Prayers
5 times daily; call for details.

Pentecostal
Queensway Cathedral
*1536 The Queensway, at Kipling
Avenue, West End (416 255 0141/
www.queenswaycathedral.com).
Subway Kipling then bus 44.*
Services 10.30am, 6pm Sun.

Presbyterian
Knox Presbyterian Church
*630 Spadina Avenue, at Harbord
Street, Harbord (416 921 8993/
www.knoxtoronto.org). Bus
94/streetcar 510.* **Services** 11am,
7pm Sun. **Map** p276/p280 C5.

United
Metropolitan United Church
*56 Queen Street E, at Church Street,
Dundas Square (416 363 0331/
www.metunited.org). Streetcar 501/
subway Queen.* **Service** 11am Sun.
Map p280 G7.

Safety & security

Toronto is a safe city but
exercise common sense.

● Don't walk around with
valuables. Leave them in
a hotel safe, and get a receipt.
● Pulling out a map on the
street makes it obvious you
don't know where you are –
not a good signal to give off.
● Most homeless people
collecting change on the streets
are harmless. The majority sit
on the street and never move.
Still, it pays to be cautious, so
stay away from anyone who
gives you a bad vibe.
● Don't carry all your cash
or cards with you at one
time. Travellers' cheques are
accepted almost everywhere.

Smoking

A comprehensive no smoking
law came into effect 1 June
2004 in Toronto. Basically,
if you want to light up, you're
going outside. In bars, clubs

and restaurants you can
no longer smoke. Some
enterprising bars advertise
'private events' at which
'members' (ie anyone who
walks through the door) can
enjoy an evening of indoor
puffing. Heat lamps are
sprouting on patios around
to keep patrons warm on
winter nights.

Study

Universities

To study in Canada, foreign
students need a study permit.
Depending on your country of
origin, a temporary visa may
also be required. Applications
are through your local
Canadian embassy or high
consulate (*see p258*).

Ryerson University
University *350 Victoria Street,
at Gould Street, Dundas Square
(416 979 5000/www.ryerson.ca).
Streetcar 505/subway Dundas.*
Map p280 G6.
Students' union *RyeSac, 380
Room A62, Victoria Street, at Gould
Street, Dundas Square (416 597
0723/www.ryesac.ca). Streetcar
505/subway Dundas.* **Map** p277/
p2280 G6.
Although it is often sneered at by
those at the city's older and stuffier
universities (it only became an
official, degree-granting school
in the 1990s), Ryerson draws on its
background as a polytechnic institute
to deliver first-rate hands-on learning
in the heart of city. The school is best
known for its journalism, fashion
and computer programmes.

University of Toronto
University *416 978 2011/
www.utoronto.ca. Streetcar
506/subway St George or Spadina.*
Students' union *Students'
Administrative Council, 12 Hart
House Circle, University (416 978
4911/www.sac.utoronto.ca). Subway
St George.* **Map** p282 E5.
The closest thing Canada has to
an Ivy League institution, U of T
consistently ranks among the
country's top three schools. It's
also one of the best-funded schools
around, thanks to a highly successful
fundraising department, so it has
the best facilities for every kind
of programme you can think
of, from medicine through law
to Celtic studies.

Directory

York University

University *4700 Keele Street, North Toronto (416 736 2100/ www.yorku.ca).*
Students' union *York Federation of Students, 336 Student Centre, North Toronto (416 736 5324/ www.yfs.ca).* Both *Subway Downsview then bus 106.*
York would have a better reputation if it weren't so far from downtown and if it didn't have such an ugly, bleak campus, which is what people talk about most often when they talk about York. That said, it is well regarded and is as known as much for its lefty women's and environmental studies programmes as its more conservative business and law schools.

Telephones

Dialling & codes

Greater Toronto has three area codes: 416, 905 and 647. Generally, businesses and residences in the city have 416 numbers, while those outside the city proper (Mississauga, Richmond Hill, Markham, Pickering) have 905 numbers. The 647 code was introduced in 2001 and still draws blank stares from locals, but is slowly catching on.

Keep in mind that as well as being a local code, 905 is also a long-distance code for southern Ontario cities such as Oshawa and Hamilton. Dialling numbers in those cities means dialling a 1 before the code and paying a long-distance charge.

The following codes are all toll-free numbers. Depending on the company or service, some numbers may not work if calling the US. You must dial 1 before the following: 800, 855, 866, 877, 888.

Making a call

All calls within Toronto must be dialled by using a ten-digit number (the first three are the area code; dial it even if you share it). To make a long-distance call within Canada or to North America, dial 1, the

area code, and then the seven-digit phone number. To call overseas, dial 011, the country code, then the number (in some cases dropping the initial zero). The country code for the **UK** is 44, for **Australia** it's 61, **New Zealand** 64, **Republic of Ireland** 353 and **South Africa** 27.

Public phones

If you can find one, payphones cost 25¢ per local call. Bell and other private carriers are fighting over the loose-change business. A Bell pre-paid phonecard available from most phone shops, grocery stores and pharmacies works only in Bell phones. Dial-in phonecards, Bell's included, are widely available and your best bet for long-distance and international calls.

Operator services

Dial 0 from any phone to speak to an operator (free from payphones). Dial 00 for the international operator.

Telephone directories

To find a number, dial 411 for information from any phone. It will cost 75¢, whether the operator finds your listing or not.

Mobile phones

As in the US, Canada's mobile phone (cellphone) network operates on 1900 megaHertz. This means that, depending on their billing plan, US travellers should be able to use their usual handset (but should check their tariffs for costs). Tri-band phones will work throughout most of North America; quad-bands tend to give some additional coverage but there is still the odd area with no coverage at all. If you have a dual-band phone or think your tri- or quad-band

phone might not work, contact your service provider to find out if it has a way around the problem. For instance, some will arrange for you to have a temporary phone while away.

If none of this works for you, there are three options. If you're a frequent visitor, consider setting up your own local account, though this is unlikely to be worthwhile. A better option would probably be to buy a pay-as-you-go phone, starting at around $125. One of the local carriers, Fido, Bell Mobility, Rogers or Telus Mobility, will be able to help you with either of these options. Their outlets are ubiquitous.

Alternatively, you could rent a phone via your hotel or from a private company such as **Hello, Anywhere** (416 367 4355/1-888 729 4355, www.helloanywhere.com; credit card required) or **Cell Express** (905 812 1307/ 1-877 626 0216, www.cell-express.com; credit card or $350-$500 deposit required), which deliver phones to your hotel for $24-$50 a week ($50-$80 a month).

Faxes

Fax services are available in most corner stores, but you'll get a better price at a copy shop (*see p164*).

Time

Toronto is in the Eastern Time Zone – just like New York – which is five hours behind Greenwich Mean Time. Daylight Saving begins at 2am on the first Sunday in April and ends at 2am on the last Sunday in October.

Tipping

Tipping is expected and, for the most part, deserved by Toronto workers. Restaurant and bar staff have a lower minimum wage than most Canadians because they're expected to make up for it in tips. Generally, tip 15 per cent on pre-tax meal bills (add the amount you'd pay in tax – it's the same percentage, which makes for easy calculation), and a buck or two at the bar. Hotel cleaning staff and bellhops also deserve a buck or two. Hairdressers expect tips of between ten and 20 per cent.

Toilets

Public toilets are scarce in Toronto, so your best bet is to use one in a restaurant or coffee shop, though note that most are reserved for customers.

Tourist information

Ontario Travel Information Centre
Atrium on Bay, 20 Dundas Street W, at Yonge Street, Dundas Square (905 282 1721/1-800 668 2746). Subway Dundas. **Open** 10am-9pm Mon-Fri; 9.30am-7pm Sat; noon-5pm Sun. **Map** p280 G6.
With free maps, and helpful advice on attractions in town and throughout the province, plus a foreign exchange counter, this new street-level location is convenient to access and easy to find.
Tourism Toronto
Queens Quay Terminal, 207 Queens Quay W, at York Street (416 203 2600/1-800 363 1990/www.toronto tourism.com). Subway Union Station then streetcar 509, 510. **Open** 8.30am-5pm Mon; 8.30am-6pm Tue-Thur; 9am-6pm Sat; 10am-6pm Sun. **Map** p279/p280 F9.

Visas & immigration

Residents of Britain, the US, Australia, New Zealand and Ireland do not need visas to visit Canada. For all other visitors and for up-to-date immigration information, see www.cic.gc.ca/english/visit/visas.html.

Weights & measures

The metric system is used in Canada.

1 centimetre = 0.394 inches
1 metre = 3.28 feet
1 sq metre = 1.196 sq yards
1 kilometre = 0.62 miles
1 kilogramme = 2.2 pounds
1 litre = 1.76 UK pints, 2.113 US pints

When to go

Climate

Toronto has one of the mildest climates in the country, thanks to the moderating effects of Lake Ontario and a southern latitude of 44° north, on par with Florence, Italy. And winter is never as bad as you've heard: the city gets less snow than it used to and has seen more slush than snowbanks in recent years. Toronto gets plenty of sunshine year-round and is generally temperate.

Public holidays

New Year's Day (1 Jan; if a Sun, then holiday is the following Mon); Good Friday (Mar/Apr); Victoria Day (24 May if a Mon, otherwise preceding Mon); Canada Day (1 July); Simcoe Day (1st Mon Aug – Ontario only); Labour Day (1st Mon Sept); Thanksgiving (2nd Mon Oct); Christmas (25 Dec); Boxing Day (26 Dec). While government offices and most banks close on Easter Monday (Mar/Apr) and Remembrance Day (11 Nov), the majority of businesses remain open.

Women

Toronto is as safe a city for women as most other cities of its size in North America. Women travelling alone are unlikely to get any trouble, but it's still a good idea to use common sense and avoid deserted streets after dark. It's also a good idea to keep an eye on your drink while at the bar – use of Rohypnol (the so-called 'date-rape drug') isn't as widespread here as in some major US cities, but it's not unheard of.
For a list of helplines, *see p259.*
National Action Committee on the Status of Women
234 Eglinton Avenue E, Forest Hill (416 932 1718/www.nac-cca.ca). Subway Eglinton. **Open** 9am-5pm Mon-Fri.

Average temperatures

	High (C/F)	Low (C/F)
Jan	-1°/30°	-7°/19°
Feb	0°/32°	-6°/21°
Mar	5°/41°	-2°/28°
Apr	11°/51°	4°/39°
May	19°/66°	10°/50°
June	23°/73°	15°/59°
July	26°/78°	18°/64°
Aug	25°/77°	17°/62°
Sept	20°/68°	13°/55°
Oct	14°/57°	7°/44°
Nov	7°/44°	2°/35°
Dec	2°/35°	-4°/24°

Directory

Further Reference

Books

Fiction

Margaret Atwood *Life Before Man; Cat's Eye; Lady Oracle; The Robber Bride.*
The poet laureate of modern Toronto, Atwood's *Life Before Man* – a tense love triangle – is a terrific portrait of the city in the 1970s. *The Robber Bride* dissects female rivalry, while both *Cat's Eye* and *Lady Oracle* draw on middle-class life in the 1940s and '50s.
Robertson Davies *The Fifth Business; The Rebel Angels; What's Bred in the Bone; The Manticore.*
Davies adds some magic realism to his many portrayals of Toronto.
Timothy Findley *The Wars.*
Headhunter, which updates *Heart of Darkness*, set in Toronto
Gwendolyn MacEwen *Selected Poetry*
MacEwen evokes Toronto in the 1960s and 1970s.
Anne Michaels *Fugitive Pieces*
This multiple-award winning debut novel starts in Poland during the World War II and moves to Toronto, to explore memory, loss and landscape. Movie on the way.
Michael Ondaatje *In the Skin of a Lion.*
Born in Sri Lanka, Ondaajte's greatest gift to Toronto is his gilding of the city's seemingly quiet past. *In the Skin of a Lion* morphs landmarks such as the Bloor Street Viaduct and RC Harris Filtration Plant into places of magic, depth and consequence.
Jane Urquhart *Away*
This haunting tale by the master of what some have called 'southern Ontario gothic' tells a story that begins in Ireland and ends in early-days Toronto.

Non-fiction

Eric Arthur *Toronto: No Mean City*
Still the definitive book on Toronto's architectural history 40 years after it was published. An updated edition places the city's growth in context.
William Dendy *Lost Toronto*
This nostalgic look at the Toronto lost to the wrecking ball – food for thought for what might have been.
Robert Fulford *Accidental City: The Transformation of Toronto*
A personal look at the city's coming of age which begins, the writer argues, with the international competition to design the new City Hall.
Greg Gatenby *Toronto: A Literary Guide*
Discover the haunts of home-grown scribes and landmarks noted by visiting writers through the 1900s.

Geoff Pevere and Greig Dymond *Mondo Canuck*
This cheeky, exhaustive tell-all puts Canuck celebs in the spotlight.
John Sewell *Doors Open Toronto: Illuminating the City's Great Spaces*
A former city mayor provides architectural insights into the buildings on the popular annual tour of the city's hidden treasures.
Murray Seymour *Toronto's Ravines*
34 walks in Toronto's leafy arteries.

Films

Ararat
(dir. Atom Egoyan, 2002)
The acclaimed Toronto director reaches back to his Armenian roots in a film-within-a-film made in contemporary Toronto.
Eclipse
(dir. Jeremy Podeswa, 1994)
Tale of sexual liaisons leading up to a solar eclipse.
Goin' Down the Road
(dir Don Shebib, 1970)
Two drifters come to Yonge Street in search of a better life. A classic.
Hollywood Bollywood
(dir. Deeptha Metha, 2002)
This cheesy musical comedy celebrates the vibrant East Indian culture in Toronto.
I've Heard the Mermaids Singing
(dir. Patricia Rozema, 1987)
Tale of self-deprecating secretary who lands a job in a local art gallery.
Last Night
(dir. Don McKellar, 1998)
The apocalypse comes to Toronto, sending a multi-culti cast in all directions ruminating on the meaning of it all.
Niagara
(dir. Henry Hathaway, 1953)
The Falls are upstaged by the presence of Marilyn Monroe in this noirish murder tale with great location shooting.
Thirty-two Short Films About Glenn Gould
(dir. Francois Girard, 1993)
An innovative bio-pic about the legendary Toronto pianist.
Zero Patience
(dir. John Greyson, 1993)
The ghost of 'patient zero', the air steward fingered for bringing AIDS to North America, stalks the city.

Music

Albums

Bruce Cockburn *Stealing Fire* (1984)
The most successful album from the onetime Yorkvillian features 'If I Had a Rocket Launcher' and 'Lovers in a Dangerous Time'.

Holly Cole Trio *Girl Talk* (1990)
A pleasing set from this acclaimed local jazz singer. Later album *Temptation* was a set of songs by Tom Waits.
Cowboy Junkies *The Trinity Session* (1988)
Easily the finest album from the Timmins clan, recorded live to one microphone at the Church of the Holy Trinity in downtown Toronto.
Glenn Gould *A Sense of Wonder* (2002)
Gould's two miraculous recordings of Bach's Goldberg Variations from 1955 and 1981.
Gordon Lightfoot *Songbook* (1999)
More of the Yorkville folker than you could ever need – nearly 90 tracks over four CDs.
Jazz at Massey Hall (1953)
A legendary concert featuring Charlie Parker, Dizzy Gillespie, Art Powell, Charles Mingus and Max Roach on the only night they ever played together.
Martha & the Muffins *Far Away in Time* (1988)
The apogee of the foursome, containing the immortal 'EchoBeach'.
The Quintet *Jazz at Massey Hall* (1953)
Charlie Parker and Dizzy Gillespie together for the last time on record.
Ron Sexsmith *Cobblestone Runway* (2002)
The Toronto singer-songwriter's fifth album (his best remains his second, *Other Songs*), and includes 'Dragonfly on Bay Street', a disco song about his pre-fame experiences working as a messenger in downtown Toronto.
The Tragically Hip *Up to Here* (1989)
Start at the beginning or, because the beginning wasn't much cop, with the second album from Ontario's finest, still together after two decades.

Websites

www.city.toronto.on.ca
A comprehensive guide to all kinds of attractions, put together by the City of Toronto.
www.martiniboys.com
Decent reviews of the latest clubs, bars and restaurants around town.
www.infiltration.org/
The website of the Toronto-based underground infiltration.
www.cbc.ca
Explore the length and breath of the country as it is covered by the public broadcaster CBC.
www.toronto.com
Its slogan is 'All you need to know about TO'. Some consider it a mess.

Index

Advertisers' Index

Please refer to the relevant page for contact details

Index

Place of interest and/or entertainment	
Railway & bus stations	
Parks	
Hospitals/universities	
Neighbourhood	MOSS PARK
Subway station	**Ⓢ**
Bus route	—75—
Streetcar route	—501—
Subway route	——

Maps

Southern Ontario

© Copyright Time Out Group 2005

Toronto Overview

Rowntree Mills Park

Humber River Regional Hospital Finch Ave Site

York University

FINCH AVE-W

Arboretum

Humber College

Woodbine Centre

REXDALE BL

427

WESTON RD

400

JANE ST

Derrydowns Park

KEELE ST

Northwood Park

KIPLING AVE

West Humber River

ALBION RD

Humber Valley G.C.

SHEPPARD AVE-W

Oakdale Golf & C.C.

Downsview Dells

Downsview Airport (Canadian Armed Forces Bases)

Woodbine Race Track

NORTH TORONTO

401

WILSON AVE

CARLINGVIEW RD

409

401

Weston Golf & C.C.

MACDONALD-CARTIER EXPWY

MAPLE LEAF DR

DIXON RD

Seneca College

Lester B. Pearson International Airport

401

THE WESTWAY

ISLINGTON AVE

ROYAL YORK RD

WESTON RD

SCARLETT RD

LAWRENCE AVE-W

JANE ST

BLACK CREEK DR

KEELE ST

CALEDONIA RD

EGLINTON AVE-W

EGLINTON AVE-W

West Dean Park

MARTIN GROVE RD

Eglinton Flats

EGLINTON AVE-W

RENFORTH DR

THE KINGSWAY

Scarlett Woods G.C.

Prospect Cemetery

Centennial Park

RATHBURN RD

Humber River

Smythe Park

Black Creek

ROGERS RD

OLD WESTON RD

Etobicoke Creek

427

ETOBICOKE

Lambton G.C.

ST. CLAIR AVE-W

Earlscourt Park

MILL RD

BURNHAMTHORPE RD

DUNDAS ST-W

DUNDAS ST-W

AVE

DUPON

THE WEST MALL

BLOOR ST-W

Montgomery's Inn

JANE ST

ANNETTE ST

LANSDOWNE

DUFFERIN ST

Etobicoke Civic Centre

Islington

Royal York

BLOOR Ⓢ ST-W

Old Mill

Dundas West

MISSISSAUGA

Ⓢ Kipling

NORSEMAN RD

PRINCE EDWARD DR

Jane Ⓢ

Runnymede Ⓢ

Keele Ⓢ

Lansdowne

Kings Mill Park

High Park

WEST END

Shenway Gardens

N QUEEN ST

Mimico Creek

SOUTH KINGSWAY

Colborne Lodge

St Joseph's Health Centre

RONCESVALLES AVE

DUNDAS ST-W

QUEEN ST-W

THE QUEENSWAY

QUEEN ELIZABETH WAY

LAKE SHORE BL-W

KING ST-W

QUEENSWAY-E

QUEEN ELIZABETH WAY

BROWNS LINE

EVANS AVE

PARK LAWN

Humber Bay

GARDINER EXPWY

HORNER AVE

KIPLING AVE

ISLINGTON AVE

ROYAL YORK RD

Humber Bay Park

DIXIE RD

LAKE SHORE BL-W

LAKE SHORE RD-W

Marie Curtis Park

Humber College- South Campus

Smith Waterfront Park

Lake Ontario

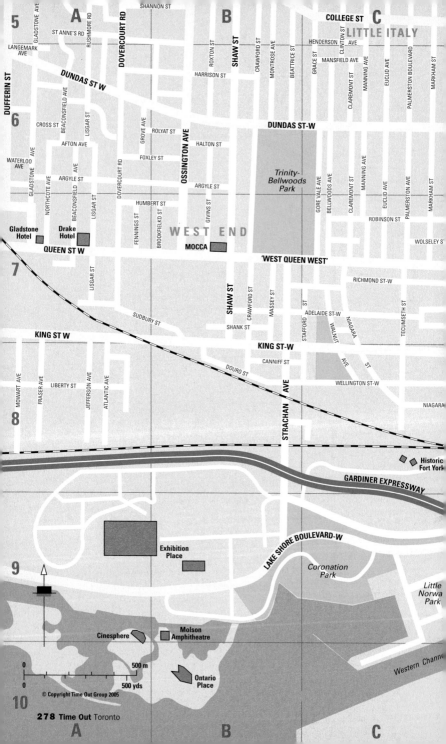

Shannon St

St Anne's Rd

Rushmore Rd

Dovercourt Rd

Gladstone Ave

Langemark Ave

Roxton St

Shaw St

Crawford St

Montrose Ave

Beatrice St

Henderson Ave

Grace St

Clinton St

Mansfield Ave

Manning Ave

Euclid Ave

Palmerston Boulevard

Markham St

Dundas St W

Harrison St

6

Dufferin St

Beaconsfield Ave

Lisgar St

Grove Ave

Rolyat St

Ossington Ave

Halton St

Dundas St-W

Gore Vale Ave

Bellwoods Ave

Claremont St

Manning Ave

Euclid Ave

Palmerston Ave

Markham St

Cross St

Afton Ave

Foxley St

Argyle St

Trinity-Bellwoods
Park

Waterloo Ave

Gladstone Ave

Northcote Ave

Argyle St

Dovercourt Rd

Beaconsfield

Lisgar St

Humbert St

Givins St

Robinson St

Fennings St

Brookfield St

Argyle St

WEST END

Gladstone
Hotel

Drake
Hotel

Queen St W

MOCCA

Wolseley S

'West Queen West'

7

Lisgar St

Shaw St

Crawford St

Massey St

St

Richmond St-W

Sudbury St

Shank St

Adelaide St-W

Stafford

Walnut

Niagara

St

Tecumseth St

King St W

King St-W

Canniff St

Ave

Wellington St-W

Mowart Ave

Fraser Ave

Liberty St

Jefferson Ave

Atlantic Ave

Douro St

Strachan Ave

8

Niagara

Historic
Fort York

Gardiner Expressway

Lake Shore Boulevard-W

9

Exhibition
Place

Coronation
Park

Little
Norwa
Park

Cinesphere

Molson
Amphitheatre

Ontario
Place

Western Channel

0   500 m

0   500 yds

© Copyright Time Out Group 2005

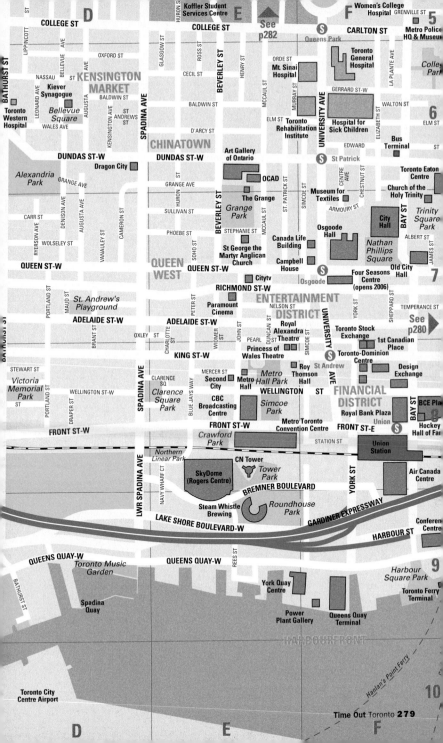

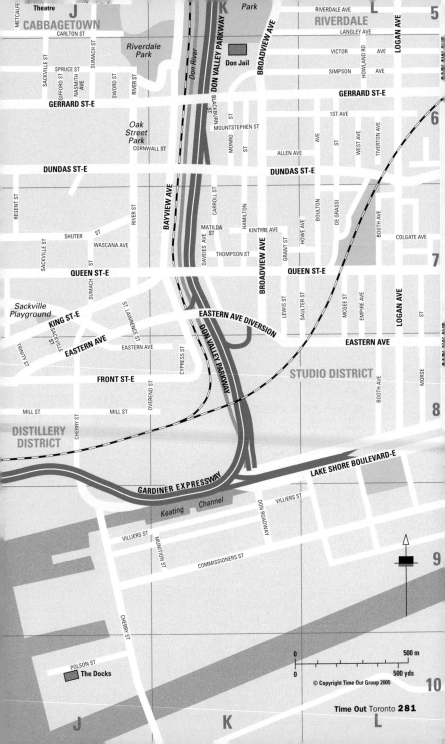

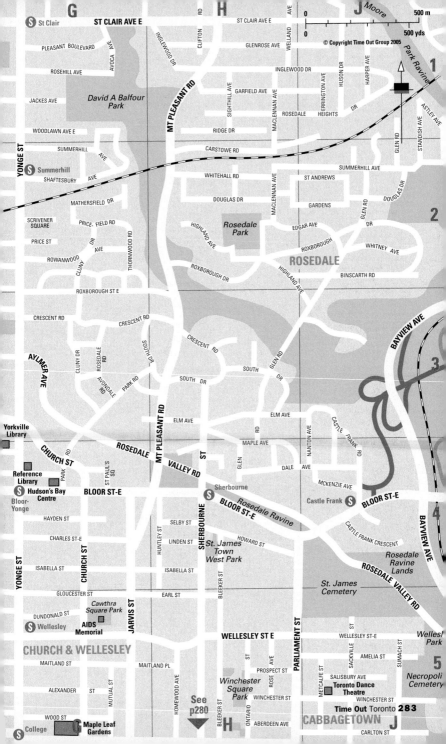

Street Index

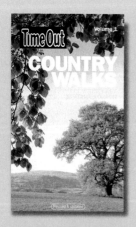

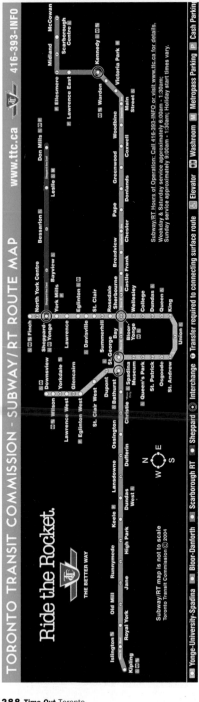

TORONTO TRANSIT COMMISSION - SUBWAY/RT ROUTE MAP   www.ttc.ca   416-393-INFO

Ride the Rocket.

THE BETTER WAY

Subway/RT map is not to scale
Toronto Transit Commission © 2004

Subway/RT Hours of Operation: Call 416-393-INFO or visit www.ttc.ca for details.
Weekday & Saturday service approximately 6:00am - 1:30am;
Sunday service approximately 9:00am - 1:30am; Holiday start times vary.

Yonge-University-Spadina   Bloor-Danforth   Scarborough RT   Sheppard   Interchange   Transfer required to connecting surface route   Elevator   Washroom   Metropass Parking   Cash Parking

Toronto Transport & Areas